Texas Monthly's Political Reader

Texas Monthly's ★ Political Reader SECOND EDITION

Texas Monthly Press
P.O. Box 1569, Austin,
Texas 78767

©Copyright 1980 by Texas Monthly Press, Inc. All rights including reproduction by photographic or electronic process and translation into other languages are fully reserved under the International Copyright Union, the Universal Copyright Convention, and the Pan-American Copyright Convention. Reproduction or use of this book in whole or in part in any manner without written permission of the publisher is strictly prohibited.

Texas Monthly Press, Inc.
P.O. Box 1569
Austin, Texas 78767

A B C D E F G H

1. Texas—politics and government—1951—Addresses, essays, lectures. I. Texas Monthly.   II. Title: Political Reader.

JK4819.T37 1980 320.9764 80-14173
ISBN 0-932012-09-4

Texas Monthly's Political Reader

CONTENTS

I.   Texas Politics: Context and Culture

    Chapter One   **Power: Texans Who Have It and Use It**

        The Most Powerful Texans by Harry Hurt III   12
        Some are politicians but most are not. (April 1976)

        Empires of Paper by Griffin Smith, jr.   22
        How three Texas law firms became the powerful institutions they are today, including a section on how they influence the politics of the state. (November 1973)

        So You Want to Be Chairman of Exxon? by Nicholas Lemann   38
        How the world's largest corporation decides who will make it to the top—and who won't. (December 1978)

    Chapter Two   **Should Texas Secede? The Cultural Context**

        Divide and Conquer by Griffin Smith, jr.   51
        Five states are better than one, when they're all named Texas. (January 1975)

        Power Shift? by James Fallows   57
        Regionalism returns to American politics. (February 1976)

    Chapter Three   **Texas and the Feds: Working With Us or Against Us?**

        The Cactus Curtain by Harry Hurt III   62
        The word going across the border is: Uncle Sam doesn't want you. (August 1977)

        Finders Keepers? by Robert Barnstone   73
        The feds are trying to get our gas again; this time they've gone all the way to the Supreme Court. (February 1978)

        The Real Governor of Texas by Paul Burka   75
        How a federal judge named Justice wields immense power. (June 1978)

        Behind the Lines by William Broyles, Jr.   84
        Two questions about school desegregation: Is busing the only way? Are integrated schools inferior? (January 1980)

II. Political Parties and Political People

    Chapter Four   **The Participants**

        Raza Desunida by Tom Curtis   90
        South Texas has had a revolution, but it's not the one José Angel Gutiérrez planned. (February 1977)

        The Case Against the Farmers by Stephen Chapman   95
        Everybody says they want to help the farmers, but nobody wants to face up to what the farmers really need. (March 1978)

Sole Brothers by Jack Keever ... 98
Can the Legislature's black caucus hang together? (January 1975)

Labor Pains by Dick J. Reavis ... 102
Second-generation refinery workers don't believe in politicians or corporations and some of them don't believe in unions. The question is, do they believe in strikes? (August 1978)

The Good Old Girls by Prudence Mackintosh ... 110
At the National Women's Conference in Houston, feminists embraced the mainstream of America. (January 1978)

Chapter Five Who Runs Our Cities and Towns?

Liberal Education by Paul Burka ... 120
Liberals finally run Austin politics instead of criticizing it. (March 1977)

Up the Creek by Nicholas Lemann ... 124
Barton Creek—to many a symbol of Austin's easygoing life—is in the hands of eager-beaver developers and a dawdling city government. (September 1979)

The People's Choice by John Bloom ... 128
Who is the mayor of Cowtown? A plumber takes Fort Worth by surprise. (June 1979)

The Second Battle of the Alamo by Paul Burka ... 132
Texas' oldest city is heading for a political showdown, thanks to some newcomers to the power game. (December 1977)

Chapter Six State Politics and Elections

Where's My Line? by Griffin Smith, jr. ... 146
Is "one man, one vote" just another numbers racket? (June 1976)

Ticket to Ride? by Paul Burka ... 149
Is the best lineup ever enough to keep the Republicans out of the elephant graveyard? (October 1978)

. . . And Still Counting by John Bloom ... 152
Why Texas' election system is stuck in the Dark Ages. (January 1979)

Behind the Lines by William Broyles, Jr. ... 154
Why Texas has one of the earliest primary election dates in the country. (May 1978)

III. Institutional Politics

Chapter Seven The One and Only Texas Legislature

The House Is Not a Home by Chase Untermeyer ... 158
What a freshman in the Texas Legislature finds. (September 1977)

The Ten Best and, the Ten Worst Legislators by Paul Burka ... 165
Texas Monthly rates the legislators, for better or worse, in 1979. (July 1979)

Six Crises by Paul Burka ... 179
It was up to the 66th Legislature to solve these problems, and we'll have to live with the solutions. (January 1979)

Big Deal by Paul Burka ... 183
Did the Sharpstown Scandal really make any difference? (January 1976)

Chapter Eight Texas Bureaucracy

Paper Tigers by Mitch Green ... 188
What a tangled web we weave when first we practice bureaucracy. (January 1977)

The Highway Establishment and How It Grew, and Grew, and Grew by Griffin Smith, jr. ... 191
It could be that the roads in Texas are going the wrong way. (April 1974)

The Firing Line by Paul Burka ... 206
The first shot in Clements' campaign to cut 25,000 state employees fells 68 casualties. (April 1979)

Chapter Nine   **Texans in Washington and What They Do There**

Buying Power by Harry Hurt III   210
The new campaign financing law takes the fun out of fundraising. (November 1976)

Grasping at Strauss by Stephen Chapman   213
For Bob Strauss, power is its own reward. (February 1978)

The Big Thicket Tangle by Al Reinert   216
Take three million acres, add politicians, lumber companies, and Time, Inc., and what have you got? A very small park, or no park at all. (July 1973)

IV. The Policy Process

Chapter Ten   **How Some Texas Bills Become Law**

Inside the Lobby by Richard West   226
These veterans of smoke-filled rooms and committee sessions do more to shape state government than most elected officials. (July 1973)

How the New Drug Law Was Made by Griffin Smith, jr.   234
In which Texas comes into the twentieth century, just barely. (September 1973)

There Ought Not to Be a Law by Paul Burka   238
Several laws that ought not to be on the books. (January 1977)

A Penny Saved Is a Penny Earned by Griffin Smith, jr.   242
Unraveling the mysteries of sales tax. (August 1976)

V. Texans and Energy

Chapter Eleven   **Energy and Government**

Pipe Dream by Paul Burka   252
How two powerful lobbies clashed over the coal-slurry pipeline. (August 1977)

So Close, So Far by Paul Burka   257
Bob Krueger almost got the gas deregulation bill through Congress, but almost doesn't count. (April 1976)

Chapter Twelve   **Slick Operators**

Psst . . . Have I Got a Deal for You! by Paul Burka   264
Oil is a slippery business. (March 1979)

Ten Giant Steps to Disaster by Paul Burka   268
How did we get into this sorry energy mess? By making sorry decisions. (August 1979)

Ask Jett Rink by Paul Burka and Nicholas Lemann   270
Straight talk about gasoline supplies, prices, and profits from Texas' most famous wildcatter. (August 1979)

The Real Story Behind the Mexican Gas Deal by John Bloom   272
Gas for a price. (November 1979)

Chapter Thirteen   **Alternate Solutions**

Behind the Lines by William Broyles, Jr.   276
What energy crisis? (June 1978)

Split With the Atom by John Bloom   278
Flipping the switch on nuclear power. (June 1978)

Solar on Ice by Robert Barnstone   280
If you are looking to the sun for an immediate solution to all our energy woes, don't look now. (October 1977)

Texas Politics: Context and Culture

PART ONE

No state in the nation rivals Texas for its raw power, distinct culture, and unique political heritage. The only independent republic to negotiate entrance into the Union, Texas has always seemed a nation within a nation, an expansive empire threatening one moment to conquer America through its mystique, power, and wealth, and the next to secede. The power within Texas is legendary and growing. While great ranches were built within Texas borders during the nineteenth century, the discovery of oil in the twentieth century fueled the growth of immense personal fortunes for yet another set of Texas elites. These land and oil fortunes have diversified into a full range of commercial activity and generated a legal and political system particularly sensitive to business interests and money. The emergence of energy as the dominant economic concern of the late twentieth century has solidified the preeminence of these economic elites and sparked a shift of national and international industry and investment to Texas. As business and commerce have shifted to the Sunbelt, so has national and international power.

The emergence of Texas as a power center has produced considerable tension within its culture and society. The old Texas of cowboys, small towns, and rodeos has become the new Texas of lawyers, big cities, and professional football. These transitions—old to new, individual to corporate, country to city, local to national—have challenged Texans to redefine themselves and integrate their self-perceived individualism into the structured reality of the corporate world. And because Texas itself is not one world, but many, the transitions have been all the more difficult.

The conflict activated by the transformation of Texas from a traditional to a modern state is clearly evident in its politics. Battles among Texas politicians end only when Texans indulge in a tendency to focus their frustrations on the national government. Nowhere in America is the tension between state and nation more apparent than in the politics of Texas. Whether the fight is over control of Texas tidelands or regulation of Texas energy resources, Texans cite the state's unique political heritage as just cause for its supremacy in federal-state relations. Some go so far as to support secession, while others would settle for the perennial dream—Texas dominance in national politics.

Power, culture, heritage—these factors determine the climate of Texas politics. To understand Texas is to understand the overriding influence of this context. The essays in Part I focus on this distinctive political environment and how it shapes the contours of Texas politics. Chapter One describes the power elites in Texas—who they are and how they operate. Chapter Two examines the culture that has spawned such power and the forces of change sweeping through Texas today that challenge the state's historical context. Chapter Three presents the imperial tendency of Texas and Texans and the continuing struggle between state and nation. These articles provide a basis for appreciation of both the state's changing character and the significance of that character for Texas politics.

Power: Texans Who Have It and Use It

CHAPTER ONE

*The Most Powerful Texans, Harry Hurt III
(April 76)
Empires of Paper, Griffin Smith, jr.
(November 73)
So You Want to Be Chairman of Exxon?
Nicholas Lemann (December 78)*

THE MOST POWERFUL TEXANS

by Harry Hurt III

The power game in Texas: how it works and who calls the shots.

Most every workday, after lunching at his favorite corner table in the Ramada Club, George R. Brown walks from the lobby of Houston's First City National Bank Building, across Main Street, and into the old Lamar Hotel, where he takes his afternoon nap. Even at the age of 78, his eyesight failing badly, he moves through the downtown crowd in slow, purposeful strides, his back erect. Short, slim, white-haired, and with striking, arched eyebrows, he might easily be mistaken for a man of only ordinary distinction—a retired congressman, perhaps, or the name partner in some regionally successful accounting firm.

In fact, George Brown was once widely recognized to be *the* most powerful man in Texas. Some ventured that at one time he was *the* most powerful man in the entire nation, and, by extension, the entire world. Even now, despite his age and declining vision, many people think he remains the most potent individual force in the politics and economy of this state and many others.

The hotel suite where Mr. Brown will nap is numbered 8F; it is a place that should be known as one of the "secret" capitals of Texas, a true historical site. There, George Brown and his late brother Herman Brown, co-founders of Brown & Root, used to meet with the likes of the great Jesse H. Jones, builder, publisher, financier, New Deal government lender, and the reigning "Mr. Houston" for over 50 years; Judge James A. Elkins, Sr., a remarkable banker-lawyer often referred to in those days as "the secret government of Texas"; Gus S. Wortham, founder of the largest insurance company in the South; and, later, Lyndon B. Johnson, longtime beneficiary of the Brown political largesse and President of the United States.

These men, who became known to themselves and to other prominent people as the "8F Crowd," called the shots on most major business and political developments in Texas during the Thirties, Forties, Fifties, and much of the Sixties. They would gather in 8F to relax—to drink and play poker—but also to talk politics, exchange ideas, make business decisions, and choose the candidates they would support for public office. ("Lyndon," one or the other would reportedly command, "go fix me a scotch.") Though each member of this all-male crowd was a strong-willed individual, they were, at the same time, a cohesive, like-minded group. Their blessing was the blessing of "The Establishment." Their rule was a virtually unchallenged and—they would emphasize—very "civic-minded" gerontocracy.

Though hardly the hive of activity it once was, 8F still bears the vestiges of that era. On the walls and around the suite are dozens of plaques and personal mementos, including a large picture, taken in the living room, that features the Browns, Jesse Jones, and other members of the 8F Crowd. Otherwise, the place where George Brown naps is a rather typical old hotel suite: two-bedroom, three-bath, with a formal dining room, a living room, kitchen, and hall, permanently rented to and paid for by Brown & Root. "Actually, 8F is probably one of the least attractive of our private suites because it's never been remodeled," says Lamar Hotel manager Edward C. Davis. "But that's the way Mr. Brown wants it. He says, 'Don't touch it. Just leave everything the way it is.'"

That sentiment bears more than a little irony, since of all his contemporaries, George Brown has recognized most clearly that the old 8F days, however memorable, have definitely passed. The government, economy, and population of Texas have grown too large and become too diverse to be controlled by a hotel-room clique, no matter how sagacious or civic-minded. This is not to say that everything now operates openly, just that private individuals and a mere handful of men cannot attain the kind of near-total economic and political dominance that was possible years ago. And no one knows this better than George R. Brown. "You know," he said in a recent interview, "all that power they say I have is just a myth." That, too, may be going a bit far, but the essential question remains: now that Texas has become a modern, urban state, the third-most populous in the nation, who does wield the greatest power and how do they wield it?

A popular method of answering this sort of question is to take a poll asking for the names of "The Ten Most Powerful People in Texas." However, in an

informal survey, more than 30 prominent Texans found themselves hard put to come up with any such definitive list. Significantly, though, several names did keep recurring. They were:
- George R. Brown
- Retired American General chairman Gus S. Wortham
- John Connally
- University of Texas Board of Regents chairman Allan Shivers
- *Houston Post* publisher Oveta Hobby
- First International Bancshares chairman Robert Stewart
- Republic of Texas chairman James Aston
- Texas Instruments founder and former Dallas mayor Erik Jonsson
- Democratic Party chairman Robert Strauss
- Real estate developer Trammell Crow
- Oilman Ed Cox
- First City Bancorporation chairman James Elkins, Jr.
- Banker-developer Walter Mischer
- Former Special Prosecutor Leon Jaworski

A number of younger men also received frequent mention as "up and coming" power holders. Among the most notable of this group were Texas Commerce Bancshares chairman Ben F. Love, Riviana Foods chairman William H. Lane, and Hunt Oil Company heir Ray Hunt.

Beyond this nucleus, the names mentioned encompassed a wide range of corporate executives, entrepreneurs, government officials, labor leaders, and even Baptist ministers and open-heart surgeons. Not too surprisingly, the majority of people nominated as "powerful" live in Houston; Dallas power was often described as "up for grabs" on a local level, while most Dallas potentates—with a few significant exceptions—were judged "not in the same league" as their Houston counterparts. Power brokers in other Texas cities were scarcely mentioned, although the name of San Antonio contractor H. B. Zachry did come up several times. At the same time, it was consistently pointed out that many of the state's most influential citizens—Wortham, Hobby, and Jonsson, for example—are now over 70 years old, and that while they retain considerable potential power, they have generally withdrawn from the very active political and economic roles they once played.

To some extent, these results may reflect the enduring corporate legacy of Houston's old 8F Crowd and/or what many see as a "power vacuum" in the upper echelons of the Texas Democratic Establishment. But they also may show how power has become diffuse and diversified since the end of World War II. In fact, as many of the people contacted in the poll pointed out, it has become extremely difficult to define just what the term "power" means today. Does it simply imply having more money than other people or does it also entail the ability to control votes and public opinion? Is someone powerful just because other people think he is? And what about people who possess special knowledge or technical skill in certain critical areas? One popular Texian notion is that power implies the ability to "get things done"—usually in business and politics—whatever obstacles there may be. But even this definition is vague. Does the ability to get things done in Houston necessarily translate into the ability to get things done in Diboll? How can a Houston power broker be compared, for example, with Arthur Temple, Jr., from Diboll, who owns a controlling interest in Time, Inc.? And, finally, is mere ability to do things enough? Particularly among the younger generation of powerful Texans, the issue is also whether they have the "will" to use their power. Potential power, in other words, may be no power.

There are also some social and historical complications. Prior to World War II, economic power generally dominated political power in Texas, which, in turn, usually held sway over special types of power like labor power and religious power. This is still essentially true, but in recent years groups whose power is rooted in the political process (labor unions, minorities, women, environmentalists) have been sapping power from the state's conservative economic elite. The actual dimensions of their gains is a subject of endless debate, but it is clear these newly franchised groups have at least established their political strength, as the election of Fred Hofheinz as mayor of Houston, the defeat of San Antonio developers in the recent aquifer dispute, and the defeat of the Trinity Canal and other recent Dallas political developments have shown.

At the same time, however, what might be called Big Corporate Power has been extending and strengthening its influence. Big Corporate Power is the highly structured, intricately interwoven brand of economic power held in and wielded through Texas' major banks, corporations, and law firms. These institutions do not just provide fat paychecks for wealthy and potentially powerful executives. They are also our major employers, our major taxpayers, our major product providers, and, alternately, our major troublemakers and civic benefactors. In short, the ascendancy of Big Corporate Power is perhaps the central fact of our postwar economic and political lives. The postwar boom, accelerated recently by the formation of multi-bank holding companies, has displaced older, stereotypically Texian types of power like that of the landed ranching families, the oil-rich wildcatter, and the free-wheeling entrepreneur. Many members of these family groups still retain considerable wealth and influence, but they have gradually become joined with—and in many cases, subordinate to—the Big Corporate structure. Meanwhile, the relocation of national corporations in Texas and the growth of home-based companies have made the dynamics of power within the Big Corporate world more and more complex. The result has been less power to relatively independent personalities like the Murchisons and the Marcuses and more power to institutionally oriented power teams like those centered around the great Dallas banks and the family and corporate descendants of the 8F Crowd.

One of the best ways to make sense of all this is to examine the overall pattern of connections, or "interlocks," between the state's largest corporations and bank holding companies (see chart, page 77). Unfortunately, this approach has been so abused by "investigative" journalists and polemical sociologists that the most useful insights it provides are often overlooked. It is wrong to assume that every director or board of directors always has an effective say in the operation of a particular company. And it is just as wrong to assume that an interlock between two corporations or between a corporation and a bank necessarily constitutes evidence of a dark conspiracy or antitrust violations. Big corporations *need* to do business with big banks because small banks generally do not have adequate capital for their enterprises. And if it so happens that the executives or directors of at least five oil and gas companies sit down at the same table every time Houston's First City Bancorporation holds a board meeting, they can even more easily get together at a men's luncheon club or on the golf course. Still, a look at the relationships between the twenty largest Texas-based corporations and the state's seven billion-dollar bank holding companies can reveal a great deal about who wields power in Texas, provided a sense of history, social context, and actual business practices are kept in mind.

For example, it is immediately apparent that Big Corporate Power in Texas arranges itself along a well-defined Houston-Dallas axis. Nineteen of the twenty largest Texas corporations and six of the seven bank holding companies with assets over $1 billion are located in either Houston or Dallas. Ten of the twenty largest Texas corporations, including Shell and Tenneco, the first and second largest, have their headquarters in Houston. Nine of the twenty largest corporations, including the third, fourth, fifth, sixth, and seventh largest, are based in Dallas. The Tandy Corporation, the state's twentieth-largest corporation, is the only one of the top twenty not based in one of these two cities; its headquarters are in Fort Worth. Nearly all these major corporations are "linked" through a common director to one of the state's billion-dollar bank holding companies. Six of these billion-dollar banks have their main bank in Houston or in Dallas; the other is located in Fort Worth. In the past five years, as these bank holding companies were formed and began acquiring other banks, they made the Houston-Dallas axis even more solid. Large Houston banks like Houston National now are part of Dallas-based holding companies, and vice versa. As Robert Stewart, chairman of the state's largest holding company, First International Bancshares, puts it: "The holding companies have brought the state together. I'm now down in Houston frequently and I have an interest in the city I never had before."

What may not be so readily apparent from simply charting these interlocks is that much more Big Corporate Power emanates from Houston than from Dallas. For example, although the numerical breakdown of the state's twenty largest corporations is about even between the two cities, the ten corporations based in Houston have combined annual sales of roughly $20.5 billion, while the nine corporations based in Dallas have yearly sales of $15.8 billion. Houston also claims more Big Bank money and more total bank deposits than Dallas. Dallas, with the state's two largest billion-dollar bank holding companies, First International Bancshares and Republic of Texas, counts total Big Bank assets of about $10.2 billion. Houston, with four of the state's billion-dollar bank holding companies, has total Big Bank assets of nearly $11 billion. The case for Houston's predominance as a center of power finds even more support when factors like population growth and economic diversity are considered. Not only is Houston already larger and getting larger faster, it also claims solid bases in energy, agriculture, and manufacturing, and the third-busiest port in the nation. Landlocked Dallas, with so much of its business centered around retailing, insurance, and light technology, is not nearly so well blessed.

The deciding factor, however, may well be Houston's giant law firms ("Empires of Paper," TM, November 1973). Houston boasts three of the six largest law firms in the country—Vinson, Elkins, Searls, Connally & Smith; Fulbright & Jaworski; and Baker & Botts. Each now employs about 200 lawyers. Three other smaller Houston firms—Andrews, Kurth, Campbell & Jones; Butler, Binion, Rice, Cook & Knapp; and Bracewell & Patterson—also rank among the largest in the country. Neither Dallas nor any other city except New York has such a formidable legal armada.

The role these big firms play as coordinators, executors, and brokers of Big Corporate Power can hardly be overestimated. In a state where power is seen as the ability to "get things done," they are the place to start. Twelve of the twenty largest corporations in Texas, including at least two based in Dallas, are represented fully or in part by one of the big Houston firms. So are hundreds of other important Texas and national companies. Besides handling every conceivable corporate legal problem, the Houston firms exercise hefty political clout, especially in state government. Their power may be largely derivative—that is, it may originate with their Big Corporate clients—but the lawyers are often the actual power wielders, particularly when power involves getting things done by or through government. Seldom, however, do the partners in the big firms stoop to take so visible a role as public office. Instead, they operate in an unseen way as mediators between their clients and those already in office. They also screen and approve political candidates, allowing—or denying—them access to the true sources of wealth, their Big Corporate clients.

However, the greatest source of power for some of the big Houston firms—and a real key to their role in the overall structure of Big Corporate Power—is their relationship with banks. In Houston, unlike in other cities, the law firms dominate the banks. The most notable of these arrangements involves Vinson, Elkins and First City Bancorp; and Fulbright & Jaworski and Southwest Bancshares. Baker & Botts, the third largest of the Big Three Houston firms, has great influence over many mid-sized banks. In these cases, the power exercised is in no way derivative—it is direct and pervasive.

Given all this, it is not so surprising that the majority of the people most frequently mentioned in the poll as being "the most powerful" in Texas live in Houston. This becomes even less surprising when the historical roots of Big Corporate Power in Texas are explored. At least four of the state's twenty largest corporations and two of its billion-dollar bank holding companies trace their beginnings right back to Houston's 8F Crowd. The key figures initially were Jesse Jones and Judge Elkins. In addition to his many other business exploits, Jones founded the National Bank of Commerce, which ultimately became Texas Commerce Bancshares, the state's fourth-largest bank holding company. During his tenure as Federal Loan Administrator and Secretary of Commerce under FDR, Jones also lent out money that was used to found Tenneco, now the second-largest corporation in the state. Judge Elkins, meanwhile, founded the First City National Bank, the main bank in what is now the state's third-largest bank holding company; he also built his adopted law firm of Vinson & Townes into the great paper empire of Vinson, Elkins, Searls, Connally & Smith. These men soon found themselves with a protégé: Gus S. Wortham, founder of American General, first an insurance company and now a massive multipurpose conglomerate that ranks as the tenth-largest corporation in the state.

However, as George Brown describes it, the real turning point for the 8F Crowd—and the turning point for Big Corporate Power in Texas—came just after World War II when he, Wortham, Charles Francis (of Vinson, Elkins), and others founded Texas Eastern, now the state's twelfth-largest corporation, by buying the Big and Little Inch pipelines from the U.S. government. "We just formed one corporation after another after that," Brown recalls, adding wryly, "Business was more fun in those days."

Indeed it must have been, for the 8F Crowd had by that time gained unequaled influence in state and national government. Through aggressive campaign funding and organizing they launched, elevated, and at times even destroyed the careers of dozens of politicians. Their key cronies were the famous duo of Sam Rayburn as Speaker of the House and Lyndon Johnson as majority leader in the Senate. Later, John Connally took over the Governor's Mansion and LBJ moved into the White House.

The most notorious beneficiary of this politicking was Brown & Root. The company's more famous government-sponsored undertakings include building the NASA Manned Spacecraft Center, drilling the Mohole Project aimed at penetrating the earth's mantle, and building, in a construction consortium, most of the U.S. facilities in Viet Nam, a $900 million cost-plus contract that was the largest ever awarded in the history of the U.S. government. These contracts were just the tip of the iceberg. The 8F Crowd and their friends also cashed in on all sorts of secondary bonanzas stemming from such things as the location of the Space Center (built by Brown & Root on land once owned by Humble Oil) and the offshore drilling experimentation done in the Mohole Project. In 1962, George Brown sold Brown & Root to the Halliburton Company for a reported $37 million. Brown also gained a great deal of stock in the much larger Halliburton and a seat on the board of

THE TOP TWENTY

James Aston, Dallas

George Brown, Houston

John Connally, Houston

Edwin Cox, Dallas

Trammell Crow, Dallas

James Elkins, Jr., Houston

Oveta Culp Hobby, Houston

Ray Hunt, Dallas

Leon Jaworski, Houston

Erik Jonsson, Dallas

William Lane, Sr., Houston

J. Hugh Liedtke, Houston

Ben Love, Houston

Walter Mischer, Houston

John Murchison, Dallas

Allan Shivers, Austin

Robert Stewart III, Dallas

Robert Strauss, Dallas

Gus Wortham, Houston

M. A. Wright, Houston

POWER: TEXANS WHO HAVE IT AND USE IT   15

directors; Brown & Root, meanwhile, continued to operate independently. Later, Brown's longtime associate Herb Frensley joined him on the Halliburton board. The Dallas-based arm of the 8F Crowd's legacy in Big Corporate Power, Halliburton is the state's fourth-largest corporation and the world's largest supplier of oil well equipment.

Today George Brown remains extremely active. He still serves on the boards of Halliburton, Texas Eastern, First City Bancorp, and ITT. He operates at least one of his oil companies, Brownco, and he donates generously to favored political candidates across the state and around the country. But he no longer plays a day-to-day management role at Brown & Root or in many other parts of his economic empire. Power in other portions of the 8F legacy has also become diffused. Judge Elkins' non-lawyer son, James A. Elkins, Jr., sits as chairman of the board of First City Bancorp, but he does not exercise the kind of influence his father did. The dominant men in the law firm of Vinson, Elkins have become John Connally, managing partner A. Frank Smith, and noted tax authority Marvin Collie; Connally sits on the board at First City Bancorp, Collie at First City National. At American General, Gus Wortham's successor, former Chamber of Commerce president Ben Woodson, is already training his successor, Harold Hook. And the Jesse Jones empire is now divided among the Jones family heirs; Houston Endowment (a foundation that owns the *Houston Chronicle*, the Lamar Hotel, and much else); and Texas Commerce Bank, the main bank for Texas Commerce Bancshares.

Meanwhile the political power of the 8F Crowd and its descendants, though still considerable, has apparently been on the wane. The 8F group can still draw on the talents of premier lobbyists like Houston lawyer Searcy Bracewell, but LBJ is dead and gone, the Bentsen candidacy has faltered, and the Texas congressional delegation no longer has the all-white-male-conservative character—or the number of key committee chairmanships—it once held. If certain demographic factors promise to keep increasing Texas' representation along with that of other "sunbelt" states, it is equally significant that the internal dynamics of Texas' national power have become more fragmented and complex. This in and of itself would not present an insurmountable problem save for the fact that the 8F Crowd—like the Democratic Party—hasn't produced a leader who can organize and direct their economic legacy and unite the various political factions.

"The 8F people would really like to have John Connally become their new team captain," observes one Vinson, Elkins lawyer, "but he's more interested in running for president." Worse, Connally must now run as a Republican. But despite the Nixonian blemishes he suffered in his bribery trial, Connally remains, as many Texas businessmen and power brokers put it, "in a class by himself." More charismatic than LBJ ever was, Connally commands a ready conservative political following and draws support from an even larger group of money men. He also possesses a business acumen LBJ never had. "John Connally is *the* man in Texas—both publicly and behind the scenes," declares a high-level business source. The same could never have been said of Lyndon Johnson. Unfortunately for Connally and his supporters, his political party switch may yet deprive him of the one thing (besides more money) he covets: that trip to the White House.

While Connally has "gone national," Walter Mischer, a man of different talents and much more recent ascension, has joined the 8F group. Mischer, 53, is a native of Karnes County who, as a friend put it, "came to town and hustled those city boys pretty good." Though his empire is relatively small by Big Corporate standards, Mischer exercises a personal control that even the most potent Big Corporate executive would envy. Having built his fortune on real estate development, he moved into banking circles, and until recently chaired Allied Bancshares, the state's most profitable bank holding company. He also commands some of the best organized, most aggressively financed political clout in state government (some have called him the "Water District King"). Newer to power, he remains more candid about it. For example, when asked what his support for Ben Barnes had cost him in the fall-out of the Sharpstown Scandal, he reportedly answered, "One hell of an investment in good government." A personal friend of George Brown, Mischer has made frequent visits to suite 8F. "He got so big they had to let him in the club," said one highly placed business source. "Yeah," replied another, "but he doesn't sit on the front row." Whatever the case, Mischer does not quite fill the apparent leadership vacuum in the upper echelons of the old Texas Democratic Establishment.

Instead, the actual exercise of power has fallen to the armies of "nameless" technocrats who man the big law firms and the giant corporate offices. None of these men individually rival a Walter Mischer, but collectively their influence is of unequaled importance in the routine functioning of the economy. These technocrats are now in the midst of a generational transition—some say, feud—which is particularly evident within the big Houston law firms. For years, the middle bracket—men now in their fifties—was passed over as power remained closely held by much older men or was delegated to bright young up and comers. But with the fading of the older generation, the men in the middle bracket have taken the reins and guard their new status jealously. They promise to remain at the top for years to come.

The result is that the power group descended from the 8F Crowd, while still perhaps the most powerful subgroup in Texas Big Corporate Power, is no longer the monolithic supra-Establishment it once was. And George Brown, while still perhaps the most influential man within that faction, no longer wins every battle. The continuing story of Texas Eastern's massive Houston Center project illustrates both the potency and the complexity of George Brown's power today. First, Brown bought up an undeveloped 33-square-block area adjacent to the core of Houston's central business district. Then he persuaded the city fathers to let him build over the streets, obtaining, in the process, the rights to millions of cubic feet of municipally owned air space for what opponents of the project charge is hardly a fraction of its true value; the office and residential complex he is building there will be twice as large as New York's World Trade Center. This was operating that rivaled the Space Center project in style. Later, though, Brown was unable to have Houston's multi-million-dollar sports arena, The Summit, built at Houston Center; instead, The Summit wound up at developer Kenneth Schnitzer's "suburban" Greenway Plaza, an outcome that would not have been possible years ago.

Another well-connected Big Corporate Power group in Houston is the one anchored by Southwest Bancshares, the state's fifth-largest bank holding company; Anderson, Clayton, the state's fourteenth-largest corporation; and the law firm of Fulbright & Jaworski. The central figures here include Leon Jaworski, who sits on the board of both the bank and the corporation, and A. G. McNeese, a former partner in the law firm who is chairman of the board of the bank. They have a very close—some say too close—relationship with the $45-million M. D. Anderson Foundation, of which Jaworski and several of his law partners have been both trustees and lendees. Jaworski's aging law partner John H. Freeman is the director of the M. D. Anderson Foundation; he also sits on the board of the First City National Bank. Jaworski also used to sit on the board of Coastal States, which, despite its LoVaca gas troubles, ranks eighth among the state's twenty largest corporations.

But even in light of the immense prestige he gained as Special Prosecutor and his obviously lucrative bank-law firm interlock, some of Jaworski's close friends said that he should not be counted among the ten or twelve most powerful men in the state. "He's certainly in the top twenty," said one, "but I wouldn't place him above that." Though clearly a potent and persuasive man, Jaworski's subgroup and his own role within it do not match the 8F group and the parts played by men like Brown and Connally. (An interesting sidelight is the animosity resulting from Connally's bribery trial. Months afterward, Connally and his supporters remain embittered because Jaworski did not put a stop to the whole affair before it ever reached the trial stage.)

Of course, from a slightly different perspective, the most important subgroup in Big Corporate Power is neither 8F nor the Jaworski group nor the Dallas banks, but Big Oil. Six of the top ten and eleven of the twenty largest corporations in Texas, including the first and second largest, deal primarily in oil and gas or related industries. Eight of these Big Oil corporations have their home offices in Houston. Exxon, the world's largest corporation, is not strictly considered a Texas-based company, but its largest subsidiary, Exxon USA (formerly Humble Oil) headquarters in Houston. With Tenneco, the state's second-largest corporation, Exxon is probably the most active in the politics and economy of the state, a major real estate owner and lobbying force as well as a multinational concern. "When Exxon hollers 'froggy,' everybody else jumps," declares one well-connected Houston oil and gas attorney.

Of course, the 8F group does exercise leverage over Big Oil. Exxon USA and three of the six oil companies among the state's ten largest corporations have officers or directors who serve on the board of directors of First City Bancorp. George Brown himself sits on the board of two of these companies. Tenneco and El Paso Company share directors with Texas Commerce Bank. Alfred C. Glassell of El Paso Company sits on the First City Bancorp board, and Exxon USA is represented by president M. A. "Mike" Wright, who also sits on the board of the parent Exxon corporation. There are matrimonial ties as well: First City Bancorp chairman Jim Elkins is married to Margaret Wiess, a daughter of Humble Oil cofounder Harry Wiess. Exxon presidents and chairmen come and go, passing in and out of office like corporate politicians, but these connections remain.

Ironically, Shell, the largest Texas-based corporation, is probably the least interested in local and state affairs. Having just moved its headquarters to Texas in 1970, Shell is controlled by Royal Dutch/Shell in the Netherlands. Its primary concerns are national and international. Its major Houston-based project consists of a 544-acre real estate development near the Astrodome called Plaza del Oro. Outgoing Shell president Harry Bridges is perhaps the best example of how power in much of the Big Corporate world resides in the office, and not in the man. A wiry, soft-spoken Englishman who worked his way up through the company ranks, Bridges theoretically controls the greatest single Big Corporate institution in Texas. "But in reality, his job is more like a PR man's," observed a close friend who is the chief executive of another not quite so large Texas corporation. "He's done a great job for Shell, but he doesn't know what's really going on throughout the company. And there's no way he could. It's just too big." Unlike George Brown, Bridges is not an executive who holds a controlling stock interest in his own corporation, and is thus much more at the mercy of stockholders and executives. Bridges must step down this spring because he will reach Shell's mandatory retirement age—60. If George Brown had been forced to retire at that same age, he would have missed out on the Manned Spacecraft Center, the Mohole Project, the Halliburton deal, and the entire Johnson presidency. In the game of Texas power a man 60 years old has barely finished his rookie season.

Another notable Houston power group consists of Republican oilmen J. Hugh Liedtke, William T. Liedtke, and Robert A. Mosbacher. Generous Nixon contributors, the Liedtke brothers were temporarily the subject of national news early in the Watergate scandal when it was discovered that a large portion of the money in Watergate burglar Bernard Barker's bank account had been flown from Houston to Washington on Pennzoil's corporate jet; somewhat less publicized was the fact that both the brothers and Pennzoil were later cleared of any wrongdoing by Representative Wright Patman's subcommittee and by a federal grand jury. The Liedtkes' claim to fame in the Big Corporate world is less clouded. With now CIA chief George Bush, they made an old-fashioned postwar fortune from oil discoveries in West Texas' Permian Basin. Then, as Bush entered public service, the Liedtkes engineered a startling series of mergers that eventually created the giant Pennzoil, currently the state's eleventh-largest corporation. Also an influential Republican contributor with family and financial ties to the East, their friend Robert Mosbacher has made his money in independent oil operations from Texas to the Philippines. He currently serves as President Ford's campaign finance chairman; his brother, America's Cup sailor Emil "Bus" Mosbacher, was President Nixon's chief of protocol. But while Mosbacher and the Liedtkes share most of the basic values of the 8F group, their officially Republican affiliation sets them apart from the mainstream Democratic Establishment. Consequently, many feel their clout in Washington is far greater than any power they could hope to attain in their own home state. The Liedtke brothers thus received frequent mention in the poll, but were usually described as "not quite in the top ten."

At the Dallas end of the Big Corporate axis, power is much more scattered and, generally speaking, more local in nature. There are few men in Dallas whose status as state and national power wielders really compares with that of Houston potentates, and Dallas businessmen, despite their overarching civic-mindedness and municipal boosterism, will privately admit it. "Houston is just more outward looking than Dallas," says a longtime Dallas Establishment leader. "The oil business and the port force Houston to look beyond its borders—that's one reason we built DFW airport. Dallas, on the other hand, is a more conventional business center based on banking, insurance, and retail. Landlocked cities usually look inward and Dallas is no exception. The Texans with national and state power—the Cabinet members, the ambassadors, the governors, the senators—none of them seem to come from Dallas."

Big Corporate Power in Dallas revolves primarily around the big banks, First International and Republic of Texas, the state's first and second largest holding companies. Before holding companies hit Texas, their root banks— First National and Republic—formed the cornerstones of one of the most tightly knit municipal Establishments in America. Self-made, small-town-born men like Nate Adams of First National and Fred Florence of Republic not only built their own banking empires, they also guided the development of the surrounding oil fields, the growth of local corporations, and the overall destiny of the city. With R. L. "Bob" Thornton, Sr., of the Mercantile Bank, they also formally organized the Dallas Establishment when they founded the Dallas Citizens Council. Through that organization and the larger, more conventionally political Citizens Charter Association (CCA), Dallas' influential bankers and other corporation heads joined together to control virtually all major political and economic developments in Dallas from 1937 up to the present.

Today the big banks remain the foremost centers of power in the city, and their top men are still among the most widely respected leaders in Dallas and in the entire state. At First International, the mantle has been passed to Robert H. Stewart III, a smooth, well-tailored 50-year-old whose grandfather also served as chairman of the board. Groomed for power since he was a young man, Stewart was named more frequently than any other Dallasite as one of the "most powerful" people in Texas. On a day-to-day basis, he shares internal bank responsibilities with president Dewey Presley, but he is clearly the top man. "There can be no discussion of it," a well-known Dallas developer observed. "In Dallas, Bobby Stewart is *it*." Equally influential in the eyes of many is Republic chairman James Aston, a transitional figure between the second and third generations of Dallas bankers. At the age of 64, he has delegated some measure of authority to four younger men—James Keay, Charles Pistor, James Berry, and William Hatfield—but he remains the father figure, the unifier, and the scion of the public good. "Our purpose," Aston has said, "is to build the country, not just to make money." Aston is famous for being able to raise large sums of money almost effortlessly, most often for his favorite charity, Southwestern Medical School.

Unfortunately for Dallas, however, other traditional elements of Dallas power, particularly retail, have suffered an actual decline in power in recent years as absentee owners have bought out some great local institutions. The Neiman-Marcus chain, for example, is now a subsidiary of Carter, Hawley, Hale of New York; Sanger Harris belongs to Federated Department Stores, and Titche's to Allied Corporation of New York. The *Dallas Times Herald* has become a part of Otis Chandler's *Times-Mirror* empire, and in nearby Fort Worth, Amon Carter, Sr.'s power base, the *Fort Worth Star-Telegram* is now owned by Capital Cities Communications of New York. Meanwhile, the advent of single-member districts has eroded the political power of the CCA. In fact, for the first time in recent memory, no candidate for mayor or city council in the upcoming special city election even wants a CCA endorsement (see "Reporter," page 14).

"I think the disaffection for the Establishment is a little exaggerated," says one longtime Dallas potentate. "The CCA is interested in the good of Dallas and that's all. If they have to take a back seat in an election, they will. I know that sounds too goody-goody, but it's true. Still, I don't think there's any doubt that there has been a significant diffusion of power here." One of the most dramatic illustrations of the changed nature of Dallas power was the defeat of the Trinity River Canal project, Dallas' proposed link to the Gulf of Mexico, despite the all-out efforts of Establishmentarians like food chain executive Robert Cullum, insurance man Ben H. Carpenter, and second-generation Fort Worth magnate Amon Carter, Jr.

The character of power in Dallas is further illustrated by the men who help form the connections between the city's big banks and major corporations. Most have bases independent of the Big Corporate structure and remarkably little interest in exerting leverage over it. Trammell Crow, a man said to own more real property than any other individual in the United States, represents this type. Crow sits on the boards of First International, Zale, and Campbell Taggart, but his money and power come from real estate development. He possesses numerous high-level political connections—in fact, when President Ford last visited Dallas, he spent some time at Crow's house—but, as a friend of Crow observed, "Trammell sticks pretty much to his own business. He'll give big political contributions but he doesn't get involved much beyond that." The same holds for independent oilman Edwin L. Cox. A director of both LTV and First International, Cox owns some of the greatest oil and gas production outside the majors. "No one really knows how much money Ed Cox has," says one Dallas business leader, "but he's definitely in the Big Rich." Still, Cox does not normally exercise the potentially political clout his wealth provides. Instead, he devotes what might otherwise be political portions of his time to his activities as chairman of the board of Southern Methodist University, and to raising funds for charity.

Of course, Dallas does boast an important national power in Robert Strauss. A former member of the State Banking Board and old friend and political associate of John Connally, Strauss has both economic clout—through the legal-financial operations managed by his brother Ted—and political clout by virtue of his position as Democratic Party chairman. He can quite quickly get men like George Brown on the phone—for advice, for money, for whatever—and he knows it. Dallas also has a figure of increasing statewide prominence in Jess Hay, chairman of Lomas & Nettleton Financial Corporation, the largest mortgage company in the United States. A long-time political activist, Hay headed Governor Dolph Briscoe's 1974 campaign fund-raising effort; he is also a Democratic national committeeman, and, at the age of 45, still young enough to have a great deal ahead of him. However, despite the fact that he exhibits unusual insight into the ever-increasing importance of simply being able to get a "fair hearing" from the government bureaucracies, he has yet to attain the leadership status of Strauss and the big bankers.

Meanwhile, those great Dallas leaders of recent yesteryears—men like Erik Jonsson and developer John Stemmons—are now getting old, and, as many see it, "fading into the sunset." They could still exercise enormous power and influence if they chose, but they have gradually retired from the business and political scenes to devote their spare time to assorted "good works." In their wake, young men like Ross Perot, Jimmy Ling, and Sam Wyly come and go, shooting to great heights and falling back even faster, never really achieving the status of the established and the accepted. As one Dallas executive observed, "There's no one around today who could get another Dallas/Fort Worth airport built the way Jonsson did."

Jonsson himself—who if Jesse Jones was "Mr. Houston" has surely been "Mr. Dallas"—characteristically disagrees with this sort of dire prophecy for the future of Dallas leadership. "Building a new city hall or even a new airport is easy," Jonsson said in a recent interview. "Those are managerial problems, the sort of problems someone with corporate experience is trained to handle. The original leadership of the city ran big companies, and so had I. We were used to thinking that way. The *big* problems are people problems, and those sort of problems—take desegregation, for example—keep getting harder." Jonsson's Texas Instruments is one of the most spectacularly successful homegrown corporations, so successful, in fact, that Jonsson was named one of 29 businessmen in *Fortune* magazine's Business Hall of Fame. Jonsson built TI with the help of loans from Fred Florence at Republic, and when he was asked to run for mayor of Dallas in the wake of the Kennedy assassination, his gratitude and civic spirit made it impossible to say no. Jonsson ran Dallas like a well-oiled corporation: goals were set, plans devised, resources allocated. In the process, the city lifted its sights from the trauma of Dealey Plaza. By taking so prominent a political position, Jonsson was following in a tradition of direct political participation first set by R. L. Thornton, who was mayor in the Fifties. None of Houston's 8F Crowd ever became so directly involved in local politics. The current generation of Dallas potentates seems convinced those days are over. When James Aston, Fred Florence's successor at Republic, was asked to run for mayor in 1974, he refused. John Schoellkopf, a young Establishment investor, was the best candidate the CCA could come up with. He lost. In the days of Adams, Florence, and Thornton, that would never have happened.

No one understands better than Jonsson what the growing influence of Big Corporate Power is going to mean for

Dallas. "I can look out my window and see buildings going up all over Dallas, some of them ten, fifteen miles to the north. Those buildings represent great new power, the power of growing corporations and new corporations coming in. The people who run those corporations are going to help Dallas by helping our economy. They're going to be busy with making their corporations grow, but they're not going to be able to afford to let their headquarters city go to hell in a hand basket. That's how I'll get them to lend a hand." But other Dallas observers are convinced the new corporate heads are going to shrink away from the really thorny problems, and will instead busy themselves with pure good works. "Sure, they'll do what some of the older people like [John] Stemmons and [Robert] Cullum do now. They'll make sure the United Fund drive doesn't fail, they'll get behind the bond issues. But that will be it," says a longtime member of the Citizens Council. "But they won't be able to get anything done, and they may not even want to. People just aren't as interested in the classic Dallas sort of power anymore."

One young man who shows great promise, however, is 32-year-old Ray Hunt, an heir to Hunt Oil Company and the sole executor of H. L. Hunt's billion-dollar estate. "He's the only likely new George Brown on the horizon," said one seasoned Democratic power. Traditionally, the Hunts have remained outside the Dallas Establishment and mainstream civil affairs, as the family's cantankerous arch-conservatism and old man Hunt's myriad eccentricities offset the potential influence their money would seem to imply. But lately, Ray Hunt has emerged an apparent winner in the struggle between the children of the old man's first marriage (among them Herbert, Bunker, and Kansas City Chiefs owner Lamar) and the children of the second marriage (Ray and three sisters). He has become active with various projects at SMU, started *D* magazine, and participated in financing the Reunion project, aimed at revitalizing his city's downtown core. "Frankly, the Hunts haven't always been very good citizens," a prominent Dallas businessman observed, "but this young man Ray is really first class. He's responsive and very intelligent. I think he's really going to be a comer."

Recently, Hunt's associate Walter Human and home-builder David Fox have helped form a promising organization called the Dallas Alliance. A triracial group with a number of young Establishment members, the Alliance has come up with a desegregation plan for the city's schools. Despite initial setbacks this effort suggests that Dallas might soon find itself with a more modern successor to the old Citizens Council, but with more realistic goals and a broader political base.

In addition to the Houston-Dallas axis, the web of Big Corporate Power in Texas has an important Austin arm: the University of Texas System. Not too surprising, the importance—and power—of this ostensibly educational institution derives from money. With an endowment of over $1 billion, the University of Texas is the second-richest institution of higher learning in the world. The Permanent University Fund, itself just a portion of the total wealth, accounts for $792 million. If the University's endowment money were considered bank assets, it would rank as one of the largest bank holding companies in the state. The people who control this enormous financial empire, supposedly in trust for the people of Texas, are the members of the Board of Regents, a group endowed with almost total power over University affairs. They have the final say on everything from appointment of professors and teacher salaries to the granting of the lucrative and multitudinous construction contracts for expansion programs totaling over $700 million in the last ten years alone.

The most nationally famous member of the UT Board of Regents is Lady Bird Johnson, who herself wields considerable moral authority when she chooses; the most powerful, however, is the Regents chairman, former Governor Allan Shivers. Shivers is the quintessential Establishment figure, an old Austin banking and political crony of the 8F Crowd (even through his long feuds with Lyndon Johnson), and consistently nominated as one of the most powerful people in Texas. "Governor Shivers could be even more influential than he is now," a friend observed, "if only he chose to be." His most obvious interlocks with Big Corporate Power have been seats on the boards of two billion-dollar bank holding companies, Texas Commerce Bancshares and (until recently) Capital National Bank, both of which are located in Houston. He is currently the chairman of Austin National Bank in Austin.

Also intimately tied to Big Corporate Power is media power. In Houston, both major dailies, the *Chronicle* and the *Post*, one major television station, KPRC, and two major radio stations, KPRC and KTRK, have direct present and historical ties to members of the 8F Crowd. In fact, at one point during the Depression, Jesse Jones owned both Houston newspapers and two of the radio stations. He kept the *Chronicle* and KTRK, now the property of his Houston Endowment Foundation and nephew John T. Jones, Jr., but sold the *Post* and KPRC to his friend, Governor William P. Hobby, at a bargain price. (Hobby was then in the midst of hard times financially.)

Today Oveta Culp Hobby, the former governor's wife, still reigns as chairman of the board of the Houston Post Company. She is truly a remarkable woman who could exert great influence by the force of her intelligence and personality alone. But she also happens to have great oil wealth and a son who is the lieutenant governor of Texas. She was the only woman repeatedly nominated as one of the most powerful people in Texas. A parliamentarian in the Texas House before she married, Mrs. Hobby became the second woman in U.S. history to hold Cabinet rank; she headed the Department of Health Education and Welfare under President Eisenhower. Though not privy to the stag card games in 8F, she nevertheless shared in much of the decision making before as well as after her husband's death. Noted for her custom of wearing hats —particularly high, wide-brimmed ones and flat berets—Mrs. Hobby is said by her friends to have "a man's mind." When the management of Texas Commerce Bank recently polled the board of directors about the possibility of including a woman on the board, the directors' near-unanimous response was, "Fine, as long as it's Oveta."* Needless to say, she is a frequent luncheon companion of George Brown; Brown's interest in media power is partly manifested by his membership on the board of Southland Paper, the nation's second-largest manufacturer of newsprint.

In Dallas, on the other hand, the lever for power Ted Dealey made of the *Dallas Morning News* is seldom used by his son Joe. The Dealey family trust breaks up by law in August 1976; what will happen then is uncertain. The *Dallas Times Herald* is now owned by the Times-Mirror Corporation of Los Angeles. Its young publisher, Tom Johnson, seems determined to make his influence felt in Dallas through his editorial page instead of through active involvement in Establishment politics. Former publisher Jim Chambers, described by some observers as the most selflessly dedicated of the classic Dallas Establishment people, continues with his civic work, but even he is less personally involved than he once was.

Representatives of older, more typically Texian types of power—the second- and third-generation oil rich and the old ranch families also participate

---

* The bank position eventually went not to Mrs. Hobby but to another woman whose intelligence is greatly admired in Houston business circles, Mrs. John Blaffer. The daughter of Dallas banker Wirt Davis, a cofounder of Republic Trust and Savings Bank, Blaffer is a Phi Beta Kappa from Wellesley. Her late husband, another Humble Oil heir, was also a member of the Texas Commerce board.

in the world of Big Corporate Power. In Houston, W. S. Farish III, grandson of one of the Humble Oil Company founders, sits on the boards of both Houston Natural Gas, the state's fifteenth-largest corporation, and Capital National Bank, the main bank of Federated Capital Corporation. Corbin J. Robertson, president of Quintana Petroleum and guardian of the Cullen family interests, serves on the board of First City Bancorp and has organized recent lobbying efforts by independent oil men. In Dallas, John Murchison provides an interlock between LTV and First International Bancshares; his son John, Jr., is a lawyer at Vinson, Elkins. But despite their obvious personal and financial gifts, these types of men have generally left the more active—and certainly the more visible—political roles to others. At the same time, many of those who would like to continue as independent oil operators feel themselves stymied by the federal government and changing times. "Their frustration is enormous," observed one oil and gas attorney. "They would like to be more active, but they don't know what they can do." The old ranch families, meanwhile, are in the midst of urbanization and division, but the most alert of them have linked up with Big Corporate Power. Ambassador to Great Britain Anne Armstrong, for example, is on the board of First City Bancorporation and Robert Shelton of the King Ranch is on the board of Texas Commerce Bancshares.

The most curious quantity in Texas power is Dolph Briscoe, a second-generation rural potentate who has risen to the governor's office. He could, simply by virtue of his wealth and the position he holds, rank among the most powerful people in Texas. However, he appears uninterested in exercising even the most routine powers of his office. His list of campaign contributors—a group dominated by men from Texas Instruments and other large corporations—makes clear his affiliation with Big Corporate Power; his own preferences, however, seem to be for the clean and simple air of his Uvalde ranch and not for the urban power centers. By and large, he is irrelevant to modern Texas power and represents a throwback to an earlier, more rural state.

Almost as curious is U.S. Senator Lloyd Bentsen. An old-line Establishmentarian schooled by the great Sam Rayburn, Bentsen retains considerable economic power because of his family's wealth and his previous Big Corporate connections, but he may have burned up a great deal of his political clout in his recent bid for the Democratic presidential nomination. His vote against the oil depletion allowance infuriated his many oil business supporters, and so have other politically expedient (and no doubt temporary) shifts leftward. He will probably win re-election to the Senate—if not a place on the national ticket—but his status as a power wielder has undoubtedly been diminished. In fact, Bentsen's two principal supporters, Ben Love and Bill Lane, both younger and newer to power than the senator, were far more frequently mentioned as being among the most powerful people in Texas, especially by those in the Big Corporate world.

A native of Vernon, Ben Love came to Houston shortly after World War II and founded a paper products manufacturing plant, which he operated for seventeen years. In the mid-Sixties, he moved into banking, first with River Oaks Bank and Trust, then with Texas Commerce Bank. By 1969, he had become president of Texas Commerce Bank, and in 1972 he was named chairman and chief executive officer of both the bank and the bank holding company. Affable, articulate, and—of no small importance—a University of Texas graduate, Love, 51, seems to embody the most highly valued qualities of the new Big Corporate leader. Under Love's leadership Texas Commerce made the transition from bank to bank holding company, and now ranks as the fourth-largest bank holding company in Texas. Meanwhile, Love himself has taken an active role as a Bentsen fund raiser, and is the manager of Bentsen's personal finances, now held in "blind trust" while Bentsen holds public office.

Equally admired in Houston business circles is Love's close personal friend, Bill Lane. Like Love, the 52-year-old Lane has enjoyed an almost meteoric rise. A native of Tennessee, Lane came to Houston in 1959 as president of River Brand Rice Mills, Inc. Before long, however, he built River Brand into Riviana Foods, a multinational with emphasis on rice and specialty foods. Now twenty-sixth in size in the state, Riviana markets such diverse goods as Russian caviar and Kosher meats, the latter being a product of Riviana's Hebrew National Division. A generous contributor to conservative political candidates of both major parties, Lane was the campaign chairman for Bentsen's presidential effort.

Though real estate developers like Gerald D. Hines of Houston and Trammell Crow of Dallas may have a greater influence over the shaping of our environment, it is men like Ray Hunt, Love, and Lane who will play the greatest future individual roles in determining the underlying politics and economy. But, despite their many talents, none of them will likely attain the status of a Jesse Jones or a George Brown, and this is in no way to their detriment. As Oveta Hobby points out, "The art of running a business takes so much more time now." One can no longer set up one corporation after another as the 8F Crowd used to do, without facing a host of federal regulations and soaring overhead costs. And leverage over the political process has become ever more difficult to gain.

Along this same line, it is important to note that the overall structure of Big Corporate Power in Texas exists in the larger national and international context. Relationships on this level are even more complex, but the New York banks and the Washington bureaucracy clearly occupy central institutional roles. Texas' billion-dollar bank holding companies must look to their much larger Eastern counterparts—Chase Manhattan, First National City, Morgan Guaranty—as correspondent banks and regular sources of back-up funds. Large Texas-based corporations must also look to the big New York banks as well as to insurance companies and investment banking firms in order to obtain enough capital for many of their projects. In fact, the largest stockholders in most of Texas' largest corporations are these Eastern financial institutions. From this perspective, the Rockefeller family, who dominate Chase Manhattan and much else, should receive due consideration as being among the most powerful people in Texas, especially since the Vice President has established a partial claim to residency by virtue of purchasing a South Texas ranch.

On the other hand, the central domestic conflict of our time may well be the struggle between Big Corporate Power and Big Government. With each passing day, businessmen complain of more power being transferred from the private sector to the public sector and of ever increasing bureaucratic interference in their affairs. Once they sought to control government; now the emphasis is on a "fair hearing." At the same time, however, the public learns of seemingly endless corporate transgressions—from pay-offs for local sheriffs to bribes for foreign diplomats —and hears evidence of monopolistic concentrations in one major industry after another. While businessmen see regulatory agencies as a bungling and unmerciful "Establishment" in its own right, the private citizen often sees these agencies co-opted by those who are to be regulated, and wonders who, after all, does rule—the government or the Big Corporate bloc.

Recent Mideast oil developments have also added an international dimension to the "Who rules?" question: is it us or the Arabs? Should the Shah of Iran or some other person like Sheik Yamani now be included among the most powerful people in Texas because of their enormous influence over the state's most important industry? Clearly, their price hikes and political policies have made the state's already giant energy corporations even bigger and more crucial to the U.S. economy.

These, then, are the main outlines and many of the important faces in the structure of Big Corporate Power in Texas. If examining their interlocks does not quite include all the powerful organizations and power holders, it at least provides the essential schematics of the state's dominant political and economic force. And it is critical to understand that the state's largest corporations, banks, and law firms—whatever their internal differences—do operate as a unified force, dancers to the same tune. The source of this unity is far deeper than interlocking directors and political party affiliations. It lies instead in a more general identity of economic interests—exemplified by the eternal struggle to preserve a "good business climate"—and in shared educational and social backgrounds. For the most part, the state's most powerful men give the impression of being almost too gentlemanly, too soft-spoken for their roles. Seldom do they display the fist-pounding and stentorian tones commonly associated with being "aggressive." They don't have to. An Allan Shivers, a George Brown, an Erik Jonsson need never raise his voice; people seem to listen anyway.

While they may be business rivals, the leaders of Big Corporate Power also enjoy a common social life. Each major city has its hierarchy of men's luncheon clubs like the City Club in Dallas, and the Ramada and Coronado clubs in Houston, and a similar hierarchy of country clubs: Brook Hollow, River Oaks, Houston Country Club. These are not merely convenient places to eat the midday meal or attractive family recreation spots, but true business and political centers, and it is as such that they thrive.

"The Ramada Club is probably the new 8F," observes a senior member of one of Houston's leading law firms. Though he speaks with expected bias toward his hometown, he may well be right. There is no other place in Texas where so many people nominated as the most powerful in Texas meet so often and for such extended periods. On any given workday, the main dining room will be crowded with the state's most prestigious Big Corporate figures: John Connally may be lunching with James Elkins or Marvin Collie. Allan Shivers, Robert Stewart, or James Aston may be in town for a meeting of the board of one of their banks. There will be some major oil company executives in the room, perhaps a few Arab faces now, and a host of other Big Corporate officers. George Brown will usually be there, seated at his favorite right corner table, a vantage point from which he can face anyone who enters the room. On the occasions when he lunches with Oveta Hobby, friends can be seen passing by their table, imparting a respectful greeting and bowing noticeably. Meanwhile, in the men's grill, other executives will be eating at "the round table" or drinking and playing cards much as the old 8F Crowd did in the Lamar Hotel.

After business hours, the Ramada Club often becomes the site of more easily recognizable political activities—a candidate review or a campaign fund raiser—usually in cocktail party form. "A ticket to a cocktail party at the Ramada Club is a one-way ticket to a contribution," observed the scion of one of the big Houston law firms. He went on to point out, very much amused, that article three of the Ramada Club House Rules specifically states that "the Club shall not be used for sectarian or political meetings." But then power, in the last analysis, may simply mean the ability to break such rules, even if they are one's own. ★

EMPIRES OF PAPER

by Griffin Smith, jr.

Three of the nation's largest law firms are in Houston. They have kept their awesome power, their pervasive influence, and their closed societies out of the public eye. Until now.

Three of the ten biggest law firms in the United States are located in Houston. Two of them rank as number three and number four. In the past two months they have overtaken several Manhattan giants that were doyens of American law for decades before the men who lead the Texas firms were even born; their phenomenal growth shows no signs of slowing down. They are the talk of the legal profession.

These are the Big Three of Houston law:

• Vinson, Elkins, Searls, Connally & Smith (186 lawyers).

• Fulbright, Crooker & Jaworski (185 lawyers).

• Baker & Botts (160 lawyers).

Roughly two fifths of the lawyers in each firm are partners, meaning they are senior men who own the institution and share its profits. The rest are associates, younger men who work as salaried employees pending promotion to partnership status. There are currently 68 partners at Vinson Elkins, 69 at Fulbright Crooker, and 66 at Baker & Botts. The only firms in the country that remain larger than the two biggest Houston mammoths are the Wall Street firms of Shearman & Sterling with 226 lawyers; and Dewey, Ballantine, Bushby, Palmer & Wood with 197. No one outside New York is any longer even close: there is nothing in Chicago, Los Angeles, Philadelphia, Boston, or

Washington to match them.

Nor is there anything in Texas either. Dallas has five firms over 30, but none over 45. San Antonio, Fort Worth, and Austin trail far behind. Houston lawyers speak of an "amoeba complex" that regularly causes Dallas firms to split into separate factions just as they approach the 50 mark. It doesn't happen in Houston.

Their elaborate structure of specialized departments and sections is a far cry from the days of the country lawyer who hung out his shingle on the courthouse square. Though the labels differ from firm to firm, each of the Big Three offers specialists in corporate finance, banking, patent law, utilities, real estate, labor, admiralty, bankruptcy, tax, wills, trusts, and public law. They also have a separate breed of trial lawyers, men who would not think of trading the rough-and-tumble of the courtroom for any sort of office practice.

Houston's Big Three have a national reputation for top-quality legal work. Local lawyers may sometimes joke about the big firms' peculiarities, but no one underestimates their skill at handling the law. A successful Houston small-firm trial lawyer who opposes big firms in courtrooms all across the country says flatly, "The lawyers I face from the big firms here in Houston are the best anywhere. They're better than Wall Street, far better than O'Melveny & Myers [the top Los Angeles firm]. By and large, they've got the finest talent in the country." Even discounted for a little Texas brag, the statement is not far wrong, judging from the opinions of their colleagues in bar associations nationwide.

22 POWER: TEXANS WHO HAVE IT AND USE IT

Illustrated by Justin Carroll

The Big Six: A Floor Plan of Houston Law

There are those who will argue that Houston law is dominated not by the Big Three but by the Big Five—or, as some would have it, the Big Six. The massive bulk of the giants does tend to obscure the fact that several other firms do a similar sort of legal practice with enough lawyers to make them giants in their own right if they were located in San Antonio, Dallas, or almost any other American city.

The oldest and most aristocratic of these middle-sized firms is Andrews, Kurth, Campbell & Jones, an exclusive group of 65 lawyers with many of the attributes of a social club. Very ingrown, they seldom fraternize with other members of the Houston bar. "It's like a closed fraternal order," says a successful solo practitioner who spent several years in another of the big firms. "They go to retreats together, that sort of thing. They judge your looks and your wife before they hire you—they take only handsome lawyers. They come to work late, and they quit early."

They are also more paternal than others: once accepted into the fold, a young lawyer is virtually assured of lifetime security without the desperate competition that characterizes the ladder of success elsewhere. Andrews Kurth once shared the cream of the Houston practice with Baker & Botts, but after the death of its driving force, Colonel Frank Andrews, in 1936, it threatened to wither on the vine.

In the past fifteen years, however, it has come back strongly and is now generally regarded as having one of the finest collections of legal ability in the city. It is also considered suffocatingly conservative, even by conservatives. Political involvement is strenuously discouraged, with a conspicuous exception for Hall Timanus, the onetime chairman of the Wallace-for-President forces in Texas. For years the firm's biggest client has been Howard Hughes's Hughes Tool Company. Among their other major clients is the Missouri Pacific Railroad. The dominant figures in the firm today are Mickey West and Harry Jones.

Although the firm of Butler, Binion, Rice, Cook & Knapp comprises 85 lawyers, it has been described as "a small firm that happens to have a lot of people in it." Formed in the 1940s, it has never gone in for representation of large corporate clients whose work requires concentrated teamwork, and therefore has developed into a collection of feudal fiefdoms instead of a monolithic empire. Each lawyer reputedly has his own set of articles of incorporation, for example.

One consequence of this informality, individualism, and lack of tradition has been a certain unevenness in the quality of the legal talent there. The firm has some very able lawyers at the top, and others who are not so able. "They've got 50 per cent good lawyers and 50 per cent bad lawyers, and they don't know which are which," is the harsh judgment of a lawyer in the Big Three. Their attrition rate is admittedly high; good lawyers like Bob Singleton, Bill Wright, and Percy Williams have departed for greener pastures. On the other hand, no major Houston firm has a more distinguished record of elevating its partners to the bench. James Noel, a federal district judge in Houston; Malcolm Wilkey, circuit judge on the U.S. Court of Appeals which heard the White House tapes appeal; and state district judge Bill Blanton, are the most notable. As might be expected from such an individualistic firm, Butler Binion is far more tolerant and flexible about the political involvement of its members. Partners and associates are readily granted leaves of absence for political work. Steve Oaks, a partner, currently serves as executive assistant to Lieutenant Governor Bill Hobby, and Jonathan Day acted as campaign manager for Houston mayoral candidate Fred Hofheinz. Since the November 1972 death of the firm's remarkable managing partner, trial lawyer Jack Binion, its dominant figures have been B. Hunter Loftin and the "name" partners, Frank J. Knapp, Cecil N. Cook, and George W. Rice. It continues to do vast quantities of probate work, and counts among its clients the Bank of Texas.

With the Big Three, Andrews Kurth and Butler Binion make up Houston's traditional "Big Five." But the explosive growth of another business-oriented firm, Bracewell & Patterson, has stirred talk of a new "Big Six." It has more than doubled in size in the last four years and now stands at 42 lawyers. Plans are being made to hire 15 more next year. "It's a supergrowth firm, just going like crazy," says a wide-eyed solo practitioner. B&P's aggressiveness has clearly (and probably understandably) not met with the favor of the older, larger firms—in particular not with Baker & Botts, from whom B&P alienated the affections of an exceptionally able lawyer, Ed Marston, to strengthen their corporate department. The older firm steadfastly refuses to acknowledge B&P's aspirations to major firm status. They dealt the upstarts a gloved karate chop this spring, when Bracewell & Patterson audaciously offered one of their partners, Hal DeMoss, as a candidate for president of the Houston Bar Association. The Bar Association, it seems, has a cozy tradition that a partner in one of the "big firms" will serve as president in odd-numbered years and someone from the small firms can have the job in even-numbered years. Except for Fulbright Crooker, the large firms never do much with the office, but they guard the honor jealously. Baker & Botts scowled that it was their turn this time, and besides, that Bracewell bunch wasn't a big firm anyway. The contest became a colossal grudge match with both firms fighting for their self-esteem. "The activity at Baker & Botts was unbelievable," recalls one young associate who lived through the experience there. "Nobody seemed to be doing any work for a while—the associates

" 'They've got 50 per cent good lawyers, and 50 per cent bad lawyers, and they don't know which is which.' "

certainly weren't. We were all on the phones, calling people to get out the vote. It was like saving Western civilization." Baker & Botts's resources eventually succeeded in electing their candidate, Ralph Carrigan, but not without some hard feelings all around. In 1975, B&P may try again, and may win.

Bracewell & Patterson, like Butler Binion, is a firm of uneven quality—a situation due in part to its rapid growth. Unlike the other big firms, it is willing to hire experienced lawyers, men who have practiced elsewhere, to shore up departments that have grown faster than the firm could manage. Politically, it maintains a moderate conservative tone that occasionally slides into super-conservatism. With Butler Binion, it shares the distinction of being the only major firm still directed by the men who created it—in this instance, Harry Patterson and the two Bracewell brothers, Fentress and Searcy. The latter is well known as a former Harris County state senator, present-day lobbyist for the utilities during legislative sessions, and one of the handful of authentically powerful figures in the downtown Houston conservative political establishment. (During the furious last days of the 1971 Legislature's congressional redistricting fight, things came to a brief but firm halt while the members awaited a precinct-by-precinct map of the Harris County congressional districts prepared by Bracewell. It arrived with instructions that the legislators were not to change it by one iota. They didn't.) Among the firm's more prominent clients are the Houston Independent School District and Parker Brothers (the shell dredgers, not the manufacturers of games).

There are some areas of the law that the big firms will not touch, principally divorce work, criminal defense work, and plaintiffs' personal injury cases. Mention to a partner in one of the Big Six that you would like him to handle your divorce, and he will react as though he has just discerned an unpleasant odor in the room. In rare instances involving a valued client, a personal friend, or an extraordinarily enticing fee, this rule may be suspended, but for the general public the big firms will politely suggest taking your divorce elsewhere. Percy Foreman is the acknowledged grand sachem in the divorce field.

Criminal defense work is regarded as far, far worse, a sullying pastime if ever there was one, and ... well, not very lucrative either. There is no point in a criminal defendant's ever stepping aboard the elevator to one of the Big Six unless he happens to enjoy heights, or he has, by the luck of the draw, been assigned one of their lawyers by the court because he is indigent. (This sometimes happens, and occasionally a big firm lawyer whose practice is exclusively civil will acquit himself—and his client—brilliantly. Leon Jaworski at Fulbright Crooker argues forcefully that lawyers should welcome the professional duty of representing accused indigents, and has done so himself in state court cases.) The day-to-day criminal law practice, however, is handled by a largely penurious cross-section of specialists. Percy Foreman and his motorcycle-riding, pipe-smoking rival, Racehorse Haynes, are the most prominent criminal defense lawyers in the neighborhood.

Representation of plaintiffs in personal injury lawsuits is potentially the most lucrative branch of the law, but the big firms are effectively precluded from entering it because they already represent the defendants—manufacturers, railroads, insurance companies—who are being sued. It is a feast-or-famine business, but the feasts are regal indeed. One Houston lawyer who specializes in products liability cases (injuries caused by defective products) has two verdicts of more than $1.5 million to his credit, one over $1.6 million, and fifty over $100,000. The usual fee for successful representation in a personal injury case is about 30 per cent of the recovery, plus expenses. Handsome. The firm of Kronzer, Abraham & Watkins is generally regarded as the top personal injury firm in town, but Joe Jamail, the driving force behind the tiny firm of Jamail & Gano, is unquestionably the leading individual personal injury lawyer.

Any member of a bar association grievance committee will confirm that the vast majority of unethical practices are committed by lawyers on the fringes of divorce work, criminal law, and personal injury work. An observer of the Houston scene laments the reluctance of the big firms to become involved in these branches of the law (or at least in divorce and criminal cases, where no problems of conflict of interest arise). "If the large firms came down and got involved, the overall quality of the work would improve dramatically, I'm sure," he says. "They have the ability and they know what an ethical lawyer is supposed to do. But they're not interested because they're afraid they'll get themselves dirty. It's a vicious circle. And the reputation of all us lawyers, good and bad, gets hurt by it."

A variety of excellent smaller firms specialize in more or less esoteric branches of the law. Dixie, Wolf & Hall is the leader in the field of labor law on the unions' side and Neel & Hooper is highly regarded on the employers' side. Royston, Rayzor, Cook & Vickery is the top admiralty firm; like Butler Binion it is notably proficient at producing federal judges, including Carl Bue, a district judge, and John Brown, colorful chief judge of the Fifth Circuit. Arnold, White & Durkee take their hats off to no one in patent law. Sheinfeld, Maley & Kay are excellent in bankruptcy cases. And there are several outstanding firms approaching twenty lawyers with a more general civil practice, including Hutcheson & Grundy; Childs, Fortenbach, Beck & Guyton; Liddell, Sapp, Zivley & Brown; Sewell, Junell & Riggs; and Foreman, Dyess, Prewett, Rosenburg & Henderson. Each is competitive with the giants, and each feels the pinch on legal business that the big firms' domination causes. There are, in addition, a number of solo practitioners and three- or four-man firms who vigorously defend their way of doing things. Many of them—too many to mention—are quite able. But the Big Three remain the striking, dominant feature of the Houston legal landscape.

Baker & Botts: Doing the Deity's Work

For many years Baker & Botts was the largest and most prestigious of the Houston law firms; until the late 1920s it held a virtual monopoly on the city's desirable law business, except for the share claimed by Andrews Kurth. From this commanding position it has now slipped in size to a somewhat distant third. But it has lost none of its classy reputation.

There is something remote... foreign... even *Yankee*... about Baker & Botts, despite its undeniable pedigree in the Houston establishment. From its earliest days it has been the East Coast's team in southeast Texas, representing Northern brokerage houses, utilities, lumber companies and other absentee landlords, and railroads. From the 1870s to the 1930s, when the Southwest was just another province in an economic system that was centralized in the East, these interests required trustworthy lawyers to cultivate their Texas gardens, and they found them. Baker & Botts grew with its clients. One of their most prized documents is an original handwritten $10,000 retainer from a corporate predecessor of the Southern

" 'Baker Botts plays golf; Vinson Elkins plays tennis; Fulbright Crooker hunts.' "

Pacific Railroad, dated 1872, six years after the law firm was founded in the wreckage of the war-torn South. The partner who handles Southern Pacific's business today preserves it in his files.

None of the other Houston firms has anything like this sort of tradition. It sustains the B&B lawyer in his serene detachment, a detachment that in turn goads other lawyers to mutter sourly of "the Baker-Botts halo" and dream of puncturing the self-righteous aura that surrounds the firm. Ask a member of Baker & Botts about his competitors and you will hear a scornful series of Olympian thunderbolts, two-thirds serious, concerning everyone but Andrews Kurth, the one firm to whom B&B graciously extends full diplomatic recognition because (some say) it is the only group of lawyers not suspected of scheming to lure away a valued client or two. He views his firm as national rather than regional, the equal (which in many ways it is) of practitioners in New York or Philadelphia.

Lawyers at Vinson Elkins and Fulbright Crooker are equally convinced of the superiority of their own firms, but they do not express their feelings with the same self-assured air of patrician certainty as the B&B man does. He seems satisfied to believe that his soul remains in Wall Street, Greenwich, Westchester, or Cape Cod, while his body has been temporarily assigned to these steamy Gulf Coast marshes in furtherance of the Deity's inscrutable barristerial design.

A strict sense of legal professionalism is the dominant concept—critics would call it an obsession—at Baker & Botts. More than any other of the Big Three, the firm scorns partisan political activity. Young associates are rigorously chosen for their grades and rank in class ("mental gear," says one). It is the firm least likely to be caught in a conflict of interest. It is also the firm least likely to have welcomed retiring Governor John Connally into its fold—in fact, they instinctively wouldn't have done it. "We have a very formalized set of procedures around here," remarked one B&B member. "To bring someone in from the outside—anyone—just upsets our traditional way of doing things."

Secrecy about the firm is almost a fetish; the managing partner never bothered to return calls or acknowledge letters from *Texas Monthly* requesting an interview. Said a young associate: "It's just imprudent, unwise, and very unBottsian to talk to the press." Baker & Botts prides itself on the fact that it has never sued a client over an unpaid bill. From this tight little island the severest censure that can be hurled at another lawyer is the epithet "unprofessional."

Baker & Botts's offices occupy all of the 29th, 30th, and 31st floors (and parts of two others) in Houston's tallest skyscraper, One Shell Plaza. A swift ascent in the building's famous leather-lined elevators ("Briar Patch, May 1973") deposits the visitor in a tastefully modernistic world of Vasarely wall hangings, glass tables, and stylish furniture. The rich blond wood called *prima vera* that panels the walls grows in just a single Central American country and represents (so the story goes) more than half the total world's supply. It is worth whatever they paid for it. The decor, so different from the traditional dark, intimidating law office atmosphere, provides a cheerful feeling of airiness and openness.

Presiding over this legal department store is the most able group of senior partners in the city. Baker & Botts has its share of deadwood at the top—patriarchs who make $250,000 a year and do virtually no productive work—but one of the signal advantages of a giant firm is that it can afford to put its superannuated partners out to pasture as civic front men. (Similarly, lawyers who turn out to be duds can be hidden away as workhorses who never tarnish the reputation of the firm by coming into contact with clients or the courts.) The majority of B&B's senior partners are exceptionally fine, and among them power is more diffuse than it is at Fulbright Crooker or Vinson Elkins.

Three men, however, stand out within the ruling executive committee: William Harvin, George Jewell, and John Mackin. Harvin is the mandarin of mandarins—a formidable trial lawyer who acts as managing partner. Associates view him as a frustrated corporate lawyer, a man who would be more at home in the gilded world of conference rooms and boards of directors. He keeps his cards close to his vest. Brilliant, poised, and cold-blooded, he first came to B&B as an associate whose *mother* was the firm's office manager. The anti-nepotism rules that prevented founder James A. Baker's great-grandson from joining the firm that bears his name (he went instead to Andrews Kurth, of course) did not apply to the sons of employees; and Harvin, bred in the firm as few others have been, has become perhaps its most tenaciously loyal leader.

Jewell runs the tax department. Affable and tough, he has leapfrogged over a score of older partners to reach his present position. Ability got him there.

Mackin is regarded as something of an enigma by everyone. A widely read man, he is powerful because his department (the corporate section) is itself so powerful.

Baker & Botts is now in the midst of a more or less orderly transfer of power from the men who arrived in the flush years of the late 1920s to those who belong to the postwar generation. (Only a handful of partners came in the 1930s.) Discreetly, they are fighting over the only things they consider worth fighting over: money, control, and the type of clients they will cultivate. Whatever the outcome, one thing is certain: the large clients like Pennzoil, who provide over $1 million a year in fees, will always be taken care of.

POWER: TEXANS WHO HAVE IT AND USE IT 25

"The B&B man seems satisfied to believe that his soul remains in Wall Street or Cape Cod, while his body has been temporarily assigned to these steamy Gulf Coast marshes."

Vinson Elkins: Jet-set Superlawyers

Vinson Elkins is not only the largest law firm in Texas: it is the third largest in the world and in reach of the top. If Baker & Botts is patterned after Wall Street practice, VE is the closest thing Houston has to the legendary Washington superlawyers. The analogy is not perfect, because VE spends the overwhelming part of its time on very traditional types of legal business; but the rest of the time it is political to a degree that no other Texas firm can match.

The offices that sprawl across the 20th, 21st, 22nd, and 25th floors of Houston's First City National Bank building (and parts of two other floors as well) are a surprisingly prosaic setting for the power that emanates from within. The reception area is an elevator lobby unsuccessfully disguised as a living room. Paintings of scenes from ancient Rome and antique cabinets containing finely bound but unread classic lawbooks line the walls, and the view in either direction is down long corridors oppressively reminiscent of federal office buildings, suffused with a pink light. There is an air of intense activity; young lawyers in white shirtsleeves and respectable ties dart briskly from one door to another, bearing sheafs of papers and intent expressions. In a random five-minute period one afternoon, 37 people passed in front of the reception desk.

Both the building and the law firm are a striking monument to the tenacity of one man, although others have improved upon his original plan. He was James Elkins, a county judge in Walker County, who came to Houston in 1917, allied himself with the young law firm of Vinson & Townes, and founded the City National Bank. The firm's fortunes were the bank's fortunes; they grew together. Judge Elkins had a winning combination, and he played it for all it was worth. He lived to be 93, but the legend of his strong will may outlast him by a century. Said a lawyer who knew him in his heyday: "There wasn't a man alive who could dominate anything Judge Elkins was in, except Judge Elkins."

He made all the decisions at both institutions for practically half a century, never bothering to get anyone else's approval. Lawyers work on Saturdays, he said, and a hundred VE attorneys attired in coat and tie duly trooped to their desks each Saturday morning until 1969, almost a decade after the other firms had made such appearances optional.

Lawyers wear hats, he said, and hats were worn. It is conceivable that by the mid-sixties, half the hats sold in Houston were purchased by Vinson Elkins lawyers. A young Kennedyesque associate, new to the firm, vowed he would be damned if he would wear a hat. One day as he was leaving, he chanced to encounter Judge Elkins in the elevator. Granitic stares. Uncomfortable silence. Finally: "Young man, I *see* that you do not have a *hat*." Came the abashed and craven answer: "Sir, I *did* have a hat, but somebody stole it, and I'm on my way out right now to buy another one."

Vinson Elkins, unlike Baker & Botts, built its strength on local business. In the 1930s it was a "four-client firm": the Great Southern Life Insurance Company, Moody-Seagraves, the production end of United Gas Corporation, and Pure Oil Corporation. All but the last were headquartered in Houston. Judge Elkins saw another resource, however, and exploited it brilliantly. The local independent oil men had never catered to Baker & Botts;

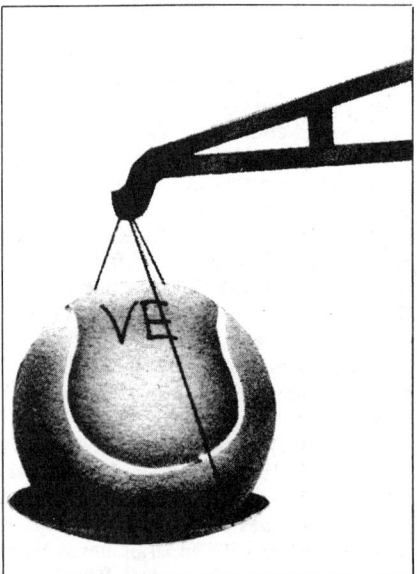

they always thought it was too close to the big oil companies and Eastern finance. The Judge, wearing his banker's hat as president of First National, gave them loans; VE in turn did their legal work. The firm prospered by carrying them on the cuff while they drilled dry holes and collecting when they finally hit. This neat little arrangement catapulted VE into the big time.

For VE's future, however, the worm in the apple was Judge Elkins's embarrassing penchant for hiring the sons of clients and judges, young men whose legal abilities were not always readily apparent. His purpose was to gain what lawyers call "client access," and it worked for a while: business boomed. But the firm became less and less able to handle that business properly. Enter, then, the second of VE's guiding lights, David Searls, whose influence grew as Elkins aged. Searls served only briefly as the official managing partner, but he was the dominant figure in the firm for over a decade, from 1960 until his death in October 1972.

Searls, a nationally known trial lawyer, recognized that the firm needed a transfusion of brainpower. He wrenched the hiring practices around to place a premium on merit. His efforts were rewarded in 1963 when VE swooped down on the University of Texas Law School and carried away practically all the top graduates of a class that is still remembered by professors as the finest in the school's history. It was an event that transformed VE and revolutionized the Houston legal scene. The new recruits set to work devising methods for winning others, and during the remainder of the decade their lavish recruiting program enjoyed success after success.

Searls gave an astonishing amount of authority to these younger men, particularly Harry Reasoner and Richard Keeton. Together they initiated most of the basic reforms that swept through the Big Three in the sixties, reforms that included sharply increased salaries for new associates, a shortening of the time required to become a partner from ten or twelve years to six, and a wider system of participation to replace ironfisted one-man rule. VE developed a reputation as the most aware and enlightened firm in town.

Searls was genuinely beloved and widely mourned. Today his picture sits on the desk of many partners, a white-haired fatherly figure alongside snapshots of their wives and children. One can talk to Houston lawyers for weeks about their peers, past and present, without hearing an unflattering word about the man.

Since his death, there is a growing feeling that the firm has begun to slip a little. Control has shifted to A. Frank Smith, Marvin Collie, and of course John Connally. Although Connally has generally been regarded as a progressive force, his busy role as presidential advisor and Republican politician has left him little

26 POWER: TEXANS WHO HAVE IT AND USE IT

"Those close to Vinson Elkins see a definite reaction against 'the liberals, the longhairs, and the fancy dressers.'"

time for day-to-day decision-making about VE's policies. As the official managing partner, Smith has increasingly set the tone. Those close to the firm perceive a definite reaction against "the liberals, longhairs, and fancy dressers." Recruitment has changed, and less say is given to younger partners and associates.

The "45-year-old bracket"—men who for years felt voiceless as Searls passed them over to share his power with the younger men—dominate Smith's executive committee. (Smith himself is 58.) Rivalry between the two groups is subdued but obvious even to the outsider. Where it will lead is anybody's guess. Worried associates observe that the 45-year-old group built up a substantial body of resentment and discontent watching the younger generation enjoy fatter salaries and swifter promotions than they themselves had been privileged to receive at such an unseasoned age; deprived of their turn at power for so long, they are unlikely to relinquish it willingly. And they are still relatively young themselves.

Whatever problems Vinson Elkins may be having with its generation gap, however, nothing has interrupted the phenomenal growth of its already high-quality clientele. The firm represents such corporate giants as Texas Eastern, Pan Am, Halliburton, and Occidental Petroleum (the last three, Connally is said to have brought in), as well as the extensive Cullen family interests. More are coming in every day, attracted from far beyond the borders of Texas by the former Treasury Secretary's reputation for thaumaturgy. "Everyone wants to hire him," smiles a VE partner, "because everyone wants to get acquainted with John Connally."

Fulbright Crooker:
Texan to the Core

Fulbright, Crooker & Jaworski is the johnny-come-lately of the Big Three, a big, gangling giant that seems as surprised as anyone else by its position as one of the nation's four largest firms. The Eastern pretensions of the other two are missing here: FC is Texan to the core. Aware that it lacks B&B's lofty tradition and VE's jet-set polish, it has stewed itself into a massive inferiority complex over the years. A lawyer at the other two who brags about his firm will simply take for granted that the listener considers it Number One; by contrast, a lawyer at FC is likely to say plaintively (as one did), "I hope you're going to be as fair to us as you are to the other two."

There is no question that Fulbright Crooker is a somewhat different genre: less sophisticated, less affected, more friendly, open, and down-home. It is much less secretive than the others. No one ever calls it stodgy. Says a former member: "Through the years, Fulbright Crooker has always wanted to hire the best, but only if they were good ol' boys." Asked for a capsule description of the Big Three, another Houston lawyer thought a moment and said, "Baker Botts plays golf; Vinson Elkins plays tennis; Fulbright Crooker hunts."

These differences provide fuel for one of the most popular (and catty) parlor games among Houston lawyers: making fun of Fulbright Crooker. "Their suits are shinier; mostly they wear Hong Kong silks," sniffs a VE wife. "They look a little bit corny, like they could wear a string

tie to work." FC lawyers absorb this sort of thing with stoic indifference; but it hurts. They respond by redoubling their efforts to make a mark in various highly visible civic and professional endeavors. It is no accident, for example, that FC always controls the Houston Junior Bar Association, nor that its senior partner, Leon Jaworski, won election as president of the American Bar Association. The firm has an unquenchable thirst to gain acceptance by its peers.

The most persistent criticisms of Fulbright Crooker involve its alleged ruthlessness and disregard for the customary rules governing conflict of interest. "They don't see a conflict of interest . . . ever," charges one of their competitors. More than any other of the Big Six, Fulbright Crooker has been touched by scandal. The Haden will contest, the Andrau airport, and the *first* Sharpstown scandal (in 1957) are oft-cited examples. Similar accusations float like wraiths around the Houston bar. "There is a constant feeling of impropriety about the firm," remarks a middle-aged solo practitioner. "Conflict of interest is not a term often heard around there."

In fairness to Fulbright Crooker, one must readily admit that it is difficult to measure how much of this criticism is truly righteous indignation and how much is just mean-spirited professional jealousy. As the solo practitioner acknowledged, "These older firms know how to use power and they are pretty proud of it. When somebody else comes along who is able to do the same thing, they get knocked."

Even the harshest critics of the firm are quick to praise the caliber of its work in many areas. FC is nationally recognized for its insurance defense trial section, headed by Newton Gresham. "They're probably the best firm in the country in that field," says a University of Texas law professor. Their labor law section, headed by Larry Clinton, is "far and away the best in town." Their admiralty work is equally fine. And virtually every department is laced with men whose legal abilities match or exceed those of their rivals in other firms. Although Baker & Botts is considered preeminent in corporate financing and Vinson Elkins in oil and gas, the overall professional quality of the Big Three is remarkably close to being even.

Fulbright Crooker has also been something of a pioneer in chipping away racial barriers and other forms of discrimination. It hired its first Jewish lawyer about fifteen years ago, well ahead of the other Big Six (one Jew did practice briefly at Baker & Botts in 1917). It is not the only firm to hire black law clerks in recent summers, but it topped all the rest by hiring a black *woman* and offering her an associateship at summer's end.

The firm is governed by a seven-member management committee, three of whom are among its most senior partners. But the dominant figure is Leon Jaworski, known to all as "the Colonel," who has been the committee's chairman for years. His rule is not the monolithic kind Judge Elkins practiced; other partners, particularly Kraft Eidman and Newton Gresham, possess real influence. Gibson Gayle is an up-and-coming figure. But Jaworski is the man that matters.

His corner office on the eighth floor of the Bank of the Southwest Building is cheerful, comfortable, and decorated as discreetly as possible with the avalanche of photographs, awards, and other memorabilia he has received during

> "Aware that it lacks B&B's lofty tradition and VE's jet-set polish, Fulbright Crooker stewed itself into a massive inferiority complex."

several decades of civic activity. (Students of the Houston skyline who associate elevation with status have noted that Baker & Botts looks down from its lofty perch on both of the other two, while Vinson Elkins has at least the satisfaction of looking down on Fulbright Crooker.) Sobriety is the keynote of the firm's reception area, where leather chairs and oriental vases are balanced by bookcases containing rare editions of Smollett's *History of England* and bound volumes of *The Spectator*. The mood of traditionalism and affluence is enhanced by portraits of Jefferson and Marshall along with an original landscape painting or two (of English pastoral scenes—not Hill Country bluebonnets).

It is impossible to dislike Jaworski. A winning blend of Legal Lion and small-town chamber of commerce booster, he never gives you a chance. His enthusiasm for Fulbright Crooker is infectious. Although he has never been fully accepted by the old Houston legal and social establishment, he is exempted from the reproofs that they sometimes levy against his firm. "The Colonel," says one, "is still a man who has *judgment*."

"Our really phenomenal growth has been in the last decade," Jaworski says. From 56 members in 1955, the firm grew to 108 in 1965 and has reached 185 "as of today." He recalls that a meeting of the entire firm two years ago had to be held in the auditorium of the Humble Building, five blocks away, because there was no room large enough to hold everyone at the Bank. (If they had all marched down there together, one supposes they would have needed a parade permit.)

He is convinced that the big firms will keep on growing. "There's not a psychological barrier at 200," he says. "Years ago I said that when we reached 100 lawyers we ought to put on the brakes because we'll be getting too unwieldy. I could not have had a more complete misconception. Either you keep growing or you run the risk of stagnation."

Fulbright Crooker got its start in 1919 through the liaison of John H. Crooker and R. C. Fulbright, an expert in tax and transportation who spent much of his time in Washington, D.C. (The firm has had an office there from the beginning.) Their principal client was Anderson Clayton & Company, a cotton compress firm which had the perspicacity to corner the world market in cotton after World War I. As far as the firm's vigor was concerned, having Anderson Clayton for a client was like having a lifetime supply of Gatorade. The company is an even bigger giant today, although it has switched to food processing, insurance, and vegetable oils. After a merger in the years following World War II that brought in a large amount of high-quality insurance defense work, FC began to grow in earnest. Clients included legendary oilman Glenn McCarthy, the M. D. Anderson Foundation, and the Second National Bank, now the Bank of the Southwest.

Jaworski surveys his firm as a benign father might contemplate his happy family. "I have never seen a team work together like these boys do," he beams. "Why, the way these boys pitch in and help when someone else's ox is in the mire is amazing. They'll even stay down here at night." It is like being captain of the world's finest steamship.

Most vivid of all, perhaps, is his obvious, pardonably Texanish pride in the sheer *bigness* of it all—how it is booming, going great guns. "We've got men going all over the world," says the man who began his career when Houston was just another provincial city never dreaming that it might one day be a seat of the mighty. "We even have an office in London now." Did you send someone over there to run it? he is asked. "No, we didn't have to. About a year ago we got a man from Mobil Oil to head up the operation. He was already familiar with that part of the country."

How the Big Firms Got That Way: They're Big Because They're Big Because . . .

Why has Houston produced these immense law factories? The question is really two-fold: *Why did they become so big? And why do they stay so big?*

The conventional answer to the first question is that they grew because of their intimate associations with the big banks. This holds true for Vinson Elkins and Fulbright Crooker; for Baker & Botts, less so. But it is not far wrong with B&B, either. The banks generated a lot of business for their allied firms, and, more important, they *sent* a lot of business upstairs. Houston's banks have traditionally done business with a single firm, in contrast to those in Dallas, which have parceled their business out and played one set of lawyers off against another. These different modes of operation were partly foreordained by the unusual way some Houston banks happened to develop: Judge Elkins's dual role as banker and lawyer is only the most obvious example.

An even more important reason, though, was the sheer forcefulness of the personalities who ruled the Big Three in their formative years. Men like Judge Elkins, John Crooker, and Captain Baker at Baker & Botts held the firms together by the strength of their own wills in the crucial 1920s and 1930s. The centrifugal forces that have held sway in Dallas—where the Turner firm reached 45 or 50 and split, the Carrington firm 30 or so and split—were held in check by these extraordinary men at precisely the time when their firms were still small enough to break apart. By avoiding the break then, they insured that it would probably never come.

As a partner at Vinson Elkins observed, "There comes a point of 'critical mass.' Beyond a certain point—perhaps fifty or so—large firms are so much more profitable because of the size of the clients they can attract and the specialization they can bring to bear." A group of partners could conceivably have walked off with half the clients of one of the Big Three in the twenties; now they never could. One does not walk off with Texas Eastern, Pennzoil, or Anderson Clayton. They are too big to put in one's briefcase—and their loyalties now are to the firm itself and not to the lawyer who handles their business (or part of it) at a given moment. The real reason for the Big Three's size is to be found in history, rather than in anything that is happening today. It is no riddle to say, "They are big . . . because they are big."

This is not to deny that there are other forces helping to *keep* them big. Some of these are common to law practices in other major cities: the sustained boom in legal business for the past decade, dumping more work than they can handle on the major firms; Houston's own growth; and, fascinatingly, the introduction of the jet airplane. By making Washington and New York as accessible as Austin, it has opened up new vistas in branches of the law heretofore monopolized by firms along the Eastern seaboard—representation of clients before federal agencies like the Federal Power Commission and the Securities and Exchange Commission, for example. As VE partner Evans Attwell observes, "As late as the fifties, the only way you could get up there was by taking a three-day train trip or flying an uncomfortable DC-6. Now you can leave in the morning, be in D.C. by noon, have your conference, and be home that night. It's opened up a whole new world of federal practice to us."

There are also forces peculiar to Houston that help keep the big firms big. Foremost among them is the special

" 'Through the years, Fulbright Crooker has always wanted to hire the best, but only if they were good ol' boys.' "

status, the patina of prestige, that they have acquired in social and legal circles. A lawyer loses it if he leaves. In Dallas no one would care; in Houston they do. A lawyer who severs his ties with one of the Big Three must face the fact that he is choosing to be an outsider from then on; it is not an easy thing for some men to do. Leaving that elite peer-group relationship takes a bite out of his ego.

If he is a partner, it may also take a sizable bite out of his bank account. The lawyer on the move is always under economic pressure: the house always costs $10,000 more than he can afford. For a partner to abandon the built-in security of the big firm is usually judged to be a pretty poor gamble. Some of the firms have penalty clauses in their partnership agreements, requiring the departing ingrate to forfeit the value of his partnership interest, which can be substantial, and refrain from competing with alma mater's business for as long as five years. All in all, it is easier to stay put.

Besides, most of the people in the big firms *like* what they are doing. It is a simple thing, but it escapes most of their critics, who reason that lawyers in large firms must somehow be miserable. "The cement that's kept the big firms together," says a lawyer at Vinson Elkins, "is the fact that they mediate the economic life of Texas. They resolve the most intriguing problems a lawyer can imagine, and they do it every day." Another young associate puts it even more simply: "I like large firms," he says, "because I can work on interesting problems with qualified people . . . for money."

Is Big Best?
The Large and the Small of Things

If you're looking for a lawyer to handle your business affairs, should you head for a big firm or seek out one of the smaller ones? It depends, naturally, on whom you ask.

Hank Webeldor (a pseudonym) is a promising young associate at Baker & Botts, wise beyond his years. He argues persuasively for the big firms. "Let's face it," he says, "they've got brand-name confidence. The client knows he's not going to get fly-by-night legal service. But even more important, he knows the big firm has as much to lose as *he* does if things aren't done right.

"You can find outstanding, brilliant lawyers who practice alone or in small groups. Look at their work and you can see they're worth their fee. But when you find an organization which is able *as an institution* to bring off work comparable in excellence to that of a brilliant, charismatic lawyer, then you've got a remarkable situation."

Webeldor concedes that big clients stand to gain the most from hiring a big firm. "A very big client can count on the firm to have all the available manpower he needs. Say you want to merge two companies and do it right. You'll have to merge their pension plans. That's intensely complicated. But there'll be a man in the big firm who does nothing but pension plans—and he'll be ready and available to talk to the client. The same thing goes for antitrust questions, securities, and so forth. If it's a big deal, you'll probably have two antitrust guys, four corporate guys, two tax guys, a patent-trademark guy, and some real estate guys. The whole thing can be done in one place without winding up in the soup."

But what about the little man, the small businessman who just wants to set up a corporation and doesn't need all that expertise? What's the point of his going to one of the giants? Webeldor's answer sums up the big firms' self-perpetuating success story: *"A blue-chip law firm gives instant credibility to a new business."*

Ray Needham, an energetic and articulate young labor lawyer who has put his chips in with the four-man firm of Schlumberger, Hinsley & Westmoreland, sees, on the other hand, a new breed of businessman developing—one who doesn't want the same kind of relationship to his lawyer that his father had.

"Houston business was created by gunslinger types," he says. "They were happy with the big firms because they'd grown up with them. But now their sons are taking over, and *they* want someone they can call 'their lawyer.' They want a guy whose advice they can trust, somebody who's not just a narrow specialist. They want a real person they can see, not a vast, anonymous structure.

"They've been going to the big firms by default, because they know they can get good work done there; but they know the big firms are always going to give first attention to their big clients, and they'd much prefer to work instead with someone they *know*—if he's good. You're going to see things loosening up around here as they take over."

There are hazards for the small practice, though, attitudes which alarm solo practitioner Brooks Pollard (a pseudonym). Pollard was associated with one of the Big Six for several years; now on his own, he agrees that many good clients are intimidated by the larger firms. But he worries about some of them.

"You have a lot of businesses who don't particularly *want* the kind of professionalism the big firms represent," he says. "There are lots of lawyers in Houston making bundles of money with an eighth-rate practice. A client calls and says, 'I want a contract and I want it now and I want it on one page'—so the lawyer does it. It's gross, horrible, sloppy—but he does it. And the client is happy because he controls the lawyer.

"A large firm has the ability to maintain its professionalism and resist client wiles and manipulations much better than someone who depends on that client for perhaps one fourth of his total income."

You pays your money and you takes your choice.

Life in the Firm:
The Bonds of Affluence

An article in *Forbes* magazine two years ago neatly capsuled the economic realities of a large law firm: "Economically speaking, a law firm is a very simple structure. It buys brainpower wholesale—by the year, that is—and sells it retail—by the hour."

Less than half the members of the large firms are partners. The rest are associates, working long hours for a fixed wage and waiting for the day when they may be allowed to "make partner." The typical starting salary for someone fresh out of law school who goes to work for one of the Big Three is now $15,400 a year. This figure has risen dramatically in a short time. In 1967, $7500 was considered good; in 1969, the going rate was $13,200. Compensation for this wholesale brainpower increases by about $2400 each year the associate remains with the firm; about the time he is getting nervous about being made a partner, six or seven years after he arrived, he can expect to be earning in the neighborhood of $25,000 to $30,000.

This may seem like a lot of money, but it is actually only a small fraction of the revenue he *produces* for the firm. Therein lies the rub, as far as many an associate is concerned. Billing clients by the hour for his work, he may bring in $80,000 to $100,000 in annual receipts. His overhead is perhaps $10,000, and the remaining $40,000 or so (after his salary is taken out) is siphoned into the coffers of the firm, to reappear at the end of the year in the pockets of the partners. This difference between the money an associate produces

and the cost of hiring him—billing cost versus talent cost—is what makes the big firms roll.

Obviously it is in the partners' interest to squeeze as much profitable labor as possible out of their associates. The associates don't get paid extra for doing more; the partners keep the revenue. "The only way they make so much money is for the associates to overproduce," says a bright young lawyer who left one of the Big Three.

To the outsider there is something chilling about the cynical ways associates are induced to "overproduce." Long hours are expected and demanded; it is not uncommon for a young associate to be at work before eight-thirty and come home after nine at night. Work regularly spills over into Saturdays and Sundays. Wives, families, and outside interests are neglected; the firm is an all-consuming thing. Some lawyers often work sixty- and seventy-hour weeks. "There is a moral imperative to spend long hours at the office," says an associate at one of the Big Six.

Fear is what keeps things going—fear of not being made a partner, fear of being resented as a laggard by one's peers. As an ex-Marine figuratively put it, "It's like basic training: if one guy falls behind on laps, the whole group has to do them over." An associate who tries to live a normal life is plagued by gnawing fears that one of his friends is back at the firm doing something he himself ought to be doing, and cussing him for it; or that displeased partners are preparing a package of switches and ashes for him at promotion time.

"The older men want to take too much out of the firm," says a young associate who left one of the Big Three, considerably disillusioned. "By the time they draw a hundred-and-fifty, two-hundred, two-hundred-and-fifty thousand a year, they are rich men. But they derive satisfaction out of pushing it higher and higher, even though it's ordinary income and taxes take a huge bite. It hurts the firm and it discourages the associates. But it's a way of explaining to themselves that the treacherous climb to the top was worth it."

The firms are ruthless about exposing idlers who do not carry their share of the excessive load; conversely, they make certain that those who work themselves dizzy are properly rewarded—with praise, of course, not money. Baker & Botts annually circulates a sheet ranking the associates according to the number of hours each has billed during the year: woe betide the young man whose total slips much below 1750 hours, and 2000 is a safer figure. If an associate did nothing but "billable" work eight solid hours every workday, fifty weeks a year, he would barely reach the mark. Since, in the nature of things, it's impossible (ethically) to bill a client for every minute he spends at his desk—six billable hours out of eight is doing well—most associates work nights and weekends to make up the difference. Others skip their vacations. Vinson Elkins is even more domineering: the billing totals for each lawyer are circulated each *month*. The sheets are reviewed by older partners who worked even harder in *their* day and don't take kindly to young whippersnappers who fail to appreciate how lucky they are. They know if you've been bad or good, so be good for goodness' sake!

The physical working conditions are, of course, superb. Messengers, day and night secretarial shifts, comprehensive libraries, even (at Baker & Botts) desk switches that open and close office doors by remote control. "You don't have to bother with the details of running a law office," says a happy associate. "You can concentrate on the law."

But the price for these advantages is steep, and it must be paid in the coin of personal independence and freedom. The firms regiment their members' dress, their access to clients, even the decor of their offices. A story now making the rounds in Houston tells of a young associate at Vinson Elkins who decided that his north-facing office did not need curtains; "Heresy," said the office managers, and they hung the curtains anyway. For a decorative plant he chose a hanging basket instead of one that sat on the floor like everybody else's; soon he was summoned by the managing partner and ordered to take it down. Except at Fulbright Crooker, which has a reputation for leniency, political activity by associates is notoriously restricted. They can vote for whomever they please, but to take an active role in a campaign is courting disaster unless the management approves. In the opinion of a VE partner, a lawyer is taking an "active" role if he receives calls about the campaign through the firm's switchboard during the day.

Even more burdensome to the self-

"'If you thought something needed to be done in Houston, the managing partners of the big firms would be the place to start.'"

respect of some proud associates is the knowledge that they are virtually forbidden to discuss their work—the major portion of their life—with their best friends outside the firm. It is not a matter of disclosing professional secrets or confidential client relationships; no reputable lawyer will do that. They know that the censorship imposed on them is broader; if they are observed talking about even the most innocuous matters, like the leadership of the firm or its history, their trustworthiness is made suspect and their advancement threatened.

This writer has interviewed political dissenters in Czechoslovakia and "banned" African revolutionaries in South Africa, meeting them in obscure cafes and parked cars to avoid detection. By all odds, associates in Houston's Big Three are more reticent and fearful than either. One old friend who did talk (but not about his firm) was obviously distressed by his sudden loss of freedom to discuss his work; he kept returning to the subject, trying to explain his predicament as the inexorable consequence of choosing to go to work there—like volunteering for the Army (a recurring image). "You obey orders in the Army," he said, "even if you're told to paint the tanks pink. You can question them logically, but if you're told to go ahead, you do it. The whole training of a lawyer in the big firms is to *know your place in the organization*—to avoid being presumptuous. One shines in one's work—not in extracurricular things. You don't talk about the firm unless you've been authorized to do it, any more than you allow a default judgment to be entered against your client. At all costs you have to avoid whatever can be seen as indiscreet."

Other young lawyers who come in contact with their friends at the big firms wonder out loud why they don't mutiny. "Why do they put up with it?" asks one. "Why don't they go on strike? Why don't they get the hell out? I've never understood it."

The answer, not surprisingly, is the alluring promised land of a partnership. "Make partner" and your income almost doubles right away—suddenly you're a sixty-thousand-dollar-a-year man, and right at Christmastime, too. It *is* delicious. Who would risk taking a chance at losing that, especially when the firm is ominously dotted with graying fifty-year-old relics who were judged a little too rambunctious in their day and were therefore kept as permanent associates, *pour encourager les autres?* When the alternative is finding yourself on the street, deprived of the monthly check and forced to develop a private practice or drown, most associates shudder, hurriedly clamp the lid on the abyss, and return to the warm glow of their respective firms. They are hooked. Predictable rationalizations ensue: their overworked existence is no longer thought of as exploitation, but rather as a prudent system of "forced savings," a way of depositing in the bosom of the firm a comfortable income for their future years, a kind of upper-middle-class Social Security.

Left unspoken to themselves and their families is the recognition that, like Social Security, the system depends upon steady, even increasing, contributions by the associates who succeed them; that it is premised on an ever-expanding economy and law business which may or may not materialize. Thus their fears become the same as those of their elders who hold them down: what if, when *I* become a partner, the associates demand their share at once? At that point, cynics say, they are ready for a partnership.

With so much riding on a partnership, there is agony as the time approaches. There is no appointed hour, just a minimum number of years (it varies from firm to firm) below which no one will be considered. But once that time passes, an associate begins to get the message. A year or two later, it is obvious to all that he is in trouble.

He can pack and go, or stick around and take his chances. The firm has very little incentive to kick him out: after all, he has eight or nine years' experience, he is bringing them perhaps a hundred thousand dollars in billings, and his replacement would be an inexperienced fellow fresh from law school. "Maybe he will improve." For those who remain, the suspense often becomes almost unbearable. One lawyer from a small firm vividly remembers the tension he has witnessed. "A fine young attorney at Baker & Botts got passed over when he should have made partner two years ago. His friends took him to lunch to console him, but he got sick. Next year the same thing happened, only this time he passed out in the street. Soon afterwards he moved to Dallas."

Merit is the main criterion for promotion, and the continuing quality of the big firms' work over the years indicates that their executive committees (whose list is almost never overruled by the full partnership) know what they are doing. Still, there is a measure of truth to the saying that "the only way you get to be a general is by not offending the generals." Every firm has those senior associates who have paid for their independence.

An element of caprice also enters in. In some firms, an associate is assigned to work with a particular lawyer; his advancement is sometimes unjustly affected by how highly the other partners regard his supervisor. In other cases the partner decides how many billing hours he will credit to himself and how many to his associates when they have worked on a project together. "How many billing hours I get to show depends on how good a guy he is," says an associate. "And yet his decision rules my career."

The high degree of specialization in the Big Three gives some associates a running head start on others. "At Fulbright Crooker, the patent section is the way to dusty death," says a former associate there. Baker & Botts is dominated by the trial and corporate departments, whose

---

**Bricklayers and Attorneys:
An Earnings Comparison**

A lawyer who becomes an associate in a large law firm will begin at $15,400 a year. He is expected to bill 1800 hours of legal work a year, which he can do by working approximately 2400 hours. His hourly wage is thus $6.42. After six years, if all goes well, he will be making $30,000 a year, or $12.50 an hour.

A high school classmate who becomes a bricklayer's apprentice in 1973 starts at $4.25 an hour. In four years, when his friend is between college and law school, he will have become a journeyman earning $8.50 an hour, double for overtime. By the time the young attorney is ready to begin working, his peer will have earned $130,116 (if he puts in the 2400 hours per year that the lawyer must). We are assuming present-day pay scales for comparison.

By the time he becomes a partner after six years in the firm (the minimum waiting period) the associate will have made $140,400, assuming his salary goes up $2400 a year. The bricklayer working the same hours would have made $272,916 by the same time, or $132,516 more. The lawyer will not catch up in total earnings, even after he is making $60,000 a year as a partner, until he is almost forty. If union pay scales rise faster than lawyers' salaries, he might not catch up until he is in his late forties; perhaps he never would.

> "A VE dinner for six law students held at Austin's prestigious Headliners Club was the single most expensive meal ever served there."

strength is demonstrated at promotion and profit-sharing time. Says a disgruntled associate: "If they make a trial man a partner, they almost have to make a corporate man a partner. If you're in, say, oil and gas, your partners may be fighting for you, but they just don't have the same clout."

Ironically, a partner's life often turns out to be more of the same. The trappings change—they sell their homes in West University and Southgate to associates and move to Tanglewood or River Oaks —but they find themselves working harder than ever. Ingrained habits are hard to change. Some new partners tend to relax and coast, but most don't; they identify themselves completely with their firms. Partnership brings its own set of competitions for rank and power.

Alcoholism and the divorce rate are both high among the middle-aged partners, evidence of discontent and frustration that will not go away. In the Big Three, a partner finds that unless he sits on the firm's executive committee, he is still not likely to have much voice in its policies. "It would be very unusual for the partnership not to go along with the management," says Leon Jaworski, "but it can happen." For those so inclined, a struggle for influence within the firm replaces the struggle for promotion.

Why then do people do it? What do the big firms have to offer that make worthwhile the struggle to win a niche in a giant organization and the loss of personal independence it entails? Part of the reason is the excitement and exhilaration of the big firms' type of law practice; there are those who are happier—*professionally happier*—in a big firm than they could ever be outside. For most, however, it is money, security, and social prestige. Money, because there are few Houston lawyers who make more than the top partners of the big firms, and those that do won their stripes in a very risky world where the losers outnumber the winners. Security, because a partnership carries with it a lifetime relief from fears of financial reversal. Social prestige, because those who have not previously moved in establishment society find the big firms an irresistibly easy path to acceptance and status.

These insights are not lost on recruiters who leave the big firms each year and fan out to law school campuses in search of the ablest talent they can find. They know their winning cards.

Students on Pedestals: The Dazzle of Big-time Law Recruiting

As recently as ten years ago, a law student who aspired to work for one of the Big Three went to their office, credentials in hand. All that has changed. Active recruiting now occupies a considerable portion of several partners' time, year in, year out. With more law business than they have lawyers to handle it, the big firms find themselves engaged in a bruising, escalating competition for top law graduates. And like college football stars at the height of the old AFL-NFL rivalry, the graduates love it.

The University of Texas Law School in Austin is the principal battleground for capturing this legal talent. While the old Texas prejudice against Ivy Leaguers has largely faded (each of the Big Three sends a recruiting team to Harvard), the old Ivy League prejudice against Texas hasn't, with the result that these sallies to New England are not notably successful. The big firms persist in showing an icy indifference to most graduates of other Texas law schools, including Baylor, the University of Houston, and to a lesser extent, SMU. But almost any second- or third-year law student in the top 10 per cent of his class at UT can, if he wants, savor the opulent delights of big-time law recruiting.

There is a round of parties in the fall, timed to coincide with a football weekend, and another in the spring, to coincide with the Law Review Banquet. These are nothing if not lavish, and Vinson Elkins (which started it all) is universally regarded as the most lavish of all.

A third-year law student who was invited to one of VE's parties this fall was numbed by the experience. "There was this giant buffet at Green Pastures [a mansion-style restaurant in Austin]," he said. "It was huge—spread out through two or three rooms. And an *incredible* amount of liquor: I've never seen anything like it. An open bar beforehand, they kept filling your drinks while you ate, then Irish coffee. Amazing! Then they invited you up to their suite for *after-dinner drinks*! I never knew lawyers could drink that much." A moment later he added pensively, "You know, I don't think people today are as impressed by that sort of thing as they were a couple of years ago."

Like the Russian army mobilizing for war, Vinson Elkins sometimes sends as many as thirty young associates, partners, and their wives to Austin for a recruiting weekend. Each is fully briefed in advance on the salient details of the four or five law students for whom he has assumed particular responsibility. At "structured" parties, each couple may be assigned a specific prospect to entertain and shepherd around, usually without the prospect's prior knowledge. The atmosphere is reminiscent of fraternity rush—in some ways it is simply a continuation of fraternity rush—and in unguarded moments members of the big firms frequently slip back into the Greek terminology (rushee, rush party) until, grinning sheepishly at the outsider, they catch themselves.

The big impetus toward lavish recruitment came after the famous VE class of '63 had settled into the firm; the other firms were virtually forced to follow. The emphasis at VE has always been upon a bountiful, conspicuous extravagance: the finest foods, the finest wines, a life of stylish prosperity. One young lawyer who went to VE describes the process as "an attempt to sway impressionable law students, an appeal to their ego. 'Here we are in Maxim's wine cellar; this is the life of the young VE lawyer.'" A Vinson Elkins dinner for a half dozen students held at Austin's prestigious Headliners Club in 1971 was, according to Club officials, the single most expensive meal ever served there.

Fulbright Crooker and Baker & Botts pursue the same pattern with varying degrees of success. The unreal atmosphere of a cocktail party, however, does not afford a congenial home court advantage to the aloof lawyers at B&B, and despite their punctilious observance of all the proper rules, they sometimes trip over their feet when stepping down from their pedestal. A 1973 Law Review graduate of UT argues, "VE gives the best parties because they hire the best cocktail party people. [The recruiting technique at] Baker Botts is just awful, clearly the worst—they send people up to Austin who don't have any idea what to do at cocktail parties and that turns some guys off." He adds, "Of course, that may mean they are better lawyers. I've never thought good cocktail party people and good lawyers were particularly compatible."

Fulbright Crooker, as always, is honored more for their folksiness than their finesse. A typical FC recruiting weekend might feature a rock band at the Party Barn in Austin. A central Texas lawyer who was rushed by the big firms recalls that on his trip to Houston he and his wife went to see *Lucia di Lammermoor* with Beverly Sills at the Houston opera, courtesy of Vinson Elkins. "Fulbright Crooker," he says half-seriously, "would have taken us to the Astrodome." He neglected to mention that VE, keeping all its options open, has reserved a block of seats behind home plate.

Until recently, the most ferocious recruiting always took place within the Texas Law Review, a prestigious group of second- and third-year students who earned their positions strictly on the basis of their grade-point average. But in late 1972 the Review began to admit members on an internship system that emphasized such things as legal writing ability; only fifteen (instead of forty) positions are now determined solely on grades. At about the same time, the Law School administration forbade firms to restrict their campus interviews to an exclusive group like the "top 10 per cent" or "Law Review only." They must now interview any student who asks to be interviewed.

The result of these reforms has been to make the grade-conscious Big Three increasingly suspicious of the students they interview on campus, with a correspondingly greater reliance on off-campus informal party impressions. There are no more blanket Law Review invitations to parties, either; admission is now by individual invitation only. "It's a lot more like rush than it used to be," says one recent graduate. "If you are shy, introverted, don't talk easily, you are likely to suffer. You just don't have the chance to make the same impression. Good people have been hurt this way, especially with Vinson Elkins, who've been getting more and more toward the good ol' boy syndrome in the last year or so."

One of the most reliable methods the firms have developed to measure the abilities of a prospective associate is the system of "summer clerkships." Students whom the firm is interested in hiring are given a chance between their second and third years in law school to do legal research at the firm, to pick up a little cash at $250 a week, and to show their stuff. Ostensibly it's just another summer job, but the firm and the clerks both regard it as a sort of trial run. In some ways it is deceptive (the clerks leave at five and don't see the young associates still working at ten-thirty), but each learns enough about the other that solid offers are frequently made, and accepted, for employment to commence after graduation. Some students thus return to law school for their final year already employed, in effect, by one of the Big Three. At least two of the big firms, and possibly the third as well, quietly provide expense accounts for them to entertain and recruit selected fellow students who are still uncommitted.

A third-year student who is being pursued by one or more of the Big Three can expect to receive a first-class trip to Houston at the firm's expense. One who recently returned from such a visit recalled that he and his wife were flown down and given a choice of staying in any hotel they desired. While he toured the office and met a succession of partners, his wife was taken on a tour of the city by several firm wives. During lunch at Neiman-Marcus the wives discussed the merits of housing and the Houston schools. Meanwhile he was having lunch at the Hyatt-Regency Windowbox with a few young associates. "There was no hard sell about it," he said. "Their attitude was, 'This is what we've got; be sure it's what you want.' " In the afternoon he continued to make the rounds of partners, impressed that the top lawyers in the firm would stop what they were doing to visit with him. His wife was also taken to meet several of the principal partners. "When it was over I was told that if I wanted an offer, I could have one," he said. "That was all there was to it, except we had dinner with some associates that evening. The rest of the weekend we were free to do as we wished; they made it clear we could stay as long as we wanted at their expense, but I had to get on back to school." A "moderately generous" check for taxis, meals, and miscellaneous expenses arrived at his Austin home a few days later.

The recruiting battle is fueled by the traditional feeling at UT that anyone who doesn't go to work for one of the big Houston firms probably isn't much good. The firms scrupulously strive to preserve their status by impressive recruiting tactics and generous gifts to the Law School Foundation. (Each of the three has endowed a $100,000 professorship.) By and large the strategy works: an offer from one of the Big Three is regarded as proof of professional ability even by their most cynical Naderesque classmates; like the winner of a Rhodes Scholarship, the recipient can never again be regarded as just another face in the crowd.

The firms' recruiting luck varies from year to year. Baker & Botts adroitly manages to spirit away a few of the highest-ranked students almost every time. Vinson Elkins dazzled the legal profession by snapping up great gobs of top graduates in the late 1960s, but their last vintage year was 1971. Fulbright Crooker outstripped the others in 1972, when they got four officers of the Law Review. A large proportion of the Class of 1973 opted for judicial clerkships, perhaps expressing a measure of distaste for the sort of work done by the Big Three. The current class talks even more radically than their predecessors, but at graduation they very likely will head for business-oriented firms.

If that doesn't happen—if the Big Three are spurned by yet another crop of activist, reform-minded UT law graduates—the firms may well be forced to reappraise some of their policies. One which is long overdue for some reexamination is their attitude toward legal work *pro bono publico,* lawyers' Latin for professional services provided free of charge to causes the lawyer deems worthy. Lawyers are traditionally even more tight-fisted than doctors when it comes to giving away their services for free, but this resistance has increasingly come under attack by young lawyers chagrined at the lack of legal representation available to poorly financed consumer, environmental, and civil rights causes. In many of the larger New York and Washington firms, a substantial fraction of a lawyer's time may be devoted to *pro bono* work for which the firm receives no income. The failure of Texas firms to follow suit has made them something of a joke among Ivy League law students at recruiting time.

None of the Houston firms has a *pro bono* program worthy of the name. There is a story, possibly apocryphal, of a much-sought-after Harvard law senior who was being recruited by Vinson Elkins. His hosts happened to take him to the office of one of the firm's grand old men, a prominent insurance lawyer. Looking at the youngster, the senior partner said, "So you want to work for Vinson Elkins."

The young man acknowledged that he thought that might be nice, and the two chatted amiably for a while about the many splendors of the firm. Finally the student asked, "By the way, do you do any *pro bono* work?"

"Any *what?*"

An explanation ensued in which the student, somewhat taken aback, explained to the old gentleman that nature of that particular form of legal generosity. With an indulgent smile came the partner's response: "Well, son, I'm sure it's all right for you to do that, just as long as you do it on Saturdays."

A recent UT graduate who is well acquainted with the *pro bono* policies of Washington law firms was discussing them with several of the top partners at VE during a recruiting interview. "I was talking about one D.C. firm—one of the two or three best—that has a written firm policy that twenty per cent of the firm's time shall be spent on *pro bono* work. No ifs or buts—it's a written policy, and it's not just something nominal, it's twenty per cent. The bigwigs at VE just flatly refused to *believe* it. What can you say?"

Vinson Elkins is by no means the worst offender in the matter of *pro bono* work, although their progressive reputation in the sixties makes their lack of initiative more conspicuous. Baker & Botts seems to discipline associates who stray too far from the moneymaking path by denying them promotion to partner year after year, regardless of the merit of their outside work. At Fulbright Crooker, managing partner Jaworski was obviously discomforted by questions involving *pro bono* work. There, as at the other big firms, the crunch comes when an attorney is asked, say, by environmental groups like the Sierra Club or the League of Conservation Voters to contribute his time in a class action suit on behalf of citizens seeking to stop industrial pollution or freeway construction.

"How," Jaworski asks, "would a client who pays us a retainer react if he found that one of our boys was sitting on the other side helping to agitate a lawsuit against him? We can't trample on our clients' interests by turning one of our boys loose to foment litigation."

Most lawyers would acknowledge that he has a point. In one form or another, this is the persistent dilemma of the big firms: conflict of interest. A junior partner at Vinson Elkins candidly admits: "Most of our clients have environmental problems. We can't represent both sides in an environmental lawsuit any more than we can in any other kind of suit, even if we represent one side for free. If someone wants to handle environmental litigation, he shouldn't come to a big firm." He means, of course, handling environmental work for the *plaintiff's* side, since the big firms defend such cases for their clients every day; they are happy to latch on to a young lawyer who knows environmental law, provided he wants to use his expertise in behalf of corporate defendants.

But lurking in the background is the realization that conflict of interest is not as final an answer as it seems. There are many environmental cases that even a lawyer in the Big Three could handle without placing himself in direct opposition to one of the firm's clients. What the big firms know, however, is that if one of their lawyers succeeds in winning a tough environmental ruling today in a case that does *not* involve one of their clients, the law thus made may be used tomorrow as a precedent in a case that *does*. In this sense, "conflict of interest" is a convenient excuse for refraining from doing anything that would impair the interests of corporate defendants *as a class,* regardless of whether there is an ethical conflict in a particular case. Critics of the big firms would regard this as a telling example of the way they confuse their own responsibilities as lawyers with the very different interests of the clients they serve.

Still, the Houston firms sense that something new is in the wind, and one suspects that they are preparing for the necessity of allowing *pro bono* work when and if they have to. Their desire to keep getting the top graduates is ultimately stronger than their distaste for *pro bono* work; if their favored graduates consistently start going somewhere else in pursuit of the greater personal opportunities that such a program offers, the Big Three will doubtless devise one of their own to win them back—but not until. Meanwhile, Houston managing partners do have fewer illusions than lawyers in other Texas cities about the nature of *pro bono* work. The graduate who had such difficulty convincing the VE brass that Washington firms actually did require *pro bono* work recalls: "At least the people in Houston know what the words mean —even if they are damned sure they aren't going to *do* any of it. At one of the biggest Dallas firms they said, 'You betcha we do *pro bono* work: one of our senior partners helps run the United Fund campaign every year.'"

Lawyers' Wives: The Loneliness of a Closed Society

Most wives find that the firm dominates their lives as well as their husbands'. Emily Lowry (a pseudonym) is attractive, dark-haired, thirtyish. Her husband recently became a partner in one of the Big Three. Seated in the den of their comfortable two-story home in a fashionable neighborhood of Houston, she analyzes their climb.

"The first thing you have to understand about being a lawyer's wife is that it's very similar to being a doctor's wife. The first few years are hard and lonely. He's working long, long, hard hours—twelve to fifteen hours is not unusual, for days at a time. You'll raise your family almost single-handedly for a while."

Whatever dreams a law student's wife may have, they probably do not include an image of herself sitting around an empty house day after day as the sun sets, the dinner hour passing unmarked and preschool children wanting to be cared for and entertained, while her husband works on downtown. The young lawyer's wife knows the firm's night number by heart. To combat the inevitable loneliness, the wives seek out others in the same situation. "They'll group together," says Emily. "For instance, they'll go over for a cocktail at five-thirty and pass the time with each other's children until eight or so. But it gets a lot better after a while."

Social life tends to revolve around the firm—about 50 per cent of the time, Emily estimates. "These are the men your husband is working with, so it's just easier that way." For the first three or four years, young lawyers are expected to shoulder the recruiting burden. When they do this sort of entertaining, whether at home or somewhere else, the firm picks up the check. Emily recalls "one of the more exuberant" parties during her husband's second year with the firm. "We went to the Petroleum Club; there were thirty of us, plus the rushee and his wife. So you see there's an advantage to entertaining—it's a very nice fringe benefit. The disadvantage for the wife, if she's only on her own budget, is that you have to have very nice clothes in order to go places with your rushees."

After the husband becomes a partner, he and his wife begin to entertain the firm's clients instead of prospective associates. For the wife this is often an emotional trial, since she is the one who is expected to see that things go smoothly. The degree of entertaining depends on the type of work her husband does. If he is in real estate, securities, or some other kind of predominantly office practice, the burden may be light. But if he is in trial work, especially insurance trial work, entertaining is a permanent part of their lives. If the wife does not like it—or if she doesn't like the people she is expected to entertain—"that can be a real problem," says Emily. "You will be constantly socializing with insurance people, going to meetings with insurance people, traveling here and there. You just have to say, 'I don't like 'em, but this is my job,' and go out and *do* it. And that isn't very pleasant, especially if you've had a hard day with six screaming children."

If the husband's line of work requires him to know a wide circle of other lawyers, his wife becomes a useful agent to help him establish and develop contacts. She may be expected to join and participate in a variety of women's clubs, civic projects, or charitable activities. If she balks, his advancement in the firm may be impaired.

When wives are so important to their husband's and the firm's success, it is not surprising that the firm scrutinizes them coldly but inconspicuously during the recruiting process. The associates' wives are often asked for their opinion of a rushee's spouse, although their judgment seems to carry weight in inverse proportion to the prospective young lawyer's grade-point average. "If you're talking about a guy with super grades," says Emily, "then he'd have to have a pretty bad wife to lose out." But it does happen. "I remember a Harvard boy who had married an actress from New York, a former prostitute. If she'd been able to cover all this up—not the actress part, but the former prostitute part—then I guess it would have been all right. But she didn't. She came to the firm and was quite loud, fairly obnoxious; and he was not offered a job because of her. They later got divorced."

"A good wife is rather unobtrusive," muses Emily. "She should be someone who can help entertain, to a degree. And yet there are some excellent lawyers whose wives you never see socially." Their husbands, presumably, had super grades. For the rest, feminine subordination to the husband's career is a basic premise of their life together. In the firm's eyes, the wife's activities are his activities, and the same ground rules apply to both. A wife conspicuously active in radical politics, for example, would be an unmitigated disaster for her husband. Life in the big firms is still very much a family affair, and the firm's threshold of embarrassment is low indeed.

An incident that occurred near the end of the interview forcefully (and unexpectedly) drove this point home. The telephone rang, and Emily's precocious seven-year-old daughter answered it. "Mommy's talking to the tape recorder," she told the caller, who turned out to be Daddy. His curiosity metamorphosed into great ire when Mommy told him she had been discussing the life of lawyers' wives. This writer took the phone to reassure him that the interview had begun with an understanding that neither Emily's identity nor the firm's would be disclosed. Unmollified, he insisted that the firm be supplied with a copy of the transcript and allowed to delete anything it did not want printed. He was told that this would be impossible, but that the writer would be happy to clear up any misconceptions about the terms of the interview on his visit to their offices the next day.

A somewhat shaken Emily returned to the sofa and continued the discussion, but her animated manner was gone. About five minutes later the phone rang again. Daddy's message was unambiguous, *ex cathedra*: I have told the managing partner what you are doing, and he has ordered you to stop the interview. "I guess you'll have to destroy the tape," said Emily as she sat back down, stunned.

A few minutes of pleasantries were exchanged to save embarrassment all around, but the interview was over. Emily grew visibly unnerved by the occurrence, changing the subject every couple of minutes to say, "I suppose I should have checked with them first, but I never *thought* . . ." And her voice trailed off. Explanations were offered—"It's just a misunderstanding, we'll straighten it out tomorrow"—but one had the distinct impression of being present at a moment when another person realized for the first time the true extent of her confinement. A man for whom she did not even work, sitting in an office building five miles away, could casually *order* her to stop talking to someone else about her life. He not only could, he *had*, without even bothering to ask first what she had been saying. It was a sobering experience, and it spoke volumes about the way the Big Three firms sweep lawyers, wives, and families into their all-encompassing embrace.

Hidden Mandarins: The Law Firms and Political Power

The extraordinary edifice of power erected by the Big Three is built on two secure cornerstones: politics and economics. Their political power is enormous, but it is not displayed in the manner that the general public has come to expect. Seldom does a partner manage a campaign, even locally. Almost never does one seek public office. Judges, too, come from someplace else. There is no tradition of public service in the big Houston firms, no *noblesse oblige*. Their sense of dignity clashes with the realities of politics as they perceive it: politics is not a gentleman's game in this state; therefore gentleman lawyers do not sully themselves by becoming politicians. This distaste extends to other forms of public service as well. Dillon Anderson of Baker & Botts, who served as special assistant to Dwight Eisenhower, and John Crooker, Jr., of Fulbright Crooker, who took a leave of absence to assume the chairmanship of the Civil Aeronautics Board, are exceptions to a very rigid rule. Much more typical is John Heard at Vinson Elkins, who declined John Kennedy's request to serve as Commissioner of Internal Revenue because his firm objected.

The big firms, of course, cannot please their critics either way. The very people who deplore their unwillingness to share the responsibilities of public service would be furious if they decided to do so, considering the possibilities for conflict-of-interest charges that could be levied against a legislator whose law firm represented the multitudinous clients of the Big Three. In any event the question of direct political participation is academic. As one lawyer remarks, "The big firms are conceived and bred like thoroughbred horses for one purpose: the practice of law. That is the end of their collective existence."

The political power is instead *derivative*. It flows through the big firms—and from them—but is not generated by them. It belongs to the people who have the money: those who rule empires of insurance, lumber, shipping, petrochemicals, utilities, and banking, to name a few. It belongs, in other words, to their clients (except in the case of the banks, which are often run by the lawyers themselves).

The big Houston firms act as mediators between these men with money and the men who hold (or want to hold) public office. "If you thought something needed to be done in Houston," muses a partner at Vinson Elkins, "the managing partners of the big firms would be the logical place to start." The firms' endorsement is a sort of imprimatur that gives credibility to a candidate, a proposal, or an idea; their power comes primarily from the fact that their judgment is trusted.

"Nothing big is going to happen in Houston unless Houston Lighting and Power, Humble Oil, *et al*. want it to happen," a liberal-minded trial lawyer insists. "And they're all represented by one of the Big Three. They go to their lawyer and have their lawyer tell the mayor." Not all the firms, however, have equal political clout. Baker & Botts seems at times to take a perverse pride in losing politically tinged battles like the recent contest for cable TV franchise rights, as though a certain degree of ineptness in dealing with politicians was the hallmark of a truly professional lawyer. Fulbright Crooker (which clobbered Baker & Botts in that fight) has a record of backing winners in political races without much regard to whether they were Republicans or Democrats. A study of the "Houston Establishment" last year placed FC at the apex of its pyramid. Vinson Elkins has for many years been the most politically astute of all, if one measures astuteness by success in seeing one's allies elected to public office; but their greatest impact has been on state, not local, politics.

To the outside observer, the role of the big Houston firms in state politics is a masterwork of subtlety. In essence it is a screening system that approves candidates and enables them to tap the great resources of establishment wealth.

"All the state officials go down and see them, hat in hand," says a wealthy, aristocratic former state legislator. But why bother with the lawyers, he is asked: it's the clients who have the big money. "Of course," he says. "But that's not the way it works. You have to go through the firm before you get to the client. You have to run the gauntlet first. In the old days you went to see Judge Elkins, or old man Crooker. . . . Now it's one of the other partners, but the routine is just the same. If the firm approves, you've got access to the client. Unless you could get their blessing, you couldn't get the money from the client. And the firms would charge their clients fees commensurate with the heat they'd taken off them."

The last Texas governor who was not the candidate of the big firms (or substantially acceptable to them) was James Allred. He left office in 1939. The firms also take an abiding interest in the races for state treasurer (held by Jesse James since 1941), attorney general, the Railroad Commission, and of course, the Texas Supreme Court. Occasionally a candidate slips up on them, as did John Hill, a trial lawyer who made his reputation on the opposite side of the docket from the big firms and squeaked through to election as attorney general in 1972. Hill's strategy was simple: he announced his candidacy at the last minute, preventing the big firms from fielding a third candidate who would split the anti–Crawford Martin vote. Hill has continued to be independent of them.

By reputation the Big Three have a hefty say in the selection of judges, particularly local judges. Partners in the firms seldom deign to accept judgeships themselves, but there is no doubt they keep close watch on those who do. Younger lawyers outside the big firms claim to see the malevolent hand of self-interest at work: "Get a judge who doesn't know the law," says one aggressive young newcomer, "and he has to depend on the reputation of the attorneys in the case . . . or of their firms." The quality of trial judges in Harris County is considered uneven, to say the least, but the appellate bench is exceptionally able for a state court. In the opinion of some experienced attorneys outside the big firms, it is at least the equal of the state Supreme Court in character, integrity, and legal scholarship. There is no real evidence that the Big Three actively attempt to maneuver mediocre minds onto the bench, although they do frequently get the benefit of the doubt in mediocre judges' decisions.

Members of the Big Three candidly admit that the firms hold a virtual veto over Harris County judicial appointments. (Although judicial positions are elective in Texas, most vacancies occur by death or resignation and are filled by gubernatorial appointment. The new judge then runs at the next election with whatever advantage an incumbent might have.) One prominent trial lawyer views judicial appointments as merely another example of the comfortable, symbiotic power relationships between big law firms and their prosperous clients. "Say you have a governor who got oil money the last time he ran. The law firm has a guy they want to see appointed judge. All they have to do is pick up the phone and call the chairman of the board of one of those companies, who just happens to be their client, whom they've just happened to keep out of trouble in the courts, and ask him to mention to the governor that so-and-so would make a fine judge down here. I'm not saying it's dishonest. I'm saying they use the political tools available to them."

Once on the bench, moreover, a Texas judge faces a lifetime of reelection campaigns if he wishes to remain there. While it is true that incumbent judges are hard to beat, very few are reckless enough to risk their positions by ignoring the political niceties. And the indispensable ingredients for a political campaign—publicity and finances—are conveniently available through the big firms and their corporate clients.

No one familiar with the practice of law in Houston seriously contends that the judges who win appointment or reelection in this fashion put on their robes and step into the courtroom determined to disregard the law in order to reward the lawyers and litigants whose influence helped them get there. But the idea that some lawyers and some clients exercise a disproportionate influence over the accession of judges has an insidious effect on the confidence other lawyers feel for their courts. Like so much else, it perpetuates an "us and them" attitude in the Houston bar.

Power Is Where the Money Is

The economic power of the firms is even more impressive than their political power. It can be traced to their special relationships with major Houston banks. National Democratic party chairman Robert Strauss, a Dallas lawyer, observes that while in most cities the big financial interests dominate the big law firms, in Houston the situation is reversed. And there is nothing at all derivative about that power.

On paper, the interpenetration is impressive: Jaworski is chairman of the executive committee of the Bank of the Southwest, and FC senior partner Hugh Buck also serves on the board. The firm also represents Houston Citizens Bank, where two other partners, Newton Gresham and John Crooker, are on the board. Vinson Elkins is practically synonymous with First City National Bank, where senior partners John Connally and Marvin Collie serve on a board chaired by Judge Elkins's non-lawyer son. Baker & Botts has its share of partners on various local boards, but it has no major "captive" bank of its own. Paradoxically, however, this situation has given them special influence over many medium-sized banks. As a giant firm with the largest corporate clientele of all, they automatically fall heir to much banking business, and the other banks tend to prefer doing business with them because they are *not* identified with Bank of the Southwest or First City National.

Economic power flows both ways, of course; the answer to the question of who controls whom is often murky. But the influence of lawyers from the Big Three is obviously substantial. The banks have channeled a disproportionate amount of their legal business to their allied law firms, in sharp contrast to the Dallas banking tradition of spreading the work around. Houston law practice is rife with tales of heavy-handed banking tactics. In effect the firms can use the banks to promote their own business. Lawyers from the small firms insist they often do.

Nor is the alliance of lawyers and banks limited to the downtown giants. Because the Texas Constitution prohibits branch banking, there is nothing comparable to California's vast Bank of America with statewide offices. Instead there is a plethora of small suburban "community" banks, each ostensibly an independent business enterprise. But the names of directors at the big banks appear with uncanny regularity as proposed directors for community banks seeking operating charters from the State Banking Board in Austin. An observer who has watched the Banking Board for years says, "When an application comes up, you can always tell which big bank is interested in it, just by looking at the names." Through this system of interlocking directorates, the big banks have dominated the Texas banking scene far more than the casual observer might suspect.

This informal procedure came roaring out into the open after the Bank Holding Company Act was amended in 1970 to permit, in effect, the development of bank holding companies. More and more "downtown" Texas banks are acquiring direct control of community banks through this device, which enables them to dominate numerous smaller institutions without running afoul of the letter of the constitution. There are now twenty multibank holding companies in the state with 122 subsidiaries. They control almost 40 per cent of the total deposits. Two of the top four are First City Bancorporation of Texas and Southwest Bancshares. The lead bank in the former is Houston's First City National; in the latter, Bank of the Southwest. Even as this new technique flourishes, however, the quest for bank charters continues.

A bank charter is a very valuable piece of paper. "It's the next best thing to a Coors beer franchise," one lawyer quips. Charters are adjudged to be so valuable, in fact, that they are granted not by a single individual but by the three-man State Banking Board, one member of which is called the banking commissioner and is appointed by the State Finance Commission. The second member is appointed by the governor for a two-year term, and the third is the state treasurer himself. A majority vote is sufficient to award a charter. And a majority of the Board is, of course, composed of one elected official and one direct appointee of an elected official, both of whom have been required to mount expensive statewide campaigns every two years.

The cooperation of the big law firms has traditionally been central to the success of gubernatorial candidates and Treasurer Jesse James. A disillusioned former member of the Banking Board sums up the situation thusly: "Millions of dollars in state funds are lying around in banks at very low interest rates. James has the authority to put the state's money pretty much where he pleases, and a lot of it winds up in Houston, at banks associated with law firms that have helped him stay in office. I'm not suggesting there's been any wrongdoing, but I am suggesting that they [the big Houston firms] understand his problem, and he understands theirs." A big transfusion of state money that can be invested at a profit is, of course, a very useful thing for a bank to have.

Lately the economic importance of the Big Three, especially Vinson Elkins, has been showing definite signs of going international, in a way that has very little to do with banks. The American oil industry, centered in Houston, is not without its influence in the Middle East. Most of the big companies already rely on their lawyers for advice that often transcends the merely technical. If the energy shortage worsens, American policy in that ticklish, oil-rich corner of the world may be affected even more by the judgments of oil men and their lawyers. Firms in New York have for decades influenced the development of American foreign policy, sending partners to counsel presidents and even to serve as Secretaries and Undersecretaries of State. Now it seems to be Houston's turn.

There is another little-noticed basis for the big firms' power. They are *enduring* institutions. A partner at Vinson Elkins reflected this when he remarked, "If you are going into Texas politics, you can assume that VE will be there throughout your career"—adding as an afterthought, "for good or ill, of course."

In a young city like Houston, their age and apparent permanence stand out sharply from the surrounding landscape. In one very real sense they are more powerful than their clients. A lawyer in government service muses on the relationship between Baker & Botts and their pollution-troubled client, Champion Paper. "They've been around longer than

Champion Paper and they'll be here when Champion Paper is gone," he says. "The judges on the bench are there because of Baker & Botts, not because of Champion Paper. Whatever happens, B&B will still be here: it's just like the government itself. They're going to suffer when their clients suffer, but they're going to bounce back."

The examples could be multiplied endlessly, but the message is the same. The big firms abide while other things change.

What the Future Holds

Where are the big firms headed? Despite their apparent immutability, they are actually at the threshold of a potentially dangerous transition. Control is passing inexorably from an older generation of generalists who had diverse knowledge of the law to younger specialists who have spent their professional lives in one narrow section of their huge firms. "There is a generation of lawyers coming up who cannot try a lawsuit or set up a small corporation," says a worried freshman associate at a Big Three firm. The fear is that such men may make mistakes their seniors would never have committed because no one will be around to see the overall picture. Whatever may happen, it is clear that the trend toward specialization makes big firm lawyers even more dependent on their institutions, more than ever unable to leave if they are dissatisfied. A lawyer who does nothing but write pension plans is eventually trapped by his own expertise.

The big firms long ago reached a size where the day-to-day demands of managing their affairs became a full-time job for one or more partners. The relentless inroads of bureaucracy continue. Many lawyers who have left to set up practice on their own did so because they felt the management techniques placed an unacceptable barrier between them and their clients. "Time sheets, billing, all the mechanical details began to dominate," said one emigrant who gave up a successful partnership at a Big Six firm. "I kept sending the stuff back, or 'forgetting' to do it, and they put up with my idiosyncracies because I brought in a hell of a lot of money every year. But that's the only reason I got away with it. Maybe they have to be formalistic, but there's nothing in a time sheet that reflects the *quality* of the work you do. After a while you fall into the trap of working for your firm instead of your client."

A great lawyer has to have a certain individualistic spirit; the giants of the profession are not technicians. But the big firms put no premium on that quality. Those of their senior partners who have it began their careers when the firms were still small. If the big firms expect to see it twenty years from now, they will have to pursue it by conscious choice.

As yet, however, they show every indication of moving in the opposite direction. Exhibiting the abundant caution of men who have already got what they want and are determined to keep it, their instinct is to play things safe. The really exotic corporate finance creativity lately, for example, came out of Wynne, Jaffe & Tinsley, a Dallas firm that represented James Ling in his conglomerate sorcery. Could it happen in Houston? Probably not; the tendency is not to be terribly bold. An inventive young lawyer who left one of the Big Three recalls an incident that helped him make up his mind: "We had a client who did business on the Ship Channel. He was worried to death about a proposed new Treasury regulation that would have required him to report under-the-table payments to captains of foreign vessels—something that was pretty standard in his business. They were kickbacks, really. He didn't mind *reporting* them because they were deductible anyway. But the captains, who weren't reporting them as income, didn't want the government to have any record of them. Our client knew that his competitors would just ignore the regulation, so that if it were adopted he would lose all his customers because the captains would just deal with his competitors and not with him.

"He was an honest man, and he was about to lose his shirt. So I went up to Washington and testified at a hearing in opposition to the regulation. I must have been persuasive, because they didn't adopt it. After I got back I told the head of my section what I'd done. I thought he'd be delighted. Instead he was alarmed, and he told me in a stony tone, 'We *do not testify* on behalf of, or in opposition to, legislative matters, without the firm's approval.' What he meant was, 'If you go around changing the law to help one of our clients, you may hurt another, bigger client.' But if the firm had said, 'No, don't testify,' where would that have left my client and me?"

The eternal incubus of the big firms, conflict of interest, subtly depresses their lawyers' creativity and sometimes stifles the free-swinging battling for the client's interest that all lawyers like to believe is their stock-in-trade.

For all their far-reaching involvement in the political and economic life of Texas, however, the big Houston firms are strangely insular places. Their power paradoxically isolates them from the society they oversee. They inhabit a curious high-rise world, peopled by men of undoubted power whose influence they share and sometimes even create, but disquietingly detached from the human consequences of the decisions they make. A person who eventually will be affected by something they do may be strolling along Main Street twenty stories below, blithely unaware that his future is being determined in some small particular by a lawyer intent on "the most intriguing legal problem imaginable," to whom he is a negligible abstraction. It happens all the time. The big firms take justifiable pride in their ability to resolve the most intractable legal problems and keep the engines of the Texas economy running smoothly for their clients. One looks in vain for a complementary sense of awe at the power they hold over other men's lives.

"They are law machines, my friend," said the trial lawyer who went on to praise them for being the finest concentration of legal talent in the country. He felt, quite rightly, that their ultimate justification lay in that fact. By their own professional lights, there is nothing wrong in siphoning off the best intellects they can find and reshaping them into men whose first loyalty is to the well-being of the institution for which they work, rather than to the society of which they are citizens. If the firm's interest ever conflicted with the good of society, they tell themselves, we would of course defend the latter; but such is their perception of society's needs that that day never comes. And so the big Houston firms feel no sense of urgency to offer leadership in the reform of law, to improve the quality of the judiciary, or to elevate the tone of public life.

The source of the malaise is politics, and the inability of the big firms to reach a reconciliation with it which they can regard as suitably professional. These thoughts were on the mind of a lawyer at one of the Big Three.

"What is a lawyer?" he asked. "Is he a professional man, an officer of the court? Or is he a tradesman who has mastered a lucrative craft? What the hell *is* a lawyer? Traditionally a professional man was respected because he was not just 'in it for the money'; he was a leader in the community and he took time away from his moneymaking to do it.

"Now, to a rather blatant degree, lawyers have become the tools of the propertied class. Instead of lawyers being the best read and wisest people in the community, they've become technocrats. Since you don't want to alienate your clients, you begin to think like them and act like them.

"Politics makes very cautious people out of us. When I think of the leadership that is lost to the community when lawyers are inhibited by these things, I become very discouraged indeed. We have a lot more to offer than we give, and we are the ones who are tying ourselves down."

The clients of the big Houston firms gain excellence, of course; but the loss to the rest of us is considerable.

EXXON
CHAIRMAN OF THE BOARD

SO YOU WANT TO BE CHAIRMAN OF EXXON?

by Nicholas Lemann

Or maybe you don't.

In May of this year Woody Dinstel sat down at his desk in Houston to write a letter. First he looked at the watch. It was a gold Hamilton Masterpiece, slim and heavy. On the back was engraved WOODY DINSTEL UPON RETIREMENT FEBRUARY 1, 1978, EXXON.

He was writing to Dr. Tom Barrow, senior vice president of Exxon Corporation in New York, the highest-ranking geologist in the company and a hero to the older generation of explorationists, an emblem of the best in the company. Dinstel had once made a presentation to Barrow in England and had been very impressed; he thought perhaps Barrow might remember him.

The letter was an appeal for help, for Dinstel was having some serious problems with the company. It had been his plan to take early retirement from Exxon—to receive a pension of $611.13 a month and perhaps in a few years to move to the country house he and his wife own in Mississippi. For a while, it had appeared that there would be no problem with that. Dinstel had signed all the requisite papers, had had his farewell lunch at a fancy restaurant in Houston, and had received the gold watch. But at the last minute the company had changed its mind, perhaps because it had learned that Dinstel was planning to take another job at higher pay with a smaller oil company, and called the whole thing off. Either stay on or quit with no early retirement benefits, Exxon had told him. "My best recourse," Dinstel wrote Barrow, "is to contact someone I know as high up in the corporation as possible. Perhaps that executive will react by thinking, 'This guy had 23 years with the company; did we give him the shaft?'" Dinstel told Barrow his story, and ended his letter this way:

"I deserve to be an annuitant; it is my right; I have earned it.

"I used to love Exxon.

"Your consideration of my situation will be appreciated."

Barrow never wrote back. Woody Dinstel, who was so loyal to Exxon that he drove around with the company's marketing symbol, a plastic tiger tail, attached to the gas cap of his car, had lost his loyalty and was going elsewhere, so the company's loyalty to him was at an end.

This is a story about success and failure in the world's largest industrial corporation, and about loyalty and love too. It's a Texas story, and not just because Exxon's domestic operations are headquartered here or because 15,000 Texans work for Exxon. This is a state that has drawn much of its sense of itself through success stories—the taming of the land, the discovery of oil and gas, the growth of businesses, the building of cities, even the victories of football teams. One of the classic success stories is that of the founding of Humble Oil & Refining Company in the oil fields of the Gulf Coast by a roughneck, a storekeeper, a banker, and six other men, who ventured into a new area, took some risks, and built the state's biggest oil company. These men rose through strong individual, entrepreneurial achievement. They broke new ground and, through determination and talent and effort and luck, built something that hadn't been there before.

Now Humble is Exxon USA, the largest subsidiary of Exxon Corporation, headquartered in a Houston skyscraper, a symbol of how success in Texas is changing—and with it, our identity. The men who run Exxon are not entrepreneurs; they are managers. Success or failure in Texas is no longer linked to venture and risk. Increasingly, it means rising or not rising through the ranks of a large, established organization. That will mean that different kinds of people will rise, on the strength of different skills. And it will mean

Illustrated by Stephen Durke

POWER: TEXANS WHO HAVE IT AND USE IT 39

RUNNING ON THE FAST TRACK AT EXXON

AGE 25

You've got your engineering degree and your MBA, and you've been with Exxon a couple of years. You had a good first job in the Baton Rouge refinery and a good second one at Exxon USA headquarters in Houston. You've gone through special company training in refinery engineering. But be careful: you're being watched closely by management. The next few years will determine whether you'll be chosen to rise in the company.

that those who do succeed will draw their sense of pride and self not from what they have built so much as from how they have risen in the organizations that selected them and shaped them to lead. That's why, in a corporation with 128,000 employees, loyalty and love are operative concepts, strongly felt by those who have succeeded, painfully absent for those who have not, like Woody Dinstel.

And it's why top executives of Exxon, by and large a tough, calm, competent breed, wander into emotionalism when they talk about how they feel about the company. Back in the days when Exxon was Standard Oil Company (New Jersey), its chairman, Monroe J. Rathbone, told a reporter from *Fortune,* "Working for Jersey has been a great thing for me. I've never in all these years been disappointed in this company. It's been an exhilarating experience." Ten years later, Clifton C. Garvin, Jr., Exxon's present chairman, asked by *Forbes* how he felt about being in charge, said, "I think of it as a proprietary relationship. Like running a company of which I am the owner. It is just my duty, but my deep personal desire is to keep it in the best shape possible for the men who will come after me." When Garvin was named chairman in 1975 and Howard C. Kauffmann president, Monroe Rathbone wrote them a note. "Your job right now," he said, "is to develop some more Garvins and Kauffmanns."

These are company men who obviously feel strongly about the organization and about the importance of developing more company men to run it in the future. The reason the feelings are so strong (try to imagine a government bureaucrat saying those things) is that what Garvin said about a proprietary relationship is, in a way, true. Certainly the people who run Exxon are in name managers, not owners, but the nominal distinction obscures the true nature of most large corporations. The owners of Exxon are diffuse and almost invisible. The board of directors is made up mostly of men who may not be founders, but who have been with the company for thirty years or more, since they were 22 or 23, rising up from the oil fields and refineries. The six senior men on the board own close to $8 million in Exxon stock and are paid salaries ranging downward from Garvin's $485,592 (with benefits, $729,267). They run a company with operations in more than a hundred countries and gross revenues larger than the annual GNP of Mexico or Australia. No wonder they feel proprietary.

Of course, most bureaucracies in the United States are staffed by a career service; the best-known examples are the civil service and the military. But in those a person can rise only so high through the ranks, and the policy decisions are made by outsiders, appointed secretaries of Defense or State. The job of the career service is to see that these policies are carried out. Exxon, however, is a self-contained world, where the career service provides everything. It doesn't hire hot young vice presidents away from Union Carbide. It doesn't bring in smooth investment bankers to run the show. Until 1966, the company's board was made up entirely of employees (now they hold eight of seventeen seats on it). Other companies farm out much of their legal work to law firms; Exxon, for the most part, relies on its in-house legal department. Other companies, when they want to raise money through a bond sale, let an investment house arrange it; two years ago, Exxon shocked the financial world by underwriting and distributing a $54.9 million bond issue itself, via a rare procedure known as a "Dutch auction." Other companies have career systems of varying sorts, but Exxon's (along, perhaps, with AT&T's) is known as the most carefully run and the best at providing talent and continuity.

One result of the career system is that, while there are no old-fashioned, overnight wildcatter success stories at Exxon, rises from rags to riches almost as dramatic as in the old days are still possible. The company is run by engineers and

AGE 35

Five years ago you made it onto the fast track, and now you're in the middle of one of the company's four-year high-potential development plans. You're married now (happily), with several kids and a nice house. But don't get too settled in—you're going to be moving a lot these next few years. Right now you've just finished your company management course and you're running a division in the public affairs department. You may be an engineer, but you have to be able to manage anything.

geologists, most of them from small towns and state universities—men who couldn't be more different from the leaders of the oil business of two generations ago, but who share with their predecessors enough drive and hunger to have done what is necessary to get to the top. Most people think the positions of greatest responsibility in the dominant institutions in this country are held by members of a loosely knit establishment made up of people from privileged backgrounds who know and tend to help one another. At Exxon, that notion just doesn't apply.

For that reason, the personnel system is of paramount importance to the company, the key to its continued health. In effect, it is the company's reproductive system too, doing for Exxon what pistils and stamens do for flowers. Exxon has to be absolutely sure that within the last five years it has hired someone right out of school with the talent to assume the chairmanship one day and do well at it. In part that's a matter of faith, but there are good reasons why the faith in the personnel system is so strong. The system is meticulously planned and operated and absorbs considerable amounts of time and effort and money. One company publication recently said Exxon spends $203,000 on each employee every year. The company carefully recruits and trains and rates people. Those who, for reasons of ability and temperament, aren't suited to a high position in a major corporation stay in the middle ranks, and those who do rise are the ones who have shown themselves to be so suited. Those tough, calm, competent men in the boardroom weren't just born that way. They were shaped.

The personnel system deserves much of the credit for Exxon's continuing vitality. For more than a century, since the days of John D. Rockefeller's Standard Oil Trust, Exxon has probably been the most significant and successful corporation in the world. "In the history of U.S. business," *Dun's Review* wrote five years ago, "the company's success has been truly singular. Of the huge industrial companies that were begun before 1900, only Exxon survives with anything like its original preeminence." Over that time, Exxon has also probably been the most hated company in the world, and the personnel system is partly to blame for that too. Exxon is a closed society, unfriendly to outsiders—an organization good at the oil business and bad at explaining itself to the public.

Exxon would not cooperate with this story. When I was beginning my research, I went to the Exxon USA public relations office in Houston and explained that I was interested in writing about the company's personnel system. Exxon has a rule that none of its employees can talk to the press without first clearing it with public relations, and public relations won't clear anything unless it has sized up the writer's intentions and made a decision to cooperate. In this case they decided not to—not to let me do any interviews with Exxon employees, not to answer a list of factual questions I submitted, not even to comment on a draft of the story. For several weeks William Broyles, the editor of this magazine, and I discussed our case with various Exxon officials, but to no avail.

I found that the majority of former employees of Exxon, especially those who left happy, wouldn't talk either. "A man who's held the position I've held with Exxon," explained Charles F. Jones, a former president of Humble Oil, "isn't going to go against the wishes of the company." A few former employees were willing to talk for the record, but most either wouldn't say anything or asked first for solemn guarantees of their anonymity. "As long as you're still in the oil business," one man told me, "Exxon can put the big hurt on you." Some people agreed to interviews and then got cold feet at the last minute and backed off. One man who had left Exxon spoke bitterly about the company for fifteen minutes on the phone, and I arranged to see him in person in Houston. But when I called him up on the appointed day, he didn't want to meet after all, only to

AGE 45

You're back at the Baton Rouge refinery, but now you're running it. It's a demanding job (and well paying), but you still find time to serve on the board of the local Community Chest. You're hoping the company will send you to the Harvard Business School for the thirteen-week advanced management course. After that, maybe New York, where, if you're lucky, you'll be executive assistant to a member of the board.

emphasize over the phone "how well I love the company."

Fear, the obvious answer, can only partly explain why the company and its employees were so reticent. The reasons for the company's stubborn refusal to give its side of the story about a personnel system of which it is extremely proud are, I think, more complicated than that. The company's explanation to us was that it didn't consider *Texas Monthly* an "appropriate forum" for such an article, and, while my strong initial inclination was not to believe that, I later came to understand Exxon's reasoning. I think it is probably very difficult for people who have spent their whole adulthood living the Exxon life to explain it to outsiders.

It's generally agreed, among those who love the company and those who don't, that the successful Exxon executive is a person (almost always a man) of a particular type. Above all, he is extremely able; the system is good at weeding out incompetents. Like many men who have risen in our large corporations, he comes from a stable, middle-class background, usually not a big city and usually not the East or West Coast. He's a family man, happily married to an attractive woman and the father of several children. He and his wife take care to be active in respectable community affairs. He's not an eccentric, a maverick, or an entrepreneurial type. He's not a flashy or sloppy dresser. He's bright, aggressive, good with numbers, less good with people. Very likely he is a veteran of the military. He's willing to relocate frequently (though this is becoming less the case) and to work hard on any assignment he's given. "The people who did best there," says one former employee, "were those who kept plugging, who never questioned authority, who said, 'If this is what the company wants, I'll do it.' Anyone who said, 'Why the hell am I staying up all night Sunday to finish this when nobody needs it till Thursday?' didn't have the right spirit."

The particular skills required of the successful Exxon manager are more those of the corporation than those of the oil field. It's important to learn how to deliver an impressive presentation to management, how to write a good memo, and how, if you've got an unappreciative boss, to circulate carbons of your memos to *his* boss. It's helpful to develop a knack for getting assigned to fast-rising supervisors, who can take you along with them, and to winning teams—it's better to work in the North Sea, where Exxon is finding oil, than in the Destin Anticline, where the company paid the federal government $316 million for leases and drilled seven dry holes. It's bad to get too emotional, to become too attached to a project to be able to accept its rejection. Exxon is a company famous for doing everything by committee, so it is crucial to be able to operate that way. The top manager at Exxon is the model of the successful organization man, hardworking and committed but, above all, a member of the team.

Most of the time, Exxon finds him on a university campus. The company doesn't make public any figures on what schools its people come from, but it is commonly felt around the placement offices at the University of Texas that UT provides more of Exxon's professional employees than any other school; whether or not that is so, UT is a good case study in how Exxon recruits. With the exception of law students, people getting degrees at UT can make more money with an oil company than with any other employer, and Exxon is regarded as the best and the highest paying of the major oil companies.

Exxon, in turn, is looking for the best people, people in the top quarter or even tenth of their class, people who are active in some leadership-demonstrating activity outside the classroom, people who are steady and responsible—people who, as one student says, "embody the ideals of American business." They must be technically trained in a field where Exxon needs experts, like geology, engineering, accounting, geophysics, or petroleum land management. Even among

AGE 55

At last, you're on the board, a vice president in charge of refining. These last few years have been busy—New York, then Europe, then back to Houston as president of Exxon Chemical. Now you're hoping they'll pick you as president of Exxon Corporation, because that's what you have to be before you can be chairman. But it has to happen soon: no matter how good you are, at 65 you're out.

MBA's Exxon prefers those who have a technical undergraduate major. Only Mobil, of the major oil companies, has a reputed interest in undergraduate liberal arts majors; last year UT's liberal arts division had a career symposium for its students, and Exxon declined to send a representative.

In some of the departments from which Exxon hires, virtually every student is headed for the oil companies, and the companies keep a fatherly eye on those departments. They contribute money and equipment to the engineering and geology departments through special foundations (called Industrial Associates and the Geology Foundation, respectively), which supplement the departments' regular budgets from the university. Last year Exxon gave the geology department at UT a seismic truck. It's hard to look at these practical and businesslike arrangements without feeling some twinge that college really ought to be for reading Shakespeare, but increasingly the liberal arts are viewed as a luxury. For those who are going to need jobs immediately after graduation, the pre-oil majors are perhaps the best guarantee of success.

Unlike the big Houston law firms, the oil companies don't wine and dine students. Some of them hold informal sessions over beer and nachos, but Exxon doesn't, and doesn't have to. "They just crook their finger and everyone comes running," says one geology student. During the spring and fall hiring seasons, Exxon dispatches teams of interviewers to UT to have half-hour talks with the dozens of students who sign up for them. Those who fare well may be asked to Houston, where they'll have a day of interviews at headquarters and perhaps go out to dinner with a bright young manager. The company stays faithfully in touch with these people, calling and writing them occasionally until they've made a final decision about where to work. Also, says one placement officer, the recruiters sometimes take a friendly professor out to lunch and pull out a list of names over coffee, hoping to find out who's really good.

The only reason a promising pre-oil student might turn down a job with Exxon would be to work for a smaller independent company. There, a very outstanding student might be offered more money, more responsibility, and the opportunity for quicker advancement. But Exxon is reliably well paying, secure, and an excellent training ground. A student getting an undergraduate degree in petroleum engineering could reasonably expect a job with Exxon to carry a starting salary of more than $20,000—in many cases, no doubt, more than the student's parents make.

Once at Exxon, a young professional immediately comes under an intensive and complex system of evaluation. Once a year each manager in the company rates all the employees under him (anywhere from 25 to 70 people) on a one-to-five scale. One is for water-walkers; a 2.5 means you're above average; and a 5 means termination, although, as one employee puts it, "you'd have to assassinate somebody to get a five." There is a forced distribution system for the ratings, so that only a small percentage of the company's employees can get ratings of one. Each manager also does what's called a seriatim listing of the employees under him—a ranking, in numerical order, according to performance. And these numbers are reviewed by more than one supervisor. As a result, Exxon avoids some of the problems endemic to other bureaucratic personnel evaluation systems. In the Army, for instance, an officer's career depends completely on the Officer Efficiency Reports he gets from his supervisor, and these are only nominally checked by others. So, much more than Exxon employees, Army officers talk about there being an ironclad rule that, no matter what, you don't piss off the boss. Another problem in the Army and many other bureaucracies is grade inflation: there's no reason for a supervisor not to give out lots of very high ratings, thus rendering them nearly meaningless. But at Exxon, the forced distribution system prevents that.

Supervisors also fill out more detailed forms on employees, evaluating their performance and suggesting areas for improvement. And each employee fills out a form on himself, saying how he thinks he's doing and what his goals are. With those in hand, employee and supervisor meet face to face and discuss their findings. This is the only part of the whole evaluation process that many employees know about, and, depending on the boss, the performance review sessions may be a healthy exchange of views or completely pro forma. "Often my boss would tell me what he said on the form, and I'd just say yessir, yessir, yessir and sign it," says one former employee.

The last and most important step in the process is a rating of potential that managers give their employees. At Exxon, as in the civil service, people move up through a series of numbered grades, with pay tied to the grade. A college graduate in a professional job will usually start as a 22. Above the numbers is a second series of lettered grades leading all the way to the top. So if you're a 22 now but show a good deal of ability, your boss might list your potential as 29. If you get a 31 or 32 or are judged to have the potential to "go into the letters," then you have a good chance of becoming a "hi-po," a member of a special high-potential group.

Upper management in each department culls all the evaluation reports and picks out the employees who seem to have high potential. These people are divided into two groups—those with just plain high potential and those with extra-high potential, the ability to become a corporate officer one day. Of the 28,000 employees of Exxon USA, several hundred might be in the first of these groups and as few as 25 in the second. The hi-pos get a great deal of attention from management. At Exxon USA, each hi-po has a special four-year development plan, and his progress is regularly reviewed by a group whose members include the president of the company, Randall Meyer. Even at the pinnacle of Exxon Corporation in New York, the employee members of the board (who make up an "inside board" that meets more frequently than the regular board) spend much of their time talking about where to move particularly promising employees.

You are never told straight out that you are on this fast track, but you can tell. You get paid in the upper end of the scale for your grade. You get promoted rapidly. You switch jobs a lot. In the elevator, vice presidents whom you've never met greet you by name. For every significant job at Exxon there is a replacement list—a roster of possible replacements for the job's present holder. Fast-track people, who tend to be on these lists, get the jobs when they open up. People are chosen for the fast track very young—often in their first five or six years with the company, almost never after age 35. That means their intelligence and ability are more important than their specific experience in winning them a rendezvous with destiny. Where management chooses to steer the fast-track people shows what experience it thinks its top executives need to have, and, by extension, what it considers most important to the continued prosperity of the company.

A typical fast-track career might go like this: after graduation with a BS and an MBA, your first job would be with Exxon USA, somewhere in the field—either at a district office near drilling sites or at a refinery. Exxon has myriad divisions and specialties, but, in broad outline, the most important kinds of work are exploration and production ("upstream"), and transportation, refining, and marketing ("downstream"). Of these, the most reliable producers of top executives—and, therefore, in the company's mind, evidently its most important functions—are production and refining. Of Exxon's many companies, the main supplier of talent for the corporation is Exxon USA. It is the work of drilling for and refining oil and gas that is at the center of what Exxon does (more so, interestingly, than finding the oil), so that's what the company rewards. More than anything else, it is in the business of efficiently processing vast quantities of its product.

After the initial field job might come a tour back at headquarters in a staff job, doing financial analysis and planning. Field jobs are the meat and potatoes of the company, and it is important to show that you can meet a production schedule, stay within a budget, and meet deadlines. But when any organization becomes large, staff work is also crucial, and a staff job provides the opportunity to learn the skills of the office, to meet executives, to make presentations to important people, to make yourself well known. Following the first headquarters job might be a second tour in the field, this time in a supervisory capacity. All during this time, in addition to doing your work, you will attend company training courses, both in the techniques of your field and in broader skills, like public speaking or negotiating. It's good for Exxon that Clifton Garvin is impressive in congressional hearings, on television, and at annual meetings, and the courses he took are one reason why he is.

After five or six years in his specialty, an employee on the fast track might spend another four or five years moving through staff and supervisory jobs in other specialties. The idea behind this is that a really good manager has to learn how to manage *anything,* even if he doesn't have any expertise in it. Often a promising middle manager trained in chemical engineering will find himself challenged by being put in charge of a unit in, say, land management, whose work he barely understands, supervising people who have the expertise he lacks. At this point, a rising employee might attend a company course in the techniques of management.

After some time in another field it is important to get back to your original specialty, whether it was geophysics or accounting (to move on to another new one can be fatal), but in a position of real responsibility. In the field, the hierarchy of such jobs would be coordinator, then district manager, then division manager, and finally operations manager. In production, for instance, a district manager might run everything out of the Corpus Christi office; a division manager might be in charge of all production in the central United States; and an operations manager would oversee all domestic production. Interspersed with these field jobs would be more time back at headquarters, ideally as assistant to some very high-level official. If all these hurdles are cleared, the next step would be a vice presidency and then a whirlwind of executive vice presidencies, executive assistantships, and presidencies of minor Exxon companies. As an example of the relative status of such jobs, a few months ago the president of Exxon Pipeline was promoted to the position of executive assistant to Exxon Corporation's president, Howard Kauffmann. Schooling during this final polishing period might take place outside the company at a special course at some prestigious university—for instance, Harvard Business School's thirteen-week advanced management program. At the end of the road would come a place on the board in New York.

A look at the histories of the high executives mentioned so far sheds some light on the route upward. All of them but Barrow are engineers. Garvin is a chemical engineer who graduated from Virginia Polytechnic Institute and is the son of a district manager for Safeway in Portsmouth, Virginia. Kauffmann is a mechanical engineer who went to the University of Oklahoma. Monroe Rathbone was a chemical engineer from Lehigh University. Garvin, like Rathbone, spent his formative years rising up the ladder at the Baton Rouge refinery, Exxon's largest and a traditional breeding ground for high executives. Garvin also served in two other common fast-track jobs—vice president of Humble (predecessor of Exxon USA) and executive assistant to the chairman of the board. Refining is the greatest producer of board members, followed by production, then by exploration, and finally by marketing. But by the time a man gets to the board his experience is never limited to one field or one place. When he ascended to the chairmanship, Garvin had already worked in Baton Rouge, Tulsa, Midland, Houston, Los Angeles, and New York, and had been president of Exxon's chemical company as well as a refinery manager. Like many Exxon executives, he had become vaguely a citizen of the Sunbelt, perhaps more of Texas and Louisiana than anywhere else, but really he was a citizen of Exxon.

Of course, this world of the successful is completely alien to most Exxon employees. For them, the hi-pos are confident, well-spoken young men and, ever so rarely, women who whiz through their offices for a year or two on their way to somewhere else. The average middle manager in the company isn't on the fast track, doesn't know personally anyone who is, and has no idea how to get on it. Even people in the high-potential group often have to reconcile themselves to the harsh realities of the promotion system: on each succeeding step up the ladder there is room for fewer people, and even some of the best have to be left behind. "Exxon likes to hire only potential presidents," says one employee, "so there are an awful lot of unhappy people around."

A good number of these people leave for the ample outside opportunities that are available to any presentable Exxon employee. Some completely give up trying and become deadwood; right now Exxon has a de facto tenure policy for all but the most blatant malefactors. One female employee told me that a male Exxon manager could, starting tomorrow, do nothing at work but read the newspaper and would probably last seven more years, and that a woman, in these affirmative-action times, would probably last ten. The company will spend long hours counseling anyone who seems unproductive or unhappy in an effort to get him back on the track.

But most people at Exxon who are no longer advancing neither leave nor completely give up. Some are craftsmen who can contentedly study fossil formations for thirty years. More stay on because it's their best option. They stay for the thrift fund, to which they can contribute part of their salary and have it matched by Exxon. They stay to become eligible for a pension. They stay for the Employee Stock Ownership Plan. They stay because they have heart trouble and Exxon provides excellent medical coverage. They stay because it's a secure job, because the raises keep coming, because there's always the possibility that something will change. Their attitude, despite what the oil companies say about the distinctiveness of the free enterprise system, is one that's no less common at Exxon than in the civil service, probably even in the Kremlin.

Woody Dinstel was one of those people. After he got out of the Army in 1946, Dinstel enrolled in geophysics at Lehigh University, figuring that would be a way to combine his love of the outdoors and his talent at mathematics. When he graduated (with honors) he went to work for Conoco, doing seismic testing and subsurface mapping on field crews. In the next three years he worked in Rock Springs, Wyoming; Limon, Colorado; Durant, Mississippi (where he met and married his wife, Ruth); Billings, Montana; Ponca City, Oklahoma; Pecos, Texas; and Sterling City, Texas. At the end of that time he quit Conoco. He wasn't getting promoted, and, because he is a small, feisty, talkative man from New Jersey, he had trouble getting along with the laconic Southwesterners who populated the crews and, for that matter, the oil business in general.

The Dinstels drove from Texas to Ruth's parents' house in Durant with their infant son and all their possessions, and Woody sat down and wrote a lot of letters to oil companies. He got a positive response from Carter Oil, an Oklahoma-based company owned by Standard Oil of New Jersey that was sort of a miniature Humble. He started with Carter in Shreveport, where he stayed six months; then went to the Jackson office; and then overseas for nine years. At that time Jersey owned dozens of companies, all operating in different places and under different names, but New York coordinated their operations and finances, and it was common for personnel to be "loaned" back and forth among them. Dinstel worked for a year in Calcutta in the employ of Standard-Vacuum (a Jersey-Mobil joint venture), for three and a half years in Caracas for Creole Petroleum, and in London for five years for Esso Petroleum.

"All these years," Dinstel wrote Tom Barrow much later, "were my glory years with Exxon and its affiliates. The geology was big, unknown, fascinating, and challenging. I worked with small staffs, had promotions, raises, and recognition. To top it all off, it gave me great satisfaction that a fellow alumnus of Lehigh University, M. J. Rathbone, had reached the top with Jersey." Dinstel's job was to interpret seismic records as part of the effort to decide where to drill. For the most part, the areas he studied were previously uncharted. When he made a presentation, it was usually to a high-ranking executive. Sometimes he also supervised other geologists and geophysicists.

In 1965 Dinstel asked for a domestic assignment because he wanted his kids (there were three of them by now) to grow up in the United States and go to American schools. The company moved him to Tyler, Texas, and that was when the glory years ended.

Dinstel's new employer was the Humble Oil & Refining Company, but not the *old* Humble. To anyone who used to work for it, the distinction is important. For forty years, Humble was the class of the Texas oil and gas business—the best paying, the best staffed, the best at finding oil, and a *Texas* company, founded by Texans and headquartered in Texas. In the early fifties, when Dinstel was working for Conoco, if his seismic crew ever moved to a town where there was a Humble operation, all the crewmen would sneak over and ask for jobs. "Humble was the finest corporation ever created," says Nick Woodward, petroleum land management program coordinator at UT and a loyal Exxon alumnus too. "Everybody wanted to work there."

Since 1919, two years after Humble's founding, the majority shareholder in Humble had been Standard Oil of New Jersey. But for decades Humble was Texas-managed; its relationship with Jersey was arm's length, in keeping with the parent company's longstanding policy of decentralization. Humble often sent executives on to Jersey, but Jersey didn't send bosses down to Humble.

In the late fifties, however, Jersey began to centralize. In 1960 it sent out a tender call for outstanding Humble stock and its ownership became almost total. Then it merged all its domestic oil and gas operations—including Carter, Dinstel's old company—into Humble, which suddenly became a huge corporation, with $3 billion in assets, six refineries, the largest fleet of tankers under the American flag, and gas stations in 43 states. In 1963 Jersey sent John Kenneth Jamieson (later a chairman of the board of Exxon) down to Houston to assume Humble's presidency and begin a consolidation process that eventually cut the Humble work force by 20 per cent. In 1966 an executive vice president of Jersey (and a Carter alumnus), Myron A. "Mike" Wright, became Humble's first outsider chairman, and its last—in 1977, when Randall Meyer became the head man at Humble, it was with the lesser title of president. On January 1, 1973, the process was completed with the changing of Humble's name to Exxon USA.

These changes may seem only to have made explicit the already existing relationship between New York and Houston, but their symbolic significance was enormous. Even people who liked the new Jersey-controlled Humble better than the old independent one say that Humble somehow had a family feeling that was lost in the early sixties. And for the majority who didn't like the change, the memories of those years are bitter ones. "Humble changed from a very personal company into an impersonal one," says one man who left the company in 1973 after 28 years. "We lost our names and became numbers and fitness reports. We had wonderful esprit de corps at the old Humble. It was like being on a winning football team. You knew everybody. You could be outspoken and critical. Then all of a sudden top management came in and we lost our identity. It changed from a vibrant oil company to a banking situation."

The transition was so strongly felt by Humble employees partly because it was the most readily available symbol of the change in Texas from the era of the family business to the era of the giant corporation, and partly because it came at a time of other momentous shifts in the oil business. The sixties were the years of too much oil. All the major companies had huge fields in the Middle East and Latin America–big enough, it seemed, to guarantee decades of cheap crude. The problem the companies faced was not how to get oil, but how to produce and refine it efficiently and sell it in sufficient quantity—hence the free-steak-knife deals that proliferated at gas stations in those years.

So, in the exploration end of the business, particularly in the continental U.S., the sixties were bleak years. The fate of the independents, whose only job is finding domestic onshore oil and gas, is an example: between 1957 and 1973 their numbers shrank from 20,000 to 10,000. Among the majors, Gulf practically announced that it was no longer interested in domestic exploration because of its tremendous reserves in the Persian Gulf. Texaco concentrated on putting gas stations in all fifty states. Only Exxon, of the majors, was reasonably farsighted —Rathbone insisted on continuing to plow money into domestic exploration in Alaska and other places and was considered an eccentric for it. Even so, the times were such that at Humble the emphasis shifted somewhat, away from exploration (which is, really, the source of almost all the romance and legend of the oil business) and toward refining and marketing.

Woody Dinstel stayed in Tyler for two years, until the office was closed down in the centralization process and he was transferred to Houston. Right from the start his work was different from what it had been overseas. He was doing, he says, work that a guy just hired would do—mapping areas in East Texas that were easy to plot and had been mapped before. Dinstel was 39 years old and bored. He tried to find another job, but, those being bad years for explorationists, he couldn't. He began to think about early retirement. The policy was that if you were at least 50 and had been with the company at least fifteen years you could, subject to Exxon's consent, leave and receive an annuity comparable to what you would be eligible for at 65. In those years, in exploration, the consent was pro forma. So for Dinstel, that meant a little more than ten years of waiting.

The work was even worse in Houston. After six months Dinstel was made a velocity specialist, which he remained for the rest of his time with the company. Velocity is a small subdivision of geophysics in which a scientist does mathematically roughly what a bat does instinctively: measures the speed of waves, in this case seismic waves, as they move through the earth. Variations in the speed of the waves can sometimes indicate the presence of hydrocarbons, particularly natural gas. For six years Dinstel was a velocity specialist for the Gulf of Mexico, and for four years for the Gulf of Alaska. It was monotonous, almost clerical work. "I wanted to be directly associated with an oil or gas discovery," he says. "To me that's the measure of your success. You've got to feel like you're worth something. And I didn't feel like I was worth anything at Exxon."

For ten years Dinstel told his supervisors in his fall performance reviews that he was bored, stale, wanted a transfer. He asked them whether Exxon wanted him to quit. He went back to school at the University of Houston and got his master's. He published an article in *Geophysics,* the magazine of the Society of Exploration Geophysicists: "Velocity Spectra and Diffraction Patterns," by Woodrow L. Dinstel. None of it helped. He was in his forties, too old for the fast track, working for a man who wasn't going anywhere either. His supervisors told him he was smart and hard working but too impulsive.

He became increasingly depressed and frustrated. His marriage began to go sour. He advised his son, who was in college at Baylor, to pick a career in some field other than geology. More and more, he looked forward to the day when he could retire. "I knew there were interesting jobs at Exxon," he says, "but I was on the shelf, and once you're there, there you stay. I hung on for ten miserable, stinking years, thinking, 'Boy, when I'm fifty, I'm gone.' "

Woody Dinstel turned fifty on November 7, 1976. On December 21, 1977, he put in for early retirement. For a year, in his words, he "stumbled around." After all those bad years, it was harder than he thought it would be to leave Exxon. Part of it was the hope that if he stuck it out a little longer something might change, but another part was that, while in his head he knew Exxon was just a huge corporation, in his heart he wanted it to tell him he was a success, not a failure.

What made him finally take action was that the oil business was changing again. The days of cheap, plentiful foreign oil were gone. All over the world, oil-producing countries were nationalizing, raising prices, increasing their share of the take. At gas stations, the steak knives gave way to spartan self-service pumps. Domestic exploration was important again, and explorationists—from students to men in their fifties—were a hot item. Dinstel's friends in the company were leaving in droves for better paying, more challenging jobs with smaller companies. People the company badly needed were taking advantage of the early retirement program, which was designed to ease out middle-aged deadwood.

At Mobil the exodus has been so serious that this year the company took Superior Oil to court for stealing its people. At Exxon USA, a chart the company sent its employees this summer showing the number of employees in various age groups shows a deep valley in the 35-to-45 range, between the twin peaks of 25 to 29 and 50 to 54. The company will rejuvenate itself, of course, simply by bringing along the younger generation more quickly, but it has been constantly increasing public relations efforts aimed at its own employees. It publishes magazines, newsletters, even an employee TV show called *This Week at Exxon*, all stressing the company's broad range of activities, its generous benefits and pensions, its concern for the environment, and its place in the free enterprise system.

The happy reports from his friends who had left encouraged Dinstel to make his break, and in August 1977 he began to send around his résumé. He was still confused about his intentions. One side of his plan was that after he had gotten another job and put in for early retirement the company would realize the error of its ways toward him and give him a transfer and a raise. On the other hand, a couple of recent events had pushed him the other way. The man who had hired Dinstel at Carter and the man who'd been his first boss there had both been district geophysicists, an important and respected position. But with the consolidation of the sixties their careers had taken a downward turn. For years these proud men drifted slowly lower in the company, filling less and less responsible jobs. The man who hired Dinstel took early retirement and six months later shot himself. On Christmas Eve of 1977 Dinstel's first boss got out his gun, killed his wife, and then killed himself.

A few days after that Dinstel had his retirement lunch and went home to use up some of his vacation time before leaving the company. After a couple of weeks his boss called him at home and said there had been some problem and his early retirement might not come through. Then he called again and told Dinstel he had better come back to work. He did, and a few days later, two of his supervisors called him in and said that management had decided not to grant him early retirement after all. They told him that if he wanted to he could go see John Loftis, senior vice president for exploration, and talk it over with him.

Loftis told Dinstel that he had decided to exercise his option of turning down the requests for early retirement of people who wanted to leave Exxon to work for other companies. Dinstel could either stay on at the same level or quit. Dinstel said that he had been stagnating for ten years, that he had looked forward to early retirement for all that time, that he was tired of sitting around drinking coffee all day. "Stay on and we'll motivate you," Loftis said. Dinstel went back to his office and cleared out his desk.

When Ruth Dinstel heard the story, she called up Randall Meyer himself and was put through to Meyer's assistant. She had been a loyal Exxon wife for 23 years, she said. She had defended the company when people criticized it. She felt betrayed by the treatment of her husband. Meyer's assistant said they'd get back to her.

A few weeks later Loftis called Mrs. Dinstel. He was very polite. He said Meyer had referred her phone call to him and apologized for taking so long to get back to her. He said Exxon would love to have her husband back, but if he wanted to leave, the company wouldn't give him early retirement. Exxon couldn't afford to subsidize other oil companies, he said. So it was over.

Dinstel thought about the whole affair a lot later, about what the had done wrong and what he had done wrong. He should have done a lot of things. He should have retired a few months earlier, when early retirement was still being freely dispensed. He should have told his son to become a geologist. He shouldn't have told the company he had another job lined up. Months later, it finally came to him what his central mistake had been. "One time a friend of mine was complaining to me about how bad the company was," he says. "How unfeeling it was, how cold. I said to him, 'You know what your problem is? You want the company to love you.' And that's what I realize now. I wanted the company to love me, too." ★

Should Texas Secede? The Cultural Context

CHAPTER TWO

*Divide and Conquer, Griffin Smith, jr.
(January 75)
Power Shift? James Fallows (February 76)*

DIVIDE AND CONQUER

by Griffin Smith, jr.

All Gaul was divided into three parts. Thanks to a little-known law, Texas can do even better.

New States of Convenient size, not exceeding four in number, in addition to said State of Texas, and having sufficient population, may hereafter, by consent of said State, be formed out of the territory thereof, which shall be entitled to admission under the provisions of the Federal Constitution. . . .
—From the Joint Congressional Resolution providing for admission of Texas to the Union, 1845

Bob Gammage, the freshman state senator from Houston's south side, sips coffee at his desk in the Bellfort Legal Center and thinks that one over. "The strongest argument in favor of it in my mind," he says, "is that it would give us a great deal more clout on the national scene. We would automatically increase from two to ten U.S. senators."

Gammage and his friend Dan Kubiak, a state representative from Rockdale, may introduce a resolution to carve up the state when the Legislature meets this month. People have been talking about that for better than a century, but obviously nobody has gotten around to making much headway. Gammage and Kubiak lofted a trial balloon during the Constitutional Convention last summer. Now, the first thing anybody asks when you propose to divide the state is, "Which way are you going to divide it?" So Kubiak and Gammage, who are less interested in drawing lines than in kicking the idea around, had to come up with a Plan.

One of their states was called North Texas; it extended from the Dallas–Fort Worth area all the way to the New Mexico border. A Lubbock newspaper immediately opined that being in the same state with Dallas had been bad enough when there was only one state to be in; keeping the two together after a division would add insult to injury. That is the problem with offering your Plan; everybody starts finding things wrong with it and wants to talk about *their* Plan instead.

That, in a nutshell, has been the problem all along, ever since Texas was admitted to the Union in 1845 under the widespread expectation at home and in Congress that division, as it came to be called, was only a matter of time. If a random Rip Van Winkle among the Texas leaders who approved that Joint Congressional Resolution should suddenly awaken in Austin today, he would be astonished that only one state with one capital existed. Throughout the lifetime of anyone who remembered the War for Texas Independence, division—some time, some way—was simply taken for granted.

Between the 1840s and the 1920s not a single decade passed without some halfway serious effort in that direction. More than once, division missed by no more than a hairbreadth.

Issac Van Zandt, a popular Democrat, ran for governor in 1847 on a platform calling for immediate division into four states. He seemed headed for victory, but he died. So did his division plan.

Conflict between East and West Texas simmered throughout the 1850s. The 1852 House considered—and finally defeated, 33–15—Representative Peter Flanagan's resolution to split the state along the Brazos River.

Flanagan was back again in the Constitutional Convention of 1866 with another resolution to segregate 38 counties east of the Trinity River into the "State of East Texas." This time he got no farther than a favorable committee vote, but the Radical Republicans were listening; when they got rid of the Confederate-tainted leaders and began Reconstruction in earnest, division was at the top of their agenda.

Tantalized by the knowledge that five separate states would mean five times as many offices to occupy and five stockpiles of patronage plums to distribute, the carpetbag/scalawag delegates to the 1868 Constitutional Convention set to work chopping and slicing maps in every direction. The only thing that prevented prompt division was disagreement over how it should be done. Of all the plans, the one that came closest to adoption called for division into just three states—"East Texas," "Texas," and "South Texas." It used the Trinity and the Colorado rivers as the boundary lines. This so-called Congressional Plan would have bisected Travis County and turned Austin into an obscure country town; it would also have severed Houston and Galveston from their natural East Texas hinterlands.

Proponents of the plan declared that, among other things, "it embodies the highest wisdom in giving Sea-coast to each state as a base for offensive and defensive purposes." Other delegates favored surgery in different directions, and a few thought Governor Elisha Pease had the right idea when he suggested selling the Panhandle and the Trans-Pecos to the U.S. government for an Indian reservation. Even though a majority of delegates favored some sort of division and succeeded in passing a general resolution to that effect, parliamentary jockeying produced a stalemate.

Radical Republican governor E. J. Davis pushed hard for division plans in the 1871 Legislature. One of these, the four-state idea submitted by Representative Robinson of Bowie County, comes closer than anything else in the long succession of division plans to making sense a hundred years later.

The Radical Republicans' self-serving fervor for division succeeded in giving the idea a bad odor for the rest of the century. Nevertheless, division talk surfaced in Texas or in Congress in 1888, 1906, and 1909, with prohibitionists doing most of the

TEXAS MONTHLY PLAN 1975

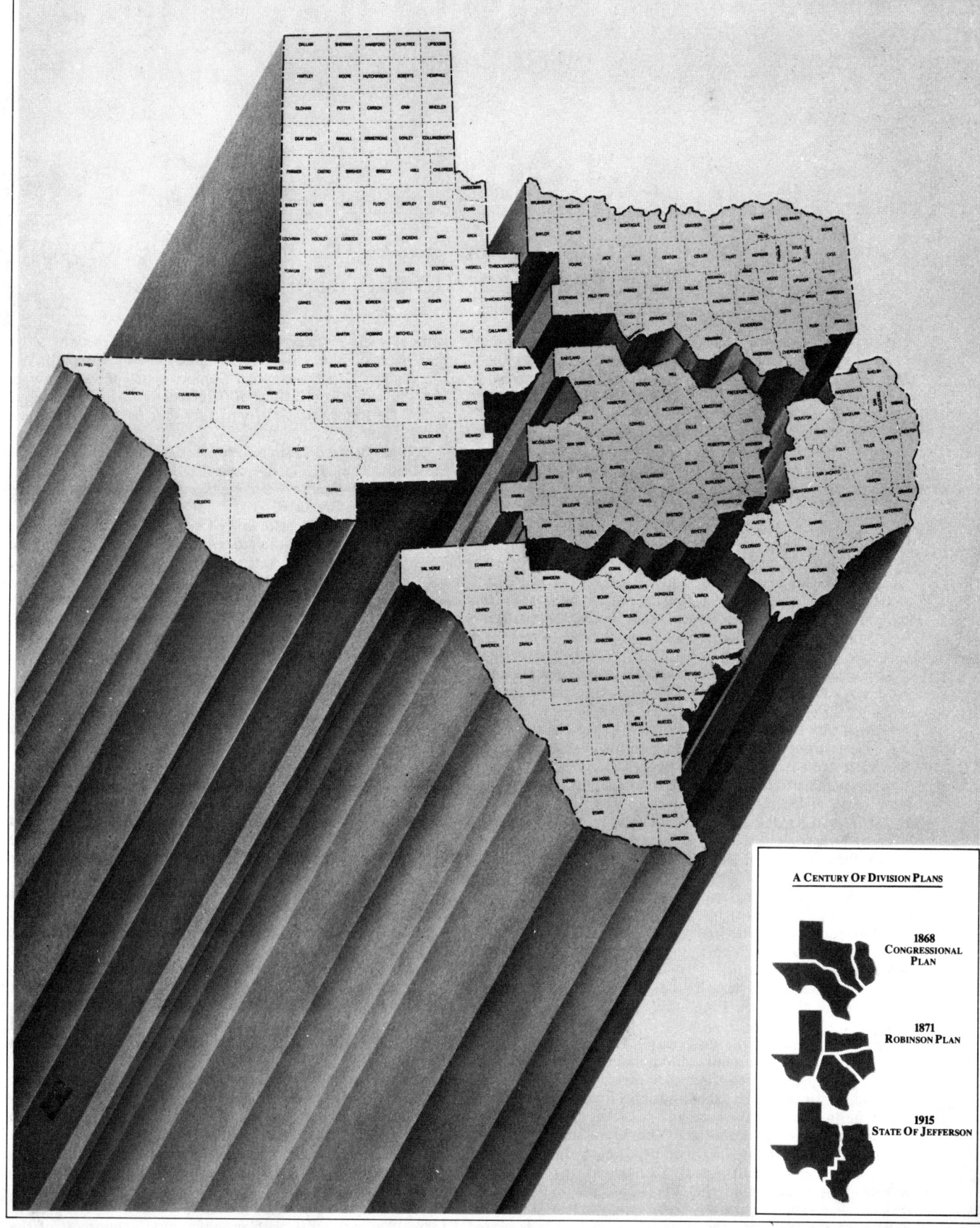

A Century Of Division Plans

1868 Congressional Plan

1871 Robinson Plan

1915 State Of Jefferson

52 SHOULD TEXAS SECEDE? THE CULTURAL CONTEXT

Illustrated by Don Stalinsky

N

NORTH TEXAS

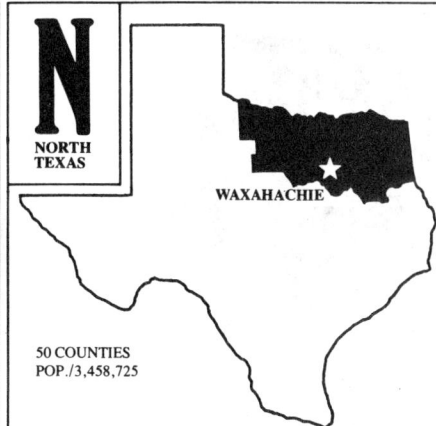

WAXAHACHIE

50 COUNTIES
POP./3,458,725

North Texas includes the Dallas–Fort Worth "Metroplex," kept together because the area is now too much of an economic unit to break up. Twenty years ago the two cities might each have dominated states of their own; today, things like the DFW Regional Airport symbolize the fact that they are stuck with each other. Upper East Texas—Tyler, Marshall, Texarkana—belong with Dallas, just as Fort Worth's back yard belongs with it. Wichita Falls is the problem. We have put it with Fort Worth instead of the Panhandle.

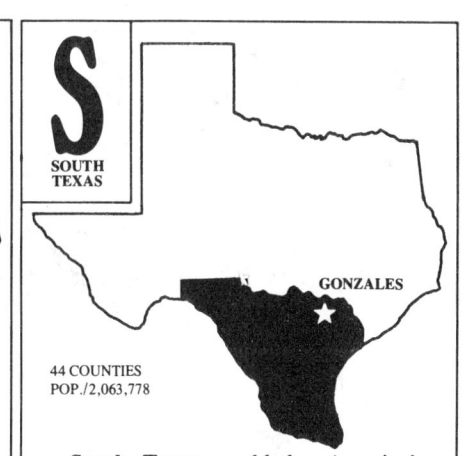

S

SOUTH TEXAS

GONZALES

44 COUNTIES
POP./2,063,778

South Texas could be America's Quebec, a state of different language and culture from the rest of the nation. Combining San Antonio, Corpus Christi, and the Rio Grande Valley, it has a substantial Spanish-speaking population. To the west it reaches just beyond the Pecos River.

talking the last time around.

West Texas discontent over the Legislature's failure to reapportion itself after the 1910 census, coupled with the feeling that too few state institutions were being located out there, produced an abortive effort to create the "State of Jefferson" in the 1915 Legislature. Even the critics of that plan, like the *Austin-American*, were still calling division "inevitable" sooner or later.

Governor Pat Neff's 1921 veto of a bill creating "West Texas A & M College" produced the last brief flare-up of division sentiment. For a few days the spirit of sedition reigned in, of all places, Sweetwater. But the outcome was just a manifesto of grievances, not a divisionist crusade.

The five-states idea became the personal property of John Nance Garner over the next decade, who occasionally pulled it from the closet and rattled it, skeletonlike, at his colleagues in the U.S. House of Representatives who showed too little respect for the power of Texas. It seems to have died with him; Texans who reached maturity after World War II think of division as only a historical curiosity, if they think of it at all, never realizing that it was a lively and recurring theme in their state's first hundred years. Oh, the late San Antonio senator V. E. "Red" Berry, an advocate of pari-mutuel gambling, proposed division into North and South Texas in 1969 to protest his northern colleagues' opposition to horse racing—but neither Berry nor anyone else took his resolution seriously.

Senator Gammage himself is an appropriate person to bring it back. His ancestors came to Texas in the days of the republic; his great-grandfather served in the 21st Legislature; and the walls of his office are decorated with yellowed family land grants. Acknowledging that Texas has been kept all in one piece as much by sentiment as by politics ("Who will give up the bloodstained walls of the Alamo?" typified the cries of nineteenth-century opponents), he thinks a divided Texas should remain a "commonwealth." By that he means any division plan should provide in advance for placing such things as the university system, the dedicated funds, and the rich public lands under a single administration. Each new state would draw a proportional share of what is now public land revenue, and each would contribute proportionally to services, like education, that would operate in common. This done, the new states could go their separate ways on everything else. The plan has a lot of obvious bugs to be worked out, Gammage admits. But he thinks it would bring government "closer to the people" and have just as much sentimental value as the present boundaries: "Now that the republic is gone I have no difficulty identifying with any other political entity that might take its place."

Gammage is careful to disclaim any serious intention—for now—to take up where Garner left off. "For the time being it's a tongue-in-cheek idea with me," he says. "But the more I think about it, the more rational it seems." And though he expects the public reaction to be negative at first, he has a feeling that the idea just might catch on. "The ordinary Texan feels used and exploited by Eastern finance; this would be sort of a political equalizer."

One afternoon when the editors of *Texas Monthly* were sitting around feeling used and exploited by Eastern finance, we pulled out a road map and started dividing Texas up ourselves. The result, after some gerrymandering and several days of haggling between factions, is the five-states plan shown here.

We began to wonder what would happen if Texas *tried* to split itself up. If Gammage or somebody else a few years from now got serious about it, what sort of political scurrying and shaking would arise?

Any division plan would meet with determined opposition from the lobby, which presently has things comfortably in hand. Texas' vast distances virtually insure that a candidate for statewide office must have better than a quarter million dollars before even considering a race, and a million has sometimes not been enough for victory. There are not many places to get that. The impact would be felt first in Houston, where industrial interests that have always counted on legislators from the boondocks to protect them from corporate income taxes and other

E — EAST TEXAS
RICHMOND
28 COUNTIES
POP./2,866,881

East Texas is dominated by Houston. It is also dominated politically by labor-liberals from the huge petrochemical complexes along the Houston Ship Channel, at Texas City, and in Beaumont-Port Arthur. Even the rural vote in the southern Piney Woods has populist tendencies. For East Texas, division means liberation from the shackles of a business-dominated Texas government; it also means a corporate income tax, strict pollution controls, and a political bonanza for organized labor.

W — WEST TEXAS
MARFA
93 COUNTIES
POP./1,696,591

West Texas has traditionally been the most separatist section of the state, a collection of independent souls who would prefer to have as little as possible to do with Austin unless the matter at hand was Water. The plan brings the Panhandle and the Permian Basin together in one state, along with Abilene, San Angelo, and the Trans-Pecos. El Paso tags along, not because it has a lot in common with Lubbock and Amarillo but because it has no place else to go.

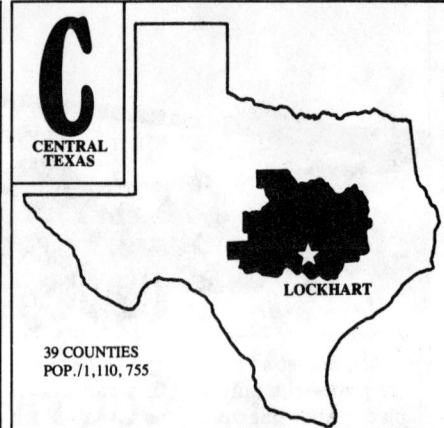

C — CENTRAL TEXAS
LOCKHART
39 COUNTIES
POP./1,110,755

Central Texas encompasses most of the state's historic German areas, from Brenham in the east to Fredericksburg in the west. The plan brings together the Hill Country and the Baptist heartland around Waco; the result, frankly, is the smallest and least convincing of the five states. Even though Central Texas is distinctly different from its neighbors in every other direction, a *four*-state division plan would certainly start by cannibalizing this one.

---

schemes attractive to Southeast Texas' predominantly liberal electorate would suddenly find themselves boondockless. "The establishment would be terrified," chuckled former state senator Don Kennard.

But if the Legislature somehow overcame all that, passed a resolution dividing the state, and sent a copy to Congress with a note saying, "We decided to take you up on that offer you made last century; please arrange for eight more desks in the Senate"—what then?

"I think 49 other states would drag us straight into the Supreme Court of the United States," says Gammage, grinning impishly. "They'd be scared to death of the clout we'd have in the Senate."

Scholarly opinion is divided over whether the 1845 Five States Clause would be upheld; one of the strange things about the whole century-long discussion is that nobody has ever tried very hard to resolve the potentially thorny legal questions. Was the clause valid at the time? Did the Civil War change anything? How about Reconstruction? If Texas finally decides to divide, does Congress have to consent again?

If the Supreme Court ruled against the division of Texas, it would probably give as its reason Article IV, Section 3 of the U.S. Constitution, which forbids the creation of any new states from the territory of existing ones without the mutual consent of that state and of Congress. But those who say that the Five States Clause was, and remains, perfectly constitutional simply argue that Congress has long ago given its half of the required consent, and all that's left is for Texas to go ahead and act.

Gammage is sure of one thing. If Texas did try to divide and the Supreme Court said no, things could really get interesting. The old republic gave up its sovereignty with the understanding that it could divide at will—there is absolutely no doubt about that—and if the Articles of Annexation that allowed this are unconstitutional, then Texas might legally be an independent republic again.

"When the courts deal with questions of constitutionality," he says, "the unconstitutionality of just one part of a law doesn't nullify the whole law—*provided* the law includes a 'severability clause.' If there is *no* severability clause, one unconstitutional part automatically nullifies the whole subject. I find no severability clause in the Articles of Annexation. So under their own precedents, if they said the portion granting Texas the right to divide was unconstitutional, then the entire document would be unconstitutional. And Texas would revert automatically to the status of an independent republic under the Constitution of 1836."

James Nance, the reigning expert at the Texas Legislative Council's informal committee to study division of the state, agrees. "Texas agreed to join the Union on those terms," he says. "If Congress couldn't offer them, why then there wasn't any meeting of the minds. Legally, everybody knows you couldn't have an agreement like that without a 'meeting of the minds.' That's fraud."

So oil-rich Texas may, it seems, have the United States over a barrel. Give us ten senators, or we join OPEC.★

A PLACE IN THE SUN

If at first you don't secede, try, try again.

Ah, but let's be realistic. The rest of the country will never go along with that five-states stuff. Trouble is—if the armchair lawyers are right—the only way they can stop it is to throw out the Articles of Annexation that brought Texas into the Union in the first place. And that means the Lone Star State will have to pick up where it left off in 1845. Independent.

Independence? . . . Not secession, mind you, just good old hard-earned sovereignty. Battled for at Goliad, won at San Jacinto, and . . . well . . . never relinquished after all. Not such a bad idea, independence; not half bad. You say we can't divide? Please, don't throw us in that briar patch.

There are currently 158 countries in the world, give or take a South Sea island or two. An independent Texas would rank 33rd in size and 45th in population. That is enough to give the republic some clout at the U.N., where Texans already have an inside track because they speak one of its five official languages. Or is it two?

In the number of daily newspapers, Texas would rank a respectable 16th. But in some other areas Texans are not as well off as they think they are: The ratio of physicians to population works out to about 30th, behind most of Europe, Argentina, Mongolia, Iceland, and Nauru. And quite a few countries can top Texas in educational expenditures.

Economically, an independent Texas would have a lot going for it, as the following tables show. (Figures for the United States have been adjusted to exclude Texas.) The Organization of Petroleum Exporting Countries (OPEC) would have a new face at its next summit meeting: President Dolph Briscoe.

And somebody in the Southwest Conference could win a national championship practically every year.

SHOULD TEXAS SECEDE? THE CULTURAL CONTEXT

CHECKING THE EXCHEQUER

COINS

The United States has the penny, Mexico the centavo, and West Germany the pfennig. When Texas withdraws from the United States, it must also cut its ties with the American dollar; without Texas oil, the American economy and its dollar are certain to collapse. Our proposal for the republic's currency system:

The basic coin: the **Cowchip**
100 cowchips: one **Bevo**

Gross National Product

(Non-communist nations only)
1. United States
2. Japan
3. West Germany
4. France
5. United Kingdom
6. Italy
7. Canada
8. India
9. **REPUBLIC OF TEXAS**
10. Australia
11. Brazil
12. Netherlands
13. Spain
14. Sweden
15. Mexico

Gross National Product Per Capita

(Non-communist nations only)
1. United States
2. Sweden
3. **REPUBLIC OF TEXAS**
4. Canada
5. Kuwait
6. Switzerland
7. West Germany
8. Denmark
9. Norway
10. France

Petroleum Production

1. USSR
2. Saudi Arabia
3. United States
4. Iran
5. **REPUBLIC OF TEXAS**
6. Kuwait
7. Venezuela
8. Libya
9. Nigeria
10. Canada

Cattle

1. India
2. United States
3. USSR
4. Brazil
5. China
6. Argentina
7. Australia
8. Ethiopia
9. Mexico
10. Colombia
11. France
12. Pakistan
13. **REPUBLIC OF TEXAS**
14. Sudan
15. West Germany

Cotton Production

1. USSR
2. United States
3. China
4. India
5. **REPUBLIC OF TEXAS**
6. Pakistan
7. Brazil
8. Turkey
9. Egypt
10. Mexico

Telephones In Use

1. United States
2. Japan
3. United Kingdom
4. West Germany
5. USSR
6. Italy
7. Canada
8. France
9. **REPUBLIC OF TEXAS**
10. Spain

Number of Television Stations

1. United States
2. USSR
3. Canada
4. Japan
5. Mexico
6. **REPUBLIC OF TEXAS**
7. United Kingdom
8. Poland
9. (tie) West Germany
    Ecuador

Registered Motor Vehicles

1. United States
2. Japan
3. West Germany
4. France
5. United Kingdom
6. Italy
7. Canada
8. **REPUBLIC OF TEXAS**
9. Australia
10. USSR

Beer Production

1. United States
2. West Germany
3. United Kingdom
4. USSR
5. Japan
6. Czechoslovakia
7. France
8. East Germany
9. Canada
10. Australia
11. Mexico
12. Belgium
13. Spain
14. **REPUBLIC OF TEXAS**
15. Poland

56 SHOULD TEXAS SECEDE? THE CULTURAL CONTEXT

POWER SHIFT?

by James Fallows

Worried New Yorkers are saying that Texas has all the power now, but we know better.

Barely one week before Congress left Washington for its Christmas vacation, the U.S. Census Bureau released a report which started talk going on the East Coast political circuits and had several congressmen looking nervously toward their futures. The Bureau had completed its mid-decade estimates of population changes since the 1970 Census, and it concluded that a trend which had developed slowly over the last twenty years was suddenly gaining speed. The "shift of the American population away from the industrialized North and toward the South and West," the *New York Times* said in its front-page story on the report, "has accelerated greatly in the last five years." While the total American population had grown by 4.8 per cent between 1970 and 1975, steady internal migration meant that the South and West were growing nearly twice as fast as the nation as a whole. The *Times* spelled out the implications that many Northern politicians saw: "Congress will be reapportioned on the basis of the 1980 Census, and today's figures point toward a tipping of the balance of political power toward what some have called the 'sunbelt.'"

The notion of a growing, prosperous "sunbelt" seems destined to become one of the political catch phrases of the next few years. The "sunbelt" means the southern third of the nation, the area between California on the west and Virginia and North Carolina on the east, that part of the country whose wealth is based not on steel, automobile manufacture, and the other heavy industries of the late nineteenth and early twentieth centuries, but on the more highly technological industries of the post-war era: computers, aerospace, petrochemicals, and the like. The recent Census estimates made clear just how popular the region is becoming. The population of New York state actually declined by 0.7 per cent during the last five years; Rhode Island lost a full 2.4 per cent of its people. As a whole, the Northeastern states grew by only 0.8 per cent, which was less than one-sixth of the national rate. The North Central region, which includes Ohio, Illinois, Michigan, and the upper Midwest, had a growth rate of 1.9 per cent. Meanwhile, the sixteen states of the South, which includes Texas, were growing by 8.4 per cent, and the thirteen Western states by 8.7 per cent. The rate of growth within Texas itself was 8.8 per cent. The Texas rate was not the highest in the nation—that honor went to Arizona, whose population increased by one-quarter within five years, closely followed by Florida, with a 23 per cent growth rate—but the absolute increase in this state's population (more than one million, from 11,199,000 in 1970 to 12,237,000 last July) was one of the largest. By itself, Texas accounted for 10 per cent of the total national increase during the last five years.

The reason these demographic trends have captured such attention in the East —and the probable explanation for the term "sunbelt" in the *Times*' story—is the appearance of a new book called *Power Shift*, written by Kirkpatrick Sale, one of the more simpleminded and ridiculous pieces of political argumentation to appear in quite some time. Its argument, in brief, is that a "Cowboy" mentality prevails in the country's prosperous (and, to Sale, homogeneous) "Southern Rim"; that the "Cowboys" are grasping, dangerous, and venal; that their culture is typified by "The Three R's—Rightism, Racism, and Repression"; that they rose to power with the "two cowboy Presidents," Johnson and Nixon, whom Sale finds virtually indistinguishable; and that they were beaten back only by a determined "Yankee Counterattack," led by the likes of Archibald Cox and Lowell Weicker. Even now, the dark Cowboy threat persists; near the end of his book, Sale asks rhetorically whether "Rimian political power remains undiminished, only gathering below the surface in some shifting and incremental mass, seeking to break through wherever the crust is thinnest, the opportunity greatest?"

The book requires mention for two reasons, the first—and most alarming—being that it has met a favorable response in the East. In a front-page article in the *New York Times Book Review*, Robert Lekachman of the City University of New York called it a "powerful and persuasive polemic," and a son of Texas, Robert Sherrill, got into the act with the following effusion on the book's back cover: "Kirkpatrick Sale, one of our very best . . . analytical writers, finally comes forth with the book that he should have written for us five or six years ago to help ward off the horrors of the Nixon era." The second reason that *Power Shift* demands

Illustrated by Ben Sargent

attention is that, in his blunderbuss way, Sale has redirected national attention to the ongoing changes in population and wealth, trends which have slipped from the limelight since first being mentioned by Kevin Phillips in *The Emerging Republican Majority* several years ago. If Sale's political interpretations are finally unpersuasive, they do at least raise questions about conditions in this part of the world. From the Texas perspective, the two most interesting questions are whether the state will continue to prosper under a benevolent federal government, and whether there is any real identity of interests between Texas and the other states in the "Southern Rim."

During the era of LBJ and Sam Rayburn, the principle that power in Washington meant profits at home was an obvious truism, at times almost a joke. NASA went to Houston, Brown and Root became construction agents to the world, military contracts streamed into Fort Worth and Dallas. Even after the passing of LBJ, congressional stalwarts like Olin Teague and George Mahon ensured that the state would not be forgotten—as the F-16 contract award last year illustrated so well. But apart from these overt manifestations of regional interests, there are two subtler but equally important ways in which the national government has blessed (and occasionally cursed) the state.

One is by regulating its economy. The two major businesses on which the state's prosperity rests, agriculture and energy, are the two where control by the federal government is most all-encompassing. The oil industry has flourished under the depletion allowance and restrictions on foreign imports; depending on your point of view, these were either outrageous subsidies or sensible incentives to continued growth. At the same time, the natural gas industry labored under the government's interstate price ceilings. Within the last two years, forces outside of Washington's control have made the state's energy resources far more valuable than they had seemed before; but just how valuable, and on what terms to Texas, are decisions that still rest with the federal government. A multitude of energy fights have been brewing—over price controls, tax incentives, and distribution of energy from state to state—and in them one can see the clearest sectional battle since the Civil War taking shape.

The questions are less starkly posed in agriculture, but the same principle of federal control applies. The success of each year's harvest may depend on irrigation, fertilizer, and God, but its profitability is largely determined by Earl Butz and his minions at the Department of Agriculture. When Texas cattlemen were slaughtering their herds to avoid bankruptcy two years ago, they did so because of political decisions about price controls and agricultural subsidies; and when the state's grain producers enjoyed record profits, they had the grain deals with Russia to thank.

The federal government has not only regulated the state's economy, it has pumped money into it. For most of the last few decades, Texas has received more from the federal government than it has paid in. In 1972, for example, Texas accounted for a little less than 5.6 per cent of the country's total population, but paid only 4.9 per cent of the total federal taxes (about $10.3 billion). That same year, Texas received a full 5.8 per cent of federal outlays, some $12.6 billion. Viewed from a profit-and-loss perspective, the state made a $2.4 billion profit out of its participation in the federal system, or about $230 for every person in the state. Naturally, some of this "profit" is explained by the widespread poverty in the state and the federal programs designed to correct it. But another explanation may be Texas' traditionally large share of some of the government's largest treasure chests: defense, agriculture, highway-building, and space. In 1972, $5.1 billion flowed into Texas from the Defense Department, which represented 8 per cent of the Pentagon's total budget. Only California—with 70 per cent more people—got more. California was also the only state ahead of Texas in appropriations from NASA and the Department of Transportation; Texas received $300 million from NASA, or about 9.7 per cent of the total, and half a billion dollars from DOT. Texas is also second on the list for United States Department of Agriculture appropriations—the leader, surprisingly, is New York—and high on the list for money from the Veterans Administration and the Departments of Justice, Housing and Urban Development, and Health, Education, and Welfare.

For these and other reasons, Texas is now in Fat City—or so it must seem to states in the East. Another recent congressional report, this one from the Joint Economic Committee, recently divided the United States into three economic categories: the "farm states," mainly in the upper Midwest (Texas could easily be included), whose prosperity is based on the worldwide demand for food; the "energy states" (which include the coal producers as well as Texas and other Southwestern petroleum states), who are benefitting even more fully from the changed world economy; and the eighteen depressed states, where high unemployment and sluggish business activity have thrown state budgets entirely out of whack. (Since this last group includes California, Florida, the Carolinas, and several other members of Sale's rich "Southern Rim," it indicates one of the shortcomings of his simplistic geographical categories, and suggests one of the ways in which Texas' interests diverge from those of other Rim states.) But despite this apparent good news, several trends bode less well for the state's continued prosperity—or at least the part of it which depends on political power.

To begin with, the federal assistance figures have begun moving in an unexpected direction. In 1974, for the first time in years, Texas received a smaller share of public monies than its share of the population—5.4 per cent of total federal outlays, compared with 5.7 per cent of the population. Granted, the state paid only 5.1 per cent of the taxes in 1974, and so still received a small "profit"; but the margin was tighter than ever before. Some of this decline undoubtedly represented the state's relative prosperity, but it may also be connected with a trend that runs counter to the *Power Shift* theory—the waning of Texas' political power.

Texas may well pick up another congressman or two after the 1980 census, but at the moment the congressional delegation is weaker in terms of raw power than at any time since the New Deal. One of the reasons is simply the passing of a generation. The permanent congressional fixtures who made the South so influential—men like Russell of Georgia; Fulbright, McClellan, and Mills of Arkansas; Eastland and Stennis of Mississippi; Ellender, Long, and Hebert of Louisiana; and Rayburn, Johnson, Mahon, Patman, Poage, et al. of Texas—are either vanished from the stage or in their closing scenes. While liberals have often complained that the seniority system has a permanent bias in favor of Southern conservatives, the generation about to profit from it is the generation of Northern liberals—Proxmire, Kennedy, Bayh, and Church.

A second reason, which affects the Texas delegation more directly, is the change in the nature of our representatives. "Back in the days of Speaker Sam Rayburn, the state's delegation consisted almost entirely of conservative-leaning Democrats from rural and small town districts," say the authors of *The Almanac of American Politics*. "Many had been county judges before they took office.... They considered a congressional seat ... the pinnacle of their careers, and they stayed in Washington a long time and amassed great seniority." Barbara Jordan, Alan Steelman, Charles Wilson, and others have come to the Congress young enough to be the Mahons and Patmans of the future, but already they are showing signs of impatience, boredom, or ambition. Wilson and Steelman have their eyes on a Senate seat, and Barbara Jordan, when asked recently whether she would like to be appointed to the Supreme Court, said that she would prefer to be making the appointments.

A third and more dramatic reason for

the decline of the Texas delegation is the active hostility of their colleagues. During the House of Representatives "freshman rebellion" last year, the big losers were Texans—notably Wright Patman, kicked from his chairmanship of the House Banking Committee amid cries of "senility," and W. R. "Bob" Poage, deposed as chairman of the Agriculture Committee. (That committee is now run by Thomas Foley of Washington, though those who have seen it work say that Poage still pulls the strings.) Miraculously, George Mahon of Lubbock, who was born in 1900, survived as the chairman of the House Appropriations Committee, but the crown will not sit easily on his head if many of the freshmen are reelected this fall.

The battles this diminished regiment will be called upon to fight will concern not only energy and agriculture, which have already put Texas' representatives out on a limb, but also a less familiar topic, which may isolate the state even further. Texas, home of the Alamo and the wide-open spaces, is fast becoming one of the most urbanized states in the U.S., with its own galaxy of urban problems. Texas is the only state to contain three of the nation's ten largest cities; according to the Census Department's latest figures, Houston is number six (and about to pass Detroit to be number five), Dallas number eight, San Antonio number ten. Nearly 60 per cent of the state's people live in the five largest urban centers (Houston, Dallas–Fort Worth, San Antonio, El Paso, and Austin). Promoting the interests of such a state will require something more complicated than an alliance with the representatives of the urban centers of the North, for the problems of Houston and Dallas are significantly different from those of New York and Chicago. Transportation is the most obvious example: the established, relatively compact cities of the North may need more and better subways, but it would cost more to send a man through a subway system in Houston than to send him to the moon. If the people of Houston and Dallas are not going to be suffocated by exhaust fumes in one last apocalyptic traffic jam, some different way must be found to move them. No one is sure what that way is right now—and the congressional representatives of New York and Chicago feel no great urgency to find out. Employment, education, housing, and other basic urban problems all wear a different face in the cities which have grown up since the invention of the automobile. This will call for a different sort of lobby than Texas—and, in fact, the Congress—has seen before. And it suggests that despite Northern worries that *Texas über alles* will be the next national anthem, the state may be fighting its future battles in true cowboy style—alone. ★

Texas and the Feds: Working With Us or Against Us?

CHAPTER THREE

*The Cactus Curtain, Harry Hurt III
(August 77)
Finders Keepers? Robert Barnstone
(February 78)
The Real Governor of Texas, Paul Burka
(June 78)
Behind the Lines, Desegregation, William
Broyles Jr. (January 80)*

THE CACTUS CURTAIN

by Harry Hurt III

*Take back your tired, your poor,
your huddled masses yearning to breathe free...*

The marchers converged on the Black Bridge over the Rio Grande before the Border Patrol could figure out what was happening. The first column, which numbered nearly one hundred, came from El Paso. The second column, which had swelled to over two hundred, came from Juárez. Some of the marchers wore military-style uniforms or paper masks; others were more simply dressed in jackets and jeans. Both groups carried signs and shouted slogans of *revolución*. They were headed on a collision course for the middle of the bridge.

David Morales marched from the U.S. side. A tall, serious Chicano with horn-rimmed glasses and a wide, round face, Morales had grown up in the barrios of South El Paso and briefly attended the University of Texas at El Paso. A self-described "indigent," Morales devoted his time to the Committee for the Development of Mass Communication and to the dream of creating an independent Chicano state in the Southwest.

José Luis Cervantes López, a 59-year-old former paramilitary guerrilla, led the contingent of marchers from Juárez. A short, balding man with a thin, black moustache, Cervantes had been a *paracaidista*—a member of a group in the Mexican land-reform movement that got its name by descending upon a tract of land as if "parachuting" in from the

Illustrated by Mike Hicks

TEXAS AND THE FEDS: WORKING WITH US OR AGAINST US?

sky. Now he was associated with the *Alianza* of Juárez, a coalition of activist groups ranging from revolutionaries to mainstream socialists. A man of byzantine connections, Cervantes was rumored not only to be a close friend of the governor of Chihuahua but also to be wanted by Mexican federal agents.

The ostensible purpose of the march was to protest the deaths of two young Mexican nationals allegedly killed by the U.S. Border Patrol. One of the youths, Manuel Soto Flores, had met his death on the Black Bridge. A favorite crossing point for illegal aliens, the Black Bridge was no more than a Santa Fe Railroad trestle with black steel sides. In addition to being a hazard for illegal aliens, it had claimed the life of one U.S. Border Patrol agent who slipped through an uncovered gap in the ties and fell into the concrete channelized riverbed below. The meeting at the Black Bridge also marked the coming together of the Juárez *Alianza* and the Chicano activist groups of El Paso, a symbolic show of ethnic and ideological solidarity. "We talk a lot about our common homeland, but sometimes the *mexicano* thinks we have sold him out," David Morales would explain afterwards. "At the Black Bridge, we decided to meet halfway. We wanted to show that we don't recognize political boundaries, that we can cross back and forth at will."

As usual, the Black Bridge was guarded by a small contingent of green-uniformed Border Patrol regulars. Since the announced parade routes of the demonstrations had not included the bridge, the agents had been caught unprepared. They were armed with guns, sticks, and a few riot-control helmets, but a hasty call for reinforcements had managed to swell their numbers to only about ten.

When the marchers reached the middle of the bridge, they exchanged greetings and pledges of allegiance and began to mix. Behind them, on the north side of the river, rose the bank towers of downtown El Paso and the graffiti-engraved peaks of Mount Franklin, the lower tip of the San Andres Mountains. Behind them, on the south side, the Juárez commercial district ran into the red-light district and then into the slum colonies—the *colonias*—which spread from the riverbank to the foothills of the Juárez Mountains. A few yards down the river the routine traffic of cars and people crossed the high-arching Paso del Norte Bridge. After a few words, the crowd split into two groups and began to leave. The group returning to the U.S. side ran smack into the Border Patrol.

"The minute we made eye contact, we knew it would be the stick," David Morales recounted later. "The Border Patrol wanted to show who was boss. They just assumed that some of the people were crossing illegally. They tried to sort us out. They started shoving, then some rocks started flying, and then they brought out their sticks."

Battle of Black Bridge: in March, dissidents from both sides of the river clashed with Border Patrol as the once peaceful border threatened to erupt.

The riverbank went wild. The demonstrators charged across the bridge shouting, *"¡Muerte la migra!"* ("Kill the Border Patrol!") and *"¡Es nuestra patria!"* ("This is our country!"). The Border Patrol managed to shove a handful of the demonstrators into a waiting van, only to stand by as the mob kicked in the sides of the van, smashed the windows, and freed the prisoners. A call for help went out to the El Paso police, but there was no immediate response. Rocks and dust and sticks were flying everywhere. The fight raged for nearly a quarter of an hour—just about the same length of time as the charge that won the Battle of San Jacinto. Finally, a quick, disciplined stick surge by the Border Patrol forced most of the crowd back across the bridge.

By the time the air cleared, one Border Patrol agent had been seriously injured in the head by a rock, and two Border Patrol vehicles had been badly damaged. The number of casualties among the demonstrators was never officially estimated, but there was only one arrest: José Cervantes López, the United States' newest illegal alien.

Cervantes warned that if he were not released, he would give the signal for 20,000 of his supporters in Mexico to charge across the river to rescue him. Cervantes was not released and no Mexican invasion occurred. A few days later, with the help of an influential El Paso attorney, Cervantes was deported to Mexico.

The battle at the Black Bridge took place on March 9, just about the same time the national news magazines were focusing on our Mexican immigration problems, Leonel Castillo was being confirmed as head of the INS (Immigration and Naturalization Service), and news of the Carter administration's amnesty and tight border proposals was leaking into print. Dale Swancutt, chief of the El Paso Border Patrol station, called the situation "explosive" and pleaded for more men, more money, and a seventeen-mile concrete-posted fence-and-canal system to help keep illegal aliens out. The incidence of violence along the once lackadaisical border has increased ever since.

What was a few months ago a "border crisis" precipitated by a "silent invasion" of illegal aliens now shows signs of escalating into an undeclared border war. Mexican aliens have attacked the Border Patrol with rocks, sticks, shovels, tools, and steel ball bearings fired from slingshots. Small bands of agitators regularly roam the southern bank, and there is some sort of confrontation nearly every week. Although Border Patrol agents, regular illegal river crossers, and local activist groups dispute the specific facts of many of these cases, all agree that the river has become a battleground. There has been a general decline in fear of, and respect for, *la migra*. One Border Patrol agent has already fired his gun to scare off a group of rock throwers he claimed had him pinned down. Some agents now say it will only be a matter of time before they will be forced to kill in self-defense.

Meanwhile, the press of people against our southern border continues. Last year, the El Paso Border Patrol station apprehended just under 125,000 illegal aliens, more than 90 per cent of them Mexicans. Nationwide, the

The Santa Fe Railroad trestle: hundreds daily attempt to cross this dangerous passageway from Juárez to El Paso.

figure was approximately 875,000. This year, the El Paso station reports that arrests are averaging 12,000 to 13,000 per month, and officials expect that the national total for 1977 will exceed one million. There is simply no way of telling how many get away. But using arrest rates as at least a rough indicator of the traffic flow, Border Patrol officials estimate that the number of illegal aliens already in the country is between four million and eight million and growing. Rapidly.

The overwhelming dimensions of this influx are exceeded only by the overwhelming frustrations inherent in any attempt to stop it. Indeed, a typical ride along the Rio Grande with the Border Patrol merely underscores two facts that many El Pasoans have long taken as common knowledge: (1) stopping or even slowing the flow of illegal aliens into this country without spending millions of dollars and imposing quasimilitary conditions along the border will be almost impossible; and (2) stopping or significantly reducing the flow of illegal aliens could have seriously disruptive, if not devastating, effects on El Paso and its sister city, Juárez.

Ray Russell swung his light green, government-issue Ford Custom up the gravel embankment of the levee and turned west toward downtown and the ever-shimmering sun. Off in the distance, in the gap that formed between the Franklin Mountains and the Juárez Mountains, the glass bank towers of El Paso and the huddled old buildings of Ciudad Juárez seemed to run together as if they were simply disparate slices of the same city. But here by the river's edge, just above the tiny and ancient community of Ysleta, the demarcation line was clearly visible.

"That's the mighty Rio Grande," Russell smirked, as he motioned out his window. "You can see what an obstacle it presents to someone who wants to come across."

The stretch of river he pointed at was a green, winding line about thirty feet wide and, by the looks of it, perhaps three feet deep, about the dimensions of an average-sized bayou or a large drainage ditch. The riverbed and banks were lined with concrete. An open grassy space a few yards wide ran between the riverbank and the levee, but there were no barriers of any kind. On the Mexican side, the land was flat and overgrown with scrub and high weeds. To our right, across the border highway on the U.S. side, a strip of run-down adobe houses blended into a cluster of steel-pipe petrochemical stacks, which led to the red-brick tenement rows of South El Paso's *segundo barrio*. The only sign of life was a brown-and-black mongrel trotting purposefully after scraps of food in the trash and paper along the near bank.

"All the cities west of here have fence," Russell complained as he continued up the levee road. "But along this stretch there is only the river and the river is no deterrent at all."

Russell spoke from experience. A slow-moving, weather-beaten man with a potbelly and a yellowed smile, he is a career Border Patrol agent. After working the Canadian border, he spent thirteen years in Chula Vista, California, the busiest crossing point, where he became patrol agent in charge, the Border Patrol's equivalent of a front-line field commander. Like most of his fellow men in green, Russell has been pushing for the construction of a fence-and-canal system along the heavily populated strip between El Paso and Juárez.

"If we had some kind of barrier, at least we'd have a chance of stopping 'em from coming across," he declared. "The way things are now, they just blend into the neighborhoods as soon as they leave the river. It's ridiculous."

Just then a covey of dark-haired figures scurried across the road about fifty yards ahead. Russell depressed his accelerator and reached down for the radio. "Forty, forty-eight, eighteen to any unit in the area: looks like we've got five or six wets down by the garbage disposal plant," he announced to the microphone. The speaker crackled, but there was no reply. Russell drove faster.

By the time he pulled up to the area by the domes of the garbage disposal plant, six teenage boys in jeans and T-shirts were scrambling down the steep bank on the U.S. side. Meanwhile, two other men on the Mexican side were in the process of rolling up their pants legs, two older women and a middle-aged man were sitting along the bank on the U.S. side as if enjoying a picnic, and a woman in a flower-print dress and a wide, white hat was attempting to wade across, carrying a blue bag in one hand and mindfully securing her hat with the other.

TEXAS AND THE FEDS: WORKING WITH US OR AGAINST US?

The Rio Grande: a cool respite from the heat and the only barrier to illegal immigration from Mexico to the U.S.

"*¡Váyanse para atrás!*" Russell shouted at the teenagers. "Go back across!"

The two stragglers of the group smiled back and waved, then hurried toward the river. The woman with her hand on her hat kept coming. Russell started down the road again. "Forty, forty-eight, eighteen to any unit in the area," he radioed again. "We just ran a bunch of 'em back. They'll probably try again in fifteen minutes."

The scene repeated itself about every half-mile. Five or six Mexicans were about to cross, another ten or twelve were fleeing for the cover of the barrios a little further upriver, and three more were wading in the water, eyeing the green Ford as it rolled past. By the time he reached the Chamizal Island area, Russell had shouted back at least 25 people trying to cross the border in broad daylight, most of them dressed in casual shopping clothes or jeans.

He pulled up near the pillars of the high-arching Cordova Bridge and gestured across the arid flats to the left and the barrios to the right. "This Chamizal area is part of the land that President Kennedy agreed to give back to Mexico after the river changed course," he said. "They had to rechannel the river and relocate about three thousand people. In the early morning, this is one of the busiest crossing points for illegal aliens. You can see forty or fifty at a time lining up to come across. We can always get a few of 'em, but when they run in all directions at the same time, it's impossible to stop 'em all."

Russell drove on past the railroad yards and the new Bowie High School and the warehouses and the downtown buildings on the right and the adobe houses of the *colonias* on the left. Along here, near the downtown area, a cyclone fence ran for about two and a half miles, and a concrete canal with deceptively deep and swift water paralleled the fence a few yards closer to the highway. However, the fence was battered and riddled with large holes in many places, and the canal, where several suspected illegal aliens had already drowned in the last year, turned away from the Rio Grande after only a mile or so.

Russell pointed to the black railroad trestles on either side of the Paso del Norte Bridge. The first trestle was blocked by a high white gate with skirts that overlapped each side of the railing. The second trestle, the infamous Black Bridge, was wide open. A light green Border Patrol van waited at the U.S. end. That very day the Santa Fe Railroad, which owned the bridge, was in the process of losing a suit brought by the INS to have the railroad put up a gate.

"You see, once they make it over the bridge, all they have to do is hop a freight train," Russell explained. "Then they're gone to Chicago or anywhere. I've seen as many as a hundred and fifty people lined up to cross at the Black Bridge. The taco vendors come out and it gets to be kind of like a carnival. Unfortunately, since the recent incidents of rock throwing and so forth, the carnival atmosphere has kind of disappeared."

A few moments later, Russell stopped at the Franklin headgates to check in with the agent on duty. Here the river was barely a hop, skip, and jump: about fifteen feet wide and only a foot and a half deep. There was a canal behind the river on the U.S. side, but no fence. Six young people, three males and three females, were sitting by the water on the Mexican side.

Russell talked briefly with the agent, then drove on slowly until we came to the western edge of the city where the river turns north and the borders of Texas, New Mexico, and Mexico come together at two brick plants. To the west there is little but arid flats and low sand hills dotted with scrub, a few clusters of houses and low buildings, and the bleachers of Sunland Park racetrack.

The border is marked only by a series of short, white pointed markers spaced half a mile apart. Except for an occasional ranch fence and the fences at the cities, there is no significant barrier from the brick plants to the Pacific Ocean. Instead, the Border Patrol has installed Viet Nam–vintage electronic sensors along the U.S. side. Though Russell and other agents believe in their usefulness, these sensors are tripped off by everything from rain drops to passing cows, and they merely detect movement across the border, they do not prevent it.

"We have 360 border miles and 84,795 square miles in the El Paso sector," Russell said, looking into the distance.

66 TEXAS AND THE FEDS: WORKING WITH US OR AGAINST US?

"The brutality of the U.S. Border Patrol is a subject of legend in Mexico and in the barrios of South El Paso."

An easy wade across the river for an afternoon of shopping, a day's work on a nearby farm, or a long ride in a U-Haul to a job in a northern factory.

"We engage in all types of activity except boats. But our total force is only about 280 active agents. With vacations and sick leaves, that works out to about 40 men per shift for the entire area. I need that many men just to patrol the river."

At this point Russell spotted some movement at the edge of some nearby sand hills. He stopped the car, got out, and walked back a few yards toward a little gully. All he could see was scraps of trash paper swirling in the wind. He shook his head, climbed back into the car, drove twenty yards, and stopped again. This time he started up the side of one of the hills. All of a sudden, two heads emerged from behind a rock, and two teenage boys in jeans and light jackets came walking down the hill. One wore a blue cap, the other a red bandanna. Russell said something in Spanish and motioned for them to get in the car. They obeyed docilely.

"It's a good thing they didn't try to run," Russell said with a grin as he got back in the car. "I probably never could have caught them."

As it turned out, the boys had been headed for Anthony, a small town on the Texas–New Mexico line, where they hoped to find work as pickers. Both said they had been arrested once before, one of them only the previous day.

"*Mala suerte,*" Russell chuckled in an almost fatherly tone.

"*Sí, mala suerte,*" one of the boys replied. This was "bad luck" indeed.

The brutality of the U.S. Border Patrol is a subject of legend in Mexico and in the barrios of South El Paso. Long before the recent border violence, there have been regular complaints that agents randomly beat aliens, that they hassle attractive Mexican women, and that their fabled midnight raids and frequent spot checks are based on no more probable cause than the fact that a suspect has dark skin and brown eyes. But these two teenagers seemed calm, not hostile or scared, just tired and disappointed.

The statutory offense for entering the U.S. illegally the first time is a misdemeanor punishable by six months in jail and/or a $500 fine. Entering the country illegally a second time is a felony that carries a penalty of two years in jail and/or a $1000 fine, but as a practical matter the boys did not face anything so severe.

"They know we're not going to do anything to 'em except book 'em and bus 'em down to Ysleta where they can go back across," Russell said as he drove back toward the Paso del Norte detention center. "We've got so many that the U.S. magistrate doesn't even want to take the time to prosecute them unless they've been caught three or four times before."

Had they been smugglers of illegal aliens the story might have been different. Those who harbor or transport illegal aliens face a penalty of not more than five years in prison and not more than $2000 fine for each illegal alien.

Russell conceded that there had been isolated incidents of Border Patrol misconduct in the past, but he denied any systematic viciousness. "We've already processed over eleven hundred aliens in the first four days of this month in the El Paso area alone," he pointed out. "When you consider the number of men we have and the volume of traffic we handle, we have a much better record than any police department in the country even if you assumed that every allegation made against us were true."

A short time later, Russell turned into the parking lot of the tan block building that houses the Paso del Norte detention center. He led his two captives into the booking room, a cool, dark green corridor with a wire partition at one end and two simple cellblocks along one side. Along the other side were several gray metal desks manned by agents interviewing the most recent arrestees. Only a handful waited behind the wire partition and inside the two cellblocks.

Russell left the two boys in the custody of one of the agents on duty and returned to the car.

"I'm sure we'll see those two again," he sighed. "They'll probably try to come back across again tomorrow. You know, sometimes when I think about it, I don't even want to come to work in the morning."

It is easy to appreciate Russell's frustration. What we saw was merely a sampling of the midday traffic. The rush hour actually begins, if it is indeed possible to pick a beginning and an end, in the predawn darkness around 2:30 when the busboys, bartenders, and barmaids who work the U.S. side start to make their way back to Juárez, and the farm workers and ranch hands arrive at their pickup stations in the gray parking lots near the Paso del Norte Bridge. All night the bushes are alive with people ducking, darting, crawling, crouching, and running toward prearranged meeting points with "coyotes"—the professional people smugglers who pack their cargo tight inside U-Haul trailers and truck them north to factories in Denver, Saint Louis, Boston, and Newark. By dawn, the maids and cooks and gardeners, the professional workers, and the freelancers bound for points north line up at the bridges forty, fifty, and a hundred at a time, some in the white uniforms of domestic servants, others in suits and ties or dresses. Indeed, by the time Russell dropped off the two teenagers at Paso del Norte detention center, the

TEXAS AND THE FEDS: WORKING WITH US OR AGAINST US? 67

Once across the border, Mexican nationals scatter and are swallowed up by South El Paso's segundo barrio.

flow had come full circle. The farm workers and ranch hands had begun to return from the fields carrying their jackets and extra shirts, and the bartenders and barmaids had just started to come across for another night's work.

Attempts to characterize the typical illegal alien are hampered by the basic difficulty of identifying and counting all of them. Judging by those who are caught, most who enter the country illegally are agricultural or domestic workers, who, like previous streams of immigrants to America, come virtually penniless. But increasing numbers are doctors, professionals, and skilled and semi-skilled workers who carry several hundred dollars with them, even after paying several hundred for a coyote to smuggle them across. Most of them are bound for the interior U.S. and, in 70 per cent of the cases, for one of seven states: Texas, California, New York, Illinois, New Jersey, Massachusetts, or Florida.

In El Paso, as in other Texas border towns, illegal aliens are an integral part of the lifestyle and work force. Indeed, from the days when Apaches roamed the land around the river, through the days of the Spanish conquerors and the first Anglo settlers, the flow of goods and people between El Paso and Juárez was cyclical and fairly unrestricted. It was not until the 1880s, when the railroads brought in carloads of Chinese laborers, that the border began to be tightened. Soon afterwards, considerable attention was aimed at stopping the flow of European immigrants through Mexico—a move largely directed at Arabs, Irish, and Jews—chiefly by means of literacy tests. Mexicans, however, were not impeded by the simple literacy test. Many entered the U.S. and soon found work on the surrounding ranches. Ironically, many of El Paso's prominent Arab and Jewish commercial families entered the country illegally via Mexico.

The first great wave of Mexican immigration occurred between 1910 and 1914, during the Mexican Revolution, when an estimated four million people streamed across the Rio Grande. But for the next fifty years, U.S. labor cycles determined the northward flow. Dr. Ellwyn Stoddard of UT-El Paso has identified the major influxes prior to the current one that were stimulated by U.S. economic needs. The first was during World War I, when a shortage of labor led to a temporary open border policy. Large numbers of Mexican workers soon appeared on the farms and ranches of the Southwest. However, when the Depression hit, most of these workers were kicked back across the border.

World War II brought Mexican workers back to the United States in the greatest numbers since the Mexican Revolution. According to Stoddard, some three million Mexican aliens entered the country while the U.S. was at war with Germany and Japan. Then, in the late forties returning servicemen swelled the job ranks again, and in the early fifties the government began Operation Wetback, an unprecedented human round-up that resulted in the deportation of almost three million people in three years. The Eisenhower administration attempted to improve the border situation by formalizing the *bracero* program, which had been in effect off and on since 1942. Under this plan, hundreds of thousands of Mexican workers were brought into the country on a temporary basis with the approval of the Labor Department and the INS. The hope was that they would learn skills they could take back to Mexico to improve conditions there while at the same time serving the needs of local farms and ranches. However, in 1964, Congress ended the program after persistent pressure from organized labor claiming that illegal aliens were taking jobs away from Americans.

The illegal alien situation has been unmanageable ever since. With the termination of the *bracero* program, the flow of people across our southern border ceased to be governed by our economy and our labor needs. Now the impetus to move north comes ever more strongly from Mexico. With the world's highest birthrate, Mexico grew from forty million to over sixty million people in just ten years. Unemployment remained over 30 per cent, and neither the archaic *patrón* system nor the burgeoning bureaucracy could provide basic food, clothing, housing, education, health care, or jobs. Mexico soon had a world-record national debt to go with her world-record birthrate. Out of fear and frustration, the rich began sending their money out of the country. Out of hunger and desperation, the poor turned to America.

Though the vast majority of illegal aliens who enter the country at El Paso are bound for the U.S. interior, an estimated 60,000 have chosen to remain in the El Paso area. In a city of 400,000, where over half the people have Spanish surnames, illegal aliens constitute a hefty 15 per cent of the population. Not surprisingly, they blend easily into the culture and commerce of the city, receiving both tacit and active support from institutions ranging from local business to the Catholic Church.

With the notable exceptions of the U.S. Army and clothing manufacturer Willie Farah, practically every major employer in town is known to make a practice of hiring substantial numbers of illegal aliens. In addition, the greater portion of the farms, ranches, and food-and-drink establishments in the area are run on the strength of illegal alien labor. As INS Criminal Investigator W. F. Mayberry put it in a recent interview, "We could spend all our time just busting bars and restaurants."

Most illegal aliens in El Paso are employed as maids, gardeners, and domestics. According to INS estimates, there are at least 15,000 illegal maids in the El Paso area, and, if the testimony of local householders is to be believed, there could be twice that many more. "Practically everyone in El Paso has an illegal maid," declared one prominent local attorney recently. "And every illegal maid has her own maid in Juárez."

In the old days, El Paso's economy was built on the four Cs: cotton, copper, cattle, and climate. Today, the city's economic stability also relies on cheap labor, and illegal aliens are clearly the cheapest of the cheap. The INS estimates that about 30 per cent of the illegal aliens employed in the area make over $2.50 an hour; the rest generally make much less. The average wage for farm and ranch stoop labor is said to be about $1.75 per hour. The going wage for an illegal maid is about $25 a week. But then, as many are quick to point out, this is about twice to three times as much as the same workers would earn in Mexico—if they could find jobs at all.

For illegal aliens who rise from poverty, El Paso offers considerable advantages and opportunities. For one thing, it is one of the most integrated cities in the U.S. A large portion of the poor Chicano and illegal alien population is clustered in the barrios south of Interstate 10, but better homes are available to Mexicans and Mexican Americans who can afford them in virtually every part of the city. The same holds for the city's blacks and other minorities. The U.S. military presence at Fort Bliss (over 10 per cent of the city's work force is on the military payroll) and the nearby scientific community of White Sands, New Mexico, have exerted a nationalizing, homogenizing influence on this otherwise isolated desert oasis. The city is by no means free of discrimination, but the days of the "No Mexicans or Dogs" signs are gone. Bilingual education and busing to improve the ethnic balance in the schools are still emotional issues, but Chicanos and Anglos seem to get along with each other much better than in cities like San Antonio and Houston. Ray Salazar, the city's Chicano mayor, was elected not because of his ethnic background but because of his experience as a CPA and his opposition to higher utility rates. The kingmakers of old El Paso—families like the Schwartzes and the Youngs—still exert influence over what happens economically and politically, but with the recent advent of single-member districts, their power is clearly on the wane. As a result, many second- and third-generation descendants of illegal Mexican immigrants have carved comfortable niches in the social structure as businessmen, professionals, and university professors.

Still, the subject of illegal aliens has always had class, economic, and racial overtones. Nowhere is this more apparent than in the well-appointed homes of El Paso's Coronado district, where a newcomer who suggests that there might be problems or hypocrisies with using illegal alien labor may be backed into a corner, where his logic will be tied into hopeless knots. Ironically, once the infidel has been defeated, the discussion has been known to degenerate into a bragging contest over who pays his maid the least.

El Paso National Bank president Sam D. Young, Jr., has expressed the old El Paso point of view several times in the press: he recently declared that Mexican women are good workers at tedious jobs. Though his comments enraged local Chicano groups, Young claims he actually meant nothing derogatory. A second-generation El Pasoan who grew up on a ranch, Young learned Spanish before English; his teacher was the family's illegal alien maid. "I employ an illegal alien maid now, and I see nothing morally wrong with it," Young declared in a recent interview. "These people come looking for work, and they are willing to do jobs no one else will do. Labor has priced itself right out of the market. Where else do they expect industry to turn but abroad?"

Here the debate begins. Local labor leaders, like their national counterparts, claim that illegal aliens do take local jobs, and they say that they think U.S. industry should look homeward. "We

Caught today; they'll be back tomorrow. 10,000 arrests a month won't stop them.

need to take care of our own people before we start worrying about Mexico," says Luis Rosales, a Mexican American who is president of the Central Labor Council. "I feel sorry for these people. My own bloodlines go back to Mexico. But we can't be expected to feed the world. The idea of America as a nation of immigrants might have been good a hundred years ago when we needed bodies to fill the plains, but now we have an overflow of bodies. Right here in El Paso, the unemployment rate is really bad. The Texas Employment Commission puts it at 12.9 per cent, but that's not counting construction workers. By my estimates it's closer to 15 per cent. Illegals are taking jobs our people need."

In the past, the local media have been rather perfunctory in coverage of the illegal alien issue, generally avoiding the sort of investigative reporting that would upset the status quo. Lately, however, the newspapers have seemed to join the forces of organized labor in emphasizing the problems created by illegals. Recent stories have held wetbacks accountable for everything from rising crime to rising taxes. The *El Paso Times*, for example, reported that the cost to taxpayers of holding illegal aliens in the city jail was $45 to $65 per taxpayer, or about $4.9 to $9.2 million per year. Other stories in that same paper have blamed illegals for rising crime in the Sunset Heights district and for swelling the welfare rolls.

Local Chicano activists decry this as racism. "The media in this town regard illegal aliens as criminals," complains David Morales. "These so-called illegals are simply undocumented workers who want jobs. They are like every other group that has immigrated to America. They are more like refugees that have in one way or another been separated from their homes because of war." Morales says he thinks the United States should end all immigration quotas, rather than strengthen the Border Patrol. "The way the government is going at it," he says, "is like trying to solve juvenile delinquency by beefing up the police force."

Of course, the most common reaction to this issue in El Paso has been to point a finger at Mexico. "We're not going to get anywhere toward solving the illegal alien problem until they clean up their act down there," says a prominent local attorney. "Not only do they have enormous social and economic problems, but they also refuse to accept bilateral foreign aid, they put limitations on foreign investment, and they do just about everything they can to stay backward. About the smartest thing the government does is encourage the traffic of illegals, chiefly by not bothering to do anything about it."

Arturo Castellanos shook his head vehemently. Mexican law, he explained through a translator, specifically forbids the smuggling of illegal aliens into the United States. Anyone who does so, either for himself or for others, can be punished with two to ten years in prison and a fine of 10,000 to 50,000 pesos. As chief of the Mexican immigration office in Juárez, Castellanos had considered this matter many times before. "The problem," he continued, as he got up from his large wooden desk and started toward a stack of metal file cabinets, "is that we have to catch them."

Castellanos would seem to be in a very good position to do that. A clean-shaven, baby-faced man in his early thirties, he works in a well-equipped modern government office building at the southern end of the Stanton Street Bridge, a location that puts him right in the middle of the border traffic. Unfortunately, as his own records showed, Castellanos and his men had been able to make a total of only five cases against illegal alien smugglers in the first half of this year.

"The big problem over here in Mexico is jobs," Castellanos continued in between shuffling papers. "Mexico is trying to solve this problem. But the American government should also punish the employers of illegal aliens in the United States who pay low wages to the illegal aliens for hard labor.

"We have a problem here with people who sell counterfeit green cards which permit entry into the United States," Castellanos said as he smoothed the front of his embroidered yellow shirt. "But we also have many complaints from people who say they were abused by the American Border Patrol."

Castellanos gestured toward a map of Mexico on the wall. "You must also understand," he said, "that we have our own illegal alien problem. People come into Mexico from Panama, Guatemala, and many other countries. Just here in Juárez we're talking about twenty-five to fifty people per month. Right now, we are investigating everybody who comes in from the south to see if they have enough money to stay as a tourist or if they can work. If not, we are returning them in buses."

Ciudad Juárez dramatically demonstrates the dimensions of his country's immigration problems. Since the mid-sixties the city's population has nearly doubled. Now Mexico's third-largest city and biggest border town, Juárez officially contains half a million people, plus many more the official census takers miss.

Meanwhile, many of Juárez' roles are changing. The border town was once one of the world capitals for abortion and quick divorce. However, changes in U.S. abortion laws and government directives from Mexico City regarding issuance of divorces have caused these formerly lucrative dealings to wane. In its efforts to bolster the border economy and to attract more tourists to Juárez, the Mexican government has instituted the *Programa Nacional Fronterizo*, or ProNaF, a border revitalization program that in Juárez consists of two large industrial parks and a cluster of air-conditioned shopping malls.

Apart from the lush green islands of the old ornate mansions in the central city and the sweeping Japanese and French provincial and neo-cubist architectural flourishes of the homes in the *campestre* district, the common element of Juárez is brown dust. Adobe *colonias* rise out of the sand hills and stretch up into the arroyos south of the city. Most of the housing is unspeakably overcrowded. In a nine-by-five room, ten or twelve people sleep in rows across the floor. In some parts of the city, conditions are more miserable. At the Juárez garbage dump, for example, over three hundred people make their homes in shanties, scrounging for food among piles of rubbish.

The poverty of Juárez is eloquent testimony to the magnetic attraction of the border. Of the thousands of new immigrants into the city from the interior, only a fraction make the crossing into the U.S. economy and—for them—undreamed of prosperity. The Irish ports during the great exodus of the nineteenth century must have been something like this. Unemployment is already over the Mexican national average of 30 per cent and growing higher with every new person. Each successive wave of people from the south further crowds housing, streets, hospitals, and jails. With the devaluation of the peso,

both personal and municipal economies went into a tailspin, as new and old citizens found that their money could buy only about 60 per cent of what it could last August.

The best thing the Mexican government has done in an effort to provide long-term employment along the border is the *maquiladora* or "twin plant" program. Initiated in 1965 shortly after the U.S. terminated the *bracero* program, the *maquiladora* program now includes over 85 foreign corporations, many of them prestigious outfits like RCA, AMF, and General Electric. The companies operate under a special law that exempts them from the usual prohibitions against foreign ownership and allows them to own and control 100 per cent of their investments and the land on which their plants are built. Companies that manufacture items like TV and radio components, for example, can send the "raw materials" into Mexico and assemble the finished products south of the border without paying a duty. Going back into the U.S., products made in the plants are taxed only on the basis of value added rather than on the basis of their full price.

So far, the *maquiladora* program seems to have provided long-term jobs. The plants currently employ 25,000 people in Juárez and 10,000 people in El Paso. However, even with an annual payroll of $72 million, the 25,000 employees in Juárez average less than $2500 a year in individual salaries.

In the meantime, the great mass of people who make even less grows more restive every day. Crime, violence, and burglary have increased dramatically, according to local officials, and there is the potential for a major social upheaval. Appropriately, in a city that is named for a revolutionary and that has many streets named for past rebellions, the word most often spray-painted on the public walls is *revolución*.

Just as the tendency in El Paso is to assign blame for the city's ills to illegal aliens, the tendency in Juárez is to scapegoat the local chapter of the *23 de Septiembre*. An organization with a history of violent acts all over Mexico, the *23 de Septiembre* has an estimated 400 members nationwide, but only four "commandos" in Juárez. Although clearly a symptom, rather than a cause, of the city's problems, the Juárez chapter has done its share of troublemaking. In recent months, for example, members of the group have taken credit for the killings of a Juárez policeman and a plant supervisor at the Sylvania installation in the *maquiladora* industrial park. Lately, both Mexican and U.S. officials have blamed the *23 de Septiembre* for the increase in violence on the border, an accusation that sources close to the group steadfastly deny.

"It's oversensationalizing," said El Paso activist David Morales shortly after the battle at the Black Bridge. "The newspapers said that José Cervantes López was a member of the *23 de Septiembre*, but he is not and never has been. Neither are most of the other activists in Juárez."

The group to which Cervantes and most other Juárez border activists do profess allegiance is the *Alianza*. Headed by Dr. Vasquez Muñoz, a Marxist physician with two Mercedes and a house in the *campestre* district, the *Alianza* claims roughly 150 active members. Unlike the *23 de Septiembre*, the *Alianza* is basically nonviolent in orientation. Its revolutionary activities consist mainly of demonstrating locally for or against specific issues and organizing farm and factory workers. But as the meeting on the Black Bridge showed, the *Alianza* has developed increasingly close ties to activist groups in El Paso and has taken a strong interest in the plight of people attempting to enter the United States illegally. Asked recently if the *Alianza* also included organized agitators bent on promoting conflict along the Rio Grande, Dr. Muñoz gave an enigmatic and unsettling answer: "In the pejorative sense, no; in the political sense, yes."

Through men like Cervantes, a former guerrilla leader, the *Alianza* maintains at least indirect ties to the country's land reform movements and to the revolutionaries scattered throughout Mexico. Recent reports from the Mexican interior compare the country to a dormant volcano, and American businessmen with operations deep in the heart of Mexico say they are moving their interests closer and closer to the border in anticipation of some sort of eruption in the not too distant future. Dr. Muñoz, for his part, will only say that he expects something to happen "soon."

In Mexico, arguments about illegal aliens go back and forth, just as in the U.S. Some contend that the continued flow of people to the United States is the last safety valve on a new Mexican revolution. Pointing to INS estimates that at least six million illegal aliens (or roughly 10 per cent of the population of Mexico) are living in the U.S., they reason that this translates into 10 per cent less unemployment and 10 per cent fewer people to feed, house, and clothe. More important, it translates into direct cash benefits. Exactly how much is hard to say, but it is said that one need only look at the Saturday afternoon *líneas de viudas*—"lines of widows"—that form at post offices in the villages of the interior to receive money from relatives in the U.S. to know that the flow of funds is considerable. According to estimates by several independent and government study groups in the U.S., the annual dollar flow from illegal aliens to relatives in Mexico amounts to between $1.5 and $3 billion per year. This is more than Mexico's total annual tourist revenue and roughly 10 per cent of the country's total gross national product.

On the other hand, Dr. Jorge Bustamante, the person recognized as Mexico's leading expert on illegal alien migration, maintains that the number of illegal aliens living in the U.S. is much smaller and more cyclical than U.S. experts believe. He estimates that there are only about one million now in the U.S. and says that about 85 per cent of these stay only twelve months, while less than 5 per cent stay longer than sixteen months. Bustamante contends that because of the high cost of living in the U.S. and because few aliens earn over $800 per month, they actually send back a relatively small amount of money, more in the neighborhood of $0.5 to $1 billion, rather than the several billions calculated by U.S. experts. Moreover, he says that, despite the relief their absence may offer Mexico's overburdened social systems, the flow of illegal aliens into the United States costs the country its youngest, most able workers.

Perhaps the only point of agreement is that, for better or for worse, illegal aliens who come to the United States usually do get jobs and usually do make more money than they would in Mexico. As immigration *jefe* Arturo Castellanos put it, for that reason and that reason alone, "the *mojados* will always come."

Leonel Castillo knows why they come as well as anyone in Washington. Although he is a second-generation U.S. citizen born in Victoria, he grew up with scores of wetbacks. His parents, who were also born in Texas, say they are unsure how Grandfather Castillo entered the United States except that "he probably paid someone a nickel to get across." Now as director of the INS, Castillo must deal with the plight of legal and illegal Mexican immigrants and supervise the activities of their arch enemy, the Border Patrol. To a certain extent, his hands are already tied.

"President Carter has instructed me to get control of our border," Castillo reported in a recent interview. "He feels that we have to do that first."

An amiable, soft-spoken former city controller from Houston, Castillo does not think that the U.S. can ever completely stop the flow of illegal aliens. However, he does believe that it is possible to reduce the traffic by 75 to 80 per cent. "As best I can determine, that will cost about fifty million dollars per year," he said. "This figure includes not only enforcing the law on the border, but also policing the international airports all over the country."

Although he feels that a plan to tighten the border without a lot of other programs would have a negative effect, Castillo maintained that Carter's "control first" approach makes "a certain amount of sense." "I think we'll see a gradual tightening of the border," Castillo predicted. "Hopefully, it will be done so that people can enter at official entry points with dignity. We don't have a system to accommodate even that yet."

Castillo also pointed out that as head of the INS he inherited a considerable legacy of administrative problems, which, like the border itself, he must get under control as quickly as possible. "We're still at the basic level of getting computerized," he said wearily. "We have eighteen million files and they're still operated manually, if you can believe that. We have no way of knowing, for example, if a student stays in the country after his student visa expires, because it's too hard to check under the present system."

At the same time, Castillo said, the Carter administration will continue to consider a variety of ancillary programs aimed at the illegal alien problem. In the past several months, the air has been filled with trial balloons testing various approaches from criminal penalties for employers of illegal aliens to a blanket amnesty for illegal aliens already in the U.S. The latest formulations emerging at the time of the interview included a campaign against the coyotes who smuggle illegal aliens for profit; civil penalties for U.S. employers who hire illegal aliens; and some sort of "nondeportable" status, rather than a blanket amnesty, for illegal aliens now in the U.S.

"There are some serious problems with a blanket amnesty," Castillo explained. "You have persons from Mexico who have been waiting five years to enter the country legally, persons from the Philippines who have been waiting seven years, and persons from Hong Kong who have been waiting ten years. It would be unfair to them to simply let all the illegal aliens become citizens just because they managed to enter the country without getting caught. The way it looks now, persons who have been living here illegally for less than seven years will probably be given 'nondeportable' status. After they have stayed here seven years, they will be allowed to apply for permanent resident status."

Should this program be enacted, it would avoid two other commonly cited problems connected with blanket amnesty. Illegal aliens would not be eligible for welfare benefits and could not bring other members of their immediate families into the country as they could if simply granted citizenship.

At the same time, Castillo said, the government is considering a "guest worker" program, which would permit Mexican labor to be imported on a temporary, cyclical basis, much as Switzerland and Germany import labor from Italy and Turkey. Though this idea has some similarity to the old *bracero* program, it is different in that the worker is not tied to a particular employer and would be free to change jobs. "No one wants to talk about *braceros*," Castillo said with a chuckle, "but the term 'guest workers' seems to be a little more palatable."

In his short tenure, Castillo has already shown a certain flexibility in this area. In June, he and President Carter got together to permit the admission of 809 Mexican farm workers to help bring in the onion, cantaloupe, and pepper crops in Presidio. Claiming that the crops would rot in the ground unless harvested quickly, Castillo issued an order stating that it would be "tragically wasteful for the nation as a whole, as well as a grievous financial loss for the farmers, if no way can be found to hire workers to harvest the standing crops." The government arranged for these workers to be paid $2.30 per hour minimum.

But for the near future, most of Castillo's attention will turn to the monumental task of enforcing the immigration laws. At least some of the border-fencing proposals will likely come to pass. "A fence the entire length of the border is definitely out," Castillo said. "But I think there will probably be fences constructed in the more heavily populated areas like El Paso and San Diego where essentially people run back and forth between neighborhoods. Those two cities are about fifty per cent of my problem. They have the greatest number of illegal entries and the greatest number of violent incidents."

The reaction to these proposals in Mexico and El Paso–Juárez has been overwhelmingly negative. "The United States is looking at illegal Mexican migration as if it were simply a domestic problem," Dr. Bustamente told the *New York Times* recently. Bustamente predicts that the Carter proposals, taken together, could result in a sort of whipcrack effect. He says that news of an amnesty program, or of the granting of "nondeportable" status, will prompt thousands more to rush to the U.S. in hopes of gaining citizenship. But upon reaching the border, they will be pushed back by a beefed-up Border Patrol or turned away by employers unwilling to hire them for fear of prosecution. As a result, the class of restive unemployed workers already populating Mexican border towns will increase and so will slums, violence, and crime.

Dr. Stoddard's view is different, but hardly more optimistic. "When the U.S. needs labor, we will bring people in; when we don't need them anymore, we will send them back," he said in a recent interview. "It's just about that simple." Stoddard says that the recent incidents of violence along the El Paso–Juárez border are merely isolated reactions. He also contends that in carrying out this latest decision to clamp down on illegal aliens, Castillo and the INS will be more flexible and selective in their enforcement policies than many suspect. "My sources tell me that the Border Patrol has already gotten the word from the top not to raid the big farms and ranches in the area," Stoddard said.

Many of El Paso's citizens do not seem so assured. They fear that tightening of the border will have much the same effect as hardening of the arteries. The decline in sales suffered by downtown merchants after devaluation of the peso was the latest illustration of the interdependence of El Paso and Juárez, and it comes as little comfort that Castillo predicts the new Carter border policies may have a similar impact on other Texas border cities. More than anything, El Pasoans worry that the net effect will be the creation of a "cactus curtain" along the country's southern border.

"We don't want a Berlin wall between our two cities," says El Paso Mayor Ray Salazar, echoing the sentiments of El Paso citizens, of Mexican immigration *jefe* Castellanos, and of many others on both sides of the river. "Besides, a seventeen-mile fence won't keep illegal aliens out. They'll just go to the end of the fence and come in around it. If the fence runs the entire two thousand miles from Chula Vista to Brownsville, they'll just cut holes in it. There's no way a barrier like that can be maintained without spending millions and millions of dollars. And the only result is going to be increased hostilities between neighbors."

The nature and ramification of any hostilities remain to be seen. But nearly everyone from Leonel Castillo and Ray Russell to Ray Salazar and David Morales agrees on one point: fence or no fence, those who attempt to cross the border in the future will encounter more resistance than ever before. The battle at Black Bridge and the incidents that have followed it are merely the first skirmishes in what may be a long and costly seige. ★

FINDERS KEEPERS?

by Robert Barnstone

Everyone from New York to California is waiting anxiously for the Supreme Court ruling on a certain piece of Texas land.

It isn't every day that the states of California and New York can agree on something. But when it comes to getting more gas out of Texas, the chorus of demand from Northern and Western states is loud and getting louder. Orchestrating this chorus is, of course, the federal government. Because Texas producers are increasingly reluctant to sell their gas out of state, a key element of the Carter energy package is new authority to the Department of Energy to divert supplies of gas from Texas to other states. But while this proposal is being debated in Congress, the Supreme Court is hearing a case that could give the federal government the power to claim vast amounts of gas currently dedicated for sale wholly in Texas.

The origins of the case now before the Supreme Court (*California* v. *Southland Royalty,* a Fort Worth oil and gas concern) go back to 1925 when Gulf Oil leased the right to produce and sell gas from the Waddell Ranch for a period of fifty years. Southland Royalty and a group of other investors own the ranch, which is in Crane County south of Odessa. Gulf Oil, the leaseholder, sold that gas to El Paso Natural Gas, an interstate pipeline company, who committed it to customers in California. Gulf's lease expired in 1975 and the oil and gas rights thus reverted to Southland, the property owners. El Paso panicked; they had been selling 30 million cubic feet of gas per day from that field to their out-of-state clients and they weren't going to give it up without a fight. They, along with the State of California, petitioned the Federal Power Commission to help them out. The FPC has long ruled that once gas from a certain field is committed to the interstate market, it must stay there until the term of the lease runs out. But now they have gone a step further. In July 1975 they ruled on the matter in El Paso's favor and declared that gas once committed to interstate pipelines is *irreversibly* committed—no matter what the owner says. "That ruling gave Gulf the right to dedicate something it didn't own," says John Brumley, Southland's president.

Southland, upset at losing their right to dispose of their own gas in a manner they saw fit—and obviously they sought the higher prices their gas would bring inside Texas—challenged the FPC ruling and won in the Fifth Circuit Court of Appeals. El Paso was tenacious. Now joined also by the State of New York, who saw the chance for a principle that would mean more gas for them, they brought a suit against Southland to the Supreme Court where the outcome is presently pending.

But John Brumley wasn't the only one who thought the FPC ruling was a bit too cavalier; Texas Attorney General John Hill has joined the suit on Southland's side. Other producing states —New Mexico, Oklahoma, and Louisiana, who together with Texas produce over half of the nation's supply of natural gas—realized the suit's importance for them and joined as well.

Because of federal price controls on interstate shipments of natural gas, almost two-thirds of the new gas being discovered in Texas is being sold within the state. The federal government is always seeking new ways of keeping Texas gas flowing into the interstate pipelines, and this suit is an opportunity for just that.

How much is riding on the court's decision? For Southland it is substantial. The difference for them between the regulated interstate price and the free market rate amounts to about $5 million a year, or about $2.5 million net, which is 8 per cent of its earnings.

But, theoretically, the ruling shouldn't affect El Paso one way or the other since, like a public utility, its earnings are regulated to be a percentage of total investment. If El Paso has less gas to sell, then it charges its customers a higher rate to get an adequate return on investment. Why is El Paso a litigant, I asked A. M. Derrick, vice president of gas supply, if there is no financial gain or loss involved? Derrick told me, "Our gas supply is dropping and we need all we can get for our California customers." To be sure there is a measure of public spirit in El Paso's position, but the vehemence with which they are pursuing this case suggests that more is at stake than public interest. One industry observer noted that El Paso sees the handwriting on the wall: with everdwindling amounts of gas going through the interstate pipelines, their transmission charges will increase beyond what the public is willing to pay.

Derrick played down the landmark nature of the case to me and stressed its uniqueness. "Very few leases are writ-

Illustrated by Kirsten Soderlind/Lonestar

ten for a fixed term," he said, "most leases are in effect for the productive life of a field. There isn't that much gas riding on this decision, other than the Waddell Ranch and a few others."

But if there really wasn't much gas at stake, the suit would have hardly garnered the litigants and attention it has. The Waddell Ranch property alone is not that vital to the States of New York and California, or the State of Texas for that matter. What is really being sought here is a new loophole through which the federal government can demand that more Texas gas go to Northern and Western cities. While it is true that most leases run for "the life of the field," there is often more than a single field on one tract of land. As John Hill put it to the Supreme Court, a producer might have a well on a small corner of a property, commit it to an interstate pipeline, play it out, and shut the field down. The "productive life" of that field is now over, and the lease on the land officially expires. But this new FPC ruling means that any new producer who might come along later to lease the same property would have to commit its gas interstate as well.

Pieter Schenkkan, a lawyer with the Attorney General's office, told me, "We have traced the history of gas leasing in two Texas counties. In the instances we reviewed, the average gas property was leased nine different times. If any one of those leaseholders sold gas to the interstate market, then under this FPC ruling, gas from that property would be under the jurisdiction of the FPC forever." I wondered how much of Texas' gas could be claimed by the interstate market. "There's no telling," said Schenkkan, "but indications are that it could be a majority of what we now consider intrastate gas."

In the argument that John Hill made before the Supreme Court, he asked that even if the court were to rule against Southland, that it do so on a very narrow basis. Granting that term leases, as opposed to life-of-the-field leases, are rare, he asked that the decision be limited to the former. Any broader definition of the FPC's authority, anything extending to all expired leases, he claimed would be unjust and confusing to landowners who would not know what encumbrances existed on their land and mineral rights.

To John Brumley and other landowners the issue is more fundamental. As James Watt, a former FPC commissioner, said in his dissent on a ruling in a similar suit: "As in the Southland Royalty case, the commission has exceeded its authority and ignored established property laws. I must dissent to a decision contrary to the laws of our nation and quite probably to the Constitution."

SUGARLAND NOT ALL SWEET

Does Gerald Hines have the Midas touch? As the developer of Houston's Galleria, one of the most successful commercial real estate developments in the world, and a host of other landmark office and industrial buildings, it is hard to argue that he doesn't. But the Ford Foundation has been in partnership with Hines for five years and has reason to doubt that Hines can turn dirt into gold just by lending his name.

The project that involves Ford and Hines is the subdivision and sale of some land 22 miles southwest of Houston, near Sugar Land. In 1972 the Ford Foundation went into partnership with Gerald Hines and Cousins Properties (an Atlanta-based real estate developer). Each received a one-third interest in Sugarland Properties, a corporation set up to buy 7000 acres of farmland from the Kempner family. With Houston's population doubling every twenty years and the cost of land in the area going up even faster, any real estate development looked rosy, but this project had more than Houston's growth going for it. Sugarland Properties had two of the biggest names in real estate —Hines and Cousins—and the Ford Foundation's ample financial resources to back it.

Both Hines and Cousins apparently went into the deal as it was first structured for little more than their sweat. The Ford Foundation, for its part, paid $4 million for its one-third interest in Sugarland Properties. On top of that, according to John McGrath, real estate investment officer at Ford, the foundation agreed to lend Sugarland an additional $10 to $12 million. That sum went to cover predevelopment expenses, including engineering, planning, and ecological studies, and interim interest on the property before the principle payments became due in five years; the looming $40 million debt for land purchase was a big incentive to get the project off the ground well before 1978. In turn both Hines and Cousins pledged their stock in Sugarland to the Ford Foundation. That way, if the project fizzled, Ford would be in a position to claim total ownership of remaining assets. If the project succeeded, presumably Hines and Cousins would have well earned their one-third interests.

The project hasn't exactly been a roaring success. Original projections called for the sale of lots to begin in 1976, with heavy sales in 1977. Instead, as of the beginning of 1978 not a single residential tract had been sold. What caused the delays? Craig Overturf, president of Sugarland Properties, blamed the holdup on lengthy predevelopment planning, but the real kicker came unexpectedly. In 1973 the Department of Housing and Urban Development produced a map showing that about 60 per cent of Sugarland acreage was within the 100-year floodplain.

Federal legislation went into effect in 1974 that ruled out most residential construction in floodplains. The law effectively prohibits any federally insured financial institution from making loans on property located in floodplains, and it is HUD that determines what is or isn't a floodplain. And recent howls of protest from local governments and property owners in Fort Bend, Brazoria, Galveston, and Harris counties demonstrate widespread disagreement over the data HUD is using to make their determinations.

After long negotiations HUD agreed that if Sugarland bolstered an existing levee, only about 6 per cent of the property would still be considered floodplain, an acceptable amount that could be used for public areas and parks. By then, Ford had been forced to increase its loans to Sugarland by another $10 million, for a total of $20 million. The additional loan to Sugarland was due "on demand" by Ford. Sugarland has also been borrowing large amounts from several Texas and Eastern banks.

In 1977 with no lots sold yet, "Sugarland was still behind on interest payments [to Ford] and we foreclosed on Cousins' stock," says McGrath. "But why foreclose on Cousins and not Hines?" I asked McGrath. "We thought Mr. Hines' experience and prestige were a great help to the project. Cousins, on the other hand, didn't have the time or energy to devote to the project." Two other factors surely played in Ford's decision: (1) Cousins had also been having financial problems with Ford on other projects, and (2) Ford needs someone in the area to be the developer, since as a nonprofit organization they can't do it themselves. Despite Sugarland's problems, Hines is still the best developer on hand.

Ford continues to bet Hines will pull off a successful development. "This isn't a white elephant," says John McGrath. "There is plenty of money to be made on this project." But even though some lots will finally be put on the market early this year, Sugarland still has serious cash problems. The original purchase of the acreage called for "interest only" payments for five years and beginning this year, for ten years, a yearly reduction of principle by $4 million. McGrath alluded to ongoing negotiations between Sugarland and the Kempner family—presumably to gain more favorable payment terms. McGrath also suggested that Hines' role was the subject of negotiations. Since the first block of lots will go on the market this year it seems that the outcome of those negotiations will be influenced greatly by the pace of sales. ★

The Real Governor of Texas

by Paul Burka

No one cast a single vote for him, but everyone in Texas lives beneath the power of a solitary judge in Tyler.

Mary Jane Blakley could hardly believe what she was hearing. She had driven into Bay City that late summer day in 1972 to handle the routine transfer of her son Mark from the Van Vleck school system to Bay City High. It was something she had done for the last two years without encountering the slightest problem. After all, Mark wanted to study pre-med in college, and Van Vleck's tiny high school just didn't offer the advanced science and math courses that were available in Bay City. It was routine, just routine, something Mark's older brothers had done on their way to becoming nuclear engineers, something people did all the time. This time, however, a clerk was telling her that there would be no more transfers, that what she wanted was impossible. No, the school board hadn't changed the rules. Bay City, and in fact the whole state, had been ordered not to accept such transfers by a federal judge sitting more than 250 miles away in Tyler, a judge with, Mrs. Blakley thought, the unlikely name of Justice, whose name she'd never heard before and who undoubtedly had never heard of her. What in the world was he doing in her life?

Judge William Wayne Justice of the Eastern District of Texas has entered the lives of a lot of people in his ten years on the bench: parents, politicians, police, school administrators, timber barons, hardened criminals, youths gone astray, environmentalists, illegal aliens, and just about everybody who lives in and around Tyler. He has been called a dictator and a tyrant by some, a hero and a godsend by others. The State House of Representatives, in a show of support for a legislator enraged by one of the judge's rulings, passed a bill to establish a halfway house for wayward juveniles next to the judge's tree-shaded home. He is the most active, and consequently the most powerful, of the 22 men who serve as federal district judges in Texas—a group of men who are appointed for life and who must answer to no one except other federal judges.

In many ways these men, with Judge Justice foremost among them, are the real governors of Texas. They make far more decisions that touch people's lives and influence the course of events than Dolph Briscoe, John Hill, or a score of legislators. They decide where and with whom your children go to school, who you can vote for and how much weight your vote will have, and many less cosmic but nevertheless vital public issues, such as whether commuter airlines can use Dallas' close-in Love Field or San Antonio can build an expressway through a public park. Nationally, federal judges have laid low a president of the United States, caused IBM stockholders to lose more than $5 billion in a week, enjoined drilling for oil and gas off the East Coast in the face of a national energy emergency, restructured professional sports by striking down contracts binding players to their teams, and, of course, done more to change the course of relations between the races in the South than the might of the Union Army.

Despite their immense power, federal judges are largely anonymous and, if they can stay away from controversy, are likely to remain so. Chances are that no layman and only one Texas lawyer in a thousand could recite the roster of federal judges sitting in Texas. Hundreds of thousands of Houstonians knew that Joe Campos Torres had drowned in Buffalo Bayou after being beaten by police, but Ross Sterling was virtually unknown outside the legal community until he set off a series of demonstrations by handing down a benign one-year sentence to policemen convicted of violating Torres' civil rights.

Wayne Justice is undoubtedly better known than any of his Texas colleagues (especially now that Sarah Hughes, who administered the oath of office to President Lyndon B. Johnson, is in semiretirement), but he is hardly a public figure. His impact on the state in the seventies, particularly in school desegregation, has been greater than any other public official's, yet his name, face, and deeds remain unknown to most Texans. Except in the relatively few school districts where desegregation suits have been filed in local federal courts, he oversees all school integration in Texas to this day. The Texas Education Agency has had to create a special division just to administer his orders. Judge Justice has ordered school districts to consolidate, ruled that Mexican Americans must be considered a separate racial group, appointed entire school boards, and banned transfers between school districts that affect racial balance. (It was this last provision that ensnared the Blakleys of Van Vleck.) His decisions have been front-page news locally from Tyler to Del Rio.

He has also had a profound effect on local politics. He forced reapportionment of a number of East Texas city councils and commissioners courts and cast the decisive vote on a three-judge panel that threw out multimember legislative districts for more than four million Texans in Dallas, San Antonio, Fort Worth, Galveston, Corpus Christi, and other metropolitan areas. Only recently he hit the timber industry right in the pocketbook with a decision

> "'I'm a conservative judge,' Wayne Justice insists. 'I've followed the Supreme Court in every instance. If they change, you'll see my decisions change. I'm a professional.'"

The story of William Wayne Justice is in many ways the story of the revolutionary developments that have taken place in American politics in the quarter-century since *Brown v. Board*. The balance of power among the three branches of government has shifted: the executive branch has been wounded by Viet Nam and Watergate, Congress has been floundering for years, only the judiciary has flourished. Wayne Justice has been in the forefront of this judicial revolution. But the story of Wayne Justice is more than just the story of another activist judge. It is the story of how the law works, for the judge himself contends steadfastly that "in every one [of his controversial decisions] the law was clear—I had no choice." It is a political story, for Wayne Justice is one of the last of his generation, the Ralph Yarborough liberals, still in power. And it is above all a personal story: a story of the bitter conflict between an old Southern town committed to a set of values and a way of life, and a judge no less committed to different values and a different way of life; a story of how lives of ordinary people like Mary Jane Blakley are touched by the law.

It is hard to imagine a less likely spot for an activist federal judge than Tyler, a picturesque town of 63,000 located just outside the giant East Texas oil field and just inside the Piney Woods. Proximity to trees and money can do a lot for the appearance of a town, and Tyler has made the most of both. It is best known as a rose-growing center, but if statistics were kept on such things, it might also be famous as the Texas city with the most $100,000 homes per capita.

The south side is the wealthy half of the city, with subdivisions like Oakleigh Woods, where oil millionaires have built homes that resemble Ramada Inns in size and, alas, architecture. The central city, memorable for its red-brick streets, is economically dormant, the better retail stores having abandoned the area for shopping centers south of town. The square has been left to the banks and the Smith County Courthouse, but the spiritual center of town is a short walk away, an intersection where two of Tyler's most influential institutions occupy adjacent corners: the First Baptist Church and the federal courthouse, facing each other like fortresses across the Rhine.

Wayne Justice grew up only 35 miles to the west, in neighboring Athens, but he is still considered an outsider, and for good reason: Athens is a universe away, with a different geography and a different political tradition. Athens is outside the Piney Woods, in the Post Oak Belt; in the judge's youth, it was farming country and not such good farming country at that. Athens is in Henderson County, the home of longtime liberal leader Ralph Yarborough and

that has halted clear-cutting (a harvesting technique that means just what it implies: indiscriminate leveling) in national forests. In another long-running case he ruled that the way the State of Texas treats juveniles in its custody amounts to cruel and unusual punishment; many suspect he is about to say the same thing about the state's prison system in a case currently before him. The juvenile decision forced sweeping changes in the Texas Youth Council, and a ruling against the Department of Corrections (regarded as the best prison system in the nation by some authorities and as one of the most provincial by others, but undeniably the most economically efficient) could cost the state millions of dollars. Another decision with possible consequences for the state treasury was his recent ruling that Tyler schools may not charge tuition for children of illegal aliens—an order that could still be extended to the rest of the state.

A single federal judge exercising this much power over the affairs of a state would have been inconceivable a generation ago. Until recently, business in the federal courts was pretty much limited to suits between citizens of different states, federal criminal cases (automobile theft, mail fraud, and the like) and matters of federal law, like bankruptcy, antitrust, and labor relations. Civil rights cases were rare, and most of those were summarily dismissed. Any school child, for example, who complained in federal court that the principal made him cut his hair would have been laughed out of court and his lawyer summoned into chambers for a tongue-lashing about wasting the court's time. Structurally nothing has changed: the district courts, where Wayne Justice does his work, are still the bottom rung of a three-tier system, the level where cases are actually tried. Above them are ten circuit courts (Texas is in the Fifth Circuit), which consider appeals from the district court and either affirm (uphold) or reverse (overturn) the trial judge's decision. At the apex of the triangle, of course, is the Supreme Court. But the rather placid life district judges enjoyed a quarter-century ago has been swept up in the turmoil that followed the Supreme Court's fateful *Brown v. Board of Education* decision on school desegregation in 1954. Southern resistance to desegregation pushed judges into using unprecedented powers to obey the Supreme Court's mandate to eliminate segregation "root and branch." It is not a long step from ordering school boards to adopt busing plans to telling states how to run prison systems. Inevitably, the declaration in *Brown* that separate but equal is "inherently unequal" meant the recognition of other civil rights, leading to an explosion of litigation: in 1960 around 200 civil rights cases were filed in the entire country; by 1977 the number had ballooned to 17,000.

> "One case quickly took on a larger significance. The issue was who ran the schools—the students or the administration. The answer, of course, was Judge Justice."

76 TEXAS AND THE FEDS: WORKING WITH US OR AGAINST US?

> "Outside the courtroom he has never tried to make his peace with the local citizenry. If someone devised a litmus test for good old boys, Wayne Justice would flunk it."

one of the cradles of Texas populism. It is also yellow dog Democrat territory; George McGovern was the only Democratic presidential nominee in a hundred years who failed to carry Henderson County. On the other hand, populism and its instinctive support for the underdog never touched Tyler. Tyler was a city of influence: it produced three governors and a United States senator before World War I, and its businessmen and bankers were statewide political kingmakers in the days when Texas was still primarily agricultural. The Depression changed nothing, for it arrived about the same time as the East Texas oil boom. While farmers were going broke around Athens, new oil millionaires flocked to Tyler to escape the rigs and roughnecks and were assimilated into the local gentry. The city continues to be dominated by the same oil and mercantile families who have run things as long as anyone can remember. Tyler is one of the few cities where hustlers and hucksters are on the outside: real estate developers, ambitious young lawyers, car dealers, promoters have little political impact. The business oligarchy has stuck to a deep philosophical conservatism of the old school that asks little from government; they are people who are used to having things their own way and they look upon outsiders like Wayne Justice with suspicion. Tyler regularly votes Republican in presidential elections; the last Democrat to carry Smith County was Harry Truman in 1948.

Even though both towns were soul South—Athens was totally segregated as late as 1964—race relations followed the same pattern as politics. "There's no meanness in Henderson County," says a lawyer who's tried cases for twenty years all over East Texas. "Blacks get more than justice. There's a feeling that whites shouldn't be allowed to overreach or take advantage of blacks. It's paternalism, but it's better than Tyler, where you've got the oil mentality of whatever happens to you is your own hard luck. There's no sympathy for the underdog. But even Tyler is better than Longview or Marshall. Over there, if you're black, you're wrong."

Wayne Justice was raised in the Henderson County populist tradition. His father, Will Justice, ran unsuccessfully for Congress in the thirties, but he was best known as a country lawyer of near legendary stature. He won so many improbable cases, civil and criminal, that a joke began to circulate that "there is no justice in East Texas but Will Justice." Those who remember him say he was a mesmerizing orator, a seat-of-the-pants lawyer with an intuitive feel for people, especially potential jurors.

Will Justice lived for a time with Charles and Nannie Yarborough in nearby Chandler; their young son Ralph would run for state attorney general in 1938. Wayne was only sixteen that year, but he campaigned for his father's friend; eventually, of course, Yarborough ran three losing races for governor and became the central figure in Texas politics of the fifties—years when Democratic Governor Allan Shivers endorsed a Republican presidential candidate, years of walkouts and rump conventions and fights between liberals and conservatives that got so rough liberals were once locked out of a state convention by armed state troopers. Wayne Justice was a loyal member of a group who called themselves the coon hunters—all liberals, mostly lawyers, and Yarborough's closest political friends.

Justice went to UT law school in the early forties, where he was, in his words, an undistinguished student who was more interested in politics than law. The *Texas Law Review*, where hotshot students publish their legal research, contains no mention of his name. As a lawyer he turned out to be very different from his father: he had less instinct for people and little rhetorical ability, but he was a careful worker who probably knew more about the law. The difference between father and son carried over into politics. When Wayne Justice learned his law partner (and wife's brother), Mike Rowan, was supporting the hated Shivers for governor over Yarborough, he demanded to know how Rowan could be for "that Republican son of a bitch." Will Justice, though, would pick up the newspaper and needle Rowan gently about Shivers' latest statements. Rowan soon left the firm; he lives in Tyler now, but the political animosities linger.

Wayne Justice's closeness to Ralph Yarborough and his loyal service to the liberal cause paid off after the Democrats recaptured the White House in 1960. Yarborough was United States senator by this time, and he used his patronage to get Justice appointed U.S. attorney for the Eastern District of Texas. The job was situated in Tyler, but Justice chose, significantly, to live in Athens and commute. His record as U.S. attorney gave little indication of what lay ahead after he stepped up to the bench. He was not known as a crusader against either racial discrimination or political corruption, though there was plenty of both in East Texas. His biggest impact came when he successfully prosecuted slant-hole oil well drillers in a very complex and difficult case. The trial was highly publicized in the area and Justice won it, but to no avail. The judge made it clear from the beginning he didn't think much of the whole proceeding. His light sentence was a slap on the wrist for the defendants and a slap in the face to the prosecution; above all it was a clear demonstration of the power of a federal judge. Several years later the judge died, and after some infighting between Yarborough and LBJ, Justice got his seat. It was just in time. Wayne Justice was in the last batch of Lyndon Johnson's judges to be confirmed by the Senate in the spring of 1968.

> "The judge got unsigned hate mail, obscene phone calls, and the silent treatment on the streets of Tyler. Cars displayed 'Will Rogers never met Wayne Justice' bumper stickers."

Soon after Justice took the oath of office, lawyers in the Dallas civil rights division of the Justice Department speculated about what kind of judge he would be. Those fresh out of law school doubted that he would be particularly friendly to the government, since his record as U.S. attorney didn't point in that direction. But the head of the office felt otherwise. "I know this man," the veteran lawyer told his staff, "and I have a feeling that if we give him the right case on school integration, he'll go with us in a big way." The thesis wasn't long in being tested. Desegregation had been proceeding pretty well in East Texas in the late sixties. In most instances no court action was necessary: HEW simply negotiated contracts with local districts on how to desegregate. But Richard Nixon's election gave hope to recalcitrants. Perhaps desegregation wouldn't be necessary after all. In September 1969 the Tatum Independent School District fifty miles east of Tyler decided to ignore its contract and substitute a freedom-of-choice plan: students could go to whatever school they wanted, but the local board would take no affirmative action.

Seldom have the wheels of justice turned so fast. The Justice Department learned on a Thursday that Tatum had reneged. By the following Wednesday they were in Tyler asking for a restraining order. Two days later there was a hearing where Judge Justice made clear he would hold the school board in contempt of court. On Monday school opened on an integrated basis.

The Tatum decision had no impact in Tyler, but it was a harbinger of things to come, in both result and residual ill will. Although they had no legal leg to stand on, some community leaders in Tatum felt they had been bludgeoned into compliance. Judge Justice's first clash with Tyler came when he presided over the local desegregation suit in late 1969. Though integration was inevitable, the school board was sullen and uncooperative. The litigation did nothing to improve the judge's standing with his new south Tyler neighbors. (The Justice family at last moved from Athens when he was named to the bench.) But the real fire storm began in 1970. In the space of little more than a year, Tyler was racked with the same kinds of controversies that were popping up all over the country: disputes over long hair, school discipline, racial discrimination.

It all started when a professor barred a twenty-year-old student at Tyler Junior College from taking a final exam in a government class because his hair was too long. Soon afterward three students were not permitted to register at the college because their hair did not comply with the college's dress code. In the spring of 1971 racial trouble flared up at northside John Tyler High School over a cheerleader election; more than two hundred blacks were suspended for taking part in a demonstration on school grounds. Meanwhile, in another lawsuit that would turn out to have important ramifications for Tyler, Judge Justice effectively took control of school desegregation for the entire state; his order against transfers affecting racial balance was aimed at the substantial number of rural whites who regularly sent their children out of predominantly black rural schools into larger, whiter urban schools. The final blow came late in 1971 when the Texas Education Agency, acting under orders from Judge Justice, forced southside Robert E. Lee High to abandon its confederate theme: no rebel flag, rebel mascot, or "Dixie" as the school song. It looked for a while as if the rebel cannon had to go too, but when research uncovered the fact that it was actually a U.S. Army artillery cannon of Mexican War vintage, use of the cannon was declared proper. (It is not recorded whether Mexican American students protested the decision.)

Each of the controversies quickly ended up in Judge Justice's lap. These were not just ordinary lawsuits; larger issues were at stake and everyone knew it. Emotions ran high; school board meetings drew standing-room-only

Order in The Court

Texas' best federal judges are both newcomers to the bench.

If federal judgeships were advertised in the Help Wanted section of the daily newspaper, they'd look pretty attractive. There's unbeatable job security: lifetime tenure, with removal only by impeachment, and that hasn't happened since 1936. The pay is good enough ($54,500), though not in a league with earnings of partners in big law firms. Side benefits include two law clerks to do research and all the prestige and social status anyone could ask for. And where else can one truly be his own boss? The advertisement should include a warning, however, that judicial appointments are political and only applicants with close ties to a United States senator will be considered.

There are 22 of these choice jobs in Texas, and fortunately almost all the people who fill them have the essential qualities of a good judge: a sense of humility; the ability to recognize the social consequences of a decision; and the capacity to rule by the law as it is, and not as one would like it to be. Former trial lawyers usually make the best judges, provided they don't suddenly have a lapse of memory about how important they once believed judicial protocol and professionalism to be. Common sense is as valuable as legal knowledge, and it helps to have an intuitive sense about when people are telling the truth. One other thing: judges should be as free as possible from partisan political involvement. The two Texas judges who come closest to measuring up to these standards are **Finis Cowan**, 48, Houston, a Carter appointee, and **Patrick Higginbotham**, 39, Dallas, a Ford appointee.

Cowan is a rarity: a genuinely nonpolitical judge. He left the blue-blood Baker and Botts firm, where he was their top trial lawyer, for the bench, probably taking a salary cut in excess of $100,000. As a lawyer he worked fifteen hours a day, a habit he's continued as a judge, including regular hearings at 7:30 a.m. Once when he scheduled some business for twelve o'clock, a lawyer inquired with apparent seriousness whether the judge meant noon or midnight.

Seldom has a judge come to the bench with higher expectations from his colleagues or lived up to those expectations so rapidly. Cowan's quick action on two controversial cases that had dallied for years—stopping the proposed Westheimer breakaway from the Houston Independent School District and insuring that black students attending Prairie View A&M could register to vote in redneck Waller County—won him immediate respect. Cowan has an unerring instinct for justice, a scholar's love for the law, and a lawyer's love for the courtroom: so far, he has been exactly what a federal judge should be. "He's going to be the greatest federal judge who ever came down the pike," says an old courtroom rival.

Higginbotham is a very thorough and intellectual judge, the latest in a long tradition of good Republican judges stretching back to Eisenhower, when Texas had no Republican senator and the administration was free to pick judges on merit. On more than one occasion Higginbotham has impressed lawyers with his references to cases that were still unpublished—indicating that he makes a habit of

Finis Cowan: superb performance lives up to credentials

Patrick Higginbotham: rare judge who'll admit his mistakes

John Singleton: a throwback to the days of imperial judges

John Wood: the kind of judge Nixon was looking for

keeping abreast of the latest developments in the law, something few lawyers or judges do regularly. He has been known to reverse himself and confess that he was wrong, something federal judges do about as often as baseball umpires. Lawyers who find themselves deadlocked over secondary points have learned to expect Solomonlike split-the-baby rulings from Higginbotham, who is frequently mentioned as a possibility for the Fifth Circuit Court of Appeals—a position Wayne Justice also covets.

At the bottom of the scale no one can match the excesses of the late Ernest Guinn of El Paso. Before his death in 1974, Guinn had compiled an astonishing record of reversals by the Fifth Circuit; once the appellate court overturned three of his decisions on the same day. Although liberal Judge **John Singleton,** 60, Houston, a Johnson appointee, has a reputation for volatile outbursts and imperial behavior, the judge more likely to fill Guinn's shoes is **John Wood,** 62, San Antonio, a Nixon appointee.

Wood was schooled in the dog-eat-dog world of insurance law, an arena that rewards greed on one side, toughness and insensitivity on the other. Wood, a hard-nosed defender of insurance companies, has never seemed able to discard that long-cultivated lack of compassion on the bench. Bonds in marijuana cases in San Antonio—most of which are set in Wood's court—average close to $200,000 (compared to $15,000 in Austin, 78 miles away). His sentencing procedures are equally harsh; once he used his contempt power to tack 29 years onto a 15-year sentence. The Fifth Circuit often reverses Wood on constitutional questions: one case it described as a judicial "believe-it-or-not" and a "constitutional fossil"; he was also overturned for allowing intimidation of witnesses. In short, he turned out to be exactly the kind of judge Richard Nixon and John Mitchell were looking for.

crowds, and letters from readers swelled the newspaper. Many people said the issue was discipline, but the fight was really over something far more fundamental: the community's sense of virtue and propriety. The things they'd seen on television—riots, demonstrations, drugs, all the traumas of the sixties—were at last on their doorstep, and they were determined to keep them out. In their minds the only thing that could thwart their will was a single federal judge.

The junior college hair dispute was weighted with this symbolic importance. Tyler Junior College was the pride of the community. It was one of the oldest junior colleges in the state, and the administration, which ran it, in the words of one former student, "like a military operation," seemed to mirror community mores. At the hearing, college officials contended the hair regulation was essential for maintaining discipline and a proper educational environment. On the last day, Judge Justice appeared on the bench with a number of open lawbooks. These proved to be cases supporting his yet unannounced decision, which he handed down promptly without apparent deliberation—against the college. Community leaders were dismayed at the ruling ("This will destroy the college," one of the city's leading lawyers glumly predicted), but they were infuriated by the judge's failure to contemplate, to give the appearance of taking their arguments seriously. Technically Judge Justice was blameless: he had had plenty of time for research, there was ample precedent to support his conclusion (including a decision by a Houston federal judge involving San Jacinto Junior College), and the college had presented more emotion than evidence. But for someone who had spent so much of his adult life in politics, Wayne Justice displayed an astonishing lack of political finesse.

It was a characteristic that would surface again and again; even his staunchest admirers lament the fact that he has never attempted outside the courtroom to make his peace either with the citizenry or the local bar. Shortly after the controversies at the junior college and the local high schools, a local politician saw him having coffee alone at the old Blackstone Hotel. The politician sat down at the table, a rare gesture in itself, and said, "How's my friendly neighborhood school administrator?" William Wayne Justice was not amused. If someone devised a litmus test for good old boys, Wayne Justice would flunk it. He never fraternizes, seldom speaks to Tylerites on the street unless spoken to first, and remains to this day a shy, courtly, formal man. He is a member of the Tyler Petroleum Club (dating back to when he was U.S. attorney) but when he lunches there, he might as well be invisible. No one speaks to him and he speaks to no one, while handshakes and greetings swirl around him in the room.

If the junior college hair case drew the battle lines between judge and community, the two high school imbroglios ended all possibility of rapprochement. The black protest at John Tyler erupted when the school administration distributed cheerleader ballots identifying candidates by race and stipulating that students vote for four whites and two blacks. (The white-black ratio at the school was 62-38.) A black walkout quickly led to a demonstration, suspension of all participants, stringent readmission rules, and a lawsuit. Once again the case took on larger significance. The issue was discipline—who ran the schools, the students or the administration? The answer, of course, was Judge Justice. He barred the school district from suspending the demonstrators; that alone was enough to irk many people, but he really seemed to cross the line separating adjudication from administration when he ordered the school to choose two more cheerleaders, one black, one white, more accurately reflecting the racial ratio.

The politically well-connected minister of the First Baptist Church still regards this decision as devastating to the moral fabric of the community. He holds Judge Justice primarily responsible for the breakdown of discipline in the schools, and to prove his point he told me sadly, "Little girls are afraid to go to the bathroom." Of course that same fear can be found in Dallas and Houston, among other places, but the judge's antagonists cannot believe that it would have happened here regardless. "You see, this man's a socialist," the minister added. "He wants to tear down what we have and replace it with something else."

Oddly, the dispute that sealed the isolation of Judge Justice from the community never even reached the lawsuit stage. When the Texas Education Agency ordered the school board to abandon the Southern theme at Robert E. Lee High or face the loss of accreditation and $800,000 in state funds, many Tylerites saw the threat as going after a fly with a sledgehammer. Since Judge Justice had ordered the TEA, in the statewide school integration case, to investigate complaints about school symbols that threatened racial harmony, he naturally got the blame.

"There's a difference between being proud of your Southern heritage and being racist," says Bill Clark, a local lawyer and state legislator. From the school cases of 1970–1971 forward, Wayne Justice has always been viewed by much of Tyler as an outsider bent on destroying everything they hold dear. The judge got unsigned hate mail (". . . if you want some more black school districts to integrate, why don't you move to Africa . . ."), obscene phone calls in the middle of the night, a few personal threats, and the silent treatment from people on the streets. He raised the insurance on his home and increased security at the courthouse. For a time the stairway to his courtroom was sealed off. Phrases like "undeterred by community hostility" began to appear in his written opinions. Tyler's leading beauticians refused to do Mrs. Justice's hair, and a repairman walked off the job when he realized whose home he was working on. In lighter moments the anti-Justice crowd joked that the court clerk ought to amend the daily incantation of "God save the United States and this honorable court" by substituting *from*. Local cars displayed "Will Rogers never met Judge Justice" bumper stickers. High school students went door to door collecting signatures on recall petitions, though you can no more recall a federal judge than you can reverse the flow of the Mississippi River. Inevitably, one unsuspecting volunteer rang the judge's doorbell and asked Mrs. Justice for her signature. A not-so-distant cousin wrote a letter to the Tyler paper professing shame at being related to the judge.

Much of the open enmity of the early seventies has been calmed by the passage of time. The petitions disappeared and the obscene phone calls have stopped. Sue Justice no longer has to have her hair done in Athens. Tyler Junior College wasn't destroyed after all, and the Lee Red Raiders are no less beloved than were the Lee Rebels. But the underlying social antipathy in this very social town continues unabated. Wayne Justice is such an avid follower of UT football that Darrell Royal once had him sit on the bench during a game, yet when Tyler honored hometown Heisman Trophy winner Earl Campbell last winter, the judge was not invited to the festivities. The usual plaques, certificates, and photographs that clutter the offices of most public figures are missing from his chambers; the sole memento is a football autographed by the 1972 Longhorns.

The judge's admirers—his former law clerks, old friends from Athens, the Ralph Yarborough coon hunters—have a simple explanation for the venom directed at him: he broke the stranglehold of an entrenched conservative gentry on a closed town, and they couldn't abide it. Undoubtedly that was a contributing factor, but it doesn't explain the depth of the anti-Justice feeling. I talked to secretaries and schoolteachers who shared the sentiments of oilmen and establishment lawyers. These are people who ordinarily couldn't care less who runs Tyler, but there is something about a judicially ordered transfer of power that people find upsetting and disorienting, because it is beyond their reach. "People in Tyler," says Smith County Judge Billy Williamson, "like to think that a judge is supposed to guarantee fair play, not be a player himself." The law is so pervasive, so powerful, so much at the heart of how society is organized, that people instinctively want it to be permanent and predictable—and the judge who determines it to be neutral. As usual, myth is not reality: the law is not static and justice is not blind. But no one really likes to be reminded just how arbitrary the process is—how easily precedent and language can be shaped to arrive at almost any conclusion. One eminent jurist has estimated that nine-tenths of the cases that have been decided in the highest court of England could have gone the other way with no violence to the common law. Wayne Justice's real problem with the people of Tyler is that he wasn't politic enough to shield them from the sad truth that the law is as arbitrary and human as the rest of society.

What happened in Tyler reveals a lot about Wayne Justice as a person—sensitive to injustice but sometimes insensitive to people; courageous in the face of hostility but with a footnote, for he was unburdened by any fondness for the community or any desire to be accepted by it—but, more important, it helps explain why Wayne Justice is in the forefront of the judicial revolution. A number of judges might have struck down the Tyler School District's peculiar readmission procedures for suspended black students, but it is hard to imagine anyone other than Wayne Justice ordering the election of two new cheerleaders. What makes Wayne Justice different from most other judges is his willingness to go all the way with a remedy once he's decided an injustice exists.

In case after case, Wayne Justice has issued orders of a scope unknown and undreamed of as recently as fifteen years ago. In school desegregation cases, he insists on "true integration as opposed to mere desegregation." After ruling that juveniles in state custody have a constitutional right to treatment, he went on to specify exactly what that meant, including which IQ test the state must use and what kinds of psychological and psychiatric services must be available. In discrimination cases, Judge Justice repeatedly has not only found for the plaintiff, but also awarded substantial attorney's fees.

His penchant for sweeping remedies is no secret, of course, and lawyers know how to maneuver cases into his court by a time-honored practice known as forum shopping. (Judge Justice is hardly oblivious to this ploy: he jokes that the case load in Tyler has seen a remarkable increase since he came on the scene.) It works like this: Texas is divided into four judicial districts, one for each compass direction; Wayne Justice is one of three judges in the Eastern District. In theory, jurisdiction follows geography—an equal opportunity suit against, say, a Lubbock contractor couldn't be tried in Tyler—but in some cases that limitation has little significance, particularly in major cases involving the state. In the juveniles' suit against the Texas Youth Council, for example, the presence of one institution in the Eastern District (the rest were in the Western District) was sufficient to get the case before Judge Justice.

When liberals decided to challenge the legislative redistricting law of 1971 for not measuring up to the one-man, one-vote standard, they ignored flagrant abuses in places like Dallas and San Antonio, and instead pored over figures and maps for days trying to find something wrong in Judge Justice's segment of the Eastern District (Justice holds court in Sherman, Paris, and, of course, Tyler). "The whole outcome turned on forum shopping," chortles an attorney for the liberals. "We couldn't be sure he'd rule for us, but we knew if he did, he wouldn't let an election take place under an unconstitutional law. Other judges might have found for us, but they'd have said, 'Yes, it's unconstitutional, but we're not going to interfere until the next Legislature has a chance to correct the problem.'"

That is why Wayne Justice is a judicial revolutionary. He is no Brandeis or Cardozo, authoring brilliant, incisive legal principles that will live for ages. Instead he is one of a handful of judges —the best known is Frank Johnson of Alabama, whose health prevented him from becoming head of the FBI—who have grasped the lesson of *Brown* v. *Board*: ultimately the remedy is more important than the substantive decision. Judges have always been part of the power equation of American politics— few powers are more potent than the ability to strike down laws as unconstitutional—but until recently their power has been mostly abstract. No longer: judges run school districts, prison systems, mental hospitals, and state property tax administrations.

Perhaps the best illustration of this judicial revolution, and Wayne Justice's place in it, is the legal battle that grew out of a squabble between two school districts 400 miles from Tyler in Del Rio. No one in that border city could have suspected that a lawsuit brought by the U.S. Justice Department in 1970 to eliminate nine all-black school districts in East Texas would end up setting off a legal donnybrook in their remote corner of Southwest Texas. When the East Texas case began, it appeared to be nothing more than an effort to force consolidation between the black districts and their white counterparts. Many of the white districts didn't even contest the suit; several didn't bother to hire lawyers. It had all the earmarks of a minor case whose outcome was preordained. True, the Texas Education Agency was also a defendant in the case—by supplying the black districts with state funds they had contributed (and, said the feds, consented) to the dual districts—but lawyers for the state regarded that as merely a formality.

That illusion didn't last long. Once Judge Justice had jurisdiction over the TEA, he ordered it to be responsible for eliminating segregation in the entire state—a responsibility that, needless to say, the Texas Legislature had never assigned it. (The idea actually originated with the Justice Department, but the judge embraced it with enthusiasm.) Suddenly a minor regional case had statewide ramifications.

Part of the judge's order was the ban on transfers that impede integration— the provision that thwarted the Blakleys of Van Vleck. In Del Rio the controversy soon involved the whole town. The area had two school districts, Del Rio and a small one on the edge of town known as San Felipe, encompassing mostly Mexican American neighborhoods. But San Felipe also took in Laughlin Air Force Base, and that's where the trouble began. For years the air base had bussed children of military families into Del Rio to avoid the overcrowded, understaffed, and educationally weak San Felipe schools. When the base learned, in the spring of 1971, that Del Rio would not accept any more transfers, a number of Anglo officers exploded with rage. A lawyer then with the state attorney general's office recalls that a high-ranking official vowed he'd close the base before he'd send his daughter to San Felipe. The bluster was sufficient to cause civic leaders to worry that Del Rio might actually lose the base or, at the very least, some government funds handed out to areas with large federal installations.

No doubt Del Rio Anglos would have been happy to perpetuate the dual school districts, but the conflict cast things in a different light. Del Rio wanted that air base and its payroll at all costs. So the school district decided the best way out of the controversy was to absorb San Felipe. But San Felipe wouldn't cooperate. They didn't want to consolidate; their schools might not be good, but at least they were *theirs*. A larger, wealthier Del Rio would obviously control the merged district. So if Del Rio wanted consolidation, it would have to go to court to compel it, and that meant going before the judge who had jurisdiction over the Texas Education Agency and thus over school integration for the whole state. No one in Del Rio knew anything about this man named William Wayne Justice.

A school board lawyer asked the state attorney general's office for advice (Crawford Martin was still AG) and was told, "*Don't* go to Tyler. Whatever you do, stay out of Tyler." They had seen Judge Justice manipulate one school case; there was no telling what he'd do with this one.

Undeterred, Del Rio asked Judge Justice to consolidate the districts. San Felipe fought back, even hiring skilled Odessa trial lawyer Warren Burnett, but to no avail. Burnett presented one of his classic jury summations, but there was no jury, only Judge Justice; no sooner had Burnett concluded his analysis of why the court couldn't consolidate the districts than the judge announced that he could and would. That was the good news for Del Rio. The bad news was that the district had to submit an equal educational opportunity plan for the court's approval, including extensive bilingual and bicultural programs. The old Del Rio board (the judge had also named a new consolidated school board) howled that this was far too costly and unworkable besides: there weren't enough bilingual instructors in the whole state, they claimed, to meet the judge's standards. So the new board worked out a compromise with the federal government, but that was torpedoed when San Felipe representatives, still smarting over the loss of their schools, claimed they'd been excluded from secret negotiations. The situation degenerated rapidly and Judge Justice lost his patience. It is never advisable to test the patience of a federal judge regardless of his ideological bent, and Wayne Justice is no exception. He charged the Del Rio people with acting in bad faith (a claim Del Rio lawyers vehemently denied) and handed down what an assistant state attorney general of that era still calls "the goddamndest cradle-to-grave order in legal history." It was a complete program for running the Del Rio schools, dealing with everything from preschool programs for three-year-olds to curriculum for every grade to parental involvement. So comprehensive was the bilingual plan that it even called for Anglo children to learn Spanish.

Ironically, little of this ever came to pass. The districts consolidated, all right (and the air base continued to pump millions into Del Rio's economy) but the rest of the order was never enforced. Perhaps its scope was too much for the appellate judges on the Fifth Circuit Court of Appeals: although they did not reverse Judge Justice outright, they shifted administration over the order closer to Del Rio, where it wound up in the San Antonio court of Judge John Wood, probably Texas' most conservative federal judge. The Department of Health, Education, and Welfare, which had actually drawn the order, failed to follow it up, and Wood dismissed the whole proceeding. But that does not vitiate the importance of the case for students of judicial activism. A federal judge had handed down a ruling that neither of the original combatants, San Felipe or Del Rio, had wanted; the outcome was one of the most sweeping, comprehensive, detailed orders any judge had ever issued—and it had been affirmed by an appellate court. No one understood what that meant any better than William Wayne Justice.

William Wayne Justice turns out to be an unlikely revolutionary. Unlike many Texas liberals of his generation, he is neither naturally gregarious nor gone to seed. He dresses conservatively ("my protective coloration," he once told an aide)—dark suits, white shirts, plain ties, often a hat—and lives a spartan existence: seven days a week at the office, jogging four miles at least five times a week, and a diet consisting mostly of yogurt and salad without dressing. The social ostracism leaves him unaffected—it's conceivable he prefers it that way—though his wife has been deeply hurt by it. There is virtually nothing about the man to suggest he is one of the leading judicial activists in the nation—except, of course, his decisions.

Indeed, even when he talks about the highlights of his years on the bench, Wayne Justice doesn't dwell on his rulings. His greatest source of pride is an obscure statistic: he went almost ten years before the Fifth Circuit overturned one of his rulings in a criminal case. He has a professional's pride in his work, prefers research to running a trial, and loves to talk about procedural innovations he's developed to make a case run more smoothly. His father, Will Justice, was an expert at what his son calls the "pitfall theory of justice"—digging traps for the unwary opposition, objecting to evidence, springing surprise witnesses—but such tactics have no place in Wayne Justice's courtroom. The judge utilizes an elaborate pre-trial order that all but eliminates the surprise factor; his courtroom is a place for professionals, and most lawyers—there are exceptions—appreciate it.

If he is biased (and most lawyers would agree that all judges are; the only question is to what degree) then sensitivity to abuse of power is no doubt at the heart of Wayne Justice's judicial philosophy. The politics of the fifties continue to have their impact on him, for he spent the decade as an Out; the state and its apparatus were the province of the enemy, and he was never a part of the world that accepts the necessity and value of bureaucratic convenience. He is passionately strict about proper procedure, the formal dance of justice. His own criminal trials are a model of correctness; he goes through the entire litany with defendants—"Do you know you are entitled to a lawyer? Are you aware you do not have to make a statement?"—and expects no less of state judges and administrators. To Wayne Justice, there are few offenses more serious than failing to play by the rules. In reaching his decisions, for example, he is more careful than many judges to touch the obligatory bases of evidence and precedent. His opinions are buttressed with excerpts from trial testimony, and his most controversial actions—the Tyler Junior College hair case, the confederate symbols at Lee High, even his ruling that juveniles in the custody of the state have a constitutional right to proper treatment—followed squarely in the footsteps of other judges.

But ruling on the law is only one of the functions of a judge, and in civil rights cases, at least, it is probably the least important one. Most civil rights suits eventually turn on how the judge interprets the evidence (usually the province of the jury, but partly because Congress didn't trust Southern juries, there is no jury in civil rights cases). The stratagem hasn't always worked the way it was supposed to, because many Southern judges excel at a charade Wayne Justice calls "playing the game." Faced with, say, a massive school bussing suit, a judge will blandly declare it has no merit and throw it out of court, knowing he'll be reversed by a higher court. (The Dallas school integration case has bounced back and forth to the Fifth Circuit so many times it sometimes appears they're playing catch.) In the meantime, the judge can continue to enjoy golf at the country club, and when the appellate courts at last make him crack down, he can say his hand was forced. Judges appointed for life may be insulated from political pressures, but few are as oblivious to social pressures as Wayne Justice.

No one can accuse Wayne Justice of ducking the tough ones. If anything, he goes to the opposite extreme. After a routine hearing in the early seventies, a young lawyer from the Justice Department was part of a group talking shop with the judge when the conversation turned to the future course of constitutional law. Wayne Justice said he felt juveniles and mental patients incarcerated by the state had a right to proper treatment; in fact, he added, if the case were before him, that's how he would rule.

A couple of years later, the Texas Youth Council refused to let some youths meet with their attorneys, the lawyers responded with a suit for access, and the case ended up in Judge Justice's court. But it soon took on greater significance, as cases in that court have a tendency to do. This time, though, the way it happened was a little unusual. Judge Justice called the Justice Department lawyer and told him, "Remember that discussion we had on right to treatment? I think I've got a case for you." He followed that with a letter, the Justice Department eventually contacted the kids' lawyers, the lawyers agreeably broadened their lawsuit and asked the Justice Department to intervene. Sure enough, the judge ruled that juveniles had a right to proper treatment.

Some would say that in molding the shape of cases in his court, the judge exceeded the bounds of propriety; others would defend it as no less than his duty. Regardless, it is something not all judges would condone and still less would do: another example of how Wayne Justice uses the full extent of his powers. But the real issues raised by this kind of judicial involvement transcend Wayne Justice. Where does it all end, and, ultimately, is it a good thing?

There are some signs the judicial revolution has already reached its peak. The Supreme Court has been cutting back on federal court interference with state criminal prosecutions, and it has also found more and more excuses to defer to states in other areas of the law. Indeed, most judicial activism today is pretty much limited to the civil rights arena, but that's still a huge area.

Closer to home, the Fifth Circuit has begun to look long and close at Wayne Justice's decisions. He has such an unflagging reputation as an activist that conservative appeals judges (and the Fifth Circuit splits close to even in philosophy) make a habit of sending their clerks to inspect his rulings. Last fall in reviewing the TYC case the appellate court didn't exactly reverse him on the right-to-treatment issue, but they sent the case back to him for reconsideration, an unusual procedure. And that wasn't all. They sent along a warning that the judge's order was "excessively detailed" and reminded him that there is more than one constitutional way to run a rehabilitation program. The significance of the opinion did not escape Wayne Justice. "I'm a conservative judge," he insists. "I've followed the Supreme Court and the Fifth Circuit in every instance," he says. "Yes, I've been in full sympathy with the decisions I've cited. But if they change, you'll see my decisions change. I'm a professional and I don't like to be reversed."

Does this herald the end of an era in Texas jurisprudence, the decline of Wayne Justice's influence over the state? Probably not. Federal judges are too much a part of the political process of modern America. The way Americans look at their government has changed radically in the last half-century; they have come to see the government as provider rather than policeman. The law has adapted to the change: judges used to direct the government *not* to do things; today judicial activists are telling government what *to* do. Nothing the Fifth Circuit says can turn back the clock or reverse the relationship between people and government. The Fifth Circuit's message to Wayne Justice was to slow down, not change direction.

Perhaps the clear-cutting case sheds some light on what may be expected of a somewhat tempered Wayne Justice. He could have handed down one of his sweeping rulings, finding that clear-cutting was so harmful that it must be banned forever. Or he could have barred clear-cutting on the grounds that it endangered the survival of a rara avis. Instead, he based his decision on narrow procedural grounds; the ruling simply requires a delay for a proper environmental study. That may not be very dramatic, but it was sufficient to stop the cutting and more likely to be upheld on appeal.*

Whatever the future of judicial activism, its past should be seen in perspective. Wayne Justice has opposite-minded counterparts on the other end of the judicial spectrum. If he is inclined to be sympathetic to civil rights complaints, there are other judges—John Wood in San Antonio, for example—who are likely to dismiss them unheard. And there is always the specter of the late Judge T. Whitfield Davidson of Dallas, who once threw the Dallas school integration suit out of court with the comment that "the *real* law of the land is the same as it was on May 16, 1954"—just before the Supreme Court's decision in *Brown* v. *Board.*

Nor should the kind of wide-ranging orders typical of Judge Justice be dismissed solely as power plays. Judges learned the lesson of desegregation the hard way: when courts spoke in general language like "with all deliberate speed," there was no way to enforce an order. The more hostile the state authorities are—and every state agency Judge Justice has had in court was initially hostile—the more detailed and specific orders have to be if a judge has any hope of their being obeyed, or of making a contempt citation stick.

Undoubtedly judicial activism can take credit for most of the political advances of the last twenty years. Judges broke the legal stranglehold of segregation on the South. They made legislative bodies more representative; they brought the vote to the disenfranchised; they protected the rights of people whom state authorities had trampled on unchecked for years. But it was not without cost. Tinkering with machinery may solve one problem but create hidden stress elsewhere; in the case of the political mechanism, the vulnerable spot has proved to be the legislative branch. Politicians like to scream about judicial interference with their territory, but the truth is that many have discovered political advantages in letting judges take the heat for tough decisions. In Alabama, for example, the Legislature was so delighted a federal court had finally forced revision of the property tax system—an issue they had wrestled with for years—that the state didn't even appeal the decision. What happens to a democracy when the creativity of its legislative branch is stifled? Defenders of judicial activism would respond that, yes, it would be preferable for the legislatures to act, but since the legislatures have defaulted on their duties, then the courts must fill the gap. It's an argument Judge Justice himself has used. But it begs the question. The real issue is, Did the legislatures have a duty in the first place? (And how do we find out? Why, the judges will tell us.)

Ultimately, though, the real problem with judicial activism is not its effect on the system, but its impact on individuals who are left without recourse. The legal system can resolve narrow controversies between individuals, or general conflicts between interest groups, but it can't seem to do both at once. There is no way to prove the valid exception to a judicial ruling without a long, tedious, and expensive process: hearings, briefs, arguments, research, and that's only one case. What if, as in the case of Judge Justice's order banning transfers, hundreds of people want exemption? Of course, a court can always delegate some decision-making power to a state agency like the TEA, but inevitably a bureaucracy under the watchful eye of a federal judge armed with contempt power will not have flexibility uppermost in its mind. People like Mark Blakley always get caught in the net.

Oh yes. Mark Blakley never did become a doctor. He never did even finish college. He dropped out after a year and works for a soft drink company. Somehow, he says, he never felt the same about school after a federal judge entered his life. ★

*It wasn't, though. Just before press time, the Fifth Circuit reversed the decision.

BEHIND THE LINES

This December, four of the largest school districts in Texas were deeply involved in desegregation decisions that would shape their destiny in the eighties. Fort Worth was putting the finishing touches on an agreement to cut back busing and restore neighborhood schools. Houston was also on the verge of ending its long stay in court, without busing and with its neighborhood schools intact. Dallas and Austin, however, faced court decisions that, particularly in Austin's case, seemed likely to require the most ambitious busing plan yet seen in Texas. The natural question, of course, is "Why?" Why are students in one Texas city to be bused and those in another Texas city not to be? Why are children in one school district assigned to neighborhood schools without regard to their race and those in another city assigned to distant schools *because of their race?*

No wonder the ordinary citizen is confused. Dr. Martin Luther King, the saint of the great movement to desegregate American life, expressed the goal so well: "I have a dream that my children will live in a nation where they will not be judged by the color of their skin but by the content of their character." In Austin and Dallas today, in the name of desegregation, his children would be judged by the color of their skin. More confusion surrounds the fact that a national commitment to eliminate segregation in schools has ended up with the courts' ruling that suburban districts—whose all-white schools are havens for white flight—are in compliance with the Constitution (basically because they had no blacks to segregate) and that their neighboring urban school districts—with almost no schools that are all white—are not. And year in, year out, those urban schools become more and more segregated.

These contradictions have sapped our national will to end segregation, and the sad thing is they are not inevitable. A desegregation plan that serves the best interests of its community should accomplish several major goals: it should eliminate any vestiges of the dual school systems that assigned black and white students to separate schools because of their race; it should improve educational opportunities for all children; and it should foster understanding and cooperation among races and ethnic groups. To meet these goals, a mandatory busing plan is the least desirable approach. It assigns students to schools by race, just as the dual system did. It disrupts education by taking children out of their neighborhoods against their will. And it increases racial tension by placing the onus for that disruption on minority children. Better solutions are possible, and school boards and minority leaders with vision have worked to find them.

Houston's desegregation plan emphasizes neighborhood schools and voluntary integration. Thousands of Houston students do ride buses to schools outside their neighborhoods, but they are bused *because they want to be,* because they and their parents think it is better for their education. The student and his parents are, after all, the real parties in these desegregation suits. A plan that gives them the freedom to improve integration by improving their education is destined to be more successful and more stable than a mandatory busing plan that relies on coercion. The Houston experience has shown that such a voluntary plan can produce integrated neighborhood schools whose students consistently surpass their supposedly superior suburban counterparts on standardized tests. It can produce, in short, better education, which is what all parents—black, Mexican American, and white—want for their children.

Minority parents don't like mandatory busing much more than white parents do, but they are placated by their attorneys, who explain that they insist on busing because it is "the law of the land." That's simply not true. When it comes to desegregation plans for specific cities, there is no such thing as a clear and consistent law of the land. The desegregation plan of a given urban school district is nominally a response to the Constitution of the United States, but it is even more the result of the school administration's diplomacy, the attitudes and personality of the minority plaintiffs, and occasionally what the U.S. district judge had for breakfast. The final character of a school district's plan (provided the U.S. Justice Department or national civil rights organizations stay on the sidelines) is largely the product of how much vision the minority plaintiffs' attorneys and the school board have, and how well they get along.

Plaintiffs in Houston and Fort Worth, for example, have been willing to accept desegregation plans that are considerably less stringent than the courts might require. Weldon Berry, the NAACP attorney in the Houston case for more than twenty years ("too damn long," he says), gives that district good marks. "There is little overt racism here," he says. "The school board is making a sincere effort. Nobody in Houston wants busing. Blacks don't like it any more than whites, since blacks are usually the ones that end up being bused. What we need to do here," he continues, "is get more whites back in the district. We need to revitalize inner-city neighborhoods and build housing young couples can afford." Berry is philosophical about the future: "I'm no longer asking them to do the impossible. Everybody is more realistic now."

That same sort of positive, cooperative spirit has evolved, after years of enmity, in Fort Worth, where the NAACP and the school board have found a common interest in preserving a strong neighborhood school system. (In the process they finally laid to rest the old myth that to be in favor of neighborhood schools was to be against effective desegregation. Precisely the opposite is true today.) But in Dallas and Austin the minority plaintiffs and the school board seem to be always at each other's throats. The plaintiffs' attorneys, for their part, seem determined to get their pound of flesh now that they have the upper hand at last. "In a lawsuit that's in such an adversary situation," one plaintiffs' attorney told me, "you start wanting to win. And then you start wanting not just to win, but to beat your opponent, and beat him good." At the moment of such victory, as in Austin, the plaintiffs' attorneys can lose sight of their community's best interests and, with a snap of their fingers, demand that thousands of schoolchildren be bused; or they can work for a voluntary solution. The choice is entirely theirs. Seldom do private individuals, accountable to no one, hold such power. The best plaintiffs' attorneys exercise it wisely and without vindictiveness. Others, human nature being what it is, do not.

Minority plaintiffs, however, are not alone in polarizing the issue. In desegregation, as in dancing, it takes two to tango. Some school boards have fought every desegregation order and made few efforts to enhance the educational opportunities of minority children. In contrast, the Houston School Board decided in 1971 that they would accept the court-ordered desegregation plan without further appeal and simply take the heat for the decision. The heat was so intense that those school board members were virtually driven from public life (although one, Eleanor Tinsley, was recently elected to the Houston City Council). But by their statesmanship they gave Houston almost a decade's lead over other Texas districts that kept their cases tied up in court. In 1975 their successors implemented, without waiting for a court order, a comprehensive plan of magnet schools (specializing in a wide range of programs, from engineering to performing arts) that were designed to improve desegregated education in 54 schools. One plaintiffs' attorney involved in several cities' suits described that move as a "positive, voluntary step that showed a sincere commitment to desegregation." That same attorney, however, had no good words for the school boards in Dallas and Austin, and therein lies much of the reason for the harsher desegregation plans those cities now face.

Practically speaking, the relative number of white students in a district also has a great deal to do with how comprehensive the desegregation plan will be. Big-city districts like Dallas, Houston, and San Antonio have been steadily losing white students, but to attribute that loss entirely to white flight is a mistake. School districts in these cities' best-known suburbs—Highland Park, Spring Branch, and Alamo Heights—have also lost students; in the past six years, for example, Spring Branch's enrollment has declined by 20 per cent, partly because its population is aging, partly because white birth rates are down, and partly because young parents can't afford houses that close to the central city. As a result of similar factors, both Houston and Dallas have around 30 per cent white students, down from more than 50 per cent in both districts a decade ago. There isn't a great deal of desegregation that can be accomplished with so few whites. Even if whites were distributed evenly among the district's schools, it is hard to maintain the legal fiction that a black child in a 90 per cent minority school is segregated while one in a 75 per cent minority school is not.

Austin, on the other hand, is one of the few urban districts that still has a white majority. But as a plaintiffs' attorney in another district said about Austin, "It's tempting for the plaintiffs not to worry about whites fleeing the system when you've got a white majority. When you get down to thirty per cent or so, however, you start worrying about keeping the whites *in*." Although a few minority activists *want* whites to flee the city schools so they themselves can have more power, the simple truth is that when whites retreat to private schools to avoid busing, they tend to become foes of the public schools. They begin voting down bond issues and taxing authority, and, in no time at all, a healthy public school system can be destroyed. "The time for moderation," the plaintiffs' attorney continued, "is when you still have the whites, not after you've lost them."

Too often overlooked in this confusion over desegregation is the true central question: what kind of education are these schools providing? For the past 25 years parents have been influenced by two powerful but contradictory myths about integrated education. Whites have regarded integrated education as inferior, while blacks have seen it as superior. As a result, whites have fled from integrated education just as determinedly as blacks have pursued it. There is, however, absolutely nothing that destines predominantly black schools to be inferior, and a growing number of blacks have come to consider racist and insulting the myth that their children can learn only if they are in school with whites. They believe that, given good teachers and sufficient resources, their children can learn as well on their own. Even more important, more and more black parents are insisting on strong schools in their neighborhoods to hold their communities together. Mexican Americans have similar concerns, intensified, if anything, by their strong neighborhood identifications and their desire for bilingual education programs. The statistical evidence is fairly neutral: in some schools minorities do better in integrated classes, in others they do not.

But the myth that integrated schools are inferior to all-white schools is easier to puncture. The tenacity of that myth, spread by suburban educators and realtors, has led young parents who want the best education for their children to suburban districts. Those districts, however, do not necessarily have better schools. Recent test results show that children in the 33 Houston elementary schools most like those in the highly touted Spring Branch suburban district scored a full *seven months* ahead of the suburban children, and *four* months ahead of students from Cypress Fairbanks, Humble, and Alief. All but two of those Houston schools have enrollments that are between 10 and 75 per cent minority children, yet test scores for these schools were significantly higher than those of all-white schools in the suburbs. A rational parent, black or white, choosing the best school for his child would have to pick one in Houston. The same clear superiority of the Houston schools is evident when their students are compared to those in other urban districts, to other students in gifted and talented programs, and even to other students in disadvantaged schools. Across the board, Houston students score as well as or better than comparable students anywhere.

The lesson in these test results, and in the many innovative programs that a large district like Houston can support, is that middle-class parents who sincerely want the best education for their children should send them back to urban schools. To choose private or suburban schools may be to shortchange their children, not simply in terms of the somewhat abstract benefits of a multiracial experience, but also in terms of the concrete advantages of superior education. Until Houston stopped worrying about desegregation and started worrying about excellence in education, about all the district could do to defend desegregation was to tell parents it was good for the nation for their children to go to Houston schools. Now they can say it is good for the children. Most cities have not expended as much effort to improve integrated education as Houston has, but with good leadership, parental support, and cooperation from their desegregation plaintiffs, they could. The fact that integrated schools can be superior, as they are in Houston, is a sign that urban education can work. There are few greater signs of hope in America today★

William Broyles, Jr.

Political Parties and Political People

PART TWO

Texans are as varied among themselves as they are distinct from non-Texans. The lives of Anglo, black, and Chicano Texans are often worlds apart, united by nothing more than a shared, fanatical devotion to the Cowboys and the Oilers. The growing influx of non-Texans has generated considerable distrust between the natives and the carpetbaggers. Texas women, gaining momentum from the national women's movement, have entered the business and political arenas, where they threaten to outshine the men. And the expansion of Texas industry has created a deepening gulf between business and labor.

Historically, much of the diversity among Texans has failed to translate into competitive electoral politics because state electoral laws and political traditions have operated to exclude minorities and inhibit the development of a strong, competitive system. As Texas has changed in other ways and as the federal government has moved to insure equal access to state and national elections for all citizens, electoral politics have changed. Statewide dominance by the Democratic party has declined, as has the conservatives' control within that party. Today, Texas politics reflect an increasingly diversified electorate—one characterized by the birth of La Raza Unida, the rise of a competitive Republican party, and the increased participation of cultural and economic minorities within the Democratic party.

The emergence of these new political forces is most apparent at the local level. From Crystal City to Austin and San Antonio to Fort Worth, the towns and cities of Texas have witnessed dramatic upheavals in politics-as-usual. Some of these local revolutions were forgotten almost as soon as they occurred; others have produced extensive and lasting alterations in the local balance of political power. All demonstrate the political turmoil engendered by the pervasive changes occurring within the state and the capacity of these changes to restructure the political landscape.

At the state level, shifts in the electoral balance of power have come more slowly. Yet the emergence of a more diversified electorate also affects the struggle for state power. Within the Democratic party, conservative incumbents find that they are no longer assured of renomination; rather, they frequently face stiff and sometimes successful challenges from moderate and liberal opponents. Together, La Raza Unida and the Republican party have fielded statewide slates that have challenged Democratic hegemony in the general elections. And in the late seventies, Texas voters elected the state's first Republican governor in a century.

These changes in the nature of the Texas electorate and in the fortunes of political forces are restructuring state politics. The chapters in Part II detail some of the intriguing behind-the-scenes stories that add color and life to the broad transformations in the state's electoral arena. Chapter Four looks at the personal side of electoral change, focusing on some of the activists in this new era. Chapter Five records several of the more dramatic local battles. And Chapter Six analyzes the on-again, off-again nature of statewide electoral change.

The Participants

CHAPTER FOUR

Raza Desunida, Tom Curtis (February 77)
The Case Against the Farmers, Stephen Chapman (March 78)
Sole Brothers, Jack Keever (January 75)
Labor Pains, Dick J. Reavis (August 78)
The Good Old Girls, Prudence Mackintosh (January 78)

RAZA DESUNIDA

by Tom Curtis

José Angel Gutiérrez' dream turned out to be a nightmare.

Long before his current troubles started, back in the days when Anglos were still in power in Crystal City, José Angel Gutiérrez told his followers an old chestnut:

An Anglo fisherman on a coastal jetty has caught a bunch of crabs and has put them in a shallow bucket near him. When he turns his back on the bucket to return to crabbing, the people next to him cry out warnings that the catch will escape. "It's OK," he reassures them. "These are *Mexican* crabs. They'll pull each other back down."

The story sounds like a candidate for the Earl Butz Award for Ethnic Humor, but Gutiérrez knew that it represented the conventional wisdom among Anglos that Mexican Americans were, as Gutiérrez wrote, "unorganizable, easily divided, apolitical, and emotional." Gutiérrez knew better. Even as a young graduate student at St. Mary's University in the late sixties, Gutiérrez could see that Mexican Americans in South Texas were a sleeping giant, a huge majority of the regional population. They needed only the right person and the right vehicle to wield them into an unbeatable, unified political force.

Martin Luther King he isn't, but José Angel Gutiérrez also had a dream. It was, he'd tell you a couple of years ago, to transform a "colony in captivity"—the impoverished Chicanos of America in general and South Texas in particular—into a "nation within a nation" that could redistribute the wealth of the region for its people. He started trying to implement it seven and a half years ago when as an articulate, aggressive graduate student in his midtwenties he came home to Crystal City in Zavala County, the heart of the fertile "Winter Garden" vegetable growing region of South Texas, 114 miles southwest of San Antonio. Through a third political party that he helped to found, La Raza Unida, he began organizing Mexican Americans (85 per cent of Zavala County's 11,400 people) to overthrow the Anglo oligarchy that had ruled them for generations. Between 1970 and 1974 the party successively swept control of the school board, city council, and county commissioners court. The new Chicano administrators brought in an estimated $20 million in federal aid to upgrade education, build homes, pave streets, and provide health and other services. People began to look at the dusty town of 8000—known previously, if at all, as "the spinach capital of the world"—as a prototype for Chicano self-determination.

José Angel Gutiérrez and wife Luz in better days, before the trip to Cuba.

Somewhere along the road, a year and a half ago or so, the *Cristal* movement began to go awry. The intense, almost totalitarian discipline that held La Raza Unida together was snapped in a direct challenge to Gutiérrez' rule as the party's maximum leader. Many among his top party and governmental lieutenants and staunchest allies split with him in a power struggle over whether they or he would control jobs and other patronage in their political domains. He denounced them as ungrateful, as a "middle-class influence" with narrow, selfish aims; they reviled him as a dictator who was interested only in personal power and who had been appropriating the movement to advance his own political and financial ambitions.

The internecine Raza struggle that ensued made its earlier "eliminate the gringo" phase involving demonstrations, economic boycotts, intense political organizing, and propagandizing look like so much Little League play. As Father Sherrill Smith, Crystal City's diocesan Catholic priest put it, "All of these skeletons that had been neatly stacked in the closet came out and began clattering around." Both sides were playing for keeps. After a 4–3 split on the school board led to the firing of a *Gutierrista* superintendent, each of the local factions tried to bring criminal charges against the other. Gutiérrez reportedly told a crowd that the 25-member Barrio Club, a self-described "social betterment organization" and a hotbed of anti-Gutiérrez agitation, had infested the schools with drugs that they sold to the students; the club's members responded with a $3 million slander suit against Gutiérrez. And so it went. The game was rough even by extraordinary South Texas standards, where the tradition of playing hardball politics is perhaps best epitomized by the incident early in this century when an election day shoot-out at a polling place launched the Parr dynasty in Duval County.

This struggle was not to launch a dynasty but to end one. The Anglos, who own almost all the land and most of the businesses but had been in political eclipse since Gutiérrez was elected county judge in 1974, joined with Gutiérrez' Chicano opponents to hand him defeat after defeat at the polls, beginning with the city council and school board elections last April. In November, Gutiérrez managed to hang onto his last electoral dominion, the county commissioners court, when his candidate survived a write-in challenge by nineteen votes. But La Raza's candidate for sheriff was trounced by a Mexican American running on the Democratic ticket. Subsequently, voters turned down Gutiérrez' plan for a half-million-dollar bond issue to develop a lakeside park by a two-to-one margin. And Governor Dolph Briscoe threw a monkey wrench into Gutiérrez' plan to use an already-awarded $1.5 million federal grant to start an export-import business

90 THE PARTICIPANTS

Photography by Alberto Farias

and an agricultural cooperative—the latter of which smacked to Briscoe of "a little Cuba."

By December, when I last visited there, the once united race in Crystal City seemed split beyond hope of repair. Zavala County had ceased to look like a prototype for brown self-determination; it looked more like a Custer's last stand for La Raza Unida, which was already moribund elsewhere and has been further demoralized by the arrest on marijuana smuggling charges of its two-time Texas gubernatorial candidate, Ramsey Muñiz. Crystal City seemed destined to take its place in the footnotes of history some place between failed nineteenth-century utopian experiments, such as the Brook Farm and Oneida communities, and Tammany Hall.

Thirty-eight miles north of Crystal City, Uvalde's first Mexican American county commissioner tells about the time 25 years ago when he was a shoeshine boy outside a local cafe. Gilberto Torres remembers asking a passing Anglo if he wanted a shine. "He said, 'Yeah, come inside,' but when I did the owner came over, yanked me up by my hair and collar, and carried me over to the door. A sign there said, 'No Mexicans, No Dogs Allowed.' Then he pushed me back out on the sidewalk." Torres, whose upholstery business has been boycotted by Anglos because of his political activity, says that before the federal Voting Rights Act was extended to embrace Mexican Americans in Texas, local Democratic officials met Mexican American voter registration drives with a welter of technicalities. Such charges were commonplace across South Texas. But not all Mexican Americans were discouraged from voting. Equally ubiquitous was the tradition of the *patrón*, the Anglo landowner or boss who would pay the poll taxes and deliver en masse the votes of the Mexican Americans under his protection to candidates he supported. It was out of that tradition that the nefarious Box 13 scandal in Alice occurred in 1948. There, 125 miles southeast of Crystal City, political lieutenants of the late George Parr recanvassed the results long after other statewide returns were complete. The recount showed 202 additional votes for senatorial candidate Lyndon Johnson and only one for his opponent Coke Stevenson—enough to give Johnson the Democratic nomination by 87 votes. Later inspection of the poll lists showed that Box 13's voters had remarkably cast their ballots in alphabetical order. Such practices gave South Texas a reputation for vote stealing comparable to that of the worst northern big-city machines.

Unlike the urban machines, however, the rural Anglo machines did little to better the lot of the people on whose votes they depended. Though there are isolated cases of philanthropy and generosity, there was virtually no political patronage doled out, and little concern with social progress. Education is a case in point. Anglo insensitivity or unconcern with language and cultural problems of Mexican American youngsters —along with their poverty—tended to push these youths prematurely out of school. As recently as ten years ago, it wasn't uncommon in South Texas to find Mexican Americans dropping out before high school graduation at rates of 80 per cent or more. In Crystal City, the Anglo cultural domination went so far as to make it a punishable offense for students to speak Spanish in public school halls or on playgrounds.

When José Angel came home to stay in the summer of 1969, the salad days of Chicano radicalism, he was fresh from a year's tenure as chairman of the Mexican American Youth Organization (MAYO), an activist group he and four other students had founded two years earlier. Despite his own middle class origins—his father, after serving in Pancho Villa's medical corps during the Mexican Revolution, had become a Crystal City physician—Gutiérrez had little empathy with the then-prevalent theory among political scientists that Mexican Americans' best hope lay with gradualism. He scornfully referred to members of middle class organizations like the moderate, officially nonpartisan League of United Latin American Citizens (LULAC) and the more liberal, partisan Democratic Political Association of Spanish-Speaking People (PASO) as "the leaders of tomorrow." The political science master's thesis he submitted at St. Mary's in 1969 was written on "The Empirical Conditions for Revolution in Four South Texas Counties"—Zavala among them. He found conditions in those counties "strikingly similar to Latin America" and the Chicano movement "but one step from the actual outbreak of violence to achieve its desired goals," goals of radical if unspecified "changes in the social order, especially in the basic institutions of government, labor relationships, and social status."

Written in the seemingly apocalyptic late sixties—days of student protests, black power, urban riots, and rhetoric charged heavily with hyperbole—the thesis reads like an exercise in maumauing, perhaps unconscious posturing for the benefit of Gutiérrez' MAYO comrades and his activist professors. Running against the grain of its insistence on revolution, however, is an interesting passage in which Gutiérrez mentions the surprise election in 1963 of five Mexican Americans to the city council in Crystal City (accomplished, as he did *not* say, with the organizing help of the Teamsters Union, which then represented workers at the local Del Monte packing plant). Although the Anglos had recaptured control of the council just two years later, the precedent impressed Gutiérrez deeply. "Never in the history of the state of Texas," he wrote without irony, "had such a significant event taken place."

Of course, there was good reason to take that election seriously, because it proved what was possible within the political structure. In most of the nation, even in most of Texas, a Chicano political party was a futile hope for winning control: a minority can't win an election by itself. But South Texas was different. In Zavala and 25 other counties, Mexican Americans are the majority. If they could be organized, which most folks felt they couldn't, then they would win.

In Crystal City, Gutiérrez started with unconventional political methods that were even more offensive to Crystal City's Anglos and conservative Mexican Americans than was the idea of a third party. He used the polarizing techniques of community organizing refined by the late radical Saul Alinsky. It didn't take him long to find an issue around which to build a movement. Late in 1969, the high school's ex-students association promulgated a rule that their homecoming queen had to be the daughter of parents who had graduated from Crystal City High School, a grandfather clause which had the effect of excluding all but a handful of Chicanas from consideration. On December 9, their leaders primed by Gutiérrez, 700 high school students walked out of classes and rallied outside the school. Parents supported the students as that single issue boiled over to include a range of grievances. Within a week the strike spread to junior high and elementary schools. The revolution in *Cristal* was on.

The chief revolutionary, José Angel Gutiérrez, seemed almost a messiah to many of his followers. Smart and quick, he miraculously proved that Chicanos could beat the Anglos at their own games. "He was the most unselfish man you could imagine," recalls San Antonio attorney Jesse Gamez, a longtime neighbor and friend who later broke with Gutiérrez. "He would go around the country making speeches and would come back and put the money he made from honorariums back into the movement by paying rents and telephone bills." He taught his people the nitty-gritty of precinct organization, how to register voters, how to be a poll watcher. Although he baited the Anglos and seemed genuinely committed to helping Crystal City's poor and largely migrant (60 per cent) population, like most politicians he wasn't specific about long-range goals. Few Chicanos, however, doubted his commitment to create a social revolution in

Crystal City.

In the spring of 1970, candidates running on La Raza Unida slate won control of the school board. Gutiérrez himself became board president. Campaign posters reflected the new party's theme of the need for unity. One showed a hand clutching a bar of soap. Translated from Spanish, the text read, "You Can't Wash Clean with One Hand." After the Raza slate took office, most Anglo or non-Raza Unida teachers were fired or quit, and pro-Raza people took their places. Raza emblems and murals and pictures of Gutiérrez and other board members went up in the schools. Bilingual programs were instituted and English abandoned as a first language in elementary schools. During football halftime ceremonies, members of the Crystal City High School band marched in formation to spell RAZA on the field and held clenched fists aloft. Before long, almost all Anglo parents and many of the more conservative Mexican American parents pulled their children out of the public schools and started a private one, the Crystal Community School; almost half its enrollment was Mexican American. They said they were protesting not only the politics but also what they claimed was an erosion of the authority of teachers and administrators.

Whatever one thinks of the methods, the Raza administration of the schools achieved results. A $2.7 million bond issue was approved to build much-needed new schools. The new school superintendent applied for and got numerous federal and foundation grants for bilingual, reading, teacher training, and other programs, creating more jobs in the bargain. The dropout rate plummeted. More than 80 per cent of Crystal City High School graduates—better than twice the statewide average for Chicano youth—were going to college, helped along by new counselors who were good at lining up scholarship aid and receptive colleges.

Gutiérrez met the obstacles he found head on. When the schools had trouble finding certified Chicano administrators, the district applied for and won a grant from the Carnegie Foundation to train them. The trainer, at $11,500 per annum, turned out to be Gutiérrez himself, but he did the work and nobody in the movement begrudged him the money. In 1972 Gutiérrez' wife, Luz, also went on the public payroll as the $16,000-(now $20,000)-a-year administrator of a county health clinic.

Later, Watergate testimony would show that the Nixon White House used the grant for the clinic to "neutralize" Mexican American votes that normally would have gone to George McGovern. Gutiérrez went along, putting out the word to Raza faithful to boycott the presidential race, and Nixon carried the county 1288 to 1122 while 1490 in Zavala County chose not to vote for president. Gutiérrez didn't apologize for the deal. "The Democrats and Republicans are just two fingers on the same hand," he told me later.

Theoretically, the controlling mechanism of Crystal City's Raza administration was supposed to be Ciudadanos Unidos, a committee of about 400 families that served as the political arm of La Raza Unida. The group met on alternate Sundays to get an accounting from public officials, rule on policy questions, and even make recommendations on the hiring and firing of public employees. Because of his preeminent stature, Gutiérrez almost always prevailed before the group.

The trappings of participatory democracy aside, Ciudadanos Unidos was basically a political machine, lubricated by the spoils system, and Gutiérrez was a political boss. Despite all the talk about "a colony in captivity," the practice wasn't all that different from the machines invented by Irish Catholics in nineteenth-century America when they too were blocked by language, poverty, and discrimination from joining the mainstream. Like earlier bosses, by his lights Gutiérrez was doing well by doing good: from a Falstaff beer distributorship, speaking fees, his Carnegie program salary, and his wife's salary from the health clinic post, his family income totaled close to $50,000—or about ten times the average in Zavala County. Meanwhile, he was working towards a PhD in government at UT-Austin.

In 1974, La Raza Unida consolidated its hold on local government by winning control of the Zavala County Commissioners Court. Gutiérrez himself defeated incumbent County Judge Irl Taylor by a vote of 1968 to 1760. But the victory only served to underscore the party's predicament. It had political power, but except for the jobs government could control, no economic power. Since La Raza's victories began, in fact, the county had begun to stagnate economically. No new businesses came in, and Gutiérrez made clear he wouldn't look kindly on employers who exploited the area's main resource, cheap labor. This may have been a calculated decision, because the Raza revolution was built on the votes of the large migrant population, which couldn't be fired for political activity as locally employed Chicano activists elsewhere had been. Still, there was a need for jobs. Gutiérrez talked about bringing a rug factory to town, but that never happened.

He had another plan, this one more relevant to the migrant population. He wanted to create a cooperative farm that could provide local people with year-round employment. This was crucial to the movement's success for two reasons: it would give La Raza additional patronage jobs as well as develop economic power to countervail that of the Anglo establishment, which had a virtual lock on economic opportunity. Plans for the farm were begun with a $50,000 grant from the federal Community Development Administration.

Before the plan was developed, Gutiérrez and ten other party members, including Crystal City's school superintendent and city manager, set out in April 1975 for a two-week tour of Cuba. The trip proved to be a watershed for Gutiérrez. Although other Americans had visited Cuba—Senator McGovern left the day Gutiérrez arrived—the trip rankled local Anglos anew and even startled some of Gutiérrez' more conservative Raza followers. Cuba proved to him, he said, that "socialism doesn't have to be all dull, gray uniformity." He marveled about the nation's successes in education, housing, and health care. But most of all, he seemed to be impressed by the high level of party organization—"down to the street level"—and that everyone seemed well versed in ideology and intimately acquainted with Castro's speeches. "We want to emulate their discipline and intensity," he told me shortly after the visit, "so we can lift ourselves out of poverty."

"After he got back from Cuba, Angel was so excited, so enthused by what he saw," Ninfa Moncada, secretary of Ciudadanos Unidos at the time, recalled later. "He doesn't get carried away by just anything, but he told us they had no problems, no crime." A growing number of followers began to doubt him. They didn't know much about Cuba, but they were pretty sure it was no Utopia; what's more, the main thing they did know was that it was run by a dictator, and if Zavala County had to model itself after Cuba, they knew who was going to be the local Castro. Some of Gutiérrez' followers questioned whether his motives were still benevolent, and Gutiérrez did nothing to dispel such fears by announcing plans for a *comité de nueve*—committee of nine —to make policy and hiring-firing decisions for the party. Like others now at odds with him, Mrs. Moncada says Gutiérrez came back with a Cuban plan to add discipline to the *Cristal* movement. (Gutiérrez insists that the committee was planned before the Cuba trip and simply amounted to a condensation of a larger 27-member group of department heads and others. But many of the Raza Unida faithful saw the *comité de nueve* as transferring power from the broad-based Ciudadanos Unidos, the policy-making committee of 400 families, to a narrower base that Gutiérrez could control.) Rudi Paloma, who runs Crystal City's urban renewal program and is a member of the Barrio Club, says club members "saw Gutiérrez

MEANWHILE, BACK IN THE MAINSTREAM...

La Raza Unida never made much headway among the 85 per cent of Texas' Mexican Americans who live in the big cities, though it unquestionably raised their political consciousness. Here's what's going on elsewhere:

• *Mexican American Democrats* (MAD). Founded in December 1976, this is a caucus of 500 or so elected officials, organizers, and other activists. Its mainspring is former San Antonio State Senator Joe Bernal, who recently served on the Carter transition team.

• *Political Association of Spanish-Speaking Organizations* (PASO). Born from the Viva Kennedy organization, PASO gets out the brown vote in Houston and El Paso. A Dallas chapter is being organized.

• *Communities Organized for Public Service* (COPS). A grass-roots coalition of San Antonio citizens' groups, COPS' membership is 98 per cent Mexican American. COPS is radical in the sense that it strikes at root issues, particularly the conflicting interests of San Antonio's fast-money suburban developers and inner-city residents who want to preserve and upgrade their neighborhoods.

---

was politicking" to stack the membership of the committee, "so we did too, and we won." That ended any desires Gutiérrez might have had to use the committee, but it was only the beginning of his troubles.

The next crisis was the firing of the school superintendent, who had injudiciously queried the Texas Education Agency about several cases of nepotism involving anti-Gutiérrez members of the school board. The vote was 4–3, and each side accused the other of making political capital out of the issue. Three of the four anti-Gutiérrez votes worked for Paloma at the urban renewal agency, as Gutiérrez never tires of pointing out. Arturo Gonzales, a former Raza mayor of Crystal City who works as a security guard at the school district, voices a frequent complaint that Gutiérrez tended to bring in outsiders like the school superintendent who depended on Gutiérrez for jobs and were less likely to challenge his authority than were people from Crystal City.

What followed the firing was almost a parody of the stereotypes about Mexican American factionalism and divisiveness. The superintendent filed criminal nepotism charges against three of the school board members. When the district clerk—a Raza member who happened to be married to the superintendent's replacement—didn't prepare the jury list for the trial fast enough to suit Gutiérrez, he demanded her resignation. Pro-Gutiérrez school administrators resigned en masse to take jobs with the county or the clinic, aggravating an accreditation crisis that ultimately resulted in the school district being put on probation by the Texas Education Agency. The anti-Gutiérrez faction retaliated by handing over evidence from school files to a local grand jury, which promptly indicted several Gutiérrez allies, including the fired superintendent, who was charged with felony theft in cases involving consultant fees. Ciudadanos Unidos split into two factions, pro- and anti-Gutiérrez, each proclaiming itself the *real* Ciudadanos Unidos, each having its own officers and meetings. Each even published its separate versions of *La Verdad*—The Truth—the Raza Unida newspaper. It was almost a relief when, during a short-lived, Gutiérrez-inspired school boycott, protesting students wore *Gutierrista* T-shirts. At least then you could tell the teams without a program.

Gutiérrez' opponents zeroed in on apparent contradictions in his governing style. Felipe Flores, a former school district deputy business manager, complained, for example, that Gutiérrez required the school district and other government agencies to buy books and supplies through the Winter Garden Publishing Company owned by Gutiérrez' ally Adan Cantú. Flores said prices often were double and sometimes triple those listed in catalogs from which the goods were ordered. Many times, Flores said, the district could have qualified for a lower price if it hadn't routed purchases through the Gutiérrez-designated middleman.

"I'm not necessarily against people making money," says Crystal City's City Manager Esequiel Guzmán, referring to the Winter Garden arrangement. "But if it's brown capitalism you're into, say that, and don't try to identify yourself with the Third World. That stuff isn't helping poor people."

Father Sherrill Smith, who came to Crystal City five years ago as a partisan of Gutiérrez' movement, also became disenchanted over what he viewed as Gutiérrez' high-handed methods. A lean, gray, ascetic-looking man of 55 who has spent almost half his life in social action pursuits, Father Smith said Gutiérrez failed to consider the fundamental implication of his revolution: "If you're going to elevate people, you're going to have to deal with them once they've been elevated." Instead, Father Smith saw Gutiérrez' approach as "totally Machiavellian"; instead of sharing his power, the priest said that he was acting "kind of like a dictator."

In any Mexican American community, the Roman Catholic Church is an important social and political institution. In Crystal City, Father Smith's stature was enhanced among Chicanos when, replacing a priest who sided with the Anglos against Gutiérrez, he demonstrated his support for "the movement"—support that cost Smith virtually all of the nearly two-dozen Anglo parishioners who were members of the Sacred Heart Church when he arrived. Nonetheless, after Gutiérrez saw that the priest was sympathetic toward his opponents, the Gutiérrez version of *La Verdad* slashed him recklessly. The attack, in a cartoon that implied the priest was both a liar and a coward, further demonstrated Gutiérrez' widely perceived tendency to go for the jugular. Ruthlessness is an impolitic quality, especially toward priests. It is particularly ill-advised in somebody like Gutiérrez, who got elected county judge only by a couple of hundred votes. As that "ruthless" view of him widened, the big, close-knit extended Mexican American families that once served as one of Gutiérrez' best organizing tools became instead a liability as whole *families* of friends became enemies.

In the April 1976 school board elections, the anti-Gutiérrez candidates—Father Smith calls them *los inocentes;* Gutiérrez, *las oportunistas*—won by margins of about 300 votes. A week later, the city council elections went the same way, although the margin of victory was down to 200 votes.

The November 1976 general election saw most of the independent Raza voters bolt from Gutiérrez. In the hotly contested sheriff's race, a Democratic Mexican American with strong Anglo support rolled over the Raza Unida candidate, 2081 to 1431. Even in Mexico Chico, a poor neighborhood near the health clinic thought to be a bastion of Gutiérrez support, the Raza candidate for county commissioner defeated a write-in opponent by only 19 votes. Rudi Paloma, who was an anti-Gutiérrez poll watcher in that precinct, claims that the Gutiérrez candidate survived the write-in challenge only because the election judge threw out enough write-ins "where the intent of the voter was obvious" but which were technically flawed. The election judge was Luz Gutiérrez, José Angel's wife. The episode provides still more irony to a city and a movement already overburdened with it: in an early organizing tract, *A Gringo Manual on How to Control Mexicans*—the same work where he set down the parable of the crabs—Gutiérrez told how gringos had stayed in control by relying on technicalities in write-in elections.

Last spring the private Crystal Community School closed its doors; in the fall many of its students returned to the public schools. In short order the Texas Education Agency lifted the district's probationary status, ending the threat of losing accreditation. Gutiérrez complained with his usual exaggeration that the schools were "back where they were in 1969." It is true that Raza indoctrination is out; it is also the case, as Gutiérrez says, that the schools "have erased Raza murals on the walls and have put up pictures of Donald Duck and Pluto instead." But more than 75 per cent of the students continue to head to college, the bilingual program remains intact, and almost all of the students, administrators, and teachers are Mexican American.

Gutiérrez seems to be grasping at straws, and the last one is the $1.5 million federal development grant, which was reapproved by the Ford Administration following objections by Governor Dolph Briscoe. The grant plan also included an export-import business and a financial institution such as a savings and loan association, but most of Briscoe's fire was aimed at the cooperative farm, which the governor called "un-American and un-Texan" in a letter last December to President Ford. Briscoe noted that 42 per cent of the total grant would go for administrative expenses and also said that the $84,000 budgeted for consultant fees seemed excessive; he further pointed out that the nonprofit farm corporation would simply buy and supplant what is currently a working farm and for that reason challenged whether it would really create many new jobs. Assuming the matter drags into the new administration, it's anybody's guess whose chips will be better with Jimmy Carter's Washington bureaucrats.

In early December, a three-man contingent of Texas Rangers rolled into town fresh from probing the blatant corruptions in Duval County. They set up shop in an office provided rent-free by the Zavala County Bank and are intent, one of them told me, on "investigating county government." Although they can expect some help from anti-Gutiérrez Chicanos and from the Anglo community, which remains almost apoplectic about Gutiérrez, the Rangers aren't likely to uncover massive thefts of public funds comparable to those that existed in Duval County government.

So the outlook for the short term in Zavala County is for a protracted, ugly struggle, rather like the latter phases of a messy, contested divorce. Fifteen months ago there still might have been a chance for a reconciliation between Gutiérrez and his opponents, had he agreed to share power with them. Now they are convinced that he is wholly unprincipled, and he remains adamantly insistent that he must be in total control. "I do think that I'm smarter than anybody else here," he acknowledges, adding: "I know more, I have better contacts—that's why they followed me for seven years. Now they think they're grown up and can run things; they can't. We still need to have one leader."

Gutiérrez isn't telegraphing whether he'll seek reelection as county judge in two years when his present term expires. County Commissioner Frank Guerrero, Jr., a Democrat with close ties to the Anglo community, says he doubts that Gutiérrez will run. "Losing would add insult to the injury he's already sustained," says Guerrero, who says that philosophically he himself is a Republican but would have no chance of being elected as one. Rancher Chester Kiefer, chairman of the Zavala County Democratic party and secretary of the virulently anti-Gutiérrez, overwhelmingly Anglo Zavala County Taxpayers Association, says the Democrats have learned a lesson and will field a Mexican American against Gutiérrez. Right now, he says, Guerrero would be the logical choice. But Kiefer hopes that there will be just one opponent to Gutiérrez. "If we don't watch it, we'll split the vote," he says, "and then Angel will get in again." Kiefer reflects the prevailing Anglo view in Zavala County that the Raza administration has been an unmitigated disaster, "a traumatic experience we've been through, same as a drastic hailstorm or terrible flood. It's going to take us some time to get back on our feet."

To Ninfa Moncada, who has become one of Gutiérrez' most thoughtful and articulate critics, it is obvious that La Raza Unida is dead as an effective political force in Crystal City. To preserve a chance for Chicano self-determination locally, she would like to see those who made up the third party take over the Democratic party. "We wouldn't have to change our philosophy or our politics or how we educate our kids just because we call ourselves Democrats," she reasons. "A name is a name. Right now no group has enough votes to win an election—Angel's doesn't, the gringos don't, and we don't. The gringos supported us in the school election, or we would never have won. We supported them, but not openly, in the sheriff's election. But if we weren't divided, we wouldn't need them."

The revolution in *Cristal* was built of the stuff dreams are made on. Its undoing has been, in some measure, testimony to the enduring power of human qualities such as ambition, vanity, greed, and envy; in part it has reconfirmed the truism that you can't go home again, in part it has shown the dangers of a community organizer and a community leader being the same person.

Gutiérrez himself refuses to analyze his revolution's failures, except to insist, rightly, that "I don't want to give you anything furthering the stereotypes that Mexican Americans can't stick together—that's a bunch of crap." My view is that Gutiérrez came to believe in, and was finally trapped by, his own high-blown rhetoric. A county in Texas, in the United States of America, cannot, after all, hope to become "a nation within a nation." As a county judge Gutiérrez lacks the sanctions such as prisons, firing squads, and the ability to expropriate land with which dictators from Generalissimo Franco to Fidel Castro have enforced the discipline of their regimes. Perhaps Gutiérrez felt forced to cast himself in the role of a maximum leader because he had failed or been unable to imbue his followers with the purposeful ideology required to attempt a more democratic move toward county-based socialism. But from the beginning, Gutiérrez had stressed cultural nationalism ("eliminate the gringo") and self-determination, and, as a result, for many *Cristaliños,* the revolution was over once Chicanos had replaced Anglos in public jobs.

If Gutiérrez has failed to establish socialism in Zavala County, he has at least succeeded in establishing democracy, something almost as revolutionary in South Texas. He deserves credit for having given the people of *Cristal* the tools to dispose not only of "the gringo," but also of himself. A final paradox he faces may be that the only way he can stop what now seems nearly certain two years hence, a coalition of old allies and old enemies to get rid of him, is to step aside. If he means what he has said about Chicano self-determination, Gutiérrez may find that the only way to preserve the movement he started is to leave it. ★

THE CASE AGAINST THE FARMERS

by Stephen Chapman

How can you keep 'em down on the farm after they've seen parity?

Several thousand farmers descended upon Washington in January to press the cause of their nationwide farm strike, and by the time they had been in town a few days they were good and mad. "You got the key to the belly," boomed a Georgia farmer to a rally on the Capitol grounds, "and if they don't give you what you want, put the key in your damn pocket and keep it there!" The farmers, most of them wearing duckbill caps emblazoned with WE SUPPORT AGRICULTURAL STRIKE, roared when a Texan proclaimed that driving his tractor 1700 miles to Washington was "a lot cheaper than farming under the conditions we've got now." Another speaker warned ominously, "The news media better get the word out to the consumers that we're serious. If we don't plant, they don't eat!" Invigorated by their own vehemence, the farmers then paraded down Independence Avenue to the Department of Agriculture, where they occupied Secretary Robert S. Bergland's office, demanding a meeting. They got it the next day, but they got no concessions from the Administration, and by the end of the week a Colorado man was being cheered wildly for telling the House Agriculture Committee that farmers who didn't cooperate with the strike might be "shot out of the cabs of their tractors."

The mood of the farmers was notably ugly, but their complaints were the same ones that have sparked every farmers' movement for the last one hundred years: low crop prices, rising production costs, large debts, high markups by middlemen, little sympathy from city people. Occasionally farmers have resorted to agricultural strikes, refusing to grow or market crops in the hope of creating food shortages, raising prices, and forcing the federal government to help them out. None of the strikes, at least up to now, has worked.

The angry farmers who are supporting American Agriculture, a grass-roots network of local organizations concentrated in the Western wheat belt and the drought-striken Southeast, are the latest victims of the nation's perennial "farm problem," which has stubbornly resisted the federal government's attempts to solve it. Fifty years ago agriculture accounted for nearly 10 per cent of national income; in 1976 the figure was 2.6 per cent. Back then one out of every five U.S. workers labored on a farm, compared with one in twenty-five today. As agriculture's share of the national economic pie has shrunk, farm people have left the land. During the sixties, a million people left the farms each year. By 1970, the farm population was down to 9,712,000—half what it had been fifteen years before. Those who stayed behind have consistently made less money than their city cousins, with per capita farm income running about one-fifth lower than the level off the farm.

The proposed farm bill is a burning issue for farmers; they prefer parity.

Like the rest of American industry, the farm has changed considerably in the last century. The small subsistence farm has given way to the large, family-operated commercial farm, and in some cases to the large-scale corporate enterprise; the sturdy yeoman has been replaced by the independent businessman or the faceless board of directors. Increasingly the farm resembles a heavily mechanized business with a large cash flow, requiring sophisticated management and shrewd planning. Instead of hauling his produce to market himself, the modern farmer sells his goods to food processing companies, national grocery chains, and commodities trading corporations. These changes have made the American farmer the world's most productive—and the world's wealthiest. But a lot of farmers, like those who came to Washington, think they're getting a bad deal.

Among the Texans who brought their case to the capital was Maxine Jones, a wiry, square-jawed woman in her fifties, who with her husband, Jake, has been farming for 31 years. They grow milo, cotton, and soybeans on their farm near the small Panhandle town of Kress, in the heart of the Texas strike country. Their story is fairly typical of recent farm history. After years of renting their farmland, the Joneses bought 400 acres in 1972 (they still rent an additional 1100), just as the market in grain was beginning to boom. Milo was selling for $3.25 per hundredweight when they bought their place, and within two years the price had climbed to $5.75. They thought they were in good financial shape until the fall of 1975, when the U.S. signed an agreement with the Soviet Union restricting grain sales, a move intended to quell consumer anger at high food prices.

"When the government ordered the embargo," says Mrs. Jones, "the price for our milo dropped a dollar and a dime in one day. That was in October, when we were just finishing the harvest and were just about ready to sell. It dropped a dollar and a dime and it just kept dropping, all the way down to

Photography by Carlos Orsorio

THE PARTICIPANTS 95

$3.90." Because of rising costs the Joneses lost $22,000 on their 1976 crop. The next year was even worse: the price of milo fell to $3.30, and they had to suspend payments on the land they had bought. "In 1976, we had to start selling some of our cattle. We sold enough to pay off that $22,000 indebtedness, and we had to sell the rest the following year," she says. "Next year, if things don't get better, we'll have to start selling land." Besides the low prices, they suffered two hailstorms —one in May, which destroyed their cotton crop, and another in June, which wiped out the soybeans they had replaced it with. Their crop insurance paid for only about half the damage.

Mrs. Jones figures that without a government guarantee of substantially higher prices for their crops, they and many of their neighbors will have to give up farming within two years. The only solution Mrs. Jones can see is higher prices than those offered in President Carter's farm bill. They would allow her and her husband to keep farming for as long as they're physically able. The Joneses' sons have already left the farm. "Our oldest son told us when he got out of school that he didn't know what he wanted to do, but he wasn't going to farm. He'd seen all the pressure his daddy had to live with, and he didn't want it," says Mrs. Jones. She smiles ruefully, "You have to love it to do it."

If most of the farmers didn't feel the same way about their occupation, they probably would be doing something else. I asked one young farmer from Manor why he kept farming in spite of all the problems, and he offered a typical answer: "We're in farming because we want to be. I enjoy the hell out of it." All the same, these farmers voted to plant only half their normal crop this spring unless they get what they want. If enough farmers follow suit, they believe, the nation will soon face a food shortage, forcing Congress to give in.

American Agriculture's principal goal is a government guarantee that all crops will be sold at no less than 100 per cent of parity. Under present commodity programs, the government provides farmers with loans and direct payments when crop prices fall below specified levels. The "parity price" of each product is derived from a complicated formula intended to calculate the purchasing power of a single unit (say, a bushel of wheat) in relation to the prevailing prices in the period from 1910 to 1914, a sort of golden age for American farmers. If prices were at 100 per cent of parity, the theory goes, a bushel of wheat would buy as much now as it did back then. Since it seems only fair that the farmers' purchasing power should remain at least stable, the demand looks reasonable on the surface, just as the farmers' complaints sound legitimate.

But whatever sympathy one may feel for the problems of the farmers, their demands are no solution. Many of their problems—chronic overproduction, the competitive disadvantages of small farmers, soaring land prices—are the result of their long-standing reliance on the federal government to protect them from the hazards of the marketplace. No sector of the economy has received more government assistance than agriculture, and the result has been costly to consumers and taxpayers and harmful to most farmers. The small farmers who can barely scratch out a living have little to gain by prices fixed by law at no less than 100 per cent of parity. Their best hope lies in the elimination of government-fixed prices for agricultural commodities, leaving them free to compete on an equal footing with the big boys. When the prices of their products were skyrocketing five years ago, farmers were perfectly happy with the free market; now that their prices have dropped, they think it isn't serving them well. Like United States Steel and Lockheed, many farmers believe fervently in their right to make profits and just as strongly in their right not to suffer losses. Like those corporations, they have turned to the government to bail them out.

Despite their recent troubles, the farmers have made substantial progress. Their average income has risen sharply in the last four decades. In 1934, the typical farm dweller had to scrape by on a bare $163 a year—less than a third of what his city counterpart earned. By 1960 he still earned only about half what the average nonfarm person did. But in 1976 per capita farm income was 81 per cent of nonfarm income, and in 1974 actually exceeded nonfarm by 9 per cent. Furthermore, the Farm Credit Administration reports that so far this year loan renewal and collection rates for farmers are normal.

The 1972 to 1974 boom, which saw big spurts in the prices of wheat and feed grains, produced a bonanza for many American farmers. Unfortunately, it also induced many of them to buy additional land (at sharply inflated prices) and invest heavily in new equipment to increase production and further boost profits. Worldwide droughts had greatly increased demand for American products, but when demand fell back to normal levels after 1974, the boom ended, leaving farmers with dashed hopes, a taste of wealth, and a lot of machinery and improvements that may never be paid off.

Faced with these problems, farmers have embraced parity as the solution to all their woes. But parity is practically meaningless as a measure of farmers' income, as the Department of Agriculture concedes. The reason is that it ignores the rapid improvements in agricultural productivity over the last 65 years. Producing 100 bushels of wheat between 1910 and 1914 required 106 man-hours of labor and seven acres of land; in 1970 it took only nine man-hours and about three acres. If a modern farmer gets the same real price per bushel of wheat as his 1910 counterpart, he will get a lot more for his total crop, since he can produce so much more. Setting farm prices at 100 per cent of parity would make the boom last forever. Holding prices artificially high, however, virtually guarantees overproduction. "If the price of wheat is set at $5 a bushel," says a Washington reporter who covers agriculture, "you can bet every farm in the country will be growing wheat." Even at current price support levels, which the strikers say are too low, government grain reserves are growing.

Preventing the accumulation of huge surpluses requires massive government intervention to restrict production—intervention that is not always successful. Restricting the acreage planted in a given crop through acreage allotments, for example, doesn't reduce production as much as one might think, since it encourages farmers to idle only their worst acres and increase the use of fertilizer, pesticides, and machinery on the land planted. A 20 per cent reduction in acreage can be expected to reduce production by only 10 or 12 per cent. Marketing quotas, which restrict the amount of the product that can be sold, work better, but are so unpopular with farmers that they are seldom used.

Holding all farm prices at parity would be an expensive proposition for the nation's consumers. American Agriculture itself concedes that retail grocery prices would rise by as much as 25 per cent. Chase Econometric Associates of Philadelphia predicts that if the farmers get what they want, a loaf of bread would cost seven cents more than it does now, a pound of hamburger 38 cents more, a gallon of milk 22 cents more. Naturally, the burden of these price increases would fall most heavily on the poor and the lower-middle-class, who spend a large portion of their income on food.

Consumers will be making these sacrifices primarily for the benefit of relatively wealthy farmers. The biggest farms stand to gain the most from guaranteed parity prices, just as they have hogged most of the benefits of past price support programs. A farmer who produces 10,000 bushels of wheat gets roughly ten times the benefit from a minimum price as one who produces 1000. A study by economist James Bonnen determined that more than half of the benefits of federal commodity programs go to the top 20 per cent of far— s, while the bottom 20 per cent ...eager 5 per cent of federal bene-...

...programs favor big farmers ...ll ones in other ways as well. ...ng farming more profitable ...uld be in a free market, price ...ve inflated the price of farm-...iting expansion by small ...making it next to impossi-...farming without inherited ...t ten years, the value of ...eased by 182 per cent, ...nsumer price index ...That's what one ...talking about ...ver sell out, ...ack in. It ...e farm-...rice ...of ...

...for higher guaranteed prices would prevent a natural shift of money, labor, and capital from farming into other sectors of the economy. In an advanced industrial society, the demand for food grows only about as fast as the population, much less rapidly than the demand for other goods and services. Consequently, even though the total output of the farm sector may grow, its share of the national economic pie will shrink steadily. This continuing decline, combined with increasing productivity, means that a sizable number of people will have to leave the farms each year. Even the federal government's programs to raise farm income have not been able to stop millions of people from migrating from the countryside to the city in the last half-century. It's a good thing, too, since without that migration, farms would be glutted with too many people, while factories and offices would go begging for employees.

Many of the farmers involved in the strike like to portray themselves as small, embattled family farmers fighting off rapacious agribusiness corporations on one side and powerful food chains on the other. The picture appears to be mostly a public relations ploy without much basis in fact. Very few of the strikers could be classified as small farmers; many own several thousand acres or more. Corporate farms still make up only a minuscule fraction of the nation's total, and a large percentage of those are family corporations. Agricultural economist D. Gale Johnson of the University of Chicago scoffs at the supposed power of the firms involved in the transportation, processing, and marketing of food. "The levels of profitability in those sectors have been on the low side for a long time."

In fact, it is not small farmers but big ones who will benefit most from the guaranteed parity prices proposed by American Agriculture. Government price supports have promoted the expansion of farms by making success less dependent on efficiency than on volume of output. If prices of farm goods are held artificially high by government policy, farmers will be most concerned about simply increasing their production by any means possible, even if growing in size will make their operation less efficient, since a little inefficiency will not jeopardize their financial survival. Price supports take much of the risk out of farming. "A small farmer can handle risk better than a big one," says Johnson. "He has fewer cash expenses, he uses mostly his own labor, and he has less investment in capital."

Regardless of the success or failure of the strike, the financial position of grain farmers is bound to improve in the coming year. One reason is that if times are as bad as the farmers say they are, some of them will give up farming, thus reducing total output. A second is that demand is likely to pick up. Beef herds, which were greatly reduced in response to the high price of feed grain during the boom, are expected to be built back up, which means stockyards and cattle ranchers will be buying more grain. If the strike succeeds in reducing production, of course, prices will rise accordingly. The present pains of the farmers are partly the symptom of agriculture's shrinking share of the Gross National Product, but more directly represent the natural valley on the other side of the peak.

At the root of the problems cited by American Agriculture, and of those that have afflicted American farmers for decades, is the fact that U.S. agriculture suffers from a chronic condition of excess capacity, which keeps prices below what farmers would like. The reason farmers produce too much is that the federal government encourages them to do so, by guaranteeing minimum prices on their goods. Holding prices at parity would simply exacerbate this condition: the idea that it would not is roughly comparable to the belief the government can set artificially low prices on natural gas without causing shortages. Prices fixed too low lead to shortages, fixed too high lead to surpluses. Giving the strikers the high fixed prices they demand would create more problems—for farmers and for the rest of us—than it would solve.

One of the most heartening trends in Washington in the last few years has been a growing recognition of the limits of government solutions to economic problems. In such sectors as commercial air traffic, trucking, and the legal and medical professions, policymakers have begun to discard some regulatory powers in favor of letting buyers and sellers work things out freely in the marketplace. In light of the failure of half a century of intensive federal efforts to solve the "farm problem," we ought to let federal farm policy take the same road. (Of course, a free market in agriculture will work best if the government promotes freer competition in other subsidized and protected industries as well.) There are difficulties with this course, particularly in the short run, but on balance they are less serious and less costly than continuing the present pattern of federal farm policy. Moreover, these difficulties can be reduced considerably by removing present restrictions on agricultural exports. Inefficient producers, perhaps a great number of them, will be forced out, leaving farming to those who can produce cheaply enough to make a profit at prices the nation's consumers will pay. People will continue to leave the farms at a fairly high rate, since there is no realistic prospect of providing a place for everyone who would like to farm. The best-run farms, however, would survive and prosper. And the impact of these adjustments could be softened by supplementing the income of those farmers who are hurt by the transition.

Neither these problems nor the likely benefits of freer competition should be underestimated. Reducing the federal government's role in farming would leave considerably more room for the men and women it supposedly has been trying to help. It also would strip the big farmers of the protection they have enjoyed under the system of price supports and production restrictions, and enable the small farmers to make full use of their natural advantages. It would also eliminate most of the incentives for farms to expand beyond the requirements of efficiency, which would most likely lower land prices to more reasonable levels and thus make it easier for those who are genuinely hard-pressed—the very small farmer, the tenant farmer, the young would-be farmer—to survive and prosper. It would substantially reduce costs to consumers and taxpayers, while encouraging a more efficient allocation of people and capital. But a freer market in agriculture for farmers is no panacea. It is more like what Churchill said of democracy—the worst system except for all the rest. ★

THE PARTICIPANTS 97

SOLE BROTHERS

by Jack Keever

Like other legislative alliances, the black caucus sticks together — sometimes.

Everyone knows Barbara Jordan now. Her work on the House Judiciary Committee during the impeachment hearings won nationwide praise. But early in her political career she was famous for another reason: she was the first black woman senator in Texas history and the first black of either sex to serve in the state Senate since Reconstruction.

"You didn't have any trouble picking me out down there," she reflected later. "I became part of the sightseeing tours of the Capitol. There were people who would stand outside the Senate chamber and say to the doorkeeper, 'We understand you've got something new inside.'"

In 1967 Jordan and two state representatives became the first black members of the Texas Legislature in the twentieth century, breaking a 72-year drouth. She stayed in Austin long enough to carve out a congressional district for herself in 1971, and then moved on to Washington by easily defeating Curtis Graves, one of the representatives who had cracked the legislative color barrier with Jordan four years earlier. Other blacks profited from reapportionment as well. (But not in the Texas Senate: the price for Jordan's congressional seat was the loss of a predominantly black senatorial district.) Eight new black House members, the only blacks among 181 legislators, came to Austin in 1973. Most were in their thirties or late twenties, and all were elected from the new single-member districts that the Legislative Redistricting Board had reluctantly provided for Houston, Dallas, and San Antonio under federal court prodding. All eight won reelection in 1974, and a ninth black representative, Wilhelmina Delco of Austin, will be sworn in this month. The novelty of blacks in the Legislature is over.

The eight blacks decided early to join together. Forming a bloc seemed only natural: it had been done in Congress, and Graves urged them to stick together for their own good. In December 1972, before any of the new members had actually taken office, they met at Eddie Bernice Johnson's Dallas home to form the Black Legislative Caucus.

The caucus can point to some impressive accomplishments during its first two years. The group first made headlines by demanding an investigation of the administration at Prairie View A&M College, a predominantly black school near Hempstead in Waller County, following student allegations that the college president was receiving kickbacks from teachers. The caucus managed to push through a resolution to investigate campus life at Prairie View, despite heavy lobbying by Texas A&M, Prairie View's parent institution. The caucus also secured an extra $7.5 million in state funds for Prairie View and Texas Southern University in Houston, reversing a long-lived legislative habit of neglecting black colleges. Caucus members were instrumental in establishing a committee to study prison reform and in passing a bill creating single-member districts for the Dallas school board—virtually guaranteeing representation for blacks and Mexican Americans on the board. And during

Jack Keever is a Capitol correspondent for the Associated Press.

The black caucus in 1973, left to right: Ragsdale, Hall, Thompson, Washington, Sutton, Leland, Johnson, Hudson

the Constitutional Convention, the caucus stood firm, voting 8-0 against the proposed new constitution when the document needed only three more votes to be adopted. "Racism lurked in every article except maybe the preamble and bill of rights," said G. J. Sutton of San Antonio, the caucus chairman.

The caucus has also been an inspiration to many of Texas' two million blacks, who often write caucus members for help rather than their own white representatives. In a sense, therefore, caucus members have two constituencies: their own districts, which they have to themselves, and an amorphous at-large district consisting of all Texas blacks, which they share. Caucus members often end up competing with each other, trying to become the first black to get a coveted committee appointment or Democratic party position. Often they appear too eager to accommodate white political leaders, and some caucus members seem to spend more time seeking personal political power than on caucus projects—acting, in other words, like most white politicians. Indeed, that is the main problem facing the caucus. Some of its members have become politicians first and blacks second, while others have retained the hardened edge of militancy.

The caucus can be roughly divided into two cliques: the militants, consisting of Sutton and Senfronia Thompson of Houston; and the politicians, who at one time or another include the other six, but generally consist of Craig Washington and Mickey Leland, both of Houston, and Eddie Bernice Johnson of Dallas. The other three are Sam Hudson and Paul Ragsdale, both of Dallas, and Anthony Hall, Houston. In addition to the cliques, the caucus is divided in all the ways that associations of politicians, or any people, for that matter, can be divided: by age, background, ideology, ambition, and personal antagonism.

At the first caucus meeting in 1972, Johnson nominated all three officers—Sutton as chairman, Thompson as vice-chairman, and Leland as secretary. She excluded herself because, a caucus member said, she didn't want to be "associated with anything that might be a mess." Sutton, by far the oldest of the group at 65, was a compromise choice, someone who would not threaten the others' political ambitions. Profiting from compromise was an unusual experience for Sutton, who has picketed and marched since the thirties for civil rights for blacks. He detests compromise with whites. "When we do what they call compromise, we're selling out," he says. "A compromise presupposes that you're sitting as equals. But we are not equal, we are on the bottom rung. When we give in, we're selling out."

Sutton comes from an amazing family. He was one of fifteen children, twelve of whom reached adulthood, and all twelve earned college degrees. His brother Percy is borough president of Manhattan and could become mayor of New York in 1978. Sutton has been through it all: He has been jailed a dozen times for picketing, and once during a demonstration in the sixties he was run off the grounds of the Capitol, where he now has an office. He collected funds for lawsuits to integrate the University of Texas and to allow blacks to register to vote in Texas.

Sutton is an established politician with a lifelong cause. "Unless we settle the racial issue," he says, "we'll never get anything settled. That's America's number one problem. Any black who tells you he doesn't have some bitterness is lying or else he's inhuman." Ironically, despite Sutton's outspoken militancy, he is the only black legislator to represent a white-majority single-member district (55 per cent).

His closest caucus ally is Senfronia Thompson, whose hostile appearance masks attractive features. "Militancy is more than wearing a dashiki or an Afro; that doesn't mean anything," she says. "Militancy is dedication to the black cause and trying to alleviate the problems that you know exist." One of those problems, she believes, is the attitude of white legislators toward blacks, as exemplified by one of the cause célèbres of the 1973 session, the Kit Cooke incident. Thompson had gone to an office building near the Capitol for a free lunch offered daily by the Texas Trial Lawyers Association, a potent lobby organization. About 25 persons were in the room and, as Thompson tells it, Cooke, a young representative from Cleburne, greeted her appearance by saying loudly enough for all to hear, "Here comes my beautiful black mistress." She snapped back, "I'm not your black mistress." But Cooke persevered, "You mean to tell me you won't have sex with a white man?"

Thompson's thoughts raced "back in history, to the white man with the two families, the black family and the white family, the white man who had the slave woman—and I was overwhelmed with anger, with disappointment, and with the fact that he did not want to respect me as his counterpart, as a representative, and he did not want to respect me as a woman, especially a black woman. I could have just gone over and beat the bloody shit out of him."

But she spun and strode straight to House Speaker Price Daniel, Jr. She told Daniel she wanted to make a personal privilege speech, but he said that according to House rules she could not. She decided to bypass the rules by going on television, and the word got to Daniel. "He sent for me very quick, and he told me I could give that personal privilege speech," she recalls.

Thompson told House members of the incident, without naming Cooke, despite warnings from a few white legislators that "they [other House members] are going to kill your legislation, they're going to hate you for it." Thompson thought Cooke should have been censured. Sutton said Cooke would have been reprimanded if he had been black and Thompson white.

"Senfronia is hostile to anyone in a leadership position," says a caucus aide, recalling Thompson's reaction to Governor Dolph Briscoe's first speech to the Legislature. "She said she certainly was glad the governor was for adult education because some of his staff obviously needed it." The aide adds, "Her role will always be to raise issues that other people are afraid to raise."

The rest of the caucus members are more difficult to evaluate than Sutton and Thompson, not because they are less militant but because they are more ambitious. And no one of them is more ambitious than Craig Washington, the eloquent, flashy legislator who moved near the top of the House pecking order in his very first term. His white colleagues respect Washington as the ablest black legislator, indeed, as one of the ablest of all legislators. In his element on the House floor, Washington smiles confidently, ignoring a House rule to announce that Hank Aaron has just tied Babe Ruth's home run record, or kidding Johnson, "Get yourself some watermelon and celebrate—it's June-teenth." He occasionally saunters into the House chamber wearing a wide, white hat and high-heeled shoes, with a leather handbag dangling from his shoulder. His dress is calculated, he says, "so the next time a white man sees a brother on the street he'll look at him for what he is and not judge him on his clothes."

As a college student at Prairie View, Washington showed little of the ability that would later earn him accolades as a politician. He received over thirty grades of F as an undergraduate, because grades were tied to class attendance and he continually skipped classes out of boredom. "I accept the F's I made, because that's my badge of courage for rebelling against the system at Prairie View," he says.

Finally Washington made it to law school, at Texas Southern, where he was determined "to prove to my detractors that I was not a dull student." He graduated with the second-highest average in the history of the law school, had the top grade in thirteen of thirty classes, never finished lower than third, and was elected president of the student bar. Eddie Bernice Johnson says that "Craig has the capability to sit on the Supreme Court of this country some day," but for the moment, at least, his ambitions are somewhat more modest.

Washington makes no secret of the fact that eventually he would like to be Speaker of the House, and he has adapted his style accordingly. He downplays racial and philosophical differences with whites on legislative turf and uses his intellect subtly, appearing humble. (But two caucus aides, when asked to describe Washington succinctly, blurted "arrogant.") The highlight of Washington's first term actually came at the very end, in the last moments of the last day, when he delivered a poor-boy-from-the-wrong-side-of-the-tracks address directed primarily at his white colleagues. Reduced to the written word in the House Journal, it seems trite even for a political address, but those who were there will never forget it: Washington's soaring, sincere delivery, the standing ovation, the embraces and tears on the House floor—a perfect valedictory for the first year of the black caucus.

Leland's style is altogether different. Outgoing and charming, he jokes about his reputation as a radical. "I favor the violent overthrow of the United States government," he says, grinning. Leland regards himself as a revolutionary in the same way Washington viewed cutting classes: it is his badge of honor. "I still adhere to a lot of the same philosophy," Leland said of his militant younger days, "except I know we have to do it another way. Otherwise, I would have been killed by now. Many of my friends have gone to jail, and some of them have been killed."

Leland was a ghetto street fighter in Houston's Fifth Ward northeast of downtown, one of the poorest areas in the city. Later he went to Texas Southern, after his mother refused to let him accept a football scholarship. "Texas Southern gave me a lot," he says. "It taught me to be militant about my people; it taught me to be sensitive about the needs of my people." He leaped on tables at the college coffee shop to denounce black complacency and would not wear a tie to classes. That refusal got him thrown out of school, but Leland retaliated by leading a demonstration that resulted in the ouster of the dean who had ejected him.

Friends convinced him that his revolutionary activities were futile, that he was headed for jail or an early grave, so he sought Jordan's advice on running for the Legislature. She told him he should do it and added, "That ought to be fun." If she was thinking that Leland would startle his white colleagues with his revolutionary views, it didn't turn out that way. He has even walked the streets of the Fifth Ward with Dolph Briscoe and has toned down considerably in every respect except his sartorial habits. Leland doesn't wear clothes, he models costumes—bright colors, large plaids, shoulder bags—and says he always has: "I just begged to be different. I was in constant protest. I called myself black before most people would admit they were black."

Despite—or perhaps because of—his move toward moderation, Leland is the only member of the caucus who has a legislative passion, an issue other than race that he considers vitally important. That issue is health care—Leland was a pharmacy instructor at TSU—and his archenemy is the medical lobby, the Texas Medical Association, which two years ago blocked his proposal to set up Health Maintenance Organizations that would provide a wide range of medical services for a fixed monthly fee. "The HMO bill is not just a piece of legislation," says Leland. "It's a whole social movement." A caucus aide agrees: "Mickey Leland is working his ass off for one thing that truly is potentially significant."

A close ally of Washington and Leland, Eddie Bernice Johnson has replaced Barbara Jordan as the legislative prototype of the modern, educated black woman. Her education includes two degrees—a nursing diploma from Notre Dame's sister school, Saint Mary's College, and a degree in psychiatric nursing from TCU. She was hired sight unseen at the Veterans Administration hospital in Dallas in 1956, and judging from subsequent events, sight unseen was the only way she could have been hired. When she reported for work, she found, inexplicably, that her dormitory room had been reassigned, and she was therefore forced to commute to work. She lived with a black family and rode the bus, but often found upon arriving at the hospital that the work schedule had been changed and it was suddenly her day off. She was the first black professional to work at the hospital, and she endured these petty harassments to become a supervisor at 23; later she helped organize the psychiatric unit and was named coordinator of the day treatment center. (She is now a consultant in the personnel office of Neiman-Marcus.)

In 1972 Johnson became the first black woman from Dallas County to seek a House seat. After winning the Democratic primary in May, she made headlines a month later when she was elected vice-chairman of the state Democratic convention—the first black woman to hold such an exalted party position in Texas. Within a year she was back in the headlines again, even more prominently this time, as a central figure in what became known as the Calvert Incident. Three legislators, including Johnson, filed complaints with the U.S. Equal Employment Opportunity Commission alleging that state comptroller Robert S. Calvert's office of 1162 employees was lopsided with white *men*. Johnson filed on behalf of *women*, not blacks, but Calvert referred to her as a "nigger woman." Informed of this racial slur, Johnson called a press conference to demand that Calvert adopt fairer hiring practices or resign—or she would call for his impeachment.

Johnson's sudden prominence was accidental. Another caucus member, Paul Ragsdale of Dallas, had originated the project and needed a woman to join in the complaint. He first sought out white representative Chris Miller of Fort Worth, an avowed feminist, but Miller anticipated a formidable reelection challenge in 1974 and was hesitant to take the risk. Johnson was Ragsdale's second choice and reaped the benefits of Miller's refusal. Miller did win reelection to a second term; the only loser was Calvert, who at 81 decided to retire, partly because of public reaction to the incident. He told Johnson he got five thousand hate letters.

Johnson, who at forty is the second-oldest caucus member, has been blessed with political luck: both the party appointment and the Calvert Incident occurred because she happened to be in the right place at the right time. But there are those close to the caucus who say she has spent far too much time in the wrong place at the wrong time—the wrong place being Speaker Price Daniel's office and the wrong time being right after caucus meetings, reporting everything that had transpired to the Speaker. Her critics claim that Johnson has let ambition get the best of her, that the woman who once described herself as "a little crusader" is now more interested in her own political future than in causes. One embittered caucus aide with a careless eye for gender describes Johnson as "the biggest Uncle Tom in the caucus" and adds, "You couldn't trust Eddie four feet. She is an opportunist in every sense of the word." Daniel says only that Johnson "always helped me when she could."

Johnson's friendship with Daniel underscores the fundamental dilemma facing caucus members: Where do one's loyalties lie? To the caucus? Or to a sympathetic Speaker? Can the caucus expect to command fidelity on issues not directly related to race? All of these questions are piled on top of the daily agonies every legislator, white or black, must face in trying to strike a balance between principle and his or her own political future.

Paul Ragsdale, Sam Hudson, and Anthony Hall are all mavericks, not really falling into either the Sutton-Thompson clique or the Washington-Leland-Johnson camp, and certainly not constituting a group of their own. Ragsdale is the most complex of the threesome, perhaps of all eight caucus members. Like Leland, he can get overly emotional, but he also has a dogged tenacity and persistence, which two caucus aides say put him "head and shoulders above anyone else" in effectiveness. His major legislative accomplishment was passage of the bill providing single-member districts for the Dallas school board, but he also has a long history of involvement in black causes dating back to his college days in the early sixties. He had been the outstanding orchestra member at Austin High School, but was told politely that there was no need to apply for a musical scholarship at the University of Texas. He went anyway.

"It was quite a cultural shock," Ragsdale says now. He picketed segregated dormitories and attempted to play basketball for the Longhorns, but, he says,

"They wouldn't let me out on the floor." Since becoming a legislator, Ragsdale has been quoted in the UT alumni magazine as saying, "I'm going to do everything I can to cut funds for the university until we teach those bastards a lesson."

After he had graduated from college, Ragsdale once stopped by a bar in Dallas that had been recommended by a white friend, only to find that blacks weren't welcome. He says he filed the first three public accommodations complaints in the state after the passage of the Civil Rights Act of 1964. That was in 1968, when Dallas was "stormy as all outdoors," Ragsdale says. Apartment managers turned him away when he tried to visit white friends. Eventually Ragsdale went to work at the city-sponsored Crossroads Community Center in predominantly black South Dallas. After missing out on a job promotion at the center, he released a report accusing the city of racial discrimination. Despite a 21-day suspension for insubordination, he subsequently released a second report alleging that city officials had falsified records at the center.

Still, he was the only caucus member who was forced into a runoff to win reelection in the 1975 Legislature. One black aide says Ragsdale will always have trouble getting elected.

"Talk to anybody in Dallas, and none of them have a high regard for Ragsdale. Time after time, Paul is referred to by black businessmen, civic people, clergymen, as a weird person. That doesn't bode well for him." That image hasn't helped any when Ragsdale, who has no employment other than his $400-a-month legislative job, applied for food stamps. Caucus members call Ragsdale "Headliner," an allusion to his habit of seeking publicity.

Unlike the other caucus members (except Sutton), Sam Hudson and Anthony Hall each have ties to prominent black families. Both of Hudson's parents are college graduates, and his father was president of the Dallas Negro Chamber of Commerce. Hudson recalls that as a little boy, "I can remember him always having to go to meetings and appearing on behalf of the needs of my people. That's something I've grown up with. I've just known that type of dedication all my life." Some people, he admits, vote for Samuel Williams Hudson III thinking that they are voting for his father. Hudson's own résumé of jobs, honors, and education fills four pages, and he is a good friend of Ray Hunt, son of the late ultraconservative oil billionaire H. L. Hunt. His legislative career, however, has been something less than spectacular. The most favorable comment came from an aide who described Hudson as "just a slow learner, quiet and studious." A caucus member, on the other hand, jokes that Hudson doesn't count toward a caucus quorum, claims that he sleeps through caucus meetings, and says he has no legislative interests. "He accepts freebies and votes liberal only because he fears repercussions from the caucus if he does otherwise," the member says. "His supporters are ashamed of his performance."

Caucus watchers characterize Hall as a conservative maverick in a group of black liberals. Conservatism, of course, is a relative term; it means one thing when applied to a West Texas rancher and quite another when used to describe a Houston black legislator whose father-in-law is J. E. Middleton, one of the most powerful black labor leaders in the state. Nevertheless, one caucus aide says, "Hall has been the one black most ready to desert the caucus for the conservatives from the beginning." Hall indicated he had independent thoughts at the first caucus meeting when he warned that "we shouldn't make ourselves so black that it would restrict us." That doesn't mean Hall hasn't been an effective legislator on black issues; as the only caucus representative on the powerful Appropriations Committee, he was instrumental in persuading his colleagues to allocate additional funds for Prairie View and Texas Southern.

There are other personality clashes as well. Ragsdale and Johnson don't swap many compliments, since they face a possible political race against each other. Leland has been accused of undercutting caucus opposition to racial policies at the University of Texas with his friendship with once-omnipotent UT regent Frank Erwin. And Hall has incurred the wrath of the other caucus members in meetings with Briscoe by singling himself out from the rest of the caucus with comments like "That's not my position, Governor."

Oddly, there is little animosity between the two cliques, Sutton-Thompson and Washington-Leland-Johnson—only a vast difference in style. Leland, for example, admires Sutton for being a black man who made money and nevertheless stayed involved. (A friend estimates that Sutton, a mortuary owner, is worth at least $250,000—"he buries only the *best* blacks.") The real threat to the caucus lies in the confrontation between people of similar ages and ambitions—the same danger that threatens every political alliance anywhere.

Two other factors will also have a considerable impact on the future of the black caucus. One is how the attitudes of black legislators will change over the years. Craig Washington, for example, has mellowed considerably in only one term. "I respect the views of people that three years ago I would have thought of as ultraconservative mossbacks," he says. "If you spend too much time worrying solely about black interests you miss too many things that are generally important. I think being a state representative means you represent the whole state." For once, Hall and Washington agree. "You're just playing with yourself to assume that unless you're talking about a Martin Luther King birthday or something like that, you're not serving black people," Hall says. "I'm not opposed to that, obviously, but that doesn't help feed anybody, that doesn't help anybody with jobs."

The second question is whether white politicians will continue to undercut the caucus, consciously or unconsciously, by following what one black who knows Washington well calls the Head Negro syndrome: "The prevailing attitude of most white politicians is that they want a Head Negro—they want to deal with one Negro—and if you've got Craig Washington, you don't need the caucus chairman or other blacks."

Sutton recognizes the problems but dismisses any idea that the black caucus will crumble. "We're treated as a group so our problems are the same," he says. "There's no difference in Houston or Dallas or San Antonio. On black issues, there's no way to split."

Perhaps. But the problem for the black caucus is to decide what those black issues are and whether to push them aggressively. For the moment, at least, not many issues seem to qualify. ★

LABOR PAINS

by Dick J. Reavis

On the eve of battle with a mammoth oil company, an old union boss gets a new message from the rank and file.

Five working men and a union officer huddle around a conference table in a room at the Ramada Inn near Houston's Hobby Airport, playing nickel-ante stud. Down the hall three company executives, who long ago cast off their coats and loosened their ties, are calculating the costs of meeting the union's demands. In the hallway two federal mediators stand ready to carry messages between the two caucus rooms. Today is the tenth day of contract negotiations between Olin Corporation and Local 367 of the OCAW (Oil, Chemical, and Atomic Workers International Union), which represents hourly workers at the Olin plant in nearby Pasadena.

Though the current contract expires at midnight, progress is stalled as time runs out. Nobody expects anything different. "We have to negotiate right down to the wire," an OCAW official says, "because otherwise, no matter what we come out with, the men will say we could have got more if we'd stayed in longer." Twenty minutes before midnight the mediators recommend that the clock be stopped until the night's talks are finished. The union men wearily agree.

Roy Barnes, the head of Local 367's bargaining team, already knows about how far the company will go in the Ramada talks, because he has studied the outcome of recent Olin negotiations with other locals. He also knows that Olin's Pasadena workers are in no position to force an exceptional settlement. The

102 THE PARTICIPANTS

company's fertilizer plant is too small to put a dent in multinational profits. During the past nine months Olin has laid off 50 workers at Pasadena, and only 330 are left on the payroll—a number small enough to make recruiting strikebreakers merely an inconvenience. Barnes knows that eventually his men will have to accept far less than the $1.25-an-hour increase they sought when the talks began; already they have reduced their stated goal to $1 an hour, and privately Barnes would settle for 85 cents. His men have no leverage; even though they make a full $1 an hour less than hourly workers at the nearby Shell refinery, they haven't struck since 1949.

By midnight the union men are tensionless and bored, waiting for the company to respond. The answer comes at 3:30 a.m.: Olin insists on holding increases to 60 cents an hour. But Barnes knows this is not the final offer; Olin granted more to Louisiana workers last February. The men return to their card game.

At 10:30 a.m. the two sides reach an agreement. Olin offers an increase of 75 cents, a dime less than the union men swore they would accept, but they take it. At the union hall that night, Barnes tells the workers, "Men, this isn't the best contract the OCAW has, and you all know that. But it's the best we could get by talking. We either take it or we hit the bricks." Only a dozen hands go up in opposition; the new contract is accepted. Roy Barnes shakes his head and sighs. He doesn't like losing; he doesn't like bargaining from weakness. He remembers that the big one comes up in January, when the Shell contract expires. It will be different then. Maybe.

One of the new breed of workers, Pat Kelly likes his freewheeling affluence.

At night from afar the mammoth Shell petrochemical complex on the Houston Ship Channel looks like a fairyland. Up close it seems like . . . Hades. Flames leap thirty feet out of hissing flares into the smoky orange sky, and on the ground, shadowy figures drag about with their shoulders hunched, as though Satan already had them in his chains. Pipelines and tubing spread across the ground and entwine in steel lattices overhead, forming a metallic jungle where workers often seem to lose their way. Smoldering distillation towers spit out wet steam, creating a foggy atmosphere that hovers over the complex. Pockets of the plant reek of sulfides and ammonia, and the roar of giant compressors sets off vibrations everywhere.

When the sun rises, the managers gather in the soundproof, vibration-free administration building, the only brick structure of any size inside the plant gates. They run the largest refinery in the Shell system, the plant that produces a third of Shell's national output—a responsibility they share, however grudgingly, with Local 367 of the OCAW.

Petrochemical plants are ideal recruiting grounds for labor unions. Their surroundings are somber and overwhelmingly impersonal; the work is at times dangerous, at times tedious. The OCAW is a strong union, and Local 367 is strong at Shell. That strength is due for a severe test, however, in the months ahead, for most Shell contracts with the OCAW expire on January 9, 1979. If the rhythm of past OCAW walkouts means anything, 1979 should be a strike year. The last walkout was in 1973, and only once has the union gone more than six years without strik-

Photography by Joe Baraban

If Roy Barnes leads the OCAW off the job at Shell, the entire nation will feel it.

ing Shell. The likelihood of a walkout is enhanced by the belief of OCAW leaders like Roy Barnes that strikeless unions atrophy.

Roy Barnes is one of the most powerful men in Texas, though it is unlikely that many Texans who work more than two miles from the Houston Ship Channel have ever heard of him. He is the secretary-treasurer of Local 367 and its sole salaried official. Eight petrochemical firms in the area have contracts with the Local, and the men Barnes represents are responsible for 10 per cent of the state's petrochemical output—and Texas produces more than a quarter of the nation's petrochemical goods. In addition, Barnes is chairman of the OCAW's Shell policy committee, which determines the union's nationwide strategy against the company, including, of course, strikes. If Roy Barnes leads his men off the job, the whole nation will feel it.

Although past performance points toward a strike, a lot has changed since Local 367 last walked out on Shell. Previous strikes against the company occurred before the Arab embargo, which makes them ancient history in the petroleum industry. Many of the hourly workers who struck with the OCAW in 1962–63, 1969, and 1973 have retired. Most of the 2300 hourly workers on Shell's Deer Park payroll today are under thirty, and, as unionists put it, have never "hit the bricks." In terms of race and sex they are a far more diverse lot than their predecessors, and, though they have joined the union and have no fondness for company management, they also have a more relaxed and affluent lifestyle that may not bend to the discipline of a strike. No one can predict how the new generation will respond in a prolonged strike, not even veteran OCAW leaders like Barnes. If the OCAW walks out in 1979, the union could be plunged into turmoil, with the older membership struggling to maintain control. Or the strike could weld the union together in a way that meetings and exhortations cannot.

A crisis between generations is common to many unions today, but nowhere is it more evident than in the petrochemical industry. From 1941 to the end of the Korean War, demand for petrochemical products surged with the incentives of war and an expanding economy. By the mid-fifties, however, the market leveled off, and at the same time automation began to take its toll. Shell started laying off workers in 1958; the labor force at the complex, which in two decades had increased fivefold to 3000, was cut to 1500 by 1963. Because the union protected workers with seniority, most of those who got the ax were younger employees. Even after the layoffs, management felt the industry was still oversupplied with labor, and a bitter eleven-month strike starting in 1962 failed to persuade them otherwise. By 1970 more than half the refinery hands in the U.S. were between the ages of 50 and 55—Roy Barnes' bracket—and the statistic held true at Deer Park. Then the embargo changed everything.

In 1974 Shell began a $1 billion expansion project at the Deer Park complex, which will diversify production and considerably increase plant capacity when construction is completed later this year. Some new units are already into operation and payrolls are fat again. Since 1974 Shell has created 600 new jobs for hourly workers; meanwhile, 200 hourly workers have retired and another 350 have been promoted to salaried ranks. More than half the plant's hourly workers were not on the payroll four years ago; three-fourths were not at Shell in 1970. Yet their plant supervisors and union leaders are all nearing sixty.

Age is only part of the difference. Before 1968, blacks at Shell worked in one segregated department. Shell employed very few Mexican Americans at Deer Park between 1938, when Mexico nationalized Shell's holdings south of the border, and 1965, when the company put equal opportunity guidelines into effect. Today, however, 18 per cent of the plant's hourly employees are black, 8 per cent are Mexican American, and nearly 6 per cent are female.

No one is more concerned about the implications of these changes than Roy Barnes. Barnes resembles Ernest Borgnine and, like the actor, seems too big to fit comfortably indoors. Barnes came to the Houston Ship Channel from Oklahoma in 1948, working first as a construction hand, then for fifteen years as an hourly worker for Shell. In 1970 he passed up a pension from Shell to run for the job he currently holds. Even company men acknowledge that he is well suited to leadership. Barnes speaks softly and with studied consideration, like a priest. Nothing about him hints at Teamster sleaziness. He doesn't have a police record, nor does he tote a gun. He says he has never pummeled a strikebreaker, and veteran union members say that he has always rejected any recourse to sabotage suggested by striking workers. Yet no one speaks of Barnes as the kind of insipid leader

"Though Pasadena projects a cowboy image, it is an industrial suburb to its core, a blue-collar town that has more in common with Dearborn, Michigan, than Abilene."

Mary Anderson earned approval from male workers without aid from the union. "What is most important to guys on the job is that everybody do his own part."

often found in the labor movement these days—the aptly named "business agent" of building-trades locals, who beams when he reports that he has never gone on strike and boasts that his children have graduated to medicine or engineering. Roy Barnes trudged a picket line for eleven months in the 1962 strike, and his son gave up an engineering job for a higher paying hourly slot at Shell. In union financial affairs, so often the source of corruption, Barnes has a reputation for openness and honesty. When I asked him how much he earns, he had to look up the figure: just under $28,000, which is roughly what he would be drawing at Shell had he not left. In the process, he let me see the books, not exactly the behavior one anticipates from a union boss.

Like a career soldier who believes the Army needs a war every so often to keep in shape, Barnes thinks strikes are necessary to keep a union alive. "A man needs to be in at least one strike to get a good education in unionism," he says. But most of Local 367's younger generation have not yet walked a picket line and many have little desire to. They rarely vote in political elections, either, and most do not see why they should. "A man has to be about forty before he can really participate in his

THE PARTICIPANTS 105

Union leaders consider Oran McMichael a radical, but they tolerate him.

union, his church, or his community," Barnes told me. But he knows that the OCAW can't wait fifteen years for the new workers to reach maturity. The deadline comes in January.

Petrochemical work is a lot like guarding a prison. Most jobs at Shell are sedentary. The workers keep watch on pressurized, highly volatile products. The prison guards' main worries are that their charges will escape or revolt; petrochemical workers' primary concerns are seepage and explosion. While moving crude oil or distillates from one compound to another, refinery workers open and shut valves, just like guards handling cellblock gates. They routinely inventory the contents of tanks and look for cracks in the walls, but between tasks they simply sit, sometimes reading or playing cards on the sly. They can be reprimanded for idleness or gaming, or ordered to perform make-work jobs. Foremen with bully mentalities often take advantage of the intermittent nature of the workers' duties, if only because ordering men around relieves their own boredom. It is not surprising that the chief complaints of petrochemical workers are that there is too much harassment from the higher ranks and that job assignments are made on the basis of favoritism.

To these complaints add the issues of job safety and workman's compensation and it becomes apparent why workers join unions. Indeed, the union got its start at Shell in 1933 after negotiations broke down over demands for, among other things, a new ambulance, gas masks, and compensation for widows of men killed on the job. By 1935 union organizers had signed up 80 per cent of the plant's six hundred hourly employees. Despite forty years of union activity, federal regulations, and a 1973 strike over working conditions, on-the-job accidents are still common enough to warrant both company and OCAW safety crusades. Two Shell pipe fitters were killed in a 1976 explosion, and two other workers were severely burned in a flare-up last spring.

Wages, of course, remain an issue, but earnings at Deer Park are attractive: a base rate of $9.23 an hour for an operator, which adds up to $19,240 a year. Unskilled laborers like janitors make $7.50. Most workers can count on overtime or night pay to push their take over $20,000, and the union will be after more in January. As one younger worker put it, "The company is making more profits these days, so we've got to make sure we get better wages. Getting our share of the pie is what the union is for."

There are more subtle reasons why people join the union. The union gives workers today what lodges gave their grandfathers fifty years ago. It has a hall where they can meet, shoot pool, and call each other by titles like "committeeman" and "chaplain"; it also gives them lapel pins, pencil clips, and matchbooks with insignia, just as the Elks and Odd Fellows do. In short, it provides a feeling of solidarity and a sense of identity. The union, like the lodge, also imposes its own code of ethics. One Shell veteran told me about a co-worker who broke the picket line during the 1962 strike; no one would speak to him after the settlement, and fifteen years later the strikebreaker is still ostracized.

Whatever their motives for joining, 95 per cent of the eligible hourly workers at Shell are members of the OCAW —a noteworthy statistic in a right-to-work state, where Texas law prohibits making union membership a condition of employment. Dues aren't cheap: $18.50 a month, or a little more than 1 per cent of base pay.

In other unions, a man of Roy Barnes' rank might call all the shots, but power in the OCAW is more diffuse. Barnes is the dominant figure during contract talks and on all large policy issues. He is an authority on everything from carcinogenic chemicals to the fine details of every OCAW contract in the industry. But the daily union work at Shell—usually grievances against foremen and complaints about safety—is handled inside the plant gates. At the base of the union structure are 112 shop stewards, 9 of them women, who handle minor grievances and recruit for the union. Above them and far more potent is the workmen's committee, which formulates contract demands, bargains with management, and calls the Local out on strike.

Ten unionists, five from the chemical plant and five from the refinery, sit on the workmen's committee, which meets every Thursday at the Local's office on South Tartar in Pasadena. The committee processes grievances that

106 THE PARTICIPANTS

"Shell's second-generation workers are restless. They have lost the faith of their fathers in the political process. Striking is the only weapon they believe in."

Bible reading and rock music: John Patterson links the new union with the old.

Dolores Miller: the union saved her job.

cannot be settled by stewards at the shop-floor level, and committee members meet monthly with management teams. The presence of a committee member is also required under the current contract whenever Shell calls a worker on the carpet.

Everyone on the committee has been a member of the Local for at least eight years, which means all are strike veterans. Six are in their late thirties or forties and consequently provide a link between the men of Roy Barnes' generation and the unseasoned work force hired since 1974. One of these men in the middle is John Patterson, 37, whose slender build, red face, curly hair, and full beard make him resemble a lanky Falstaff. Patterson is said to have ambitions for higher union office, and his personal tastes suggest a fondness for compromise. Like the older generation, he often wears pointed-toe cowboy boots; like the younger men, he is partial to pastel T-shirts. The older crowd is notorious for its affinity to pickups. Patterson drives a Malibu, but, like his older peers, he is a devout Bible reader. His musical preferences run more to rock than to country and Western, and he reads contemporary fiction in addition to the Scriptures.

Patterson grew up in nearby Galena Park but now lives in Pasadena. His father was a nonunion construction worker who was killed in an on-the-job accident. A few days after Patterson was hired by Shell in 1968, Local 367 walked out. Though he had not yet joined the union, Patterson honored the picket lines.

"By then I had enough experience with companies to know what unions are for," he said. "And I'd been at Shell long enough to know that without a union I wouldn't want to stay there." Three years ago he was elected to the workmen's committee, and since then union work has taken up most of his spare time.

Patterson is a good example of the transformation occurring in today's union membership. He is a step removed from the men of Roy Barnes' generation. I talked to a recent Shell retiree named R. C. Blair who came to the Ship Channel in 1948. He'd been a barber in Throckmorton, northwest of Abilene, before World War II, but when his postwar income didn't measure up to his expectations, he headed for the city in search of industrial work. To his delight, he found not just a job but a niche. "It was just like home," he recalled. "We were all just ol' country boys and ex-GIs."

Today's Shell worker is more likely to have grown up along the Ship Channel than in West Texas. Many are second-generation industrial workers. Though Pasadena superficially reflects a cowboy image, it is an industrial suburb to its core, a blue-collar town that has more in common with Dearborn, Michigan, than Abilene.

The more union members I met—affluent young whites, women intensely aware of their minority status, radical blacks—the more I was struck by their remoteness from Roy Barnes and the union men of his era. If Patterson is one step removed, they have taken several leaps. That doesn't mean they are in open rebellion to Barnes' leadership, but it does mean that they have different values and don't necessarily share his reverence for union, church, and community. I found myself wondering as I visited in their homes whether such diverse people could hold together under the stress of a long strike.

When Karl Marx said that workers had nothing to lose but their chains, he reckoned without men like Pat Kelly. Every workday morning, 27-year-old Kelly leaves his $23,000 Pasadena home and climbs into a Datsun 280-Z for a twenty-minute drive to Shell. It is true that older unionists have known a degree of prosperity (R. C. Blair could cash in his home and four rent houses for about $150,000, an average net worth for refinery workers his age), but few of them pursue the good life with the fervency of Pat Kelly.

When I visited Kelly, he was reclining on his Herculon couch, dipping Skoal from a round tin and spitting it into an empty milk carton. A dishwater-blond beard hid part of his face, pink-tinted sunglasses shielded his eyes, and his pastel T-shirt displayed the name of rock singer Jackson Browne. Soft rock music was playing on the stereo.

Pat Kelly grew up in Pasadena. His father was a union worker at Shell until the 1962 strike, when he quit to take a job overseas. After high school, Kelly enrolled at local San Jacinto Junior College, even though he never cared much for academics. When he drew a high number in the 1969 draft lottery, he decided to turn in his books and go to work. Shell hired him as an operator, a job that requires shift work. Each 24-hour day is divided into a daytime, evening, and late-night or graveyard shift, and workers spend about a week on each, with two days off between shifts. At the end of this cycle, they get four days off. Roy Barnes told me the men enjoy shift work because of the mini-vacation; this may be true of family men, but younger unmarried workers dislike it because they are on the job many weekends and nights. Because of the company's seniority system, Kelly spent four years on shift duty. As soon as he could, he applied for a pipe fitter's job, involving days only. The change probably pleased Shell as much as it did Kelly, because his attendance record quickly improved. "I didn't think twice about calling off if I had plans for the weekend," Kelly said. "Shift work tears up your single life." Shift workers get a pay premium for evening and graveyard shifts; consequently they average $100 a month more than their colleagues who work only straight days and no overtime. Kelly, however, didn't mind the pay cut. He earns about $20,000 a year, and after his house payment there is still plenty left over for his all-important social life. He spends his leisure playing poker, hunting, fishing, and carousing with other plant workers who, like him, are unmarried and prosperous.

Kelly did not attend the union meeting at which workers voted to strike in 1973, but he did not complain when walkout orders came. "I had enough money saved up that I didn't mind it a bit," he shrugged. "It gave me a vacation. I partied for four and a half months and that's about it." But the strike wasn't just a lark for Kelly. He says that he first thought about unionism while walking the picket line. "I never gave it much consideration before. Belonging to the union was just something I did because the older men wanted me to. But when you're out there on the picket line and those scabs go through the gates like nothing is going on and don't even look up—it gets to you. They're going in there, getting your job, and getting your money. That's enough to make anybody burn."

Six months ago, Kelly volunteered for an opening as a union steward in the pipe-fitting shop. Even in his new capacity, Pat Kelly is not all that Roy Barnes would have hoped for in a union member. He rarely attends steward's meetings or other union functions and he despises politicians and does not vote; he does, however, contribute to the OCAW's political war chest and, as steward, he sells the lottery tickets that fund it. But he adamantly ignores OCAW's continual exhortations to go to the polls: "Two years ago, I did volunteer work in a local election and got all of politics I need. I don't like anything about politics. It's just like the plant without a union. Who gets elected is whoever has the most money or the most pull or does the most brownnosing. Politicians are just like foremen."

In lifestyle and political cynicism, Kelly is firmly in the ranks of the new generation, but in his feelings toward the company, he is a thoroughgoing union man. If anything, he disdains foremen more than politicians. They are salaried workers, the lowest rung on the management ladder, and though many are former unionists, the promotion sets them apart. "I've seen too many guys ruined by it," Kelly says. "You make them foremen, and suddenly they think they're different. I wouldn't be a foreman for any amount of money. I can be myself the way I am now."

Last spring Mary Anderson, 27, another Shell hourly worker, made plans to attend a "safety dinner" to celebrate a year's work without a lost-time accident in her department. Shell policy allows employees to bring dates to such activities, and Mary did not want to miss the party. When Pat Kelly transferred into her unit, she decided to ask him out. Since then the two unionists have been dating.

Mary, whose father worked for Sinclair, is a second-generation refinery hand like Pat. Before she came to Shell, she worked at the usual women's jobs—typist, Dairy Queen attendant, Fotomat clerk. She doubled her income when she came to Shell two years ago. Reasons beyond money brought her to the job. "I went there to lose weight. I wanted to do something energetic, and I have. When I started, I weighed 165. Now I'm down to 135. I'll probably stay at Shell the rest of my life."

Mary does not take easily to unionism. "I have a hard time seeing what it's good for," she says. But she is not as outspoken as Vickie Schmelzle, a tank-farm worker. "I joined the union, but against my will. If you're not in the union and you get in trouble, you won't get any help from the other workers. They won't look out for you unless you're in the union." Like Pat and Mary, Vickie has never voted; unlike them, she has also declined union appeals for political contributions. She even ignores meeting notices. "I don't even know where the union hall is," she told me. Vickie Schmelzle was the only Shell worker I spoke to who didn't know who Roy Barnes was.

Before starting at Shell eighteen months ago, Vickie was a vocational nurse. Her new job gives her certain luxuries nursing did not afford: she goes camping on long weekends and has taken up photography. She keeps her nursing certification active "in case of a strike" and also because she is hesitant about making a career of refinery work. "For one thing, I have chronic bronchial inflammation from breathing fumes. For another, I am finding that plant work is not so different from nursing. One of the reasons I quit nursing was that there was so much backstabbing and gossip among the women. I never knew men were the same way until I started at Shell."

The attitude of Shell women toward the union seems to depend on how well they've been accepted on their jobs. The harder they've had to fight for acceptance, the more likely they are to support the union. Mary Anderson earned approval without turning to the union. "Sometimes there's a lot of teasing and butt grabbing," she said. "You've got to learn to put a stop to it." Mary's job required driving a forklift, loading 460-pound resin drums onto pallets. It tested her five-seven frame, but she refused offers of help. "What is most important to the guys on the job is that everybody do his own part. A woman at Shell can get guys to do her job, but that's not good for"—she stumbled over a phrase that did not come easily for her—"well, I guess you might call it women's liberation."

But sometimes doing a job right is just not enough. Dolores Miller says the union saved her job: "I had one foreman who made it very clear he didn't think a woman belonged out there. He wanted to take me to the gate [union slang for getting someone fired]. The union got me removed from his unit. Women are stronger members than men, because we know we're out there by the grace of somebody besides the company." A staunch union partisan, she is a steward and a telephone volunteer at election time. Her resentment of male workers, who, she says, "have to be taught to behave," has touched off two moves to recall her as steward. Both failed.

Sexual discrimination is undoubtedly a touchy subject, and could get touchier, but race is the issue that could tear the union apart. It has once before: in the eleventh month of the 1962 strike, a rumor circulated among black workers that Shell would concede to the union's economic demands if the union would agree to promote blacks into skilled jobs. The blacks, who were then confined to unskilled work, decided that the union was prolonging the strike not to win economic demands but to maintain segregation. Thirty black workers crossed the picket lines to demonstrate their lack of faith in the union leadership. Fifteen years later, the barriers against blacks in skilled jobs have been eliminated, but lack of faith among black workers is as strong as ever.

In two years as an OCAW machinist, Oran McMichael, 27, has raised the ire of union leaders on numerous occasions. As he refinished a floor in his newly bought South Houston home, he told me why: "I haven't been afraid to say what I think of the union's policies. The union has not really tried to include blacks. They'll take a grievance on anything but discrimination. If they get one, they may take it, yeah, but call it something else."

His differences, McMichael claims, are not with white co-workers, but with the union leaders. "Race relations are really at a new point. Whites invite blacks over to their homes after work and vice versa. It's usually pretty stiff and formal, and the friendships usually break down after a few visits, but at least the effort is being made. A few blacks have moved into Pasadena, and they haven't met the hostility that we expected. Things are getting better."

Last year McMichael led a dozen blacks and Mexican Americans to a union meeting with a demand that the Local censure Shell for slowness in promoting minority workers. Roy Barnes opposed the measure, which also called for a program aimed at improving race relations within the union. The proposal failed, but ten of eighty white workers present voted with McMichael.

McMichael also assails Roy Barnes and the OCAW for routinely endorsing Democrats. "Younger folks are seeing the swindles and scandals that have come out since Watergate, and that's one reason why they're turned off politically. The other big reason is inflation. The union is misleading folks by saying the Democratic party is all we have. Union leaders won't call for the formation of a party that is really in the interest of working people."

McMichael is a member of the Trade Union Educational League, which he describes carefully as "an organization that stands for the interests of all working people." It could more accurately be described as a socialist labor group. Organized labor in this country, despite a leftish public image, is in many ways quite conservative, not at all like European unions that band together to form socialist political parties. The OCAW constitution forbids membership to communists—an undefined term that at other times in American history has been broad enough to encompass whatever and whoever its detractors wanted. In the years just after World War II, Local 367's leaders secretly cooperated with an FBI informer whose job was rooting out radicals at the Shell plant, and since that time there have been no open communists or socialists in the union. One steward warned me that McMichael was convinced the OCAW hated blacks and that he was "probably a communist," a term he seemed to use as a convenient synonym for "radical troublemaker."

In other times and other unions, Roy Barnes and his cronies might have moved to expel McMichael. Instead, they have decided to tolerate him in the interest of avoiding racial strife. McMichael recently won election as a shop steward on his unit, with the support of white co-workers, and the Local issued certification papers under Barnes' signature without delay or protest. "Now that Mr. McMichael is a steward," Barnes says, "we are hoping that he'll take a different attitude."

McMichael has also had second thoughts about his approach to Barnes. "I don't think we'll ever agree about a lot of things, like union democracy and politics. But it's in the union's interests to keep all its members united, and Barnes knows that."

And McMichael is right. It is political attitudes that most sharply divide the old and new memberships. Despite the differences in sex, race, and lifestyle, there is little question that the younger members are pro-union and that they support the notion of striking.

Roy Barnes believes that the union has two weapons at its disposal: politics and striking. An autographed portrait of Ralph Yarborough hangs in his office. But the younger members of Local 367 wouldn't vote for a Ralph Yarborough or anybody else. They have lost the faith of their fathers in the political process. Striking is the only weapon they have confidence in; if anything, they are more strike-happy than their elders.

Nonetheless, Shell executives are not particularly frightened by strike talk. They see a 1979 strike as an opportunity to test the OCAW in new circumstances and, possibly, to weaken it. Most of them would like to believe that union power in the petrochemical industry has crested and will now decline.

"In the past few years, the OCAW has won larger wage gains than many of us in management thought were justified," says Deer Park employee relations chief Dave McClintic. Shell would like to halt that trend in 1979 and it has other objectives as well. "This Local bargains hard on a variety of issues besides wages. So we are now looking at the current union contract to see what restrictions in it we might want removed," says McClintic. Talk of "removing restrictions" does not sit well with Roy Barnes. "I wouldn't put it past Shell to provoke a strike if it wanted. An untimely strike could hurt the union," he says.

A short strike would probably be good for Local 367. It would give the green recruits a picket-line education and would pull members into union meetings. Even if they won only minimal concessions, the strike would affirm the faith expressed in the old union song: "The boss won't listen when one guy squawks, but he's got to listen when the union walks." It would establish the new generation at Shell as a work force not to be tempted.

But Local 367 can't determine how long a nationwide strike will last. If all OCAW locals with Shell contracts walk out together, workers at Deer Park cannot return to their jobs until national demands are met locally. Further, if the OCAW walks out, it gives Shell the option of forcing the strike into extra innings. Strike funds are limited. Roy Barnes estimates that the OCAW nationally and Local 367 could provide only about $20 per week for no longer than five months. Economic hardship might force some workers to cross picket lines or seek other employment.

But most would not. Local 367's younger generation, despite its inexperience and material comfort, should not be regarded as soft. The union's newer members may spurn politicians and second-guess their union leaders, but only a few give credence to Shell. Their fathers sought and found prosperity in the refineries, but they take affluence as a starting point for their economic lives. They do not compare their standard of living with Depression-era poverty; they look not to what was but to what could be. They know petrochemical firms are doing well and they want a share of Shell's good fortune. The attitude typical of the younger worker at Deer Park is described in Ecclesiastes: "The sleep of a labouring man is sweet, whether he eat little or much: but the abundance of the rich will not suffer him to sleep." Shell's second-generation workers are restless, not because they are poor, but because others are rich.★

The Good Old Girls

by Prudence Mackintosh

Texans didn't exactly run the National Women's Conference, but they made it work.

I knew I wasn't exactly the cutting edge of the movement when a Houston friend's first question on hearing I was going to the National Women's Conference was, "What are you going to wear?" Surely that was not the right question for a feminist gathering. (As it turned out I was wrong, but not for the reason one might expect.) I was certain that across the country women were just tossing a T-shirt, a pair of jeans, and some sandals in a canvas bag and hopping a plane for Houston while I was eyeing my new wool dirndl skirts and trying to decide if I could make it through airport security with my hair drier. I opted for a little of both—jeans and black turtlenecks and skirts and neat blouses; I reasoned that at a Mississippi delegation caucus some lipstick and a straight hemline might serve me better than media credentials. However, taking two wardrobes made my luggage so cumbersome that, in spite of the collapsible carrier I had bought to get me independently through the airport, my typewriter proved too much and before I boarded the plane at Love Field I had already enlisted the services of two gentlemen. Settled in my seat, I tried to assume the proper feminist perspective. My male seat companion was a big help: he spent the better part of the flight, with no encouragement from me besides an occasional nod, telling me how indispensable he was to his company and how he was getting nationally known for his race-car engine rebuilding. I wondered to myself how long it might take for a professional woman to develop such a monumental ego.

I had been instructed by some jaded reporters that to cover a convention, it was necessary to write your story before you arrived, then afterward change the things that didn't go as you expected. But I hadn't had enough dealings with the women's movement to do any predicting. The cab ride into Houston gave me time for some theorizing, however. While Texas women, as all women, have had to contend with unequal pay for equal work and inequities of that nature, I was of the opinion that the reason the feminist movement didn't sweep Texas like a storm in its early days is because it concerned itself with certain things that many Texas women had taken care of a long time ago. Maybe it's our frontier heritage; after all, it was the frontier states that first granted women suffrage in this country (Texas was seventh). Maybe our great-grandmothers were just too important to everyone's survival to take much put-down from their men. All I know is that growing up in Texas it never once occurred to me to think of myself as inferior to men. Indeed, in Texas high schools the strong tradition of football tended to short-circuit the academic energies of the good old boys while we good old girls who didn't have the legs for baton twirling were busy making the honor roll, editing the school newspaper, and running the student council. Chauvinistically, I wanted to believe that the leaders of the women's movement had set this conference in Texas because we had a tradition of resilience and effectiveness that other women could learn from. Although I knew its goals were more specific, perhaps in a psychological sense this would be the Texanization of the women's movement.

This gathering of women in Houston was bringing together nearly 2000 delegates elected in meetings in every state and territory of the United States. In the next three days, November 18 through 20, the women would forge a 25-point program aimed at eliminating barriers to equality for women. The National Plan of Action, which would include economic issues as well as the controversial issues of the Equal Rights Amendment, abortion, and lesbian rights, will be presented by the conference commissioners to Congress and President Carter by March 21.

Since I was in town a day early, I wanted to get a look at the behind-the-scenes preparations. I saw women acting as security guards, floor tellers, microphone facilitators; they ran first-aid stations and information booths; they acted as interpreters for foreign visitors and non-English-speaking delegates; they signed for the deaf, typed braille for the blind; they provided transportation, housing, and child care, registered the press, and coordinated special events at the Albert Thomas Convention Center and throughout Houston. Most were Texas women and experienced workers coming out of such organizations as the YWCA, League of Women Voters, American Association of University Women, and National Council of Jewish Women.

The press would be looking for radical, braless, denim-clad feminists and, although it would certainly find them, it would also find blue-haired grandmothers, young club women in well-cut suits, and female executives from federal agencies—all being led by Mary Keegan, the chair for the Houston committee of the IWY (International Women's Year) Commission. Mary, who has headed many volunteer efforts in Houston, would be responsible for over two thousand of the volunteers, a job few corporate executives would consider taking on at top salary and which she did without pay.

At the IWY office, the scene was like any campaign headquarters the day before an election—confused. The difference was that women running a national convention like this for the first time are defensive about being called disorganized, so I was quickly taken aside and shown the overall structure for reassurance. With only one day left before the torch from Seneca Falls, New York, would be relayed to Houston, last-minute decisions had to be made, but at this crucial point the lines of authority were becoming tangled between the Texas volunteers and the mainly Eastern IWY staff. Only two days before, the national IWY staff from Washington had descended on the Houston headquarters. I sensed that the transfer of power to Bella Abzug, presiding officer of the conference, and her paid staff had not been entirely smooth. While the transition between advance staff and permanent staff is undoubtedly difficult in any large organization, the East/West cultural differences in this exchange of power served to accentuate inherent problems.

The two women who did the most to help smooth out these differences, as well as a host of other seemingly insurmountable obstacles, were Houstonians Poppy Northcutt and Helen Cassidy. Each time a crisis was resolved, I heard the names of these two extraordinary Texas women. They had been hired in late September by the national IWY staff to act as "special conference consultants." According to Helen, all the national staff had done in Houston at this point was reserve the meeting halls and hotels for the actual convention dates. No thought had been given to the sort of details that for most national conventions of any size are planned five years in advance.

Helen and Poppy had six weeks to accomplish miracles. Their previous experience with the National Organization for Women conference three years ago in Houston would prove invaluable, as would their friends and contacts throughout the city. Helen, a lawyer, and Poppy, a trajectory analyst and the first woman in Mission Control at NASA and more recently an account executive with Merrill Lynch, had recently left their jobs to establish Women's Advocate, Inc., in Houston. The two agreed from the start of their involvement with this conference that Helen would deal with the people and Poppy would deal with things.

Some of the tasks seemed enormous. For example, the Sam Houston Coliseum leased for the conference had no bathroom facilities for the handicapped. Poppy was able to get an additional stall added in each bathroom, but in order to do it, one regular stall had to be narrowed. "Anybody with hips measuring more than thirty-six who got in line for that one was bound to be embarrassed," Helen said. Braille information for blind delegates and par-

Betty Friedan (l.) with Mary Keegan, who organized Texas volunteers

THE PARTICIPANTS 111

ticipants had to be put up in various places in the hotels and convention center. Sometimes the job had to be done twice. While touring the meeting halls, one commissioner confided to Helen, "I saw this very right-wing-looking young woman pasting some sort of secret code up in our elevators at the Hyatt. You'll be relieved to know I went around behind her taking them down." A wrestling match had been booked into the coliseum the night before the women's conference was to open. That left only the early-morning hours for setting up the convention floor plus a press room complete with phones, teleprinters, and typewriters.

One of Helen's many people jobs was acclimating the national IWY staff to Texas modus operandi. "We had the most problems with the New York women. I told them before they got here that in Texas, we say 'please and thank you and yes, ma'am.' They weren't too sure about ma'am. 'Isn't that how people in England address the Queen?' they asked. I assured them that any courtesies they might afford the Queen would be standard procedure with any women from Texas or the rest of the South. The New York women wanted to pride themselves on being the roughest, toughest, most outspoken women on the earth, but I assured them although we might be quiet-spoken and polite, we could be vicious when crossed. I suggested that they reread *Gone with the Wind* before they came."

Due in large part to the efforts of Helen and Poppy, what didn't happen at the conference was as noteworthy as what did. As it turned out, there was no major dissension between the national staff and the Houston volunteers —just an interesting contrast in approach. I saw an example of one type at breakfast Thursday morning in the Hyatt Regency coffee shop. I invited myself to join two very busy members of the national staff who were arguing, even before their orange juice was served, over who was to blame for a proposed demonstration by the militant handicapped from California. "You knew we'd have a demonstration on our hands. I told you to put that paraplegic woman from California on the committee, but you vetoed my recommendation. You should have anticipated this move. The militant handicapped from California could ruin us. I hear we don't even have ramps to the podium if one of them should speak. Who's responsible for this kind of foul-up?" "Foul-up? What about the dog show that got booked in the press room?"

So much talk of "power moves" and "confrontation" so early in the morning almost made me choke on my grits. By contrast, late that afternoon I met Texan Ann Britt, the convention center decorator, who was directing dozens of

Ann Richards of Austin epitomizes the good old girl style of politics.

Some friendly persuasion by Texans softened Utah's anti-feminist stand.

Wichita Falls' Arthur Bea Williams knows how to get people to listen.

Irma Rangel found Hispanics divided.

Texas journalist Liz Carpenter's speech brought women to their feet.

Two Houstonians rescued the NWC from trouble: Poppy Northcutt . . .

. . . and Helen Cassidy, who handled details the national staff ignored.

112 THE PARTICIPANTS

union laborers without raising her voice. Ann Britt, who grew up in Carthage with a bunch of brothers, is every bit as tough as the women I had met that morning. The difference was in style. Ann Britt was wearing a frilly dress, her hair and makeup were perfect, her nails were polished, and her voice was right out of *The Last Picture Show*.

"Some of these women I'm dealin' with don't have no more sense than a waltzin' pissant. In Texas we grew up knowing that if you really wanna get somethin' done, you first ask politely and you communicate just as clearly as you know how what you want. I'm the only woman convention decorator in this city and a lot of people don't think it's a job for a woman. But I'll tell you, I've never had a bit of trouble with my guys. Getting these teamsters to work this convention could have been a real mess; I work with the guys who think we all oughta be barefoot and pregnant, but they respect me and do what I tell 'em. Lookin' nice is part of it, I guess. My mama raised me to care what I look like, and rolling up my hair at night doesn't mean I can't demand top wages in this business." All the women behind the scenes were having to deal with conflict, and it seemed to me that the Texas women who had never lost their ability to communicate with the good old boys who install telephones and unload chairs would deserve a lot of the credit for bringing off this conference.

By the time I returned to my hotel Thursday afternoon, new conflict was developing. Delegates from every state and territory and their luggage were beginning to create an impasse in the lobbies of the Sheraton and Hyatt Regency. If the male desk clerk at the Sheraton had ever contemplated a sex change, surely it was now. The women were bunching up around the desk and polite inquiries about room reservations had degenerated to "What the hell is going on here?" when it became clear that the hotel would be unable to house even those with confirmed reservation slips in their hands. Everyone seemed to have a different explanation for the hotel snafu and rumors swept the lobby. Some said that the Sheraton and the Hyatt simply overbooked for Thursday. Both hotels had offered the IWY reduced rates because they did not anticipate much business the week before Thanksgiving. Others hinted that when a lumberman's convention at the Hyatt opted to stay another day at full rate, the hotel was reluctant to evict them. Rumors also spread that right-wing groups had called in and canceled entire blocks of rooms reserved weeks in advance by state delegations. After the conference was over, I thought back on the lobbies full of tired women sitting on their luggage singing "Show me the way to go home, I'm tired and I wanna go to bed," and I couldn't help but wonder how much more contentious the conference might have been had the energies of so many women not been initially spent in fighting for space to sleep.

On Thursday I attended my first press conference with Bella Abzug presiding. Again, I realized I had been wrong to assume that "What are you wearing?" was an inappropriate question for the National Women's Conference. Indeed, Bella met the press at that first briefing in a pink suit. Of course, she wore her trademark, a floppy-brimmed hat, but this one was a complementary shade of pink. Everybody had apparently given appearances considerable thought. Knowing that Liz Carpenter had been worrying about what to wear for her speech at the opening session—the rose Ultrasuede or the new Molly Parnis—some of her Austin friends sent her a telegram that read: RE: IWY MEETING. MOLLY PARNIS SUIT. MUST CHANGE PLANS. I OWN SAME SUIT. BOUGHT IT FIRST. PLAN TO WEAR. KNOW YOU'LL UNDERSTAND. PHYLLIS SCHLAFLY. "In the early days," said Jane Hickey, a delegate from Austin, "it was a big deal that you *didn't* dress up. I don't know why, except that it was a lot more comfortable —no panty hose, just old tire-tread sandals. But at some point, I guess about three years ago, somebody noticed that nobody listened if they were looking at your dirty feet. I guess the return of dresses indicates a greater degree of political sophistication. We don't want to just be right anymore. We want to win."

In keeping with that sentiment, as Bella introduced various members of the IWY Commission, she said more about their children and grandchildren than about their professional achievements. She emphasized that many of the issues of this conference would go right to the heart of the grass-roots American woman, the homemaker— Social Security laws that discriminate against her, inheritance laws that may reduce her to poverty when her husband dies, displacement when she tries to enter the job market when her children are grown. Phyllis Schlafly across town at the Astrodome certainly had no monopoly on so-called pro-family issues. A cynical *Washington Post* reporter leaned over to me during Bella's press conference and whispered, "I wish they'd get off this motherhood stuff. For the first time at a feminist conference, I'm beginning to feel disenfranchised."

Any national convention is a circus and it seemed to me that this one had more than three rings. I could have spent the entire four days simply looking at the 2000 women on the convention floor. The diversity in their ages, ethnic origins, and dress alone made the conference a reporter's feast. There were Oriental women with delicate flower-imprinted buttons bearing the slogan "Lotus Blossom doesn't live here anymore," Midwestern matrons in polyester pantsuits with yellow ERA scarves proclaiming "Women's rights is as American as apple pie," California delegates as varied in appearance as their sign indicated: "Imagination rules the world," Indian women in tribal dress, Nebraska women swinging bras over their heads with a sign saying "We never burned 'em," Alabama women in their Sunday best demurely needlepointing Christmas ornaments, Guamanian and Hawaiian women in bright muumuus with tropical blossoms in their hair, and of course young women in traditional feminist uniform—jeans and T-shirts.

The diversity in the press gallery was a microcosm of the larger group. For part of the conference I sat beside a delightfully unjaded reporter named Brenda from Springdale, Arkansas. "Oooh, I just can't believe it," she squealed, "Barbara Jordan is my idol and I'm hearing her right now in person." And sometimes I ended up between the more cynical journalists from the East whose entire store of nouns, verbs, and adjectives derived from a certain Anglo Saxon verb that still retains some shock value in these provinces. At one of the evening sessions, after listening to more than eight hours of floor debates, I wearily remarked to my female press companions that I thought the cause of women's rights might be better advanced if we all turned our voices down about fifty decibels. "I know it's heretical to say, but I've about had it with women today. I don't care what Gloria Steinem says. I am not missing 'the part of myself that society has repressed.' What I'm missing is men, particularly my husband." My companions shrugged coolly, and later when they asked me to save their seats, I asked, "What paper are you with, just in case the press aide tries to seat somebody here?" They grinned and one offered me her card; it read *Lesbian Times*.

Those "exotic issues," as former Democratic Chairman Bob Strauss used to call them, occupied one ring of the circus. My friends back home might feign some interest in the parliamentary maneuvers that brought about the passage of the minority rights resolution, but the main thing they'd want to know was "Did you see any lesbians or prostitutes?" Of course I did. I went to the press conference held by the National Gay Task Force. Jean O'Leary, a commissioner for the IWY, was the spokeswoman for the group and for the record

THE PARTICIPANTS 113

she does not have green hair and horns. In fact that press conference was one of the least sensational I attended. The motto for the lesbian participants was "We Are Everywhere," and out-of-the-closet lesbians proudly displayed their unity by wearing bright orange happy face buttons proclaiming "It's fun to be gay." From a group that sometimes calls to its defense the homosexual artistic geniuses of the Western world, I found the happy face buttons a real letdown.

The prostitutes showed more imagination. Their group, COYOTE (Call Off Your Old Tired Ethics), described as a "loose women's organization," wore buttons or T-shirts that read "The trick is in not getting caught." At their press conference I presumed the major issue would be decriminalization of prostitution, but before I knew it I was drawn into a pragmatic exchange on such subjects as zoning of red-light districts, the exploitation of prostitutes by massage parlors, the economic necessity of getting rid of pimps, and the need for massive VD screenings. "It's about time everybody quit blaming the whores for venereal disease," the spokeswoman said. "It's the teenagers who pass that around, and it's bad for our business."

In my attempt to soak up all the diversity of the conference, I missed one of the major events, the last lap of the torch relay that had begun in September in Seneca Falls, the birthplace of the women's rights movement in this country. It must have been impressive; I heard a man say later at the ERA fund raiser that it was the only time in his life that he was sort of sorry he wasn't a woman. Sometimes it was difficult to take seriously a conference that was trying so self-consciously to be historical. Bella and the other presiding officers were banging a gavel once used by Susan B. Anthony, tape recorders were set up in the Convention Center for delegates and participants to record for posterity their musings on the days' events, and conference memorabilia would be tagged and shipped to the Smithsonian. However, I confess to getting teary-eyed at the opening session in the midst of the drum and bugle corps, the trooping of the colors, the comely young women with the torch, the three first ladies, and the Battle Hymn of the Republic.

Texas had a strong grip on the opening sessions. Helen Cassidy, again behind the scenes, also had to hire a band for the conference. By that time she was so harassed by the out-of-staters (she now referred to them as "the aliens") that when the bandleader asked about music, she said she told him to play standard convention fare—"You know, 'The Yellow Rose of Texas,' 'The Eyes of Texas,' 'Texas Our Texas.' " When the Equal Rights Amendment resolution passed, the delegates found themselves singing "The ERA was passed today [clap clap clap clap] deep in the heart of Texas." But more than the music, there was the presence of Texas women on the platform—Lady Bird Johnson and daughter Lynda Robb, IWY commissioners Gloria Scott and Liz Carpenter, and keynote speaker Congresswoman Barbara Jordan.

Liz Carpenter's speech to the opening session was full of her characteristic humor, dramatic flare, and remarkable timing. Convention speeches are traditionally ignored, but everybody listens to Liz. "The President of the United States and the Congress have asked us to assess our needs, assert our worth, and set our goals for filling the legislative gaps. I thought they'd never ask!" she opened. She traced the role of women in America from Queen Isabella, who put up the money to discover it (the Native American Indian caucus would take Liz to task for that later), to Sacajawea who led the pale-faced men to the Pacific. She spoke of women's traditional role as mothers and nurturers but also of the reality of their role as breadwinners: "I have known the warmth of a baby's laughter and, as a journalist, the satisfaction of a newspaper byline." She had strategically stationed delegates of diverse backgrounds on the platform behind her and proceeded to rally the audience like a tent revivalist. The women stood as she related their stories. "Eighty-five-year-old Clara M. Beyer of Washington, D.C., retired government worker of sixty years, protégé of Justice Brandeis, teacher at Bryn Mawr College, one of the handful of valiant women who with Eleanor Roosevelt and Florence Kelley pushed the reform of child labor, mother of three sons and twelve grandchildren. Would you deny this senior citizen mother the Social Security rights due her, or deny women like her inheritance rights?" The crowd roared, "NO!" "The delegate from Minnesota —farm woman Mary Ann Bruesehoff, who runs her own poultry farm on Route Two near Watkins. She was butchering ducks when I called. 'I'm just a chicken picker,' she says. While her husband raises pigs, cattle, and sheep, she just fell into raising three thousand broilers, ducks, and geese each year because, 'We like good old-fashioned food that's uncontaminated.' Everyone else did too and it helps pay the college tuition of three children. Would you keep this woman out of business because she wouldn't get equal credit to run a business?" Again the crowd exclaimed, "NO!"

And then there was keynote speaker Barbara Jordan. You know the voice. One cannot escape feeling a little like Moses receiving divine instruction on Mount Sinai when she intones the Scrip-

The Ladies

They left home to lobby to stay in it.

On the morning that Betty Ann Peden set off from Hondo to attend the National Women's Conference, Bob Peden woke her and presented her with a bouquet of red roses and a freshly brewed cup of coffee. It wasn't a gesture of farewell, however. The Pedens had hired a babysitter to mind their two boys and some temporary help to run their drugstore (they are both pharmacists), so Bob could escort Betty Ann to Houston. "You see, my darling husband knew I was nervous about coming," explained Mrs. Peden.

Mrs. Peden, who is 36 but looks about 20, even when she's dressed up in her heels and stylish pin-striped suit, had been offended by the cutoff jeans and dirty language of some of the women at the state conference in Austin last summer. How was it, she wondered, that the feminist majority could approve resolutions favoring lesbians and reject those concerning motherhood? She expected the Houston convention to be rancorous ("like two thousand kitty cats in a bag," she predicted), if not downright dangerous, but somebody had to stand up for conservative and rural women.

"I'm not opposed to women's rights at all," she insisted. "I've been working since I was thirteen—as a clerk, a receptionist, a waitress, and at a hospital and a nursing home. I was one of two women in my pharmacy class at UT. I know how hard it can be for a woman trying to make her way outside the home." Still, she said, she can't support any program that relies on the federal government for solutions.

The Pedens are Methodists and traditionalists. The husband is the head of the household, "because it's more convenient that way," explained Mrs. Peden. "I help him at work and he helps me at home. We share both things because we love and understand each other."

"We have a benevolent dictatorship. I get to be king if she says it's okay," her husband said.

Mrs. Peden was one of the rural women recruited by an anti-feminist member of the committee that organized the Austin conference. The feminists who controlled that meeting included a few token opposition delegates—including Betty Ann Peden—on their official slate of delegates. "I'm really very bashful, but I campaigned and shook a bunch of hands, and I was elected to go to the national meeting," she said.

Mrs. Peden took on the role of peacemaker in the 58-member Texas delegation. "None of us are really pro or anti anything," she said at the caucus meeting. "You couldn't get three women to agree on the color of the dress I'm wearing. But we've got to get something positive out of this meeting. The news media is itching for us to get into a fight. I want us to try to find something to agree on."

During the long days on the convention floor, she and the other five Texas delegates who described themselves as "pro-family" sat together on the last row of the Texas delegation, close to a dozen like-minded Mormons from Utah. They found some concerns to share with the rest of the Texas delegation—the need for new rape legislation, equal financial credit for women, better job training for welfare mothers. But on the linchpin issue of the conference, passage of the federal Equal Rights Amendment, the six pro-family women stood in lonely opposition to the majority. "I question whether we need the ERA, whether it's redundant. It could open the door on a lot of things," Mrs. Peden said. "I wish they had been willing to hear the other side. That's my only complaint."

Token anti-feminist Betty Ann Peden went to Houston with husband Bob.

Although few women changed their minds on the issues, many found they could at least communicate with the opposition. "My preconceived idea that any woman in Texas who was for the ERA was anti-family and anti-God was wrong," Mrs. Peden said. "I found out that the pro-ERA women resent the fact that they've been called bad mothers just like we resent the fact that we've been called Ku Klux Klaners and Nazis."

Three days with the sisterhood did not make a feminist out of Betty Ann Peden, but it made her a stronger woman. Being elected a delegate reminded her of the time Edith Bunker was called for jury duty on *All in the Family*. "Just like Edith said, 'Nobody ever *asked* me before what I thought.' A year ago I wouldn't have stood up to vote against ERA. I would have just sat there and kept quiet. This conference has made me look at myself for the first time in my life. The fact that my friends wanted me to come to Houston as their representative gave me a sense of identity, a sense of worth."

The conference had no such redeeming value for Minnie Maloy, a friendly Waco grandmother who has been a leader in Catholic women's groups for many years. Mrs. Maloy ran as a delegate because of her deeply felt opposition to abortion. She sided with the majority on many of their resolutions and she had hoped that feminists would break ranks and vote with her against the abortion resolution. They didn't. "That vote was the culmination of the whole meeting for me, and it was a bitter pill to swallow," she said. "I went off the floor and was physically sick. It was about forty-five minutes before I could come back. It does bother me that rights were granted to so many people and there were no rights granted to the beginning of creation. I feel no bitterness toward anybody, but I'm so disappointed. I'd like to go back to Duval County where I grew up and sit under a mesquite tree and not even think for a while."

Mrs. Peden and Mrs. Maloy are rather moderate representatives of the anti-feminist backlash that has stopped the Equal Rights Amendment three states short of ratification. While they were flying their colors amid the feminist majority at the women's conference, about 11,000 pro-family advocates were holding a counterconference seven miles away in the AstroArena. It fell somewhere between a tent revival and a George Wallace rally. Families came from all over the South (twenty busloads from Tennessee alone) to save both church and country. The polar viewpoints drama-

Feminists held ranks and Minnie Maloy failed to stop the abortion resolution.

tized by these two gatherings have been described as feminist versus anti-feminist, religious versus secular, traditionalist versus modernist, states' rights versus federalism, conservative versus liberal. For many of the folks at AstroArena, it was nothing less than the forces of good versus the forces of evil.

The Sunday-dressed families carried Bibles and signs condemning "Women's Lip" and "Immoral Women's Year." "God is a Family Man," one banner declared. All of the elements of the national pro-family coalition were present. There were Southern Baptists, Mormons, and members of the Church of Christ, the American party, the John Birch Society, and the Republican right wing. A platoon of the newly formed Freedoms Heritage Society stood at attention at the entrance of the arena. One member of the group explained that their black uniforms symbolized America's sinful society, while the gold braid stood for the light of Christ.

The rally was organized by Lottie Beth Hobbs of Fort Worth, president of Women Who Want to Be Women; Phyllis Schlafly, president of Stop-ERA and *Eagle Forum*, a national right-wing newsletter; and Dr. Mildred Jefferson, president of Right to Life, one of the major anti-abortion lobbies. Mrs. Schlafly, the Gloria Steinem of the right, thanked her husband for "allowing" her to attend the rally. "I love to say that because it irritates the women's libbers more than anything else."

The audience sat straight in their folding chairs and unanimously passed resolutions against abortion, the ERA, and any federal intervention in family life. The gathering ended with a prayer and a vigorous rendition of "God Bless America."

Kaye Northcott

THE PARTICIPANTS 115

tures, "Who can find a virtuous woman for her price is above rubies . . ." Who could munch popcorn while she demanded, "What will you reap? What will you sow?" Other speeches may have contained noble thoughts, but with a convention crowd it's delivery that counts, and the Texas speakers knew how to deliver.

But the Texas influence extended even beyond the podium. I do not think it was accidental that the Texas delegation was seated on the presiding officer's right at the very front of the convention hall beside microphone number one. Although some might argue with validity that this delegation was not entirely ideologically representative of the state as a whole, few delegations could claim such nearly perfect ethnic or age balance. Delegate Owanah Anderson of Wichita Falls had presided over the Texas state meeting last June with a tomahawk. First names like Lupe, Pokey, Melva, Nikki, Hortense, and Hermine only hint at the diversity of backgrounds confirmed in last names like Glossbrenner, Tobolowsky, Rodriguez, and McKool. The delegation had its well-known faces, such as Nikki Van Hightower, Houston's former women's advocate under Mayor Fred Hofheinz; Eddie Bernice Johnson, regional head of HEW; and Sarah Weddington, now general counsel to the Department of Agriculture, who gave the seconding speech at the convention for the controversial abortion resolution. But within the delegation of 58 Texas women, there were politically astute women that I had never seen before.

I followed Irma Rangel, the first Mexican American woman elected to the Texas Legislature, to a Hispanic caucus one evening between two sessions. Irma has been a teacher in South Texas, South America, and California. Since graduating from Saint Mary's law school in San Antonio in 1969, she has served as a law clerk and assistant district attorney and now maintains a private practice in her hometown of Kingsville. With no education, her father rose from farm worker to barber's apprentice to barbershop owner and finally to landowner and entrepreneur. Her mother also began as a field worker, but by the late forties she was running her own dress shop. Irma is one of three successful daughters. One is a pharmacist, the other a teacher. She told me, "Because my mother and father had to work so hard as equal partners to get where they did, I guess my mother was always 'libbed up.' We grew up so accustomed to racial discrimination, I don't think it ever occurred to us to think that we were also being discriminated against as women." Although raised a Catholic, during her stint as assistant DA in Corpus Christi, Irma saw enough suicides and illegal abortions resulting from pregnancies caused by incest and rape to have no qualms about her affirmative stand on the abortion resolution at the conference. Irma's decision to run for the Legislature was prompted in part by the Women in Public Life Conference at the Lyndon B. Johnson School of Public Affairs two years ago. "I saw that there were plenty of black women moving into elected positions, but no Chicanas."

The Hispanic caucus, composed of Cuban, Puerto Rican, and Mexican women, was exasperating to Irma. The room was crowded and noisy. Some of the delegates did not speak English, so the parliamentary process was slowed by the need for occasional translation. "¡Hermanas, por favor!" shouted the presiding delegate in an effort to restore order. Although these women all wear the *Viva la Mujer* button of Hispanic solidarity, I was amazed at the rivalry and difference of opinion within a group that most Anglos would presume monolithic. Adopting the blanket term "Hispanic" had consumed the better part of one caucus. "Get to the point, Graziela!" yelled one delegate as a Puerto Rican woman basked in the attention afforded her by chair recognition. "We have one hour to come up with an amendment that meets all of our needs. I want to get goddammit down to work."

Irma worries that many of her *hermanas* know so little about parliamentary procedure. "If they would just read the rules," she says, but then mellows. "Most of them have so little time to read anything and at least here they can learn by doing." I had seen presidential assistant Midge Costanza at a previous Hispanic caucus. When asked if she thought the Latino representation at the convention was adequate, she candidly replied, "No, I don't, but what is happening here today—women becoming vocal and organizing—assures that it will never happen again."

I had breakfast with another member of the Texas delegation, Arthur Beatrice Williams of Wichita Falls, who in 1970 was both the first black and the first woman to be a bailiff in Texas. Once a domestic worker, she is currently the secretary to the Wichita County judge. Arthur Bea's main concern at this conference is child care. Having raised a child without a father, she knows the hardships and needs of working mothers. She is a self-assured and able spokeswoman for her causes. "I don't know what it is about me, but I know that people listen to me in Wichita Falls."

When I first talked with Arthur Bea, she was unsure how she would vote on the issues of lesbian rights ("sexual preference") and abortion ("reproductive freedom"). When I talked to her later, she admitted she surprised herself on both of them. "I was tempted to vote against the lesbian resolution, but then I said to myself, 'Arthur Bea Williams, look at your black face. If these women say they've been discriminated against for something they were born with, how can you vote against it?'" On the abortion resolution, she said, "I voted against it. Oh, abortion isn't what bothers me. It's the government paying for it that I don't want. I call it 'sin tax.' I think the decision to have an abortion is a heavy enough burden without asking somebody else to pay for it. But my main concern is that it will siphon money from other medical care. I just have a soft spot for children and old people. I want them cared for first." When I asked Arthur Bea about the value of the conference for her, she said that she'd made some friends and allies. As a member of the mayor's committee on the status of women in Wichita Falls, she hopes with the help of these new contacts to get a rape crisis center established.

The face of a third Texas delegate, Travis County Commissioner Ann Richards, may be well known in Austin, but I had not met her before the Houston conference. On Saturday, Ann would second the primary resolution of the conference, the Equal Rights Amendment. In her seconding speech, she said, "I rise in behalf of my two daughters who cannot find women in the history texts of this country. I also rise in behalf of the men, the contemporary men of America in thirty-five states who had the guts to stand up and ratify this Equal Rights Amendment. And I also rise on behalf of the men who are keeping our children tonight so we could be here." She later told me that she called her husband after the speech. "I told him I had done a little takeoff on the Abigail Adams famous entreaty to her husband, 'Remember the ladies.' I said, 'Remember the men.'" "That's nice," her husband replied, "I just watched Phyllis Schlafly do the same thing on television tonight. She thanked her husband for letting her come to Houston."

Ann Richards is said to look a little like Betty Grable or Mitzi Gaynor but she also has a sort of Texas frontier woman swagger. Actually, she reminds me of Barbara Stanwyck in *The Big Valley* ordering rustlers off the place. When she belted out "guts," every journalist within earshot scrambled for her pen and asked, "Who is that woman?" Ann has been active in politics since her days as a Young Democrat on the University of Texas campus. When she and her husband lived in Dallas she vented some of her frustration at being kept out of the mainstream of politics ("Alphabetizing cards was about as far as we got in those days") by writing and producing satirical skits with the North Dallas Democratic Women, her first successes as a fund raiser. When the Richardses moved to Austin, Sarah Weddington called. "She was planning to run for the Legislature but was a political neophyte. It was perfect timing. I needed something, and she needed something I could offer." Ann ran several successful campaigns, for Sarah and other people, before launching what I've been told was a textbook campaign against a long-time incumbent for her present position as county commissioner.

I asked her about women politicians and how they differed from the men she had worked for before. "Well," she said, "women tend to be more receptive to instruction, they don't have to be the boss, they are more interested in new approaches, and they are hesitant to attack." The combination, according to Ann, is a very good package. "Most good women candidates come across as honest, sure of themselves on issues, but also as gentle and as people you can work with." Having observed the Texas delegation in a caucus the night before, I was curious as to where those women gained their political expertise. It seemed to me that a lot of the women in the delegation were club women, business and professional women, members of the American Association of University Women, or perhaps past PTA presidents. She agreed that was true in the beginning, but now Texas women were becoming a political force in their own right. "We looked on our early victories as miracles or accidents, but our subsequent victories have been very calculated, planned, and are not accidents at all. We know now that it takes skill and very hard work."

Ann is the mother of two sons and two daughters. She says that her feminist concerns are in part the result of her position as a daughter and a mother. Her mother belonged to the Rosie the Riveter generation, women who learned during World War II that they could do men's work. "Those women," said Ann, "just like the ones at this conference, did not go back to their homes the same."

But it isn't just what she inherited from her mother, it is also her concern about her own daughters that explains why she's here. Jill Ruckelshaus, the 1976 IWY presiding officer, had said earlier of her generation, "We were raised in the tradition of our grandmothers, but we are living in the tradition of our daughters." Ann agreed. "When my oldest girl brings home a paper from school saying that she can be on the drill team or the pom-pom squad only if her bust does not exceed a certain measurement or if she's not too tall, I am beginning to ask why."

Even before the first plenary sessions, Ann Richards clearly recognized that this conference would be a chance for women to demonstrate their political skill and discipline. She and many of the Texas delegates would work hard with the Pro Plan caucus dedicated to keeping the agenda moving at all costs. Seated so near the microphone, the Texas delegates knew well the power of the parliamentary phrase, "Madam chair, I move the question."

This National Women's Conference is, of course, unprecedented, but occasionally during the four days I had the feeling that in some small way I'd been there before. The American Legion Auxiliary will probably deplore this comparison, but sixteen years ago I was a delegate to Bluebonnet Girls State in Austin. Although the Girls State Conference was ostensibly designed to teach us the workings of state government, the majority of us haven't set foot in a caucus room since. At both conferences, the mock and the real, I remember being overwhelmed by the talents and energies of women. Absurdly, bathrooms were an issue at both conferences. Opponents of the ERA have repeatedly suggested that the ratification of the amendment will deny our rights to privacy in public bathrooms. At Bluebonnet Girls State, because our conference was held at the Texas School for the Blind, we were housed in dormitories that had open shower rooms and no doors on the toilet stalls. Sixteen years ago we never thought to question why our male counterparts at Lone Star Boys State were housed conveniently close to the Texas Capitol on the University of Texas campus, a campus on which many of them would later build political careers.

At both Bluebonnet Girls State and the National Women's Conference we trooped the colors, swayed to "God Bless America," talked about the greatness of our country, and listened to government officials, but unlike my mock convention of 1961, this time the listeners were from every possible female walk of life: homemakers and prostitutes, government officials and domestic workers, rural farm women and urban lesbians, experienced club women and women who had never stayed in a hotel or attended a meeting run by parliamentary procedure in their lives. The delegates to my mock convention were from the Valley, the Panhandle, and deep East Texas—a more diverse group than most states could muster—but at the National Women's Conference delegates were of every color and ethnic origin in the United States and its territories. Their concerns ranged from the Eskimo woman's dire dependency on whaling for subsistence to the feminist artist from Manhattan who wanted to know why "art" is what men do while "craft" is the term for the creative efforts of women and natives. And perhaps the big difference between this conference and the one I attended sixteen years ago is that the government officials and influential speakers this time around were all women.

The real nitty-gritty of this National Women's Conference was not about the destruction of the American family (although due to the late November timing of the conference, I suspect there were quite a few Thanksgiving turkeys that didn't get thawed) or abortion or lesbian rights—as Phyllis Schlafly told her followers—nor was it just a confused, disorderly women's wrestling match—as perhaps some of the television coverage implied. It was about women and power, and if every item on the agenda had failed, the impact on the women who participated would not be diminished. A black woman from Alabama could not go away untouched by Barbara Jordan's cadence, "We would not allow ourselves to be brainwashed by people who predict chaos and failure for us. Tell them they lie and move on." Nor would a Puerto Rican domestic worker who sat in a Latino caucus with presidential assistant Midge Costanza be quite the same when she picked up her broom on Tuesday. Young women found role models in women past sixty. At the very least we all had a few new names to drop. I met Sally Quinn of the *Washington Post*.

The impact of the conference will be felt in the organizational abilities and compromise skills that women acquired and demonstrated in the caucuses the television crews never saw. And the power boost for women will come not only from the passage of legislation that may emanate from this convention (Secretary of HEW Joe Califano has already appointed a task force to study the discrimination against women in Social Security). It will also, and perhaps principally, come from the gradual linking up across the country of "good old girls" as Ann Richards called them, the bright and potentially powerful women who know how to raise money and get grants, women who have perhaps heretofore only talked to each other on the telephone, but now have spent four days and a few sleepless nights face to face. ★

Who Runs Our Cities and Towns?

CHAPTER FIVE

Liberal Education, Paul Burka (March 77)
Up the Creek, Nicholas Lemann (September 79)
The People's Choice, John Bloom (June 79)
The Second Battle of the Alamo, Paul Burka (December 77)

LIBERAL EDUCATION
by Paul Burka

When Austin elected a "progressive" city council, some folks said the millennium had arrived. Turns out it's still a ways off.

With local elections only a few short weeks away, there is good news and bad news for the liberal majority on the Austin City Council. They have kept most of their campaign promises, compiling a solid record of achievements that has aroused little substantive opposition. In the process, they have helped unify a city that a few years ago threatened to become increasingly cleft along ideological lines. That, of course, is the good news. Now for the bad: folks in Austin seem united not *for* the council, but *against* them. From one end of the political spectrum to the other, Austinites seem disenchanted with—indeed, fed up with—the council, not so much for what they have done as for the way they have done it. How the first unabashedly liberal body ever to control a major Texas city managed to squander its political capital offers a lesson in politics and government that won't be found in any textbook.

To understand Austin politics today one has to go back two decades, before the baby boom hit the University of Texas, before the state bureaucracy became inflated, before Austin itself began the explosive growth that has seen its population almost double in the last twenty years. In those simpler times, politics was simpler too. The town was roughly divided into two camps: on one side were old families, established bankers, and downtown merchants who thought things were just fine the way they were; on the other were the hustlers —builders, building supply companies, land speculators, developers, aggressive new bankers—who wanted the city to grow and make them rich in the process. The old guard held the upper hand through most of the fifties, but their philosophical differences with the fast-money boys rarely flared into open warfare. They were differences of degree, not kind; both sides recognized that, except for the State, Austin was a one-industry town. Homebuilding and construction were the economic life blood of the community. Austin had to grow. The only issue was How Fast? So the requests for zoning changes were granted; the neighborhoods were converted to apartments; the buildings sprouted taller and taller, obscuring the Capitol; the subdivisions marched north and south; and the bulldozers began eating away at the hills.

The developers finally gained complete control of the city in the early sixties. One of their own was in the mayor's chair, an employee of the largest building supply company in town. The city planning commission overflowed with builders, who channeled the city's growth in directions that would benefit their holdings. Meanwhile UT doubled in size; soon it would almost double again. The Legislature created new state agencies like the Water Quality Board and expanded most of the old ones. Lyndon was in the White House and the virtues of the Texas Hill Country—and Austin—were on every front page. Jobs and people were everywhere: it was a builder's dream.

Control of the city nominally changed hands in 1967 when a moderately liberal council took office. But the issue of uncontrolled growth that would dominate the politics of the seventies was still only dimly understood in the sixties. The new council did take on the real estate interests, but on an entirely different battleground: an open housing ordinance that was overwhelmingly rejected in a citywide referendum. That fiasco, plus growing student unrest at UT, produced in 1969 one of the most unflinchingly conservative councils in Austin history. The basic direction of the city had never been challenged; the so-called "quality-of-life" issues that would gain prominence a few years later were never raised.

After repeated imbroglios with protesting students—one such incident ended with the council getting their wrists slapped by a federal judge—the archconservatives gave way in 1971 to a new council widely hailed as moderate. The mayor was a smooth-talking car dealer, banker, and land speculator named Roy Butler (now Austin's Coors beer distributor). It was the early sixties all over again; building and development interests were in complete control and the Austin boom seemed limitless. By Butler's second term, Austin ranked eighth in the country in the number of building permits issued—ahead of, among others, Chicago. But the new mayor soon had something to contend with his predecessors had not.

Austin had long held the reputation as the most liberal city in Texas (there weren't many other contenders), but its staunch Democratic loyalty and keen political awareness were often misread as liberalism. When eighteen-year-olds were given the vote, however, the myth suddenly became reality. In a single stroke Austin gained more than 30,000 potential new voters, and at least three-fourths of them could be counted on to cast their ballots in a bloc. The campus has since become more moderate, but those were the years of the environmental crisis, of bitterness and disillusion with government, of Richard Nixon. Added to blacks, browns, intellectuals connected with UT or state government, and what little organized labor there is in Austin, the students gave liberals a theoretical majority.

By the spring 1975 council elections,

120 WHO RUNS OUR CITIES AND TOWNS? Illustrated by Ben Sargent

the students had become the linchpin of the liberal coalition. Their leaders were far more politically sophisticated than the idealists who had led the student uprisings in the late sixties. At election time their organization turned out huge majorities in liberal boxes for most of the slate candidates, who had been carefully picked in a series of meetings with various elements of the coalition.

The resulting victory of five liberals (out of seven seats on the council) was widely interpreted as irrefutable evidence that Austin was now a liberal city. But another factor was at work as well. The students had revolutionized Austin politics not only by changing the numbers drastically, but also by striking a responsive chord in those longtime residents of Austin who had always looked upon their city as the closest thing to Paradise. The students were the first to raise the quality-of-life issues: the need for preserving Austin's past, its environment, its neighborhoods. The people who had already bought homes in the hills were ready to listen: they didn't want any more development out there that might spoil *their* view. The Butler council had too obviously cast its lot for unchecked growth and expansion. Now the pendulum was swinging back the other way. Perhaps sensing that his days were numbered, Butler opted not to run for reelection. When the ballots were counted, the only conservatives on the council were Betty Himmelblau, who split the student bloc by venturing onto a hostile campus and luring away female votes, and holdover councilman Lowell Lebermann, who had the dual advantage of a moderate political reputation and weak liberal opposition.

This was the new council majority:

• Mayor Jeff Friedman, young progressive, ambitious, and the sole liberal with previous council experience (as a maverick under Butler);

• Margret Hofmann, a German immigrant and committed environmentalist whose tree-saving campaign propelled her into the limelight;

• Emma Lou Linn, a psychology professor at St. Edward's University and a doctrinaire liberal;

• Jimmy Snell, a black activist from East Austin;

• John Trevino, part of a clique of young Mexican American politicians known locally as the "Brown Mafia."

A black, a brown, two women, and a young Jewish mayor: a balanced ticket, to be sure—almost *too* balanced. Austinites joked that they had the only city council in the country that complied with federal equal employment opportunity guidelines. The council was vulnerable to the charge that they had been picked by political bosses as expedient symbols rather than for any individual talents they might have. If things went well, that wouldn't matter, but if things didn't go well, this would not be a council that had a reservoir of good will to draw on. And almost from the start, things didn't go well.

It was the unhappy fate of the new council to inherit a number of thorny issues left over from the Butler years. They were the kind of problems seasoned politicians dread: short-range emotional issues that have little to do with the common weal but leave lingering bitterness in their wake. There was the matter of 19th Street, for example, which the Butler council had renamed Martin Luther King Jr. Boulevard—it is the main route through predominantly black East Austin. But it also runs for a short distance just south of UT, and white merchants there objected violently to the change. And there was the irksome matter of Mo-Pac, a new northwest expressway so named because it parallels the Missouri Pacific Railroad's main line. Upper-middle-class residents of West Austin pleaded with the council to shut off access to the expressway at three points; at stake, they said, was nothing less than the integrity of their neighborhoods—which was precisely what the new council was sworn to preserve.

Seasoned politicians, liberal or conservative, know there is only one way to deal with such issues: whatever you do, you've got to do it fast and get it behind you; don't let it fester and give people a chance to get still more emotionally involved. The council ignored this elementary political axiom time and again. In the case of Mo-Pac they sat through acrimonious public hearings, went to neighborhood meetings, hired consultants, and generally agonized for weeks on end. The decision was finally made for them when the Texas Highway Department announced that the city had no legal authority to close the ramps even if it wanted to. For the first time, but not for the last, the council had looked ridiculous.

The failure to deal decisively with emotional issues soon became a trademark of the new council. Previous councils had twice before submitted referendums on nuclear power; the last time Austin had gone nuclear by 700 votes when then-Councilman Friedman refused to take a stand. Later, as mayor, he decided the city should sell its share of the proposed project and voters got a chance to reconsider. This time the margin was three-to-one in favor of nuclear power.

Issue after issue, the council muffed its opportunities. One of the worst blunders came on a vote to permit city workers to participate in a dues check-off plan—a necessary prerequisite to unionizing public employees. All the liberals were committed to it, though there is no doubt the idea was anathema to the city as a whole. (The proposal came up during New York's fiscal crisis, for which unions got a heavy share of the blame.) The worst thing that could happen was for the fight to become long and protracted, filling the newspapers for weeks. But that's exactly what did happen, because Friedman, Linn, and Trevino decided to back one of the two unions that were vying to represent the workers. The liberals looked as though they were making a payoff, and at the same time they handed the competing union a ready-made issue: the council was, after all, management. In the end, the favored union lost and the liberals had once more risked their political necks for a cause that was doomed from the start.

If anything, the council handled people worse than they handled issues. Systematically they antagonized group after group in the city. They browbeat ordinary citizens who came to council meetings, ignored the work of special commissions they had appointed, and refused to consult with their strongest supporters. A case in point was the hiring of a new police chief. It was the issue most crucial to the black community, one that called for close contact between the council, particularly Friedman, and black leaders. Instead, the mayor avoided them, failing to show up at their meetings or even to notify them that he wouldn't be coming. Rumors spread that Friedman favored promoting someone from the ranks—a course blacks strenuously opposed. The city ended up hiring the person everyone agreed was the ideal candidate for the job, former Dallas police chief Frank Dyson, but by that time relations between the mayor and the black community ranged from chilly to hostile. Friedman and Mayor Pro-Tem Snell hardly spoke for weeks.

Friedman is a smart, hardworking man and an excellent rhetorician, but he is also someone who doesn't really enjoy talking with—as distinguished from *to*—people. He blusters frequently and launches into speeches, even in one-to-one conversations. People find him hard to talk to and harder to know; many misinterpret his aloof and withdrawn nature as a sign of arrogance. The new mayor had been a first-rate adversary on the Butler council; he felt he knew what was wrong with the city and didn't lack for ideas about how to correct it, but now he was a legislator thrust in an administrator's role, and it was a part he did not play easily or particularly well.

Meanwhile, his fellow liberals on the council weren't helping matters any—particularly Margret Hofmann. "Probably more effort was expended on her election than any candidate in the history of the coalition," grouses one liberal strategist. "And the first thing she did was publicly disavow that we elected her. She truly believes that she was elected by virtue of the people's desire for Margret Hofmann to serve." Of all the council members, she seems to have the least perception of politics. ("She's in over her head," sighs a liberal leader who didn't want to be quoted by name. "She's a good person, she means well, she has integrity; she's the kind of person who would have made a good council member thirty years ago.") Hofmann couldn't be counted on, ever: she repudiated a campaign promise to support single-member districts; she helped string out the controversial unionization issue; and her vote (along with Trevino's) torpedoed Friedman's effort to give city workers an across-the-board pay raise instead of a percentage raise.

Emma Lou Linn had the exact opposite problem: she was nothing if not predictable. Travis County Democratic Chairman Ken Wendler, the city's leading moderate, calls Linn "an absolute disaster. She will not confer—you cannot discuss an issue with her." Linn was rigid, uncompromising, and flamboyant—a pure ideologue.

(Snell, by contrast, was no less liberal, but whereas Linn voted and talked, Snell just voted—and made virtually no enemies.)

The list of the alienated could go on and on; it includes just about everyone who has come in contact with the council. The students grew disenchanted when the council backed a $162 million bond issue that included huge outlays for new water and sewer facilities—which, students feared, were stepping stones to more growth. A more politically adept council might have defused student objections, but this one never learned to deal with opposition that way. By the time the bond election campaign gained momentum, students were determined, in the words of one liberal leader, "to teach those sons of bitches a lesson." The bond issue lost—another defeat for the council, another vote of no confidence.

Defenders of the council—and there remain many—argue that their record outweighs their political shortcomings. Certainly the record is an impressive one. Regardless of what happens in this year's elections, it is indisputable that the council has had a lasting effect on Austin politics.

In the area of human relations, for example, the council has brought minorities into the government in unprecedented numbers—not just as employees, but as appointees to city boards and commissions. For the first time within memory, a council is spending bond money in East Austin as fast as in West Austin. The council can claim credit for a popular police chief, a public accommodations ordinance, an equal employment opportunity ordinance, and a city budget for social services that is twice as generous as the Butler council's.

In the touchy area of growth and environment—probably the main reason the liberal majority was elected two years ago —the council has repealed a complicated scheme through which the city actually subsidized development. Under the old system the city built and paid for large mains and refunded to developers the cost of smaller pipes that hooked up with the city's facilities. Now the system is designed so that developers must recoup their costs from home buyers, not city taxpayers. The council also passed a billboard and sign ordinance, adopted a Lake Austin master plan, and passed a tree ordinance: a good environmental record.

Finally, there was an assortment of actions which can best be described as "good government" reforms: a tough lobby registration law, a comprehensive financial disclosure law, and more equitable valuations of homes (wealthy West Austin had been grossly undervalued).

Just about all of the council's changes are here to stay, mainly because no one really opposes them. Though he is doing everything in his power to beat Linn and Hofmann this time, Ken Wendler admits, "I'd have voted with the majority at least eighty per cent of the time, and on the rest I'd say the council has gone just an inch too far." One of the young businessmen who is leading a conservative resurgence says, "No one issue is a problem. My objection is that they don't know how to run a city."

How to run a city: even more than how to deal with people, this was the dilemma the council never solved. Austin operates under a council-manager form of government. Theoretically the council's function is to set policy and hire a city manager to carry it out. In practice things rarely work that way. As we have seen, councils can't always agree on policy. In any event, there is no way a part-time council with a staff of seven can cope with a full-time bureaucracy with a staff of 6700. Ultimately the council must rely on the figures and information it receives from department heads. And in Austin, at least, that information is not always reliable.

It is commonly accepted around city hall that the administration misled the council about the need for the $162 million in bonds that went down to defeat. The council was given inflated need projections justifying new water and sewer systems; what's more, the capacity of the proposed systems was underestimated. In short, the city would have built more facilities than necessary to meet a need that didn't exist. Council members had so little confidence in data supplied by the electric department to a special commission studying utility rates that they hired a consultant: sure enough, the information was faulty. Perhaps coincidentally, the electric department had shown little enthusiasm for the council's ideas about rate reform.

Very well, one might say: why didn't the council just fire the heads of the offending departments? There's the catch. In a council-manager government, council members aren't even supposed to *talk* to department heads, much less *fire* them. Only the city manager has the power to hire and fire. The council's only recourse is to take their complaints to the city manager, and if he won't act, they can always fire him.

This may sound like horse-and-buggy government, but the fact is that not long ago the council-manager system was viewed as a reform; indeed, in some quarters (the League of Women Voters being one) it still is. Its purpose was to get politics out of government, and it does do that. The only trouble is that in a modern city, the two can't really be separated. The council-manager form is perfect for a compact city of, say, 150,000 or less whose population is basically homogeneous—just what Austin was twenty or thirty years ago. It is based upon the premise that government primarily involves housekeeping functions: keeping the traffic flowing, the garbage collected, and the water pipes from leaking. It is an anachronism in a big city; no doubt that is why Dallas is said to be the largest city in the world with a council-manager government.

It has been suggested only half jokingly that the council-manager system would be improved if the public elected the manager and he appointed the council, instead of the other way around. But setting aside theoretical disputes about what structure is best for Austin, practically speaking the council had two options when they took office: they could fire respected city manager Dan Davidson and replace him with someone whose views about the role of city government were more in line with their own; or they could ride herd on Davidson and his staff, forcing them to bend to the council's will. In fact, they did neither. With the sole exception of Betty Himmelblau on one issue—mismanagement of city-owned Brackenridge Hospital—there was no one on the council to confront the bureaucracy, to ask hard-nosed, penetrating questions. The council was full of ideas but low on toughness—a weakness bureaucrats instinctively know how to exploit. Liberals who dealt with the city were outraged that the council docilely submitted to what amounted to sabotage; conservatives were horrified at the thought of a bureaucracy out of control. Not only did the departments feed the council distorted information, but also they couldn't get their own houses in order. A conservative leader expresses amazement that the electric department, a major source of city revenue, doesn't even use a uniform accounting system. Transportation head Joe Ternus can't seem to get Austin's traffic lights synchronized; he also effectively scuttled a council project for a downtown trolley by announcing, after a trip to Europe, that no suitable streetcars could be found. One elected official who has worked with Ternus calls him "a walking Aggie joke." And though the council made great strides to improve emergency medical services, Brackenridge Hospital and its administrators have been under fire for months.

Meanwhile the council wrung its hands and bemoaned the city charter provision that forbids the council from communicating directly with department heads. "The charter be damned!" explodes one former Friedman admirer. "Do you think Roy Butler worried about the charter when he wanted something done? He'd get someone on the phone and put the fear of God in them. He ran this city the right way for the wrong side."

The immediate future for the liberal majority is a struggle for survival. Snell and Trevino, the two minority incumbents, are safe, but Hofmann, Linn, and Friedman will have to fight for their political lives. For awhile it looked like Friedman might escape a serious challenge while moderates and conservatives concentrated their fire on the fiery Linn and the ineffectual Hofmann. But at press time Friedman had two opponents and Roy Butler was leading an effort to find a third.

Even if the liberals lose (and it is far from certain that they will), the new council won't be anything like the archconservative group that followed Austin's last liberal council a decade ago. The political spectrum in Austin has shifted perceptibly to the left, and nothing could be more indicative of that fact than the slate moderates and conservatives have recruited to oppose incumbents and fill the seat Lebermann is giving up. It is sprinkled with people who would have been considered moderates, maybe even liberals, by the standards of the Butler years. There is a passing of the torch underway in the conservative camp; the developer-builder types still kick in the money, but they have been supplanted by a coalition of young businessmen, lawyers, bankers, retailers, and managers at Austin's "soft" industries like IBM and Texas Instruments. The new breed of conservatives is sensitive, if not committed, to issues like environmental quality and revitalization of the central city. But where they most differ from their predecessors is their attitude toward minorities. Unlike the conservatives of the fifties and sixties, they have no philosophical objections to talking with blacks and Mexican Americans—or, for that matter, to spending a few tax dollars in East Austin to pave the streets and operate day care centers. They are far more interested in taming the city bureaucracy and establishing a stable political climate for business. And, of course, they'd like to know that land management—zoning, growth—is consistent with their interests.

The liberal coalition, meanwhile, is showing signs of stress. No one knows whether the campus machine can crank out the vote as it did two years ago; many of its old operators have left the city, and in any case, more than half the undergraduates weren't around for the last election. Students seem to be getting more conservative (the central UT boxes supported Gerald Ford over Jimmy Carter) and, equally important, apathetic. Then there is the matter of how long and how faithfully blacks and Mexican Americans will support white liberals. Minority politicians have many higher priorities than the quality-of-life issues white liberals hold so dear. For blacks and Mexican Americans, growth and heavy industry suggest not Paradise Lost but jobs. "Clean air," snorts one black politician. "Don't talk to me about clean air. We've lived next to the dump and the sewer and the rendering plant all our lives."

If the growth issue is threatening the alliance between white liberals and minorities, it is also starting to cause a split among white liberals themselves. An increasing number are beginning to believe that growth is one of those difficult problems that defies political solutions. Certainly the present council has tried: a drive around the periphery of Austin reveals open fields, broken only by an occasional trailer park or junkyard. The stream of subdivisions appears to have been dammed. But this is only an illusion. Beyond the city's extraterritorial jurisdiction, subdivisions are springing up as fast as ever. They have jumped over the undeveloped doughnut, toward Round Rock to the north, past Anderson Mill to the northwest, Buda to the south. Many of these homeowners work in Austin and use city facilities but pay no taxes. Some left the city because of white flight and high utilities, but many came to Austin because there are jobs to be had, and there was simply no new housing closer. The irony is that the most anti-growth council in Austin history may have done more to bring about urban sprawl than did any of the pro-developer councils that preceded it. Over 75 per cent of the homes built in the Austin metropolitan area last year were outside the city's extraterritorial jurisdiction.

Such ironies are familiar by now. The liberals on the councils cut their political teeth in the McCarthy-McGovern years. They came to office believing in openness and discussions and consultations and commissions, but they found that democracy and government don't always mix. The ticket that was supposed to be so representative of all segments of the community rarely exhibited any understanding of people. In the end, the failures of the most liberal, most ideological city council in Texas were not their policies, but their politics. ★

Politics

by Nicholas Lemann

Drains are for sewers, not creeks.

UP THE CREEK

Barton Creek—to many a symbol of Austin's easygoing life—is in the hands of eager-beaver developers and a dawdling city government.

One day in June, Ellie Rucker, the popular consumer-advice columnist for the *Austin American-Statesman*, printed a letter from a lady in Wisconsin who said she was thinking of moving to Austin but wanted to know first about "costs, insects, scorpions, or rattlesnakes, and other problems" she had heard about. Rucker told her that she should be sure to stay away, because Austin is full of not only scorpions and rattlesnakes, but also ticks, chiggers, alligators, coral snakes, roaches, and many other unpleasantries. "We have sky-high utility bills," Rucker wrote, "too many developers, too many bridges under construction, and enough people."

That column loosed a flood of mail to the *Statesman,* all of it, aside from a prissy rejoinder from the chamber of commerce, wildly enthusiastic. Readers called Rucker witty, brilliant, and courageous; they nominated her for mayor, city manager, and editor of the *Statesman*; and they bitterly decried what they saw as the fast-proceeding decline and fall of Austin. "May your detractors be banished to Houston," one man wrote, "where they can become rich beyond the dreams of avarice and wallow in the quagmire of overcrowded humanity."

Austin is the Texas city that people find it easiest to fall in love with, and for reasons that would make a Houston or Dallas booster blanch. When the case for Austin is made (as it is to the point of obsession by its residents), it's made on the basis of the city's physical beauty and its easy, pleasant pace. Words like dynamic, new, and big, which spring naturally to the lips of people in Houston and Dallas, are seldom heard in Austin.

Meanwhile, however, Austin is booming every bit as much as its larger sisters. Because of its location, its comparatively low cost of living, and, indeed, its pleasantness, it has become a mecca for light industry, and its population is supposed to increase by about 35 per cent in the next dozen years. This prospect greatly disturbs much of the local citizenry, and Austin has become a hotbed of that most un-Texan of civic sentiments: opposition to growth. When the Michelin Tire Corporation put off its plans to build a new plant on the north side of town this summer, there were joyful letters in the *Statesman*. When the American Cities Corporation announced plans to pull down 48 acres of old and mostly seedy

Austin's cliff-hanger: will all of Barton Creek become an apartment alley?

124 WHO RUNS OUR CITIES AND TOWNS?

Photography by Jeff Rowe

buildings downtown and replace them with a "revitalization" package of offices, hotels, and apartments, there were groans all over town—so many, in fact, that the project now appears to be dying. Lots of people in Austin don't want their city to be like Houston and Dallas. They don't want any ladies from Wisconsin moving to town. They think it's time to pull up the ladder.

The particular issue that has most engaged these general passions is the development of the area around Barton Creek, which rises in the Hill Country south and west of Austin and winds its way down to Zilker Park and the Barton Springs swimming pool. The pool is the universal symbol of what there is to love about Austin. (See "Barton Springs Eternal," TM, August 1978.) It's an eighth of a mile long, fed by cool natural springs and banked with shady lawns, a democratic summertime hangout for students, hippies, lawyers, bankers, housewives, little kids—in short, everybody in town. If anything should happen to Barton's, the feeling is, something precious will have been irretrievably lost to Austin.

To the untrained eye, the pool still looks wonderfully clean and fresh, although true aficionados say the water is just a bit cloudier than it was five or ten years ago. But it's obvious to everyone that the environs of the pool have become a hot development area. In 1972 a former Kansas state legislator named Sid Jagger, who had come to Austin a decade earlier and gotten into the real estate business, built an apartment complex called Wind Ridge on the bluffs overlooking Barton Creek. He set off a small boom, and now there are 1300 apartment units either built or planned in the creek's watershed just above Zilker Park. The threat these developments pose to the pool is partly visual and partly environmental. Although the pool is fed not by the creek but by an underground river called the Edwards Aquifer, the creek and the aquifer join forces at several points upstream. So if the creek is polluted, which in itself would be unfortunate, it might also pollute the pool.

Most residents of Austin think that development in the Barton Creek watershed should be severely restricted or stopped entirely. The developers naturally don't want that, and they say that if they own land they ought to be able to build on it.

That puts the ball in the city's court—its job is to balance the preservation of the creek against the property rights of the developers. The city has botched it magnificently. It could have come up with some plan to restrict development. It has not. It could have bought up land in the watershed—for four years it has even had money put in its coffers by the voters and the city council to do just that. It has not. The government of Austin has, in other words, so far completely failed to preserve the city's best natural resource.

To its credit, the city has temporarily (but not permanently) stopped a proposed bridge over the creek and turned down shopping-center zoning on one plot of land. But, on the other hand, besides not mounting any overall effort to protect the creek, the city has given the developers a long string of victories. It has okayed the placement of a sewer line right beside the creek, and the building of a million-square-foot shopping mall a little way upstream on land Jagger sold to an Indianapolis developer. The city is also on the verge of approving rezoning that would permit development of a ten-acre plot very near the pool owned by the Knights of Columbus.* The city has allowed substantial development to take place in the watershed; at several points along the creek, concrete gullies collect the water that runs through the streets and gutters of the subdivisions and direct it into the creek. In July the city council passed a moratorium on new zoning and sewer hookups in the watershed within the city limits, but this was an act with little practical effect since those who already have zoning and sewer permits are allowed to go ahead and build.* On an issue where even a lot of pro-growthers want to control growth, growth has won resoundingly.

Five miles or so upstream from the Barton Springs Pool, the Barton Creek watershed is impressively beautiful and wild. The creek is shallow and clear, with occasional spectacular limestone cliffs rising up on one side or another. About four miles from town, two bridges cross the creek at the site of a huge development called Lost Creek. On the east bank is the Lost Creek Country Club, with a golf course right on the creek's edge; on the west bank are expensive houses and newly bulldozed roads, an unpleasant jolt to the eye after the preceding wilderness.

Downstream from Lost Creek the creek is undeveloped again for a couple of miles, and runs a little muddier through empty private land. At a few places along the way there are small waterfalls and swimming holes. Two miles from the pool a highway called Loop 360 passes over the creek, right near the future route of the extension of the MoPac freeway and the site of the new shopping mall. Just past Loop 360 there is a sign announcing the beginning of the City of Austin's Barton Creek Greenbelt.

On the day I walked down the creek the first thing I saw after the greenbelt sign was a big yellow bulldozer sitting

*At press time, the Knights of Columbus withdrew their request to rezone, and the city council extended the moratorium to slow down some growth, but ten major developments in the watershed were not affected by the extension.

squarely in the middle of the creek bed, which was dry at that point. Once I got around a bend and out of hearing range of some pneumatic jackhammers that were chugging away nearby, I felt I had returned, more or less, to the bosom of nature. I came across a few reminders of civilization: a rusted-out car chassis, a washing machine full of bullet holes, a rubber dildo strapped to a tree, a boulder on which the name of a fraternity had been painted, even two naked men in passionate embrace. Occasionally an apartment complex or a fancy house with picture windows would peek over the edge of the cliffs fifty feet above me. Down near the pool, some hippies were taking the air next to a swimming hole. But for the most part I didn't see anybody, and the cliffs were pretty and the woods untouched, and for a three-hour walk near the middle of a city that's saying a lot.

In 1975 the voters provided $875,000 in bond money that the city council earmarked for buying up and therefore protecting some of this land. (Later $725,000 more was added.) At the time the talk was that the city could buy a belt of land all the way up to Lost Creek. But four years later, the city has spent only $75,000 of the money, and bought only 8.4 acres, while in the meantime land prices have skyrocketed and the city's purchasing power correspondingly plummeted. At current rates the remaining bond money would buy, at the outside, 100 acres, which is less than a sixth of a square mile. Although there's talk of another bond election in November to finance more land-buying, for all practical purposes the opportunity for the city to buy up a significant amount of the creek for a park no longer exists.

City officials say the land-buying has gone slowly because the creekbed is difficult to survey, negotiations with landowners are delicate, appraisals take time, and the parks department is understaffed. All that may be true, but the buying of land was clearly at the bottom of the city staff's list of priorities. The effort made has just not been impressive.

In 1976, realizing that it was time to size up what was happening to the creek, the council ordered a $59,800 environmental study of the entire watershed, 125 square miles. The study, by Espey, Huston, and Associates, wasn't completed and delivered until three years later, in June of this year, and it concluded what environmentalists have said all along: that "there is serious hazard to the [Zilker] park area if runoff from upstream developments is not strictly controlled." Now the city government is going to study the study in order to decide what to do, a procedure unlikely, given past performance, to be very speedy.

Mindful of the danger to the pool, the

WHO RUNS OUR CITIES AND TOWNS? 125

city spent $300,000 in 1975 to construct a bypass for the creek. The idea was to prevent the creek from filling up the pool with silted-up (not to say polluted) water after every heavy rain, by building a culvert next to the pool and directing the creek through it. Now, in normal times, the creek runs right up to the pool, then into the culvert, then emerges aboveground again past the end of the pool. But after a heavy rain, the creek still sometimes floods the bypass and fills the pool with silted-up water—not as often as before, but often enough to mean that the whole project was less than completely successful.

During the period of these good-hearted but half-baked attempts to preserve the pool and the creek, the city council allowed a group of developers led by Jagger to build, at their own expense, a sewage lift station to service the new developments in the watershed. This they did with a speed and skill far greater than the city's, putting the station under the Barton Springs parking lot. Then the developers asked Curtis Johnson, the director of the city's water and wastewater department, and several other officials if it would be okay for them to install new equipment that would double the capacity of the lift station, paving the way for more development. Johnson and company said fine, go ahead—without bothering to ask the city council, which should have made the decision. Even Johnson's boss, city manager Dan Davidson, says he didn't find out about it until more than a year later.

To the conspiracy-minded, all this would indicate that the city has nefariously plotted to let building in the watershed proceed at full steam while at the same time deliberately screwing up any of its assigned tasks that would slow down development activity in the area. Even to the non-conspiracy-minded it might seem odd that the Austin government, so good at delivering basic services like water and roads and emergency medical services and police, would be so bad at buying land and getting studies delivered. Davidson, after all, is widely regarded as an efficient, professional administrator.

Not being conspiracy-minded myself, I think the answer to the riddle lies in the nature of Austin politics. To oversimplify a little, most city governments have two jobs: to provide services and to determine through zoning and sewer-building how land will be used. The first of these tasks is completely non-controversial, a matter of efficiency. Everybody wants good services. Everybody will look kindly on a city government that provides them and unkindly on one that doesn't. But governing the use of land requires making decisions between competing interests, resolving often bitter disputes, making policy. Austin has a weak-mayor, strong-manager system of government that emphasizes professional staff over elected politicians, and therefore technical proficiency over policymaking. That's one reason why Austin can make things work but can't firmly decide between the wishes of various constituencies on the direction in which the city should move.

The constituency in favor of growth is the group that has traditionally run Austin—bankers, lawyers, entrepreneurs, and, most of all, people in the real estate business. These people have a personal stake in the increasing population and prosperity of the city. Because the decisions of the city council and staff are likely to affect their lives more directly than anyone else's in town, they stay in touch with their local government. Much of the staying in touch is just the day-to-day contact with city officials that is a fact of life for anyone in a business like building or engineering, but it also involves providing political support. By far the biggest campaign contributors in this year's Austin elections were Bill Milburn, John Wooley, and Gary Bradley, all developers, all with some holdings in the Barton Creek watershed. (Milburn and his wife spread $4000 among five candidates, as did Wooley and Bradley, who are partners.) Among the environmentalists, Norman and Betty Brown, leaders of the save-Barton-Creek fight, were almost alone in giving at all, and they gave only paltry $25 contributions to two candidates. Members of the council know that when it comes time to run for reelection, it will be the pro-growth crowd that pays the bills, and this may help explain its failure to ride herd on the city staff about Barton Creek.

Pro-growth people run most cities, of course, and in Texas they reign unquestioned in Dallas and would in Houston, too, if that city would make it worth their while to take an interest in city government by instituting zoning laws. What makes Austin different is that it has a large population that has no personal stake in growth. These are not blacks and Mexican Americans, who tend to be for growth because they're for jobs and upward mobility. The anti-growthers are usually white and middle-class. Many of them are employees of the state government and the University of Texas, people whose economic fortunes are tied to the public payroll, not the local economy, and who hence have nothing to gain from growth. Some of them are students, ex-students, hippies, craftspeople, even lawyers and doctors—people who have come to Austin because they've decided, in pursuit of a pleasant life, to be less personally ambitious than they could be, and who want the city to make the same decision. In Dallas or Houston the average Joe in the street probably feels that his city's boom is going to help him personally; in Austin the average Joe probably feels that the boom is going to make his life more harried and uncomfortable.

The influence of the anti-growth constituency on city politics is sporadic. When it gets fired up about something and either votes or seems likely to vote, it has as much power as the pro-growth people. On an issue like Barton Creek, even generally pro-growth people have signed on in substantial numbers. But in the slack periods, the environmentalists go to sleep. Day in and day out, over the years, it's the businessmen and developers who maintain the strongest interest in city politics and who have the most power. Fired up in 1975, the anti-growth constituency, in coalition with the minorities, elected Mayor Jeff Friedman and a liberal council; quiescent again in 1977, it had very little influence in electing Mayor Carole McClellan and the current council. So while the council has its liberals, it has no reliable anti-growth votes. Of the liberals, John Trevino represents Mexican Americans and Jimmy Snell blacks. As a candidate, Richard Goodman encouraged the environmental constituency to think of him as one of their own, but now he is thinking of running for mayor, and if he does, he will need the developers and their money on his side, so he has been voting with them more and more.

Not only is the council divided in its loyalties and weak as Austin councils go, but it also has very little of the traditional source of power for government officials—patronage. Austin's government is set up so as to maximize continuity and technical proficiency in the city staff, and as a result the council presides over a manager appointed two mayors ago and a set of department heads far more loyal to him than to the council or the voters. It's as if President Carter presided over a Cabinet whose members had been appointed by Lyndon Johnson and who planned to be in Washington long after Carter was gone. There's little built-in incentive for the staff to satisfy the council's every whim.

The staff has some degree of natural bias toward development, for two reasons. First, like the members of the council, members of the staff are likely to be in near-daily touch with developers, and out of this develops a genuine empathy, perhaps edged with a sense that these are powerful people, the obstruction of whom might result in the loss of one's job. Second, it is in the interest of the city staff to see the city grow. Steady, outward-moving growth means regular annexation of new lands, and therefore an increasing tax base, and therefore a dependably increasing city budget. If, on the other hand, the city starts restricting land use, that ultimately means fewer taxpayers. If, God forbid, it were to place severe limits on development, that would mean people settling outside the city limits and paying their taxes to some other town government. If the city were to start taking over vast swatches of land by eminent domain, it would have to pay immense, budget-ruining sums of money for them. All of the natural budget-preserving impulses of bureaucrats work against their keeping Barton Creek undeveloped.

However, the movement to save the creek has by now struck fear into the hearts of the council. Every council member is on record as favoring preservation of the environment in the Barton Creek watershed, and every member voted for the moratorium. When an issue touches a nerve the way Barton Creek has, politicians respond. Even the developers, sensitive to the way the wind is blowing, have now fallen in love with the environment. Milburn says he is planning no new deals in the watershed. Wooley and Bradley let the head of the Austin Sierra Club use their office as his downtown base of operations. Herman Bennett and former lieutenant governor Ben Barnes, the big Brownwood homebuilders, have put the development of their 1467-acre tract in the watershed in the hands of young realtors who talk about keeping the land as beautiful as it is now. Sid Jagger is building a home and office for himself on the bluffs above the creek and otherwise turning his attention to building apartments in Houston and Dallas. He serves on the city planning commission, where he often votes pro-environmentalist, and he says that he is now "very frankly not proud" of his early apartment complexes above the creek.

As for the fate of the creek itself, the couple of miles nearest to Austin, lined with apartments already, will probably be developed even further—it's too late to stop that now. Further upstream, most likely there will be large home lots and the city will ease its curb-and-gutter requirements to reduce urban runoff, and the watershed will be a beautiful and expensive residential district, similar to Westlake Hills just east of the Barton Creek watershed. Politics and the resistance of the city staff to spending money being what they are, it's extremely unlikely that the city will ever acquire much more land in the watershed than a narrow greenbelt along the creek. The Barton Springs pool will probably stay relatively clean and fresh, if only because it's so beloved that whichever council let it get polluted would meet with a swift and merciless demise on the next election day.

Ellie Rucker, by the way, says she has been getting periodic calls from realtors. They want to get in touch with that lady in Wisconsin so that, alligators notwithstanding, they can sell her a house in Austin. ★

REPORTER
BY JOHN BLOOM

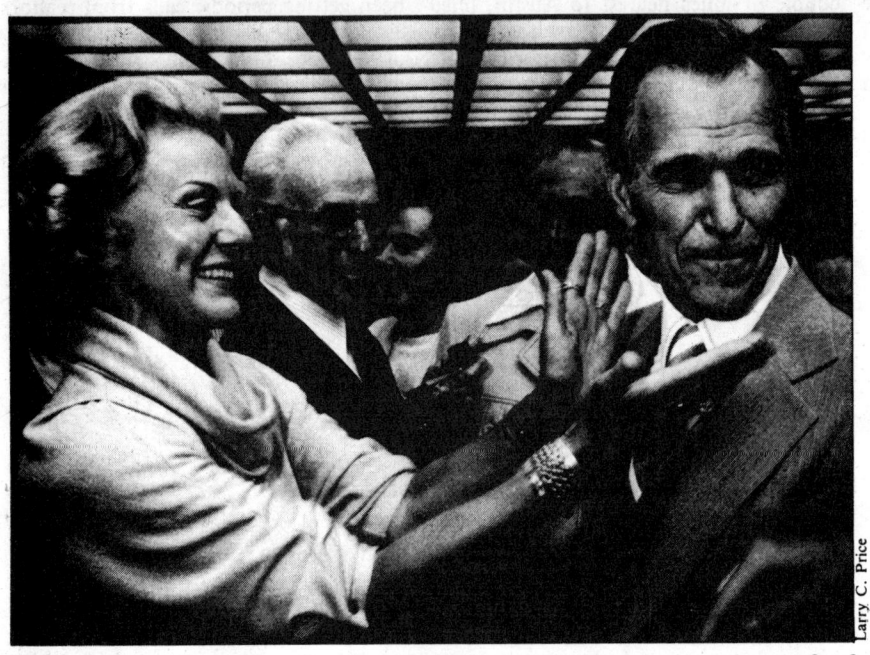

Woods (r.) with loyal fans after the runoff: doesn't this man have an honest face?

The People's Choice
A plumber takes Fort Worth by surprise.

The new mayor of Fort Worth, Woodie Woodrow Woods, is a plumber who owns a fleet of trucks painted with an image of Woody Woodpecker holding a pipe wrench. That alone should be enough fodder for the Dallas residents who still bother to joke about Cowtown, but there's more to come. Woods is also Fort Worth's first politician to run on the George Washington "I cannot tell a lie" ticket, the only mayor elected after a runoff in a two-man race, and a man so flustered by the presence of television cameras that he almost failed to deliver his victory speech because he couldn't find his glasses. One of his first pledges to the public was: "I'll take help from anybody that'll offer it to me." The people of Fort Worth have spoken.

The election of Woods to lead the state's fifth largest city was not, as you might expect, a statement of working-class solidarity. In fact, it's indicative of the way Fort Worth works that Woods, a plumber, was widely perceived as the candidate of the establishment upper class, while Hugh Parmer, the Yale-educated incumbent who owns a million-dollar marketing firm, was the candidate of the downtrodden masses. This campaign had less to do with class and power than with suspicion and petty hatreds. Parmer, the most activist mayor in Texas, tried to hold together the same alliance of blacks, Mexican Americans, and working-class whites that propelled him into office two years ago. But many thought him arrogant, abrasive, and too ambitious to lead a city so recently emerged from the feudal control of wealthy businessmen. Woods had a better alliance—working-class whites and rich whites—and used his plain-vanilla country-boy image to sneak up on Parmer and beat him, first by a mere 23 votes, then, after a complicated appeal, by 10,700 in the runoff. More than 50,000 people turned out to vote in the runoff, yet it's difficult to say how many of them voted for Woods, as opposed to voting *against* Parmer.

In the tangled web of Fort Worth politics, the first rule of statesmanship is to befriend your enemy's enemies. And Parmer's two-year term was littered with the resentment of city officials (twelve department heads resigned, many because they thought Parmer was eroding the city manager system and abusing his power), utility companies (he aggressively fought their rate increases), and politicians (he wrote and ramrodded through the council an ethics code tougher than that of any other Texas city). Plumbers, on the other hand, don't ordinarily make enemies unless the toilet overflows.

Woods ran a campaign so devoid of issues, or even rhetoric, that it can be summed up in three words: peace and harmony. A lean, middle-aged man who wears his hair like Porter Wagoner, Woods was raised on a farm, dropped out of school in the seventh grade to peddle the *Fort Worth Press* on street corners, and distinguished himself in World War II by installing the only indoor bathroom on Okinawa. Afterwards

Parmer makes his living running other pols' campaigns. But he lost his own.

128 WHO RUNS OUR CITIES AND TOWNS?

Lettering by Flat Lizard Graphics

he parlayed that expertise into a thriving plumbing contracting business and married the second of four wives. Asked to describe his politics, he is apt to say, "I'm an average American." His very lack of style may be his greatest political strength. In person, he is awkward, nervous, and shy, but somehow those qualities, when exhibited before 100,000 television viewers, come across as sincerity.

Hugh Parmer, on the other hand, is the very exemplar of style. At the age of 23 he was the Texas Legislature's youngest member (losing a second term because he supported the Civil Rights Act), and he has devoted the intervening sixteen years to perfecting the art of politics. His Parmer Marketing, Inc., grossed over $1 million last year, much of it made by running campaigns for candidates in other states. He employs pollsters, speech communications experts, and political strategists who are counted among the best in the business. He has trained his boyish visage to look directly into the TV camera at just the right moments; he is blessed (or afflicted) with a neon Jimmy Carter grin; and his evenly modulated voice is as reassuring as that of the six o'clock weatherman. As the city's first liberal mayor—a liberal being anyone who can sweep the minority precincts—he was anointed the populist reformer of the future after upsetting wealthy businessman Clif Overcash in 1977. The so-called Seventh Street Gang, Fort Worth's dwindling oligarchy of businessmen and political puppeteers, thought at first he was bent on making the city another Cleveland. But Parmer sought conciliation, notably by helping attract American Airlines to the city and developing a downtown revitalization plan.

If ever a man appeared to be in control of his career, Parmer did. Neither the business community nor the press nor the council believed he could be beaten, least of all by an unsophisticated amateur like Woods. Woods had served two terms on the council, but his first victory in 1975 was viewed as a fluke resulting from an alleged financial scandal linked to his opponent. What Parmer and everyone else failed to realize is that populists come in more than one shape. Parmer played Jerry Brown to Woods' Howard Jarvis, and this is the year of Jarvis. In fact, Woods is better at antigovernment crusading than Jarvis; in his four years on the council he became the very incarnation of ineffectual (and safe) leadership. By most accounts, Woods got worked up only twice—once when he proposed an antipornography ordinance ("Being a professional plumber, I recognize sewage when I see it") and again when he insisted that a new landfill be built in a middle-class East Side neighborhood. Ironically, Woods and Parmer were close voting allies before this latter issue, but when Parmer voted with the East Side residents their alliance began to fall apart.

When Woods decided to run for mayor, partly at the urging of Seventh Street, Parmer's most visible flaw—his ambition—became apparent. People in Fort Worth enjoy the delusion that there are politicians seeking power who don't really want to use it. Woods fit the image; Parmer didn't. Parmer aides, drunk with their 1977 victory and polls that showed them 22 per cent ahead of Woods two weeks before the election, talked frequently of congressional seats or even a governor's race in 1982. And when it came to the most significant crisis of Parmer's career—the frenetic weekend in April when Parmer seemed to have lost by a measly 23 votes—he suddenly looked like a desperate man. It was not so odd that he sent a crew of aides to city hall on Palm Sunday to recheck tally sheets (a perfectly legal exercise exaggerated into a "secret meeting" by the media), nor was it unexpected when Parmer challenged several votes as illegal and demanded a recount. But the mayor may have written his political death warrant on the day that has come to be called "Black Friday."

On Black Friday—the thirteenth—the council met to officially canvass the election returns. Normally this is a rubber-stamp ceremony, but in the closest race in Fort Worth history it was *the* crucial procedure. At issue were 30 write-in votes, some frivolous, some serious, 22 on hand, 8 others recorded on tally sheets but mysteriously missing. If all 30 were approved, then Woods would fall 3 votes short of a majority and a runoff would be necessary, but the city attorney advised the council to accept only 22.

Parmer, as the presiding officer at the canvass, announced that for ethical reasons he wouldn't vote on the matter. But the council wouldn't decide it for him. Four voted for 30 votes; four voted for 22. The vote was taken twice, and no votes were changed. Parmer waited for a long moment after the second vote, then gave his support to the 30-vote faction. "The chair votes aye," he said, and there were shouts of "dictator" in the chamber.

Parmer was virtually forced to vote. If

An angry crowd confronts Parmer on Black Friday—the day he forced a runoff.

Woods' first pledge to the people of Fort Worth: "I'll take help from anybody."

WHO RUNS OUR CITIES AND TOWNS? 129

he had not, the votes could not have been canvassed and no legal election would have occurred. Sooner or later a court would have forced Parmer to vote so that the election results could, at the very least, be challenged in court. No one knows exactly what went through Parmer's mind at the moment of truth—but he certainly would have been better off waiting for the courts to force his vote, or for a councilman to change his mind.

The resulting runoff began with Parmer's own polls showing him behind 68 to 32 per cent. That was too much to make up in two weeks, and Parmer was widely regarded as a frustrated opportunist at that point anyway. He lost by 10,700 votes, but it would have been much worse had the minority precincts not given him heavy support.

Woodie Woods is not the worst thing that could have happened to Fort Worth. As reporters constantly remind the public, he *is* an honest man, and the city will be more tranquil when he's in charge. But some wonder how the new mayor—who admits "I'm not much of a speaker"—can effectively promote Fort Worth's vision of equality with Dallas. For fifteen years the city consistently lost population and languished in the shadow of its sister to the east. Then came the opening of DFW Airport, the resurgence of downtown, and the wooing of companies like American Airlines to diversify the economy. Hugh Parmer was instrumental in most of those movements, but on election night 1979 he was beaten by a man he considered a throwback to frontier days. Thirty minutes after the polls closed, the landslide was apparent, but Parmer waited two hours to concede. By that time he appeared to be exhausted, and his words ran together like molasses. "I want to tell you something," he announced to the TV cameras, his eyes batting slowly. "Woodie Woods is my friend." He paused and rolled his eyes. "A loooong time. But to the people who have taken back our city, I just want to say: we'll be watching you!" Seventh Street lives again.★

132 WHO RUNS OUR CITIES AND TOWNS?

THE SECOND BATTLE OF THE ALAMO

by Paul Burka

When a group of Mexican Americans learned how to fight city hall, they touched off a revolution that may engulf all of San Antonio— themselves included.

The rain began late Wednesday afternoon, a slow soaking that lasted through the night. When he awoke on Thursday morning and saw that the rain was still falling, Andres Sarabia knew that it would be a bad day for San Antonio's heavily Mexican American West Side. Soon families on Inez Avenue, a few blocks south of Saint Mary's University, would be packing up their belongings and seeking refuge on higher ground; every time there was a big rain, the giant Mayberry drainage ditch behind their houses would turn into an immense thrashing lake. Muddy water lines on the houses ominously marked the extent of the most recent floods: two feet, sometimes three feet, high on the white frame exteriors.

Closer to town, Elmendorf Lake couldn't hold the water that was streaming into it, and neither could Apache Creek, which wound east and south from the lake toward the stockyards and packing houses southwest of downtown. Apache Creek was a killer; few rainstorms hit the city that the creek didn't claim a life or two, usually kids trapped on the side away from home by the sudden overflow.

Sarabia shook his head and allowed himself a short, bitter smile. People said this was an act of God; well, he knew better. There was just too much water with no place to go. Aside from a major thoroughfare or two, no street on the West Side had any drainage. You could drive for miles on curbless streets without seeing a storm drain. Even the huge ditches, some as wide as a river, that were supposed to carry off the water were choked by high grass, trees, and everything from grocery carts to old washing machines. None had even been cleared, much less channelized. Instead the water just seeped into the ground until the ground couldn't hold any more, then it flowed down the streets toward the drainage ditches until *they* couldn't hold any more, then it just stayed where it was, sometimes for days. Sarabia got into his car and began to pick his way through the flooded streets toward Kelly Air Force Base, where, like thousands of West Siders, he was employed as a civil service worker. Something had to be done. But what?

South of the stockyards Beatrice Gallego watched the river flow in front of her home and asked herself the same question. Actually that wasn't a river; it was Winnipeg Street, but heavy rains turned it into a muddy torrent. She thought about her oldest child, Terry, whose trophies for beauty contests and softball tournaments were all over the house, walking to school barefoot, ankle-deep in mud. Perhaps she should ask one of her women's clubs to send another petition to the city; maybe the city would do something this time.

The city would do something, all right, though not this time. On that rainy September day four years ago, Sarabia and Gallego couldn't have foreseen—they didn't even know each other —that they would help change the face of the city, not only physically but also politically; that they would become the leaders of the most unlikely political organization any Texas city has ever seen; or that they and their followers, most of whom earn less than $10,000 a year, would decide how the nation's tenth-largest city spends hundreds of millions of dollars.

Today their organization, known as COPS (Communities Organized for Public Service), is firmly established in San Antonio as a major political force —some would say *the* major political force. It has won victory after victory,

Illustrated by Tom Ballenger

WHO RUNS OUR CITIES AND TOWNS? 133

everything from large drainage projects and neighborhood parks to single-member city council districts, and yet its importance transcends any or all of these. For COPS has proved that you *can* fight city hall; it has challenged the basic assumption that pervades municipal government in every major American city: that ordinary citizens should leave things to experts, interest groups, and politicians. And, perhaps most important, it has unleashed San Antonio's majority (and politically long dormant) Mexican American population, a fact that has in turn panicked the Anglo North Side, where people speak openly of a city divided into two camps and a Second Battle of the Alamo for political control of the city.

For most of the last quarter century, the quest for power in San Antonio was a triangular struggle among the staid Anglo business and social establishment, an increasingly large and vocal group of fast-money Anglo land developers and other outsiders who wanted action and lots of it, and an ambitious Mexican political clique trying to shoulder its way into the game. (Local folks of both ethnic groups use Mexican as shorthand for Mexican American, just as Bostonians talk about the Irish, rather than Irish Americans.) Most of the time the old-money gentry held the upper hand, and the standard interpretation of San Antonio politics has been that this ruling class sought and exercised power out of a sense of noblesse oblige, while the fast-money boys sought power mainly to further their own interests. It didn't really matter why the Mexicans sought power because they never got any.

All that has changed now. The political arm of the ruling establishment, the Good Government League (GGL) is in ruins; the developers' hegemony, after four stormy years, has been shattered, and the Mexicans can no longer be ignored. It is anybody's ball game—literally anybody's; the rise of Andy Sarabia and Beatrice Gallego is proof enough of that. What a strange place for all of this to be happening: stuffy old San Antonio, the only city in the U.S. outside of New Orleans where social status is determined by men; a city where what club you belong to really *matters*, not just socially but politically and economically; a city that somehow missed out on the economic miracles that transformed Houston and Dallas—something its self-conscious citizens have never accepted and can't understand. And here it is, the first city in Texas to experience the ethnic political upheavals that will someday surely come to Houston, Dallas, and the rest: from noblesse oblige to the Second Battle of the Alamo in five years.

White Man's Burden

Asked if San Antonio is in fact headed for a Second Battle of the Alamo, a local Mexican activist snapped, "Yes—and this time we're going to win." They won the first time, of course, but no one, Anglo or Mexican, thinks of it that way. The Alamo is where it all started, this century and a half of ethnic tension that has gripped and shaped and at times even blessed San Antonio, giving it a unique character and depth no other Texas city can approach. Seldom has that tension been pushed far into the background: not in the years immediately following Texas independence (Mexican national troops intermittently occupied the town between 1836 and 1848); not by the time the railroad arrived in the 1870s (Germans began to control the town's banking and commerce and had replaced Mexicans as the town's dominant ethnic group); and certainly not in the first half of the twentieth century, when San Antonio neighborhoods were segregated by deed restrictions, San Antonio schools were segregated by tradition, and even downtown was tacitly segregated by Flores Street.

But seldom has the city been as divided as it is today. With the 1970 Census, Mexicans are again a majority of the population—a fact that by itself would be enough to make Anglos uneasy. Enrollment in the San Antonio Independent School District is 70 per cent Mexican and only 14 per cent Anglo; the school board is in Mexican hands and the eleven-member city council is headed that way. It has five Mexicans and one black, giving ethnic minorities a majority, and crucial votes often split right down the ethnic line—a development that delights some of the Mexican councilmen and dismays others. For the first time the central fact of San Antonio's existence—its ethnic diversity—is reflected in its politics, and though there is an almost universal sense that this is healthy, no one seems to know where to go from here. Like Europe before 1914, San Antonio appears headed for a war nobody wants and nobody thinks can be avoided. There is no ground swell for bridge builders, though one of the Mexican councilmen, University of Texas at San Antonio professor Henry Cisneros, is ideally suited for the role. For a time he seemed destined to be the city's first Mexican American mayor in over a century, but events may have overtaken him.

Even Anglos of goodwill—and there are many in San Antonio—are starting to be afflicted by the same kind of doubts that plagued sympathetic white Southerners during the civil rights movement. What is wrong with these aliens in our midst? Why can't they become "Americans?" Why can't Mexicans do what the Germans and the Irish and the Italians and the Jews did when they came to this country?

There is no one answer to such questions. Some say the discrimination has been greater; some point to the psychological burden of being a conquered people (going back long before the Alamo, all the way to Cortés); others talk of vast cultural differences, theorizing that the Protestant ethic so basic to the Texas character is missing from the Mexican's heritage. But at least part of the reason rests on something so basic as geography. When the Germans, the Italians, the Jews, came to America, they came in great waves—and they stopped. There was an ocean between them and the Old Country. They had to assimilate; there was nothing else to do.

The difference between the European and the Mexican is the difference between an ocean and a river. There was no single wave of Mexican immigration; rather it was a steady trickle that began in the early years of the twentieth century, when South Texas was cleared for agriculture and revolution broke out in Mexico. There were always more Mexicans arriving, more family to be cared for, and though the front end of the community disappeared into the melting pot, the back end never seemed to diminish. The constant tension between front and back tugged on the middle and never allowed it to break loose from its past.

Meanwhile most Mexicans had little to do with the political or economic life of San Antonio, mainly because they were too busy trying to survive; tens of thousands got through the Great Depression by shelling pecans for a few pennies a pound. Who had the money to throw away for a poll tax?

A few Mexicans, though, were very much involved in politics. From the twenties through the forties San Antonio was run by a strong and corrupt political machine that stayed in power by handing out municipal contracts and city jobs. During the height of the Depression opponents charged that there were 3000 mattress inspectors on the city payroll; the machine hired city employees for their political connections and expected them to deliver their friends and relatives on election day. To this core the machine added the small ethnic vote on the Mexican West Side and the black East Side. No racial ideology was involved; the machine simply bought the loyalties of a few key organizers with favors, and these henchmen in turn bought poll taxes for their minions. Usually the favors involved protection for vice: West Side political meetings took place above the brothels on El Paso Street, and every prostitute had a poll tax.

The machine gave way to the Good Government League in the fifties, and politics began to open up a little for the West Side. A Spanish-language newspaper editor's son named Henry B. Gonzalez ran for city council and won; he survived a turbulent term when the city went through 48 councilmen in two years to win again. For the West Side Gonzalez was the right man at the right time. As basic as drainage was to be in the seventies, the issue in the fifties was more basic still: it was philosophical and political acceptance of the Mexican American as a part of San Antonio. Gonzalez symbolized that acceptance, but just as important, he was worthy of it. He took no money, he cut no deals, he spoke out for what was right, and his people revered him for it. He shattered his constituents' own stereotypes about corrupt Mexican politicians and eradicated the memory of the whores with their poll taxes. That is why even today there are hundreds of people on the West Side like the old man who runs a gas station on Zarzamora Street, proudly showing visitors a frayed, yellowed letter Henry B. wrote him twenty years ago.

The GGL began as a reform movement, bent on bringing professional city government to San Antonio ("a copy of the American corporate structure applied to politics," Walter McAllister called it; he would become mayor in 1961, at the age of 72, and serve into his eighties). For a century, ever since the early Germans had been too busy making money to pay much attention to politics, San Antonio's leading citizens had shunned city hall, but now they invaded it to run the town as it had never been run before: everything from paving long-neglected streets to bringing the city a world's fair and a branch of the University of Texas.

And yet, underneath the smoothly running exterior, all was not well. From the start the GGL made no effort to cultivate new Mexican political talent and develop a critical mass of West Side support. Instead, like the old machine, it chose to deal with the West Side through a few handpicked intermediaries—although in keeping with the changing times, its contacts were Mexican American businessmen, not vice peddlers. As a result there was no political outlet for ambitious young Mexicans: no spots on the city council, not even appointments to city boards and commissions. As for other electoral races, that didn't sit well with Gonzalez, who by the time McAllister became mayor in 1961 had gone off to Congress—but not before spreading the word around the West Side that "there is only one politician here and that is me." The only refuge left for Mexican political hopefuls was whatever liberal Democratic organization happened to be functioning at the time: Viva Kennedy, PASO, Mexican American Democrats. The names changed but the clique didn't. They sat around, drinking and complaining and talking of the days when they would have power and cutting each other up, as liberals will. Some went on to become lackluster state legislators; others, even now, are waiting their turn, laying plans to reap the spoils of the Second Battle of the Alamo.

Ambitious Mexicans weren't the only ones who felt excluded by the GGL. San Antonio's council-manager system had gone to great lengths to keep politicians from making money out of government. (Two crucial city departments, water and electric utilities, were governed by self-perpetuating boards completely free of council control.) But no system could erase the fact that money was there to be made. Fortunes depended on where the city built water mains, how it enforced subdivision regulations, and what it decided about zoning. Builders and land developers yearned for city policies that stimulated growth, but the GGL was composed primarily of Chamber of Commerce types—downtown businessmen and merchants, many from old families, who had little incentive to tilt city policies in favor of suburban growth. These natural economic tensions were heightened by the social conflicts between the GGL's old families and developers with nothing but contempt for bloodlines.

After McAllister finally stepped down in 1971, no one could hold the GGL together. The telling blow was delivered by a maverick GGL councilman named Charles Becker, son of the founder of the Handy-Andy grocery chain and a member of an old San Antonio family. Despite his GGL ties, Becker had far more affinity with the fast-money boys than with the stodgy old downtown crowd who, said Becker, spent their time "lollygagging" around the San Antonio Country Club and the Argyle Club, pruning their family trees. When the GGL needed the West Side votes, they weren't there, and suddenly the GGL was O-U-T. Familiar names on city boards and commissions were replaced by Becker allies; before long, the president of the Greater San Antonio Builders was in charge of the planning commission and a major developer was chairman of the powerful water board.

Becker loved to talk about his feud with the GGL; his favorite saying was, "I'm gonna kill me some snakes." But, it turned out, that was all he did; he destroyed the old order but built nothing new to take its place. When he quit in 1975, his legacy was a power vacuum.

Old Story, New Ending

In the fall of 1973, about the time Charles Becker was busily killing snakes, Father Edmundo Rodriguez was listening to yet another plan for organizing San Antonio's Mexican American community. A pudgy, gentle Jesuit priest in his late thirties, Rodriquez looked more like the ideal person for the part of Santa Claus in a secular Christmas pageant than a crusading reformer. But his visitor, himself a bulky 200-pounder, knew he had come to the right place. Working out of the fading red brick Our Lady of Guadalupe Church on the near West Side, not far from the old Missouri Pacific Railroad Station, Rodriguez had been active in numerous causes: U.S. Civil Rights Commission hearings in San Antonio, bilingual and bicultural committees, and a drive to get the Bexar County Hospital Board to respond to patient grievances. Equally important, Rodriguez was active in interfaith organizations and knew who might be willing to back their sympathy for the poor with cash.

Rodriguez wasn't optimistic. There always seemed to be another social activist with a plan for organizing the West Side. He had watched them talk to people in the barrio about the obvious issues—racial discrimination, bilingual education, police brutality, unemployment—and had seen lots of heads nod in agreement, but somehow the organizers never made any progress. People didn't seem to *care*, at least not enough to act.

Nevertheless, Rodriguez sensed that this one was different. His name was Ernie Cortes, he was a native of the West Side, and he had a solid grasp of how power worked in San Antonio. Furthermore, his bulk gave him an air of authority that made him hard to ignore. Cortes, thirty, had gotten his formal education at UT in economics, his political training on the Bexar County Hospital Board as an appointee of County Commissioner Albert Peña, and his practical experience as an economic development specialist for the Mexican American Unity Council. (It was as a member of the hospital board that he had first met Rodriguez.) Moreover, Cortes had received training earlier that year as a community organizer at the late Saul Alinsky's Industrial Areas Foundation in Chicago. Alinsky, a self-described radical whose goal was to bring power to the powerless, first came to national prominence in the thirties as a friend of labor boss John L. Lewis; he later organized Chicago's Back of the Yards area (Upton Sinclair's *Jungle*) and led the fight against Eastman Kodak on behalf of Rochester's ghetto blacks. Alinsky was no idealist or social

" 'The trouble with this town is that it has too many old rich and too many new poor. They're just alike. They're lazy and idle and contribute nothing. Give me the nouveau riche every time.' "

The main stream is a drainage canal; the tributary is a flooded street, but in this West Side scene from pre-COPS days, it's hard to tell the difference.

Harvard/Aggie-educated Councilman Henry Cisneros may be the first Mexican mayor of modern San Antonio if he doesn't get caught in an ethnic maelstrom.

Banker Tom Frost admires COPS; they see him as symbol of the establishment.

Jim Dement and other developers can't figure out why COPS doesn't like them.

136 WHO RUNS OUR CITIES AND TOWNS?

dreamer; he was a hard-core realist who wrote extensively about how to overcome the weaknesses of the poor by exploiting those of the rich and powerful.

All this Rodriguez knew. But what most impressed him was that Cortes didn't seem to be just another hustler looking for no-strings-attached dollars from the church. He wanted money, to be sure, but Cortes agreed that it should come from an ecumenical sponsoring committee that would closely monitor the project and hold the staff accountable for the money. (Several San Antonio churches had already been stung by self-appointed organizers who had little to show for their efforts—including financial statements.)

Rodriguez agreed to try to raise the money. It wasn't easy, but he was able to pry loose some contributions from Church of Christ, Methodist, and Episcopal sources, and to win the essential support of San Antonio Archbishop Francis Furey. The money would be doled out in stages and could be cut off at any time. Only Rodriguez could sign the checks. The sponsoring committee, made up of churchmen from the donating denominations, was formalized in January 1974 and hired Cortes as the organizer at a salary of $16,000 a year. The movement was uninspirationally labeled the Committee for Mexican American Action, and Cortes went to work.

He started at the churches, asking pastors for the names of parishioners who were leaders, whether churchgoers or not. Cortes wasn't interested in people who were active in politics; he was looking for those who organized church socials, ran PTAs, or perhaps were union stewards. *Natural* leaders, he called them: not people who were showy, but those who got others to show. He found a woman in a public-housing project who spent Saturdays cooking food for shut-in senior citizens; later, when the neighborhood organization tried to get a bridge across a creek for schoolchildren, she had no trouble getting people to turn out in support—they trusted her. He found Andy Sarabia, the chairman of the community life committee of Holy Family Church, who was already spending much of his time finding out what the parish could do about problems in the area. And he found Beatrice Gallego, a PTA leader and Head Start volunteer who was also involved with senior citizens and Catholic women's groups. Cortes looked for anyone who had a following, and he found them in every Mexican neighborhood, people with no history of political involvement.

After identifying who to organize, Cortes' next problem was to find what to organize them around. Instead of picking the obvious civil rights issues that had mesmerized previous organizers, Cortes took the simple but crucial step of asking his new contacts what mattered to them. The answers were startling: drainage, high utility bills, chugholes in the streets, sidewalks for their children. There was not a single mention of any of the more glamorous causes traditionally embraced by minority politicians.

Rodriguez was elated. It was, he said later, like one of those light bulbs that suddenly appears in cartoons. No wonder previous efforts had failed. They had been on the wrong track. The myth that Mexicans could never be organized, that they didn't really care about social issues, had been repeated so many times he had almost begun to believe it himself. Many of his parishioners did believe it. But the problem had been with the technique, not with the people. It was so obvious; why hadn't he seen it earlier? For the first time he allowed himself to think that this thing might actually work.

Cortes went from parish to parish during the winter and spring of 1974, recruiting leaders, weeding out the weak from the strong, researching issues, and setting up independent neighborhood groups organized around parish churches. It took him seventeen phone calls before Beatrice Gallego would even agree to a meeting. By the summer he was ready to take the crucial step: bringing the area groups together under one umbrella organization. Cortes and Rodriguez knew that this was where previous organizing attempts had been undercut by jealousies and personality conflicts. Certainly the potential was present for that to happen again. Neighborhood leaders would be vying for power in the central organization, and only a few could succeed. People who had spent their whole lives fighting for their own neighborhoods were suddenly going to have to shift their efforts on behalf of other areas. Yet without a strong umbrella, the local groups would have no clout. Projects like drainage were too big and too costly for one parish to attack.

Cortes and Rodriguez did the groundwork for the changeover. They taught their inexperienced troops that in politics, size is power. They explained about trade-offs: you help this parish get a park and they'll help you get drainage. They promoted a merit system for leaders: those who produced rose higher; those who didn't were limited. They talked to people about their fears and learned that most didn't worry about losing jobs, or what their neighbors would think, but that they would be made fools of in public by people who knew more than they did. So Cortes helped them learn how to do research: where to look for answers and what to ask for when they went to city hall. The area leaders met in midsummer at a parish social hall to form their new union. There was a tense moment or two while the group debated what issues to focus on—a sizable contingent, incensed over spiraling utility bills, wanted to go to war with the city's natural gas supplier, Lo-Vaca Gathering Company—but Cortes channeled the discussion toward whether anything could be done. Gradually, the group perceived, unhappily, that the utility crisis was in the hands of the courts, the Texas Railroad Commission, the Arabs, the energy companies, and, locally, the independent CPS (City Public Service) Board—none of which could be affected much by what some angry citizens in West Side San Antonio had to say. But drainage was different; it was localized, focusable, in the hands of a city manager, a city council, and, ultimately, voters, who had to approve bond issues.

The leaders settled on drainage ("*We* couldn't tell them," says Rodriguez. "It had to be understood and agreed on by the people themselves"), and Rodriguez breathed a sigh of relief. The center had held. Now it was time for a meeting with City Manager Sam Granata. But first, there was one more thing to do. That insipid name, the Committee for Mexican American Action, had to go. In a strategy session for the confrontation with city hall, someone jokingly suggested the name COPS: "You know, they're the robbers and we're the cops." Someone else, still bitter about those utility bills, pointed out that "PS could stand for public service, just like CPS, only we really mean it." And the group that would fill Charles Becker's power vacuum had its name.

Ask and Ye Shall Receive

When Ernie Cortes called, Beatrice Gallego knew what he wanted—word passed quickly on the West Side, even though nothing had appeared in the news media about Cortes' organizing efforts—but she didn't want to talk to him. She had heard it all before, young radicals talking about confronting the system, full of socialism and kill the gringo, trying to convince her that she should get involved. Get involved! What about Head Start, the PTA, the church, substitute teaching? Those were the things that really mattered; who cared about another march to protest police brutality? There wasn't any time left for politics, even if she'd been inclined that way. Besides, like most of the women she knew, even the most active, she considered home her first priority—her three children and her husband Gilbert, a hardware salesman who had built their house in a modest middle-class neighborhood called Palm Heights.

There was another reason she didn't want to talk to Cortes. The whole idea of radicalism appalled her. The youngest of seven children, she had wanted to be a nun until she met her future husband. Like many Mexican Americans, she had been raised in a strict family atmosphere and been instilled with a respect for authority (though occasionally her father shocked her with bitter complaints about the city's Anglo leadership and their neglect of the West Side). Long after her name had become a household word in San Antonio political circles, she recounted to him a small victory she had won at a public hearing New Braunfels Congressman Bob Krueger had arranged to hold in San Antonio. As she described Krueger's reactions, her father interrupted his youngest child, "Baby, did you call him Krueger? You shouldn't say that. He's *Congressman Krueger*."

At the urging of a priest, Gallego finally met with Cortes. He asked her about problems in her neighborhood. "I had to laugh," she recalls. "What wasn't a problem? We had no drainage, no sidewalks, no curbs, no parks, we were cut in half by an expressway, we didn't have enough water pressure to water the yard and draw bath water at the same time."

She was still skeptical, though, as the fledgling organization prepared for its showdown with the city over drainage. COPS tried to arrange a West Side assembly with Granata; he refused to come. So they took their plea for a meeting to city hall, jamming into the small council chambers in such numbers that one councilman was reminded of Travis' famous message from the Alamo: "I am besieged with a thousand or more of the Mexicans." The council took one look at the crowd and ordered Granata to meet with the West Siders. The session was set for August 13, 1974, at a West Side high school.

Cortes and Rodriguez were worried about the upcoming confrontation. They knew that turnout was critical; COPS had to make a good showing. More important, they wondered whether their people were psychologically prepared for what lay ahead. Most, like Gallego, had been brought up to respect authority. The Alinsky approach did not require breaking the law, but it did not shirk from bending it a little. Its guiding principle was to encourage and focus the latent anger of the poor by showing how the system worked against them. But everything was predicated on that anger; it had to come naturally. Just how angry were these homeowners and church-goers? Angry enough to forget their upbringing? Angry enough to implement the Alinsky tactic that "ridicule is man's most potent weapon"? Angry enough to overcome the lack of confidence and fear of ignorance they all were sure to feel? Another of Alinsky's cardinal rules was "Never go outside the experience of your own people." Was militance itself a violation of that rule?

Cortes did the best he could to prepare his people. At training sessions they rehearsed the confrontation, anticipated the double-talk bureaucrats excel at, and drilled on pinning the city manager down to yes or no answers.

Poor Sam Granata. Not only was COPS laying for him, but also the sky was about to fall on him. On August 7, just five days before the meeting and practically a year after the destructive 1973 rainstorm, the heavens opened again. Forty families were forced out of their homes, and on Inez Street floodwaters drove an old woman with a 105-degree fever out into the mud. A bridge across the Mayberry ditch caved in, and streets all over the West Side were impassable. COPS didn't have to worry about the turnout anymore; 500 angry people showed up. "That bolstered our faith in God," said Sarabia of the rain.

Granata was greeted with slides showing typical West Side scenes after a storm. The city manager was on the defensive from the start. COPS researchers had uncovered histories of drainage projects that had been authorized by the council but never funded—the Mayberry project had been part of the city's master plan since 1945—and others that had been funded in bond elections but never implemented. COPS wanted to know why, and the only answer the beleaguered Granata could come up with was "We dropped the ball." In the audience, Beatrice Gallego could hardly believe what she had heard; her last doubts about COPS' tactics melted away. The authorities weren't so smart after all. Why, COPS knew more about drainage than the city manager! These people weren't worthy of her respect. Now she *was* angry. Granata made matters worse by lamely defending the city's inaction with an explanation that would come back to haunt the city: "If you want something, you have to ask for it." Beatrice Gallego vowed to herself that no one would ever have to say that again. She went home that night and started drawing up lists.

Granata's ill-advised admission that San Antonio government operated by the squeaky-wheel-gets-the-grease method did more to politicize COPS' membership than all their careful training. It exploded the myth most of them had accepted for years—that the city in its wisdom would take care of them in good time. The battle lines were drawn for keeps.

The aftermath of the Granata confrontation was immediate victory. When he refused to promise any action on drainage, the meeting ended in a shouting match, and COPS returned to the council chambers. Becker, who eventually would turn against COPS when the organization began sniping at developers, professed astonishment that the Mayberry project had been neglected for thirty years and told the city staff to come up with a plan for financing it. That fall the council drew up a $46 million bond issue that passed in November—the same month that COPS held its first annual convention, formalized its structure, and elected Sarabia president.

Perhaps more than any other person in COPS, Sarabia epitomizes the idea of a natural leader. When he talks about city politics, his eyes bore into you like lasers, with the fierce intensity of focused anger. He is outwardly calm, with none of the gestures of the polished speaker, but the listener is transfixed by the eyes. It is only later that you realize he is quiet and softspoken. He seems to shout without raising his voice.

"We got into COPS because we cared about our neighborhoods," he recalled recently. "We weren't looking for any handouts—we're taxpayers, and we found out our tax money wasn't working for us. They'd promise us projects and then they'd use the money for something on the North Side. We found case after case of it. It made us angry. Then we found that they were incompetent. When you learn something emotionally, I guarantee you, you never forget it.

"You're educated to become one of *them*. If you want to make it, you have to leave your neighborhood, move to the North Side, forget what you left behind. It doesn't just happen; the city's policies are planned that way. Ignore the old, subsidize the new. But what if you don't want to move to the North Side? What if you'd like your children to stay in your neighborhoods?"

COPS invited the city council to its first annual convention so they could learn about the needs of the neighborhoods. None showed up, so COPS decided to go over their heads to the symbolic leaders of the business community. They tried to arrange a meeting with the head of Joske's ("We had lots of charge accounts with him, so we assumed he'd help us," said Sarabia, who is no longer so naive as to assume anything of the sort). The counteroffer came back: would Sarabia meet him alone? No deal. Sarabia took 200 people to Joske's, and they spent hours examining fine dresses, trying on expensive coats, asking sales personnel about jewelry—and buying nothing. With 200 Mexicans and a half-dozen TV cameras clogging the store, Joske's didn't do much business that day. The next day Sarabia led the group to the Frost Bank, the city's largest. Again they broke no laws but merely lined up at tellers' windows to exchange dollars for pennies, then moved to the adjacent window to trade pennies for dollars. Upstairs, Tom Frost, Jr., agreed to meet with a COPS delegation, admitted they had legitimate complaints about the way the city had neglected their neighborhoods, but declined to say it publicly. The next day, however, the head of the Greater San Antonio Chamber of Commerce appeared at COPS' shabby West Side headquarters. All he learned was that next time he'd better make an appointment first. Cortes refused to see his unannounced visitor.

Not surprisingly, the tie-ups caused a storm of protest in the city about COPS. Bewildered North Siders couldn't understand what these people wanted; hadn't the city responded to their requests with a bond issue? They didn't understand that COPS was interested not just in projects but also in power—a permanent share of the decision-making process. But not all the protests came from the North Side. One Mexican on the West Side recalled her reaction to the tie-ups: "I couldn't believe the church was involved. They're always saying, 'Mind your manners.' How could they support such things? It was just horrible, walking over people like that. I can't figure out to this day what made me change my mind and join COPS." But she did.

Who Are Those Guys?

Occasionally there are moments that capture perfectly in one insignificant incident the unending historical tension between past and future. Such a moment came to San Antonio in early 1975 at, of all places, a hearing on how the council should spend $16 million in federal funds. COPS was there in force, with more than 200 supporters, presenting its case for putting the money into old neighborhoods for parks, drainage, and streets. But Mrs. Edith McAllister was there too, the daughter-in-law of the ex-mayor, soliciting $300,000 for the San Antonio Museum Association to renovate the old Lone Star Brewery. It was clear that COPS didn't think much of her request when there was water standing in the streets, and it was equally clear that she didn't really comprehend why all these people were up in arms. How could she make them understand? She summed up her plea to the room: "Man does not live by sewers alone. He also needs museums."

From the beginning Anglo San Antonians have had a difficult time understanding just what COPS is. Their perplexity is understandable, because COPS is an organization built on paradoxes and contradictions. It is a radical organization made up of people whose personal style is intensely conservative. It is a political organization made up of people who have no use for politicians. It is an organization made up mostly of Mexican Americans, but it has nothing to do with traditional ethnic issues.

Yet someone with as long and proud a record of public service as former Mayor McAllister can say, in all seriousness, that "I haven't got any use for a communist organization." And lest that be interpreted as just the bitterness of an 88-year-old man, John Schaefer, one of the city's leading developers and the chairman of the City Water Board, says, "To be kind to them, I'd say they're socialist. Their philosophy is straight out of the communist manifesto: from each according to his means, to each according to his needs." A local oilman has a somewhat more charitable view: "They're just looking for a handout. I bet most of them are on welfare."

In fact, most of them detest welfare. Carmen Badillo, COPS vice president, tells how her father bought cheap land near a creek rather than go into a housing project. The home cost $2500 and consisted of four walls—he had to build the inside walls himself—no sewers, no running water; it took him twenty years to pay for it. But it was better than public housing. "There are a lot of people on welfare who shouldn't be," she says. "It's gotten to be the thing to do. But it's wrong. It robs you of your dignity. Welfare people don't participate. They don't get angry." So antagonistic is COPS toward handouts that its charter bars the organization from accepting federal funds. (Although in its early years COPS relied heavily on religious foundations, it is now entirely self-sufficient, financing its $100,000 annual budget through dues and an advertising booklet that brought in $47,000 in four weeks.)

As for economic philosophy, the COPS ranks are not exactly crawling with Marxists. A case can be made—as one area leader said—that "we're more conservative than Tom Frost." (Frost, who actually has considerable respect and admiration for COPS—"They're good people and they're good for the city," he says—seems to be the organization's favorite symbol for the Anglo power structure, even though he cannot accurately be called a power broker.) "Let me tell you what kind of free enterprise system they believe in," says Andy Sarabia. "It's only free for themselves. *Our* taxes pay for *their* free enterprise."

Most Anglos have been unable to make the distinction between radical *tactics*, which COPS enthusiastically embraces—shouting, intimidation through numbers, rudeness, threats of mass action against politicians and financial institutions—and radical *people*, which it should be obvious by now are few and far between in COPS. Some might say there is no difference, but that is a terribly shortsighted view with terrible consequences for San Antonio. For there are Mexicans in town who do not share COPS values, who, though they do not use radical tactics, do aspire to control the city in a way COPS does not.

One of the things least understood about this organization is its contempt for politicians—all politicians, Mexicans included. Before major elections COPS holds "candidates' accountability nights," when office seekers are asked to give their views on issues COPS regards as crucial. COPS permits only yes or no answers—a tactic not so admirable when practiced by, say, the AFL-CIO, but the difference is that both COPS' issues and its membership are broader based than the usual pressure group's. And while there is much disagreement in town over COPS' tactics, there is no dispute over its power at the polls. COPS will not endorse particular candidates, but it will raise unholy hell about those who openly oppose their goals. One unfortunate Mexican politician came to accountability night a little too full of booze and macho; he said no to their questions and they walked the streets to beat him at the polls. On two important citywide referendums—one over halting development on the Edwards Aquifer northwest of town, the other on single-member city council districts—COPS showed its muscle when both propositions passed. During the single-member districting election, word got out at midafternoon that the West Side turnout was too light and in three hours of working door-to-door, COPS boosted the turnout high enough to help districting squeak through by 2000 votes.

The only people in town who seem to have figured out that COPS has no political ambitions beyond its issues are the politicians themselves. Several councilmen complain privately (they wouldn't dream of saying so publicly) that COPS never gives any credit to politicians who help with their projects.

As an organization, COPS views all politicians as the same. "A politician is a politician," Gallego is fond of saying; they would all rather make a speech than a commitment. Undoubtedly there are COPS members who emotionally would like to see the city elect a Mexican American mayor, but once the votes were counted, ethnic ties would make no difference. Earlier this year COPS attacked the Anglo majority on the school board for voting to spend $1.6 million on a new administration building instead of refurbishing rundown schools; the April elections produced a Mexican majority and COPS promptly attacked them on another issue. That produced a phone call to COPS the next day: "What's the matter with you people? Don't you realize we have to stick together?"

Of all the things about COPS, this disinterest in personal or ethnic political power is the hardest for other San Antonians to believe. Many people thought that when Sarabia voluntarily gave up the presidency last year (to be succeeded by Gallego), he was preparing to run for county commissioner. He didn't, he says, "because then I'd have to face all these crazy people." Sarabia talked about why he could never have switched over to politics:

"If anyone really thought that, it proves they didn't understand COPS. Politicians don't matter—people matter. The whole basis of this organization is a tremendous faith in people.

"Can you imagine what it was like in the beginning? *Nothing* was easy. We got calls in the middle of the night: 'Why don't you go back to Mexico?' We were awed when we went to city hall. We didn't know anything about a single issue. All we had was our own anger—and trust. COPS started as a blind trust; it was *built* on trust. Now no one wants to violate it."

"Let San Antonio Grow"

High up in one of San Antonio's tallest bank buildings, The Lawyer made it perfectly clear *he* didn't trust COPS. He had tried to understand them, tried to deal with them, but it was useless. He had even suggested that his clients, some of San Antonio's biggest land developers, read Alinsky's manual *Rules for Radicals*, but demand was so high local bookstores couldn't keep it in stock. Meanwhile, COPS kept attacking his clients even more fiercely.

"I can't understand it," The Lawyer said. "There's only one answer to the West Side's problems, and that's better jobs. Who else in this town besides the developer pays double the minimum wage? If we don't build houses, what's left here economically except the military."

The Lawyer proceeded to reel off a dismal litany of statistics. Houston's building permits are up 40 per cent; San Antonio's down 2 per cent. San Antonio's unemployment rate is twice that of Dallas. Houston has 122 home-based companies listed on the New York and American stock exchanges; industry-poor San Antonio by comparison has only 11. Manufacturing accounts for only 13 per cent of the labor force, compared to 27 per cent nationally; almost all of that is concentrated in products for local use, or in the needle trade—businesses that pay minimum wage: $2.30 an hour, $92 a week, less than $5000 a year. More than one job in four is on a government payroll; only Washington, D.C., has a higher percentage. The federal government alone accounts for a third of San Antonio's total wages. The picture is not a good one, nor, says The Lawyer, is it an accident: "Before we got involved in politics, there was *nothing* here. The dumb bastards that ran this town did everything they could to keep industry out and build a wall around this town. They didn't want outsiders here."

One outsider they particularly didn't want was Henry Ford. Long before World War II he wanted to build an automobile assembly plant in the city, but the local gentry didn't exactly greet him with open arms. It is said that they tried to snooker him on the land deal and otherwise made it known he could take his factory and his labor unions elsewhere without being terribly missed. When Ford finally realized he wasn't wanted, the story goes, his parting shot was "You people are crazy."

But the business leaders of that era didn't care. After all, the banks were full of cattle money and oil money—but no one stopped to consider that little of it ever seemed to be plowed back into San Antonio. Instead it was invested in the oil patches and grasslands of South Texas. Its owners had no stake in the city's economic vitality. The economy came to rely increasingly on the military—another group, like cattlemen and oilmen, without a permanent stake in the community. No one paid much attention in 1933 when a small company named Frito picked up and moved to Dallas; no San Antonio bank would advance it the capital for expansion, so it had to look elsewhere. But the loss of that company, which now employs 17,000, typified the complacent attitude of the business leadership. True, the city made some nominal efforts to attract industry—the council even voted tax dollars to help support the local Chamber of Commerce—but the Chamber was dominated by merchants who benefited from the abundant supply of cheap Mexican labor. When a new plant was lured to the city, it usually turned out to be something like Levi Strauss, another nonunion minimum-wage shop. And despite the city's gloomy economic statistics, some of the city's leading figures, like former Mayor McAllister, still maintain that San Antonio shouldn't go after heavy industry.

"We broke that up," The Lawyer says. "*Anything's* possible here now. Where do you think COPS would be if we hadn't opened things up? I can't figure out why they hate us."

The Lawyer leaned back in his chair, locked his fingers behind his head, and inspected the ceiling through fashionably large glasses. "The trouble with this town," he summed up, "is that it's got too many old rich and too many new poor. They're just alike. They're la-zy and i-dle"—he drew out the first syllables contemptuously—"and contribute nothing. Give me the nouveau riche every time."

There was a time, when the GGL was falling apart in the early seventies, that astute San Antonians involved in politics thought the alliance of the future would unite the Hungries (Anglo developers and Mexican West Siders) against the Satisfieds (old families and downtown interests). Similar coalitions have sprung up in other cities—Austin, for one, where ethnic minorities broke with the no-growth policies favored by students and other liberals. But such predictions reckoned without COPS.

Once COPS realized that money had been diverted from projects planned for older parts of town, they looked to see where it went. They found, for example, that the widening of Pleasanton Road, a major South Side artery, had been approved in a 1970 bond issue—but when the road builders went to work, it was San Pedro Avenue on the North Side that got their attention. More often than not, that was the pattern: the diverted funds went to build a water main extension to a new subdivision, to pave streets or build drainage systems in the newer parts of town. Issue after issue came down to who would get the money, new or old, and it became clear that city policies, intentionally or not, usually favored the new. The consequences were obvious: people wanted to live where the roads were, where the drainage was, where the money was spent.

Other city policies benefitted not just suburban areas generally, but their developers. COPS was particularly outraged at City Water Board procedures, instituted after developer John Schaeffer became chairman, that called for the city to provide auxiliary water main materials free to subdividers. The materials may have been free to developers, COPS protested, but not to inner-city taxpayers who continued to cope with substandard mains and low water pressure while their tax dollars were handed out to developers in the form of subsidies. Furthermore, COPS noted, developers were supposed to reimburse the city for the much larger suburban mains the city built out to their subdivisions—but in practice both the developers and the city generally ignored the debt. That, of course, amounted to another subsidy. Now COPS had the ammunition to challenge the most basic of assumptions about the modern city: that the decline of the core and the sprawl of the fringe are inevitable.

So the developers became the enemy. They were in power; they were the ones shuffling money around to encourage growth outside of town. Nothing underscored their attitude—and their power—more clearly than their reactions to a study by an upper-level city planner suggesting that all growth in San Antonio for the next 25 years could take place within Loop 410. During a public hearing, a developer on the city council threw a copy in the trash can, proclaiming vehemently, "That's where it belongs." Soon the author was canned too.

The feud between COPS and the developers broke into the open in July 1975 when 250 shouting, boisterous COPS supporters jammed a small room at the City Water Board to protest a proposed rate increase. But COPS wasn't there just to protest; its style is always to have an alternative. Stop subsidizing developers—make them pay for their own water mains—COPS said, and you won't need a rate increase; and they hauled out facts and figures to back it up. Eventually the board agreed to change its subsidy policies and consented to a compromise on the rate increase. COPS had proved that it was not just a powerful neighborhood organization, but a force to be reckoned with citywide.

A few months later COPS successfully challenged the developer crowd again. The city council narrowly voted to buy a suburban golf course from a developer for a price considerably above appraised value; for added controversy, the council planned to finance the deal with federal funds earmarked for the inner city. Beatrice Gallego vowed publicly that if the purchase went through, she would make a national scandal of it. The city was spared when COPS was instrumental in getting federal officials to veto any diversion of the funds.

But even more important than the individual victories COPS was winning was the political change that was taking place in the city as a whole. People were getting fed up with the developers. Subsidies, sweetheart deals, insider transactions, stacked boards and commissions—COPS had helped put San Antonio city government under the microscope and people didn't like what they saw. The developers suffered an overwhelming defeat when COPS and Anglo environmentalists forced a referendum on a council decision to allow construction of a shopping mall over a thin slice of the Edwards Aquifer northwest of town. Environmentalists managed to portray the fight as a clean water issue, but COPS *knew* the real issues were growth and power. Voter turnout trebled expectations, and the developers—who had run newspaper ads warning that COPS was trying to take over the city—were routed by a 4-1 margin. The developers' brief rule was in serious trouble, and suddenly they began showing up at council meetings wearing buttons pleading "Let San Antonio Grow." But they were finished. A year later, in March 1977, another referendum ushered in single-member council districts and in the April election, developers were routed all over town: their candidates were beaten not just on the West Side and South Side, but North and Southeast as well.

Curiously, despite the fact that COPS has publicly insulted them and contributed greatly to their loss of political power, some developers hold a grudging admiration for COPS—much more than for the old guard that once ran the town. Perhaps it is because, despite Anglo fears of an ethnically divided city, there is still a large reservoir of goodwill in San Antonio. John Schaeffer—though he considers Sarabia "definitely radical," thinks that COPS is "out to take over the city," and says COPS members have threatened him personally—nevertheless bought a $1000 spread in COPS' fund-raising ad booklet this summer. Jim Dement, who helped finance Charles Becker's 1973 mayoral campaign and this year made an unsuccessful council bid himself, is similarly ambivalent. He accuses COPS of "fostering hatred and real problems," but he concedes, "They had to do something drastic to get the attention of the public." And he adds, "I see dedication to San Antonio that wasn't here three years ago. There's more hope and conversation in this town than in a hundred years. And I love it. This is a town where you can have nothing and be somebody. Now don't tell me COPS is bad."

A Call to Arms

On a warm October night Henry Cisneros interrupted dinner with an old friend to speak to one of several Anglo citizens' organizations that have sprung up in San Antonio with hopes of emulating COPS' success. It had not been a good week for bridge building—the council had split twice along ethnic lines amid much controversy—and Cisneros was a little nervous.

It was a Friday, so a lot of parents and most of the students were at high school football games. Nevertheless, about forty members of the CDL (Citizens for Decency through Law) showed up at a small church to hear Cisneros talk about the spreading menace of pornography in the city. It is an issue that truly outrages Cisneros—a few days earlier he had walked into a West Side convenience store with his two young daughters to discover a tabloid on the counter featuring the story How to Rape a Woman—but despite this affinity between speaker and audience, something didn't click. Cisneros can call on a pretty rousing speaking style, but on this night he was subdued, content to rely mainly on homilies that are the ultimate refuge of every politician. He closed with a rhetorical question—"What can a small group of people do?"—but it soon became apparent that this small group of people was unlikely to do very much.

Someone asked Cisneros, "What can be done by the city council?" and he quickly flipped the ball back: "You people who have studied and worked on the problem need to come up with a plan to present to the city." Hah! COPS would never have let him get away with that. They would already have had a plan. Then someone complained that the Witte Museum was displaying pictures of naked women. Cisneros bravely tried to point out that political organizations are more effective when they stick to things a large number of people can agree on, but the zealots persisted. It was another mistake COPS would never have made, another trap they would have avoided. It is inconceivable, for example, that COPS would embrace a cause currently popular among Hispanics in the U.S. Northeast: bilingual law courts. COPS stays sighted in on targets that are carefully chosen—so carefully chosen that in a recent poll, 70 per cent of San Antonians said they agreed with COPS *goals*, despite the general unpopularity of COPS *tactics*.

Finally a white-haired lady at the back of the room caught on. "I don't approve of COPS," she told Cisneros, "but they certainly know what they're doing, don't they?"

They do indeed. The truth is that the CDL felt the same anger about pornography as COPS felt about drainage. It is a fair guess that everyone at the church that night was more affluent and better educated than 99.9 per cent of COPS' members. Yet, if that meeting is any indication, CDL is unlikely to approach COPS' success. COPS has managed to do the one thing that is essential to success in politics—or in business, athletics, or just about anything else. It has discovered the elusive formula of how to build an organization that works.

Not that anyone would want to use COPS' organization chart for a model. It looks like a map of the New York subway system. Technically COPS is an organization of organizations—the only time individuals are counted is when attendance is added up at the annual November convention—but no one can say for sure how many groups are part of COPS at any one time. It depends on the issue and who's paid dues recently. Right now there are 33 primary organizations, known as locals, with another three or four on the periphery. Most are Catholic parishes (which on the West Side is the same thing as a neighborhood organization, since neighborhoods there are defined by parish boundaries), but there are also block clubs and churches from other denominations: a small Anglo COPS chapter in the northeast, which joined because the area couldn't get city help for their drainage problems, and a growing black East Side COPS group.

Each local is virtually autonomous in choosing its own neighborhood issues. If, for example, Andy Sarabia's Holy Family local wants a park, a footbridge for schoolchildren, or some vacant lots cleared of weeds, it plans its own research and strategy—though obviously its chances will not be hurt by operating under the COPS banner.

There has to be a central organization, however, to set policy, raise money, and hammer out compromises on citywide issues like drainage priorities. COPS has managed to come up with a structure that allows everyone to take part without hampering the ability of a few skilled leaders. How this works is too complicated to be explained in detail, but it involves an executive committee (composed mostly of citywide leaders), a steering committee (composed mostly of neighborhood leaders), and a delegates' congress (composed of any member of a COPS local who shows up to vote). In theory the committees recommend and the delegates ratify, but in practice the power lies with the committees. If this sounds too labyrinthine, try substituting *management, directors, shareholders,* and *General Motors* for executive committee, steering committee, delegates' congress, and COPS.

One important omission from this bureaucracy is the Alinsky-trained organizer. This is no oversight. The organizer's primary job is to spot new natural leaders in the community—to provide the group with a continuing supply of new blood. In the beginning, of course, Ernie Cortes did that and far more: he plotted strategy, helped lead actions, trained the Sarabias and Gallegos and other emerging leaders. It was too much, and to his credit Cortes had the wisdom to see it; to last more than a year or two, COPS had to be run by the people themselves. So Cortes left for Los Angeles in August 1976, to be replaced by someone who is as different in temperament and background from Cortes as Cortes is from Tom Frost. Cortes is from San Antonio, Mexican, and Catholic; Arnie Graf, his successor, is from upstate New York, Anglo, and Jewish, and for that matter doesn't speak a word of Spanish. Nor was Graf well versed on COPS' central issue. When he was interviewed by Beatrice Gallego, she inquired what he knew about the 39 Series; all he could think of was, "Didn't Cleveland win?"* She was asking about drainage, not baseball, but Graf's record as organizer of a white working-class Milwaukee neighborhood eventually carried the day and got him the job.

The Alinsky connection is probably the least understood, and most feared, aspect of COPS among San Antonio's Anglo community. Many see it as the cause of the trouble. They pointedly mention that Father Rodriguez, Sarabia, Gallego, and other COPS leaders have gone to the Industrial Areas Foundation for training, and former Mayor McAllister bluntly calls the IAF "Saul Alinsky's communist school in Chicago."

Arnie Graf chuckles at the unlikely sight of Beatrice Gallego, mother of Miss Teenage San Antonio, earnestly watching a demonstration of how to make Molotov cocktails, or studying the Bolshevik Revolution. "Most businessmen could go to Chicago and get something out of it," Graf says. "You learn how to read a city budget, how to deal with the news media." Rodriguez says the most important subject is how to run a meeting, for that is where most organizations fail—either by having the same people make all the decisions, or by falling into endless unresolved debate. So the IAF teaches such mundane skills as how to plan and stick to an agenda, and how to resolve an issue.

No, the Alinsky connection was not the secret. At most it provided a useful frame of reference. Far more important were factors unique to San Antonio. There were breakdowns in city services that even the most sheltered Anglo could agree were inexcusable. There was a power vacuum in the city's leadership, so no one could mobilize to stop COPS when it was still vulnerable. Many COPS leaders like Andy Sarabia held civil service jobs and were immune to Anglo threats of economic retribution. San Antonio's ethnic minority had just become a numerical majority, so the old argument that Mexicans were powerless no longer had any validity. And most important, COPS had the Church.

It was as much a marriage of convenience as love at first sight. The Church has traditionally maintained a paternalistic attitude toward its Mexi-

_____
* No, the Yankees.

can American subjects. Only seven local Mexican American priests have been ordained in the San Antonio archdiocese in 250 years. Many priests never mastered Spanish, still the lingua franca on the West Side. Then, after Mao booted Belgian missionaries out of China, many came to the West Side in search of other downtrodden subjects. But by the seventies things were changing. Protestant denominations had been the great force for social reform during the civil rights fights of the sixties, but the Catholic Church was catching up. In San Antonio, as the West Side continued to deteriorate and young people moved to the North Side, it became obvious that the economic self-interest of the parish church lay in keeping the neighborhood up. San Antonio is not a rich archdiocese; there would be no help from the hierarchy. So COPS became not only good politics but also good religion.

The support of the Church was the crucial factor that got COPS started and kept it going. The Church was the only institution in the community that had the widespread allegiance of the people. It provided a financial base and a sense of permanence. It was a reservoir of leadership talent, and a way for people to keep in touch. But most of all, it gave COPS something no previous movement had had: a stamp of legitimacy. That is why even today the average COPS member would rather be led into battle by Father Albert Benavides, a fiery, immensely popular West Side priest, than any other COPS leader, even Gallego or Sarabia.

The role of the Church points the way to another of the reasons for COPS' success. The organization draws on the inherent strengths of the Mexican American community—qualities like loyalty, belief in basic values, and a love for family. COPS *is* a family, an extended family in the Mexican tradition. This pays off in unexpected ways: when COPS speakers approached the podium during early confrontations, the audience, without coaching, crowded around them to give moral support. *They* knew how awed their leaders were by symbols of power, but of course the council or the water board didn't; to them these tactics smacked of intimidation. That was fine with COPS —these moves became part of the game plan.

For all of its strengths and successes, COPS is approaching a critical phase in its history, one that may well test the ability of the organization to endure as a political force. Its leaders have chosen to tackle the most basic— and most elusive—of all issues in San Antonio: economic development. They have had enough of the traditional San Antonio wage scale, skewed toward the minimum wage and ranking far below the other big cities in the state. They want to bring high-paying industries to the city and they want them located near their neighborhoods, not far out on the North Side.

This will prove to be a very different fight than anything COPS has undertaken before. In the past the battle was in the political arena; COPS was dealing with people who at least nominally answered to them. There was always the ultimate weapon of the ballot box, as more than one candidate found out to his sorrow last spring. But in economic development the enemy is better insulated. At an October training session, COPS area leaders stood beneath a wall chart eight feet high listing the names and positions of the members of the elite Economic Development Foundation that is practically a roster of the San Antonio establishment. It includes bankers, downtown businessmen, and developers, who together have personally chipped in $1.5 million in the last three years to bring industry to San Antonio—mostly without success.

COPS leaders are convinced that the EDF, like the businessmen who ran off Henry Ford, prefers smaller industries that are harder to unionize and won't upset the wage scale. Cheap labor is also a useful selling point to counter fears of runaway utility bills. The EDF vigorously denies pushing cheap labor ("Who says that?" asks Tom Frost. "We don't. I've been there. That's the worst thing you can say. Plants want skilled labor"), but someone neglected to tell the EDF's consultant to softpeddle the cheap labor issue. In a secret report COPS somehow managed to sneak a look at, the consultant warned the EDF "not to attract industries that would upset the existing wage ladder." All the evidence indicates that the EDF is following this advice to the letter. For example, the report carefully identifies the high-wage and low-wage sectors of the metal industry; one of the EDF's proudest acquisitions, Bakerline oil tool supplier, matches the description of a cheap-labor operation.

But the issue may be moot, says Frost. "Asking me if I want heavy industry is like asking a man dying of thirst in the desert if he'd like a beer when there isn't one for a thousand miles. Sure I'd like it, but we can't get it. That kind of industry locates near markets, transportation, and water, and we haven't got any of them."

COPS, of course, disagrees (and so, for that matter, do some of the hustlers on the EDF itself, like developer Jim Dement). But what galls COPS above all else is that the EDF, which is the primary group trying to attract business to the city, conducts all its business in secret. No one in the city outside of the membership has a voice in anything the EDF does. "It is our future they're determining," Gallego told the COPS training session, "and they should be determining it out in the open." So COPS is committed to bringing the EDF out of the closet.

That almost happened a year ago— or more precisely, COPS was invited into the closet. A well-intentioned EDF member offered to put up $20,000— then the price of two memberships— "so that underprivileged groups on the Mexican American West Side and the black East Side can become part of the economic efforts for progress." But the affair was bungled from the start. The offer was made in the press rather than in person; its tone was insulting; and it smacked of tokenism. Sarabia rejected the offer, also in the press, by announcing that "COPS is not for sale," and added scathingly, "By the way, we don't consider ourselves underprivileged, because we have the will to fight for our dignity. We think *they're* underprivileged."

Everything about the coming battle with the EDF points to a tough struggle. The issue is a hard one to grasp; it is hardly as easy to understand as, say, water in the streets. The first COPS training session did not go well; the area leaders were slow to respond to Gallego's attempts to draw out their feelings. Finally Sarabia, exasperated, stood up in the corner of the room. He scolded them for their lack of anger— some were even making jokes—and asked, "Don't you know what cheap labor means? They're talking about *you*. Our kids can't find a decent job here. All they talk about is going to Houston or Dallas." That subdued things for awhile, but the feeling still filled the room that this was going to be a long, long fight. One important stratagem of an organization like COPS is to keep morale up by pointing to a continuing series of successes. That is possible with drainage, but how do you show results in economic development? Even if COPS can remove EDF's cloak of secrecy, that still doesn't produce one plant or one job. The economic cards, as Frost suggests, may be stacked against the city—and even if they aren't, even if COPS succeeds as it has before, the rewards may not trickle down to the neighborhoods for a dozen years.

For once COPS may also have the wrong side of the timing. The organization is entering a transitional phase, with the original leaders gradually turning over the reins to new recruits. Perhaps it is too early to say, but the second generation doesn't appear to have the intensity or the ability of the first. Gallego and especially Sarabia are remarkable people who have an almost mystical empathy with their constituency. No one coming up seems to have that. The theory of organizations like COPS is that people grow with their responsibilities, so perhaps someone will develop. But some of the newer COPS people seem to lack that most basic of ingredients—anger. Maybe that anger is only possible for those who remember the beginning; maybe COPS has grown fat with too many successes.

The most serious threat to the future of COPS, though, is the one least within its control. It is the pace with which San Antonio is rushing toward ethnic politics. The Mexican political clique, shut off from power all these years, finally got a base when they took over the San Antonio School Board last April; their first action was to fire the district's longtime Anglo lawyers and replace them with Mexicans from their own crowd—who took exactly one month to raise the district's legal fees astronomically. The targets for 1978 include the district attorney's office and a northwest San Antonio state senatorial district. Then there are the true Mexican radicals, a small but disproportionately vocal segment of the community, who also have a power base in the form of a couple of council seats. To both groups, ethnic political control of the city is the primary issue, and the more noise they make about it, the more the North Side is coming to view that as the sole issue too. And even though that is the one thing COPS does *not* care about, it may be COPS that suffers most.

The first shots in the Second Battle of the Alamo could be fired in January, when the city votes on a bond issue that contains many of COPS' pet projects— too many, some North Side critics are already saying. The numbers aren't encouraging: despite the fact that San Antonio has become a majority Mexican American city, the bulk of the voter turnout is still concentrated on the North Side. That could be fatal to the bond program's chances, and developer Jim Dement, for one, doesn't think it has a hope of passage.

No matter how the vote turns out, ethnic tensions are sure to be exacerbated. What if COPS loses? Make that loses *again*, for a COPS-backed school bond proposal went down to defeat by less than a thousand votes last spring. When the crunch comes, will COPS vote issues or race—and if it sticks to issues, will anyone listen? San Antonio in all likelihood is in for some rough years ahead, and the direction it is moving does not augur well for COPS. In the ethnic politics of the late seventies and early eighties, the "radicals" of today may well become the conservatives of tomorrow.

But even if COPS never accomplishes another thing, its legacy is indelible.

Long after time has dulled the recently laid concrete on the storm drains and sidewalks of the West Side, long after San Antonio has had its first Mexican American mayor, the repercussions of COPS will still be felt. For the real significance of COPS is not that it has changed streets but that it has changed people—its own people. There are for the first time ordinary folks on the West Side of San Antonio who do not see themselves as strangers in a strange land. Andy Sarabia, Beatrice Gallego, and a thousand others were awed the first time they set foot in city hall; now they are no longer prisoners of the myths and stereotypes that bound them up, and neither are their children.

One family active in COPS lives beside a drainage ditch on the South Side; even a moderate rain threatens their home and leaves water standing in the street. Late one evening this fall a politician and a friend stopped in front of the house to look at the tall grass that clogged the ditch and caused the flooding. The politician was pointing animatedly when a six-year-old boy emerged from the house, walked up to the strangers, and asked, "Are you COPS?"

Five years ago he would have meant something else. ★

State Politics and Elections

★

CHAPTER SIX

Where's My Line? Griffin Smith, jr. (June 76)
Ticket to Ride? Paul Burka (October 78)
... And Still Counting, John Bloom (January 79)
Behind the Lines, William Broyles Jr. (May 78)

WHERE'S MY LINE?

by Griffin Smith, jr.

Oh, for the good old days when there was nothing to worry about except gerrymandering.

"One man, one vote." The battle seems so long ago. All those vigorous debates in the Sixties, when lawyers, academics, and politicians disputed whether congressional districts (and legislative, and county commissioners', and city councils *ad infinitum*) should be apportioned with numerical equality: the whole controversy seems so quaint in retrospect. One man one vote is like so many other issues that once convulsed the American body politic —issues like free silver, the Hawley-Smoot Tariff, the income tax, Jim Crow. Some won, some lost; but no one debates them any longer. As issues they are settled. Of *course* one man one vote: was there really ever anything else?

"Perhaps the greatest problem which any historian has to tackle," the Cambridge scholar J. H. Plumb wrote recently, "is neither the cataclysm of revolution nor the decay of empire, but the process by which ideas become social attitudes." One man one vote first forced its way into the public consciousness in the Fifties as an import from late colonial Africa; a Lumumbist slogan. By 1963 it had been elevated into an American constitutional principle by William O. Douglas, writing for the Supreme Court in *Gray v. Sanders*. Today it is simply taken for granted as part of our conception of justice—even by most of those who once deplored the Court's decision as bad politics and worse law. Try to explain to a twelfth-grade civics class what nuances Everett Dirksen and his 23 co-signers had in mind when they proposed a constitutional amendment to infringe that principle, and you will be met with incomprehension. In less than two decades the slogan has become a social attitude.

In 1971 the Texas Legislature adopted a congressional redistricting plan (Senate Bill 1) in which the deviation between the largest and smallest districts was only 4.13 per cent. Declaring this plan unconstitutional two years later, the Supreme Court explained that the deviations "were not unavoidable, and the districts were not as mathematically equal as reasonably possible." (*White v. Weiser*) The Court imposed a new plan in which the maximum deviation was less than two-tenths of one per cent, or no more than 696 people within districts that contained approximately 466,530 people each. (The largest district, Jim Wright's, contained 466,930 people in the Court's plan; the smallest, Ray Roberts', contained 466,234.)

All of this came to mind a few weeks ago, when the Census Bureau released its current population estimates of people eighteen years and older in the country's congressional districts. They revealed that the variation among the voting age populations of Texas districts has grown to 29.9 per cent. That prompted a check of the Census Bureau's most recent estimates of *total* populations (the standard used by the Court), which was hardly less arresting: it showed that by that criterion, the Texas districts now vary by more than 18 per cent, ranging from a maximum of 546,000 (Jake Pickle's district) to a minimum of 454,000 (ironically, Jim Wright's district). Three years ago, in other words, the Supreme Court discarded the Legislature's plan because it contained a maximum deviation of about 4 per cent; now the maximum deviation under its own plan is more than four times that large. Normal population shifts have already obliterated the Court's finely tuned plan before the congressmen elected under it in 1974 have even had the chance to seek another term. Nor is Texas unique: the Census figures show that Florida's deviations are 29 per cent; New York's, 30 per cent.

The question inevitably arises: what —after redistricting bills in two regular legislative sessions, a special session called solely to redistrict, and prolonged litigation in the federal courts, all producing four different sets of congressional district maps within the space of six years—was the point?

Redistricting in Texas has required enormous labors to achieve numerical

146 STATE POLITICS AND ELECTIONS

Illustrated by Tom Evans

equality; yet numerical equality has not been achieved. By the standards of one man one vote, the districts are wildly awry all over again. Was it worth the trouble? Or are we fooling ourselves?

Recall for a moment the circumstances that led the Court to rule that one man one vote applied to congressional districting. The *Wesberry v. Sanders* case (1964) arose in Georgia, where one district had been drawn to be 203 per cent larger than a neighboring one. Faced with a disparity on that scale, the Court understandably felt that the result "contracts the value of some votes and expands that of others," and (with three justices dissenting) concluded that the Constitution required that "as nearly as practicable one man's vote in a congressional election is to be worth as much as another's." The Court's implicit overriding goal was to establish fairness in representation—a goal that admittedly had not been uppermost in the minds of state legislators across the country who had allowed some districts to be as much as 352 per cent larger than others.

But in pursuing that goal during the past twelve years, the Court seems to have lost sight of what it was originally trying to accomplish. Even assuming that substantial numerical equality between districts is possible—something the new Census figures seem to refute—the effect of the Court's rigid insistence on simple arithmetic has been to emphasize one aspect of fairness at the expense of others, blindly. One man one vote as enforced by the Court focuses on certain political consequences ("unequal" votes) and ignores or intensifies others (gerrymandering, separating voters from their traditional representatives and political subdivisions, producing geographically unmanageable districts). In the name of fairness the Court has picked and chosen which kinds of fairness it cares about and which it doesn't.

Take gerrymandering, for example. In Senate Bill 1 the Legislature, struggling to conform to one man one vote requirements, snipped off 40,711 people from the northeast corner of Harris County (Bob Eckhardt's district) and gave them to Jack Brooks' district. The area had been represented by Eckhardt since 1966. True, the Legislature's selection was affected by political considerations—Brooks is less beloved in almost any other direction the redistricters could have taken him, and they wanted to protect his seat—but the significant fact is that the Legislature had to find about 40,000 people *somewhere* to "even up" his district; one man one vote demanded it. The entire legislative discussion focused on *where* they could get them, not *whether* they should. Simply letting Eckhardt's district be about 40,000 people larger than average, and Brooks' 40,000 less, was not an allowable option. Why? It is worthwhile pausing to consider. Why should 40,711 people who reside a short bus ride away from Bob Eckhardt's office in Houston be forced to obtain their congressional representation from Jack Brooks in Beaumont? In what sense did this produce "fairer" representation for them? Its principal effect was to move their congressman 70 miles away. But the Court, which indirectly had caused this gerrymander, upheld it in 1973 with only minor adjustments.

Similarly, legislative gerrymander and judicial insistence on nearly perfect equality of districts have combined to give Bexar County the short end of the stick. San Antonians have a good case when they say they are entitled to two local congressmen. But if, for whatever reason, they don't get two, how are they helped by having large areas of their city assigned to Chick Kazen of Laredo instead of their hometown man, Henry B. Gonzalez? Why not recognize that, within some realistic limits, it is better for San Antonians to be represented by someone from San Antonio even if the resulting district is somewhat more populous than the ideal?

Urban areas have not been the only losers. For the sake of numerical equality the Court removed Brewster County in the Big Bend from the Trans-Pecos district where it had been since 1887, and placed its 7780 people in a district dominated by northwest San Antonio and the Hill Country counties. As things have turned out, residents of Brewster County cannot even savor the dubious pleasure of knowing that their votes are "worth" more than they would otherwise have been: their new district, says the Census, is now 4.12 per cent too large, their old district less than 1 per cent too large. If a Supreme Court justice were invited to speak in Alpine, he would be hard put to show how his enforcement of one man one vote had provided his audience with better, or fairer, representation.

And he would probably be wise to leave Dawson County (Lamesa) off his itinerary completely. Residents there awoke one morning to discover that the Court had cut the county into two pieces in order to remove 1648 people from the district of George Mahon and raise the neighboring district of Omar Burleson just that tiny bit closer to perfect equality. "If I had to choose a congressman other than Mr. Mahon, Mr. Burleson would be my next choice, all right," says County Judge Leslie Pratt. "But we were pretty satisfied with Mr. Mahon. He's represented Dawson County ever since this district was formed in 1934." The Court's plan put most, but not all, of one precinct into Burleson's district, leaving out, Judge Pratt says, "a little strip about two miles wide and eight miles long. I don't suppose there's over ten or twelve voters in that area," he explains, so rather than redraw the precinct boundaries, "we just let them go ahead and vote in Burleson's district. Nobody challenges them." Though the Court believed it was doing all this juggling for Dawson County's own good, "It doesn't make a lot of sense to us," Pratt says. "I understood they had some accountant run 'em through a computer or somethin', and that's the way it came out. I don't know about this computin'. I hope they don't go to dividin' *people*."

In what sense are those individuals (or anyone else in Texas) better represented as a result of the Court's disregard of Dawson County's established ties with Mahon? No one argues that an incumbent congressman "owns" his district (no one except perhaps some congressmen themselves in their more extravagantly egotistical moments); but it is unrealistic to pretend that voters and their representatives do not develop personal ties that transcend mathematics: ties that ought to be recognized as an element in fair representation. Chick Kazen, whose district has been protected in the era of one man one vote by some of the most awkward gerrymandering to occur in Texas, frankly acknowledges that the contortions necessary to save his seat (in the name of ideal equality) have interfered with another ideal, that of personal contact. In the past five years, portions of ten counties have been shuffled into or out of Kazen's district, leaving considerable numbers of South Texans confused about who really does represent them. "I think the people are entitled to know *who* their congressman is, and to have some stability in that," Kazen says. "He needs to get out there and know them on a first name basis. I still get letters from people in my old counties. They can't understand why I'm not still their congressman. In some cases, I can't understand it either."

In addition to dividing 27 counties between different congressional districts, complicating the map so badly that even the *Texas Almanac* has quit trying to specify which town belongs in which district, the Court's plan intensified a problem unique to Texas and a few other western states: districts so large that congressmen cannot establish satisfactory personal contact with their inhabitants. Omar Burleson's district includes parts of 33 counties and covers 30,000 square miles, for example. Robert Krueger's district is bigger than the state of Vir-

STATE POLITICS AND ELECTIONS   147

ginia. They have ballooned to such immense size because the Court refuses to admit that vast distances can impair fair representation as much or more than variations in numerical equality. (The Court has dismissed such claims with the scornful observation that "people, not land or trees or pastures, vote.") Recalls Burleson: "When I came to Congress I had twelve counties and 230,000 people. I could tour around and visit the whole district. Now it's much, much harder just to get to see people. But people *should* know you. That is what representative government is all about."

You need not pine for the bad old days of districts that varied by huge percentages (or feel that your Santa Gertrudis should have the franchise) to recognize that an insistence on mathematical equality under the geographical conditions of West Texas may do more harm than good to the goal of fair representation. Nothing the Court can say can erase the fact that geography is a factor in Texas as it is not in, say, Connecticut; and representation here is a function not merely of numbers but also of territory—the ground a representative has to cover to do his job. If a West Texas representative had 400,000 widely scattered people in his spread-out district while a central San Antonio representative had 600,000 in his compact district several miles square, might not the outcome be fairer than the present arrangement, to all concerned? At the least, might not those 1648 folks in Dawson County be allowed to stick with George Mahon?

The conventional one man one vote answer, of course, is *absolutely not*. One man one vote rests on the basic premise that a citizen's vote has an objective "value" or "worth" which can be measured arithmetically by counting the number of people in the district where he lives. Thus, if your district contains 502,000 people, you hold a share of a congressman exactly 1/502,000ths in size, and the bigger your district gets the smaller your share gets—measurably diluting your influence on the political process. The Court has taken the position that people are hurt if their votes are diluted by a fraction as small as the 4.13 per cent in Senate Bill 1: the difference between a 1/458,581st share and a 1/477,856ths share. The best way to test this notion is to ask the voters of Austin, Brenham, La Grange, and other parts of Jake Pickle's district whether they have lately felt a vague malaise attributable to the fact that their votes are "worth" so much less than they used to be: Pickle's district, you will recall, is now the most populous in Texas, some 8.75 per cent bigger than the ideal. Or ask the voters in Fort Worth if they have sensed any special exhilaration traceable to the fact that Jim Wright's district has shrunk to 9.56 per cent less than it "should" be, giving them each that much unfair, unreasonable, extra clout in Washington. Is there anyone, in either district, who can show how these shifts have made the slightest difference to him? The truth is, nobody has even noticed them. In realistic terms of actual representation, it doesn't matter at all that Pickle has 44,000 "too many" constituents, nor that Wright has 48,000 "too few." The whole thing sounds absurd; politics doesn't work that way. Yet these are the kinds of distinctions the Court has solemnly insisted make a serious difference—indeed, make the *most* significant difference. This is what one man one vote is now all about. If the 18.31 per cent deviation between Pickle's and Wright's districts were included in a redistricting plan offered to the Court, the plan would be struck down in an instant as unconstitutional. The distinctions sound persuasive in a legal brief; they are absurdly insignificant in real life.

By pushing the broadly accepted principle of one man one vote to microscopic extremes, the Court has required legislatures and judges to expend great time and effort to eliminate slight variations—even though (1) the variations are not significant in the real world, (2) the attempt to remove them often aggravates other, equally important, problems of fair representation, and (3) as the Census figures show, they are not actually eliminated at all. As presently enforced, one man one vote has become an abstract judicial exercise engaged in for its own sake, not for the sake of the people it is ostensibly trying to help.

To the extent that the Court's policies brought an end to outrageous variations in congressional apportionment, they had a salutary effect on American politics. But are "outrageous variations" really a menace any longer? To the general public one man one vote—meaning substantial equality of districts, not microscopic perfection—has become an aspect of fairness. The public would have no patience with the sort of backwoods (and backroom) skulduggery that went on before *Wesberry*. Politicians, much as we tend to disparage them, are not immune to the attitudes of their society, of which a general feeling about fairness is one. It is not the Thirteenth Amendment that keeps our politicians from reinstituting slavery, nor the Nineteenth that prevents them from depriving women of the right to vote; it is our social attitude about what is fair and just. No matter how willing legislators are to monkey with redistricting—a subject in which they inevitably have a prurient self-interest—there are limits beyond which our contemporary social attitudes will not let them go. These limits are far stricter than most people would have dreamed of twenty years ago.† Mathematically they are probably strict enough that the Court is now protecting us against largely imaginary evils.

In any event, the historian who finally documents the growth of one man one vote from a slogan into a social attitude may well conclude that our judges' (and to a less doctrinaire degree our own) attachment to that principle is symptomatic of Americans' declining faith in any sort of organic community that overrides all our diversity and individuality. To think in terms of defending our personal 1/502,000ths share of a congressman is to admit how little we really believe that our politicians, our fellow citizens, and perhaps we ourselves, think about "the common good" anymore. Americans could not have adopted one man one vote as readily as they have unless they had first lost confidence, to a very real degree, in the ability of public officials to look beyond their own interests and those of their constituents to reach a sympathetic understanding of the needs of the entire society. ★

---

†**What are they?** Certainly *Wesberry*-style deviations of 200 and 300 per cent would offend most people's sense of fairness; *Weiser*-style deviations of two-tenths of a per cent almost certainly do not. Even the 18 per cent-plus deviations in Texas today have caused no alarm. Where, between those points, would most people draw the line?

Politics
by Paul Burka

TICKET TO RIDE?

The Republicans have their best lineup ever, but it may be destined for another elephant graveyard.

When a veteran Galveston legislator retired in 1976, a delegation of Republicans urged an ambitious local businessman named Douglas McLeod to run for the open seat under their banner. Young, articulate, affluent, with an intensely conservative record in nonpartisan local politics, McLeod seemed to be perfect Republican material. If he could be persuaded, the GOP could pick up a legislative seat in what is normally a labor stronghold. But McLeod decided to run as a Democrat and is no doubt thankful he did; today he is eyeing a Senate seat that he would have no chance to win as a Republican.

That small incident says a lot about the state of the Republican party in Texas today. Except in wealthy Southwest Houston and North Dallas, it is still regarded largely as an organization for people of principle rather than ambition. That is fine for churches, but not so good for political parties.

If ever Republicans are going to make real inroads into Democratic one-party domination of Texas politics, 1978 should be the year. The ticket is the party's best ever: John Tower, seeking his fourth term in the Senate; Bill Clements, the first Republican candidate for governor with the personal reputation and campaign budget to compete on even terms; Jim Baker, back from running the Ford presidential campaign to become the first Republican to make a serious race for attorney general; half a dozen or more congressional candidates with a chance to win; and a like number of legislative challengers. But with big effort comes big risk. If the Republicans lose—and they could get wiped out, losing everything including Tower's seat—how long will it be before the state party will recover, before other candidates of stature will be induced to run, before a Douglas McLeod finally decides that political ambition and Republicanism are compatible?

It wasn't supposed to be this way. At least twice before—once in the early sixties, again in the early seventies—Republicans thought the end of Democratic dominance was at hand. John Connally almost lost his first race for governor in 1962, but the Kennedy assassination and LBJ's accession stopped that first Republican drift. Then came Nixon, John Mitchell's "Southern strategy," and a Republican resurgence throughout Dixie. John Connally surveyed the political scene in the early seventies and concluded his future lay with the Republican party, but he seems to have guessed wrong. Though Republicans have picked up a number of seats in the Legislature in the seventies (most of them thanks to redistricting), as well as county judgeships in the state's two largest counties, Democrats, for the most part, are as much in control as ever.

Republican hopefuls Jim Baker, Bill Clements, John Tower (left to right): If the race is to the swift, then why are these candidates riding an elephant?

What went wrong? There is no shortage of theories. A frequent explanation is Watergate, which undercut Republican momentum across the country. Some Republicans complain that the party leadership has always concentrated on the top of the ticket—that is, Tower—to the detriment of everyone else from gubernatorial candidates on down. Others feel there has been a misplaced, almost European harping on the party itself, when the emphasis should be on candidates who happen to be Republicans, not Republicans who happen to be candidates. The more scientific election analysts point to the failure of Republicans to woo minority voters when the Democratic party was still segregationist; now blacks and Mexican Americans pull the Democratic lever in ever increasing numbers. But much of the explanation lies in the resilience of the Texas Democratic party, which has almost entirely reconstituted itself in the decade since John Connally's governorship. Eight years ago Democrats offered Lloyd Bentsen for senator, Preston Smith for governor, Ben Barnes for lieutenant governor, Crawford Martin for attorney general, Jerry Sadler for land commissioner, Bob Calvert for comptroller, Jesse James for treasurer; no ideological variety, no appeal. Compare that with this year's slate of Krueger, Hill, Hobby, White, Armstrong, Bullock. Only Treasurer Warren G. Harding seems out of place.

Similar things are happening throughout the South. Republicans have lost ground since the early seventies everywhere except Louisiana; in Arkansas, which eight years ago had a Republican

Illustrated by Tom Ballenger

governor, and Georgia, which almost did, Republicans have almost disappeared without a trace. As John Connally can testify, political trends are fickle. But if there's going to be a reversal in Texas, 1978 may be the Republican party's last chance for a long, long time.

Senate

Early in 1977 Congressman Charlie Wilson of Lufkin reluctantly told friends he'd decided not to try for John Tower's U.S. Senate seat in 1978. He ran through some reasons: his own rising career in the House, Democratic rival Bob Krueger's head start in raising money, the likelihood that then-popular President Jimmy Carter would turn into a burden by election day, and . . . Wilson stopped, shook his head. "Nah, that's not it," he said. "I'll tell you why I'm not running. Because John Tower's the luckiest SOB in politics."

Sometimes Tower does seem blessed by fate. He won his seat in a 1961 special election that was necessary only because Lyndon Johnson had persuaded the Texas Legislature to let him run for the Senate and national office simultaneously. To win the special election, he needed two more breaks—appointment of a lackluster successor to fill LBJ's seat temporarily, and a Democratic party rent by factionalism—and got both. When he came up for reelection in 1966, the Democrats were still split and Tower exploited the rift to win again. When Texas Democrats finally nominated a challenger with broad party support, Barefoot Sanders in 1972, George McGovern was at the top of the ticket and Tower campaigned more against him than Sanders. This year things were supposed to be different: John Tower was number one on every loyal Democrat's hit list. But that changed overnight when John Hill upset Dolph Briscoe. The same Democrats who most want to beat Tower—a coalition of progressives, moderates, and party faithful—are on the verge of capturing the statehouse and all its patronage; for them Bill Clements, not John Tower, is the Republican to beat.

Even so, Tower's luck may be tested. Late-summer polls showed him only narrowly ahead—and trouble early in the race is usually a bad sign for an incumbent. Compounding Tower's troubles, Krueger is strong in two places where Tower usually runs well: among Spanish-surname voters and in the sprawling 21st Congressional District. In 1972 Tower collected 35 per cent in Mexican American boxes, very high for a Republican. Krueger strategists, spreading the word that Tower opposed extending the Voting Rights Act to Texas, predict they'll cut that in half. As for the 21st—solid conservative country stretching from northwest San Antonio to the Big Bend—it is Krueger's district and political base.

Such small swings are crucial in a race where the main issue is who can measure up to the average voter's concept of a United States senator. With the aid of slick TV spots, Tower has always excelled at this, not always deservedly. Despite an undistinguished and often frivolous first term, he rode a brilliantly orchestrated TV campaign to his largest majority ever, 57 per cent, in 1966. Since then he has transformed himself, to the surprise of many, into one of the most powerful and respected senators on the minority side. Despite his rock-ribbed conservative reputation, he is no Strom Thurmond or Ronald Reagan and has little use for the extreme right wing of the GOP. Though Krueger will attack him this fall for his failure to author major legislation, the truth is that Republicans seldom have that opportunity in a Democratic Congress; nevertheless, just this summer Tower tacked an important amendment onto an urban aid bill, substituting formulas favorable to Sunbelt cities for a Northeast-oriented Administration proposal. Yet Tower's new Washington reputation hasn't made much more impression on the Texas electorate than his old one did. If anything, voters probably have a clearer picture of Krueger, the ambitious, intellectual former Shakespearean scholar who rose to national prominence through his advocacy of oil and gas deregulation. No doubt Tower will, as always, use TV effectively to get his message across, but if Krueger can raise enough money to fight back, Tower once again may have to depend on a stroke of good fortune.

Governor

Can Bill Clements really beat John Hill? Hardly anyone but Clements thinks so, but then at this point in the primary campaign hardly anyone but Clements thought he could beat former Republican State Chairman Ray Hutchison for the GOP nomination. The difference in the primary was money: Clements spent an unprecedented $1.8 million; Hutchison, a paltry $175,000. The multimillionaire chairman of SEDCO, Dallas-based drilling contractors, swayed the Republican electorate by reminding them of past failures when GOP candidates ran out of money and momentum in the fall and by pledging that it wouldn't happen to him.

Money isn't the only thing that separates Clements from previous Republican nominees. No Republican has ever run such a sophisticated campaign. Clements' forces have analyzed recent election returns and come up with the game plan they feel their candidate needs to win. It works like this. The last four major Republican candidates —Jack Cox in 1962, Paul Eggers in 1968 and 1970, and Hank Grover in 1972—suffered from identical handicaps. None had a name of stature, none had an effective organization; none had enough money to make an all-out race. Yet all accumulated between 43 and 47 per cent of the vote. By Clements' reckoning he is starting the race at 45 per cent.

How to make up the difference? In the past, Republicans have run well in the state's largest population centers (in the 1970 senatorial race, George Bush carried Houston and Dallas, and still lost to Lloyd Bentsen by 150,000 votes) while getting nickel-and-dimed to death in rural counties. They conceded the minority vote and made little headway with conservative Democrats content with the likes of Preston Smith and Dolph Briscoe. Clements, however, intends to concede nothing. He is particularly focusing on rural Texas, where his strategists hope to eat into Hill's lead enough to let the city vote carry the election. To this end they've snapped up Briscoe's campaign treasurer and put him to work organizing the 230 rural counties, using a lot of old Briscoe hands around the state. One Clements aide contrasts a recent showing at a function in Stephenville, where two hundred people showed up, with the old Eggers days: he remembers going into Lubbock and finding one lone supporter at a fund raiser, going into Sweetwater and finding none.

So what's wrong with this picture? Just one thing. Much of the Republican vote in previous elections—as much as 20 per cent—came from moderate-to-liberal Democrats disenchanted with the party nominee. Those folks won't be voting Republican this time. Clements' 45 per cent base just dropped below 40. And despite the much-touted Briscoe defections, their value is questionable; an Austin lawyer experienced in Democratic campaign politics says bluntly, "Clements doesn't have the *right* Briscoe people." In any event, even if Clements gets every Briscoe vote, every Hutchison vote, plus all his own primary votes, that's still less than Hill's primary total. The general election turnout is larger, it is true, but many of the newcomers are from minority groups that traditionally vote Democratic.

Despite the holes in Clements' battle plan, and notwithstanding early polls that show Hill with a three-to-one edge, it would be a mistake to write off the Republican challenger. Anyone with a television budget of around $2 million will do some damage. But will Clements' aggressive, holy-war brand of conservatism really strike a chord with an increasingly sophisticated Texas electorate? Can he really convince voters that Hill is, as Clements puts it, "a fla-a-aming liberal?" Come to think of it, that sounds familiar. Another candidate with a lot of money, fellow named Briscoe, tried that a while back.

Attorney General

Jim Baker thought he could beat Democrat Price Daniel, Jr., for attorney general, and he was right. The only trouble was that he beat him six months too soon: Daniel was so worried about Baker that he husbanded his money for the fall campaign, thereby managing to blow a 20-point lead in the polls in the last two weeks of the spring. The beneficiary of Daniel's blunder was Mark White, the little-known secretary of state who made the most of having TV time to himself. Suddenly White has emerged as darling of the conservative wing of the Democratic party and is already being touted as John Hill's successor as governor. Meanwhile, Baker, who was preparing to run a straight conservative-liberal race against Daniel, finds himself in need of a new strategy.

The new tack will focus on Baker's superior legal qualifications. Undoubtedly they are superior—Baker has spent eighteen years in the hardball atmosphere of the big Houston law firms, while White's training is mostly as a political operative—but does anyone care about qualifications except the League of Women Voters? Actually, no one knows, for there's never been a serious race for attorney general in the fall. It's just possible that the stature John Hill brought to the AG's department, building it into a first-rate law office and deemphasizing political considerations in areas like legal opinions, will linger in the minds of voters.

Even though Baker's race won't get the attention it deserves, it may be the one that has the most bearing on the future of the Texas Republican party. In the last quarter century, the GOP has competed in Texas on an almost even basis for president and U.S. Senate. They are in the ball park in most gubernatorial races. But they've never come close to penetrating the rest of the ballot. If Texas is ever to become a two-party state, the Republicans are going to have to field candidates like Jim Baker for offices like attorney general. Baker is a heavyweight with impeccable credentials, both personal (he is the great-grandson of the founder of Houston's elite Baker & Botts law firm) and political (he was President Ford's campaign manager in 1976). If he wins, or even comes close, other bright, ambitious Republicans will follow his lead. If he gets wiped out, Republicans will go back to running folks like Tom Cole, who managed 24 per cent of the vote against John Hill in 1974. Indeed, the presence of just such an unknown—Gaylord Marshall, the token Republican candidate for lieutenant governor—may hurt Baker badly on November 7. His name appears on the ballot between the Republican heavyweights and Baker; Marshall's name may be the familiar signal that voters can safely ignore the rest of the Republican contenders.

Railroad Commissioner

When former Land Commissioner Jerry Sadler rolled to a solid lead in the crowded Democratic primary race for railroad commissioner, Republicans thought they might have a chance to grab a seat on the powerful body that regulates, among other things, the oil and gas industry. Sadler, after all, had a tarnished political reputation dating back to his reprimand by the Legislature in 1969. But a statewide press barrage against Sadler boosted Dolph Briscoe appointee John Poerner to an easy win in the runoff. That was bad news for Republican challenger Jim Lacy, an independent oilman from Midland with a campaign war chest large enough to make more than a token race.

Though Poerner is a vast improvement over his predecessor, petroleum industry mouthpiece Jim Langdon, he is still no prize and in a true two-party state would have a tough time against the more articulate Lacy. But past election results hold out little hope for Lacy. Four years ago Republicans contested two seats on the commission; both GOP candidates polled around 27 per cent—approximately the hard-core Republican vote in Texas. In 1976 former Railroad Commission hearing examiner Walter Wendlandt, who had ruled against Coastal States Gas Corporation in a major case, advanced that showing by 5 per cent. If Lacy can pick up another 5 per cent, he can consider it a moral victory.

Congressional Races

Nowhere has the Republican party's failure to grow into a major force in Texas politics been more evident than in congressional races. Republicans hold just two places in the 24-member Texas delegation—the same number they had sixteen years ago. Worse, Republicans have seen three seats slip away in the mid-seventies. If ever there is to be a Republican renaissance, this should be the year, for five Democratic incumbents are not seeking reelection and three others are clinging to office in marginal districts. Democratic prospects are hardly enhanced by Jimmy Carter's low popularity in the state. But despite conventional political wisdom that off-year congressional elections are a referendum on the standing of the party in power, Texas voters have never seen things that way. They regard congressmen as local, not national, officials, and many are no more likely to vote for a Republican congressman than for a Republican county commissioner. So, although Republicans are shooting for all eight shaky Democratic seats, they are unlikely to score any hits.

Probably their best chance is in West Texas, where former Odessa Mayor Jim Reese stunned House Appropriations Committee chairman George Mahon by getting 45 per cent of the vote in 1976. But neither showed up for the rematch. Mahon retired after 44 years in the House, leaving the field to Democratic State Senator Kent Hance, while Reese lost the primary to George Bush, Jr. Bush, son of the former Houston congressman (and current presidential aspirant), operates out of Midland but is fighting an uphill battle against the bulk of the district's population in Lubbock, Hance's political base.

Other retiring Democratic incumbents include Omar Burleson (Abilene), Ray Poage (Waco), Tiger Teague (Bryan), and of course Bob Krueger (San Antonio and points west). In the spring Republicans had high hopes of taking at least a couple of these, but Democrats wouldn't cooperate: several candidates Republicans were hoping to oppose lost the nomination. Particularly galling to GOP hopes was banker Marvin Leath's runoff victory over unabashed liberal Lane Denton in Poage's old district after Denton had led the primary. Now Republican hopes to pick up a seat are focused on Krueger's former bailiwick, where the GOP candidate is 32-year-old Tom Loeffler of Kerrville, a former White House aide under President Ford. Republicans ought to have a good chance in this extremely conservative district—Krueger had to spend more money than any other congressional candidate in the U.S. to win here in 1974—but Democrat Nelson Wolff, a former San Antonio state senator, will erode Republican strength in affluent northwest Bexar County.

The three Democrats with marginal districts are Bob Gammage and Bob Eckhardt in Houston and Jim Mattox in Dallas. Only Eckhardt's district has not been in Republican hands in recent years, and the veteran liberal was hard pressed to win his primary against a conservative Democrat. Enhancing GOP prospects, all three Democrats are controversial in their own party, and Republican candidates will be well financed. But past elections have shown the advantages of incumbency to be enormous, and unless Republicans can entice conservative Democrats, who traditionally cross over only for president and senator, the beleaguered incumbents should win all three.

The Opening Line

Tower over Krueger by 2
Hill over Clements by 6
White over Baker by 10
Odds represent per cent of the total vote. ★

REPORTER
BY JOHN BLOOM

"Quit trying to figure it out, lady, the polls closed hours ago."

Politics
...And Still Counting

Exactly one week after the November general election, I sat down in the Capitol-area office of Bob Lemens and watched as he frantically excavated through several inches of paper strewn across his desk. "I hope you don't mind interruptions," he said, after discovering a lost message at the Paleolithic level. As he dialed an election judge in Abilene, I had time to study the wall-sized Texas map to Lemens' left. Half its counties had been ripped off, others were beginning to peel, and the entire state had turned a sickly yellow, as though it were slowly crumbling into chaos.

I was sitting at the very heart of the Texas election system. As head of the elections division in the Secretary of State's office, Lemens is charged with seeing that all votes are counted, tabulated, and certified. But the disorder in his office was entirely appropriate. There may be another state somewhere with a worse system for choosing its elected officials, but not in this country. Texas has not one but 254 separate systems —each controlled almost entirely by county-level officials—and every two years the horror stories recur: ballots improperly prepared, computer programs botched, votes never reported, ballots voided that should be counted or counted that should be voided. Sometimes, as in the May referendum on horseracing, even the outcome can remain uncertain for weeks. The potential for distorting an election, either by negligence or outright larceny, is nowhere greater than in Texas.

Texas elections have never been models of administrative efficiency—in 1918 several West Texas counties never bothered to report results because they (correctly) considered Governor W. P. Hobby a shoo-in—but this year the closeness of two major races made the defects more apparent than ever. Later this month the state's first Republican governor in 106 years will enter office, but it's still impossible to obtain the precise statistical data that would show exactly which voters elected Bill Clements and why. Most of what the public knows about the November election comes from either the Texas Election Bureau (TEB), a loose-knit association of newspapers and television stations with an official-sounding name, or the News Election Service, a reporting organization operated solely for the television networks and wire services. The Secretary of State, ironically, is not required by law to report any results to the public. All he has to do is enter the official returns into an enormous ledger kept in a vault in the State Capitol. If you want to know how the election turned out, you have to go to the Capitol and read it.

The root of the problem is that elections represent one of the last fiefdoms controlled almost exclusively by county commissioners. Hence Dallas County uses one kind of voting machine, Harris County another. Travis County uses computer punch cards, and Bexar County has two kinds of voting machines *and* punch cards. In Webb County (Laredo), voters use something called a Valtec optical scanner that "reads" your vote off a paper ballot, and the overwhelming majority of the counties (209) still use paper ballots only. Some counties count ballots by hand, others by computer, and even the counties that use computers don't use uniform programs.

Douglas S. Harlan, a San Antonio political scientist and twice-defeated Republican congressional candidate, has compiled the only published source for official election data in Texas, a book called *TexaStats,* which appears irregularly as the need arises. "If one wished to design an election system guaranteed to produce errors and foster inequities," he wrote in the most recent edition, "no imagination would be required. The Texas system stands as a model." He went on to cite the familiar snafus common to every Texas election—names omitted from ballots, returns not reported, canvass totals that don't equal the sum of precinct totals, precincts with voter turnouts in excess of 100 per cent, ad infinitum ad nauseam. Legislators

Institutional Politics

PART THREE

As the changing character of Texas society has transformed the electoral landscape, the actors and institutions governing the state have changed as well. Offices with a statewide constituency remain dominated by the predominantly Anglo, conservative, and male political cast of the state at large; the Legislature, however, where the state's diversity is expressed through regional representation, has experienced increasing membership by representatives of the state's ethnic and ideological minorities, women, and Republicans.

The Legislature has become a major battleground in the struggles between old and new, rural and urban, rich and poor, consumer and producer. The state's growing population, urbanization, and expanding economy continually force the Legislature to confront a wide range of new issues. Recent problems facing Texas highlight the need for legislators who take their jobs seriously and exercise informed judgment in policymaking. To solve these problems also requires an increasingly active state government.

Although Texans traditionally abhor big government, and bureaucracy in particular, the new activism of the state government has generated its own expanding bureaucracy. Texans encounter more and more red tape and bureaucratese in Austin, as well as Washington. And Texas politicians increasingly find that alliances with state agencies and relevant interest groups can help them to solidify their political fortunes. While these politicians make hay at home by railing against big government in Washington, they build political careers by nurturing big government in Austin.

The Texas politicians who successfully translate state careers into national power find plenty of bureaucracy in Washington to attack. And Washington has often found Texans to be among the most talented and influential politicians in the nation. For generations the state has exercised extraordinary power in Congress through control of committees and party leadership positions. Likewise, Texas has often produced savvy political advisors, from Colonel House in the days of Woodrow Wilson to Robert Strauss in the modern era. At times, Texas politicos find themselves leaders of opposing forces that interpret the needs and interests of Texas and the nation quite differently.

Such conflicts seem certain to continue as the state diversifies. The chapters in Part III examine the nature of the actors and institutions governing Texas, and the changing character of the political conflict among and within them. Chapter Seven looks at the Legislature, Chapter Eight at the bureaucracy, and Chapter Nine at Texans in Washington. Together, these chapters characterize the personalities and conflicting forces determining public policies and the future of the state.

BEHIND THE LINES

Most newspapers and a number of magazines routinely endorse candidates for public office. We don't. We do, of course, have a great deal to say about politics and politicians. In addition to taking close looks at virtually every major political figure in the state, we have picked the best and worst legislators, rated the Texas congressional delegation, and handicapped primary elections. But none of those is quite the same as an endorsement. The difference is one of writing about Texas politics as they are, not as we think they should be. The dangerous thing about endorsements is that they tend to obscure such crucial distinctions.

If we predict a leader in a statewide race, as we did last month, we are no more endorsing that candidate than we would be endorsing Notre Dame if we had predicted they would beat Texas in the Cotton Bowl. Even a legislator who has managed to earn a place on our "ten worst" list is not necessarily (Texas politics being what they are) worse than his opponent.

Endorsements are really a relic from another era, a time when most cities were run by political machines and the majority of voters were abysmally lacking in political sophistication. Some newspapers fancied themselves independent forces crusading in the public interest; their endorsement was a means of educating voters to the evils of machine politics and the people who perpetuated them. Other papers were mouthpieces for the machines. But times have changed. The public is no longer so politically naive, and, alas, when it comes to endorsements, many publications are no longer so concerned with the public interest. Far too many journals let their loyalties to politicians and causes interfere with their loyalties to their readers. That is why the typical political endorsement would be classified as fictional material by most public libraries. It paints in the rosiest hues all the virtues of embraced candidate A, neglecting altogether or else concentrating solely on the numerous vices of rejected candidate B. Endorsements are bad journalism, in theory and in practice.

We intend to avoid that trap; we believe our readers are capable of making their own decisions. But we intend to give you plenty to think about while you're making up your minds.

But for Lyndon Johnson's national political ambitions, we wouldn't be writing about political primaries this month. Back in 1959, Johnson persuaded the Texas Legislature to move the 1960 primary date back three months so he could wrap up the Democratic nomination for U.S. Senator and still be free to seek the presidency. Johnson ended up as John F. Kennedy's running mate, of course, and appeared twice on the Texas ballot; he would have remained a senator even if the national ticket had lost. Johnson's legacy remains with us today: Texas has one of the earliest primary election dates in the country.

The early primary has only one redeeming feature—it takes place in the spring, when the weather is livable, instead of in the intolerable heat of late July. But that is less important these days, when far more campaigning takes place in air-conditioned living rooms via television than at outdoor rallies. The minimal advantage of better weather is cancelled by a number of minuses the Legislature could not have foreseen when it yielded to Lyndon's urgings.

Despite the fact that the old primaries took place when voters had to pay a poll tax, turnouts today are consistently lower. Candidates have never been able to stir up much interest during the spring; even this year's closely contested battles for governor and senator haven't penetrated public indifference. The early primary forces the voters to focus on politics for an entire year—something most people are unwilling to do. There is a natural rhythm to American politics that reaches its peak in the fall of even-numbered years. Even though Texas has traditionally been a one-party state, our early primary is out of phase with the cycle. With the Republican party growing in strength, the general election will become increasingly significant, and it seems self-evident that the closer the primary falls to the general election, the greater public interest will be. One race that is definitely affected by the gap between elections is the Democratic primary between Bob Krueger and Joe Christie to see who will oppose Republican U.S. Senator John Tower. The match between Tower and the Democratic winner is sure to arouse strong passions in the fall, but that's more than half a year away; in mid-April, half the Democratic electorate remains undecided and uninterested.

For those insiders who do think about politics regardless of the season, the spring primary has stretched the political year into a biennium. The filing deadline is in February; fund raising and campaign planning must begin long before that. A candidate who already holds office has to choose between neglecting his job and neglecting his future. Bob Krueger is a talented congressman, but his constituents were virtually without representation for most of the last year while he toured the state in search of money and support. On the other hand, Joe Christie was criticized by his own supporters for staying too long on the job as chairman of the State Board of Insurance. Either way you can't win.

Another drawback to the early primary, and perhaps the most serious one, is that it places an undesirable premium on a candidate's ability to raise money. That problem has even become an issue in the Republican gubernatorial primary between Ray Hutchison and William Clements. The well-heeled Clements has tried to capitalize on his wealth by pointing out how previous GOP standard-bearers have run short of funds during the long campaign. Candidates who draw on big money can run forever; those with limited resources are at a greater disadvantage than ever. Money is inevitably a factor in politics, of course, but the early primary date multiplies its influence.

Texas is already the most difficult state in the nation to campaign in: the area is so immense, the population so spread out, the electorate so diverse. The early primary is an additional burden candidates should not have to bear. The Legislature should push the primary back to late August, after summer vacations, and likewise shorten the runoff campaign to two weeks from the present four. It isn't often that the Legislature has a chance to do something that benefits politicians and the public too. ★

William Broyles, Jr.

Typical election-night scene: ballot boxes sit unopened and tallying takes forever.

have occasionally been brazen enough to suggest that Texas needs a uniform voting procedure (like the all-machine states of Louisiana and New Mexico) or a state election commission to coordinate efforts, but no one has been willing to challenge the omnipotence of the county commissioners. Shortly after this election Clements announced that election reform would be one of his priorities. It will be interesting to see whether he can clean up the nation's most confused voting system without violating his pledge to curb the growth of bureaucracy.

It's no small wonder that the Texas Election Bureau has been called the slowest election-night reporting service in the country, since it must painstakingly compile vote totals from these 254 independent sources. (Some are *very* independent: a few counties still don't post returns every two hours, as required by state law, and in East Texas some counties are notorious for shutting down at 2 a.m., regardless of whether the vote count is complete.) The TEB has been keeping track of elections since 1916, operating from a long, narrow room on the fourth floor of the *Dallas Morning News* building. It was originally a subscription service for participating newspapers, but today it represents the sole reporting source for an entire state. Regardless of where you live—Monahans, Brownsville, or Houston—everything you know about the election emanates from the TEB. The vote totals are called in by volunteer county correspondents, and then computer printouts are handed to just two reporters, one from Associated Press, the other from United Press International. Election-night analysis depends on the ability of those two reporters to digest a fifty-foot computer printout in a matter of minutes, so the public has to be content with gross totals containing little information about geographic or ethnic voting patterns.

"It's not nearly as bad as it used to be," said Lemens. "We are beginning to clean up some of the most flagrant abuses. But what you have to remember is that an election is not a precise science. It's an art form. Probably the only thing that has kept our elections straight and honest up to now is that we have amateurs running them."

By the only criterion that really matters—public confidence in the system—it works passably well. But when South Texas political boss George Parr of Duval County delivered 201 votes for Lyndon Johnson in 1948, the system tottered on the very edge of legitimacy, and nothing since then has greatly improved it. The recounts requested by John Hill and Bob Krueger this year were more than exercises in futile optimism; the discovery of a single computer error in a single county could have put both of them in office. It's estimated that Texas would have to spend up to ten million dollars in equipment and employees, not to mention the hours spent revising the Election Code, just to make the system work uniformly in all 254 counties. For our peace of mind, that's cheap. ★

The One and Only Texas Legislature

CHAPTER SEVEN

The House Is Not a Home, Chase Untermeyer (September 77)
The Ten Best and the Ten Worst Legislators, Paul Burka (July 79)
Six Crises, Paul Burka (January 79)
Big Deal, Paul Burka (January 76)

THE HOUSE IS NOT A HOME

by Chase Untermeyer

In which our hero, an intrepid freshman, manages to survive 140 days of lobbyists, parties, wheeling, dealing, Christians, Lions, whites, blacks, reds, greens, and other hazards of the Texas Legislature.

November 3, 1976, 10 a.m.: A knock at the door. Still groggy from last night's bittersweet election partying, I open it to find a messenger from the University of Houston with an invitation from the president and Board of Regents to a dinner honoring Speaker of the House Bill Clayton *tonight*. The invitation is addressed to the Honorable Me. What a difference a day makes: only a few hours ago I was a Republican candidate for the Legislature in a white-socks and silk-stocking district on Houston's west side, and this morning I'm honorable. In the expansive good mood I have on this day of general GOP gloom, the state representative-elect from District 83 accepts with pleasure. So the lobbying starts this early. In the next several days I am also to receive a bronze paperweight bearing the Texas A&M seal and an application for free tickets to the remaining games in the University of Texas football season.

November 22: Today begins "freshman orientation" for the 38 newly elected members of the House at UT-Austin's LBJ School of Public Affairs. In the shuffle from conference hall to seminar room to reception, I am pleased and somewhat relieved to find that the old stereotype of a state legislator—a boozing hayseed out to have a good ole boy's good ole time in Austin—is nowhere in sight. Observers already are remarking how serious, dedicated, and knowledgeable we freshmen seem to be. Perhaps serving in the Texas Legislature won't spread too bad a stain on the family reputation after all.

December 19: Back from a three-week trip to the East Coast, I find three paper sacks full of Christmas mail. There are warm and personal messages from university presidents whom I've never met and others from people I've never heard

State Representative Chase Untermeyer is a former political reporter for the Houston Chronicle *and has contributed to this magazine in the past.*

of at all. Later, in Austin, I learn they're lobbyists.

In addition there are cards from organizations that anxiously await another time of Santa Clausery once the Legislature convenes. "When we count our blessings at Christmastime," one reads, "we think of friends like you!" It was signed the Pasadena Police Officers Association. Another card says on the cover, "To faithful old friends, to cherished new friends, and to those whose friendship we hope to earn . . ." Flipping it open, I find it's from the Texas Public Employees Association.

January 10, 1977: My last full day as a civilian. I walk from my room at the Stephen F. Austin Hotel and for the first time see my small but serviceable Capitol office. Surrounded by staff asking questions, visited by colleagues, lobbyists, and assorted other well-wishers, I have a premonition that for the next 140 days I shall never be completely alone.

January 11: The normally somnolent "Stephen F" has come alive overnight and is filled with old-timers greeting acquaintances from past legislative sessions.

"Why, looky here! Who you lobbyin' for this session?"

"Beer 'stributors."

"Boy, they sure are smart to hire you!"

"Well, I figger they didn't get where they are by bein' dumb."

I am introduced to Tom Uher of Bay City. As chairman of the House State Affairs Committee, Tom plays the role of monster man during the session, sitting on bills that members (especially the Speaker) never want to see again. In person he is one of the House's most ebullient members, and he is particularly glad to meet me.

"Another U!" he exclaims, pumping my hand. "Ain't never been another U the whole time I been up here!" We agree on the spot to form the exclusive U Political Caucus.

The caucus never gets very far, but it is much more of a reality than a larger and presumably more political associa-

Illustrated by Tom Ballenger

THE ONE AND ONLY TEXAS LEGISLATURE 159

tion with which I am affiliated, namely the Republican party. There are eighteen Republicans in the Texas House of 1977, up two from the previous session and the biggest GOP contingent since Reconstruction. But in the entirety of the 65th session we are never to have a leader or even to caucus, save for an informal and poorly attended weekly gathering at state headquarters.

Bob Davis of Irving grabs me off the street and sweeps me back inside the hotel to have breakfast. Bob is probably the shrewdest Republican in the House, acclaimed for his knowledge of its rules. He is also one of the most valued members of Democratic Speaker Clayton's "team"; by week's end he will be named chairman of the Insurance Committee.

Stabbing at a sausage, the fast-talking Davis explains why there is no Republican organization in the House. "The name of the game around here is who has the authority to compel attention, and we ain't got it. Maybe when we have about thirty members we will. But till then if we try to line up as Republicans, all we'd do is have the Democrats line up against us."

Noontime comes and with it the ceremonial swearing in of a new House of Representatives. I proceed to the House floor, which is filled with legislators and their families. This gives the House the ambience of a third-class railway coach in India—better dressed, of course, but roiling and moiling just the same. Children are crawling, screaming, poking; old people trying to look suitably composed for the occasion; and lawmakers scrounging for extra seats.

After the oath-taking and the unopposed reelection of Speaker Clayton, the House recesses for lunch. We send our families and supporters back home and return to debate the rules by which the House will govern itself. The afternoon gives birth to the best mixed metaphor of the entire session. A senior member, arguing against a rule change, protests that the proposal is "a horse of a different color that opens up a whole new can of worms."

January 13: Committee assignments for the session are announced to a House wreathed in total and atypical silence. All day there was an air of Christmas Eve expectancy among the members. Now the reading clerk, unchallenged for attention, reveals what the workaday fate of 150 legislators will be.

I am assigned to both committees I requested: Intergovernmental Affairs and Health & Welfare. The latter is chaired by John Wilson of La Grange, star of the 1975 session and a sly and capable country boy with a reputation as a populist. A few days after the committee lists are unveiled, I request an appointment with Wilson to get to know him better.

John tells me he had his choice of four committee chairmanships and chose Health & Welfare because "we're not exactly on the main line of fire like other committees are."

"What do you mean by that?" I ask.

"Well, take Energy Resources, for example. There ain't nothin' comin' out of that committee that the oil and gas industry doesn't want and that the Speaker doesn't want. At least on Health and Welfare you members can hear all the testimony and come up with a pretty objective idea of what kind of bills should be passed."

January 17: The Texas Association of Realtors throws a mass reception for legislators, and half of Austin shows up. The popular image of a legislative session is that lawmakers spend most waking hours rolling from one lavish reception to another, never once having to pay for their food and drink. After tonight's affair and a couple of others, I conclude that the typical legislative reception is a lousy place to eat, drink, or even try to talk.

A legislator invariably is accosted by someone (a lobbyist or a colleague) between the nametag table and his destination—the bar or the food—and forced to stave off pangs of hunger and thirst till a break can be made. By then, legislative staffers—the only Capitol habitués who really depend on receptions for sustenance—have done extensive damage to the shrimp or guacamole. Standard Capitol wisdom says that receptions are political musts, the place to work on getting a bill out of subcommittee or to campaign for votes for Speaker. Maybe. But they're certainly not agreeable places (in a colleague's inspired expression) "to graze."

January 19: I seek general-purpose advice from Fred Agnich of Dallas, the Daddy Warbucks of House Republicans. Fred was a director at Texas Instruments and doesn't have to worry about making do on his legislative pay of $600 a month.

"If you don't know what's in a bill," he counsels, "always vote no. You can usually justify a no vote on any bill, but it's not always easy to justify a yes vote. Hell, we've got too much damn legislation anyway."

January 24: In today's mail I receive a letter from Colonel Wilson E. Speir, director of the DPS (Department of Public Safety). Saluting me as "My dear friend" (I've not yet met the gentleman), Colonel Speir writes, "For many years it has been traditional for the DPS to provide an identification card to members of the Legislature. I am attaching your card for the current session and hope you will find it of value."

The blue card is laminated and gives nothing more than my name and title. I have long heard about these get-out-of-jail-free cards but am curious to find out just what use Colonel Speir hoped I would find for it. On a whim I pick up the phone and dial the DPS. Neither Speir nor his first assistant is in, but the public relations man is.

He greets me with the relentless cheer typical of his breed, which, however, begins to disappear when I inquire what circumstances require a legislator to present an ID card.

"Ah, there's no reason except . . . some very remote situation when . . . some emergency might arise and . . . well, some people find them handy." When pressed, he weakens steadily. "In the old days, a senator or a representative might be in a hurry—on official business, of course—and he might be stopped by a policeman and then . . . he'd just show his card and be on his way."

Later the House convenes for routine business. There are long pauses between the conduct of affairs from the dais, and I make a habit of bringing something to the floor to do during these lapses: constituent mail, the clipping service of state news provided free to legislators, or one of the many thick state agency reports. Looking up from my busywork at the several clusters of my colleagues talking animatedly, I wonder if I'm missing out by not getting up to mill around with them. Are they making deals on bills, exchanging juicy information I should know, or just passing the time in pleasant blather? Somehow they seem as if they're doing their job and I'm not.

January 25: With a minimum of trouble, I arrange for a courtesy call on the governor. Howard Richards, the governor's legislative liaison, escorts me into the private office, cluttered with Western bric-a-brac and paintings. Dolph Briscoe enters from the side and we shake hands. Briscoe reminisces about the 1972 gubernatorial campaign, which I covered as a reporter from the *Houston Chronicle*, and, with a warm smile, asks whether I like the Legislature. This permits me to drop a chestnut I've been using all week.

"Well, Governor, serving in the Legislature is a little like sex: if you admit you like it too much, you're supposed to feel guilty."

Dolph's grin grows wordlessly wider. Howard sinks deeper in his chair. I realize this was perhaps the first time in four years that *that* word had been heard in those parts. The call soon ends.

February 8: The House debates the first major bill of the session, one to divert $528 million in new funds into highways. Ever since the last session, the state highway department and the powerful "highway lobby" (construction companies, engineering firms, suppliers, and the like) have staged a mammoth public relations campaign about a "funding crisis" for the department. True, the department is far behind in fulfilling its commitments, but a lot of the backlog is due to New York City–style overcommitment by the three-member highway commission to every rural county commissioners' court that asks for a new road.

Some extra money for highways is justified, but the lobby is taking no chances on the Legislature's goodwill. They want HB 3 (the highway bill) passed intact and immediately, long before the general state appropriations bill forces the House to decide its priorities for the state budget. I join a group of liberals and some Republicans in demanding HB 3 be postponed until the appropriations bill has been considered by the Legislature. The bill's proponents want purity and they get it: the motion to postpone is tabled, 85–55. My vote becomes the one of which I am proudest all session, and before long the rammed-through highway bill becomes a constant oratorical reminder to all members of how we were bamboozled into voting first for concrete and then having to divide the remains among other needs such as teachers and mentally retarded kids.

February 12: Back home for the weekend, I attend the festivities of Involvement Day in Houston, sponsored by the Cousteau Society. It's a chance to look at some fascinating exhibits and, not coincidentally, to say hello to environmentalist friends. One of these greets me and says, "What's happening in the Legislature? You're pushing things through very early, like the highway bill." In the middle of my reply I suddenly notice that I am defending the honor of the House, explaining the bill in terms its supporters would approve—rather like a member of one of those old and decaying Southern families who quarrel among themselves but close ranks against the world.

February 16: The House takes up HB 22, which would permit farm and ranch land to be taxed on its productive (rather than market) value. The bill means a lot to rural legislators who have seen farmers and ranchers forced to sell out to developers because their property taxes got too high. It's also a bill I favor, believing that urban areas also benefit from greenbelts on their fringes, land that provides natural flood protection and a nearby source of food and fiber. Other urban legislators see the issue differently, contending that if rural residents get a tax break, they'll simultaneously get a larger share of the state's school funds under the present funding formula.

When the vote on HB 22 looks close, I take the floor in my maiden speech. "Mr. Speaker, members," I begin, in the standard opener to all speeches to the House.

The House, which is difficult to grasp as an entity when seated on the floor, becomes almost surreal from the front mike. Some members are listening, others not. Suddenly there's a burst of laughter from a group of members huddling on something totally divorced from HB 22. Beyond the brass rail that corrals lawmakers, there is a continual motion of pages, press, staffers, and members. Legislators still seated at their desks hear me in an after-lunch attitude of bored courtesy.

"This piece of legislation has been characterized as an urban-versus-rural fight," I continue. "I rise in support of this bill even though I am definitely a city boy. In fact, the largest agricultural operation in my district probably is maintaining the golf course at the River Oaks Country Club."

After a few appreciative yoks, I sketch the reasons for my support and sit down. The bill passes easily—indeed, too easily for my speech to have made any difference. For the rest of the day I feel awful, remembering things I could have said. By the end of the session I learn not to take too seriously either my own words or others' reactions to them—but also not to take the act of addressing the House so lightly that I am constantly "on the mike." Some members can kill a bill just by speaking *in favor* of it, so tiresome are their frequent trips to the podium.

February 21, 11 p.m.: Mickey Leland drops by my office, where I'm taking advantage of the quiet hours to read day-old newspapers and mail. Despite our marked philosophical and personal differences—he, a free-spirited black liberal Democrat, and I, a buttoned-down white conservative Republican—we have been friends since an unlikely dockside meeting during the 1972 governor's race.

Knowing my interest in mental health, Mickey asks whether I can support a proposed $14 million appropriation for a hospital for the Houston-based TRIMS (Texas Research Institute of Mental Sciences), a division of the Department of Mental Health and Mental Retardation, which currently rents hospital space. I reply that the mental health community in Houston fears that a TRIMS hospital might prevent other state funds from being allocated for badly needed community services. Moreover, the elite research-oriented TRIMS has always acted as if it had no special obligation to the people of Houston. If a rider could be attached to the hospital appropriation that in some way directly committed TRIMS to helping the mental health problems of Harris County, I muse, the local Mental Health Association and county officials could back the project and help quell opposition from Houston legislators.

"A legislator might be in a hurry—on official business of course—and be stopped by a policeman and then . . ."

Mickey says that whatever I want to put in the rider he'll tack onto the TRIMS hospital appropriation. It's a deal.

February 22: Using the telephone at my desk on the House floor, I call John Trimble, board chairman of the Harris County MHMR, whose wife is very active in the Mental Health Association. I mention the Leland offer and leave it up to John to propose the one thing the Houston area most desperately needs in mental health services. John later calls back with the answer: about 25 to 50 beds for emotionally disturbed children, there being no such public facility in the county.

February 23: I catch Mickey on the floor and tell him of my talk with Trimble. He says beds for children is a great idea. This evening, a Health & Welfare subcommittee will hear testimony from Dr. Joseph Schoolar, the director of TRIMS. Mickey whispers to me as I enter the hearing room, "Everybody's for what you want." Schoolar and I confer before he takes the stand, and we agree on a few items which we later repeat on the record in minstrel-show fash-

ion. If this is how multimillion-dollar budget decisions are made, it almost seems too easy.

February 25: By virtue of my high office, I have been invited to ride in the annual Houston Fat Stock Show and Rodeo parade, precipitating what my staff and I call the Horse Crisis. The invitation said I could ride my horse, their horse, or a pickup truck. I decide to concede my lack of horse and horsemanship by riding the pickup. This proves the wisest political choice, for the rodeo folks make up big signs bearing the politician's name to tape to the side of the truck—something they don't put on the horses.

I show my east Harris County colleague, Henry Allee, something Bill Buckley pointed out in a spy spoof he recently wrote: English royalty always wave as if they're reaching up to unscrew a lightbulb. Henry and I ride off into the sunrise, unscrewing lightbulbs all the way down Main Street.

March 7: The Health & Welfare Committee hears hours of testimony on a bill to permit pharmacists to substitute generic drugs without a physician's approval. To me, it's a "bad ole bill," poorly drafted and more rhetoric than remedy. There's only one catch to my deciding flatly on a no vote. The bill's author is Mickey Leland, and it's something he has been trying for three sessions to pass. If I vote against him, will he pull the plug on our agreement to put the children's services rider on the TRIMS appropriation?

As the vote nears, I lean toward Mickey and ask, "Do you have the votes to get this bill out of committee?" He nods; I vote no.

Afterwards, I ask Mickey if my opposition to his pet bill means trouble for the TRIMS rider. Still jubilant at the favorable committee vote, he claps me on the shoulder. "No, man. I'm still cool on that. We made a deal."

Drug company lobbyists rush forward to thank me for my vote as scowling pharmacy students file past. Because of my committee assignments, I tend to get a lot of lobby contact from groups interested in all phases of health care in addition to visits from policemen, firefighters, and miscellaneous "cause" crazies. Other than that, I'm astounded at how *little* I'm contacted by the infamous Big Boys of Austin lobbydom. After learning of my absolute dedication to county home rule, the Realtors have stopped calling. Never am I to meet the major oil company lobbyists, and the railroads visit me only because they're fully mobilized for the crucial debate over construction of a coal slurry pipeline.

Seldom am I asked out to a meal, and as for lobby gifts, reality once more fails to live up to legend. No one offers me a weekend in Acapulco or a night with Jacqueline Bisset. New laws limit gifts to items worth less than $10, but if the booty is less than impressive, the quantity is imposing: a Texas Motor Transportation Association plaque; two movie passes from theater owners; letter openers from the Spring Branch Education Association and the Texas Municipal Police Association; a two-pound sack of Spanish peanuts from peanut growers; two rose bushes; a half-dozen grapefruit; a fishing lure; a box of Mexican food products; a metric converter; two heavy brass belt buckles; a jar of honey; an orange Houston Astros baseball cap; a cube of rock salt; a Pierre Cardin necktie with a Texas map design divided into six regions, which few members realize represent the Southwestern Bell area codes; and a flyswatter, inscribed "good for use on flies, lobbyists, newsmen, and other pests."

March 24: Local & Consent Calendar Day. Facing us is a long list of bills that are theoretically "uncontested"—though several are at least as important as others we've debated for hours on the regular calendar. The impetus is to move the bills through all the necessary motions—fast—with members lining up to give only one-sentence "explanations" of each measure.

Clayton is a master at the auctioneer's patter required for this show, and he has developed a rhythmical slapping of the gavel that almost demands that the pace not be broken. Once today when a colleague was a little slow in coming to the front mike, the Speaker barked unhappily, "C'mon, members! Let's keep rollin'!"

As well as I can make them out, these are the magic words that the Speaker intones to move bills on "L&C" to third reading and final passage:

"Clerkill readabill!" (The clerk starts to read the bill's title but is interrupted a split-second later by the smack of the gavel.) "Izzair jection? Passterd reading!"

March 31: The House finishes a brutal three-day debate over the county ordinance-making authority bill, approving a much-amended version by twelve votes and sending the ragged creature off to die on the table of a Senate committee. Next I focus on a bill coming up in the Intergovernmental Affairs Committee to permit pari-mutuel wagering on horse racing. My district is split on the issue between the Baptists of Spring Branch and the polo players of River Oaks. I oppose the bill as a bad business deal for the state, something my horsier constituents say isn't correct.

I get a call from a horse breeder who says: "You have no idea, son, what this could mean for Texas. I had to send my prize mare up to Kentucky to be bred with a famous stud up there. It cost me ten thousand dollars—and do you know they charged a five per cent state sales tax on top of that?"

A dangerous precedent, I reply: a tax on sex. You never know where something like that may lead.

April 12: The biggest, longest, and hardest day of the session yet. At 9:30 a.m. the Intergovernmental Affairs Committee holds its public hearing on the horse-racing bill. The crowd of stylish-looking people (all wearing the uniform of the day—white cowboy hats) packs the House floor and gallery. "I sure am glad I'm a member of this committee," I lie to a colleague. "Otherwise I couldn't get a seat."

When we adjourn four hours later, we barely have enough time to gulp down a snack before the full House meets. There we spend almost six hours debating another Leland bill, which would make a state park out of a high-priced junkyard in the Fifth Ward ghetto northeast of downtown Houston. When that is voted down, we take up the indescribably complicated school finance bill.

An hour after we adjourn at 7:30 p.m., Health & Welfare convenes to hear testimony on two of the session's most controversial bills: one sought by Fundamentalist churches to exempt church-owned child-care facilities from state Welfare Department inspections; the other to restrict abortions. The committee meets in the House chamber, and for the second time today the place is packed. The church bill gets out of committee by one vote, but the abortion bill's sponsor, after more hours of testimony, does not ask for a vote on his measure because exhaustion has robbed him of some of the members he needs for a majority. We finally quit at 1 a.m., ending a seventeen-hour workday. Is this the Texas Legislature I've always heard about, a place of unrelieved gaiety and partying?

April 13: Tonight it's the Equal Rights Amendment that has filled the House chamber and kept committee members in their seats for hours. Not on that particular panel, I am free this evening to do officework till midnight. When finished, I drop by the House to see if anything's still going on. The place is empty except for a mustachioed man in his late thirties with a little girl at his side. Unaware that a legislator is anywhere close, the man grimly tells his daughter, "People here get paid money to cheat."

"They *do*?" the girl asks incredulously.

"Yes, lie and cheat. It makes me sick. Let's go home."

April 26: Just like in the Army, the troops are grumbling at the generals. The Appropriations Committee got out of control and became the scene of such widespread logrolling that the resulting budget bill is a numbing $400 million over the recommendations of the respected Legislative Budget Board. The House leadership now swears off any connection with it, which means the bill must be "written on the floor," a term of disgust that legislators apply to any measure that has been poorly handled by its parent committee. It also means that individual legislators will have to defend their special projects in the bill rather than simply rely on the leadership to push the whole package of pork.

One of these projects is the TRIMS hospital. Mickey was able to get it through the Appropriations Committee, my rider attached, by only one vote. With a $14 million price tag, it becomes a prime target for budget trimming.

Jimmie Edwards of Conroe offers an amendment to strike the TRIMS facility altogether. In a rare show of liberal-conservative Houston harmony, Mickey and I team up to defend the hospital. Deliberately skirting the question of whether the hospital is truly needed, I emphasize what the rider would do "for the children of Texas." Mickey moves to table the Edwards amendment, and the voting board lights up gratifyingly green. We triumph, 87–56.

April 27: The TRIMS hospital victory proves short-lived. Milton Fox, a fellow Harris County Republican who sits on Appropriations and was more appalled than anyone at the trade-offs that occurred there, is especially peeved about the TRIMS project. He offers another amendment designed to kill it. Still angry with the Appropriations Committee, the House is in a cuttin' mood. The Fox amendment passes, 77–69. Over in the Senate, the TRIMS hospital never survives the Finance Committee. When the two houses meet to hammer out the final budget bill, the hospital, children's beds and all, is set aside for two more years.

The budget battle lurches on. As the House debates increasing state welfare payments, Representative Chris Miller of Fort Worth takes the front mike to read a letter of support from the Baptist General Convention. Trying to get the House's attention, Chris says, "This is something that will be of interest to all you Christians—and to you Jews, too, Mr. Ribak" (Abe Ribak of San Antonio, the House's only Jewish member). A gruff laugh comes from Redneck Hollow—a section of the House floor with a heavy concentration of conservatives that corresponds to the liberals' Red Square. "Well, that may be what the Christians want," a member says, "but the *Lions* want something else!"

The Lions win today. Cuts are made in most everything that anyone is courageous enough to propose chopping. An exception is funding for the arts, retained at the Appropriations Committee's figure, itself twice as high as the Commission on the Arts and Humanities requested. With the TRIMS fight now over, I become a hidebound Lion and vote for every cut, including the arts.

May 4: The appropriations bill is now in its seventh excruciating day of floor debate. As a blessed bit of relief, the Speaker recesses the House in the early evening so members can make a couple of social engagements tonight. Among these is the gala Texas Arts Showcase, a revue by various Texas performers of everything from mariachi music and Chopin études to country and Western singing. During intermission, Milton Fox notes something interesting. The legislators who are here tonight are mostly Lions who voted to slash funding for the arts along with everything else. Where are the vaunted heroes of that fight, the cultural Christians? They're at the other event happening tonight, the boilermakers union shrimp shuck.

May 9: Three weeks to final adjournment. Attendance this morning is spotty. But the vote board is brightly lit green when attendance is called by the Speaker, thanks to the time-worn legislative custom of punching thy neighbor's button. Specifically against House rules, the practice is nevertheless so common it breaks into print only on dull days when the press has nothing else to report.

This morning, with bodies scarce on the floor, button pushing is the only thing that can get a theoretical quorum and start business. A hulking rural legislator with an eight-foot wingspan races down the aisle and simultaneously pushes the buttons of missing members on either side. A neighbor is impressed: "Boy, you workin' like an octopus on a motorcycle today!"

May 13, Friday the 13th: Appropriately enough, today the resounding rhythm of the Speaker's gavel continues past the bills on the Local & Consent Calendar and gives the same rush-'em-through treatment to bills on the regular agenda. We will pass 134 bills today. Ed Watson, a scrappy union official from Deer Park who always wears a big gold Democratic donkey lapel pin, takes the back mike to interrupt the eardrum-splitting crack of the gavel. "Mr. Speaker," Ed inquires, "is this ole train gonna slow down for crossings or is it just gonna whistle?"

I vote no wherever I have the slightest doubt about a bill, especially banking bills, remembering both Sharpstown and Fred Agnich's advice. But who knows? Maybe it will be a hospital district bill or something connected with utilities aboard that ole train which causes the next great Texas political scandal.

"Lobby gifts: no trip to Acapulco or night with Jacqueline Bisset; instead fishing lure, flyswatter, rock salt..."

May 19: As the days dwindle down, tempers grow shorter as the sessions grow longer. A phrase heard more often nowadays is "mislead this House." When a member tells another in debate, "I think you're misleading this House," he means his colleague is lying. When a member from the front mike says, "I don't want to mislead this House," he is imploring. "Please believe me."

May 23: One week to go, and things are getting meaner. Today brings another Local & Consent Calendar, chock-full of major items that shouldn't be there. Among these are election-law changes that Republicans and liberal Democrats, from years of sad experience, know are written by and for the dominant conservative wing of the state Democratic party. We Republicans summon enough signatures on a "knock-off slip" to bump one election bill off L&C and onto the regular House calendar, meaning certain death at this stage of the session. The Democrats retaliate by killing a Republican-backed elections bill. But knockers are nowhere to be found for a bill deliberately aimed at circumventing the Houston City Charter to permit members of the

THE ONE AND ONLY TEXAS LEGISLATURE 163

city council to raise their own salaries without a vote of the people.

Next session, I vow, I'm going to be more of a sumbitch. But to do so I must face the danger of not passing anything of my own. If a legislator has a program, 149 other members of the House hold his bills hostage. It's a risk few take.

May 24: Every bill is beginning to sound like the one before, "just a simple change from somethin' we did last session." I find myself agreeing with words sputtered today by the old bulldog of the House, Bill Heatly of Paducah. Once feared when he reigned unrivaled over the Appropriations Committee but now largely an amusing relic of the Bad Old Days, Heatly advises a freshman against a proposed constitutional amendment. "Why?" the member asks.

"I jes' don't think we should change a thing. We gettin' on all right."

From the front mike comes the carefully homespun oratory of Ben Grant of Marshall: "We need a law with teeth in it, and I don't mean teeth that smile at improprieties. I mean teeth that bite and chew and gnaw at wrongdoers."

May 28: Fifty-six and one-half hours till *sine die*. This term, meaning the absolute constitutional end of the 140-day session, is not pronounced in any way recognizable either by Cicero or Father O'Flaherty from the parish church around the corner. Rather, in these parts, it rhymes with "briny fly."

After weeks of rushing bills through, the House now seems in suspended animation, just as at the beginning of the session. From time to time we vote on a conference committee report or listen to a resolution commending two sergeants at arms for becoming engaged.

I wander over to the Senate to check the action, not having spent much time on the other side of the rotunda all session. After close observation this afternoon, I conclude that the only thing that makes the place more, well, senatorial, is not its smaller and self-consciously more distinguished-looking membership but the fact it has a somber green carpet while the House has one of happy-face yellow. Tom Creighton of Mineral Wells notices me and turns around to introduce himself. "You people over in the House have been sendin' us trash, just trash," Creighton says. "And you know what? We been passin' it."

May 30: The longest and last day begins with doubt as to whether it truly will be our final day. House and Senate conferees are still short of compromises on the medical malpractice and school finance bills. Especially if there is no agreement on schools, the governor will almost have to call a special session, ordinarily anathema to him.

The House today mostly waits for words from the conference committees. Members take the opportunity to introduce visiting constituents in the gallery. The champeen introducer, though, is Joe Allen of Baytown. Irritated at the silly subterfuge whereby members must inquire of the Speaker "whether it is against the rules" to introduce so-and-so, Allen gains fame by "recognizing" such absolutely absent celebrities as Anita Bryant, Nelson Rockefeller, Farrah Fawcett-Majors, and the Mormon Tabernacle Choir.

After a long late-afternoon recess, we reassemble to wait some more. The medical malpractice conferees report that peace has been reached with the Senate, and a bill that appeared doomed quickly becomes law. At 10:30 the Speaker announces that an agreement on an $896 million school finance bill has been reached but that the bill has not been "printed," a legislative euphemism for cutting, pasting, and photocopying pieces of various bill drafts. Clayton promises we won't be asked to vote on anything not physically before us.

At 11:30—only half an hour before adjournment *sine die*—Jim Kaster of El Paso takes the front mike to present the compromise school bill. Members still don't have a copy of it, only a sheet purporting to contain the highlights. Of course, with so complicated a subject and so few remaining minutes, having the full 83-page bill in front of us wouldn't necessarily mean anything. Even to take up the bill requires a suspension of the House rule mandating that a measure be in members' hands at least two hours before it is "laid out" for consideration. Kaster moves to suspend this rule, which will take a two-thirds vote, or 100 members pushing the aye button. John Bryant of Dallas, the unofficial liberal leader of the House, warns that "a special session wouldn't be nearly as costly as what this bill could cost us."

It's one of those occasions in politics when liberal conscience and conservative caution merge into the same conclusion. Along with deskmate Lee Jackson, a Dallas Republican and one of the very few House members who understands the thorny school finance problem, I conclude that it would be the height of irresponsibility to vote on an education bill costing almost $1 billion that no one has even seen in one piece.

In his racetrack announcer's accelerating voice, Clayton states the question before the House. Members, leaning forward like thoroughbreds, fingers already on the voting machine button of their choice, feel a rush of emotion and adrenaline as the board instantly becomes a Christmas canvas of red and green. From the hefty-looking number of red lights nestled among the green, we whoa-sayers know immediately we've won. The galleries and floor explode with whoops of triumph and cries of outrage. The Speaker gavels the entire chamber to silence, warning that the galleries will be cleared if order is not maintained. Then, with a laconic tone that seems divorced from the electricity of the moment, Clayton announces, "There being ninety-two ayes, fifty-five noes, the rule fails to s'pend."

A special session now a certainty, Clayton gavels the regular session to a close, and the tired members break up to shake hands ("Sure been great workin' with ya!") and to find out where the office parties are. Outside, a delegation from the Houston school district waits to find out why I voted the way I did. I gather my papers for the last time and leave the chamber to face them. In the process I forget to make a last visual sweep of the place where I had just spent 140 of the most fascinating days of my life. But no more dramatics are needed tonight, and, besides, we'll all be back. ★

THE TEN BEST AND THE TEN WORST LEGISLATORS

The triumphant homecoming of the Killer Bees: is there any political body, anywhere, quite like the Texas Legislature?

Glory bee! The world at last has gotten a glimpse of the Texas Legislature as we have come to know and love it. Thanks to the Killer Bees, the twelve senators who eluded a statewide search for four days after walking out in opposition to an early presidential primary, everybody now knows what we've been saying all along: nobody, but nobody, plays hardball quite as hard as our Legislature, nor has so much fun in the process. Imagine, if you can, a dozen gray-flanneled New England congressmen dodging the FBI, or a band of California legislators going underground in Chinatown . . . impossible.

But the flight of the Bees may have been a last hurrah for the old days and the old ways. The Texas Legislature, in its 132nd year, is going through a belated change of life. The good-old-boy approach to politics isn't enough anymore; today's Texas legislator is more at home with semicolons than six-packs. Consider the issues that tested the 66th Legislature: tax relief, new interest ceilings,

Texas Monthly's legislative coverage was compiled by a special project staff under the direction of senior editor Paul Burka.

penalties for usury, manufacturers' liability for defective products, the dilemma of how to finance and control college construction, wage levels for constructing public projects, weakening the consumer protection law, revising workman's compensation, *plus* Sunset, the Legislature's first real attempt to get a handle on the bureaucracy, *plus* the presidential primary, *plus* some perennials (school finance, appropriations, property tax administration) and some leftovers (revisions of strip-mining, clean air, and consumer credit laws).

As if that weren't enough, the Legislature had to deal with the state's first Republican governor in a century. Bill Clements asked for initiative and referendum, a ban on state income taxes, wiretapping authority for police, and some other goodies; about all he got was increased budgeting authority. Still, as Texas' best practitioner of political theatrics since John Connally, Clements managed to come out looking good despite getting virtually nothing he wanted, as opposed to his predecessor, Dolph Briscoe, who usually got everything he wanted and looked terrible.

With all this to think about, any legislator who didn't have a grasp of finance and credit, who didn't understand the state's intricate property tax system, who didn't know the law, was doomed to the sidelines. For some reason, the murkier the waters, the more lawyers seem to be able to see; and with the waters of the session muddied by so many complex issues, lawyers dominated the session. Although the Legislature's 181-member roster includes only 75 attorneys, our Ten Best list includes 8. Even the other two have attended law school; they are, not coincidentally, the hardest working members of the House and Senate.

Our criteria, as always, transcended any consideration of political philosphy, for both conservatives and liberals use the same standards to judge their colleagues. A good legislator is intelligent, quick to understand, well prepared, open-minded, and independent. He knows the distinction between firmness and fairness and makes good use of both. He is effective because of his colleagues' respect, not their fear. He thinks about what's *right*—and he is smart enough to know he may be wrong. A bad legislator is more difficult to define: indolence, stupidity, and ineffectiveness can be overlooked if a legislator has enough sense to stay indoors during emergencies. It's the driver who's so oblivious that he blocks the road who frequently ends up on the Ten Worst list along with, of course, those occasional ogres who take pleasure in running over people.

We did look closely at one nonpartisan issue in making our determinations. This was the first year of the Sunset process,

Photography by Tomas Pantin

where state agencies must periodically justify their existence. Every agency up for review this year, 26 in all, would cease to exist if the Legislature did not reestablish them. This provided a golden opportunity to make an agency like the State Board of Morticians more responsive to the public and less a creature of the industry it regulates. In contrast to issues like higher interest rates, where it was debatable where the public interest really lay, Sunset was one of those issues with the public interest on one side and taking care of your friends on the other—and we judged it accordingly.

The Best and Worst lists represented a consensus of our own observations of floor and committee action combined with interviews of legislators, staff, Capitol press, lobbyists, and state agency birddogs who keep their noses close to the Legislature. Our Best list includes six liberal Democrats, two conservative Democrats, and two Republicans—disproportionately strong showings by liberals and Republicans, but a dismal performance by conservatives. Perhaps the state's political talent, like its population, is piling up in the cities and their suburbs, but the more likely explanation is that conservative Democrats lost too much talent through retirement last season: they were like a football team whose best players had graduated—still a couple of years away from a good year. Chances for a comeback are good, because most of the freshman talent had a decidedly conservative Democratic tinge. **Ed Howard** (42, Texarkana) was in a class by himself in the Senate, and **Bill Messer** (28, Belton) and **John Sharp** (28, Victoria) were the best newcomers in the House. All are conservative Democrats. **Lloyd Criss** (38, La Marque) was the top liberal arrival, and **Ed Emmett** (29, Kingwood) led the Republicans. The Worst list was more balanced: four conservative Democrats, three liberals, three Republicans.

In addition to the Ten Best and Ten Worst, there were some near-misses in both directions. Three House committee chairmen deserve honorable mention: **Gib Lewis** (42, Fort Worth) ran the best committee in the House (Intergovernmental Affairs) and was effective on the floor—unfortunately, too often on behalf of the beer lobby; **Bennie Bock** (42, New Braunfels) orchestrated the first override of a gubernatorial veto since 1941 and guided park programs through the Environmental Affairs Committee; and **Bob Simpson** (35, Amarillo) deviated from tradition by running the Insurance Committee as something other than an arm of the insurance industry. Down in the trenches, two committee workers were exceptional: losing Speaker candidate **Buddy Temple** (37, Diboll), who instead of nursing his wounds tried to find solutions to some of the session's thorniest problems on the State Affairs Committee; and **Lee Jackson** (29, Dallas), whose urban Republicanism was a force on both tax relief and Sunset. In the Senate, **Pete Snelson** (56, Midland) emerged from the pack on Sunset and education, and **Ron Clower** (38, Garland) finally lived up to his potential by leading resistance to a separate presidential primary.

On the negative side, a couple of dirty tricksters earned dishonorable mentions. Senator **Peyton McKnight** (54, Tyler) tried unsuccessfully to get a Houston law firm to fire a woman lobbyist who dates one of his political enemies. In the House, **Tim Von Dohlen** (35, Goliad) earned the title of most distrusted member: once he used his position on the traffic-directing Calendars Committee to hold up a member's bill, already approved for floor action, for more than a month while he maneuvered to get his own bill on the same subject out of committee; when he succeeded, he slipped his bill onto the House schedule first—only to have his ears pinned back when the House voted to substitute the rival bill.

Four Bests repeated from 1977: John Bryant, Ron Coleman, Lance Lalor, and Babe Schwartz, who extended his winning streak to four sessions. Jim Nugent and three-time Best Max Sherman moved up in the world, to Railroad Commissioner and West Texas State University president respectively. Wayne Peveto, after twice making the top ten for his efforts to reform property tax administration, finally passed what remained of his much-compromised bill—alas, not very much. Lynn Nabers was a first-rate member when he was interested, which wasn't often; John Wilson, on the other hand, was always interested but never had a chance—he's running for Speaker against Clayton in 1981. As for Ray Farabee, whom we expected to replace Sherman as the Senate's best and most independent member, he still could, but first he has to try.

On the Ten Worst list, only Tom Massey was fitted for a second straight black hat. DeWitt Hale, Chris Miller, and Joe Tom Robbins were ineligible; only Hale's retirement was voluntary. Bob Davis became the first to make the leap from Worst to Best in one session. Charles Evans didn't come quite that far, but he was much improved in his new role as chairman of the House committee overseeing Sunset. House Appropriations Committee chairman Bill Presnal ran a tighter ship this session under orders from Fleet Admiral Clayton. We wish we could say that Tom Creighton and Clay Smothers were better; actually, others were just worse. And where is perennial Worst Glenn Kothmann? Well, he sent us word that he wasn't one of the *ten* worst. So be it: we accept his plea bargain of eleventh.

THE TEN BEST

Bryant: two fingers for No—not victory

John Bryant, 32, liberal Democrat, Dallas. Opposition standard-bearer in the House, the spiritual leader of the Gang of Four, whose fiery conscience was matched only by his temper. Got off to a terrible start: threw a fit at labor lobbyists, usually his allies, for their support of a utility bill he opposed; appeared to mislead the House—that's legislative parlance for lying—during the tax relief debate; then violated an unwritten code by suggesting his colleagues had been influenced by the timber lobby's lavish wining and dining.

The average member would have been banished to the back benches, if not by his enemies, then by friends eager to keep him quarantined. But Bryant had the intelligence and ability to recover, and in the session's critical final weeks he reemerged as a force—perhaps *the* force—to be reckoned with.

Realized he was too outgunned to kill business-backed legislation outright; instead shot to maim. Limited the higher ceiling on interest rates to two years' duration; attached the same time limit to a proposal giving manufacturers of defective products protection against consumer lawsuits. Took a much-criticized bill allowing auto dealers to charge a $25 documents fee and made it more palatable to consumers with a tough disclosure amendment.

Even managed one unqualified triumph: led the successful assault on a loan shark bill authorizing a 300 per cent increase in interest rates on small loans. Functioned as the House apiarist for the Senate's Killer Bees, marshaling forces against a separate presidential primary and putting the House on record against it while the Bees were in flight.

As the sun set on the last day of the session, the scene on the House floor was almost predictable. There was Bryant, looking red-faced and permanently sad, like someone too long in mourning, maneuvering virtually alone to block adoption of the appropriations bill. And

THE BEST ★★★★★★★★★★★★★★★★★★★★★★★★★★★★

there, clustered around the Speaker's podium, was fully a third of the House, trying to figure out what to do about him.

Ronald Coleman, 37, liberal Democrat, El Paso. The best all-around member of the Legislature this session. His virtues are straight from a civics textbook: intelligence, industry, independence, fairness, vision, courage, and—a bonus that must have come as a surprise even to Coleman—influence.

As a member of the Gang of Four and one of just eight members to vote against the reelection of Speaker Billy Clayton, he should have been a lonely leper; instead was responsible for the state's first equitable school finance bill. Persuaded a House committee to substitute his bill, which gave more state money to poor districts and less to rich districts, for a Clayton-backed version that would have done the reverse; then somehow managed to sell the idea to, in order, Clayton, his team, the House, and a House-Senate conference committee. On a list of unlikely achievements, a team outsider passing the most important legislation of the session has to rank alongside Idi Amin rising to become commander of the South African army.

Before the school finance battle, played his usual role as a fly attacking the flyswatter. Handed Clayton forces their first drubbing of the session by getting the House to chop (in the name of fiscal responsibility) more than half of an arguably inflated emergency appropriation for the Railroad Commission; also squelched an attempt to give the Animal Health Commission emergency funds to provide a niche for a Clayton crony. And what did Clayton's team think of all this? Said one loyalist: "He's as good as any member on the floor. I wish we had a hundred and fifty like him."

One of the most effective members of the House in floor debate. Speaks in a rasping tenor voice capable of emotion or unrelenting logic as the moment demands, then distractingly puffs on a thin cigar while his adversary struggles to answer. Put up a memorable fight against a Clayton-backed bill to eliminate the public interest advocate at the Department of Water Resources; his tough questioning so exposed the sponsor's ignorance that Clayton offered to help Coleman's one pet bill if Coleman would just lay off.

Not as visible on the floor after winning the school finance battle, perhaps because he didn't want to endanger what he'd accomplished. That makes him the rarest of all creatures in the Texas political menagerie: a liberal who knows how to win.

Bob Davis, 37, Republican, Irving. Comeback of the year: moved from Ten Worst to Ten Best in just one session, and did it without changing very much. Still one of the Legislature's most capable members—capable of anything.

The big difference: he switched committee chairmanships, giving up Insurance for Ways and Means, and in the process traded the concerns of one industry for the concerns of the entire state. The move helped Davis shed his image of being beholden to the lobby—though cynics suggested the only real difference was that instead of being beholden to just one, he was now beholden to many. They referred, no doubt, to the controversial tax breaks handed out to corporate farms and timber operators in House Bill 1060, the Tax Relief Act. But in fact HB 1060 was less a Davis bill than a committee bill, the type of consensus product that's common in Congress but rarely seen in the Texas Legislature; Davis helped shape the final bill and skillfully defended it on the floor, tax breaks and all. When John Bryant won a preliminary vote to remove timber companies, Davis made one of his now-look-members-this-just-isn't-good public-policy speeches and turned the vote around. It was Davis at his best.

Davis at his worst still surfaced now and then—most notably when he used a parliamentary ploy to adjourn his committee before they could vote for a bill he opposed. But he later helped pass the same bill with a good amendment—a sign that he has finally learned to draw his sword without throwing away the scabbard.

A presence everywhere: Clayton's most realistic advisor about what could be sold to the membership, the best in the House on the rules, a devastating opponent on the microphone, and a bulwark in conference committee, where he made certain that House views prevailed on tax reform.

But in the end, what best defines Davis is not his skill but his passion for com-

Davis: cleaned up his act—and his image

bat. On the wildest night of the session, after Davis helped break a liberal walkout and two bills he cherished passed the House in bitter floor fights, he stood at the back of the chamber, tie askew, collar open, exulting in the sheer fun of the game. A concerned colleague, remembering that Davis had suffered a heart attack between sessions, came over to inquire about his health. "My pulse rate is up to a hundred and sixteen," he gloated, "and I haven't had such fun in years."

Lloyd Doggett, 32, liberal Democrat, Austin. Leader of the Senate brigade whose determined efforts to sandbag a flood of anticonsumer bills led a

Coleman: shouldered the liberals' burden

Jones: a worker who doesn't want to lose h

168 THE ONE AND ONLY TEXAS LEGISLATURE

Doggett: on his feet, talking, as usual

disgruntled Bill Hobby to refer to them as the Killer Bees. As a tactician, rivaled Clausewitz. Knew he'd be fighting a defensive battle, so made his opponents struggle for every inch of ground he gave up. His main weapons: filibusters, threats of filibusters, and—in desperation—fleeing the battleground. A selection from Doggett's primer on legislative warfare:

Principle: the House, with 150 members, is less susceptible to lobby saturation than the Senate, with 31 members. *Strategy:* use the press to make bills you oppose unpalatable to fair-minded House members. *Execution:* mount a well-publicized filibuster against a bill weakening the Consumer Protection Act, referring to the proposal as the Consumer Destruction Act. *Result:* the House sponsor admits the bill needs improvement and includes amendments Doggett could never have passed in the Senate.

Understood perfectly the rhythm of the 140-day session—too relaxed in the beginning and too frantic in the end—and turned it to his advantage. His white tennis shoes became the most celebrated symbol of the session; their presence on his desk warned of his readiness to stand on his feet filibustering for hours. Early in the session the mere sight of them was enough to persuade restless senators to adjourn rather than sit through the night. Later, when a filibuster would mean certain death for the noncontroversial bills stacked up waiting for the Senate runway to clear, Doggett could win in the negotiating room what he had lost on the floor: for example, his last-night threat to talk to death the State Bar's Sunset bill forced bar lobbyists to accept additional nonlawyers on their board of directors.

Superb at using the power of reviewing gubernatorial appointees: paved the way for the first Senate rejection of a Clements nominee by forcing potential judge Monk Edwards to admit he assumed there was money in an envelope he delivered to then Governor Preston Smith on behalf of Gulf Oil. Rid the state of nefarious bureaucrat Hugh Yantis by invoking senatorial courtesy.

Not a member of the Senate club —oldtimers occasionally slight him by not holding hearings on his bills—and succeeds mainly through hard work and attention to detail; never parties, never relaxes with lobbyists, reads during every spare moment—even in committee meetings. A Texas politican of the modern mold—a pure technician, earnest, a bit dour, like an aging choirboy. Works seven days a week and expects his staff to do the same; once went to his Capitol office on Christmas afternoon and was infuriated to find the building locked.

Jerry "Nub" Donaldson, 36, conservative Democrat, Gatesville. The House counterpart to emerging Senate panjandrum Bill Meier. Like Meier, was the lead water carrier for the business lobby on his side of the Capitol; unlike Meier, managed not to come out all wet.

In a session dominated by complex, controversial issues, Donaldson handled three of the session's most contentious bills—raising the interest rate ceiling on home mortgages, giving the Public Utility Commission exclusive authority to set local electric rates, and authorizing auto dealers to charge a $25 documents fee—and passed them all. Accomplished this feat mainly through absolute mastery of the subject matter; as was once said of former New York Governor Al Smith, he "can make statistics sit up, beg, roll over, and bark." One faltering answer to an enemy question could have aroused the herd instinct of the House to a stampede against him, but Donaldson's competence kept his votes in line.

Unequaled at judging the effects of hostile amendments in the heat of debate, the most precarious and volatile moments in any bill's rite of passage. Knows which he can accept so as to defuse the opposition and which he has to fight in order to preserve his bill. May have saved the interest rate bill from decimation when, after losing a preliminary vote against a John Bryant amendment, he judged not to prolong a doomed fight, accepted the amendment, and helped break the opposition's momentum.

One of the few players on the Clayton team distinguished not by loyalty but by ability. Took a fairly independent voting line. "He's reasonable about any vote that doesn't hurt his district," said a black legislator. In fact, frequently supported key black issues like shoring up the school breakfast program and forcing Texas A&M to end the neglect of its stepchild institution, Prairie View A&M. Despite his reputation as a point man for the business lobby, he seldom advocated

ins; "the only senator you can always believe."

Donaldson: good old boy—very good

THE ONE AND ONLY TEXAS LEGISLATURE 169

THE BEST

their position on the microphone except on his own bills and could not be counted as an unquestioning pro-business vote. Sided with Bryant to help kill a loan shark bill; also voted against cutting back consumers' rights to sue for deceptive trade practices.

A changed man from last session, when he was frequently assailed as being petty, vindictive, and flighty. The metamorphosis was attributed by some to his desire not to alienate any potential votes this session, by others to his desire not to alienate any potential votes *next* session—when, one frequently hears (though not from Donaldson), he'll be back as a lobbyist for the savings and loan industry. If he decides to stay, Donaldson, with his technical ability and polyester good-old-boy style, has to be reckoned as a leading candidate to succeed Billy Clayton as Speaker in 1983.

Grant Jones, 56, conservative Democrat, Abilene. The Legislature's most ardent devotee of hard work; a beast of burden for whom the yoke is reward, not punishment. Spent the session, like Sisyphus in Greek mythology, pushing a heavy boulder uphill; unlike Sisyphus, actually reached the summit—then looked for more boulders to push.

Jones' record: reformed property tax administration, implemented tax relief, revised the consumer credit code, increased state tuition grants to students at private colleges, and updated state stripmining regulations. Any two would have made a good session for anyone else; for Jones all five were a mere fraction of his work load, since as chairman of the Senate Finance Committee he was also the chief architect of the appropriations bill.

The only senator who could have filled the void left by retired Finance chairman A. M. Aikin; had the unquestioned integrity and universal respect necessary to hold together the committee's collection of Senate heavyweights with easily bruised egos. Said one Senate staffer: "Everybody jives and tricks each other except him. He's the only one you can believe on every issue." An indication of his colleagues' esteem came on the first day of the sensitive tax relief conference committee: the other Senate conferees decamped to the floor, leaving Jones alone to bargain with five House members about areas of disagreement.

Played an important role early in the session by standing up to Governor Clements' demand for wholesale cutting of the budget. Said Jones: "We are a modern industrial state with modern responsibilities. If we are serious about returning power from Washington to those governments closer to the people, then states must not shy away from accepting responsibility." For a lot of legislators, the statement would have been nothing more than clever rhetoric; when conservative, sober Grant Jones said it, the impending budget battle with Clements was over before it began.

Lance Lalor, 32, liberal Democrat, Houston. A walking refutation of the idea that to succeed in the Texas Legislature you have to be a good old boy. His demeanor on the floor is straight from Isaiah—"Stand by thyself, come not near to me; for I am holier than thou"—but it doesn't curtail his effectiveness.

Represents a district that epitomizes modern Texas (the Warwick, Rice University, the Texas Medical Center, the Astrodome); fittingly, is the Legislature's leading urban advocate—a distinction, alas, for which there are too few contenders. In a body where most members' idea of urban legislation is a bill to improve the firemen's pension fund, Lalor was able to pass two bills that could have a salutary effect on the quality of city life: one earmarked around $16 million a year for creation of urban state parks, the other would help arrest the decline of older neighborhoods by providing for low-interest commercial loans backed by revenue bonds.

Effective despite the fact that he doesn't try to be liked, doesn't care if he's liked, and *isn't* liked; succeeds mainly by doing his homework (he lined up 102 cosponsors for his urban parks bill) while others are sampling Austin's manifold pleasures. Lalor's idea of a night on the town is a Wendy's hamburger followed by reading the bills on the next day's calendar. One lobbyist who talked to Lalor about a complicated mortgage revenue bond bill was impressed when Lalor asked him about a law review article mentioned in a footnote to another law review article, then was dumbfounded to discover Lalor isn't even a lawyer.

One of the new breed of liberals who opposes restriction of competition by anyone—particularly the government. Upset more traditional libs (but scored points with conservatives) by carrying the so-called Beneficial Finance bill eliminating the ceiling on the maximum number of offices one loan company may operate. His philosophy made him a natural advocate of the Sunset process: woe to the regulatory agency that wouldn't accept public members on its board or agree to put its money in the State Treasury. Probably the House member most responsible for whatever success Sunset had.

A full-time legislator, Lalor is still working. At midnight on June 4, a week after final adjournment, Lalor was sitting in his office as usual, poring over conference committee reports from the last week of the session. The 67th Legislature is a year and a half away, but for Lalor, it's time to get ready.

McFarland: ex-cop still has street smarts.

Bob McFarland, 38, Republican, Arlington. The House's high priest of conservatism, heir to the mantle of Ray Hutchison (who left the House after two sessions on the Ten Best list to run unsuccessfully against Bill Clements in the GOP primary). Has a genius for applying rational argument to the legislative process and making it stick. A strong advocate and mature adversary who doesn't hate anybody when the fight is over.

Regarded as a comer when the session began; established his arrival beyond all challenge by tackling a bill to reduce penalties for charging usurious interest. Won the admiration of liberals and conservatives alike for his even-handed performance: eliminated the old law's draconian provisions (the penalty for exceeding the 10 per cent interest ceiling on a thirty-year $50,000 loan was almost $250,000) without letting lenders off lightly. House handicappers had rated the prospects of passage at no better than

Lalor: holier than thou, better than most

fifty-fifty; McFarland was so persuasive the vote was 89-40.

Took on an even tougher assignment: finding common ground between defense and trial lawyers quarreling over the right of consumers to sue for injuries caused by defective products. Took the defense lawyers' bill and became a one-man recycling center, turning trash from both sides into a respectable bill he then passed over fierce resistance. In debate, maneuvered like a pool player: one could almost hear the *thwock . . . plop* of the ball as he rattled off his argument, racked up the point, and left himself in position for the next shot.

A member's member who has the qualities colleagues value most: doesn't play arm-twisting games (he was the only member of the notorious Calendars Committee not at the top of someone's enemies list) and is straightforward ("He'll tell you, 'I can't go with you on that'; he doesn't waste my time," said a liberal member) but not dogmatic (one of the few Republicans who voted to increase child welfare payments).

The most conservative dresser in the House—favors navy suits without a hint of pattern—he walks around the floor absolutely erect, looking exactly like the ex-FBI agent that he is. Retains an uncanny street sense which helps him judge the mercurial moods of the House, but is totally free of the macho ex-cop syndrome: even passed a bill stiffening penalties for police brutality. Said one highly regarded Capitol lobbyist: "He impresses me more than any member of the House."

Babe Schwartz, 52, liberal Democrat, Galveston. The scene: the floor, Friday, May 25, 11:00 p.m. In an hour, the 72-hour rule will take effect; any bill not passed by midnight is effectively dead. Inside the brass railing, Babe Schwartz is working the floor: telling jokes, slapping backs, counseling with the presiding officer, holding up one finger to signal an aye vote, running over to make certain a potential ally is voting correctly. It is a textbook show of how to pass a bill. There is only one thing wrong: this is the *House* chamber; Schwartz is a *senator*.

No, Schwarz wasn't lost; he was just showing why he belongs on the Ten Best list for the fourth time. He's a pro: never loses interest, never fails to follow through, never misses a trick, never has an off day; he may go down swinging but he never gets called out on strikes.

As usual, one of the Legislature's premier bill passers; so versatile that he ranked as one of the top killers as well. Turned around votes during debate to beat a bad ol' bill letting contractors off the hook for negligence in constructing public projects; also killed in the closing hours a bill he discovered could be used as a vehicle to store nuclear waste in Texas. Tackled the long-standing squabble between commercial and sport fishermen—ignoring the adage that anyone who fools with a fishing bill had better enjoy private life—and somehow managed to pass fish and shrimp conservation bills that made him the hero of both sides.

Godfather of the Killer Bees; spent the session flailing his colleagues for being beholden to the lobby with comments like "If God himself came out here today and told you to vote against this bill, you still wouldn't do it." Harangued, threatened, cajoled, and—always—lectured his fellow senators: got away with such constant moralizing by being a charter member of the Senate club. Feuded constantly with the other charter member, Bill Moore of Bryan; by harping on his old enemy's excesses and taunting him into near-fistfights, Schwartz has neutralized the Bull of the Brazos, who now has trouble passing bills.

Never free of criticism, blamed by a few for running a sloppy Natural Resources Committee, by a few more for not contributing to the negotiations on issues like consumer protection. There is some validity to both counts, but critics ignore Schwartz' ultimate role: a man to let others solve what they can already see and show them what they cannot.

Craig Washington, 37, liberal Democrat, Houston. The best natural politician in the House, as born to his medium as Mikhail Baryshnikov is to dance. Whether he's trying to kill a bill, add an amendment, or cut off the enemy's retreat with a parliamentary maneuver, Washington is the show other members most like to watch.

Provided the House with its one unforgettable moment of the session during debate over his bid to raise child welfare payments. Washington pulled out a bag of clothing and toilet articles purchased at a cut-rate store to illustrate what the current $32.58 a month can buy: a pair of cheap jeans, crepe-sole shoes, two pairs of socks, deodorant, toothpaste, and shampoo (but no food) for $27.27. "You know what that leaves?" he asked. "Pocket change. I want you to look at what you're giving your children. You'll see them again. You'll see them going to the Texas Department of Corrections. Gut up one time, members. We vote on all kinds of rotten things in the appropriations bill. Gut up this one time and you'll be doing yourself a favor." The vote: 103-37 for gutting up, the first time the House had voted such a raise in ten years.

Eloquence was only one of his weapons; foremost among the rest was an asset originally observed in Theodore Roosevelt: he had an absolute sense of political pitch that enabled him to strike the notes the chorus awaited. Was the House in a mood to duck an issue? Washington would move to postpone it, as when he scuttled a bill absolving doctors of negligence during emergencies. Was the House disgusted with the Senate? Just after the Senate passed its abysmal version of deceptive-trade "reform," Washington stalled an anti-union bill by suggesting that representatives should let the Senate cut itself up on the bill first. Was welfare being identified as a black issue? He pointed out that 57 per cent of the kids on welfare are white, only 14 per cent black.

Enhanced his effectiveness by keeping his distance from the Gang of Four. Underscored that he was a member of the House first, a black second, and an ideologue last. Refrained from attacking Clayton and the team; made a seconding speech for the Speaker and praised conservatives like Nub Donaldson from the microphone.

If he had a flaw, it was that he sometimes failed to recognize that there is a larger political arena beyond the House floor. Lost some of his welfare gains by failing to lobby the Senate; also failed to follow up a floor victory to improve permanent funding for Prairie View A&M until it was too late. Could be even better than he is, but to criticize his shortcomings is a little like lamenting that cats aren't like dogs: there is enough satisfaction in what he is without dwelling on what he is not.

Schwartz (left) with old nemesis Moore: still lecturing, moralizing—and winning

THE TEN WORST

Andujar: no political sense; the road to failure is paved with good intentions.

Betty Andujar, 66, Republican, Fort Worth. Sigh. We don't really want to do this. As one old Capitol hand put it, "She's such a good-hearted gal, you hate to criticize her." But he did—and so does everyone else.

Her basic problem: she just doesn't understand. The same theme—her lack of intuitive political sense—runs through every Andujar story. Never was this more evident than during the confirmation hearing for Joe Bishop, nominated to the University of South Texas board of directors. Andujar described him as "not a quality man," gave colleagues copies of anti-Bishop petitions signed by faculty members, and distributed a letter accusing him of improper personal conduct. If it sounds like Andujar was out to bust him, think again: she was his sponsor! Since Bishop was her constituent, Andujar could have defeated him simply by invoking senatorial courtesy, but she just couldn't do it: one senator was for him, another wasn't, it was just too confusing. "There's a great deal of politics in this," she complained. What did she expect to find in the Senate?

Political complications always seemed to baffle her. In four sessions, has never learned how to pass a bill. Rarely had the votes lined up in advance; only after she'd tried, and failed, to clear a bill for debate did she go from desk to desk to find out what the objections were. Couldn't make connections: when a colleague proposed funding battered women's centers with a $5 increase in the marriage license fee, she thought he was kidding. Very flaky: during the running battle over a separate presidential primary, she'd tell opponents of the idea, "I'm with you *this week*." Every senator reneges now and then, but they don't advertise it in advance.

Despite all the foregoing, we thought that some weight should be attached to the fact that of all the senators, she's the one who does the least intentional harm. But that was before the last day, when she killed a bill designed to prevent hospitals from denying treatment to emergency patients who can't speak English. Said Andujar, a physician's wife: "My solution is they had better learn English. If I were sick in Hong Kong, I would be in trouble." Just as we had pulled our Worst net out of the water, she jumped right into the boat.

Arnold Gonzales, 40, liberal Democrat, Corpus Christi. The archetypal legislative cockroach: the problem wasn't what he carried away but what he fell into and messed up. Ruined, among other things, any hope of meaningful Sunset legislation emerging from the House Government Organization Committee, where he was often the swing vote on a closely divided panel. Alas, Gonzales always seemed to be swinging in the same direction: away from the determined coalition of Republicans and liberal Democrats struggling to make Sunset work.

The overriding issue of Sunset—whether licensing and policing agencies like the Real Estate Commission and the State Bar would be run for the benefit of the professions or the public—escaped him entirely. Couldn't see beyond his personal experience: opposed efforts to merge the perpetually feuding cosmetology and barber boards because he likes to get manicures. Can't see the connection? Neither could his frustrated colleagues, who had counted on Gonzales as a vote for consolidation. Also reneged on forcing the State Bar to put its money in the State Treasury. "He was a complete toady for the professional groups," a discouraged committee member sighed. "All they had to do was get a Mexican American professional to call him." Like a feather pillow, Gonzales retained the impression of the last person to sit on him.

Constantly reminded the House he possesses a PhD, perhaps the best evidence that education doesn't equal intelligence. When the discussion got over his head, which was frequently, asked colleagues surly questions like "What makes you think you're so smart?" The combination of arrogance and stupidity led him to make the worst error of judgment of the entire session: a baseless accusation that a former House member, now a Dallas lawyer, had "lied under oath" to a committee while testifying about one of Gonzales' bills. Only the intervention of Billy Clayton and other intermediaries saved him from a lawsuit.

Disastrously inept at the legislative game. Asked by a group of veterans to introduce a bill, Gonzales procrastinated until they turned to his hometown Mexican American rival, Hugo Berlanga. Then when Berlanga introduced the bill, Gonzales accused him of stealing it. Spent the rest of the session sniping at Berlanga and Berlanga's legislation: forbade his staff to speak to Berlanga's and once rushed to the microphone to interrupt Berlanga and chide him for a mispronunciation, a performance that did nothing for their ability to work together effectively on common local problems. If, after two sessions, Gonzales still thinks that's how the game is played, it's time he looked at the scoreboard.

Gonzales: classic legislative cockroach

Forrest Green, 57, conservative Democrat, Corsicana. Classic furniture who had the misfortune to get into a position where he was required to do something; sure enough, he couldn't. Planned to quit after last session but came back at Clayton's request to take the chairmanship of the Agriculture and Livestock Committee. Why he wanted it remains a mystery.

As idle as a car engine permanently in neutral. Sat by and watched his committee deteriorate into the most inept panel in the House. So many Agriculture and Livestock bills were shot down on the

172 THE ONE AND ONLY TEXAS LEGISLATURE

THE WORST

Green: he lacked the sense to stay home.

floor that sometimes it seemed as though the committee was conducting a skeet shoot: bill-killers like Ron Coleman and Bob Davis would say, "Pull," and the committee would send up another clay pigeon. Among the targets: a proposal to regulate plant nurseries, a prohibition against purchase of agricultural land by nonresident aliens, and a ban on meat imports that was so badly drafted it would have prevented Texas beef that was processed out of state from being shipped back in. "When a committee loses that many bills on the floor," said a veteran legislator, "it means the chairman and the staff aren't doing their job."

Virtually invisible outside of committee—except in the House post office where, as an ex-postmaster, he liked to tell employees how to go about their business. Had no influence on the floor, where, said a colleague, "He'd vote against the roll call if he could." Shunned the microphone as though it contained colonies of fire ants.

True to character, tried to avoid holding a hearing on a farmworkers bill he opposed—but his committee objected. After the hearing Green refused to call for a vote, and without waiting for a motion, sent the bill to its death in a subcommittee and gaveled the meeting to a close. It was the worst abuse of power of the session, and from the unlikeliest source: the one time he was unable to avoid action, he got in trouble.

Bill Hollowell, 50, conservative Democrat, Grand Saline. First served in the Legislature during 1957-1967; it's changed but he hasn't. On the Ten Worst list not just for his archaic states-rights rhetoric—when he gets up to speak, members put a small Confederate flag on the podium—but also because his work on the House Appropriations Committee repeatedly required undoing by his colleagues.

Could have performed a true public service by joining the small minority of fiscal conservatives on the committee who resisted logrolling and pork-barrelling; instead, wasted his energies trying to inject his prejudices into the state budget. Succeeded in prohibiting the Commission on the Arts and Humanities from spending money on jazz festivals; the restriction was removed on the floor, but not until it became the only piece of legislation all session to be openly condemned as racist. Tried to abolish a federally funded program to encourage the use of food stamps—had he succeeded, the state would have been disqualified from the entire federal food stamp program.

Other programs Hollowell shot at and missed: UT faculty salaries (he described UT's endowment as a "slush fund"); abortions for welfare mothers who are victims of rape or incest (he made good his threat to vote against the entire appropriations bill if the state was allowed to be, as he put it, a "coconspirator to murder"); the Land Office's environmental management division ("We don't need any more management of the environment"); and the state program to combat child abuse. Hollowell was also rebuffed when he insisted that the state provide legislators with free license plates, exactly the sort of excess everyone else knew was out of step in a belt-tightening year.

Once respected—in spite of such antics—for doing his homework, Hollowell showed signs of slipping this session. Railed against an insignificant election bill because he read an analysis saying that before the law could take effect, it would have to be approved by the U.S. Department of Justice. As the bill's sponsor pointed out, this was nothing new—it's been happening since 1975,

Hollowell: hates feds and all that jazz

when Congress put Texas under the Voting Rights Act.

Like the chorus in a Greek tragedy, he kept issuing sober precepts of morality that the actors ignored. Opposed a constitutional amendment allowing churches to hold bingo games with "Jesus chased the money changers from the temple. I have no indication that Christ ever changed his mind. I cast my vote for Him." The House, perhaps with more current information, cast its vote for bingo.

Despite his outbursts, House liberals have a soft spot for Hollowell because he accepts no campaign contributions and is totally free of the lobby. It only goes to show that integrity is not enough.

Tom Massey, 48, conservative Democrat, San Angelo. Public Enemy Number One, the most hated member of the House as the result of his high-handed, arbitrary chairmanship of the Committee on Calendars. In his previous incarnation last session, Massey made the Ten Worst list for his high-handed, arbitrary chairmanship of the Public Education Committee. Unfortunately, Clayton's solution to the Massey problem was to take last session's localized disease and allow it to infect the entire House. Massey had the most sensitive job imaginable—life or death power over which bills reached the floor—and proved singularly unfit for it.

Every bill that came to Calendars for scheduling had already been approved by a working committee; yet Massey insisted that his panel was a supercommittee with the right to judge each bill anew and even force amendments—though Calendars conducted no hearings, heard no testimony, made no studies, and under House rules had a purely procedural role. The journey from committee to the floor through Calendars became the most hazardous since Viet Nam's Route 1 from Hue to Da Nang. The very first bill filed this session was approved by the Agriculture Committee on February 23 and arrived in Calendars the next day. It was never seen again.

Liked to characterize himself as a bill killer whose committee blockaded what he called "bad, sorry bills"; House members, however, characterized him a little differently: "He's a sorry, no-good liar," groused a Clayton team loyalist after Massey rescinded a promise to schedule a bill. In fact, it was bad, sorry bills that had the least trouble slipping through Massey's net; once he even interrupted a hearing to ask a lobbyist if he wanted a bill on the next day's calendar. Thanks largely to his work, an unprecedented number of bills were overwhelmingly defeated in floor debate; several got fewer than 20 votes out of 150.

So intoxicated with power that he almost lost control of his own committee

THE ONE AND ONLY TEXAS LEGISLATURE 173

THE WORST ★★★★★★★★★★★★★★★★★★★★★★★★★★★★★

Massey: handling of Calendars Committee united every member—against him.

by claiming to have jurisdiction over local and uncontested bills, which are the province of a different scheduling committee; refused the request of several legislators to look at his committee logs, forcing them to appeal under the Open Records Act, a breach of legislative decorum no less vulgar than spitting on the House floor.

By the end of the session almost no one would deal with Massey anymore. One measure of his standing came on the last night, when Massey, who considers himself something of an authority on water law, tried—with some justification—to kill a local Harris County water district bill because he had been excluded from compromise discussions. When the results appeared on the voting board—Massey lost by over a hundred votes—the House broke into spontaneous cheers.

Bill Meier, 38, conservative Democrat, Euless. The most notorious carrier since Typhoid Mary. Carried a legislative program so anti-consumer it did everything but make *caveat emptor* the eleventh commandment. Passed the session's most maligned bill, which he claimed would balance the state's deceptive-trade law; his remedy was about as balanced as the federal budget. Would also have had the second most maligned bill, but critics were silenced prematurely when he couldn't muster the votes to restrict the consumer's right to sue for injuries caused by defective products. Handled yet another controversial bill raising the ceiling on home mortgage interest rates.

Masqueraded as one who would advance the cause of conservatism; in fact, his cause was himself. Unlike John Dean's, Meier's ambition was not blind. Widely thought to covet the lieutenant governor's job if Bill Hobby moves on in 1982, and chose his legislation accordingly: his bills were backed by realtors, auto dealers, retailers, and savings and loan associations—prominent groups in every community, a natural statewide constituency. Followed a pattern he'd established as chairman of the fledgling Sunset Commission before the session began, when he gutted recommendations for more public accountability in order to score points with lawyers, CPAs, morticians, and other potential blocs of votes.

It wasn't just the bills he carried that earned Meier his stigma; it was how he carried them. Unlike House sponsors of the same bills, ignored fair play and compromise; knew which side his bread was buttered on and developed too fond an appetite for the dish. Agreed to negotiate but refused to yield, like a child who reluctantly comes out to play but won't share his toys. Knew the Senate

Meier: dined on lobby-buttered bread

was "so lobbied it was wrapped," in the words of a lobbyist who helped tie the bow; once his colleagues had committed themselves to support his deceptive-trade bill, he held their feet to the fire—even though some of them didn't like the heat. Had Meier budged just a little, his colleagues could have taken credit for improving the bill; instead, House members got the opportunity and made the most of it. Meier's intransigence won him admirers among the lobby, but some of his colleagues were not so pleased.

The sad thing is that Meier represents a double loss: not just a bad senator but a good one gone to seed. One of the Ten Best in 1973 when we praised him as open-minded, highly accessible, and never dogmatic. My, how things change.

Bob Price, 51, Republican, Pampa. If the Senate were a horse race, nobody would bet on him. Slow out of the gate, weak down the stretch, a nice guy who, true to form, finished last.

Senate staffers and lobbyists collected and swapped Price stories like old coins; most involved his work in committee, where every meeting seemed like his first. In the Human Resources Committee, he professed bafflement at the strange look of bills, with repealed language crossed out and new language underlined—despite the fact that the same procedure is used in Congress, where he served for eight years.

In idle moments staffers amused themselves by listening to a tape recording of Price presenting his bill requiring all public buildings to be accessible to handicapped persons (currently only structures built after 1970 have such a requirement). Not since Ethelred the Unready has lack of preparation presented so many pitfalls—and Price obligingly fell into each one. Asked the cost of his proposal, Price referred senators to the mandatory fiscal estimate attached to the bill. That was, as everyone but Price already knew, precisely the problem: it said no estimate was possible. Next Price offered an amendment that turned out not to be an amendment at all but a staff-written analysis of the bill. Then Price offered to make the bill apply only to buildings constructed in the future—which, as a colleague pointed out, was already the law. Finally Price moved to send his then meaningless bill to subcommittee, only to be told that, not being a member of the committee, he couldn't make the motion.

Carried some of the session's strangest bills—one required every agricultural product produced in or shipped through Texas to be labeled "product of the United States"—and cast some of the strangest votes. Remonstrated against, then voted for, a bill to increase interest rates on large bank loans; flip-flopped so many times on one utility bill that a

THE WORST

Price: not since Ethelred the Unready has lack of preparation led to so much ruin.

desperate mayor from his district brought a local TV cameraman to Austin to film Price taking the mayor's side before he changed again.

Actually succeeded in passing some farm-oriented legislation, partly because liberal colleagues appreciated his occasional don't-take-me-for-granted votes that, at apparently random intervals, put Price on their side (fellow Republicans, however, didn't; they twice chewed him out publicly) but also because they felt sorry for him. On the day one farm bill was scheduled for debate, Price told backers of the bill, "Everything will be all right as long as nobody asks me a question." Nobody did, at least not until he was over all the procedural hurdles; then a colleague inquired if he could ask a question now that it couldn't hurt anything. Sure enough, Price couldn't answer it.

Senfronia Thompson, 40, liberal Democrat, Houston. The kind of politician who would have fit right in during the heyday of Tammany Hall: concerned only with parochial ethnic issues and tarred with the brush of taint.

For most legislators, trouble with the law means difficulty understanding the statutes; for Thompson it was the real thing. The only legislator to have a run-in with a district attorney over anything more serious than setting DAs' salaries. Investigated—and still under investigation—for charging personal phone calls to her state credit card, including 47 to a Galveston funeral home and 6 to an Oklahoma real estate man. When reports of the investigation hit the front pages, Thompson vanished, going AWOL from the House for nearly two weeks.

Had earlier stretched the edges of propriety by inviting lobbyists to a January fundraiser in violation of the universally observed custom that one doesn't hit up the lobby during the session. Perhaps it never occurred to her that it's bad form to ask people for money at the same time they want something from you—but it certainly occurred to lobbyists on the invitation list; one Capitol veteran flatly described the affair as a "shakedown."

A washout as a member of the powerful Appropriations Committee. Interested only in black issues, especially funding for long-neglected Prairie View A&M and Texas Southern University; viewed other issues not on their merits but according to the you-get-yours-then-it's-my-turn-principle. Had all the subtlety of an importunate debt collector: colleagues cringed when she shouted across the room reminders such as, "See, Mr. Heatly, I'm voting with you. I'll expect a vote from you later." This brazen logrolling worked against her in the end: when the time came to trim the budget to realistic size, she didn't have the respect, and consequently lacked the clout to defend her ill-gotten gains.

Terrible on the floor: loud, blustering, and usually wrong; one who was not baffled by complexity but rather missed it altogether. Irate over the state's approval of a dump in her district, she cut out funding (later restored) for regulation of solid-waste disposal sites—ignoring warnings of sympathetic members that without regulation, even more dumps would end up in her district. Opposed a Sunset-inspired proposal to reduce the burdensome training required of shampooers with "If you went to get your hair done, wouldn't you want someone to recognize all the venereal diseases in your scalp?"

Here is Senfronia Thompson in a nutshell: appointed to the Election Code Revision Committee during the last interim, she attended only two meetings, left both early, showed up once on the wrong day, and then made a big fuss to make sure she was reimbursed.

Bob Ware, 22, Republican, Fort Worth. A freshman who, by defeating notorious incumbent Tom Schieffer, performed a public service; it was his last. A throwback to a nineteenth-century Thomas Nast cartoon, in which politicians were characterized by large bellies and small minds. Sent lobbyists fleeing with comments like, "You didn't help me in my campaign, but you can still get right."

Displayed overwhelming ineptitude in losing an innocuous bill to extend from 500 to 750 feet the distance unmanned walk-up facilities may be located from a bank. The bill had already received tentative House approval by a 69–52 vote; banking lobbyists padded Ware's cushion by persuading 11 nay votes to switch. What they hadn't anticipated was that Ware would lose 26 of his *aye* votes by privately describing his legislation as a "branch banking bill"—as ill-advised

Thompson: just like in the bad old days

Ware: as if from a Thomas Nast cartoon

THE ONE AND ONLY TEXAS LEGISLATURE 175

THE WORST

as asking in old Salem where the witches were meeting that night. Things went downhill so far and so fast that one member went to the microphone to ask Ware, at 22 the youngest member of the House, "Don't you want to have your twenty-fourth birthday in the Legislature?" Said one lobbyist thankful to be an uninvolved spectator: "It may not be the worst performance of the session, but it's got a three-stroke lead." Nobody caught up.

One of the most stoutly partisan members of the Legislature—a trait that got him in trouble with his fellow Republicans, who were deliberating how to respond to a Democratic legislator's attempt at overriding a Clements veto. Since the Republicans are still a tiny minority (23 out of 150), they feared a vote along strict party lines would isolate Clements and endanger their own effectiveness; several suggested that the Republicans split their votes, but Ware, ever blind to subtlety, took offense at the slightest prospect of defection. "He suspected the rest of us of being tainted by moderation," complained an irked colleague.

Has all the earmarks of a one-termer. Told his hometown paper that he voted against a loan shark bill, after previously supporting it, because "it was obvious the bill was going down to defeat"; went on to say he nevertheless supported the bill—thereby negating the political advantage of voting against it. During the banking bill debacle, was warned during debate that he was contributing to Schieffer's political resurrection. What did the hapless residents of southwest Fort Worth do to deserve such a choice?

John Whitmire, 29, liberal Democrat, Houston. Nicknamed Double Zero: one digit representing his ability, the other his stature in the House. The comic relief of the Gang of Four, though how he wound up in fast company like Bryant and Coleman is one of the more mystifying questions of the 66th Legislature.

Seemed to walk around carrying a "Kick Me" sign. One member, Susan McBee of Del Rio, was so eager to oblige that after two hours of refusing to answer any hostile questions about her bill to cripple the school breakfast program, she made an exception for Whitmire. Sure enough, given the opportunity to help save an important program for Texas children, he launched a series of dumb, pointless questions that benefitted neither his cause nor his reputation.

Whitmire approaching the podium was a misguided missile homing in on his own self-destruction. Offered to make peace with Clayton at the start of the session, saying he wanted to be on the team, then took the microphone to rant and rave for a rule to elect the Speaker by secret ballot—a direct attack on

Whitmire: booby laying traps for himself

Clayton. Not content to quit while he was behind, proceeded to bury himself by going back to the microphone to say he was only kidding, just the sort of humor the Speaker—and the House—appreciate about as much as brucellosis.

Plumbed unexplored depths during debate on the appropriations bill by offering an amendment to eliminate funding for thirteen assistant commissioners of mental health, after admitting he hadn't read the bill and had no idea what the commissioners did or didn't do. His justification: "I was bored to death and wanted to shake things up." A fellow liberal tried to turn Whitmire's lark into something serious by proposing to transfer the funds earmarked for the bureaucrats' salaries to child welfare. Whitmire opposed it. Craig Washington took the microphone to explain patiently to Whitmire, like a parent attempting to reason with a petulant child, that the substitute would help pass his amendment: "They're trying to help you, John." Whitmire still opposed it. The substitute passed anyway. Eventually a House-Senate conference committee restored the positions, as everyone, except possibly Whitmire, knew all along they would.

Never was Whitmire's lack of standing in the House more evident than on the final Friday of the session. With the House scoreboard clock showing 11:59 p.m. and the 72-hour deadline on considering new bills about to take effect, Whitmire stepped forward with a noncontroversial local bill providing pay raises for Harris County probate judges. The one universal legislative courtesy is that *anyone* can pass a local bill—anyone, that is, but Whitmire. As the voting board flashed red, a disgusted Houston legislator cursed himself for not suggesting that somebody else present the bill. "I should have kidnapped him," he muttered, Preferably at the start of the session.

SPECIAL AWARDS

THE THREE WORST KILLER BEE JOKES

Killer Bee Senator Gene Jones of Houston ended his telephone conversations with "I've got to buzz off now."

The Killer Bees hid from police at evangelist Lester Roloff's controversial children's home, because that's the only place the state won't inspect.

After the Department of Public Safety failed to find any of the missing senators and arrested Gene Jones' brother, the DPS became known as the Bumble Bees. State representatives who supported the senators became known as the Houseflies.

WORST SENSE OF TIMING

Craig Washington had just completed a stirring appeal to the House on behalf of Sam Hudson's bill to allow conjugal visits for prison inmates. Supporters of the bill sensed that things had swung their way; it was time to vote, *now*, before the mood evaporated. But Hudson couldn't resist the lure of the microphone: "All I have to say, members, is three little words." The House waited expectantly. "Please vote for this bill."

They didn't.

BEST REPARTEE

During a discussion of the same bill, someone asked Ed Emmett of Kingwood, "What's the Republican position on conjugal visits?"

Replied Emmett: "Why, missionary, of course."

SLEAZIEST COMMENT

First prize to Senator Carl Parker of Port Arthur, for asking a woman reporter to pick a number between one and eight. She guessed five. "Wrong," Parker replied. "If you'd been right, I'd have taken off my clothes. Now you take off yours. Let's go, baby."

Second prize to Senator Carl Parker of Port Arthur, for answering a woman reporter's question about a bill with "I'll tell you if you kiss me."

SPECIAL "FISCAL RESPONSIBILITY STOPS AT THE WELLHEAD" AWARD

House Energy Resources Committee chairman Joe Hanna of Breckenridge, when asked during debate why the Railroad Commission needed a $581,000 emergency appropriation he was proposing, replied, "It's not my prerogative or duty to question what it takes for them to do their job."

Hudson: just two little words too many

Emmett: ask him about a position paper.

Parker: kiss of fate or kiss of death?

A LEGISLATIVE LEXICON

The Legislature, like any club, has developed a descriptive language all its own. Among the more popular expressions:

bad ol' bill *n*. A bill that, in the eye of the beholder, is utterly without redeeming social value. "Members, this is a bad ol' bill," is the nuke of legislative rhetoric.

crater *v.i.* To renege on one's promises under pressure; a sudden and total cave-in. "He really cratered when his mayor showed up."

dog and pony show *n*. A staged event designed to appear real, in which participants follow a set script. Senate meetings held for the sole purpose of denouncing the missing Killer Bees were this session's classic example.

downside *n*. The unsavory aspects of a proposal. Usually well hidden and little publicized, as in a bill purporting to expand the Tarrant County civil service system. Buried deep in the bill was the downside: if a referendum on the expansion failed, the entire system would be wiped out.

flake *v.i.* To drift away by degrees from a previously stated position. "Senator, I may have to flake on that presidential primary bill." In contrast to cratering, flaking may serve to enhance the flakor's bargaining position with the flakee.

Gang of Four *n*. The hard core of opposition to Speaker Billy Clayton, viz., John Bryant of Dallas, Ronald Coleman and Luther Jones of El Paso, and John Whitmire of Houston. Blamed, like their Chinese namesakes, for all the regime's troubles.

grandfather *v.t.* To exempt current practitioners from the effect of a law. Frequently designed to give those already in business a competitive advantage, as in a bill (later vetoed) that put tough restrictions on new pawnshops and grandfathered old ones.

green board *n*. A favorable outcome for the matter under discussion. Refers to the electronic voting board in the House chamber, where a green light beside a member's name signifies he is voting "aye" and a red light signifies "no." Usually heard in the interval between the start of voting and the flashing of the final tally: "That's a green board, friends."

heat *n*. Intense pressure. Can be applied by the leadership, influential folks back home, even the press. "Senator Blackhart has really been taking the heat on his bill to quadruple interest rates."

lib *n*. Derisive term applied to a liberal who would rather make an eloquent, quixotic speech against a bill than kill it quietly in committee. Anyone who talks openly about "right and wrong" is a suspected lib.

Linoleum Club *n*. The otherwise nameless junk-food dispensary in the basement of the Capitol. The primary source of sustenance for legislators who don't go to real clubs for a free lunch on the lobby.

lobster *n*. A lobbyist willing to pick up the tab. "Let's go to the Quorum. I've found a lobster." **syn** SPONSOR

One Hundred Club *n*. Informal designation for a group of House members whose proposals have been rejected with more than a hundred votes against. Charter member was Don Rains of San Marcos, whose bill to regulate plant nurseries lost 19–106.

pissing match *n*. A spiteful, petty test of egos usually characterized by A killing B's bills and B retaliating in kind. Can bring the entire legislative process to a halt, as occurred four days before adjournment, when Dallas House members responded to a bill's death in the Senate by holding up over a hundred Senate bills in the House.

Red Square *n*. An area of the House floor where most of the desks are populated by liberal members. "Are you voting with Red Square on this one?"

sleazy *adj*. Extremely unsavory, morally offensive, lacking in merit or character. Has replaced **low rent** as the universal legislative pejorative. Additional contempt may be conveyed by drawing out the first syllable, as in "The honorable member from San Antonio is a sleee-zy sumbitch."

team, the *n*. The Speaker's support in the House. Includes both staunch and occasional loyalists; hence, has little significance except to opponents, who blame it for their legislative shortcomings. "I can't get any bills passed because I'm not on the team."

traveling light *adj*. Without a legislative program; therefore, free to resist the leadership without fear of retribution. Not to be confused with **furniture**, members whose lack of a legislative program betrays their standing as little more than the desks and chairs they occupy.

walk *v.i.* To leave the floor as a means of avoiding a vote. Usually a sign of cowardice, but may be used to help a cause by not staying around to vote against it. "If you can't vote with us, will you walk?"

water carrier *n*. A legislator who uncritically sponsors bills and amendments drawn by lobbyists; a faithful servant of the lobby.

work *v.t.* To persuade, bargain, threaten, solicit, or beg, when done by a legislator. When done by others, known as lobbying. "I've got to work the floor for the Speaker."

SPECIAL AWARDS

Cofer: best dresser, almost furniture

Head: "Pssst. Can you give me a lift?"

Cartwright: little angel for big lenders

FURNITURE

The session involved so many issues almost everyone found something to do. It was hard to be furniture—the term for the most insignificant members—but a few managed: in the Senate, Bill Braecklein of Dallas and Lindon Williams of Houston; in the House, 1973 Worst Charles Finnell of Holliday and 1975 Best Bill Sullivant of Gainesville. Perpetual furniture Jim Clark spent the session running for mayor of Pasadena (he won); it was weeks before anyone missed him. Pointer Sisters look-alike Lanell Cofer of Dallas escaped the furniture list mainly by being the most-noticed member of the House.

BIG-TIME SPENDER

During the first four months of the session, Fred Head went home to Athens (394-mile round trip) almost every night, including 25 journeys by chartered plane—costing taxpayers $3620.80.

BEST NICKNAME

Don Cartwright of San Antonio, "the Pillsbury Doughboy," a name that resulted from the happy marriage of Cartwright's cherubic face and his sponsorship of a bill to treble interest rates on small loans.

ROOM AT THE TOP

We have traditionally considered the presiding officers—Lieutenant Governor Bill Hobby and Speaker Billy Clayton—ineligible for either list. This is unfortunate for Clayton but a blessing for poor Hobby.

Clayton once again was an evenhanded Speaker who let the House find its way on every vote. He tried to avoid bloodbaths by getting opposing sides together for negotiations before issues came to the floor. His only albatross: Tom Massey, his choice as chairman of the Calendars Committee.

Hobby was hampered from the start by the retirement of four key conservative senators. Short on loyal hands, he turned to the lobby for help in passing a separate presidential primary; they wanted no part of it. Still hoping for their support, he helped the remaining conservatives break liberal filibusters to get business-backed bills passed; the lobby took but it didn't give. Hobby had lost control: of the liberals, by siding openly with conservatives; of the conservatives, by courting them so desperately. Finally he found a ploy to pass his primary bill—and that's when the Killer Bees (Hobby's own words come home to haunt him) walked out. Lesson: in politics, it's never good to want something too much. ★

178 THE ONE AND ONLY TEXAS LEGISLATURE

SIX CRISES

by Paul Burka

Here's what our legislators will be battling over for the next few months. Naturally they'll have our best interests at heart.

Uh-oh. Here it is January of an odd-numbered year again. That means it must be time to dust off all the old jokes: about the New York judge who declared, "No man's life, liberty, or property are safe while the Legislature is in session"; about the two things you should never watch being made—sausage and legislation; about the typographical error in the Texas Constitution that has the Legislature meeting every 2 years for 140 days instead of every 140 years for 2 days as intended.

Yes, the Legislature is back for its sixty-sixth biennial assault on the State Capitol. But this time something new is waiting for them—a Republican governor. The last time Texas had one of those was back in 1871, and the legislative session that year still ranks among the most tumultuous the state has ever seen. Alas, no one expects anything quite so colorful this time. After all, ol' E. J. Davis got his comeuppance for spending the state into debt, a mistake Bill Clements is unlikely to duplicate. Still, this should be the most memorable session in years, as legislators learn to their surprise that Texas really does have a governor's office. It's a new game—called two-party politics—with new rules, and neither Clements nor the legislators know how to play yet. While they learn, here are a few of the other things they will be worrying about.

Illustrated by Tom Curry

SAFETY FIRST
The products liability crisis

Pity the poor trial lawyers. A couple of years ago they were regarded as one of the two or three most potent lobbies in Austin. Then came the malpractice crisis and a legislative struggle with doctors that left both sides nursing their wounds. To make matters worse, just when it looked as though one of their own would be elected governor, along came Bill Clements, whose scornful description of John Hill as a "liberal claims lawyer" doesn't bode well for them. And now they're back on the defensive, with virtually the entire business lobby aligned against them.

It seems that a new crisis stalks the land, with the rather uninspired name of products liability. If you think the topic sounds dull, you should try studying the issues, which depend mainly on one's grasp of narrow points of law. The crux of the problem dates back to 1967, when the Texas Supreme Court made it much easier for consumers to sue manufacturers and sellers of defective products. Prior to that time, a victim could collect for a hidden defect only when the product was food—say, an exploding soft drink bottle. In recent years, however, the courts have taken increasingly dim views of unsafe automobiles, falling elevators, defective lawnmowers, and the like. Jury awards in seven figures are more and more frequent, and one recent case was *settled* for more than $6 million.

The business lobby hopes to reverse this trend by tinkering with the legal system. Unlike the doctors, whose ill-concealed distaste for lawyers hurt their own cause last session, the business coalition is slick, calm, and patient, basing its case on rational argument. (Example: if the person operating the defective lawnmower put his former foot too close to the casing when the shaft flew off, that should reduce his award—which the current law doesn't allow.) The trial lawyers appear to be in for another rough session.

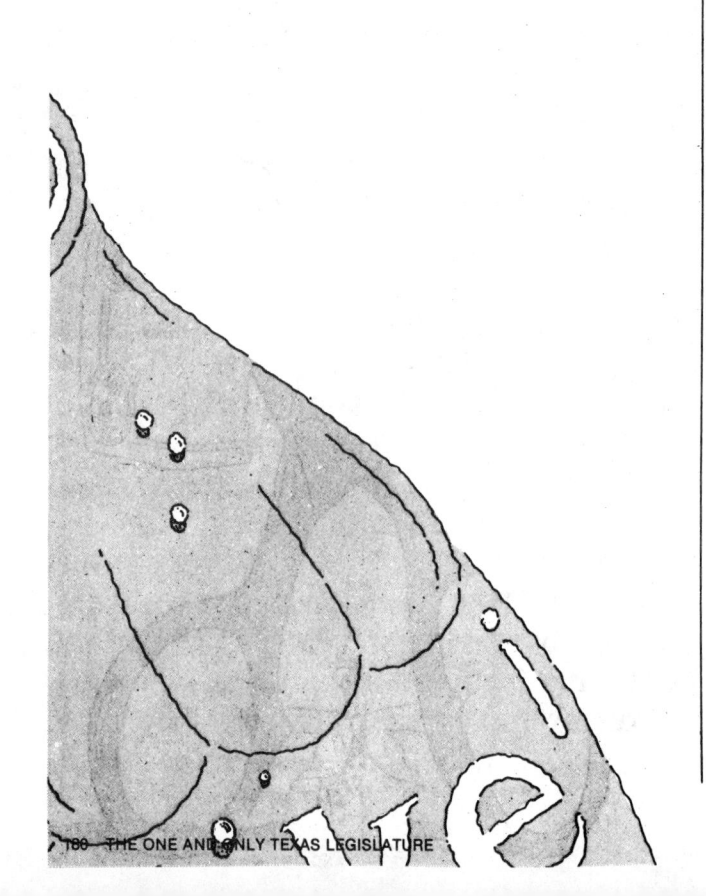

BELLYING UP TO THE BAR
The Sunset laws

When the Legislature enacted the state's first Sunset law two years ago, there was a great deal of self-congratulatory talk that the independent fiefdoms and duchies of state government would at last be brought under control. Now the time has come for the Legislature to put up or shut up.

The concept works like this: every two years the Legislature reviews selected state agencies, until after twelve years it has examined them all. Each time an agency is under scrutiny, it is automatically terminated unless the Legislature passes a new law re-creating it. In theory, if an agency has ceased to perform any useful function, the Legislature will pull the plug. In practice, however, that may be more difficult than it sounds.

Sunset is aimed particularly at the string of agencies whose primary task is to issue licenses to aspiring professionals. Many of these agencies—the State Board of Morticians is archetypal—are headed by boards drawn entirely from the regulated profession; less than eager for new competition, their guiding principle seems to be, "We're on board, pull up the ladder." Up for review this session are 26 agencies, ranging from the vestigial Stonewall Jackson Memorial Board and the Pink Bollworm Commission to agencies that control access to such professions as barbering, nursing home administration, surveying, architecture, and law. The pivotal test of how serious the Legislature is about making Sunset work will come when the lawmakers tackle the powerful State Bar of Texas. A regulatory agency that also functions as the lawyers' trade association, the Bar is a classic example of a profession running a closed shop in the name of state government. But lawyers, morticians, realtors, and other professionals are precisely the people back home who have the ear (and probably the heart) of most legislators, so making Sunset work will not be easy.

THE BLESSINGS OF AGE
Nursing home grants

Of the issues that will keep the Legislature busy in the months ahead, some, like agricultural tax relief, are perennials that arise every session. Others, like products liability and the tax revolt, will be making their first appearances. And every session something pops up that no one anticipates. This year's issue waiting to happen could turn out to be nursing homes.

It's about time. Believe it or not, after education and highways, nursing homes get the biggest slice of the state budget: $191 million, or almost six times the $33 million allotted to the much criticized Aid to Families with Dependent Children program. AFDC is often denounced as inefficient or ineffective, but as a waste of taxpayers' money it shrivels in comparison to the nursing home boondoggle. For example, community-based approaches—meals, transportation, day care for the elderly—are much less costly than institutional care (and are preferred by most recipients), but they invariably get short shrift from the Legislature. One reason is that more federal money is available to supplement nursing homes than for community services (though the latter remain a better deal). Another is that most of the state's 962 nursing homes are businesses rather than nonprofit organizations and wouldn't like to lose the monthly dole that amounts to more than $500 per patient. In fact, they would like to increase it and will be asking the Legislature to do just that. They are well organized and generous with campaign contributions; nevertheless, there will be voices raised in opposition. An important factor behind the nursing home owners' desire for more money is that they have overbuilt—out of a state total of 100,000 beds, about 20,000 are usually empty. Some legislators want to control the building and get more support for community services. As we said, it's about time.

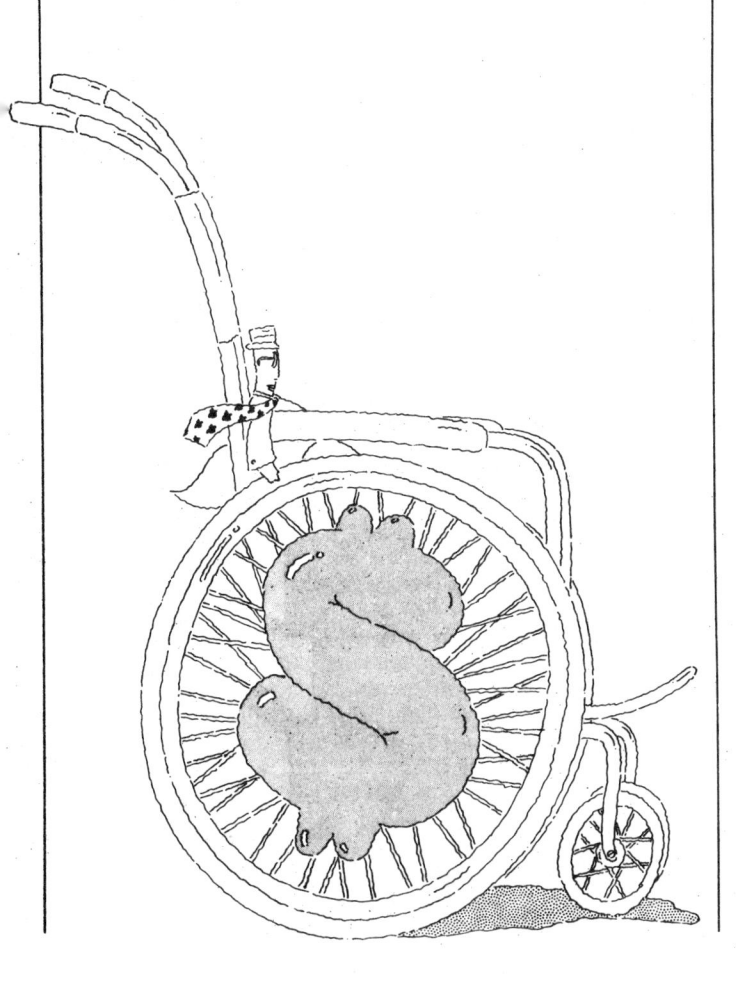

THE UNKINDEST CUT
The tax revolt

For the past six years, the Legislature has chafed under a governor whose watchword was "No new taxes." Now they find that his replacement doesn't even think much of the old ones: Bill Clements is committed to a $1 billion tax reduction on top of the $1 billion the Legislature has already kicked back to taxpayers as the result of last summer's special session. Happily for Clements, inflation and the state's continuing economic prosperity have fattened the state treasury to the extent that the Legislature has $2.6 billion more to work with than it had in 1977. Unhappily for Clements, the Legislature is just as committed to spending every last penny of this windfall as he is to tax relief.

The battle of the purse is certain to be the most important issue of the session and just may be the biggest test of Bill Clements as a governor. Clements has the veto power, of course, plus the force of public opinion on his side. But every legislator has his own pet project that requires a few million dollars, and the temptation to spend the treasury surplus is almost irresistible. Furthermore, despite the rhetoric of tax relief, most legislators know that the state tax burden here is one of the lowest in the country.

Clements is headed for a collision with Lieutenant Governor Bill Hobby, who just happens to be the governor's most likely Democratic challenger in 1982. Hobby was instrumental last summer in blocking limits on state and local spending and rejecting provisions that would handcuff future Legislatures in need of funds—all of which Clements supports wholeheartedly. The governor wants to submit local tax increases to a vote of the affected citizenry and proposes constitutional amendments barring state income taxes and requiring a two-thirds vote of the Legislature to pass a tax bill. Most legislators would prefer to remain unfettered, but to vote no will be hard in today's political climate.

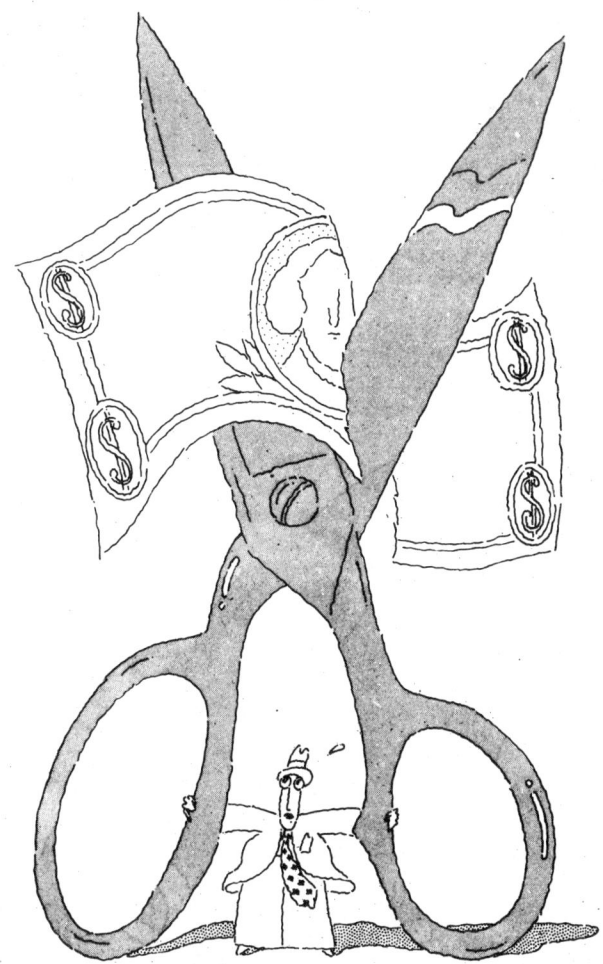

THE ONE AND ONLY TEXAS LEGISLATURE

PLOUGHSHARES
Agricultural tax breaks

Tax breaks are a lot like sibling rivalry: whatever it is you're enjoying, somebody else wants in on the fun. That means there's going to be a lot of shouting and pouting this spring before the Legislature finally decides how to implement the special treatment for rural property that Texas voters, after years of saying no, authorized last fall.

The idea is that farmers and ranchers should be taxed on the value of what their land produces rather than its market value, and the purpose is to protect mom-and-pop farmers and ranchers who can't afford to pay taxes based on skyrocketing land prices. If something isn't done, the argument goes, the family farmer, regarded in some quarters as the fount of American virtue, will be driven off the noble land into the wicked city, presumably at great social cost to the rest of us. The contention is not without merit—there are, for example, some rice farmers southwest of Houston who are barely hanging on—but it has two flaws: a vast amount of rural property in this state is owned by corporate farmers, timber interests, and land speculators who don't need any tax breaks. And, except around Houston and Dallas, most small rural property owners pay taxes that are negligible by city standards, and the last thing they need (or want) is for the Legislature to start tampering with the system.

Nevertheless, the voters have spoken and tamper the Legislature will. But how? Some members would like to limit the tax breaks to small farmers, but this is difficult to do, lexically or politically. The clamor of "me too" will echo through the chambers and will be hard to resist. The biggest fight will probably center on the timber industry, which, despite a notable lack of mom-and-pop operators, claims it deserves a break just for keeping land rural. The outcome, like any sibling (or political) rivalry, is less likely to be decided by merit than muscle.

OIL IN THE FAMILY
Energy alternatives

The Legislature would dearly love to do something about energy, if only they could figure out something to do. If they had their way, the first item on the agenda would be a prohibition against any natural gas leaving the state. Unfortunately, or perhaps fortunately, depending on whether you're reading this south or north of the Red River, there's a small obstacle known as the U.S. Constitution, which prevents states from meddling with interstate commerce. However, not everyone has given up: Bill Clements has been trying to drum up support for a tax on gas leaving the state. Since the Legislature tried this approach back in the fifties and the courts would have none of it, one would be tempted to dismiss it out of hand, were it not for the fact that Mr. Clements has earned the right to be taken seriously.

The idea, of course, is for out-of-staters to compensate Texas for the loss of its irreplaceable resources, and if Clements is serious about the idea, there are a couple of other taxes with better constitutional credentials he might take a look at. Currently Texas makes producers pay for the privilege of removing oil and gas from the ground; coal, lignite, and uranium miners escape altogether. This makes no sense, especially when Western states like Montana extract tributes of up to 30 per cent from coal operators—a charge that is eventually passed on to Texas consumers. Then there is the familiar idea of a refinery tax, which was championed by liberals in the antiquity before the Arab embargo but now has been resurrected by some of the Legislature's more chauvinistic conservatives, who would like to see it replace local property taxes. Since most of the output of Texas' 53 refineries is sold elsewhere, the refinery tax in effect forces motorists across the country to fund our state government. It may not be quite as effective as letting them freeze in the dark, but it will have to do. ★

Politics

by Paul Burka

BIG DEAL

Remember how the Sharpstown Scandal was going to change Texas politics? Well, it didn't quite turn out that way.

The scene on the floor of the House was bedlam: representatives clustered around the Speaker's desk whispering advice; others gathered at the back microphone bellowing for recognition; and smaller groups huddled at scattered spots across the giant chamber where members passed rumors or strained to hear them. It was the closing hour of the 1971 regular session of the Texas Legislature, and the legislative process had broken down under the weight of the Sharpstown Scandal. The heavy-handed tactics of Speaker Gus Mutscher, under attack for shepherding two suspicious-looking banking bills through a previous special session for discredited Houston promoter Frank Sharp, had divided the House into three groups: blind loyalists, troubled conservatives, and a coalition of liberals and Republicans known as the Dirty Thirty. A huge backlog of legislation was hopelessly stalled, and time was running out. Would Mutscher ask the governor to call a special session? Or would he order the hands of the clock turned back at midnight, extending the session while he tried to arm-twist members into passing a few of the more important bills? Or perhaps he would make a dramatic appeal to the House, asking members to put aside animosities and try to pass *something* in the little time remaining.

"May I have your attention, members?" Mutscher for once had no trouble with this request; all eyes were on him. "The Chair recognizes Mr. Nelms."

The legislators were stunned. Why Nelms, everyone was thinking. Johnny Nelms of Pasadena was only a freshman, and a mediocre one at that. What could he do? The silence was broken by the sound of a guitar. Johnny Nelms could sing, that's what he could do. And as the clock at the back of the chamber ticked away the final minutes of Gus Mutscher's hegemony over the House, Johnny Nelms serenaded his colleagues with a song the Speaker particularly liked. It was called "Everything I Touch Turns to Dirt."

It has been five years now since the federal Securities and Exchange Commission (SEC), in a neat—and not accidental—bit of timing, filed suit against Frank Sharp for a stock manipulation scheme on the very day that Governor Preston Smith was inaugurated for a second term. Supporting documents in the case indicated that Smith and Mutscher had traded heavily in the suspect stock just prior to the special session when Sharp's banking bills would be before the Legislature. The SEC, backed by a Republican Administration in Washington, expected the scandal to produce a voter reaction that would finally end Democratic dominance of Texas politics. Liberals saw Sharpstown as an opportunity to wrest control of the Democratic Party away from entrenched conservatives. Reformers decided this was their chance to change the way state government worked by making it more accountable to the people. Everyone said the scandal would be a watershed in Texas' political history.

On the surface it appears that they were right. The voters reacted by forcing one of the biggest legislative turnovers in years. Mutscher loyalists were destroyed by slogans like, "Why fire the ventriloquist and hire the dummy?" Tarnished Preston Smith sought vindication from the voters in the form of a third term; he was rewarded with a pathetic 8 per cent of the vote. Voters adjudged Lieutenant Governor Ben Barnes, the one-time Golden Boy of Texas politics, guilty by association even though he had never been tied directly to the scandal. Two years earlier Barnes had carried all 254 Texas counties, but he could run no better than a poor third in the 1971 gubernatorial primary with less than 20 per cent of the vote. Mutscher and two key lieutenants were indicted and convicted for accepting bribes, and several other legislators were successfully prosecuted by Travis County District Attorney Bob Smith for misusing state funds in their expense accounts.

The reform spirit dominated the 1973 Legislature, as new House Speaker Price Daniel, Jr., threw his weight behind a series of bills designed to clean up the mess in Austin. The package included an ethics bill, a strict campaign finance law, a lobby registration act, and requirements for open meetings and open public records. Daniel guided the bills through the House and sent them to a reluctant Senate which considered itself untouched by the scandal. Still, public pressure carried the day and forced the Senate to enact the bills into law. Sharpstown was given credit for changing Texas politics.

But did it really? We have come to view politics so much as a game between two sides—call them liberals and conservatives, Republicans and Democrats, ins and outs; it doesn't really matter—that we gauge success and failure according to our idea of how points are scored. Aha, we say, reformers must have won the Sharpstown game—

Illustrated by Ben Sargent

THE ONE AND ONLY TEXAS LEGISLATURE 183

after all, they beat X candidates and passed Y bills. The trouble is, of course, that these are only statistics, not the final score, and statistics quite often tell very little about who really won or lost. The only important question is: did it make any difference?

Randall Wood is someone who believes that Sharpstown did change things for the better. Now executive assistant to State Comptroller Bob Bullock, Wood was the lobbyist for Common Cause, a self-styled citizens' lobby, during the 1973 reform session. He points to campaign financing as one area where reform laws have had a major impact.

"Before 1974, candidates just didn't report any contributions they didn't want to report," Wood says. "They could conceal donations under the Harris County Committee for Joe Doaks and didn't have to tell who made up the committee. Or they could just list the contribution under someone else's name. Corporations gave their upper management people bloated expense accounts and generous bonuses which would then be channeled to sympathetic candidates. You just can't do that any more."

So score a point for liberals and reformers, right? Well, maybe. Some liberals paint a different picture. "The campaign finance law hurts liberals more than conservatives, there's no doubt about it," says one veteran Texas politician. "Liberals used to take money from the lobby and hide it under a committee. They can't do that now, so they can't risk taking the money. But most conservatives don't care. People figure they're supposed to be for business." Another liberal in a key administrative position says he gets calls all the time from liberals inquiring about loopholes in the campaign financing law.

No one disputes that money is harder to raise these days. But that doesn't mean that stricter reporting requirements will lead to the election of independent-minded public officials. The best test so far of the impact of the campaign financing law was Sissy Farenthold's lawsuit against Dolph Briscoe during the 1974 Democratic gubernatorial primary. She accused Briscoe of gross violations and apparently caught him red-handed, but no one seemed to care and Briscoe won in a landslide. Nor has the campaign financing law had much effect on the legislative success of politically active lobby groups like utility companies. Utilities have long been specialists in the art of concealing campaign contributions; they were among the primary targets of the new law. Yet in a year when the telephone, gas, and electric power industries were all under heavy fire, utility lobbyists succeeded in substantially watering down a utilities regulation bill.

The ethics and disclosure law can be viewed in much the same light as the campaign financing act: it sounds good but it doesn't really affect anything. "Why not let the public know who's backing you?" says House Speaker Billy Clayton, a conservative. "If you disclose a possible conflict of interest, people won't get mad at you for voting that way. They knew about it before they elected you. Disclosure really is more to the protection of the candidate than the public." A liberal legislator agrees: "Financial disclosure doesn't help our side one bit. If you're clean your opponent is going to lie about you anyway; and if you've got a conflict of interest, you can always shrug your shoulders and say, 'What's there to get so excited about? See, I disclosed all this right here.' The public doesn't really give a damn about anything that's out in the open. It's only when you *look* like you're hiding something that you get killed."

Another law of major importance to reformers was the revision of the lobby registration act. The bill placed sharp restrictions on the amounts lobbyists could spend on entertainment in an effort to stop them from feeding, watering, and clothing compliant legislators.

Well, it worked. During the 1975 session little groups of forlorn legislators could be spotted at cheap Mexican restaurants and cafeterias around Austin buying their own dinners. Meanwhile lobbyists dined together at expensive restaurants. They were delighted. Most of them never liked legislators much anyway and greatly preferred each other's company at mealtime. Lobbyists, it developed, had been feeding legislators all these years because they *had* to, not because they wanted to. The new law may even have *increased* their influence, because instead of spending money on all those mandatory meals, lobbyists can now save their entertainment funds and pour them into campaigns instead. Money still buys influence, only now the transaction is less visible. "The lobby bill has done nothing but make the lobby happy," says a high-level Senate aide. "It certainly hasn't diminished their power any."

Where Sharpstown may actually have had some effect was on the legislative process itself. Before Sharpstown, almost nothing was decided in debate. Votes were procedural necessities; the outcome was a foregone conclusion. Skilled lobbyists could work with conniving members to slip noxious provisions into bills at the last minute. If a legislator wasn't a member of the leadership team, particularly in the 150-member House, he might as well spend the session at Scholz's beer garden—and quite a few did. Many bills zipped through the Senate by a process known as floor reporting, a fanciful voting technique which in effect allowed senators to pass blank sheets of paper and decide later what to fill in. The House was more subtle. Bills piled up there till the last moment, and most could emerge only on a "consent calendar." Once a bill made it to the floor on a consent calendar, it passed automatically. True, any five representatives could knock a bill off the calendar—but their own bills would then be subject to the immediate retribution of their colleagues. Bills authored by potential troublemakers were always delayed until the final weeks. It was an intentionally corrupt system, delighted in by the leadership, which used it to cement their power, and by the lobby, which knew how to use the secretive system to slip in the harmless-looking exemptions and requirements that meant millions of dollars for their clients.

All that has changed now. Floor reporting is a thing of the past in the Senate. All bills must have a fiscal note prepared by the Legislative Budget Board setting forth the cost of a proposal. Committee hearings can only be held after proper notice is posted well in advance. Even the consent calendars are handled differently, though the potential for abuse still lingers. In the Senate each candidate for the consent calendar is individually checked by the Administration Committee as well as by the lieutenant governor's staff; consent bills are also perused closely in the House. Major issues like school finance and utility regulation make it to the floor these days instead of dying in committee as they usually have in the past. Debates and votes are often passionate and close.

Many legislators credit the change to Sharpstown. The Romans had a phrase for such fallacious reasoning: *post hoc ergo propter hoc*; after this, therefore because of this. It is equally plausible that the post-Sharpstown reforms were the inevitable result of a long trend toward a more professional legislature. As recently as 1961, most legislators had no private offices. They came from rural districts to sit at their desks on the House floor, secretaries by their side, where they received constituents and lobbyists. Beginning in 1963, legislators got offices in the Capitol, although House members often had to double up. Senators began hiring full-time lawyers for staff help in 1969, despite rules that placed a $650-per-month ceiling on salaries; at the same time House members began to raise their meager $800 monthly allotment for *all* staff salaries.

If Gus Mutscher were to return to the Legislature today, he would find it a vastly different place. Reapportionment has continued to change the makeup of both the House and Senate; they are now distinctly urban and suburban rather than rural. Single-member districts make a difference, too. No longer could Mutscher rely on the bloc support of a sheep-like Dallas delegation obedient to its downtown Establishment. He would find that senators now have expense allowances of $3900 per month, representatives $3000, and these will undoubtedly go up next session. He would notice that House members don't have to share offices anymore, and that many have lawyers, not just law students, on their staffs. He would find them more serious, and, in part because of their larger and more professional staffs, better informed. All this would have happened without Sharpstown. The scandal did not cause the change; it merely accelerated it.

To the extent that Sharpstown can be considered a reform movement, its effect never really penetrated beyond the walls of the State Capitol. The history of America since the Civil War includes three major reform movements: Populism in the late nineteenth century, Progressivism in the early twentieth, and the New Deal during the Great Depression. All sprang from the fear that the competitive process in America had somehow gotten out of whack, that the system had malfunctioned to the point where hard work no longer earned its just reward. Reform was aimed at excessive accumulations of power; it attempted to restore the balance and save the work ethic. The legislative process in Texas was in a similar predicament under Ben Barnes and Gus Mutscher: if you weren't a member of the Team, nothing else mattered—not your skill, not hard work, nothing. Today membership on the Team is still an advantage, to be sure, but a legislator's display of independence no longer automatically condemns him to a session in exile.

Aside from changing the rules of the game, however, Sharpstown has had relatively little long-term effect. Genuine reform movements in America have always brought about a redistribution of political or economic power. Sharpstown produced neither; it was a reaction, not a movement. The wrath of the electorate was vented against Smith, Barnes, Mutscher, and incumbents generally, but it was short-lived. Conservative Democrats were in control before Sharpstown; they have continued to hold power since. The liberal and Republican factions which comprised the Dirty Thirty made no measurable gains, either in the Legislature or in statewide elections. The reform laws produced no wave of activist politicians of any persuasion, and the special interest lobby still calls most tunes in the Legislature. Common Cause, the vanguard of the nonpartisan reform movement, is having trouble raising money and has been forced to release its full-time lobbyist.

Five years after the Sharpstown Scandal shook the foundations of political power in the state, the names and perhaps the style of Texas politics have changed, but not the substance. Mutscher and Barnes are long gone, Mutscher to appeal his conviction and Barnes back to Brownwood to make millions. Smith works in development and public relations for Texas Tech. Frank Sharp still has his realty company in Houston, having escaped the wrath of the SEC by accepting immunity from Judge John Singleton in return for state's evidence that didn't seem to add much to the case. Even the leading reform figures have disappeared from the scene: Daniel retired after the ill-fated Constitutional Convention to practice law and ruminate on the wisdom of volunteering to make oneself a lame duck; Farenthold lost embarrassingly in her second try for the governorship against Dolph Briscoe in 1974. Of the original Dirty Thirty, fewer than half are still in the Legislature. Meanwhile, business goes on as before—different, but the same. In short, despite impressive first-quarter statistics, reformers have yet to put any points on the scoreboard. ★

Texas Bureaucracy

CHAPTER EIGHT

Paper Tigers, Mitch Green (January 77)
The Highway Establishment and How it Grew . . . Griffin Smith, jr. (April 74)
The Firing Line, Paul Burka (April 79)

PAPER TIGERS

by Mitch Green

Meet the people who don't mind cutting through red tape — as long as they do it lengthwise.

Rolando and Eddie have been cutting hair side by side in their south Austin shop for three years. "We're a team," says Rolando. "A family will come in and Eddie will take the husband and kids and I'll take the wife." But since June something has come between Rolando and Eddie—an eight-foot opaque wall, to be exact. Why? To protect the public, of course. That's what the State Board of Barber Examiners told Rolando and Eddie when the construction crew moved in, and that is the premise on which a good deal of state government's more pointless activity is based. You see, Eddie cuts hair; he's a barber. Roland cuts hair too, but he's a cosmetologist, and to listen to the State Board of Barber Examiners tell it, the commingling of these two acts would be a threat to the health and safety of the public.

The State Board of Barber Examiners is just one of some three dozen state licensing agencies distinguished mostly by their obscurity. As far as the public is concerned, these bureaucratic fiefdoms are like vestigial organs: it's hard to know they exist because they don't seem to do much. But people fortunate enough to be in a regulated profession know better. They understand that mastering the state licensing game is more important than mastering the rules of free market competition and it pays higher rewards.

To each regulated trade, the state licensing agency is many things—all of them good. It is, first and foremost, a guarantee against unwanted competition, a closed shop for professionals sanctioned by the State of Texas. The Texas right-to-work law prohibits unions from having a closed shop, but there is no right-to-work law for prospective plumbers, new car dealers, athletic trainers, lawyers, or morticians. No one can practice any of these professions unless the State of Texas, through one of its licensing agencies, checks him out and gives its approval. The "State," in all cases, really means a board required by law to be filled either largely or totally from the regulated profession itself. Who gets to decide how many car dealers should divide the profits from this year's new car sales? A board dominated by car dealers, of course—and you can bet your monthly car payment that there won't be so many dealers that they have to resort to price wars to get the public's attention.

Theoretically these agencies were created to protect the public from assorted threats to its well-being that unregulated practitioners pose. Judging by a quick glance at some of the regulated occupations, the threat to the public is pervasive. It comes not only from barbers and cosmetologists like Eddie and Rolando, but also from doctors, lawyers, landscape architects, water-well drillers, librarians, social psychotherapists, optometrists, hearing-aid fitters, podiatrists, and many others. With so much danger lurking about, the Legislature has found it necessary to protect us by creating agencies which sell licenses for anywhere from 75 cents to $100. Like McDonald's, the state's name is supposed to guarantee a minimum standard of quality. Unlike McDonald's, if you don't like the state's hamburgers, you can't go around the corner to Burger King. All you can do is move to Oklahoma, and things aren't much different there.

Although their ostensible role is to protect the public, that charge apparently does not include the consumer as you will quickly learn if you call up with a complaint. Licensing agencies have nothing to do with how much a plumber can charge you on Sunday afternoon, with making sure that you get your money's worth for a $15 haircut, or with requiring continuing education for all professionals. Their main role in life is to protect their clients by limiting entry into the field, adopting rules which require the public to use licensees when it's unnecessary or redundant (the State Board of Plumbing Examiners is the champion at this little gimmick), and enforcing restrictions against advertising and competitive bidding (the Justice Department recently filed an antitrust action against the State Board of Public Accountancy over the board's rules against competitive bidding). All in all, it is hard to see how the public is better off than with no regulation at all—or at least that's the view of retiring Dallas State Representative Richard Geiger, who was vice chairman of the House committee responsible for keeping track of the state's dozens of bureaus and commissions and boards.

The essence of the problem is that the licensing agencies exist to serve their profession and no one else. Some are more blatant about it than others. The Motor Vehicle Commission deigns to include two ordinary citizens along with four car dealers, but only funeral home directors are eligible for the State Board of Morticians. The accountancy board isn't even allowed to adopt its own rules and regulations without first submitting them to the members of the profession for approval —this was one of the abuses that attracted the attention of the Justice Department. The bond of the soul between regulators and their clients is perfectly symbolized by a number of Austin lawyers who openly represent both the board and the professional trade association. A conflict of interest? Hardly.

188 TEXAS BUREAUCRACY

Illustrated by Mike Hicks

Robert Hughes, a respected member of the Austin legal community, has no ethical qualms about his firm representing both the State Board of Morticians and the morticians' trade association. "As far as the regulatory agency is concerned," says Hughes, "the association doesn't have any interests different than the public's. The association hasn't had a disagreement with the board in ten years." Another lobbyist, C. Dean Davis, represents both the pharmacists and the pharmacy board, not to mention the hospital association.

A franchise, then, is a valuable thing, something to be eagerly sought and fiercely protected. It is small wonder, therefore, that the Legislature touched off a minor war when it cut the barber's franchise in half in 1971.

The barbers are no strangers to regulatory battle. As far back as medieval times they were clashing with the butchers, the only other profession with ready access to sharp instruments, for the exclusive right to perform surgery. The barbers triumphed, and the bloodstained sheets which they hung outside after their ministrations evolved into the barber pole.

In more recent times the barbers have been battling not the butchers but the cosmetologists. The barbers were first regulated by the State of Texas in 1929. Dirty towels, lice, and rusty scissors all threatened the public welfare, so barbers were placed under the specially created State Board of Barber Examiners.

As far as the barbers were concerned, things were going along just fine. If anyone, male or female, wanted a haircut the law said only a barber could give it to them. Beauticians and hairdressers, licensed by the State Board of Hairdressers and Cosmetologists, were allowed to cut hair only if it was incidental to their primary service, styling. Then in 1971 the Legislature changed the Board of Hairdressers and Cosmetologists into the Cosmetology Commission and expanded their bailiwick so that cosmetologists could cut women's hair. In 1972 the law was ruled unconstitutional on the grounds that it discriminated on the basis of sex. For the next three years barbers and cosmetologists were free to cut whatever heads they found sitting in front of them. It was during this period that Eddie the barber came to work at Rolando's south Austin shop.

The court's ruling came at an inconvenient time for barbers. Long hair was no longer the exclusive province of hippies and radical students; it was generally fashionable. Yet many barbers weren't adept at the new styles. Men were getting scalped by barbers but couldn't bring themselves to go into a beauty parlor. The natural result was the unisex shop where barbers and cosmetologists worked side by side cutting hair. The public, after all, only wanted haircuts and didn't care what the person wielding the scissors was called. But the barbers did. There are more than 75,000 cosmetologists in Texas and only 18,000 barbers. "If the barbers lose the distinction of being barbers," explains their lobbyist, Austin attorney Charles Babb, "they'll be swallowed up by the beauty chains that are taking over cosmetology. Barbers are really the last small businessmen left, and if they are not kept distinct, they'll be gone."

"Anyone who believes that business is opposed to regulation," Babb adds, "still believes in the tooth fairy."

When the Legislature convened in 1975, both sides were girded for battle. The cosmetologists wanted a law saying they could do virtually everything barbers could. The barbers were prepared to concede that, but they wanted the distinct separation of barbers and cosmetologists working on the same premises. Eddie's troubles began when all parties decided to leave the details of separation up to the respective boards.

State Representative Ben Munson of Denison, the unlucky legislator whose subcommittee was saddled with the task of studying the bill, believed that the agreed-upon version did not require a total separation. That was the interpretation of the Cosmetology Commission, which last November adopted a rule requiring a four-foot partition between barbers and cosmetologists working in the same shop. But keeping barbers separate was a much more vital issue to the barber board. After several fumbling tries and in the face of numerous warnings from Representative Munson, the barber board last June decided to require the erection of an eight-foot opaque wall—plus the display of a barber pole and separate entrances for barber customers. Rolando asked if a glass wall would suffice and the board said no. "That means I'm going to have to put Eddie into a closet," complained Rolando. "How would you like to work in a closet?"

Not only unisex shops were hit by the ruling, but also the mom-and-pop shops in rural areas where barbering and cosmetology are offered under one roof not because it's stylish but because it's convenient. Munson was furious. He threatened the barber board with extinction, but the board turned a deaf ear, its courage no doubt buttressed by the fact that Munson was not a candidate for reelection. Meanwhile Rolando refurbished a storage closet and moved Eddie in.

The barbers-cosmetologists fight is the grudge match of occupational licensing, but the Legislature is besieged by such fights year after year. A committee clerk who keeps track of such things says the Legislature spent more time on haircuts last year than on the public utilities commission bill, and Austin Senator Lloyd Doggett says he got more mail about the barbers last session than anything else. Through the years the Legislature has had to referee fights between hearing-aid dealers and audiologists, individual optometrists and chain optometry stores like Texas State Optical, architects and designers, plumbers and landscape architects, dentists and plastic surgeons, doctors and chiropractors, social psychotherapists and social workers, new car dealers and used car dealers. So desirable is the state's franchise that colleagues within related fields fight over it like urban street gangs vying for territory.

In the early seventies the big brawl was between two rival groups of optometrists. The trick in such cases is to make your side appear to embody good and the other side to embody evil, so the individual optometrists started calling themselves the "ethical optometrists." They don't quite go so far as to label the other side "unethical optometrists," but the Legislature got the idea. "Ethical" optometrists are those in private practice who do not engage in advertising; their opposition generally practices in conjunction with chain stores like TSO or Lee Optical, and, as the ethical optometrists see it, advertise by virtue of their association with the frame dispensers. So far the ethical optometrists appear to have won the battle—the law allots them two-thirds of the seats on the optometry board—but you can be certain that the chain optometrists will continue to apply pressure on the Legislature.

Why should the public care? The head of the ethical optometrists warns that if his group loses control of the board, the quality of visual care will decline; naturally the spokesman for the chain optometrists denies any such thing. (Both sets of optometrists, though they belong to different organizations, have to meet the same standards.) In the end, the whole fight amounts to little more than a bureaucratic spectacle which takes up a lot of the Legislature's time to little purpose. It has also prodded the self-interests of ophthalmologists, who are eye doctors licensed by the State Board of Medical Examiners, and opticians, who don't have a board but would like one.

Some franchises are more valuable than others. Architects feel left out because their licensing law passed in 1936, gives them the right to use the title but doesn't do much else. A designer with no formal training may do anything an architect can. In practice, most large buildings are designed by architects and built under the supervision of licensed engineers. But many smaller structures are handled by designers, many of whom work for contractors. Naturally the architects think the public needs to be protected from this latent danger, and since the public may not be aware of the difference between architects and designers, it is incumbent upon the Legislature to guarantee that only architects can design buildings. So far the Legislature hasn't bought it, but at least a bill to license designers didn't get very far, either.

In recent years the Legislature has become increasingly reluctant to create new licensing boards. That doesn't keep various professions from trying; last session everyone from kennel operators to wrestlers were being considered for a closed shop. But only the social psychotherapists were successful.

What is a social psychotherapist? Texas is the only state that has them; the term was invented by the Legislature to single out the upper crust of the social work profession, the most educated and therefore the fewest in number. They fall just below psychologists and psychiatrists, with whom they were trying to share the franchise for the human mind.

Their argument to the Legislature was that an untrained person could do measureless damage to a person's psyche; therefore the state had a duty to set standards for licensing. But as usual, there was more to the story. Many federal health grants require state certification for social workers seeking federal aid. The whole social work profession was after a slice of the pie, and the psychotherapists successfully used the Legislature to get accredited with Washington—and close the pantry door on everyone else.

The audiologists were less successful. If you have a hearing problem, you go to a hearing-aid dealer, who will test you and, if necessary, fit you with a hearing aid. They perform much the same service as optometrists do for eyes. But the audiologists found this a potential conflict of interest; they argued that they were much more qualified to test and identify hearing problems. The Legislature did not agree, and that guarantees the audiologists will be back this session.

Sometimes conflicting pressures on the Legislature cause it to confuse matters further by granting the same bailiwick to two groups. For years the plumbers had the exclusive franchise for tapping into the public water supply. If you paid a contractor to build a lawn sprinkler, you also had to pay a licensed plumber to connect it. In 1973 the Legislature brought lawn irrigators under the regulation of the State Board of Landscape Architects and gave them the same connection franchise, as long as it was limited to sprinkler systems. The result has been an interagency dispute that not even the attorney general has been able to straighten out. As the law now stands, all the landscape architects who cut into water mains are violating rules of the plumbing board and the plumbers who connect sprinkler systems are violating rules of the landscape architect board.

"It sure seems like a lot of foolishness," says Representative Geiger of the maze of agencies that hide out in little cubbyholes near the State Capitol. "Not one consumer in a thousand cares whether a barber is licensed by a cosmetology board, a barber board, or a health board. These fights make people think the Legislature has nothing better to do."

Despite the apparent folly of the current system, there is only scattered pressure within the Legislature for governmental reorganization. Any legislator worth his salt will rail about an intraprofessional fight he thinks is ridiculous, but chances are he has his own pet agency he'll fight to the death to defend. Even Geiger, apparently a staunch foe of licensing, sponsored the unsuccessful effort by the architects to squeeze designers out of the picture. Still, there are a couple of reform proposals drifting around that may come up for a hearing this session. One is based on the fact that the original reason for licensing occupations was to protect the public health. Licensing agencies should therefore be placed under the Department of Health and Public Resources (or some other superagency). In some respects this would merely give new names to the same old problems, but it would at least have the advantage of putting licensing agencies under a board not dominated by individual professions.

A more creative notion has attracted some attention both in the state and out. It's commonly called sunset legislation, and it has been adopted in Colorado and approved in principle here by the Legislature during the Constitutional Convention. Sunset laws call for the automatic demise of licensing agencies at regular intervals, say, every ten or twelve years. Then, if the agency can convince the Legislature it is necessary, the lawmakers can re-create it. In theory, this makes agencies like the barber board which exist beyond the influence of the Legislature—most don't even need much in the way of appropriations, existing off their license-fee revenue—more responsive. If not, off with their heads.

Sunset legislation will definitely be introduced during the 1977 session. If it is passed, it will be good news for Eddie. Until then, he'll have to stay in his closet. ★

THE HIGHWAY ESTABLISHMENT AND HOW IT GREW,

AND GREW, AND GREW

BY GRIFFIN SMITH, jr.

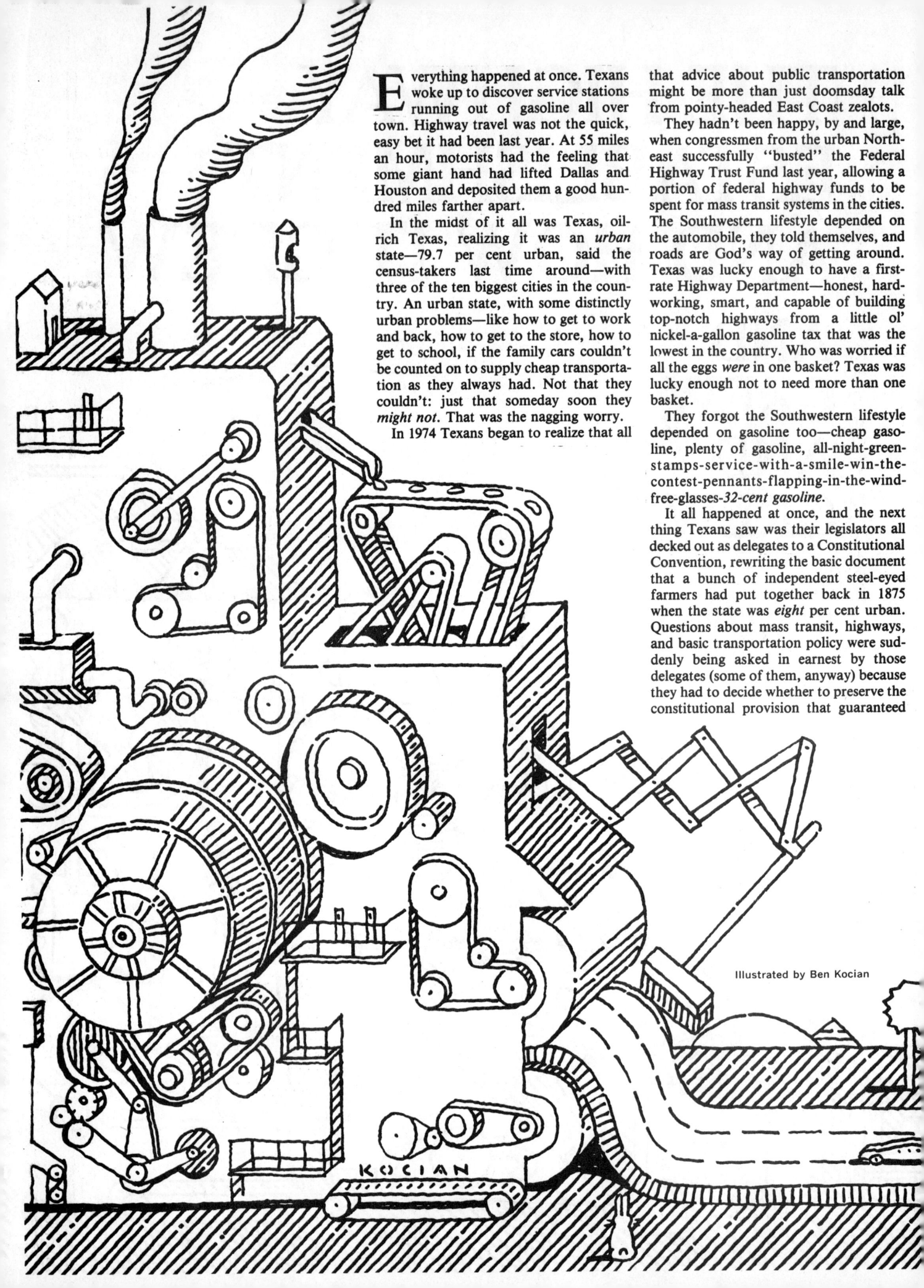

Everything happened at once. Texans woke up to discover service stations running out of gasoline all over town. Highway travel was not the quick, easy bet it had been last year. At 55 miles an hour, motorists had the feeling that some giant hand had lifted Dallas and Houston and deposited them a good hundred miles farther apart.

In the midst of it all was Texas, oil-rich Texas, realizing it was an *urban* state—79.7 per cent urban, said the census-takers last time around—with three of the ten biggest cities in the country. An urban state, with some distinctly urban problems—like how to get to work and back, how to get to the store, how to get to school, if the family cars couldn't be counted on to supply cheap transportation as they always had. Not that they couldn't: just that someday soon they *might not*. That was the nagging worry.

In 1974 Texans began to realize that all that advice about public transportation might be more than just doomsday talk from pointy-headed East Coast zealots.

They hadn't been happy, by and large, when congressmen from the urban Northeast successfully "busted" the Federal Highway Trust Fund last year, allowing a portion of federal highway funds to be spent for mass transit systems in the cities. The Southwestern lifestyle depended on the automobile, they told themselves, and roads are God's way of getting around. Texas was lucky enough to have a first-rate Highway Department—honest, hard-working, smart, and capable of building top-notch highways from a little ol' nickel-a-gallon gasoline tax that was the lowest in the country. Who was worried if all the eggs *were* in one basket? Texas was lucky enough not to need more than one basket.

They forgot the Southwestern lifestyle depended on gasoline too—cheap gasoline, plenty of gasoline, all-night-green-stamps-service-with-a-smile-win-the-contest-pennants-flapping-in-the-wind-free-glasses-*32-cent gasoline*.

It all happened at once, and the next thing Texans saw was their legislators all decked out as delegates to a Constitutional Convention, rewriting the basic document that a bunch of independent steel-eyed farmers had put together back in 1875 when the state was *eight* per cent urban. Questions about mass transit, highways, and basic transportation policy were suddenly being asked in earnest by those delegates (some of them, anyway) because they had to decide whether to preserve the constitutional provision that guaranteed

Illustrated by Ben Kocian

"The postwar infatuation of Texans...with the private automobile —a passion for individual mobility...scarred most forms of 'public transportation' with a vulgar social stigma."

the Highway Department would have first shot at the money it needed to keep on building roads.

More than any other part of the country, Texas in the spring of 1974 was the place where public officials were forced to stand up and debate about the kind of transportation policy their citizens should have—to argue whether highways ought to have first priority, whether mass transit was feasible, whether the Legislature's hands should be tied by the new document.

As a result the Constitutional Convention has been a grand show. Other states fumed, fussed, and speculated about the problem of getting around. Texans actually had to make some decisions about how they were going to cope with this new topsy-turvy world. At the Big Top in Austin, the highway lobby is out in full force, and the spotlight shines on one of the most remarkable bureaucracies in state government.

A Well That Won't Run Dry

The battleground is the so-called dedicated highway fund, a state constitutional provision that has profoundly shaped transportation planning in Texas since its adoption in 1946. It allocates, or "dedicates," most of the money the state collects from motor vehicle registration fees and taxes on gasoline, diesel fuel, and lubricants "used to propel motor vehicles over public roadways" into a special fund that must be used only for acquiring rights-of-way and constructing, policing, and maintaining public roadways. The bulk of it goes to the Highway Department. A small portion (less than ten per cent) goes to the Department of Public Safety; the counties keep a slice of the registration fees, according to a 1929 formula that strongly favors rural counties over urban ones; and one fourth of the motor fuel taxes are diverted to the public schools.

In a state with nine million gas-gulping cars, trucks, buses, and other motor vehicles, such a scheme provides the Highway Department with a massive chunk of guaranteed tax revenues. None of the other state agencies, from the Air Control Board to the Water Well Drillers Board, enjoys this special luxury. They must each shove and fight every two years for legislative appropriations to run their shops. Only the Highway Department, the public schools, The University of Texas, and Texas A&M University have the benefits of constitutionally dedicated revenue. The money is there; they know from past experience just about how much of it there will be; and the Legislature merely performs a polite ceremonial gavotte by awarding them biennially what is already theirs.

How massive is this revenue chunk? In Fiscal 1973, the Department drew $454,380,000 from the dedicated fund. That was 64 per cent of its total income; most of the rest, 31 per cent, came from the Federal Highway Administration as matching funds. By way of comparison, the total 1973 appropriation for the Air Control Board was $399,000, for the Department of Health $44.9 million, for Parks and Wildlife $39.3 million, and for the Water Quality Board $5.4 million.

By the parsimonious standards of the state budget, Texas has made a lavish commitment to one particular form of transportation. The reason can be traced to the confluence of several currents: a powerful and effective lobby, a bureaucracy that in many ways exhibits the best qualities that government has to offer, and not least the postwar infatuation of Texans themselves with the private automobile—a passion for individual mobility that scarred most forms of "public transportation" with a vulgar social stigma. Each of these currents is a matter of history.

The TGRA: Well-Drillers Extraordinaire

The adoption of the "Good Roads Amendment" by a vote of 231,834 to

58,555 in the general election of 1946 was the climax of parallel and at times consolidated efforts by two different groups. The first of these included business interests having a direct economic stake in expanded, large-scale highway construction. The second included public-spirited citizens who saw in good roads (and the general economic development they might produce) the magic key to the booming, bustling Texas they dreamed of creating. Twenty-eight years later the amendment remains intact, unaffected by all efforts to divert its dedicated funds to other purposes, and the dual motives that created it are still apparent in the membership rolls of the powerful lobby that midwifed its adoption: the Texas Good Roads Association. The TGRA brought these two groups together in the thirties and keeps them together today. It is a marvel of symbiosis and stratagem: perhaps the most fascinating lobby in Texas politics.

The combination of "economic" interests and "civic" interests lies at the heart of the TGRA's lasting effectiveness. It has always drawn the bulk of its financial backing from industries that want a transportation system dependent on the use of highways and the construction of more and more of them: the oil companies; petroleum distributors; cement, asphalt, and tire dealers; automobile dealers; bus companies; truckers; and of course the highway contractors themselves. (Highway building is the only industry in Texas that is 100 per cent dependent on government money.) Subcontractors also play an important role in highway lobby movements, as do such diverse groups as engineering firms that specialize in roads, and land speculators and developers. They are united by a common desire to preserve, perfect, and expand the highway transportation system. There is no doubt that they have been the muscle behind the TGRA since its inception. In a surprisingly candid article in *Texas Parade*, the Association's Director of Public Relations and longtime President Weldon Hart described its creation 42 years ago:

The Texas Highway Chapter of Associated General Contractors took the lead in getting a committee organized, representing the whole highway industry. [Tyree] Bell represented AGC, Ben Warden the cement industry, Lou Kemp the asphalt industry, Datus Proper the rock asphalt interests, and so on. One of the important moves was to find a president . . . and the TGRA was in business.

Significantly, the first president was a respected civic leader with no personal ties to the highway industry. His name was William Ogburn Huggins, and he was the editor of the *Houston Chronicle*. His selection symbolized the intention of the TGRA's founders to give their organization the image of a disinterested civic club supporting highways because the state needed them, rather than the image of an economically self-interested industry pleading its case. According to founder Bell, Judge Huggins carried this shrewd decision a step farther by insisting that "for public acceptance . . . the officers . . . should come from the public generally and not include anyone in the highway industry." His rule remains in force today: all of the officers are, to use TGRA's word, "laymen."

More impressive even than the "laymen" officers, however, are the "laymen" members. Among the Association's 2335 members are 54 local chambers of commerce, 46 cities and counties (some of which pay their annual dues with public funds),* and numerous individuals who are prominent in the social and political affairs of their communities. These are the opinion makers. They are crucial.

Some of them, of course, represent highway-oriented economic interests wearing another hat. Many of the local chamber of commerce officers, for example, have a personal economic interest in some aspect of road-building. Others may have a different sort of self-serving interest: very few county commissioners have ever been hurt by having a road built in their precincts, and there are still a few who stay in office by tipping off their friends about the paths of new rights-of-way. But most of the laymen are exactly what they seem: well-respected, public-spirited citizens who honestly believe that the welfare of the state depends on a good network of highways built by a Highway Department unblemished by political

---

*A spokesman for the TGRA says the $25 membership fee paid by cities and counties "doesn't even pay the cost of the material we send out. It amounts to a subscription to our publications for the information they contain. They get a bargain."

If the TGRA loses money on its $25 membership fee for nonprofit organizations, it loses even more on the $15 annual fee it collects for ordinary individual memberships. Without the fees for firms ($50) and highway industries ($100), plus additional contributions from its backers, the TGRA could not stay afloat. Its "layman" members are a dead economic loss.

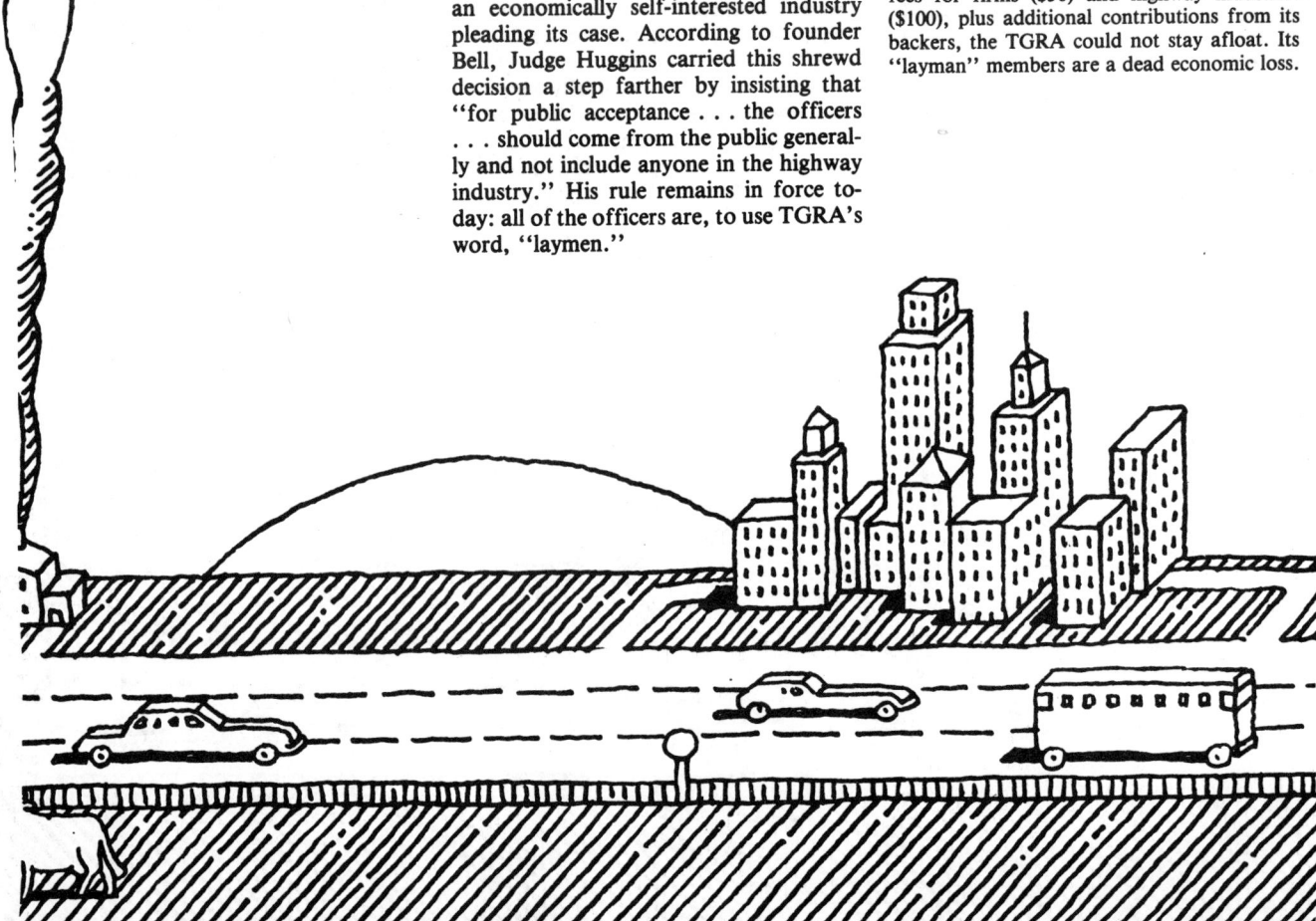

chicanery. They are not money-seekers, not crackpots; they are the bedrock Establishment of Texas. To an impressive extent, TGRA commands their loyalties.

These laymen are indispensable to TGRA's purposes. Without them the Association is naked, a straightforward phalanx of powerful economic interests. With them, it is something grander than a lobby: it is a movement, a personification of the Texas automobile-highway-mobility ethos. No other lobby in the state has so successfully camouflaged its basic economic motives.

Impressively framed on a reception-room wall in its Austin headquarters is a striking, hand-lettered gubernatorial proclamation issued by John Connally in honor of Highway Week, 1964. The visitor reads:

Highways are derived from vision, and vision is rooted in the people.

The TGRA has actually done much to create the ethos it personifies. Its relationship with the Texas news media is nothing less than amazing. From the day its founders chose an influential editor as the first president, the Association has diligently cultivated good press relations. Journalists have figured prominently in its hierarchies. Among the ablest is Weldon Hart himself, a former aide and confidant to Governor Allan Shivers whom even a political adversary described as "a brilliant writer, a genius." (He also has a sense of humor: one of his recent articles in *Texas Parade* was titled "The Glory and Splendor That Is Highway Week.") Hart ran the TGRA from 1965 to 1972. Partly as a result of his work, it now counts among its members 23 newspapers and publishing companies, including the *Dallas Times Herald*, the *Dallas Morning News*, the *Houston Chronicle*, the *San Antonio Light*, the Express Publishing Company [*San Antonio Express* and KENS-TV], the *Midland Reporter-Telegram*, the *Lubbock Avalanche-Journal*, and others from Abilene to Longview and Denison to Victoria.

When the dedicated fund is threatened, as it has been in this year's Constitutional Convention, the TGRA can expect prompt and vigorous editorial support for its viewpoint—sometimes by the very next morning in certain member newspapers. But the media can be even more cordial. A set of six TGRA advertisements praising the highway network and defending the dedicated fund was published 150 times last year in Texas newspapers as a "public service announcement," free of charge. Radio and television stations give free air time to its twenty- and sixty-second "spots." These promote rail, air, water, and pipeline transportation in addition to highways, and the message in some of them bears an intriguing similarity to the paid advertisements of oil companies that help to finance the TGRA. *Texas Parade* magazine, which was the TGRA house organ for decades, now publishes an article a month prepared in cooperation with the Association "as a valuable contribution to public education."

In the communities, the TGRA promotes the highway ethos in a variety of ways. Part of it is simply good organization work: the Association has area chairmen in forty cities and a board of directors in each of its 25 districts (the districts themselves coincide precisely with the Texas Highway Department's own districts). The directors constitute a good start toward a who's who of Texas. For the local, district, and state leaders, there is an endless round of speeches to Lions Clubs, Rotary Clubs, and Chambers of Commerce—a spreading of the gospel to revive the loyalties of fellow laymen and win conversions among unbelievers. The Association has produced a documentary film called "Turning Point," which, according to a TGRA spokesman, "has been used by television stations in most Texas cities—and is in constant use by civic and service clubs each day." Cultivation of lay support never really stops.

But organization, even good organization, has its limits. In the end the special strength of the TGRA comes from the fact that its members participate personally to an unusually high degree in the power structure of Texas. Said one former legislator: "It's not that they contribute so much in campaigns; it's more subtle than that. They belong to the right country clubs, the right power elites."

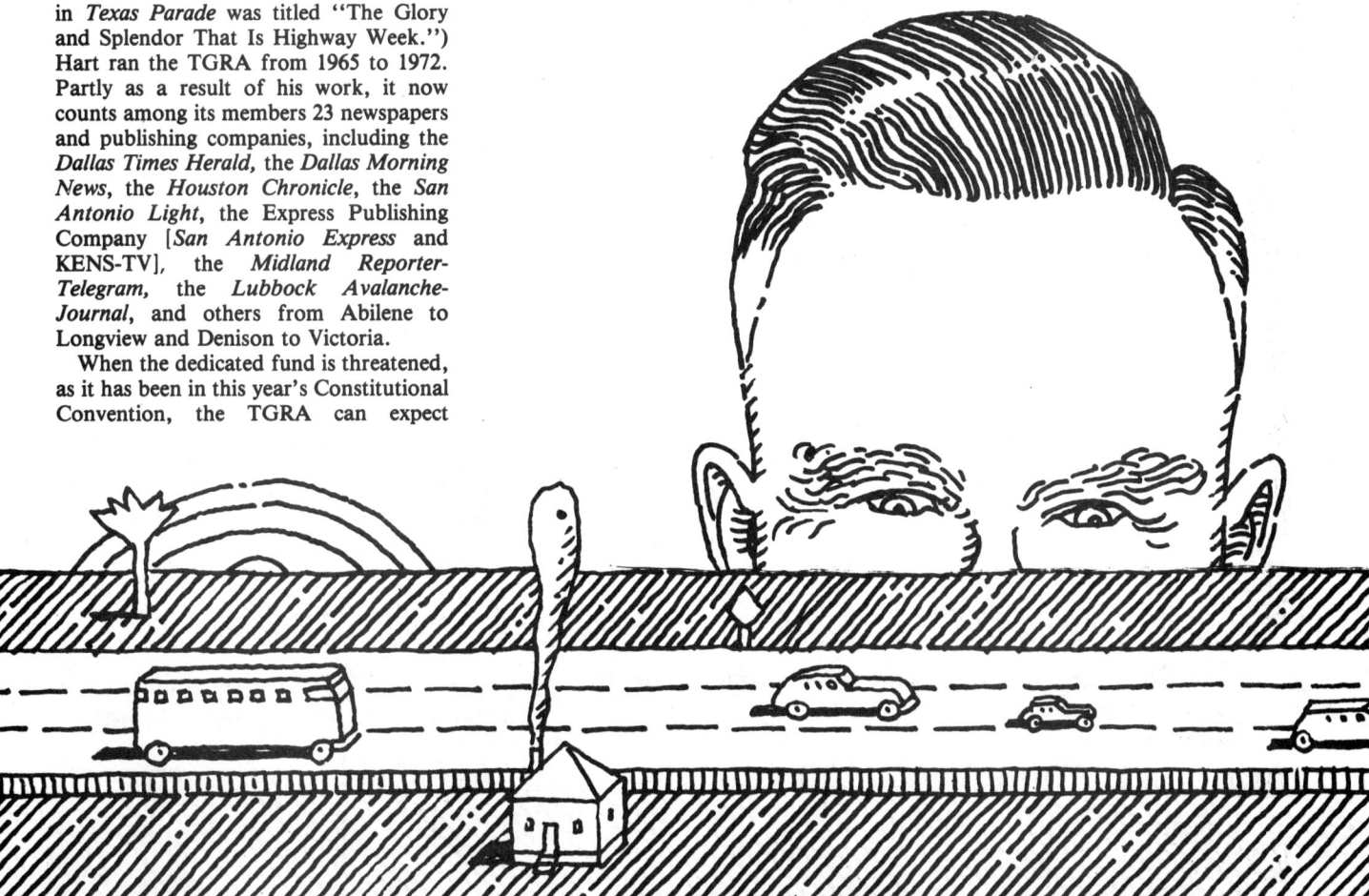

The Association's public pronouncements exist on two levels. The first is a calm, sober, and straightforward enunciation of the view that highway transportation is intrinsically good for Texas. "This vital transportation resource," says a sample TGRA resolution, "... is essential to the State's business, industry, and emergency requirements and to the mobility, welfare, and recreational needs of its citizens and visitors." Without the dedicated fund, the argument goes, irresponsible legislators would allow construction to slump into an unpredictable series of peaks and valleys. Highways, "a perishable product," require an average lead time of eight years from the planning stage to completion, and any skimping on funds one year would have an impact eight years later. The highway industry itself also likes to know the total dollar value of contracts to be awarded in a given year; the security of the dedicated fund relieves them of the anxieties that trouble other industries dependent on the uncertainties of legislative funding. Says the TGRA:

> The contractors who build the state's highways must depend on a "core of expertise" to get the job done. These are key employees who are permanent, so long as there are contracts to be executed. But if there is a drought of funds . . . then the state's major highway builders must let their key personnel go—and the loser, in the final analysis, is the highway user himself.

The Association's foremost precept is the belief that revenues collected from highway users should be spent only for "costs . . . directly related to highway construction, maintenance, and improvement." The campaign of "educational publicity" starts from this point.

But there is a second, much more emotional level, in which the dedicated highway fund is viewed as the fountainhead of all good things, and those who would change it as either anti-social knaves or starry-eyed fools ("We the People," *Texas Monthly*, January 1974). Two years ago, Eugene W. Robbins, then the TGRA vice-president, warned an audience in Gonzales that a "conspiracy is afoot in the United States to stop all highway construction. The plot was hatched in the densely populated Northeastern megalopolis but its disciples are spreading throughout the land—including Texas." He described the members of this "conspiracy" as "pseudo environmentalists, rail mass transit zealots, politicians and bureaucrats, and social planners with active support from some news media." Robbins himself, now the president of TGRA, is a mild and personable man, and a visitor to his office who hears him speaking genially and knowledgeably about the state's highway system is likely to wonder just what gets into him (and other TGRA spokesmen) when he stands behind the podium of a small-town meeting hall. Perhaps such rhetorical excess is possible because the Texas highway ethos is so pervasive, leaving the speaker with a sense of freedom to speak his mind because he feels he is among friends who think as he does, far away from the zealots and social planners who inhabit foreign territory. Or perhaps it is something more: a sudden reminder of the fundamental gulf that separates the laymen from the economically self-interested side of the TGRA, a ferocious expression on behalf of those who know that if Texas changes its highway priorities they themselves have a fortune to lose.

The gulf is there. It is too wide to paper over indefinitely, although the TGRA has done a remarkable job of doing so for the past four decades. That is why the Association prefers to speak in glowing generalities that submerge the blunt economics of profit and loss beneath the rhetoric of high public purpose.

How the Well Was Won

The TGRA won adoption of the Good Roads Amendment in 1946 by using many of the same techniques it uses today. If ever there was a broad-based effort to change state policy, the campaign for this amendment was it. Charles Simons, who was executive vice-president of the TGRA at the time, recalls that it had "virtually unanimous support" from political figures. "Governor [Coke] Stevenson was real strong for it. Allan Shivers—he was a senator then—carried it in the Senate, and Neville Colson carried it in the House."

The "layman" members of TGRA were concerned equally with making sure that the highway industry had a steady flow of public funds and with preventing monkeyshines and corruption in the Highway Department. Critics of the dedicated fund today tend to underestimate the extent to which Texans of that era feared political favoritism in the Highway Department. The farmer was still in the mud in those days; inter-city road travel left a lot to be desired; and the prospect that important highway construction would be carried out to suit the needs of some politician's career instead of the logical traffic requirements was abhorrent to many in-

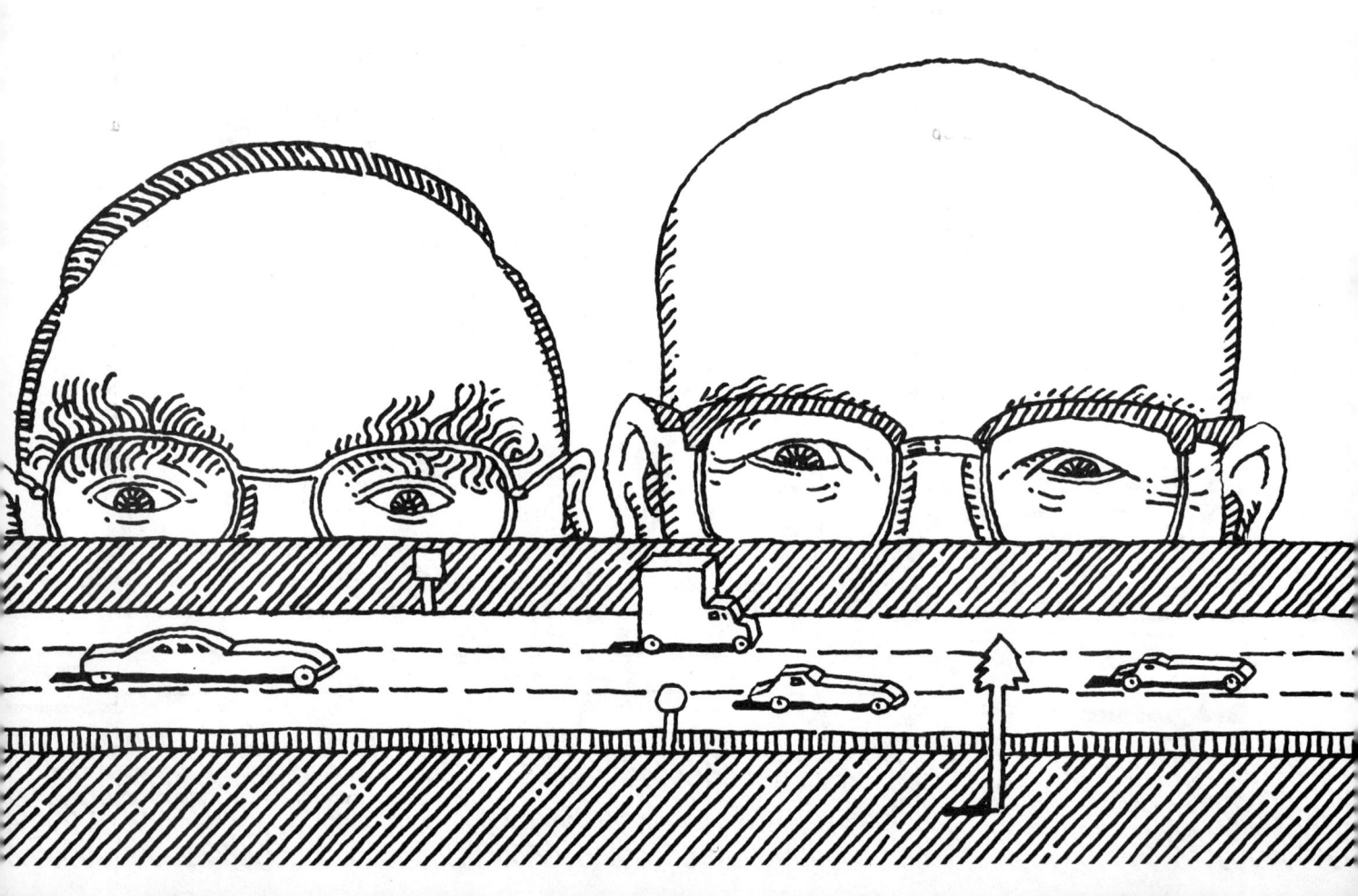

"The special strength of TGRA: 'It's not that they contribute so much in campaigns; it's more subtle than that. They belong to the right country clubs, the right power elite.'"

fluential citizens. The issue in 1946 was not whether a particular road should be two lanes or four: it was whether that road would be *paved*.

Although the Highway Department in the thirties and forties was ably run as a professional, rather than a political, operation, the squalid smell of still-recent history reminded many Texans that unless the Department's planning was insulated from the biennial legislative process, the state might just be living on borrowed time. During the administration of Governor Miriam A. "Ma" Ferguson in the mid-twenties, the Department had struggled through a bleak period of chicanery and political patronage. In a single biennium (1925-26) four different men served as highway engineer, the Department's top executive position. Ten individuals were named to the three posts of highway commissioner. All but one of the division engineers lost his job. Finally the Federal Bureau of Public Roads refused to participate in Texas highway projects because of the deteriorating system. The memory of this experience lingered long after the Department was reorganized in 1927. Not surprisingly, it spurred sentiment for the Good Roads Amendment: the Ferguson fiasco, after all, had occurred less than twenty years before 1946, making it closer in time than the passage of the amendment itself is to us today.

Securing the Highway Department's finances outside the normal appropriations process was a simple, logical, and therefore attractive panacea to allay these fears. The fact that it would also award virtually permanent protection to a particular special interest's economic needs was seldom discussed.

Most of the resistance to the amendment came from other interests who had cast their eyes covetously on the same gasoline tax revenues. County authorities, who wanted to convert one fourth of the tax into a permanent source of county income, had squelched an attempt to get an earlier version of the amendment on the ballot in 1942. The TGRA's decision to draft their 1946 amendment to preserve the existing statutory allocation of one fourth of the gasoline tax to the Available School Fund was a brilliant tactical maneuver that insured the backup support of the powerful teachers' lobby, for both passage of the amendment and preservation of the dedicated fund in future years.

Before 1946, Charles Simons recalls, "you had to continually be fighting off the brushfires" that threatened the Highway Department's funds. The voters changed all that. From the adoption of the amendment, the Department was to grow into the largest, most powerful, and in many ways the most competent of state agencies. Nineteen-forty-six was a milestone, and the years since then are the *Anno Domini* of the Texas Highway Department.

Et in Arcadia Ego: The THD

The modern Texas Highway Department (THD) has far surpassed the most optimistic predictions made for it in 1946. Its reputation is untarnished by any serious hint of scandal. It is among the least secretive of state agencies. It has developed the largest (and many feel the best) system of highways in the United States. Set apart in its own snug—but not little—insular world of engineering excellence, it has an enviable esprit de corps.

The Department's reputation for honesty is especially remarkable in view of the vast sums of public money at its disposal. Scandals of the sort that brought Spiro Agnew low in Maryland are an all-too-common aspect of highway construction elsewhere. They don't happen in Texas. The fact that highway funds are constitutionally protected has of course had something to do with this state of affairs, although not as much as the highway lobbyists and the THD would like the public to believe. Keeping highway building out of legislative politics accomplishes very little unless the department that builds the roads keeps its own hands clean. The special strength of the THD is its conscientious administrative tradition—and that is the result not of some nebulous code of loyalties but of the direct personal influence of specific men in specific positions. The man most frequently credited with developing this high standard of honesty is DeWitt Greer, a quintessential Aggie who served as chief highway engineer (in effect, the Department's executive director) from 1940 through 1967, and is currently one of the three highway commissioners. "The lion's share of the credit goes to Greer," says Garrett Morris, a highway commissioner from 1967 to 1971. "Nobody could ever point an accusing finger at him." Although an increasing number of critics question Greer's emphasis on highway transportation, he was primarily responsible for selecting generations of middle-level administrators who have kept the Department out of politics for more than thirty years.

The THD's efficiency and honesty, coupled with Texans' affinity for highway travel, has to some extent made the Department its own best lobbyist. Legislators are reluctant to place themselves at cross-purposes with an agency that is so popular back home. "It's really the fact that they do such a good job and they're so honest, that's made them into a sacred cow," says one former senator. Then too, voters by and large do not object to things they can *see* as tangible examples of governmental services. "We're really the only state agency that produces a product," says Marc Yancey, one of two assistant highway engineers. "You can't see the welfare product, or even the education product, but you can see ours all over the state. It helps."

The highway system rapidly expanded in the years following 1946. From approximately 28,000 miles in 1947, it grew to 42,000 in 1950 and 62,000 in 1960. It has now passed the 71,000-mile mark. The Department told the Finance Committee of the Constitutional Convention that 21 entire counties and 1716 communities (including 49 county seats) currently are served by no mode of transportation except the highway system. (Supporters of public transportation, of course, consider this a lamentable situation rather than a source of pride.) The 1970 census revealed that in 18 Texas counties, the number of registered motor vehicles exceeded the number of human inhabitants.

Highway building is the principal, but far from the only, responsibility of the THD. The Department provides an incredible array of services—some which directly benefit the public and others which reinforce its image as a virtual state-within-a-state. Charged with the duty of promoting tourism, it publishes a semi-annual "Calendar of Events" listing everything from the Sweetwater Rattlesnake Roundup to the Houston Livestock Show, along with brochures about historical trails, maps of every county in three different sizes, a monthly road-conditions bulletin (the January issue listed 193 construction sites, with detailed information on the location, extent of construction, projected date of completion, and even the type of road surface onto which traffic was being detoured), and the award-winning guidebook, *Texas: Land of Contrast*. Its materials have a well-deserved reputation for thoroughness and polish.

The Department's in-house publications include a slick monthly magazine, *Texas Highways*, a newsletter called "Highway News," and several other newsletters published for specific geographical districts. Various branches produce motion pictures (including a thirty-minute sound and color feature on highway beautification), answer telephone calls about emergency road conditions, run computerized data-retrieval systems that can locate any magazine article about transportation systems, distribute public service announcements to TV stations (a current "spot" tells how to enter a freeway safely), catalog the archaeological discoveries unearthed in the course of road-building, devise new techniques of highway safety (including breakaway road signs and the ingenious empty-barrel collections called Texas Crash Cushions), and print the tons of manuals, reports, and other documents the Department issues each year. The public information office distributes more than 1300 press releases annually (on the average, four or five every working day). So great is the Department's reputation and so deep the lethargy of some weekly newspaper editors that many of these are printed, unchanged, as news stories in small-town papers.

Some idea of the size and complexity of the THD can be gained from a brief glance at its internal structure.

The three commissioners are Reagan Houston (the chairman), DeWitt Greer, and Charles Simons. Houston is a San Antonio lawyer appointed by Governor Dolph Briscoe. Governor Preston Smith had the inspired idea of crowning Greer's career by appointing the retired chief engineer to a commissioner's post; it was like picking Winston Churchill to be king of England. Smith also appointed Simons, a balding, witty gentleman who looks like Sibelius mellowed by a touch of Charles Coburn. These men set the Department's policy, and Chief Highway Engineer B. L. DeBerry carries it out.

DeBerry has separated his giant bureaucracy into two parts and placed an assistant highway engineer over each one. The "operations" side of things is supervised by M. G. Goode, Jr. Its eight sections include Highway Design; Bridges; Maintenance Operations; Secondary Roads; Construction; Right-of-Way; Materials and Tests; and Planning and Research. Each is directed by an engineer. The administrative side is supervised by Marc Yancey, Jr., a likable, diplomatic ambassador for the Department who could, in meticulously chosen language, probably convince the head of a local Sierra Club that a proposed interstate highway through his living room was actually a splendid idea. Yancey's seven sections include Finance; Motor Vehicles; Travel and Information; Insurance; Equipment and Procurement; Automation; and Personnel.

The day-to-day business of the Department is highly decentralized. Only 400 of its 18,000 employees work in the downtown Austin headquarters. More than 1250 THD buildings are scattered around the state in 25 separate and largely autonomous geographical districts. Each district is headed by a district engineer who, in accordance with traditions established by Greer, is expected to handle most of his problems at that level. Interestingly, there is also a "public affairs officer" in each district, a man whose job entails more than answering questions from the public about Highway Department plans. "He keeps apprised of the economic and social conditions in his district," Yancey related. "He can tell us about the current political climate and things like that."

Because of its solid financial base, the THD has vast resources that other state agencies do not even dare to dream of. Its *Twenty-eighth Biennial Report*, covering Fiscal 1971 and 1972, itemizes the 17,989 pieces of "major highway equipment," valued at $19,900,483.50, that the Department owned at the end of August 1972. In addition to the predictable asphalt distributors, batchers, boilers, core-drills, diggers (posthole), earth-movers, graders, grass-seeding machines, guardrail washing machines (motorized), concrete mixers, power movers (gravely class), nail pickers, paint stripers, pavement breakers, power shovels, road rollers, road rippers, snow plows, mulch spreaders, tractors, trailers, trenchers, trucks, and something called an "unloading machine," the report also lists 868 passenger cars of various sizes (642 of which were equipped with two-way radios) and 3506 pickup trucks. This was a sufficient number of cars and pickups to allow approximately one out of every four departmental employees, including secretaries, janitors, and typists, to be on the road alone at the same instant. When employees of an underequipped agency like the Park Division of Parks and Wildlife hear this sort of thing, they whimper. Most of them have to use their own cars when they travel on state business.

The Highway Department is, in reality, a separate fiefdom, a veritable fourth branch of government. When asked about its relationship to the Legislature, highway commissioners and the TGRA like to emphasize the constitutional language that makes the dedicated fund "subject to legislative allocation, appropriation, and direction," but this subordination is more symbolic than real. The Department has not been forced to justify a highway expenditure to the Legislature since 1946. While the lawmakers can crack down on the THD through the appropriations process if they choose (by requiring it to pay the full cost of various expenses like rights-of-way, curbs, and gutters that are now shared with other governments), the dedicated fund revenue *must* be used for highway-related purposes. The Legislature is not free to shift it into mental health or mass transit. Even if the legislators got so mad at the Department that they refused to appropriate any of the dedicated fund for anything, the money would simply pile up and await future legislators, two, twenty, or a hundred years hence, who would eventually have to appropriate it for highways. The Highway Department has the upper hand, and the legislators know it.

Legislators are human and they enjoy the power that comes from being able to insist that an agency justify its appropriations. It is a bit galling, then, to be faced with one that is financially independent enough to get away with saying, politely of course, "We appreciate your suggestions but we don't plan to take them." This bothers the legislator who feels he ought to have the right to balance the relative needs of, say, a hundred mentally retarded children against the need of the city of Taylor to have a four-lane loop built around its outskirts. But it also bothers the legislator who just feels he ought to have a say in how the state of Texas spends three quarters of a billion dollars every year. The financial independence of the THD has caused more friction than either side is willing to admit.

This resentment rarely flares out into the open because the average legislator is reluctant to oppose a sacred cow like the Department. One occasion when it did, however, was when the THD planned construction of a ten-story, $20 million headquarters building in front of the State Capitol and across the street from the more modest building erected in 1933. San Antonio Representative Jake Johnson, an old foe of the Department, blasted the proposal in the 1971 legislative session, calling it a "monstrosity" that would make the Governor's Mansion directly behind it "look like an outhouse." He asserted that it had been designed to be so tall "in order that DeWitt Greer can look down on the Legislature, rather than the other way around." Johnson nearly blocked the building, but the Legislature eventually settled for suggesting that the commissioners find some other site. By October 1971, however, the Department had produced a 25-page, slick-paper pamphlet (at a cost of $1.60 a copy) defending the building's aesthetics, mentioning that the downtown location was convenient to the offices of the contractors who do business with the Department, and suggesting that if the structure was not built, commercial developers might buy the property and erect something even more offensive. By March 1972, the Department was contending that even the Legislature could not prevent construction of the building because it would be paid for with dedicated funds over which the Legislature could exercise no control. This struck a nerve. After a personal privilege speech by Representative Frances Farenthold in a June special session, the Legislature ordered the Parks and Wildlife Department to buy the property and convert it into a state park. Governor Smith then vetoed these instructions, leaving the matter more confused than ever.

"The price for this sort of insulation from politics is bureaucratic inbreeding. Eventually everyone begins to think alike because those who think differently are not hired..."

But when the Legislature returned for yet another special session in October, both houses overwhelmingly approved a resolution warning the THD that they were mightily displeased with the whole affair. The lame-duck governor could not veto a resolution, and the Department, sensing that they had aroused the Legislature's ire, threw in the towel and agreed to build their headquarters somewhere else.

Significantly, however, the Department has never abandoned its claim that it has the legal right to construct buildings out of its "own" funds without legislative approval. And even now, more than a year later, Commissioner Charles Simons gets a wistful, faraway look in his eye when he is asked about the legislative battle. "I really believe that our building, the way we had it planned, would have been a prime asset to that site and to downtown Austin business," he says. "It was a *beautiful* building."

The commissioners have traditionally had few qualms about putting pressure on the Legislature to accede to the Department's wishes. Most agency heads are rather circumspect about marching out and soliciting public support for their agency's position in a controversial political issue. Not the highway commissioners. In recent months they have become unabashed lobbyists for preservation of the dedicated highway fund. At a luncheon speech to a businessmen's association called "Fort Worth's Progress, Inc.," last November, all three commissioners thanked Beeman Fisher, a member of the Constitutional Revision Commission (and of the TGRA) for his successful efforts to preserve the fund in the proposed new constitution. They urged the audience to help persuade the Constitutional Convention to keep it there, and by extension, to keep roads ahead of mass transit as a state priority.

From top to bottom, the people at the Texas Highway Department have a firm faith in the value of what they are doing. But even as they bask in the sunshine of public admiration for their visible accomplishments, they display the faults of people who talk seriously only to others in their own closed circle. The conflicting ideas expressed before the commissioners at public hearings seldom penetrate the bureaucracy itself. If, as some say, the Department exhibits all the advantages of a government run by engineers, it likewise exhibits all the *disadvantages*.

Haunted by the possibility that political meddling could ruin the Department —which of course it could—the postwar leadership and Greer in particular hewed an administrative path as far from politics as possible. To administrative positions he promoted men from within the Department strictly, as he saw it, on the basis of merit. The reasoning was simple: as long as our administrators are men who have served in the Department, as long as they are trained men who have proved their competence and not "outsiders" who might be unqualified or who might rock the boat, we are safe from political interference. Greer was determined to protect the Department by quarantining it. He wanted a bureaucracy composed of engineering professionals, and that is what he got.

Except for the commissioners themselves, who are appointed for six-year terms by the governor and confirmed by the Senate, virtually all the important administrative positions in the Department are held by engineers who have been promoted through the ranks. "It's kind of like being a doctor: first you have to be an intern," says Marc Yancey. "This is one of the essentials of the type of operation we have." (Starting at the very bottom, however, is not required. Yancey himself left a career in consulting work to join the Department, but he still served six years in the Bridge Division before moving up.) The price for this sort of insulation from politics is bureaucratic inbreeding. Eventually everyone begins to think alike because those who think differently either are not hired, or, if hired, are not promoted to positions of influence. Such a rigid promotional system firmly precludes the possibility that an unorthodox thinker could become chief highway engineer. And only an unorthodox chief highway engineer could choose outsiders with fresh ideas for the middle-echelon administrative positions. It is the kind of unconscious oversight that would come naturally to a trained engineer who began his highway career in 1927 just a few weeks after the Ferguson scandals were ended, as Greer himself did. The formative experiences of this 26-year-old assistant resident engineer in Henderson County were to shape the Department's policies for nearly half a century.

This inbreeding is profoundly reinforced by the fact that the great preponderance of THD engineers are graduates of either The University of Texas College of Engineering or the Texas A&M College of Engineering. The dominant influences on Texas civil engineers flow from UT's Highway Research Center and A&M's Texas Transportation Institute; the graduates' outlooks are formed there, and, as the Texas Public Interest Research Group (TEXPIRG) has noted, those outlooks are routinely predisposed to favor highway transportation over rail mass transit and other modes.

The current semester at Texas A&M's civil engineering department, for example, includes courses in highway engineering; highway materials and pavement design; highway design; highway problems analysis; structural design of rigid pavements; roadside safety design; and highway construction. Only 1 of the 72 courses deals expressly with urban transportation. Approximately thirty academic civil engineering professors hold joint appointments as research engineers for the Texas Transportation Institute, and they spend, on the average, 60 per cent of their time on TTI research projects. Those projects are heavily weighted in favor of highway problems. At the present time the TTI is conducting 52 separate studies for the Texas Highway Department.

Even before the state's civil engineering graduates have reached the Highway Department, they are intellectually comfortable with its world view. Perhaps this is because the Highway Department has reached *them* before they reached *it*: both the Highway Research Center and the Texas Transportation Institute are partially supported by Highway Department funds.

All these influences have given Texas an established Highway Department bureaucracy of transportation professionals who think only *roads*. Like other bureaucracies, it exhibits the standard tendency to expand its needs, ambitions, and goals (by 1948, only two years after the Good Roads Amendment was passed, Greer told the Legislature that the Department's needs in the next five years would cost twice as much as the anticipated revenue). What has made the Highway Department different from other state agencies is that it has not been compelled to justify its expenditures against other, non-highway needs. The same things that have helped make it honest and efficient have also made it wealthy, powerful, and inbred. The luxury of its dedicated fund has allowed it the luxury of becoming set in its ways.

These danger signals for the future were fully apparent in 1946, if anyone had stopped to see them. No one did. The Texan's love affair with his automobile continued, raising motor vehicle registrations from 1.9 million in 1946 to 3.1 million in 1950, 4.9 million in 1960, and 8.5 million in 1972. The Department grew with them.

How the Lobby Works

The transportation interests have always been a powerful lobby in Texas. Before the highways, there were the railroads. The modern-day highway lobby begins but does not end with the Good Roads Association. True, the Association is the closest thing the highway interests have to a common flag; but the various economic groups that support the TGRA also do some lobbying on their own. Two of the most powerful are the Highway-Heavy Contractor branch of the Association of General Contractors, which represents roadbuilders, and the Texas Motor Transportation Association, which vigorously protects the interests of the truck and bus industries. Opinions differ as to which other groups wield the most power. Former Secretary of State Bob Bullock, one of Governor Preston Smith's closest advisers, insists that no one in the highway lobby has more clout than the oil industry. Other observers contend that when hard lobbying is needed, the local chambers of commerce are the most formidable force around. But everyone agrees that the highway lobby ultimately draws its strength from its diverse *combination* of interests.

Those who expect to wait around the Capitol and watch the highway lobby flex its muscles every two years are, however, in for a disappointment. The mighty highway lobbyists paradoxically do very little "lobbying," at least as that word is ordinarily understood: wining, dining, wenching, and twisting arms of legislators. They don't have to. That is the beauty of the dedicated fund, the glorious legacy of the Good Roads Amendment. So long as Article VIII, Section 7a, of the Texas Constitution remains in the lawbooks, they are safe. And *the only* way that provision can be taken out is by constitutional amendment: a process that requires a two-thirds majority of both houses of the Legislature even to get on the ballot. It is a lobbyist's dream. While the other lobbyists—the doctors, the insurance industry, the brewers, the lawyers, the pot smokers, the land developers, and all the rest—are racing around the Capitol halls trying to get their pet bills enacted or defeated step by tedious step, from subcommittee, to committee, to the floor, to the other house, to conference committee, and to the governor's desk, the highway lobbyists just sit back, act friendly, and smile. All they need is one third plus one of *either* house of the Legislature on their side, and the dedicated fund will stay safely beyond all danger. Just 51 representatives, say—or better yet, just 11 of the 31 senators. Keep those 11 little senators, and *nobody* can tamper with the dedicated fund: not the governor, not a majority of both houses of the Legislature aroused to high dudgeon, not the voters, not Saint Christopher himself—nobody. The ball, as they say, is in the other court. It is a lovely sort of life.

With such an overwhelmingly strategic advantage, the highway lobby can put out the occasional brushfires without ever bothering to take off its white gloves. Even the brushfires are rare. A 1947 attempt by Senator Grover Morris to create a farm-to-market road program by increasing the gasoline tax was successfully squelched by truck, bus, and oil industry lobbyists, who objected to any "diversion" of gasoline tax revenues (even new ones) away from arterial highways. Two years later these same lobbyists, along with the TGRA, supported the Colson-Briscoe Act financing a farm-to-market road program out of general state revenues. The dedicated fund had been preserved inviolate. By 1968 the TGRA had grown as fond of farm roads as any other kind; it buried a bill by Representative Glenn Purcell that would have, in his words, "put the money where the rubber is" by closing out the farm road program.

One of the liveliest brushfires broke out in 1965 when Bob Bullock, then a lobbyist for municipal bus companies, got a bill introduced that would have given them a rebate on the 75 per cent of their motor fuel tax that went to the Highway Department. Bullock reasoned that city buses operate on city streets, not highways. Most of the companies were on the verge of bankruptcy, and his bill would have cost the Highway Department only two or three million dollars, a drop in the bucket for them. A similar bill had been killed on the House floor in 1963, 80–61, and this time the highway lobby was ready. Bullock later recalled: "I had a hard time even finding a sponsor. Finally we got it introduced and had a hearing. Lots of mail started coming in from Good Roads members, editorials started popping up in newspapers saying 'Don't open the door: everybody will ask for rebates.' . . . It went to subcommittee and, man, it never budged at all. They beat the hell out of me."

Bullock described the lobby effort as "a very honorable fight. The oil companies lobbied over a drink. . . . there certainly wasn't any money changing hands, nothing like that. The Good Roads members contribute to campaigns as individuals, and who was I? I represented a lot of broke bus companies, some of them city owned. Face it: a contributor gets the ear of a legislator quicker than a non-contributor. The Good Roads Association is potent. They're political, and they do a damn good job."

Apart from these periodic easy battles the highway lobby has very little to do except to continue nourishing the highway ethos that envelops the legislators when they return home to visit with the constituents. Very little, that is, except for one critically important function: year in, year out, they exert decisive pressure on the selection and confirmation of the highway commissioners who set the policies of the THD. If the commissioners waver, the entire highway building superstructure is endangered. So the TGRA and the other components of the highway lobby pay special attention to gubernatorial politics. Selection of these commissioners is the summit of their lobbying. Their aim is to insure that the state's transportation leadership, like its professionals, thinks only of roads.

A number of exceptional men have served as highway commissioners over the years. Most of them have been chosen in a process dominated by the highway lobby. The TGRA's candidates are not necessarily men with an economic self-interest in roads—just as the TGRA's own officers are "laymen." But they are invariably men having a solid predisposition in favor of the TGRA's road-building aspirations.

Thirteen men have been appointed highway commissioner since the Good Roads Amendment was passed. A few, like Garrett Morris and the current Chairman, Reagan Houston, have not been TGRA candidates. Among the others are the following:

• Fred A. Wemple (1947–1953). President of TGRA before serving as commissioner, 1942–1943, and again afterwards, 1955–1956.

• Robert J. Potts (1949–1955). President of TGRA, 1947–1948.

• C. F. Hawn (1957–1963). Member of TGRA Executive Committee before serving as commissioner; president of TGRA, 1968–1970.

• Herbert C. Petry (1955–1973). TGRA director before serving as commissioner.

• J. H. Kultgen (1963–1969). TGRA director, 1947–1962; TGRA president 1951–1955. Automobile dealer since 1936. President of Bird-Kultgen, Inc., Ford dealership in Waco.

• Charles Simons (1971–present). Director of TGRA public relations, 1936–1942; Editor, *Texas Parade,* 1936–1942; TGRA executive vice-president, 1942–1947. Executive vice-president, Texas Mid-Continent Oil and Gas Association, 1947–1971.

The TGRA was unable to say how many of the remaining commissioners had been members of the Association before or after their terms of office. But it is unlikely that they would have protested the appointment of men like DeWitt Greer (1969–present), or Marshall Formby (1953–1959), who ran for governor in 1962 and distributed campaign literature describing himself as "a staunch believer in wide highways" who "helped spend more than a billion dollars for highway maintenance and construction" while serving as commissioner.

During the Constitutional Convention hearings, delegate Jim Vecchio of Dallas brought out the fact that Commissioner

Simons had recently applied for a bank charter with, among others, TGRA Board Chairman Russell Perry. Vecchio's questions implied that there might be a conflict of interest if a highway commissioner and a top highway lobbyist went into the banking business together. After Simons heatedly responded, "I don't think his being chairman of the Good Roads Association would influence me for five seconds," the chuckles echoed for days. But the truth of the matter was, Simons was absolutely right. What his critics overlooked was the fact that Simons and Perry *already* thought exactly alike on every important question about the state's transportation needs, and had for years: just as virtually every other highway commissioner and Good Roads official has thought alike for two generations. If the commissioners did not already share the Association's aims, the Association would never have consented to their appointments as commissioners.

The critics mistook an effect for a cause.

Mass Transit in Texas?

The Constitutional Convention fight over the dedicated fund has become a battle over the pros and cons of mass transit. Gasoline shortages have suddenly made the issue very real: how do you get to work if there is no gas for your car? But there is something very one-sided about the now-fashionable assumption around the Capitol that mass transit is needed just because fuel is short. For some people that is reason enough; but for many Texans who don't own a private car and never will, the problem of finding gasoline to propel one is entirely academic. Texas cities with more than about 50,000 residents are so large, geographically, that people who have no private car find it hard to get where they need to go—to work, to the grocery store, to church. For them there is a transportation shortage, not a fuel shortage.

Garrett Morris has seen the problem from both sides, first as a highway commissioner and currently as a member of the State Board of Public Welfare, and the experience has made him a firm believer in mass transit.

"For many people," he says, "the automobile doesn't provide true mobility—the young, the old, the blind, the disabled, the indigent. You've got to make good money to buy a four-thousand-dollar car and maintain it. Ever since we tore up our streetcar tracks and shipped them to Japan in the thirties, these people have had a hard time getting around."

Bob Bullock noticed the same thing when he lobbied for rebates to rescue local bus companies in the sixties. "These transit companies were a losing proposition but a necessary service," he says. "Affluent people don't realize this. I don't understand all about mass transit, but I understand something when I see a bus full of blacks and Mexicans."

This latent class bias is implicit in the attitudes of the middle-class "layman" supporters of the Texas Good Roads Association. TGRA President Eugene Robbins says, "Our objection to using gasoline taxes for mass transit is that it places the entire burden on the guy who drives his car—and he may or may not be the one who's using mass transit." The broad front of the highway lobby is distinctively white middle class, and such a person, burdened by the already high costs of running an automobile—or two, or three—sees good sense in Robbins's argument. But others are not so sure. Robert E. Gallamore, Director of Policy Development for Common Cause, recently argued to a congressional subcommittee that despite the fact that the roads themselves are usually constructed out of highway user taxes, those who use the highways still don't pay the full social costs:

> Noise, congestion, and air pollution are shared with others. Large portions of dislocation costs are borne by unfortunate people whose incomes and often whose race do not enable them to move out of the path of new freeways until it is too late to make that choice voluntarily. Gasoline is relatively cheap [this was in 1973] because all taxpayers subsidize oil companies through the percentage depletion allowance, intangible drilling cost write-offs, and foreign tax credits. . . . Local jurisdictions pay for traffic police out of general funds. . . .

The auto got us into this mess, say the mass transit advocates, and those of us who are too poor to own an auto now that public transportation has dwindled to almost nothing may reasonably think that there is nothing wrong with taxing the auto to help get us out again.

The highway lobby has kept the mass transit advocates off balance by cheerfully agreeing that Texas does need more mass transit—surely does, needs it in the worst way. The problem is, they say, that there's not enough money in the highway budget right now for highways, and besides, nobody has invented any sort of mass transit system that will work in Texas. They prefer to think of mass transit in terms of large fleets of diesel-powered, rubber-tired buses rolling over . . . roads.

The TGRA has too much political savvy to sit back and allow the increasingly popular notion of mass transit to be co-opted by the highway critics. Last November TGRA Chairman Russell Perry announced the formation of a 29-member Urban Mass Transportation Advisory Council having as its "primary function" the dissemination of information "giving Texas citizens perspective and understanding on urban transportation issues" so that the public will support "reasonable urban transportation programs for Texas cities." At its organizational meeting February 12, the group endorsed the idea of a state mass transportation fund so long as it did not interfere with the dedicated highway fund, and they suggested that the TGRA change its own name to "Texans for Better Transportation" to reflect its "broad concern with the total transportation picture."

The Advisory Council's specific recommendations must await future meetings, but it seems doubtful that its members will discover any "reasonable" programs that require fixed rails or invade gasoline tax revenues. Meanwhile they have the inestimable public relations benefit of being able to disseminate the TGRA position from a letterhead that includes the magic words "Urban" and "Mass Transportation."

Despite brave words ("We have the farmer out of the mud. Our challenge now is . . . to get the city dweller out of the traffic jam"), the TGRA's position on mass transit boils down to this: do it if you want to, but get your money somewhere else. In a letter to Governor Briscoe in January 1973, the Association listed fifteen "specific actions" they would support. Some of these, like state guarantees for transit authority bonds and passage of legislation to permit establishment of metropolitan transit authorities, were helpful to mass transit without being harmful to the Association's members. Others were a veiled way of saying "leave our money alone" (e.g., "Support of increased Federal and State funding from general funds," "Support the release of funds authorized by Congress . . . but withheld by the Nixon Administration"). The rest were clearly designed to pad out the list: "Support demonstration projects to prove new systems will work," "Support coordinated planning for all transportation modes," a proposal seemingly indistinguishable from "Support coordination of efforts by state agencies," and, finally, "Support the Texas Highway Department in its desire to help the cities achieve improved public transportation."

The intensity of the THD's desire to help the cities in this respect is open to question. It does not appear to have grown significantly since DeWitt Greer declared in 1967:

> I do not believe mass transit is the answer in Texas. . . . Texans are oriented to the use of the automobile. It would take a generation to break Texans of the comfortable and convenient habit of riding in the automobile. If we are to please the taxpayers . . . then we must develop more adequate thoroughfares in the urban areas.

> *"When it gets to be too inconvenient and too costly to drive downtown, [the auto user] will use public transportation. When gas is 50 cents a gallon people will go back to buses."*

To the extent that the Department does set its collective mind to considerations of mass transit, it thinks only of buses and roads. Asked about the THD's plans, Commissioner Charles Simons mentioned Houston's heavily traveled West Loop 610 as evidence that the Department is already "the biggest public transportation system in Texas." Of the auto user, he said, "When it gets to be too inconvenient and too costly to drive downtown, he will use public transportation. When gas is fifty cents a gallon people will go back to buses. We're gonna help them because we have the facilities over which those buses roll."

Today gas is over fifty cents a gallon and there are few buses for Texans to go back to. In the past generation, bus service has been discontinued at the rate of one city per year in Texas, declining from 36 cities in 1955 to 18 cities today. The systems that remain are a pale shadow of comprehensive public transportation.

There are two fundamental problems facing any urban mass transit system in Texas. They figure prominently in every TDH and TGRA statement on the subject, and even the advocates of mass transit do not deny them.

One is residential *density*. Texas cities grew fastest in the era after automobiles had become the primary mode of personal transportation. Therefore they sprawl: unlike the closely packed, high-rise cities of the East Coast, where population densities exceed 20,000 persons per square mile, residential neighborhoods in Texas are spacious, with densities in the vicinity of 3000 persons per square mile. How, ask the mass transit critics, can a bus or fixed rail network serve enough riders within walking distance of each stop to make the whole thing attractive?

The other problem is commercial *decentralization*. Traditional mass transit systems are designed to handle suburb-to-central-business-district movement quite well, but the Shopping Center Society of 1974 spends most of its travel time going places other than the downtown area. Commissioner Simons estimates that only five to seven per cent of all trips in Dallas County have downtown destinations. How, ask the critics, can a mass transit system take urban Texans where they want to go?

Density and decentralization are the favorite themes at TGRA gatherings where mass transit is discussed. They are treated as insuperable barriers to a mass transit system, at least within the lifetime of the audience, and thus they take on the character of a rhetorical fail-safe system against threats to divert the dedicated fund. If mass transit is impossible, only fools would waste money on it. Especially highway money.

One illustration of this phenomenon occurred at the joint meeting of the TGRA and the Houston Chamber of Commerce last November. The speaker was Dr. R. W. Holder, Associate Research Engineer at the Texas Transportation Institute. He discussed the density and decentralization problems and concluded that "no rapid transit system in use today appears to be directly applicable to Texas cities. Our urban forms are so different from those of cities in the North and East that we faced a different set of problems." By this, said Holder, "I do not mean to imply that we cannot solve this problem.... We must search for mass transportation system designs that are compatible with our urban forms and"—he added significantly to his highway-minded audience—"[with] our existing urban transportation systems."

One suggestion proposed by Holder was to establish "freeway surveillance and control with priority entry for buses."

As newspaper headlines outside warned of imminent gasoline shortages, Holder concluded by telling his audience: "Texas is the greatest state in the greatest nation in the world.... I see no reason why Texas should adopt an approach of copying urban transportation systems developed for other cities.... Let us design our own systems.... Let's pioneer the way and let the rest of the world follow us."

The applause was fervent.

The density and decentralization problems are serious obstacles, to be sure. If the Manhattan subway system could somehow be inserted in the swampy muck that underlies Houston, it still would not fully solve that city's transportation problem. Mass transit advocates merely deny that these obstacles are insuperable. "*No mass transit system is feasible in Texas,*" says Buck Wood of Texas Common Cause, "if you start from the premise that everybody has to drive his car to work." Pointing to the rail commuter societies of Long Island and suburban Philadelphia, where residential density resembles Texas' and people take a bus, drive, or are driven to rail terminals, Garrett Morris remarks, "This density argument sounds good, but I'm not sure it's as valid as people would have you believe. When you've got the necessity for conservation of fuel, density is not the argument it once was. Anyway, the old streetcars worked with lower density than we have today."

Commercial decentralization is not so severe as to prevent the creation of a mass transit system serving major shopping centers as well as the central business district. If our present decentralized shopping patterns grew up in the last thirty years as a direct result of the increased mobility that private automobiles provide, is it not reasonable to expect that with reduced auto use and better mass transit our shopping patterns will swing back toward greater centralization, giving downtown stores a badly needed shot in the arm? Is that so bad a prospect?

At the moment, however, mass transit plans in Texas are hamstrung by problems far more elementary than density and decentralization. Though thousands of commuters need to cross municipal boundaries, the cities face difficulties extending their own systems across these lines. The counties lack mass transit authority altogether. An effort to establish a regional transit authority in Houston last fall collapsed in a roar of recriminations. Revenue sources are shaky. The smaller cities cannot (or will not) put together enough revenue to qualify for federal matching funds. (Since 1964, Texas has received only $35.6 million in federal aid for improving mass transit, less than one tenth as much as California, that bastion of the private car, has gotten, and far behind the $260 million for Illinois, the $210 million for Massachusetts, and the $200 million for Pennsylvania. Under the law, Texas *could* have gotten $762.5 million.) Good transit is expensive, like police, fire protection, waste disposal, and other city services. Because it was a profit-making business until very recently, the cities are doggedly reluctant to assume the responsibility of supplying it at a loss.

The Boys on the Bus: The TMTC

The authority that has been charged with helping the cities overcome these problems is the Texas Mass Transportation Commission. In a state where impotent agencies outnumber the eunuchs in a Turkish harem, the TMTC sings its soprano song to an audience of benign neglect. Established by the Legislature in 1969 to "foster... the development of public mass transportation, both intracity and intercity, in this state," but without being given funds to do so, the Commission existed for twenty months, after September 1971, with no chairman, no quorum, no employees, no money, and no telephone. In January 1973, it received an appropriation of $80,100, of which $58,000 goes to pay the salaries of Executive Director Russell Cummings and his three employees, "leaving," in his words, "about $22,000 to do all these great wonders the Legislature requires us to do."

Cummings, a folksy 48-year-old former legislator from Houston's Montrose district, is sensitive to the inconvenience that the present meager public transportation systems impose on racial and economic minorities. He is not, however, a visionary, and he talks a lot about buses. "We're not set in concrete on any particular mode," he says, adding, "—but every rail system in the U.S. lost money last year." He also takes a modest view of his agency's duties: "We are a service organization, not a regulatory authority." Unlike other mass transit advocates, moreover, he takes a hands-off approach to the dedicated highway fund, insisting that "where the Legislature gets the money is their decision. We're not seeking anybody else's funds."

Cummings's caution is understandable in view of the interests of the six appointed commissioners who hired him:

- Chairman Albert Rollins is an engineering firm member who previously served as engineer assistant for the Texas Highway Department.
- Member Joe P. Cain is president of Lake Truck Lines, Inc.
- Member Robert H. Cutler is chairman of the board of ICX Illinois-California Express, Inc., a motor freight carrier. A 32-year veteran of the trucking industry, he has held office in the Texas Motor Transport Association and is past president of the American Trucking Association.
- Member J. W. Porter is executive vice-president of Gifford-Hill & Co., Inc., manufacturers of ready-mixed concrete, Portland cement, sand, and gravel (and, for the record, railroad cross-ties).
- Member Clyde Malone is the manager of the Austin city bus system and a member of TGRA's Urban Mass Transportation Advisory Council.
- Member James W. Ward was, at the time of his appointment, chairman of the Amarillo Chamber of Commerce Traffic Committee.

Five of the six (excepting only Porter, a Briscoe man) are the legacy of Governor Preston Smith.

The selection of these particular men to establish policy on the Texas Mass Transportation Commission is compelling evidence that the highway lobby has moved as swiftly to neutralize this faint potential threat to highway dominance as they customarily move to influence the selection of the highway commissioners themselves.

So Russell Cummings sits in his tiny office on South Congress Avenue twenty blocks from the Capitol, a distance too far to walk and too humiliating to drive, and types the lead on his latest press release:

1974 is the Year of the Tiger in China, but it may be the Year of the Bus in Texas....

Shootout at the Watering Trough

With these issues, the current constitutional fight over the dedicated fund is being waged. The Texas Highway Department insists that every penny of its allotted funds, and more, will be needed to finance highway needs for the next twenty years. Even ex-commissioner Morris agrees with that. The planned reconstruction of 12,000 to 14,000 miles of noninterstate primary highways will, the commissioners say, require $13 billion. Thirteen hundred bridges are substandard, some of them "damn dangerous," according to Simons. Another 10,000 miles of farm-to-market roads are planned. The suburban loops that were being built five years ago around cities the size of Tyler (pop. 60,000) are now being constructed around Vernon (pop. 12,600), Taylor (pop. 9616), Monahans (pop. 8350), and Perryton (pop. 8100). "Towns that used to threaten to secede if we built loops now ask for us to build them," says Simons. Since the money is available, the loops are built.

The Department's philosophy of loops is interesting. Spokesman Marc Yancey explains:

If you look at history you see that . . . the cities that last longest have a radial design. The center deteriorates, but because it's practical to drive within the radial loop, the center rebuilds itself, like Montrose in Houston is now doing.

Loops have a very good purpose. Rome is a classic example. Athens, Greece, has a radial highway.

Today Athens, tomorrow Dripping Springs.

Maintenance costs are continuing to rise. In the 1973 fiscal year they amounted to $116 million, but Yancey says "costs have gone right through the roof" and the figure will rise to $132 million this year and $150 million in 1975.

Pie graphs distributed to the Convention by the TGRA show the same maintenance figures for Fiscal 1973, $116 million, along with figures for "right of way and construction" totaling $432 million. Apparently the pie graphs were embarrassing. In a season when both the gasoline supply and the dedicated fund are in danger, expenditures for "maintenance" are better public relations than expenditures for construction. The TGRA and the THD quickly began to distribute new charts for Fiscal 1974 containing a "Maintenance and Operation" category that had swollen to $296 million and "right of way and construction" categories that had shriveled to $171 million. Yancey explains that the figures originally described as "maintenance" include only routine things like mowing grass, picking up litter, and filling potholes. He attributes the increase to a simple reclassification of serious maintenance—work designed to prolong the life of a highway by resurfacing, sealcoating, or improving its base. Randall Wood of Common Cause contends that it includes the cost of four-laning existing two-lane highways as "maintenance." There is, in any event, something suspicious about a statement captioned "TEXAS HIGHWAY DEPARTMENT INCOME & EXPENDITURES" that includes $40 million for the Department of Public Safety under the category of "Maintenance and Operation" for the *Highway Department*.

A similar sort of confusion surrounds the impact of the energy crisis on highway revenues and needs in Texas. The Department has based its projections on the assumption that the number of motor vehicles will increase by nearly 50 per cent by the year 2000, and that these vehicles will consume about *twice* as many gallons of gasoline as were sold in Texas last year. Both assumptions now seem dubious, yet the Department has projected that this much traffic will need new roads, that this much traffic will tear up the roads that currently exist. Commissioner Simons says, "We haven't been affected by the energy crisis at all yet."

His confidence is shared by the Department's estimate of its income from the motor fuels tax this year. Even though gasoline stations are closing on every corner, the Department expects to collect $24.7 million dollars *more* from these taxes than it did in 1973. How can this be? The five-cent tax rate remains unchanged. The prestigious Advisory Commission on Intergovernmental Relations estimates that gasoline tax collections this year will be 17 per cent below those in 1972—a cut of about $39 million dollars for Texas. Does the Department know something the rest of us don't know? Asked about the apparent discrepancy, a THD spokesman said mysteriously that he was confident the estimates were correct and the reason would become apparent "very soon." And laying a finger aside of his nose, and giving a nod, up the chimney he rose.

In the Constitutional Convention the mass transit proponents, led by Common Cause of Texas, have argued first for elimination of the dedicated fund altogether or, as an alternative, for language that would allow some of the money to be used for public education and public transportation systems. The highway lob-

> *"'Imagine how foolish we'd look today if in 1875 the Constitution's framers had dedicated a five per cent tax on the sale of every horse to financing public watering troughs and hitching posts.'"*

by, as tactically astute as ever, has responded with a proposal of its own: a *different* constitutional provision that would dedicate one fourth of the present four per cent state sales tax on motor vehicles solely for mass transportation. This plan would provide about $50 million in state funds (matchable with 80 per cent federal funds), while leaving the half-billion-dollar highway fund intact. Both sides have claimed popular support for their positions, and each has produced the results of a poll to prove they have it.

A feeble compromise was adopted by the Convention's Finance Committee in February. Delegate Bill Sullivant of Gainesville proposed that the dedicated highway fund be preserved without change, except for a proviso that any *future* increase in the gasoline tax (above five cents per gallon) should not go automatically into the dedicated fund. The Legislature that raised the tax would, in Sullivant's plan, have the discretion to give the new revenue to the THD or channel it somewhere else. At press time it seemed likely that this proposal would be adopted by the whole convention. Certainly it seemed the most that the critics of the dedicated fund were likely to get.

The highway lobby has thrown itself energetically into this critical battle. The TGRA provided each delegate with an inch-thick book that is a tangible record of their pervasive ethos-building. It contains newspaper editorials, endorsements of the dedicated fund from dozens of chambers of commerce and county commissioners (many of whom simply filled in the blanks of model resolutions supplied by the TGRA and returned them as-is), and a not-so-subtle reminder that if all the members of all the TGRA member organizations are added together, the Association speaks for 280,500 Texans.

Governor Briscoe has cooperated by issuing a statement declaring that the retention of the dedicated fund "is essential if we are going to continue to have an effective highway system." The governor, who campaigned on a platform of aiding urban mass transit, then adds:

> Mass transit at some time—and in some form—has to be explored. But mass transportation will not reduce the need for highways. Texans are sort of independent . . . each wants to go in his own car.
> Highway building must go on . . .

The oil industry lobbyists have been conspicuously silent this year (lines at the filling stations prove that they no longer have their old interest in pushing up the demand for petroleum products). By contrast, the truckers and bussers (represented by the Texas Motor Transportation Association) have threatened to oppose the entire new constitution if the Sullivant proposal is adopted.

Despite all the talk about the virtues of the dedicated fund and the need for mass transit, what is really being fought out in the Constitutional Convention is utterly simple. It is whether the people of Texas are going to have the right to change their transportation priorities in the future through the legislative process, *if they decide to do so*. As long as the dedicated fund remains in the Constitution they cannot do so unless a two-thirds majority of both houses of the Legislature lets them. The votes of as few as eleven senators can block any change forever—regardless of urban needs, the energy shortage, or the wishes of a majority of the voters themselves. As long as the fund remains where it is, there will *always* be money for highways, and the rest of the public needs will fight it out for what is left. *Can a majority of Texans change the state's priorities?* That is what the battle is all about.

Felton West, the *Houston Post*'s Capitol correspondent, put the matter succinctly when he wrote:

> Imagine how foolish we'd look today if in 1875 the Constitution's framers had dedicated a 5 per cent tax on the sale of every horse to financing public watering troughs and hitching posts.

But then again, Governor Richard Coke had not told the press:

> Texans are sort of independent . . . each wants to ride his own horse.

Cloverleaf Without Exits

Is it endless then, a cloverleaf without exits?

The answer is suggested by the Convention testimony of Commissioner Simons. If the dedicated fund is removed, he told the delegates, the highway system will be "plunged into the heart of politics . . . instead of having highway projects based on traffic *needs*."

"Needs" is the pivotal word. Still influenced by a brief but lurid episode of corruption that flourished and died in less than a thousand days nearly half a century ago, the Department leaders constantly remind themselves of the dangers of political meddling in highway affairs, meddling that substitutes political favoritism for true highway "needs." Even though the Department's reputation is so secure today that it would surely be insulated from legislative logrolling if the dedicated fund were dropped, this fear remains its central organizing myth, its Homeric legend retold from father to son. In 1925 Troy fell. With his sturdy sailing ship, Aeneas has led his men to Rome.

Single-mindedly intent upon protecting their cherished Department from the indignity of being forced to serve counterfeit *political* needs, the highway leaders never pause to consider whether their own traditional definition of "needs" is losing its validity. To them, transportation needs and "traffic needs" are one and the same thing. Their history, their training, their manner of selection and promotion, indeed their whole experience has led them to identify "traffic needs" with "highways" absolutely. Men whose mode of thinking is bounded by rubber tires and concrete do not speculate on whether traffic needs can become something different in an urban, energy-short era.

If you imply that these external changes in the seventies have created a situation in which the Highway Department itself has begun to supply transportation that is not based on "needs," the leaders find that statement ultimately incomprehensible. Whether building an interstate or building a loop around Taylor, they are simply doing what they and their predecessors have always done. Interpreting the accusation in the light of their experience they can only think you are suggesting they are corrupt, that *they* build roads as political patronage: for in their injured pride that is the only sort of violation of "needs" they know.

It is not surprising, then, that the Department leaders tend to see the same dangers that the highway builders see—the danger of running out of funds, of not being able to plan ahead. In a real sense the interests of the highway bureaucracy and the highway lobby have become identical. And why should not a commissioner and a lobbyist open a bank together, if there is no longer a point of view to influence "unduly"?

Proposals for mass transit in Texas focus on buses not merely because buses are the only form of public transportation that can be put to work immediately, but also because the idea that transit can be "mass" is an unfamiliar, undigested one. At the very time when lines at the filling stations are demonstrating that transit may have to be "mass," and substantially so, in the very near future, public transportation is still regarded as no more than a means for moving people around whose poverty, disability, or temporarily empty gas tank prevents them from using a private car. Unquestioned is the assumption that we can rely on the automobile . . . forever.

Is there a more sensible way of getting people around than having them propel two tons of steel at eight miles per gallon? Should there be?

Texans may soon be forced to make some hard choices about their transportation policies. At the moment, because of the dedicated fund, those choices are made for them: the Highway Department will go right on building highways until someone tells it to stop or to slow down. They have the money and they define the "needs."

There is no way short of constitutional amendment for the public to redefine those needs or to force their moderation so that more money can be spent on other things. New funds can of course be created for new needs, be they mass transit or anything else. But the highway money will still be spent. And it is as much "misgovernment" to build things the taxpayers do not need, as it is to *fail* to build those things they *do* need. Even if you build them honestly. Even if you build them well. In its studied, proud efforts to avoid making the latter mistake, the Highway Department may now be in danger of making the former.

The reaction of the Department toward suggestions that it be given responsibility for all forms of public transportation, becoming a sort of state Department of Transportation, is a telling commentary on its insularity. All three commissioners told the Convention that mass transit programs should be handled by some other agency. Commissioner Simons added that putting the two together would "dilute the thrust" of the Highway Department.

Instead of saying, "We are engineering professionals; we are ready to do what the state needs. When you wanted good roads, we built the best in the country. If you want good mass transit, we can build that best too," the Department has fled from the new responsibility. Through changing times they have remained precisely what the lobby planned for them to be: a bureaucracy totally committed to roads.

Texans may or may not want a vigorous governmental effort to develop mass transit; different polls yield different results. But if they do, they cannot be optimistic when they see the Highway Department, the Mass Transportation Commission, and the penetrating influence of the highway lobby on the selection of the men who set these agencies' policies. They cannot expect the Texas Good Roads Association—even if renamed "Texans for Better Transportation"—to send forth the word to chambers of commerce and local governments that a new day is at hand. Most important of all, they cannot expect their existing transportation bureaucracy to step back and take an impartial look at other types of transportation.

If Texans want this done, they will have to find a way to circumvent the most immovable bureaucracy and the most irresistible lobby in their state. If the people want an exit, they will have to hire their own bulldozer. ★

Politics

by Paul Burka

THE FIRING LINE

When 68 employees were fired from a controversial state agency, Republicans called it good business—but it was really good politics.

Omar Harvey, the man Bill Clements picked to trim what many have called the fattest agency in state government, stood in the center of his office with his back to a clear plastic box, glanced at his watch, and began the countdown. "I don't have to look," the new executive director of the Texas Department of Community Affairs (TDCA) said proudly. "I *know* it's going to drop in exactly fifteen seconds . . . ten, nine, eight . . ." Just as he reached one, there was action inside the box: a small silver ball dropped into a gray trough and rolled along until it plunked into a hole signifying that the time was now 9:38. Omar Harvey nodded his head and smiled.

Harvey is a man who likes things to function—like his eye-catching office clock—with promptness, precision, and a bit of flair. Before he arrived in Austin in early January, the agency he now heads rarely demonstrated any of those qualities. It was, its numerous critics contended, a model of bad government: top-heavy (with 78 managers out of 258 employees), overstaffed (seven people did nothing but draw up the monthly payroll), and impossibly rigid (all managerial decisions had to be approved by an executive committee paralyzed by infighting and petty jealousies). Hostile legislators had sworn to dismantle TDCA, and even the agency's friends admitted something had to be done.

Although TDCA had been created back in 1971 to assist smaller cities and counties, the agency was frequently at war with the very people it was supposed to serve. But TDCA's bad reputation went beyond mismanagement. The agency serves as a conduit for federal grant programs—manpower training, drug abuse, housing, and early childhood education, to name a few—and there were whispers (never documented) in political circles of remarkable similarities between grant recipients and supporters of then-Governor Dolph Briscoe. Auditing was frequently sloppy. TDCA was, in short, exactly the kind of unwieldy, inefficient, do-good operation that makes businessmen shake their heads in dismay and conclude that what government needs is to be run more like a business. So it was inevitable that,

In one state agency Governor Clements' head-rolling plans are going like clockwork.

when businessman Bill Clements became governor in January, TDCA was in for a long, hard look.

TDCA wasn't alone, of course. Clements pledged to reduce the number of state employees by 25,000, a magnitude that leaves little doubt he considers most state agencies overstaffed and underworked. Unfortunately for Clements, however, there is little a Texas governor can do about such independent fiefdoms as the Department of Mental Health and Mental Retardation, where the number of workers has steadily risen despite an equally steady decline in the number of clients served. The trouble is that MHMR, like most of state government, is run by an autonomous board that the governor appoints but does not control. He can influence them only by persuasion and example. But TDCA is different. Originally part of the governor's office, it never achieved total independence: the executive director serves at the pleasure of the governor and there is no board or commission to get in the way. TDCA was ideally suited to be the Normandy of Clements' assault on the bureaucratic fortress, and Omar Harvey, Clements' Republican primary campaign chairman and a managerial heavyweight, was ideally suited to lead the charge.

Harvey came to TDCA from Dallas, where he was president of First International Services Corporation, a subsidiary of First International Bancshares, and the executive vice president of First International's flagship, First National Bank. But banking is not where his heart is. "I'll tell you what I am," Harvey said as we talked about the firing of 68 TDCA employees that made statewide headlines in February. "I'm an IBMer. I spent twenty-three years with that company, and I'll tell you, it's got the finest management philosophy of any company in the world. Everybody has individual responsibilities and set goals. At IBM, committees just give input to the person who has to make the decision, they don't make decisions themselves. I don't care if you are my brother, if you don't produce, you don't survive."

Harvey normally talks in measured, soft tones, but management theory is his passion and his thoughts were running ahead of his words. He started firing questions at me: "What's the difference between a government job and IBM? Why is banking more like government? What do banks, insurance companies, and public utilities have in common? They're all institutions with regulators looking over their shoulders. They're run by committee, everything's on the CYA principle. Cover your ass. If you want to loan me two million, the first thing you do is get fourteen signatures on that loan. And if I don't pay, you bring that piece of paper right back to the loan committee and show them all their signatures. No one is responsible. Institutions!" He shook his head sadly.

"This is not the way this country was built. This country was built on having a job to do and doing it. During Clements' campaign I had to get three hundred people together in Fort Worth on one day's notice. These are prominent people, busy people. What would you do? Send them a telegram, right? So I went to Western Union, and they said they couldn't get the wires out in time. I went to the post office, and they said they couldn't get the letters delivered. I ended up hiring three porters to hand-deliver the invitations. Everybody else wanted to hide behind regulations. Well, this agency isn't going to work that way, not anymore."

Harvey briefly outlined his plan for TDCA. It was pure IBM: delegate authority, fix responsibility, let people develop the most efficient ways of getting things done. One of his first actions was to disband the dilatory executive committee. (A program to correct housing defects that cause high winter utility bills, proposed in August, was kicked around by the executive committee until January—too late to do any good this winter.) He centralized duplicated functions like auditing and public relations, which previously had been scattered around in each of TDCA's nine divisions. He roamed through the five-story building, meeting individual employees ("Some told me the executive director had never been on their floor before"), and called the first mass meeting in their memory. His promise to evaluate performance and "get rid of the deadwood" drew sustained applause. Less than a month later, 68 employees got their pink slips.

How does a supermanager go about paring his work force by 25 per cent? In Omar Harvey's case, it was a little like a doctor helping an obese patient to lose weight by lopping off a foot, an arm, and an ear. There were no personnel evaluations ("We lost some good people," Harvey admits) and no studies to find out which divisions produced and which ones didn't. Nor was there any attempt to identify superfluous positions below the managerial level. Harvey set up a reorganization task force, adding Clements' campaign aide Pete Collumb, a personnel expert, and gave them an organization chart without names. The idea of "getting rid of deadwood," as Harvey had termed it, was abandoned from the start; the task force was told to look at positions, not people. It quickly became evident that they weren't even supposed to do much of that. Collumb decided how many people each division had to cut, called in the division directors one by one, and passed along a quota—usually between 20 and 25 per cent. As one member put it, "The rest of us just sat there. It was strictly Pete's show." There was no appeal. One director pointed out that his area had lost nineteen people in the last four years and urged Collumb to start from the beginning, examine the programs, and decide how many people were necessary to run them. No dice. "If you don't want to make the cuts, I'll make them," he was told. The director made the cuts.

In the end the reductions had no relation to a division's work or its reputation within the agency. This led to some strange anomalies: manpower, generally regarded as one of the better divisions, was left with 36 people to handle $65 million in federal funds; drug abuse, a jungle of inefficiency, emerged with 35 people to handle $7.6 million. That hardly seems the way IBM would have done it. Whatever was achieved by eliminating high-level bottlenecks may have been undone by indiscriminate quotas at lower levels.

The cuts may not have made sense from a business standpoint, but the truth is that Omar Harvey was acting not as a businessman but as a politician—one close enough to Bill Clements that he attends the governor's daily staff meeting. There may have been better, fairer, more efficient ways to handle the cuts at TDCA, but they would have taken months. Several years ago the state highway department quietly cut back its staff 20 per cent by going around the state to private engineering firms and getting jobs for people it had to let go. That took a year—a blink in the life of a bureaucracy, but a lifetime in politics. The Legislature is in town, about to become deadlocked with Clements in a test of wills over the state budget; at every other state agency piranhas are studying the governor's every move to see how serious he is about cutting the state payroll. Clements needs a symbol *now,* not next fall, and TDCA was the only available choice, even if that meant sacrificing 68 people. The across-the-board cuts at TDCA were to Clements what Proposition 13's across-the-board cuts were to California: the right thing in the wrong way. But that's the way politics is. Sometimes, if you wait to do things the right way, the moment passes, never to return. Maybe that's why businessmen who try to run government like a business never seem to succeed—and maybe Omar Harvey is turning out to be not an IBMer at heart, but a politician. ★

Texans in Washington and What They Do There

★

CHAPTER NINE

Buying Power, Harry Hurt III (November 76)
Grasping at Strauss, Stephen Chapman (February 78)
The Big Thicket Tangle, Al Reinert (July 73)

BUYING POWER

by Harry Hurt III

The dollar doesn't buy what it used to, and neither does a political contribution.

Houston oilman Robert Mosbacher tells a sexy story about the newly reformed art of political money raising. The story comes from Mosbacher's experience this year as President Ford's national campaign finance chairman and involves two "women of the street" who meet one night on a downtown street corner. The younger woman is wearing a tattered dress and an old shawl, but the older one is flashing a brand-new mink coat, brown and luscious.

"What a beautiful coat," the younger woman says enviously. "Did you have to pay for it with your own money?"

"No," replies the older woman. "I got one of my boyfriends to give me three thousand dollars, and I bought it with that."

"Oh," says the younger woman, and the two slink off into the night.

Several weeks later, the two women meet again. This time the younger one also sports a brand-new mink coat, brown and luscious.

"What a beautiful coat," the older one says with a grin. "Did you get one of your boyfriends to give you three thousand?"

"No," replies the younger woman with a beleaguered look. "I had to get a thousand boyfriends to give me three dollars each."

That may sound like the kind of story that is told at the beginning of speeches before men's luncheon clubs, but for Mosbacher and many other veteran political money men it neatly illustrates the changes brought on by the new federal election and campaign finance laws. Under these statutes, individual campaign contributors are now limited to giving $1000 per candidate per election and can give no more than $25,000 total to all candidates in any one election year. Corporate, labor, and special-interest groups may contribute through "political action committees." These PACs are limited to giving $5000 per candidate per election, but there is no aggregate limit on PAC contributions in any election year. The new laws also require the reporting of the "in-kind" contributions so traditional at all levels of politics—the free use of an office, a phone, a car, a jet—and demand much more detailed accounting and filing procedures.

With the advent of public financing for the general election, most presidential fund raising is now confined to the primaries. Here also are new limitations. This year, each candidate was allowed to raise and spend no more than $13.5 million in the primaries nationwide. The surviving candidates, Carter and Ford, then received about $22 million apiece in public funds to spend in the general election.

Many top politicos say the new finance laws have already proven to be the most important single factor in the 1976 campaign. There is no doubt that their effect has been pervasive and profound, and largely favorable to Jimmy Carter. In the past, a few big fat cat contributors like Clement Stone of Chicago, who gave Richard Nixon more than $2 million in 1972, and Houstonian George R. Brown, who gave Lyndon Johnson untold thousands during his political career, could provide seed money for a campaign war chest—and gain predominant influence—through their individual contributions alone. Now money for political campaigns must be raised from a large group of people. Big contributors have less chance to gain influence because they are limited in what they can give just like everyone else, and their donations are just part of a larger crowd. Nor can a heavily backed candidate like Richard Nixon, who officially raised over $60 million for his 1972 campaign, bully his opponent with sheer financial power.

As the campaigns of favorite sons John Connally and Lloyd Bentsen faltered, many traditional big-money political givers in Texas responded to all this by choosing to give little or not at all to the 1976 campaigns. "Frankly, they didn't see what their money was gonna buy," observed one veteran Democratic fund raiser. "A lot of them thought it was just better to sit this one out and save their money."

Ironically, the presidential candidate who did the best financially in Texas was the one who lost the state in the primary—Gerald Ford. According to Ford campaign finance officials, the President's men had raised over $820,000 in Texas by the time of the Republican Convention, making Texas his second-best fund-raising state. California, with total contributions of just over $1 million, was the only state that gave him more.

Jimmy Carter, meanwhile, collected about $400,000 in Texas, or slightly less than half of what President Ford got, according to Carter campaign treasurer, Robert Lipschutz. But reports on file with the Federal Election Commission (FEC) show that Carter also spent far less in the Texas primary—just $84,000, compared with the $500,000 spent by Ford. Not too surprising, Carter's most profitable fund-raising state was Georgia, where he collected a whopping $1.6 million.

In addition to providing money, Texas also provided some key manpower for both Ford and Carter money-raising efforts. With the waning of the state's fabled fat cats has come the rise of the Texas "thin men." The thin men are the new breed of doers, those politically interested businessmen and lawyers who somehow seem too young, too agile, and, in a few cases, not quite rich enough to qualify as full-fledged fat cats. Just as the new campaign finance laws have shifted the emphasis from the size of individual contributions to their volume, they have shifted the real power in campaign finance from the money givers to these money getters, the men who can do the sort of organizing now required of a campaign fund raiser. Among the most prominent of the senior Texas thin men in this year's national campaigns are Robert Mosbacher, the 49-year-old Ford finance chief and champion sailor from Houston, and, on the Carter side, 45-year-old Dallas business executive Jess Hay, a veteran Dolph Briscoe finance man, who is chairman of the board of Lomas & Nettleton, the nation's largest mortgage banking firm. The Carter forces also benefited from the efforts of several junior thin men, relative newcomers to the world of national campaign financing, most notably 34-year-old stockbroker John Dalton of Dallas, 35-year-old lawyer David Berg of Houston, 31-year-old businessman-attorney Richard J. Trabulsi, Jr., of Houston, and 43-year-old Conoco vice president Tom Sigler of Houston.

One of the few traditional big givers to take an active role in the actual fund raising this year was Dallas real estate developer Trammell Crow, who headed the Texas campaign finance effort for his close friend President Ford.

Many members of the Texas establishment, however, were hedging their bets on the presidential race this year by contributing to both sides at the same time. Houston oilman and developer George P. Mitchell, for example, gave $1000 to President Ford and $250 to Jimmy Carter. Henry F. Le Mieux, chairman of the board of Raymond International, and Alfred Glassell, a wealthy Houston investor who sits on the board of the El Paso Company and First City Bancorp, each gave $1000 to Ford and $1000 to Carter.

Many of the state's major corporations, law firms, and interest groups, which may contribute up to $5000 per candidate through their political action committees, also firmly entrenched themselves in both political camps. The Nursing Home Administrators Political Action Committee, for example, gave $5000 to President Ford and $5000 to Jimmy Carter. Bracewell, Patterson, one of Houston's most prestigious giant law firms, is represented on the Republican side by longtime GOP bigwig Hal DeMoss, who gave $500 to Ford, and on the Democratic side by partner John Cope, an active Houston fund raiser who gave Carter $1000, and by the firm's political action committee (the P Committee), which also gave $1000. Likewise, Houston Natural Gas (HNG) chairman Robert Herring was one of the first to join President Ford's local fund-raising committee, but he is also listed as contributing $250 to Jimmy Carter. HNG president Joe Foy, meanwhile, gave $500 to Carter and co-sponsored an important establishment fund raiser for Carter in July.

As these names attest, both Ford and Carter got substantial support from leaders of the petroleum and energy industries. Other prominent oil industry contributors to Ford (each gave $1000) include George F. Kirby, president of Texas Eastern Transmission Company; Raymond M. Holliday, chairman of Hughes Tool Company; and David C. McMahon and Walter A. Schmidt, executives of American Quasar Petroleum Company of Fort Worth. James J. Graham, a senior vice president of Exxon USA, has made a $1000 contribution, which is listed as "pending" on the latest available Ford campaign report.

Carter's list of oil industry contributors is just as impressive. On the list of $1000 contributors are Brown & Root and Texas Eastern founder George R. Brown; Scurlock Oil founder Eddy Scurlock; and Scurlock president Jack Blanton, who is also the president of the Mid-Continent Oil and Gas Association. The Houston independent oil family of Pat Rutherford, Sr., Pat Rutherford, Jr., and Mike Rutherford each gave $1000.

In some cases, however, members of the same family ended up on different sides of the fence. Hunt Oil heirs Ray Hunt and Ruth Hunt of Dallas each contributed $1000 to Jimmy Carter, but half brother Bunker Hunt gave $1000 to President Ford, thus mirroring the internal schism reportedly dividing their family. While the three Rutherfords mentioned above were Carter contributors, both Pat, Jr., and Mike also gave $1000 to Ford.

One way of increasing financial clout under the new contribution limits is the familiar method of husband and wife giving. Among the notable spouse tandems this year were Dayle and David Berg, Mr. and Mrs. Jess Hay, Mr. and Mrs. Harry Cullen of Houston, and Mr. and Mrs. Miledge A. Hart of Dallas, all of whom each gave $1000 to Jimmy Carter; and Mr. and Mrs. Edwin Cox of Dallas, Mr. and Mrs. Charles W. Duncan, Sr., of Houston, and Mr. and Mrs. Estill Heyser of Dallas, each of whom gave $1000 to President Ford.

President Ford boasted a number of luminary political contributors this year, including famed heart surgeon Dr. Denton A. Cooley of Houston ($1000); former Nixon defender Charles Alan Wright of Austin ($150); former Dallas Mayor Erik Jonsson ($750); and Howard Hughes heir William R. Lummis of Houston ($500).

The biggest name missing from the list of Ford fund raisers, however, was that of John B. Connally, who delayed announcing his support for the President until shortly before the Republican Convention. In fact, Connally even got headline publicity for contributing $300 to his law firm's political action committee, which gave $3000 to Jimmy Carter and only $1000 to President Ford.

But if one of the most interesting stories of the Republican campaign financing effort is how smoothly it went even without Connally's assistance, the hidden story of the Carter fund-raising effort is how poorly it went until the Bentsen-Briscoe people came aboard. FEC records show that by April 1, 1976, Texans for Carter had raised about $10,000 in contributions over $100 in the state; the Ford people had raised over $280,000 in contributions over $100, despite the Reagan challenge and the possibility of Connally entering the race.

Texas political donors changed their tune considerably after June 8, the day Carter locked up the nomination by winning the Ohio primary and finishing second in New Jersey. This was when the Briscoe-Bentsen people, having already been disappointed once, came on board in force. The key figure was Jess Hay, who had been a major fund raiser for Bentsen's presidential effort. At Governor Briscoe's urging, the Carter people named Hay their statewide finance chairman and later gave him a position on the national campaign finance committee. Despite his late start, Hay quickly proved his financial worth by organizing a Dallas dinner which cleared about $210,000.

The Dallas event and a fund raiser in Houston, which netted about $50,000, gave the Carter fund-raising effort a needed lift. By early July, Jimmy Carter was shaking hands and having lunch with some of the most flush Texas fat cats.

Nearly everyone from Eugene McCarthy to Senator James Buckley has been critical of the new campaign finance laws; this year's most active Texas campaign finance men are no exception. The provision subject to the most controversy is the limitation on individual campaign contributions. This is what prompted McCarthy, Buckley, and others to file a federal suit this spring alleging that the new law is in violation of the First Amendment because it limits an individual's right to express his views on behalf of a candidate or a political idea. In response, the Supreme Court ruled this spring that an individual (not a corporation) may spend as much as he likes on a candidate of his choice as long as he does not confer with the candidate and coordinate his efforts with those of the regular campaign, except to confirm the legality of his methods.

This "independent expenditure" exemption is not as much of a loophole as it might appear. It means, in effect, that you can buy as many billboards and television commercials as you wish for the candidate of your choice—but you can't have any help from the campaign staff. You may not, for example, sponsor a commercial distributed by the campaign headquarters. You can't arrange a rally at which the candidate will appear or which his staff will help organize. You can't even use the candidate's logo on your billboards. In other words, your efforts must be just what the name implies: independent. For all practical purposes, that makes it useless to both donor and donee, and its only real practical value is that it enables the Supreme Court to rule that free speech is not abrogated by the law.

Ford finance chairman Mosbacher said that the only visible effects of independent expenditure he has seen was a large billboard for Ford near the Houston Intercontinental Airport; it was paid for by Houston oil operator A. T. Stautberg. Carter fund raiser Trabulsi said he did not know of any independent expenditures on Carter's behalf in Texas. A top Carter aide in Atlanta pointed out that the language of the independent expenditure provision "discourages a lot of legitimate political activity by ordinary citizens," because even minimal expenditures for such things as homemade posters and signs must be counted as a political contribution if it involves the official campaign organization in any way.

One method used to get around the spending limits this year is to run the campaign through the regular party apparatus. Under the law, the national Democratic and Republican party committees may still raise $3.2 million for each candidate to spend in the general election. In addition, the law says that expenditures which are made by the parties on behalf of the ticket generally are not counted against the spending limit of any individual candidate; these expenditures include office overhead, rallies, voter registration, and get-out-the-vote drives. Thus, the new laws have given the old theme of party unity an important financial meaning. An example is the Carter headquarters in Houston. The office, which is listed as a Democratic party office rather than a Carter headquarters, has literature and bumper stickers for nearly all the local Democratic office seekers, not just the presidential and vice-presidential candidates; its expenses are part of the Democratic party budget, not the budget of the Carter-Mondale campaign.

Unlike Eugene McCarthy and James Buckley, most Texas fund raisers said they felt that a limitation on individual contributions was good "in principle," and that it had encouraged much wider citizen participation, but that they would like to see the current $1000 ceiling raised to $2000, $3000, or perhaps even $5000. Mosbacher reasoned that the current $1000 limit makes fund raising a difficult and expensive task. He added that he did not think a $5000 contribution by an individual would buy much influence in a national campaign.

Carter fund raiser Jess Hay, on the other hand, criticized the limitations on campaign expenditures, especially in nonpresidential campaigns, because "they place an overwhelming advantage in the hands of the incumbents." Hay observed that "the guy whose name is already known just has to deliver his message; the unknown must first worry about being taken seriously and being recognized." It is harder, he maintained, for the unknown candidate to become known. Ironically, the major criticism of the unlimited finance laws of the past was that they gave the incumbent an advantage, that the overreaching power of his incumbency made it easier for him to raise more money than his opponents. One need look no further than the Texas Senate race to realize that a strong incumbent like Lloyd Bentsen benefits from the law. Alan Steelman, who would have had little difficulty raising money except for the ceiling on contributions, has run into severe money troubles under the new law. With big Republican donors limited to $1000 each, Steelman ran short of money in September, curtailed his television ads, and pared his staff.

You can even get an argument here and there about whether the demise of fat cat contributors should be cheered or mourned. One of the mourners is Robert Allen, chairman of the Houston-based Gulf Resources Corporation. Allen has had some experience in presidential fund raising in the past. Remember the so-called Mexican money—the $100,000 that originated in Houston, passed through a Guadalajara bank, returned to Houston, and was flown to Washington and Richard Nixon, eventually to reappear in the bank account of convicted Watergate burglar Bernard Barker? Well, Allen contributed the money and was one of the men who flew it to Washington on a Pennzoil corporation jet. (A congressional committee and a federal grand jury investigated Allen and Pennzoil in 1973 but later cleared both of any wrongdoing.) Allen is still contributing to presidential and other political campaigns, but the new laws which were inspired in part by the Mexican money episode have diminished both his role and his enthusiasm.

"There's no way that an individual can really affect a campaign now, because you can only give a thousand dollars," he says. "Under the old system, a candidate was required to listen to those who supported him financially. You knew he was being advised by knowledgeable, informed people. Public financing makes candidates less responsive to these people." ★

Politics   by Stephen Chapman

GRASPING AT STRAUSS

Is Bob Strauss really one of the most powerful men in Washington? Or is his power mostly an illusion?

There are a lot of stories about Bob Strauss, but one of the best is about his swimming pool. A few years back, the story goes, Strauss built a pool in the backyard of his Dallas home. It was quite a pool: spacious, built into an interior courtyard, surrounded by dozens of tropical plants.

One day a guest, being shown around the house, complimented Strauss on his lovely pool and remarked that he certainly must enjoy swimming in it. Well, no, said Strauss, I don't swim. Then surely Mrs. Strauss uses it a lot, said the guest. Not really, came the reply, she doesn't swim much either.

"Well, then," said the guest, "why did you build the damn thing?"

Strauss grinned. "Well, at the end of a hard day at the office, I like to come home, fix myself a drink, sit out by this pool, and say to myself, 'Bob Strauss, you're one rich son of a bitch.'"

Right now Robert Strauss is also one powerful son of a bitch. As special trade representative, a Cabinet-level post with ambassadorial status, he has the weighty and highly visible responsibility of trying to improve the United States' position in the world trade arena. He is a close adviser to the President, who likes him, trusts him, and gives him a variety of troubleshooting chores—lobbying on Capitol Hill, offering counsel on political problems, and, since Bert Lance's departure, representing the Administration to the business community. His hand can also be detected in the recent resignation of Kenneth Curtis from the chairmanship of the Democratic National Committee, Strauss' last job.

All this is particularly impressive in the light of Strauss' tenuous position a year and a half ago. Jimmy Carter, it was becoming clear, would win the Democratic nomination on the first ballot, which appeared to spell oblivion for Strauss. He had made no secret of his personal distaste for Carter, who Strauss had appointed as head of the Democratic Campaign Committee. "He thought Carter was a pushy, arrogant little nobody using that position to advance his own ambitions," says one

Texan Stephen Chapman lives in Washington and has written for New Republic *and* Washington Monthly.

Bob Strauss (l.) and George Mahon: two approaches to Washington's power game

reporter who was close to Strauss then. In turn, Carter offered Strauss as a sacrificial lamb to liberals who were unenthusiastic about the party chairman; he promised to replace Strauss as soon as the convention was over, and only with some difficulty did his staff persuade him that Strauss would be indispensable to the campaign.

Jimmy Carter is known as a man who tries to keep cold reason riding herd on his emotions, and it no doubt was a sober assessment of Strauss' worth that persuaded Carter to keep him around. Given the present Democratic President and a Congress with a lopsided Democratic majority, one tends to forget the condition of the party in 1972, when Strauss took over as chairman. The emerging Republican majority looked like a lead-pipe cinch, even to such cold-eyed political operators as John Connally. Strauss got a lot of help from Watergate in rebuilding his party, but the credit goes mostly to him. Even his liberal critics readily concede his due for fusing the party's disparate elements—the McGovernites, organized labor, the Wallace people, the Richard Daley regulars—into a solid, if not uniform, block. Strauss had gained the chairmanship on the strength of his recognized performance as party treasurer, a position he acquired at a time when the Democrats were $8 million in debt and running a monthly deficit of $100,000. (Strauss' first suggestion was to take out a large life insurance policy on each DNC employee and draw straws once a month to determine who would jump out the window.)

His announced intention as chairman was to "deliver a party to the nominee, not a nominee to the party." Strauss' determination to let the party work its own will proved crucial; a chairman clearly partial to any faction would have dangerously deepened the rifts. Like a broken bone that, once healed, is stronger than before, the Democratic party that Jimmy Carter took over in July 1976 was healthier than it had been since FDR's heyday. Carter probably figured, rightly, that any man who could do what Bob Strauss did was far too valuable to lose. So Carter not only gave him a chance to demonstrate his loyalty during the campaign, but once Strauss had proven it, also took him along to the White House. Political pros like Strauss are necessary to any administration, but he is especially important because Carter's inner circle consists almost entirely of people with no experience in Washington politics. He is the consummate insider in an Administration full of outsiders.

From the looks of his resurrection, Strauss seems to be a powerful man. But this presumption rests on a one-dimensional view of power. In Washington, power takes many forms—the legislative responsibility of members of Congress; the influence of ideological and economic interests; the administrative authority of Cabinet officers; and the obscure power of the men behind the scenes—the latter group including Bob Strauss. Members of the inner circle around the President clearly often help form policy, but presidential advisers are not all alike. At one pole are the men of strong convictions who value their positions mainly for what they can be used to accomplish—advisers like Alexander Hamilton, Colonel House, Harry Hopkins, and, more recently, Clark Clifford and Alan Greenspan. Personal ambition may not be completely insignificant to such people, but it usually takes a backseat to idealistic objectives. At the opposite end are the *consiglieri*, men who, in order to be near the center of power, set aside their own views (if any) to provide counsel on the likely consequences of given actions. This second category includes Strauss, who seems perfectly content to serve whatever purposes his boss chooses; from all appearances, he has no say on policy other than its political implications. Strauss' influence is limited to how best to sell the goods. To Carter, Strauss' power is really only a reflection of the President's.

Strauss' pliability apparently extends even to occasional sycophancy. A recent incident: Strauss raises his hand at a Cabinet meeting and is recognized by Carter. "Mr. President," says Strauss, "I wonder if I could waste three minutes of your time." All right, says Carter, a notorious clock-watcher. Strauss launches into a harangue of the other Cabinet members. They're lazy, he tells them. They're not team players. They're not doing enough to push the President's fine programs through Congress.

When at last Strauss is done, Carter turns to him. "That was five minutes." A pause, and then a big grin. "But none of it was wasted."

Nobody ever said Bob Strauss wasn't a team player. Once aboard the Carter campaign, he did everything from raising money to keeping the party regulars in line. He probably saved the day in Texas, where he arranged for Lady Bird Johnson and her daughter Luci to campaign for Carter after the disastrous *Playboy* interview, which included his description of Lyndon Johnson as a liar. Strauss was named trade representative because of his unrivaled skill at fashioning compromises among apparently irreconcilable groups, a skill he honed at the DNC.

Handling the trade negotiations is a full-time job, but it hasn't stopped Strauss from shouldering other tasks when the President needs him. Lately Carter has needed him most on the Hill, where he has lobbied for the Panama Canal treaty, the cargo preference bill, and the energy program. He keeps a low profile, though, because of his lingering unpopularity with party liberals. "He's into the energy thing a lot more than he or anyone at the White House or on the Hill wants to admit," says a friend of Strauss. "If it got into the papers, all the liberals would be saying, 'What's that goddamned Texan doing over here?'" On Capitol Hill, Strauss' backslapping, horse-trading approach is a refreshing change from the self-righteous demeanor of his boss and the fabled ineptitude of Carter's chief lobbyist, Frank Moore. Strauss is adept at dealing from a position of either strength or weakness. Says National Committeewoman and Texas liberal stalwart Billie Carr, an old Strauss foe, "He's just like LBJ. If he's got fifty-one per cent of the vote, he's a tough son of a bitch, but if he's only got forty-nine, he's the sweetest guy in the world."

Strauss has also kept a hand in the affairs of the Democratic National Committee, where he still has many old friends. He was not happy with Kenneth Curtis' way of running things. (If there's anything Bob Strauss can't stand, it's a poor team player.) Instead of enforcing strict discipline on his national committee members, Curtis let them argue things out, with the chips falling where they might. That was not how Bob Strauss ran the DNC. "Before every meeting, he'd talk to every member about exactly how things would go in the meeting," says Carr, "and that's exactly how they would go." When Curtis let the committee pass a resolution that fell short of unequivocal approval of Carter's Panama Canal treaty, Strauss let him know he was no longer wanted.

It's almost impossible to picture any of Strauss' longtime cronies—say, Lloyd Bentsen or John Connally—shilling for a measure that would damage Texas as much as Carter's energy program, but Strauss apparently got the pill down without gagging. It's not clear whether Strauss simply has no ideological moorings ("Philosophically," says one admirer, "he doesn't give a damn") or just doesn't mind setting his views aside whenever there's something to be gained by it. But state loyalties plainly count for little with him. Carter, after all, has already proven himself the most anti-sunbelt president since Herbert Hoover. Besides his broken pledge to deregulate new natural gas prices, Carter has moved methodically to channel federal funds into the decaying Northeast. Most notable is his urban aid program, which HUD Secretary Patricia Harris promises will be aimed at those cities most in need—which, in Carter's terms, means those up East. And it was the West and South that would have suffered from Carter's elimination of eighteen water projects, only nine of which have been reinstated.

On a dozen different matters, the President has made obvious his intention of buttressing his strength in the snowbelt, regardless of the cost to the South and the West. With his eye on 1980, Carter no doubt figures that the South will support its native son again no matter what he does, and that the West will reject him with the same near-unanimity it did in 1976. Forsaking the old political formula of rewarding your friends and punishing your enemies, the President has embraced a new strategy: Ignore the people who love you or hate you and woo the ones who are lukewarm. Pivotal to this strategy is Bob Strauss, the Texas wheeler-dealer who can cozy up to Massachusetts' Tip O'Neill or Louisiana's Russell Long with equal ease. It was Bob Strauss, after all, who once defended his flexibility by arguing, "If you're in politics, you're a whore anyhow. It doesn't make any difference who you sleep with."

Strauss is a highly successful representative of the old Washington type, the faceless, behind-the-scenes power-seeker. The city is full of such people, who survive on their ability to shed their philosophical ideals and personal loyalties as easily as a snake sheds its skin. Try for a moment to think of one issue Bob Strauss feels strongly about, or even one politician he is genuinely devoted to. Certainly not the energy bill or free trade; certainly not Jimmy Carter. Such matters, if they concern Strauss at all, are secondary to the central aim of climbing the ladder to the top. Bob Strauss obviously relishes his position: advising the President, as any former presidential adviser will testify, can be awfully heady stuff—just as to a poor boy from Stamford, simply owning a swimming pool is a distinct pleasure, whether or not he ever gets in it.

On political matters, Strauss is clearly able to make his preferences felt, and he is even capable of purging a national chairman for insufficient servility to the White House. The new chairman, Texan John White, though not a close Strauss ally, is acceptable to Strauss and no doubt will take care not to antagonize him. But again the question is, to what purpose is all this? What goals does it serve? And the answer one arrives at is that it really serves no end but perpetuating and enhancing whatever power is held by Jimmy Carter, who will choose its ends without the advice of Bob Strauss.

One alternative to spending your life taking orders from someone else is to run for office yourself. Strauss considered running for John Tower's Senate seat in 1972 and again this year but never found in himself the drive to make the race. Since Strauss places no great value on abstract ideals, he would gain little by holding office and having the freedom to make his own decisions about which programs he favors and which he opposes. Troubling over such matters would be a nuisance. Attaining decisive power on Capitol Hill, moreover, is a slow, tedious process, requiring long hours in committee work, incessant campaigning and cultivation of congressional colleagues, detailed knowledge of specialized areas, and, ideally, integrity and a commitment to some goal besides personal advancement.

A case in point is Texas' senior Congressman George Mahon. Mahon is hardly a household word in Texas, though as chairman of the Appropriations Committee he probably holds more real power than any Texan since LBJ. He came to Washington 43 years ago from West Texas. During his tenure as head of the Defense Appropriations Subcommittee, Mahon has been generally sympathetic to the views of the Pentagon, but unlike most members who share his views, he has invariably refused the proffered favors of military contractors. In deference to his rectitude, no one questions Mahon's motives, however much they dispute his judgment. He is known as a congressman who votes on the basis of reasoned and well-informed conviction. For that reason he commands more attention than a member who simply holds his finger to the wind on every vote.

Mahon's influence can be measured in the October vote on the B-1 bomber, which President Carter ordered scrapped last July. The House canceled the project in September by the narrowest of margins, but the plane's supporters, angered by Administration talk of replacing the B-1 with the FB-111 (a clearly inferior plane), managed to bring the question to the House floor again, with good prospects of winning this time. The surprise came when Mahon rose to speak his piece. Reminding his colleagues of his unstinting support of national defense, he told the B-1's backers that they were "looking at national defense as if through a little knothole, as though the bomber was everything that was going to save us from war or win the war if it should come." His voice rising, Mahon demanded, "Does not everybody in this House know that the primary weapon of the future is the intercontinental ballistic missile? The only purpose of the bomber is to do the cleanup job. And after the atomic exchange we could probably do the cleanup in an oxcart." Minutes later the House killed the B-1 once and for all. Appropriations chairmen have a lot of sway in any case, but Mahon's power is enhanced by his character. Anyone in his position could decide the fate of bills as he chooses, but very few could affect the votes of their colleagues by mere intellectual persuasion. Mahon could have killed the B-1 appropriation in his committee but out of a sense of fair play allowed it to come to the floor, where he shot it down with an eloquent, forceful speech.

There are several lessons to be learned from George Mahon, not the least being that there is no substitute for an early start and a long life. The younger a congressman is when elected, the sooner he'll get enough seniority to make a difference and the more years he'll have to put it to use. The second is that you can't accomplish anything if you don't know your subject. Mahon has been one of Congress' most diligent students of defense issues, and his knowledge alone is enough to intimidate many of his colleagues. A lot of the matters Congress deals with are endlessly complicated, and getting to know your way around them requires years of study. The lazy and the easily bored have poor prospects for power. The last lesson, and perhaps most easily overlooked, is that integrity and a reputation for principle can carry considerable weight by themselves.

The root of the difference between Mahon and Strauss is that power is defined in large part by how it is used. Strauss' power is confined to the realm of pure politics—the fate of men. He has little say over questions of policy— the fate of nations. If Strauss valued any abstract ideals, he might be in a position to advance them; since outward success is his guiding principle, he can't really advance anything but himself. Mahon, on the other hand, has been able to make full use of his power because he sees it serving some noble purpose, and because his formal power is enhanced by his own character. After he retires from politics next year, Mahon can look back on a career distinguished by its devotion to principle, as well as its substantial achievements. And Strauss, staying in Washington to do the President's bidding, can sit down at the end of each long day at the White House and say to himself, "Bob Strauss, you're one powerful son of a bitch." ★

THE BIG THICKET TANGLE

by Al Reinert

Politicians, lumber companies, and even Time, Inc., are maneuvering to tell us what kind of park, if any, we'll have. That is, if there is any Big Thicket left by then.

Mike Buckley is reading *Sports Illustrated*. Strictly business. He had glanced through this particular issue before, but it had been only a cursory look. As a corporate officer of Time, Inc., the publishers of *Sports Illustrated,* he feels he needs to know what it's doing; he doesn't take the time to read very much, but feels uncomfortable at board of directors meetings if he can't talk about the magazines like everyone else does. When this issue first came in, he hadn't even noticed the article that now engaged him more completely than anything he had read in years.

The Union Camp Paper Company, said the article, had donated to the federal government 50,000 acres of Virginia's Great Dismal Swamp to be used as a park. *Sports Illustrated* lauded the company for their generosity and environmental consciousness and, it seems to Buckley, provided them a wealth of free publicity. Besides, he surmises, they could probably write off the donation for more than the land would be worth if sold outright. It seems like The Answer, a grand-slam solution to the one great nagging problem that has been looming over his shoulder for a decade.

Mike Buckley is the president of Eastex, Inc., a timber, pulpwood, and paper company that is one of the largest single landowners and employers in Southeast Texas. It is, as well, the most profitable subsidiary of that same Time, Inc., that publishes *Sports Illustrated, Fortune,* and *Time*. He is 63 years old and has spend the bulk of his life in the timber industry, transforming Texas pine trees into what must by now total a half-million houses and a billion tons of plywood, newsprint, cardboard, and all the other incarnations of cellulose. He loves the woods and the outdoors, hunting and fishing, and he is proudly convinced that his company is doing its level best to preserve that environment, to utilize its recreational potential while harvesting its trees. In the years he

A timber cord: ten centuries of growing

has been in the industry he has helped to introduce modern techniques of hybridization, conservation, tree farming, game and forestry management that seem to him a perfectly American blend of profitable private business and public-spirited concern for a national resource.

That's why he laughed when he first heard the proposal for a Big Thicket National Park, now more than ten years ago. He still hasn't changed that opinion much, but he won't say it in public anymore. It just seemed ludicrous to him, to take woodland wilderness and protect it, in its natural state, when those same lands could be used to build homes and the Gross National Product. His friend and fellow timber executive Arthur Temple had called the Thicket a "varmint-infested swamp," and he privately agreed with him, could see no value in maintaining it.

Despite Mike Buckley, though, the idea of preservation had grown over the years, and support for a park had spread well beyond laughing distance. Americans are all caught up in this crazy environmentalism, he thinks, and politicians who ought to know better are scared not to pander to it. It's been steadily closing in on him, this problem of taking a park out of the middle of his woods, and in recent years it has occupied more and more of his time. He has continually given ground, he feels, been willing to compromise, first with the "String of Pearls," then this fool moratorium on cutting, other things, and now the board of directors is even willing to endorse a 75,000-acre park. Since the first of the year he has been to meetings in New York, Acapulco, Austin, Chicago, Washington, some of them several times, and at all of them the dilemma of the park has been a principal topic. And now, after ten years of retreat from "a silly idea," virtually on the edge of defeat, he sees in the article a solution.

Mike Buckley hurriedly makes phone calls. New York, Washington, Diboll, Houston. Support from other timber companies is quickly secured. He calls in Ollie Crawford, his right hand, the front man for the timber industry, and prepares to dispatch him to Washington to confer with the National Park Service. About 30,000 acres, they finally decide, just *given* to the government for that crazy park. He can see it, a last-gasp come-from-behind victory over those damned conservationists. *(Jesus,* Sports Illustrated *will have to give us a story like that other one; we're both owned by the same company . . .)*

Buckley writes letters: one to John Tower, the one U.S. senator he knows he can count on (and a Republican, to help grease the rails with the Administration); and to the congressmen he feels will aid him, Charlie Wilson and Jack Brooks. He xeroxes the article and sticks the copies in the letters.

In Washington, Fred Bonavita, the

bureau chief of the *Houston Post,* gets wind of the deal . . .

It comes rolling in from the north and east, a great green cloud welling up from the gray sandy soil, rich green tiers billowing up one upon another, then cascading down again, occasionally gathered in the shape of loblolly pine or sweetgum, maple or beechwood, a soft, thick foam of green, chlorophyll gone wild. Pin oaks and massive yellow pines strain for release from the dense, dark underworld of laurel, yaupon, and magnolia while the world's greatest cypresses march jaggedly, like the soldiers of Oz, down the banks of secret steams past baygalls and palmetto bogs.

Within the soft ambience of the Thicket exists an encyclopedic range of nature's permutations, rare botanical anachronisms, some found nowhere else in North America, refuged in a whirlpool of green. And, perhaps, nested somewhere in the recess, lives one of the world's rarest creatures, the ivory-billed woodpecker, its staccato pleas in prophetic harmony with the dread cries of the Southern Pine Wolf, the Caddo and the Tonkawa Indians, the Tennessee trappers and Alabama emigrants, all those who sought to live in the Thicket's green fastness.

Resting hard on the western edge of the Southern Pine Forest, the Big Thicket has been called "the biological crossroads of North America," the intersecting point of eight wholly separate ecological systems, the only spot on the continent where subtropical and temperate vegetation overlap. The National Park Service has described it as "containing elements common to the Florida Everglades, the Okefenokee Swamp, the Appalachian region, the Piedmont forests, and the open woodlands of the coastal plains." Characterized by one writer as "a biological Noah's Ark," the area has spawned the world's largest specimens of a score of different trees, three dozen varieties of wild orchids, ferns, flowers, mosses, and fungi found nowhere else, and four of America's five carnivorous plants.

For generations the Thicket has been a woodlands Mecca for Thoreauvian disciples; botanists, zoologists, ornithologists, herpetologists—all of biology's footsore specialists have made the pilgrimage and announced their wonderment. Tom Eisner, a biology professor in the distant marble sanctum of Cornell University, helps oversee Save the Big Thicket committees on a hundred American campuses.

For an equally long succession of generations, men have sought in their

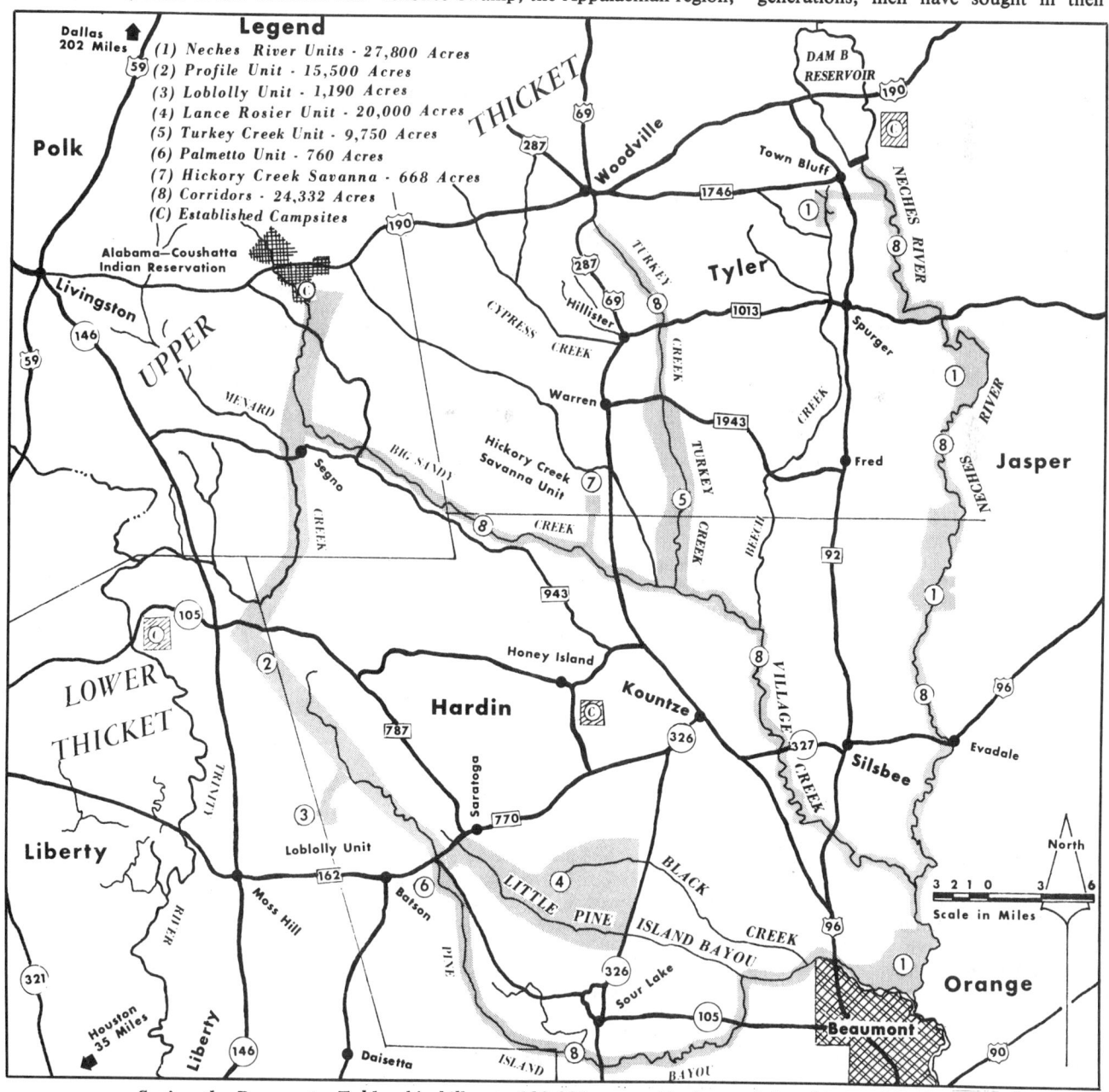

Saving the Remnants: Eckhardt's bill puts 100,000 acres (dark areas) in a National Park.

Map by Sandra Beddow

Clear-cutting: the timber stands are cut over, and the land is replanted, like corn, in long rows of pines.

various ways to exploit the Thicket's incredible fecundity and regenerative powers. The Alabamas and Coushattas, migrating west, displaced earlier Indian occupants in their search for a home that white men couldn't subdue, and peopled the Thicket. Even the railroads, rumbling precursors of Industry, found the region an impenetrable tangle of vines and swamps, and detoured to the north and south. For five generations the only white settlers were prairie iconoclasts, late-coming homesteaders, Civil War deserters, smugglers, rumrunners, trappers, and hunters.

Then finally came Industry, timber and oil companies that rode technology into the Thicket and came out with riches. The oil companies spilled their wastes in the streams and bogs, lumbermen scythed relentlessly through virgin woods, and, acre by acre, the Thicket shrank. The ivorybill hunted solitude in the deeper reaches as the buzz saw chased after it. The Big Thicket by the middle of this century was little more than a metaphor for the three million acres it had once been, and conservationists became alarmed. The only answer, Lance Rosier felt, was a Big Thicket National Park.

Known in his last years as "Mr. Big Thicket," Rosier was a self-taught naturalist, a man who struck with Nature a Faustian bargain, trading comfort and companionship for the wisdom of the woodlands. He cataloged hundreds of species of new plants, discovered specimens of life forms thought extinct or anomalous, learned the secrets of the Thicket in a way few men know themselves. In 1962 he helped found the Big Thicket Association, dedicated to the preservation of the area and intent upon creating from it a national park.

In 1966, Ralph Yarborough, who as a barefoot boy had drifted Huck Finn–like down the Neches River on homemade rafts, introduced in the U.S. Senate the first Big Thicket National Park bill. An introspective, sentimental man who rummages deep into his East Texas roots for the populist energies that still keep him going, Yarborough was the first great champion of Texas conservationists. He was the Big Thicket's first martyr.

He was defeated for reelection in the 1970 Democratic primary by Lloyd Bentsen, who went on to win the general election and occupy the Yarborough Senate seat. In the lame duck session of the 91st Congress, largely as a personal tribute to him, Yarborough's Senate colleagues passed the bill he had introduced and fought for through four years: the creation of a Big Thicket National Park of "not more than" 100,000 acres. The House of Representatives did nothing; Colorado representative Wayne Aspinall, then chairman of the House Interior Committee and a feisty opponent of environmental matters, declined to return to Washington for the session, and his committee never met.

Bentsen, now the Democratic nominee to replace Yarborough, promptly surprised the timber industry, which had avidly supported him in the primary, by endorsing the notion of a 100,000-acre park. Houston congressman George Bush, the GOP nominee for the Senate seat, upped the ante by calling for a 150,000-acre park and introducing a House bill to that end. Political expedience clearly spoke in favor of a Big Thicket National Park.

The Nixon White House, which had urged Bush to make the Senate race in the

"Charlie Wilson remembers a timber company official who told him he didn't really care about what finally happened as long as 'that damned Eckhardt don't win.'"

first place, rushed then-Secretary of the Interior Walter Hickel down to Texas to tell Texans what a fine man George Bush is. Among other things, Hickel said he was "strongly committed to the preservation of the Big Thicket" and rhapsodized at length about the fine piece of legislation that was Bush's bill.

After Bentsen won and was installed in the Senate his first action was to introduce a 100,000-acre park bill similar to Yarborough's. By this time, political sentiment in Texas was undeniably on the side of a largish (100,000 acres or more) park. One of Lyndon Johnson's last speeches as President called for its enactment and most of Texas' daily newspapers had endorsed the idea. Even the Houston City Council, which has never zealously pursued the creation of parks within its own jurisdiction, went on record unanimously in favor of 100,000 acres.

By late in the next year, 1971, it was beginning to approach election time again, and politicians were dusting off their hiking boots. Rogers Morton, who had replaced Hickel as Interior Secretary, came to Texas to tour the site of the proposed park. He spoke out eloquently on the idyllic splendors of the Big Thicket and promised to "keep the pressure on" to create a National Park. What pressure he spoke of was left rather ambiguous. His one-time, off-the-cuff, whistle-stop remark was then and remains the closest approach to positive action the Nixon Administration has made (as of late this spring) toward the creation of a Big Thicket Park.

What with his bow ties and rumpled suits, his misshapen felt hat and shaggy, forever mussed, graying hair, Bob Eckhardt seems a curious spokesman for urban Houston in a modern Congress. He is, though, of a kind with those people who have made representative democracy work in spite of itself. Eckhardt combines an intellectual affinity for the abstract with an earthy affection for the commonplace and is possessed of a keen instinct for channeling the energies of America's past to deal with the dislocations of its present. His respect for the country's traditions, of both its people and its institutions, has made him, simultaneously, a well-regarded constitutional lawyer, an avid conservationist and amateur historian, a consistent but original liberal, and, perhaps most important, a powerful and adept manipulator of the ofttimes mysterious tools of Washington politics.

Charlie Wilson, on the other hand, is a more prosaic congressman. An Annapolis graduate, he still looks like an ensign, sandy-haired and grinning, with the lanky presence of the junior varsity basketball player who only recently sprouted to six-five and hasn't yet decided how to deal with those *legs*. Young and exuberant, country affable, he has brought to Congress the back-slapping, hand-shaking, good ol' boy style of politickin' he perfected in fifteen years in the Texas Legislature and East Texas stumping. He had always been vaguely typed as a liberal in the Legislature but, as he puts it, "bein' a liberal in the Texas Legislature ain't the same thing as bein' a liberal in Congress," and he has found himself steadily compiling what can only be called a conservative voting record. He is a freshman this year, representing the East Texas district that

Congressman Bob Eckhardt

encompasses most of the Big Thicket.

Eckhardt and Wilson are, for the most part, the central figures in the parliamentary dance that will see the creation of a federally protected Big Thicket. It can be easily viewed as an interesting confrontation—the urban liberal, congressional veteran, thoughtful and intent, versus the rural neophyte, uncomfortably conservative, contagiously friendly, accustomed to the dark machinations of Austin legislating—but it would be an oversimplification. There are other characters, in many ways larger ones, who figure in the dance, some of them tapping their toes on the outskirts, counterfeit wallflowers helping to set the rhythm.

It is Wilson, probably, who plays the pivotal role; without question he is subject to the most intense pressures of any of the participants. It is within his district that the park, whatever its eventual character, would be created, and congressional protocol confers on him considerable influence for that reason alone. His predecessor in Congress, John Dowdy, had introduced a bill positing a 35,000-acre park configured in the shape of a "string of pearls." The String of Pearls proposal was the timber industry's first hesitant concession to the notion of a park and was a collection of smallish, widely scattered plots, or "units," that the experts all agreed were those most urgently in need of preservation. Dowdy's efforts in behalf of the timber lobby were, however, largely ineffectual; he was at the time under indictment for accepting a bribe and spent most of the 92nd Congress suffering "back trouble" that kept federal prosecutors from bringing him to trial.

Eckhardt was at this time (1971-72) pushing his own bill, calling for a 191,000-acre park. Texas conservationists, in the form of the Big Thicket Association (BTA), were as adamantly opposed to anything smaller as the timber lobby was to anything at all. As the BTA saw it, the Thicket had already dwindled to less than 300,000 acres and the String of Pearls was a ridiculous crumb to settle for. Their greatest disagreement, over and above the absolute size of the various units, was their determination to include streambed corridors. As conservation-minded ecologists pointed out, to preserve an isolated unit of woodlands without protecting the watershed of which it is part and parcel is to foredoom that unit to eventual destruction. The Eckhardt bill, together with bills offered by other members of the Texas delegation, again fell victim to Chariman Aspinall's general indisposition to parks of any sort; the

TEXANS IN WASHINGTON AND WHAT THEY DO THERE 219

House Committee never even held hearings and the 92nd Congress, like the three Congresses before it, expired without resolution of the controversy.

When the 93rd Congress opened in January, the atmosphere had changed and the stage seemed ready for a concluding act: Wayne Aspinall had lost a Colorado primary and the House Interior Committee was suddenly shifted in a more conservationist direction; the several proponents and opponents, almost all of them, had wearied of the steady buffeting of conflicting interests and the gentle serum of compromise had imbued them all; and Charlie Wilson had replaced John Dowdy as the 2nd District's representative in Washington.

Without exception, the conservationists cheerfully welcomed Wilson as a considerable improvement over Dowdy but, as they saw it, a disquieting cloud hovered over him. For two decades Wilson had been an employee of Temple Industries, one of the largest of the timber companies, and it had been with the active support and encouragement of the Temple family that he entered his first political race. His offices still boast a score of photographs, interspersed with pictures of the ships he served on, of sawmills and lumberyards, and he long ago earned the nickname "Timber Charlie." To his credit, it is a relationship Wilson has never ducked, and he speaks of Arthur Temple, Jr., the company president, as "one of the two or three people in my life I have felt the closest to for the longest time, not just politically but personally, too, in every way possible."

The Temple-Wilson connection is not as worrisome to park advocates as it might seem at a glance. Temple Industries, of all the major timber companies with large East Texas holdings, is the only one that is locally owned. Together with the other companies, Temple declared a voluntary moratorium on cutting in the general area of the proposed park, but their proscription was far more generous and extensive, not to mention adhered to, than any other company's. Moreover, Temple has foresworn practices that the rest of the industry has found economical and environmentalists have termed detestable: the wholesale clear-cutting of large timber stands and the razing of cut-over lands, the airborne use of herbicides and defoliants to erase underbrush. Temple has also shown a willingness to encourage slow-growing, often fragile stands of bottomland hardwoods, like cedars and oaks, that other companies have ignored in favor of quick-and-easy pine plantations.

As Eckhardt conceded, Temple has had "a generally salubrious effect on conservation in the area; they have been the most reasonable to work with of any of the industry people." There is another, more pragmatic reason for Temple's conciliatory view of the park: their holdings lie farther to the north than any other major company's, and they would be least affected by the park's creation. The company that would lose land to a federal park is the same one that environmentalists see as the most villainously obstinate: Mike Buckley's Eastex, Inc.

It was once estimated that a dozen pine trees went into every billboard.

When Fred Bonavita broke the story on Eastex's proposed donation, according to an insider at the National Park Service, "It blew the whole deal right out of the water." Corporate generosity seems somehow less charitable when it goes down in Washington's back rooms, and advance publicity about the deal scared the Park Service out of negotiations. Conservationists, who had been caught off guard, reacted with retroactive indignation; said an Eckhardt staffer: "Those sonsabitches, they nearly pulled a fast one there."

It had been but the latest in a long barrage of fast and slow ones, all aimed at the same general target: halting, or at least forestalling, the creation of the park. From the first, Eastex has been the most forceful opponent of the plan, lobbying against it at every turn. Ollie Crawford, the president of Southwestern Timber Company, a division of Eastex, has led the steadily retreating crusade against the park. Handsome and tanned in a double-knit suit, with a Jimmy Stewart kind of masculine charisma, Crawford is an impressive spokesman for any cause. The walls of Southwestern's Neches River lodge are covered with pictures of him hunting, fishing, and flying in the company of congressmen, presidents, and astronauts, photographs from his reign as the Jaycees' "Mr. East Texas," and plaques commemorating an astonishing variety of chamber of commerce-style honors.

Crawford is the timber lobby's circuit rider, scurrying from point to point to preach against the park, marshaling the diverse forces of the industry into a united front of stubbornness. (Even the *Louisiana* Forestry Association, for some reason, has seen fit to rail against the notion of a Big Thicket Park.) When the Texas House debated a resolution memorializing Congress to create a Big Thicket Park, Ollie Crawford whisked into Austin to head up the opposition.

The Texas Legislature, of course, has no constituted authority in the creation of federal parks; a memorializing resolution is roughly equivalent to writing to your congressman, with the exception that most Texas congressmen are sufficiently familiar with the nature of the Texas Legislature to pay less heed to it than to their average constituent. As Baytown state representative Joe Allen, the author of the resolution, phrases it, "When you get right down to it, the resolution doesn't mean spit, but they [the timber industry] treated it like we were going to war or something. I've never seen that kind of lobbying over just a resolution." It passed overwhelmingly, with Lufkin state representative "Buddy" Temple III, Arthur's son, voting aye.

Another manifestation of Eastex's attitude toward the proposed park has been the parent company's (Time, Inc.), resolute indifference to magazine stories dealing with the Big Thicket. *Sports Illustrated* and *Time,* according to staff writers for the magazine, have both either mangled or killed outright stories that have dealt with the area and, inevitably, Eastex's involvement. One of the most fiercely fought battles at the old *Life* magazine revolved around a story on the ivory-billed woodpecker and the adamant insistence of several editors that Time/Eastex–Big Thicket relationships be at least *mentioned*. The outcome was a barely discernible footnote and an apologetic phone call from Hedley Donovan, former *Life* senior editor and now Time, Inc., editor in chief, to Mike Buckley.

Eastex's heavily political role in the Thicket controversy has, unavoidably, made them some enemies. Barefoot Sanders, the 1972 Democratic nominee for the U.S. Senate, and Alan Steelman, a

> "The company that would lose the most land to a federal park is the same one environmentalists see as the most obstinate: Mike Buckley's Eastex, Inc."

Republican congressional candidate in Dallas, both took strong campaign stands on the side of a large park and both were denied permission to tour Eastex holdings in the Thicket. Another politician they have opposed in the past, though not so frantically, has been Charlie Wilson, who says, "I don't owe them [Eastex] anything; they've never done anything for me 'cept hit me over the head when they felt like it."

When Wilson entered the new Congress, conservationists were hopefully optimistic that he would support their new, whittled-down, 100,000-acre compromise proposal. During the congressional interim, Eckhardt had sat down with the Big Thicket Association and other members of the Texas delegation, to arrive at what he felt was a bill most everyone could support. The streambed corridors were narrowed and some of them removed, the standing units pared in size. To the conservationists, it represented their ultimate compromise, an effort to pass a bill before the Thicket disappeared altogether.

Eckhardt took the bill around to Bentsen, to Wright Patman, the dean of the Texas delegation, to other Texas congressmen. "I wasn't going to compromise beyond the 100,000 acres," he remembers, "but nobody ever said that was in question. I didn't get the impression that there was anybody at all opposed to it."

Eckhardt went to see Wilson: "I showed him our compromise bill and we talked it over and he never said a word about being opposed to 100,000 acres. I told him that, since it was in his district, he could take the initiative and I'd just sign his bill [as a cosponsor] if he had one."

Wilson's own recollection of the meeting is fuzzier but essentially the same: "I told him to just go on ahead with his own bill."

Wilson admits that, at the time of the conversation, he had an advance inkling of an event of some import to East Texans: in February, Temple Industries and Eastex, Inc., announced their intent to merge. Between them, the newly enlarged Time, Inc., subsidiary would hold over a million acres of Texas land. Rumors abounded as to the terms of the proposed merger (e.g., the Temple family was to become the largest single stockholder in Time, Inc.), but one solidly factual nub stared balefully at horrified conservationists: Mike Buckley would be the operational head of the merged interests.

The announcement, or advance word of it, may also have had repercussions in Washington. A man who is both a constituent and a close friend of Charlie Wilson's contends that up until that time Wilson was committed to a 100,000-acre park, but "the day they announced that merger, that park lost 30,000 acres." Reports came sifting out of Washington that Wilson was going to introduce a bill of his own, a park of 75,000 acres with only a Neches River corridor. Those were accurate reports.

Although less than joyful ("it's unfortunate"), Bob Eckhardt admitted that "they kind of have Wilson in the middle somewhat." Wilson was getting what he called "one helluva lot" of pressure. Mike Buckley sent him a telegram that termed the park proposals "shockingly discriminatory against Eastex," and predicted "the future of this corporation would be severely damaged with the passage of your bill as I understand it, and as a representative of all the people in this district I do not understand how you can justify discriminating against one company to the proposed degree."

Ollie Crawford followed that up with a letter even less marked for subtlety: "Certainly Mike Buckley's position is easy to understand as president of one of the largest corporations in your district which employs more than 1900 people . . . I would suggest you set up an appointment with him on your next trip to Texas to discuss the Big Thicket." It was not the kind of correspondence that freshman congressmen are pleased to receive.

There were other pressures as well. Wilson had, like all marginally liberal Texas politicians, sought and received the support of organized labor in his campaigns. When both the Sabine Area Building and Trades Council and the Beaumont Teamsters, two of the largest union locals in his district, denounced the park, Wilson started feeling a little boxed in.

There was little offsetting pressure from park proponents. Said Eckhardt, "There are a lot of selfish interests who are against the park and bringing a lot of pressure to bear. But there aren't any powerful lobby groups on the other side to counter that."

Another curious reversal was in progress. In mid-1972, Bob Eckhardt, then five long years into his labors in behalf of a park, had seen his first hopeful glimmer of a powerful ally. The National Park Service, which in typically bureaucratic fashion had been studying the proposals for seven years, showed him the working plans that would precede their own recommendations.

"I was very pleasantly surprised," he recalls. "It was almost identical with our own [100,000-acre] compromise proposal. They had everything in there we did, the corridors, all of Village Creek, everything. And it was laid out in exquisite detail, with maps and color overlays, aerial photographs."

In February and March of this year, Eckhardt met with Nathaniel Reed, the Nixon-appointed Assistant Secretary of the Interior and the Administration figure most directly responsible for developing the Park Service recommendations. "He was very encouraging," says Eckhardt. "He told me he was very concerned about preserving the watercourses. He was very adamant, very strong, about it. We were undecided about including Turkey Creek in our bill, and it was at *his* urging we did so."

By April, however, it was apparent that the Park Service recommendations, still not made public, had plummeted to less than 70,000 acres and all of the streambed corridors had been removed. Charlie Wilson was saying he had to "fight tooth and nail" just to get them to include a Neches River corridor. They had yet to notify Eckhardt of a change in plans, and no one at the Park Service or Interior Department is willing to speak for the record on what caused the switch. As Eckhardt says, "There's a helluva lot of double-talk going on here."

It is difficult to say what caused the Nixon Administration to back off so far from all those strong words by Wally Hickel, Rogers Morton, and George Bush in 1970. Eckhardt blames Senator John Tower, who, he says, "has become the major spokesman for the timber interests." A Nixon-appointed official in the Interior Department, who admits to the backpedaling, blames it on "a tight budget," but Eckhardt says the difference between the two park proposals is "infinitesimal compared to the total national budget."

For his part, Senator Tower says he is committed to 100,000 acres but that he will "probably support the Administration proposals." The fact that the Administration proposals do not square with his commitments is the sort of thing that politicians are able to talk around without ever noticing a conflict.

The House Interior Committee is expected to begin hearings this month on the various Big Thicket park bills. Eckhardt is modestly confident that, despite the opposition of Wilson, the timber lobby, and the Park Service, the committee will report out a bill more or less in agreement with his own. Wilson concedes the possibility but warns, "They'd better be prepared for one hellatious Armageddon of a battle when we get down to the mat on the floor of the Congress; I'm not gonna stand for that kinda abuse without taking every one of 'em to the wall." In East Texas, that's fightin' talk.

Charlie Wilson remembers talking to a timber company official who "told me he didn't really care about what finally happened as long as 'that damned Eckhardt don't win.' "

It's pretty much come to that. In the ten bitter years that the Thicket battle has been joined, the parameters of disagreement have steadily narrowed while individual perspectives have diverged. It is difficult to support or oppose a cause for a decade without one's own ego being confused with the rightness or wrongness of it. Again quoting Wilson, "It's gotten down to everyone just bein' ate up with who's gonna win."

The ivorybill, in the meantime, is driven nearer to extinction in an effort to find solitude. Every day, fifty acres of climax forest are lost to the rattle of chain saws and the advancing sterile columns of the pine plantations. And Bob Eckhardt's sad prophecy on the need of streambed corridors is being proven correct. Down near Saratoga, suburbia's advance guard has driven into the very heart of the Thicket wilderness. The unmarked tractors of a land developer are penetrating to the virgin cypress banks of Village Creek, and the wild tangles of laurel and magnolia are being flattened for the front yards of "vacation home sites." ★

The Policy Process

PART FOUR

Institutional politics are important, ultimately, because through institutions policies are established that affect the interests of Texas and Texans. Textbooks generally simplify policy process and impact; the reality is often quite different, particularly in Texas today.

As old and new forces collide in state and national policy arenas, the making of policy often involves intense struggles among opposing groups who view current policy decisions as determinants of future policy commitments. Such struggles focus extensive attention on the role of lobbies, and lobbyists often seem to dominate the policymaking process. In general, policy results from the complex interplay of opposing groups, politicians, bureaucratic agencies, and the like, with the resulting laws fully satisfying no one and at times failing even to address the initial question coherently. In other instances, the decision process seems remarkably responsive to fundamental issues.

Unfortunately, social change within Texas is occurring at such a rapid pace that policies are often implemented in a world quite different from the one envisioned by policymakers. Thus, as policy is put into effect, it may generate far-reaching and unforeseen consequences—possibly because the agencies implementing a law may interpret that law differently than the legislators who passed it. Also, interested groups, having lost the legislative struggle, may continue their fight during policy implementation, producing executive or judicial revisions of legislative policy.

The policy process is a complicated maze, in which interests and ambitions clash in ways that are often unpredictable, with results that are often unintended. It is a process that is rarely uninteresting. The essays in Part IV provide a glimpse of this fascinating world and allow insight into the political process as it affects lives and fortunes in Texas.

How Some Texas Bills Become Law

CHAPTER TEN

Inside the Lobby, Richard West (July 73)
How the New Drug Law Was Made, Griffin Smith, jr. (September 73)
There Ought Not to Be a Law, Paul Burka (January 77)
A Penny Saved Is a Penny Earned, Griffin Smith, jr. (August 76)

INSIDE THE LOBBY

by Richard West

On a fine spring Saturday morning in mid-May, nine days before the end of the legislative session, Bill Abington sat in the Senate gallery and nervously puffed on his cigar, awaiting the final vote on a bill that was as important to him as any he could remember.

His intelligent, pale-blue eyes moved from the list of 31 senators in his hand to the men themselves, thirty feet below him, as he tried to predict the outcome for the hundredth time.

The measure in question was the compulsory oil and gas unitization bill, and as director of the three-thousand-member Texas Mid-Continent Oil and Gas Association, he felt personally responsible for its passage or defeat.

As he gazed around the gallery, Abington spotted the Exxon boys, Gaylord Armstrong and Wade Spilman. Armstrong is a strapping six-foot-three Austin attorney with reddish-blond hair who used to travel with Ben Barnes and looks enough like him to be kin; Spilman is a former House member, an attorney, and the acknowledged expert in oil and gas, insurance, and alcoholic beverage law among the lobbyists. Their company had worked so hard for the bill's passage that during the recent committee hearings it was referred to as "the Exxon bill."

As Abington continued to gaze at his list, he couldn't figure out why he felt something was wrong. On paper everything looked good.

The bill had easily passed the House earlier in the year by a vote of 103-36. Thirteen senators, three short of a majority, had co-signed the bill when it was originally introduced. Senator Jack Hightower, a teetotaling, hard-shell Baptist from Vernon who was the bill's sponsor on the floor, was regarded as an expert and able leader.

Abington was growing impatient as the Senate plodded through regular business. Part of the trouble was that you couldn't depend on anything this session. It was *so* different. His great friend Ben Barnes, who *knew* how to run the Senate, was gone. Gus Mutscher, a little slow but always reliable, was a convicted man now living in Brenham. Even ol' Preston looked good at this point. You don't miss your water till your well runs dry.

Abington had worked long hours for months on this bill. Now, what was done was done. It was up to those 31 politicians milling around below him who, within the hour, would pass or kill the bill for two more years. Abington settled back in his gallery seat to wait.

Bill Abington is a prominent member of a group of a hundred or so men and a few women who make up the "Third House" of the Legislature. Highly paid, thoroughly acquainted with legislators and legislative procedure, they are known, for better or for worse, as the lobby.

Basically, a lobbyist is a person with no official government position who attempts to influence government decisions and policy. Lobbyists traditionally try to influence legislatures, but they may work with the executive branch as well. The name originated during Andrew Jackson's first presidential term, but the popular use derived from persons who, since they are not allowed on the floor, literally hung around in lobbies of legislatures, collaring members for lunch after adjournment.

To lobby successfully requires a great deal of energy from a man who must wear many different hats. Lawyer. Educator. Entertainer. Friend and companion. And if the occasion arises, procurer.

A good lobbyist does five fundamental things: (1) makes clear who he represents; (2) makes clear what his interest is; (3) makes clear what he wants to do and why; (4) answers questions; (5) provides enough backup material and information for politicians to be able to make a judgment.

He also never asks a legislator to vote for or against a bill; this is considered bad form. He explains his position on the bill, answers questions, and, if he is smart, warns how it might hurt back home in the next election.

A good lobbyist has a well-developed system of seeing that people in home districts who are interested in legislation are contacted and, in turn, ask politicians to vote for the bill in question.

The Texas State Teachers Association (TSTA), Texas Trial Lawyers Association, and the Texas Medical Association are the recognized experts at this "grass-roots lobbying." In a town of 50,000, the TSTA will have 300 lobbyists and husbands (or wives) who, upon command

226 HOW SOME TEXAS BILLS BECOME LAW

Illustrated by Neil Caldwell

Several lobbyists gather in the House Gallery to watch debate on the Lobby Control Bill (HB 2).

from lobbyist L. P. Sturgeon, can flood the Legislature with letters or themselves.

The smart lobbyist has this manpower working for him and remains above the nitty-gritty of pressure tactics. He is just the good guy who offers information, buys lunches every so often, and when the vote is near puts his arm around shoulder after shoulder and says, "This bill is coming up and we need the vote. I sure hope we can count on you."

Many lobbyists are former members of the Legislature and are hired not for their knowledge of the client's business, but because they know legislative procedure and the legislators themselves. Of course, being a lawyer helps, but it is not essential.

This past session, six freshman lobbyists were members two years ago: Ralph Wayne, Texas Mid-Continent Oil and Gas; Ace Pickens, Texas Medical Association; Gerhardt Schulle, Texas Association of Realtors; James Slider, Lone Star Steel; Joe Golman, Dallas Chamber of Commerce, Dallas Community College, and the National Association of Theater Owners; and J. P. Word, Texas Association of Taxpayers.

A few lobbyists learned the ropes as administrative assistants to governors or other Capitol officials. Howard Rose (Padre Island Investment Corporation) was Governor John Connally's first administrative assistant. Weldon Hart (Texas Good Roads Association) was the top assistant under Governor Shivers. Dan Petty (the University of Texas System's director of public affairs) served under Governor Preston Smith. Buck Wood was the Secretary of State's director of elections before taking his present job as lobbyist for Common Cause.

To become chief legal counsel for the Texas Railroad Association was almost inevitable for Walter Caven. He grew up in Marshall, which at that time was the shop town for the Texas and Pacific Railroad. His father was an attorney who represented the railroads, so it wasn't surprising that after serving one term in the House in 1949, Caven went to work for the Railroad Association.

Former members who have secured profitable niches representing their clients before the Legislature are many. A few prominent ones are: Reuben Senterfitt, former Speaker of the House (utilities); Terry Townsend (trucks); Bill Abington (oil and gas); Johnnie B. Rogers (insurance); George Cowden (insurance); Searcy Bracewell (Houston Natural Gas, Gulf States Utilities, etc.); Dick Cory, Jep Fuller, Buck Buchanan (beer); Robert Hughes (independent auto dealers); and Gene Fondren (Texas Auto Dealers Association).

The ways lobbyists work are as varied as the clients they represent. Their most effective work is done long before the session begins, in campaigns a full year before the Legislature convenes. For instance, there are 414 wholesale beer distributors in Texas who are members of the Wholesale Beer Distributors of Texas. When a man becomes a candidate for the House or Senate, these men find out one thing: does he drink an occasional beer or is he a high tenor in the Baptist church choir who denounces demon rum every Sunday?

It doesn't matter if he is a Commie-Red-Pinko-Symp or worships the spirit of Josef Goebbels. Will he vote wet or dry? A study on the candidate's background is sent to their chief, Turner Keith, who reviews each candidate's profile carefully before deciding yea, nay, or who cares.

A major change in lobby techniques has occurred in this area in recent years. Previously, the lobby looked at the field of announced candidates and picked out one to support. Today, a strong grass-roots organization such as the TSTA will actually recruit a young man or woman to run, particularly if the incumbent has proven an irritant.

With the crack of the gavel convening the new session, the lobbyists begin the endless round of gratuities. They drop by members' offices daily, offering to buy lunch or drinks or just to chat. Those legislators who respond to flattery are shamelessly backslapped. Those who are fiercely independent are treated at arm's length. Lobbyists know how busy most legislators are and they are always there to hold hands, lift spirits, run messages—being everything from page to lawyer.

One of the bright new lobbyists explains why this daily contact is important: "Even when nothing is happening that affects my client, I have to keep circulating because inevitably the time will come when it is critical that I know this or that particular member.

"It's like being a fireman. You spend a lot of time polishing the brass and revving up the engine because it has got to work when the bell rings." But this same lobbyist is critical of how some industries play the game. "The railroads have eight to ten men down here all session and they are all assigned certain people to take to lunch every day. John Eck of Southern Pacific has asked Hawkins Menefee every day for lunch, and here it is the last day of the session, and Hawkins ain't been yet. It's not a personal thing, but the Hawk just doesn't want to spend his noon hour with a railroad lobbyist."

It is doubtful that any member has ever changed a vote because of two or three meals. Days and nights of constant dinners, parties, attention, favors, and celebrations *do,* however, create bonds of friendship and companionship in what for many legislators is a lonely town. It is terribly hard to vote against a friend, and to some extent everyone is influenced by that personal touch. The sole reason for all this effort on the lobbyist's part is indeed to make a friend of the legislator, to gain access to his office, and once there, to make his pitch.

Lobbying is much more sophisticated today than it was in the fifties. Bourbon, beefsteaks, and blondes were three formidable weapons in the lobbyist's arsenal then. Not far out South Congress Avenue were two of the better whorehouses in Texas; many of the girls were working their way through UT and were not your average hookers. Hattie's and Peggy's were lively on a Sunday night, and lobbyists gladly followed along to pick up the members' tabs.

Today, the few hookers are freelancers whose business is going down. One young lady interviewed said, "Yeah, I get an occasional legislator or businessman, but they're older and just get drunk and pass out. I still get the hundred bucks though, don't you worry about that."

Because it's expensive and, more important, because of the Sharpstown scandal's effect on such ostentation, junketeering has been throttled the past few years. Gone are the days of lobby-paid trips to Keeneland Race Track in Lexington, Kentucky, and mass migrations to Matamoros or Juárez under the guise of inspecting the state's coastal lands or Texas Western College. This year, unless you wanted to view the Houston Ship Channel courtesy of the Chamber of Commerce, it was stay in Austin and gut it out.

Gifts to legislators have also dropped off sharply. No longer is there a flood of turkeys, transistor radios, packages of imported cheeses, whiskey.

For the legislators and for most of the lobby, the 1973 session was just unpleasant and exhausting. As a lobbyist from Houston put it: "It was an isometric session. You pulled and strained as hard as you could and got nowhere. There was never a game plan, but you kept going back every day hoping you could catch hold of what was going on." Reuben Senterfitt, the powerful lobbyist for the utility industry, was overheard saying, "I did okay this time, but I dreaded every day going to the Capitol and doing business."

What was going on were efforts by 77 new House members and 14 new senators to deal with confusion, distrust, and two presiding officers who chose to preside rather than lead—and, in the process, to pass some legislation.

In the spirit of reform, Speaker Price Daniel, Jr., announced he would be Speaker only one term. The immediate and continuing result of that pronouncement was that an instant Speaker's race was created, and from the first day forward, trust among House members was minimal at best. This, in turn, meant no floor leadership. If the Speaker doesn't provide strong direction, it must come from experienced, respected members on the House floor. Those who tried were suspected of cutting deals and furthering their own causes.

In the Senate, things weren't so bad. A slightly smaller percentage of freshmen, a lighter work load, and experienced men chairing crucial committees helped. Lieutenant Governor Bill Hobby didn't. To campaign and be elected lieutenant governor in a state whose constitution makes that Senate presiding officer the most powerful in the fifty states, and then to disavow and turn away from this authority is a waste.

No one, however, accused either chamber of laziness. House and Senate members began with a mole-like diligence, burrowing through Saturday meetings as early as March and attending noncontroversial committee meetings that often lasted until the early morning. By the session's end, the unfortunate result was a totally exhausted legislative membership. So many House members were vowing not to run again that the turnover in 1975 may be 25 or 30 more than the normal average of 47.

Despite problems, changes, and realign-

Lieutenant Governor Hobby (left) and Peyton McKnight (right), in happier days

THE LOBBYISTS

From left to right: Harry Hubbard (Labor); Dick Cory (Beer); Gene Fondren (Autos); Jim Yancy (Business); Steve Simon (Pot); Joe Golman (Dallas Chamber of Commerce and Community College, Movies).

ments of old political alliances, work was accomplished, bills were passed and defeated, and in the end, there were definite winners and losers among the lobbyists.

The reason many thousands of dollars are spent lobbying the Legislature is because the stakes are enormous. Almost without exception, every industry and business is affected by decisions made every two years in Austin. The basic rule for the lobbyist is that money is the root of all lobbying: keep the client from paying it out; pave the way to bring it in.

For the men representing the major industries—oil and gas, beer and liquor, utilities, chemicals, railroads, trucks, sulphur—the overriding task is to avoid taxation. This they did and, therefore, they were winners.

Other associations had specific battles to fight: kill this bill, pass this one, amend this one. Some did and some didn't.

One spectacular fight, one in which there were definite losers and winners, involved Bill Abington, the lobbyist for Texas Mid-Continent Oil and Gas Association, whom we left waiting in the Senate gallery for a key vote. Abington's battle contained all the elements of a good novel: forceful characters, strong developing plot, a large purse at stake, and a smashing dramatic climax.

In one corner: Texas Mid-Continent Oil and Gas Association, made up of three thousand members from almost all the independent and major oil companies in Texas, and considered the strongest industrial lobby in Texas; the Texas Manufacturing Association; twelve major chamber of commerce groups; four environmental groups; 32 Texas newspaper editorial endorsements.

In the other corner: Senator Peyton McKnight, Tyler; several independent oil men, notably Wesley West of Houston and Robert Payne of Dallas; the Permian Basin Petroleum Association, a small association of independent oil men headquartered in Midland.

At issue was the passage of the oil field unitization bill (HB 311). Unitization is a complicated concept, but basically the bill would have allowed 75 per cent of the operators in a given oil field to require all operators in that field to pay for and share proportionately the benefits of secondary recovery methods in fields where normal drilling could no longer efficiently recover oil.

Senator McKnight's opposition to the bill was well known. His view was that the voluntary unitization law in Texas was already working in over four hundred fields and that this new bill would force smaller oil operators with good producing wells into unitization with a larger field of less productive units. The energy crisis (used by supporters to gather votes for the bill) is a phony issue, McKnight claimed, because (1) the only way to solve the crisis is to find more oil reserves and increase the capacity of existing refineries, and (2) the secondary recovery method is not guaranteed to work and may not contribute a thing.

The Mid-Continent Oil and Gas boys made their first mistake early in the session. McKnight felt his position was hopeless, so he offered to work out some amendments to the bill that would help protect the small operators. Mid-Continent refused to discuss compromise with McKnight (as it later turned out, a big mistake).

The lobby had no trouble in the House. Opposition was fragmented; the bill's sponsors, Dave Finney of Fort Worth and DeWitt Hale of Corpus Christi, were both veteran, respected leaders. One seemingly innocuous amendment was tacked on, involving a relatively inexpensive severance compensation program for laid-off oil workers. This was done because of the successful work of the Texas Oil and Chemical Union president, Morris Aikins, and resulted in shifting fifteen to twenty labor votes in the House. More important, Senator D. Roy Harrington of Port Arthur, a labor man, then changed sides and supported the measure. The bill passed the House 103–36, thus strengthening the confidence of the lobby.

McKnight dug in for an all-out battle. His strategy was to delay consideration of the bill as long as possible, giving him time to explain the bill point-by-point to other senators. As the only oil man in the upper house, his words carried much weight.

He insisted on a full presentation of testimony before the Natural Resources Committee, and those hearings lasted over a month. When the bill arrived from the House, he insisted on hearings on the House amendments, then presented a series of unsuccessful committee amendments that took two more weeks. When the bill's sponsors tried to get it out of committee, McKnight surprised the committee with a rule requiring a transcript of all hearings prior to final action, delaying passage for another week.

McKnight had another opponent, one who really curled his socks. Lieutenant Governor Hobby broke his trance and for the first and only time during the session actively worked the floor for a major bill, urging his colleagues to vote aye. Hobby needlessly tweaked McKnight's nose by refusing to re-refer a minor bill from an unfriendly to a more favorable committee, a common senatorial courtesy usually granted from the floor.

McKnight fought back, refusing to back down to the presiding officer. He announced that "Billy Hobby may well have an East Texas opponent next year."

The climax came on that spring Saturday morning with the vote Bill Abington had been awaiting for a long time. Greg Hooser, Senator McKnight's aide, noticed that all 31 members were present, which was very rare for a Saturday. As he looked around the gallery, he also noticed that the oil and gas lobbyists were all there, including Mr. Abington himself. Then it struck him that this must be the day, the final try to shake McKnight's hold on the bill and to bring it out of committee for a vote. But Hooser remembered one of the recently adopted joint rules. It stated that no House bill could be brought up except on regular House bill days (Wednesday and Thursday) without a two-thirds vote of both Houses. It seemed unlikely to Hooser that such votes could occur in both Houses this morning.

Senator Jack Hightower stood up and moved to take up House Bill 311, the unitization bill. McKnight objected, citing the new joint rule. To Hooser's amazement, Lieutenant Governor Hobby overruled McKnight. Then followed a series of personal privilege speeches by fellow senators. Senators Bill Patman and Max Sherman objected to the ruling, but the dean of the Senate, A. M. Aikin, spoke in support of Hobby.

Once again, Senator Hightower moved

THE LOBBYISTS

From left to right: Bill Abington (Oil & Gas); Gaylord Armstrong (Exxon); Buck Wood (Common Cause); Harry Whitworth (Chemicals); Walter Caven (Railroads); Phil Gauss (Trial Lawyers).

to suspend the regular Senate rules and take up HB 311 for a vote. This required a two-thirds vote: 21 members out of the full 31 present. Secretary of the Senate Charles Schnabel began calling the role in his steady baritone: "Adams?" "Aye." "Aikin?" "Aye." "Andujar?" "Aye." "Blanchard?" "No." "Braecklein?" "Present."

Braecklein was the first surprise, and the first hint that McKnight might win. A wealthy man from Dallas, Braecklein had many friends in the oil business, but he thought McKnight's arguments rang true.

The vote continued down the list. The final vote: 17 for, 13 against, 1 present. The lobby had needed 21 votes. The bill was dead, short by 4 votes. McKnight had won. Knowing the personal battle he had waged against the measure since January, his fellow senators mobbed McKnight and congratulated him on his victory.

Upstairs, Bill Abington, defeated, tucked away his pen and quickly made his way out of the gallery and toward the elevators. He suddenly felt tired; the only bright thought that occurred to him was that the session's end was only nine days away. Despite all the money, pressures, and manpower, this time the lobby had lost. What had happened?

They had been overconfident. The early success in the House helped many lobbyists forget that the Legislature had repeatedly defeated the bill since 1949. Overconfidence led them to refuse to compromise, the biggest mistake of all. They also put too much reliance on their early legislative commitments. Getting 13 senators to cosponsor the bill in January did not necessarily mean the rest would follow. Because of the complexity of the bill, some senators couldn't cast a vote on its merits and had to rely on the judgment of McKnight.

The oil and gas lobby did not move quickly enough. It was caught off guard time and time again by McKnight's tactics. Each day that passed was a small victory for him because, as the session drew to a close, his colleagues did not want their own bills stymied by a potential McKnight filibuster.

McKnight proved that one senator who had enough skill and would fight hard enough could defeat, for better or for worse, the largest industrial lobby in the state.

Although Abington was a loser, the lobbyist who was the biggest winner was probably Buck Wood, a first-term lobbyist for Common Cause, a citizens' group that was focusing its attentions on the Legislature for the first time. Wood pushed his programs through against the opposition of practically every other lobbyist and many of the legislators themselves, although the strong support of Speaker Daniel and his team helped immensely.

Legislative reform was top priority for the 5500 members of Common Cause. With a new governor, lieutenant governor, attorney general, and Speaker of the House, and with a Legislature pledged to reform, Wood knew that it was now or never to put an end to the practices that had allowed the Sharpstown scandals and that in his eyes subverted the democratic process.

Wood was hired in September 1972. By late November he had drafted five bills that focused on ethics of legislators and state officials, lobby registration and reporting, expansion of the open meetings law, enlarging the public's access to government information. On December 5, a full month before the session, copies of the bills were mailed to House and Senate members as part of Speaker Daniel's reform package.

The first bill passed the House on February 8, and the rest followed in rapid succession. The Senate received them with less than total enthusiasm, and Lieutenant Governor Hobby announced that no action would be taken until his own citizens' conference convened in mid-March.

When it became clear that passing the bills would require the same grinding drudgery that must accompany the typical lobbyist's bill, Wood settled down to it, ushering the bills from subcommittee to full committee.

After countless hours of work and untold committee meetings, the key reform bills came right down to the wire on the last day of the session. Only one central aspect, a proposed Ethics Commission, bogged down hopelessly in a House-Senate conference committee and had to be abandoned for the sake of passing the whole ethics bill.

Besides the ethics bill, Common Cause secured its other goals: an improved open meetings law; tightened controls over campaign contributions and expenditures; easier public access to government records; and, most important for the lobby, tightened control over lobbyists and their spending.

Almost all lobbyists hated this part of the reform package (HB 2). It requires them to report expenditures while the Legislature is not in session. Lobbying expenses can no longer be reported in a lump sum but must be categorized. Also, individual members of organizations must now report their expenditures on lobbying. These new requirements rankle some of the lobby, but by and large they still leave the lobby with plenty of room.

One should not get the impression, however, that the old guard is completely moribund. Against Harry Whitworth of the Texas Chemical Council, the environmentalists and their legislative package didn't have a chance. If bringing up the nine reform bills didn't start a lobbyist spluttering with indignation, certainly the mention of the major environmental measures would. Virtually all the business and industrial lobby stood in ranks solidly against these bills, making their passage next to impossible.

Harry Whitworth entered the starting gate at the session's beginning riding a mule instead of his customary thoroughbred. In 1963, he had spotted a tall, red-haired, rough-edged House member named Ben Barnes and decided he was unique. As head of the powerful Texas Chemical Council, Whitworth had entrée, money, and information, all of which he gladly shared with young Ben.

Barnes's capacity to learn astounded even his most ardent admirers, and in 1965 he was suddenly elected Speaker and was on his way. Whitworth had displayed his most valuable talent: choosing an unknown out of the gaggle and staying hitched to him.

In January 1973, Barnes was building shopping centers in Brownwood, and Whitworth was awaiting the beginning of

230 HOW SOME TEXAS BILLS BECOME LAW

a new session, as he had done for many years. He had always performed well. The chemical industry flourished, and because of his efforts, they paid no special state taxes.

There were two bills that Whitworth had to kill this session: (1) HB 205 by Hawkins Menefee of Houston, which would have allowed any Texan to file suit to stop pollution of the air or water—a privilege now belonging only to the state and to those who suffer specific provable damages at the hands of the polluter. It also would have allowed suits against state agencies by persons who believed their clean air and water standards were not set high enough or were not well enough enforced; and (2) HB 646 by Carl Parker of Port Arthur, which would have set state policy on the environment and would have created an umbrella environmental protection agency to which all state agencies would have to submit environmental impact statements on planned projects. The new office would have authority to veto projects that would harm the environment.

Whitworth's work was cut out for him. The first thing was to decide who would also find this bill disastrous. That impact statement had to be a nuisance for lots of folks. He began by calling John Terrell, lobbyist for the Texas Association of Builders. Old John didn't like it at all. Certainly cities would be affected, so Whitworth forewarned the executive director of the Texas Municipal League (TML), Richard Brown. Almost every mayor and city official in Texas belongs to the TML, and it has *clout*.

The next step was to find a freshman House member, unknown, conservative, unscarred, to work the floor. To Whitworth, Pete Laney from Plainview seemed ideal. Pete put out a farm and ranch journal and was a farmer up in the Panhandle. Whitworth was interested in farming, and soon the two were old friends. Whitworth never asked Laney for anything regarding the bill; he asked him only to study it carefully and assay how much it might hurt the farm and ranch business.

Joining Whitworth, the homebuilders, and the Texas Municipal League in opposition were the Texas Water Quality Board, Texas Mid-Continent Oil and Gas, Texas Independent Producers and Royalty Owners, and West Central Texas Oil and Gas Association.

On May 2, after two crippling amendments were added, Parker angrily pronounced his bill dead. Pointing to the lobbyists in the gallery, he said, "I see the vultures up there waiting to pick the bones. They have done their work well in representing their clients."

The *Houston Chronicle* reported that the noise of the lobby leaving the gallery was so great after Parker admitted defeat that Speaker Daniel told the House to stand at ease until quiet was restored. Watching the phoning and commotion was Mr. Whitworth, as serene and secure as a moo-cow.

A similar fate killed Menefee's bill almost exactly a month earlier. A crippling amendment won passage and the bill never saw the light of day.

Sadly enough, the 63rd Session passed only a few environmental reform measures, one of which was the endangered species act. Mrs. Char White, chairwoman of Environmental Action for Texas, no doubt wishes Harry Whitworth was one of those critters included on the list under her new law. But Whitworth is still very much around and, although not in the catbird seat, still a winner.

Another winner this session, as at every session he participates in, was Frank C. Erwin, Jr., a man few people have ambivalent feelings about. Depending on

Will Davis (airlines and insurance) told Texas Monthly: *"My clients' business is not your business."*

your point of view, either he has singlehandedly ruined the University of Texas or he has pulled it up into the twentieth century.

He is a complex man: emotional, mean as a rattlesnake in a sleeping bag, defiantly loyal, shy but unfailingly polite with women. He is what used to be known as a gentleman of parts, a man who is as much at home with Puccini's *Turandot* as he is passing statehouse gossip with the coarsest representatives.

Since 1965, Frank Erwin has presented the huge UT System's budget before the House Appropriations Committee and the Senate Finance Committee and has testified for or against bills affecting the UT System.

He has a brain as sharp as an awl, and as the Appropriations Committee chairman makes his way through the several-inches-thick budget, it is very clear that Erwin has done his homework. Erwin's participation began in 1965 when one of Governor John Connally's aides recommended vetoing funds for UT's Memorial Museum. Erwin was appalled that such a thing could happen to his beloved UT.

That year the appropriation for the UT System was $77 million. Erwin has lobbied for UT every session since, and, for the 1974-75 biennial, the UT System will receive $427 million, a 453 per cent increase over 1965. Even with new institutions added in, it is an impressive figure and a credit to Erwin's skill.

"There was a considerable difference in the House Appropriations Committee this time. Many committee members were new and were unfamiliar with the institutions and their backgrounds," said Erwin.

"However, I think the appropriations bill is exceptionally good, considering the no-new-tax constraint and flexible welfare situation the committee had to work under."

He concluded: "Governor Briscoe gave us no leadership or help whatsoever. He has expressed interest in vocational education, which is fine, but he has made no pitch for higher education, either general or academic instruction, medical or dental units."

The Coordinating Board of Colleges and Universities introduced five bills to denude UT of its power. None was enacted. There were 35 or so unfriendly bills introduced, mainly by freshman members. All failed.

Erwin and UT are used to being number one. Railroads, on the other hand, are not. If his friend and fellow power-lobbyist Bill Abington was left holding the bag, Walter Caven had the other half. Chief legal counsel for the Texas Railroad Association since 1959, the tall, patrician-looking, blue-eyed Caven had the dubious pleasure of having a much sought-after bill become Governor Briscoe's first veto.

Caven's bill would have authorized special railroad agents to be peace officers, carry weapons, and move from one county to another with no legal hassles. There was no indication of trouble and Caven was confident. When Sergeant Julius Knigge of the Houston police department, lobbyist for the Texas Municipal Police Association, found out about these about-to-be 150 new peace officers, however, he fired off a letter to Governor Briscoe protesting that for the first time private industry would have its own police force.

That's all it took. In a press release announcing the veto, the governor agreed that it was a problem and a study would be the best thing.

Unique among the big four industrial lobbyists, Caven has the manpower to aid the cause. The major railroads in Texas—Missouri Pacific, Santa Fe, Southern Pacific, and Katy—send down between four and ten lobby-drones during the session to do the dirty-collar work. Each

HOW SOME TEXAS BILLS BECOME LAW 231

drone is assigned three or four House members a day for lunch. Mr. Caven looks after the Senate.

Caven vehemently disapproves of Price Daniel, Jr. ("I haven't said anything to him except hello since the session started, and I don't intend to"), calls lobby reform a false issue, and thinks the present lobby law is adequate and only needs to be enforced.

One of the strongest lobbies is the Texas Trial Lawyers Association (TTLA). The 1100 members are by profession advocates and persuaders; their business is to persuade juries. They persuade legislators, too. Phil Gauss has been the executive director since 1949 and has had two pieces of legislation on the front burner for a long time. They finally passed this session.

The two long-awaited bills: (1) A bill making comparative negligence part of state tort law, passed last session and vetoed by Governor Smith, made it this time and was signed into law on April 9; (2) a bill providing for voluntary first-party insurance. If you choose to pay an additional $25–$35, this add-on insurance will provide up to $2500 in automatic payoffs for injuries and loss—no lawsuit necessary.

Much of TTLA's strength comes from its political arm, LIFT (Lawyers Involved for Texas). Headed by attorney Wayne Fisher of Houston, LIFT contributes heavily to Texas House and Senate races.

Name any interest you want and it's a safe bet that its concerns are represented by an association or lobbyist in Austin. Below is a random sampling of persons and associations that for better or worse hang around the Capitol:

AFL-CIO—The labor movement in Texas has always had the numbers and the money. The increasing urbanization of Texas may give the labor unions the added political muscle they have missed, although union membership is not picking up rapidly. Secretary-Treasurer Harry Hubbard leads a five-man lobby delegation that worked for passage of collective bargaining for public employees (failed) and an upward revision of workmen's compensation payments to injured workers (passed).

Texas Brewers Institute—Chief legal counsel Dick Cory is the lobby's acknowledged expert on the drafting and constitutionality of legislation. A former sixteen-year House member and participant in two previous constitutional revision studies, Cory had an easy session, putting out brush fires and worrying about a future tax bill.

Texas Automobile Dealers Association —An organization of 1450 franchised new-car dealers in Texas headed by former representative Gene Fondren. On the job little over a year, Fondren knows the Legislature's whims and, along with Cory and attorney Wade Spilman, ranks among the most competent drafters of legislation.

The answer to a lobbyist's prayer: Lobbyist Frank Erwin surrounded by the most important state and federal politicos of the day: (Left to right) Richard M. Nixon, John B. Connally, Frank Erwin, Ben Barnes, and LBJ

THE LOBBYISTS

From left to right: Johnnie B. Rogers (Insurance); Terry Townsend (Trucks); L. P. Sturgeon (Teachers); Ralph Wayne (Oil & Gas); Allen Commander (U. of Houston); W. Price, Jr. (Food).

Texas Manufacturers Association—Six thousand members representing three thousand firms make up this widespread organization headquartered in Houston. Their ability to raise money has declined, as has the prestige of the executive director, Jim Yancy.

National Organization for the Reform of Marijuana Laws (NORML)—By taking polls, appearing on TV and radio shows, and persistent lobbying, state director Steve Simon provided valuable assistance to the already excellent groundwork done by former state senator Don Kennard's Senate Interim Committee on Drug Abuse. The combined efforts of the Kennard program and the activities of NORML bore fruit on the last day of the session, when the penalty for first-time possession of marijuana was reduced from a felony to a misdemeanor.

Joe Golman—One of the busiest individual lobbyists in Austin, Golman represents the Dallas Chamber of Commerce, Dallas Community College, and the National Association of Theater Owners. Golman is a popular former House member from Dallas who will commute from Dallas to the Austin office between sessions to keep abreast of legislative business that may affect his clients.

There are many, many more, ranging from the powerful Texas Medical Association and many other medical-related lobbies, to Allen Commander's efforts to work for the University of Houston in the shadow of Frank Erwin's got-it-down-pat work for UT, to shrimpers and oystermen, to every delegation and individual who visits Austin at one time or another.

The lobby is hardly a monolithic body, although its major members share certain basic interests and a certain common folklore. When it comes right down to it, the business of lobbying is the business of petitioning the government: it's trying to right wrongs, achieve a special good, or just get what you can.

Lobbyists will swear up and down that democratic government could not go on without them, particularly as the world, and governing, become more complex. Most legislators would agree with them. The legislators know how difficult it is to keep informed on issues.

The methods that the lobbyists use are pretty much standard; it is the ends that are different from lobbyist to lobbyist. The danger comes when some lobbyists spend too much time around power and come to equate the public interest with their own.

In the meantime, Bill Abington of Texas Mid-Continent Oil and Gas is preparing for another session—perhaps a tax session, perhaps the constitutional revision session this spring, perhaps the next regular session. If he could just figure some way to get around Senator McKnight . . . ★

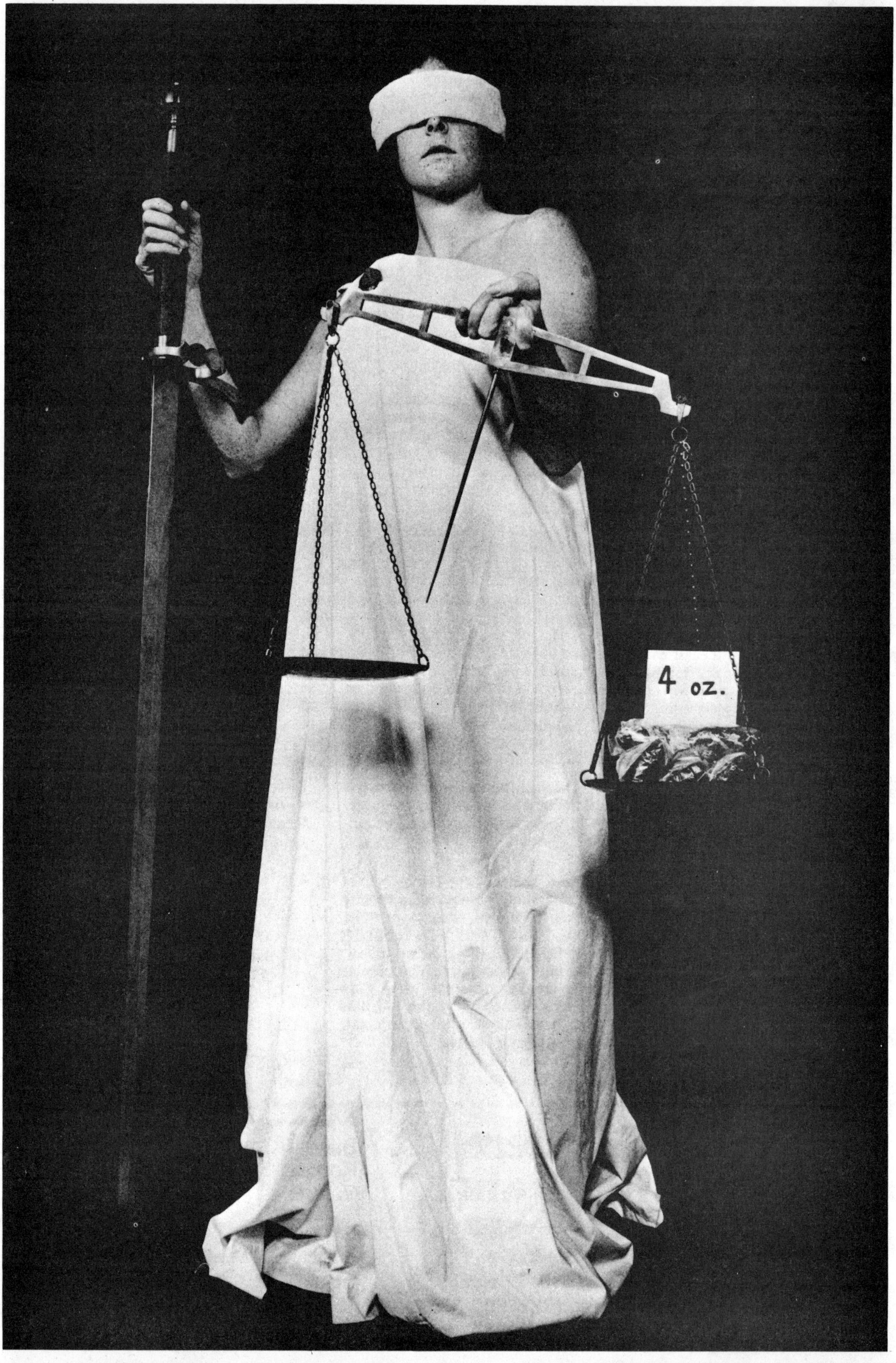
4 oz.

How the New Drug Law Was Made

by Griffin Smith, jr.

Texas' new controlled substances act regulates everything from pot and heroin to those tranquilizers in your pocket.

Texas, the next-to-last state to treat all marijuana possession as a felony (and the last to take seriously its two-years-to-life penalty) quietly succumbed to the ebbing wave of the sixties counterculture on August 27 as the Texas Controlled Substances Act went into effect. The event was duly commemorated by connoisseurs of the forbidden hemp at midnight celebrations in the privacy of homes across the state—celebrations tempered by the knowledge that even the "reform" law viewed them as deserving a few days or months behind the bars of their nearby county jail, and tempered, too, by a theatrical sense of the absurd that so much energy could have been expended by so many to pass/toughen/moderate/repeal/amend/reform a prohibition that was honored more in the breach than the observance. Connoisseurs of irony took note that this particular message-in-a-bottle was lifted from the sand on precisely that day which the more doctrinaire members of the counterculture would once have deemed most piquantly repugnant—Lyndon Baines Johnson's birthday, a new state holiday. *Sic transit gloria psychedelia.*

The law was passed because too many of the wrong kids were being arrested. The story is really as simple as that. True, before the Legislature finally approved HB 447 a scant five hours before the 63rd session was gaveled to a close on the 28th day of May, the Capitol's chambers and committee rooms had been the stage for much soul-searching, courage, foolishness, and villainy. But none of this would have happened had not marijuana crossed the tracks from the barrios and black neighborhoods to River Oaks, Highland Park, and Alamo Heights. The police in hot pursuit did not stop to notice that the rules were supposed to change too.

Griffin Smith, jr. a senior editor of Texas Monthly, served as Chief Counsel to the Drug Study Committee of the Texas Senate, 62nd Legislature. He also served as special counsel to Senator A. R. Schwartz during the House-Senate Conference Committee deliberations on the Texas Controlled Substances Act in May of this year.

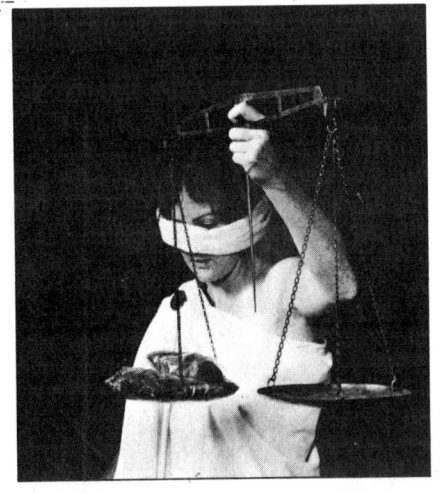

Eventually the state was peopled with good, solid, white middle-class parents who knew about that nice kid down the street, the Eagle Scout who made nothing but top grades in academics and deportment, whose parents were having to exhaust his college savings in lawyers' fees to defend him on a felony charge of having a marijuana cigarette in his car. Their anxieties were eventually, but duly, transmitted into law. The fact was not lost on the Legislature's black and Chicano members, no mean connoisseurs of irony themselves.

Marijuana is but one of hundreds of drugs regulated by the new act. It provides for a misdemeanor penalty of up to six months and a $1000 fine for possession of not more than two ounces of the stuff, and twice that penalty for possession of up to four ounces. Possession of more than four ounces is punishable as a felony, two-to-ten years in prison and a $5000 fine; identical penalties apply to sales of any amount and all but the smallest gifts. Because the judge is given the power to reduce these felonies to misdemeanors when to do so would "best serve the ends of justice," it is theoretically possible for a marijuana dealer (as well as a user) to get off with a $1 fine. Texas appears to be the only state which allows such abstract leniency for "pushers." The possession penalties now place Texas near the middle of the states.

Passage of a drug law confronts the individual legislator with a special sort of crisis. Drugs are different from almost every other problem he is called upon to "solve." Most of the time he either knows what he is doing or knows that he does *not* know; be the issue tax reform or automobile insurance or wiretapping or school finance, if he does not understand it himself he at least has some idea of where to turn for answers that satisfy his mind. He knows other people—real people he can trust, constituents at home or experts in the state bureaucracy or lobbyists out in the hall—who can tell him, in a fashion he regards as credible, "here is how it is."

With drugs he is lost on a sea of formulas and isomers and seven-syllable names for pills he has never seen; oxymorphone, bufotenine, ibogaine, methylphenobarbital, 3,4,5-trimethoxy amphetamine. What does this mean? Who is there to ask? What will happen if we make this a misdemeanor instead of a felony? There are no familiar faces in the doorway or the hall, no handy number in the Rolodex to tell him what to do. And the experts who do testify seem to disagree more often than they agree. Even for the member who wants to do right and damn the political consequences—*especially* for him—how is he to *know?*

No wonder the big electronic voting board lights up sluggishly on drug amendments in the House, as members hold back to get the drift of things in this particular chilling political blizzard, eventually huddling together like sheep in a cold wind. It is not cowardice that drives them to it, but raw uncertainty.

To be sure, part of this uncertainty is inflicted willingly by the members upon themselves; it could be avoided if they were more ready to make critical judgments about the information at their disposal, meager though it may sometimes be. During the consideration of the Controlled Substances Act, legislators were all too prone to say, "Well, the report of the National Commission on Marihuana and Drug Abuse says this about marijuana, but on the other hand Bob Smith [Travis County district attorney] says the opposite, so we just don't know *what* to think." Phony helplessness has its uses.

But for the most part their bafflement was genuine. This was luminously illustrated during the House-Senate conference committee deliberations late in the session, as senators fought to preserve key vestiges of their moderate bill in the necessary compromise with the hard-line House product. House sponsor Tim Von Dohlen, a pharmacist, had tucked away in an obscure section of the House version a provision that imposed a two-year jail term for possession of any prescription drug unless it was in a labeled bottle supplied by a licensed pharmacist.

Ostensibly aimed at penalizing distribution of prescription drugs by black marketeers in competition with legitimate pharmacists, the provision applied equally to the ordinary citizen who might take along a few pills like antibiotics or Darvon when he was away from home, rather than tote his medicine cabinet in his briefcase. Quite a common occurrence—but also a crime—as Senator A. R. Schwartz noted incredulously. "Do you mean to tell me," he demanded of Von Dohlen, "that these Valium pills I have in my pocket could get me two years in jail, just because I took them out of that little bottle this morning instead of carrying it up here in my pocket?" Von Dohlen nodded his assent. "That doesn't make any sense at all," said Schwartz. "And besides, *two years* just for possessing Valium? What's so bad about Valium?"

Heads of the other conferees bobbed in agreement: Valium, a mild relaxant, is widely used around the Capitol by legislators seeking to cope with the incredible tensions of the session. Two years for possessing Valium without a prescription, or outside the Rx bottle? It didn't make any sense to them; no sense at all. They knew what Valium was; they knew people who used it; and they were profoundly certain that nobody ought to wind up in jail for *that*.

The next morning the issue came up again. Another Senate conferee, Charles Herring, had put in his first appearance. When he heard what the House bill proposed to do with Valium, he too pulled out some tablets from his pocket and protested that the whole idea was outrageous. That afternoon a chastened Von Dohlen announced to the committee that he was willing to delete the clause that penalized possession of prescription drugs outside their original container and would also cut the penalty for possession without a prescription to no more than six months. The senators, harrumphing, agreed.

Here was a drug the legislators recognized. Never mind that Valium may be more dangerous, some experts say, than many of the mystery drugs for which these same legislators imposed penalties of ten or twenty years in prison. Finally all those isomers and seven-syllable words became vividly real, and they knew, instinctively knew, that putting people behind bars for abusing this drug made "no sense at all." Presented with something within the range of their own experience, their minds immediately began to rev up and purr with neat cause-effect relationships. A palpable wave of relief filled the room—

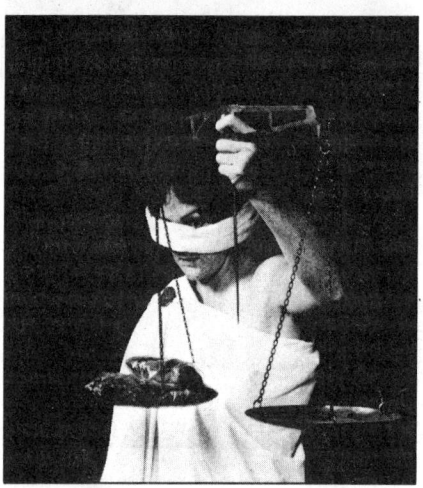

relief at finding something familiar amid all the gobbledy-gook of the Controlled Substances Act, relief at being able to deal with it in rational forms and categories.

This assurance was precisely what most legislators lacked, and knew they lacked, about most of the drugs they were being asked to regulate. It is no accident that the Legislature took every illicit drug they recognized, except marijuana, and raised the possession penalty—to life imprisonment for heroin, speed, and LSD. Penalties for the vast middle group of obscure drugs remained about the same as current law—but few members were willing to risk the political peril of seeming "soft" on anything anyone had ever heard of. Particularly in the headlong Gardarene rush to "get the pusher" on the House floor, the decision to control a drug was regarded as synonymous with slapping the highest possible penalty upon it. Precisely because the members knew the names but were strangers to the drugs themselves, demagoguery dragged debate to the lowest common denominator. A member who questioned the penalty was treated as though he was questioning whether the drug should be controlled at all—and by extension he was questioning whether it was "harmful" to the sons and daughters of Texas.

Locked into this logic it was impossible for the legislators to extricate themselves, and they were helpless to resist the lynch-mob atmosphere that required them to prove their concern by imposing the highest conceivable penalties on drugs of public notoriety. Thus a member like Fred Agnich could proclaim his emancipation from the hoary myths of marijuana by voting for its decriminalization, then moments later bellow out his approval of the amendment that punished possession of LSD by life in prison. Had he known someone who had taken LSD, he probably could never have voted as he did, regardless of the political furies. As it was, he never saw the inconsistency. Dallas Republicans use Valium, not LSD.

Had the members understood as much about the dozens of obscure drugs as they knew firsthand about Valium, the new act might well have been substantially different. Their willingness to virtually rubber-stamp the governor's irrational penalties for these drugs can be traced not so much to their constituents' pressures (how many voters have ever heard of psilocybin, ibogaine, mescaline?) as to their own deep, troubled uncertainties. They were afraid to gamble not so much because they feared retaliation as because (at least for the best of them it was because) they truly did not know what they were up against, truly feared that the half-remembered stories in the newspapers might be right, truly feared that the well-being of the people whom they governed might hinge on their mistakes. In such dilemmas are the best-intentioned men vulnerable to the worst.

The marijuana penalties met with general satisfaction among the members. They are probably close to the most reasonable that could have been passed, considering the degree to which the governor had incited the hard-liners to influence the anti-marijuana climate. (In support of his bill *reducing* the marijuana penalty, Briscoe summoned a carefully chosen parade of witnesses to tell how *bad* marijuana was, a somewhat contradictory procedure.) But the bill passed by the Senate, establishing a maximum penalty of seven days in jail for up to eight ounces of marijuana, almost certainly was far closer to the *personal* views of a majority of the legislators than was the version they finally agreed upon. Many legislators will tell you that most of their colleagues would actually prefer decriminalization if the decision could somehow be secretly left up to them.

How sobering, then, to witness the workings of naked politics on the formulation of the criminal law. If these members wore judicial robes and presided over a court of law, few if any of them

> " 'That doesn't make any sense at all,' said Schwartz. 'Two years just for possessing Valium? What's so bad about Valium?' "

would convict an innocent man in order to satisfy some public clamor. They would be affronted by the mere suggestion of such a thing. Yet on the floor of the House or Senate they could vote willingly for laws that classify as criminal certain conduct which they themselves believe should not be punished—justifying their action on the grounds that it must be done to satisfy the public clamor. There is a difference between punishing a man who has done no harm and authorizing others to punish him; but there is not much difference. We have different expectations from our judges and our lawmakers—or at least they think we do.

Observing this performance by men who knew that what they did was not enough, the practical mind is at odds with the humane mind. The practical mind says: they chose the only way open to improve the barbaric law we had; they did the best they could; they did it brilliantly. The humane mind answers: they chose the way of Pilate.

The principal question mark now hanging over the new act is whether its provisions for resentencing the current crop of marijuana prisoners will be upheld by the Texas courts. A section of the act, restrained at the insistence of the Senate conferees, allows any person who is currently serving a sentence for a marijuana offense to petition for a new sentence based upon the revised penalty structure now in effect. Thus someone serving a sentence of, say, five years for possession of an ounce could be resentenced to no more than six months. Assuming he had already served more time than this, he would be eligible for immediate release. Someone serving a sentence of twenty or thirty years for possession of six ounces of marijuana could be resentenced to no more than ten years, and less if the judge felt a shorter time was appropriate. He too would be eligible for release once he had served the substitute sentence.

Attorney General John Hill has opined that the resentencing procedure infringes the governor's clemency power under the Texas Constitution. Since a flood of petitions from the numerous marijuana prisoners was expected to begin promptly on August 27, the issue should be resolved soon. For many of the young people now in the Department of Corrections, the ultimate decision is critically important. If resentencing is upheld, the new penalties automatically become retroactive. Neither the governor nor the Board of Pardons and Paroles nor the judge himself can refuse to give a prisoner the benefit of them. But if it is not upheld, they will be forced to serve out their sentences, often of exorbitant length, as punishment for an offense which the law no longer regards as quite that serious after all. Their one hope then is for ordinary parole—but this depends on the willingness of the governor and the Board of Pardons and Paroles to grant it.

Without the board's approval, the governor is powerless to act. And the board has shown no inclination to regard drug prisoners with any special sympathy, despite the Legislature's obvious intent in passing the resentencing section. (The Senate also passed a concurrent resolution urging special parole consideration for marijuana, heroin, and cocaine offenders.) The board takes the position that regardless of the reduction in penalties, current prisoners must serve out the customary one third of their original sentence before parole will even be considered. Even then, they plan to continue their present policy of refusing parole automatically if the district attorney who prosecuted the case objects to the prisoner's release. In the words of a member of the board, "we don't quarrel with the DAs about it. That's their business, however they feel. Some of these marijuana prisoners may be too dangerous to turn loose on the streets, and the DAs know that better than we do."

For many marijuana prisoners, this is tantamount to locking the door and throwing away the key. The district attorneys unanimously agreed at their recent state convention to resist the resentencing approach to the bitter end, and they have shown little interest in bringing their past convictions into line with the new penalties. Their attitude is a sobering reminder that although the law may change, some minds do not. The president of their association, Bob Smith of Austin, noted that resentencing or parole could help those sentenced under the old law who were still serving time. "However," he said, "why help them? They knew what they were doing."

When England finally abolished capital punishment for such crimes as stealing a loaf of bread, and the king commuted the sentences of those breadstealers who had been condemned to die, there must have been a prosecutor in some benighted corner of the realm who snorted, "Why help them? They knew what they were doing." ★

THERE OUGHT NOT TO BE A LAW

by Paul Burka

Before the Legislature starts passing new laws, it should get rid of some old ones.

It's that time again. The Texas Legislature meets only in odd years—a designation some pundits swear has more to do with politics than mathematics. Two years have gone by but the Legislature is facing the same old issues: property tax reform, school finance, and just who should get their hands on the state's bulging treasury surplus.

Since the Legislature can't seem to make much progress toward solving these perennial problems, perhaps it should look at some others it can do something about. The lawmakers might start by looking at some of their own making: laws they passed which are unnecessary, undesirable, or unconstitutional—and sometimes all three.

BONANZA
The Coal Relinquishment Act

Suppose you decide to sell some land but elect to keep the mineral rights. One day oil is discovered in the neighborhood and you inform the new owner that you're ready to drill. But when you arrive with your rig, he threatens you and refuses to let you on "his" land. Do you: (a) push him aside and go about your business? (b) go to court to enjoin him from interfering with you? (c) offer to pay him a reasonable fee for the use of the surface? (d) cave in and give him half the oil in exchange for his letting you use the land?

If you're the State of Texas, you do (d). That's what happened when oil and gas were discovered in West Texas. Stubborn West Texas ranchers who had bought state land at bargain-basement prices blackmailed the state into ceding half its oil and gas interest in a 1919 law known as the Relinquishment Act. Of course, that was long ago; nothing like it could happen today, right? Maybe not. But it sure could happen in 1967. That was when the Legislature gave away part of the interest in coal and lignite, two minerals that one day may be as valuable as oil and gas. But never let it be said that the Legislature didn't learn something in the intervening 48 years. This time, instead of a 50–50 split, the state got 60–40.

R.I.P.-OFF
The Morticians Licensing Board

Almost every law that regulates a profession under the guise of protecting the public is really designed to protect the regulated profession as well. The acknowledged classic of this type is the act governing the funeral profession. In the words of one knowledgeable legislator, it is written "by funeral directors for funeral directors."

Unlike some regulatory boards, which include token members of the public, the State Board of Morticians is composed entirely of funeral directors. Ordinary citizens are not invited, nor, for that matter, are their complaints. There's no provision for consumer grievances—something the profession's had plenty of in recent years.

Most of the regulatory laws find ways to restrict competition, and naturally the Morticians Act is no exception. It accomplishes this in the usual ways—by requiring licenses and prohibiting advertising about prices—but adds an ingenious twist. Current license holders have total control over entry to the profession, because newcomers can't get a license without serving the longest apprenticeships since the heyday of medieval craft guilds. You can't even escape the mortician by being cremated. State law forbids cremations within 48 hours after death—but it requires that bodies be embalmed within 24 hours.

IT STINKS
The Polluter Protection Clause

The biggest polluter of the Houston Ship Channel is the City of Houston, which dumps 100 tons of untreated sewage into the city's bayous every day while the Texas Water Quality Board (WQB) benignly looks the other way. The city's repeated violations of state water pollution standards did come to the attention of Texas Attorney General John Hill, who was ready to take the city to court: ready, yes; able, no. Standing in his way was a law that bars the attorney general from suing a polluter without prior authorization from the WQB.

That's the same agency, you may recall, whose executive director once volunteered to be a *defense* witness in a pollution suit brought by the federal Environmental Protection Agency. That pretty well sums up the board's attitude toward polluters, whom it would rather work with than prosecute. Predictably, the WQB has not exactly kept the attorney general's office overworked with requests for lawsuits. On those rare occasions when the board finally runs out of patience, the victim is likely to be a small-time operator. It is no coincidence that the biggest judgments in pollution cases, including those against ARMCO and Champion Paper, came from suits filed by Harris County, not the state.

Some lawyers think that the restriction against the attorney general runs afoul of the Texas Constitution. "He's elected by the people to be *their* lawyer," says one. "But where pollution is concerned, he is forced to represent an appointed commission instead." Meanwhile, the Clear Creek Basin Authority grew tired of waiting for the state to act and sued the city itself. That forced the WQB to enter the case as an intervenor—along with its attorney, John Hill.

LIQUOR IS SLICKER
The Alcoholic Beverage Code

Emotional issues often produce bad laws. Some legislators will embrace almost any scheme that brings them a few extra votes—and there's always a friendly lobbyist around to suggest such a scheme. Over the years there have been few issues more emotional in Texas than the fight between Wets and Drys, so it should be no surprise that the alcoholic beverage laws are a mess. Every interest group imaginable has its own special provision: wholesalers, package stores, convenience stores, mixed-drink permit holders, hotels, restaurants . . . everyone who handles Demon Rum is represented. Some of the provisions are so blatant that you wonder how anyone had the nerve to propose them:

• Don't make the mistake of bringing your own bottle of wine to a restaurant whose wine list you don't like. That's not just bad manners; that's a *crime*. The restaurant owners thought that one up.

• In the business world, most retailers buy from wholesalers on consignment. Not in the liquor business. Cash only: that's what the law says. Score one for wholesalers.

• Don't feel too sorry for the package stores. Restaurants and clubs with mixed-drink permits would dearly love to buy their liquor wholesale—but they can't. The law requires them to buy from retailers only.

• Package stores must close by 9 p.m. That assures convenience stores which sell beer and wine three hours with no competition.

There are more, many more. In a rare moment of candor, one liquor lobbyist admitted, "They ought to repeal the whole damned thing and sell the stuff to adults just like eggs or lettuce. But we'll fight 'em to the death if they try."

"If you are feeling guilty about turning down legislative pay raises, don't. The Legislature has written itself one of the fattest, most comfortable, most outrageous retirement systems man has ever devised."

GENTLEMEN PREFER BONDS
The Skiles Education Act

This one is complicated. It involves state finance, a difficult subject at best and one few legislators understand. But those who do are really putting one over on the rest of us.

One of the more sensible provisions of the much-maligned State Constitution is its pay-as-you-go requirement which prohibits the state from going into debt without first asking permission of its citizens. In short, this means no bond issues without a vote of the people. Well, almost no bond issues. The Legislature has authorized a clever scheme which allows colleges to ignore the pay-as-you-go rule and gives them a blank check on the state treasury.

Here's how it works. Starting in 1941 with the Skiles Act, colleges have been given blanket authority to issue bonds secured by tuition. On the surface this looks all right: there will always be plenty of tuition money to pay off the bonds. But . . . if tuition is used to retire the bonds, how can the college pay its teachers and stock its libraries? Only through ordinary appropriations from the Legislature. Look what has happened in this shell game: the Legislature could not issue bonds backed by the state treasury without a vote of the people. So, it let colleges issue bonds secured by tuition, and then replaced the obligated tuition money with dollars from, yes, the state treasury. Instead of the pea disappearing, though, what got lost was your right to vote. Something else disappeared, too: about $60 million. That's how much more tuition bonds cost than state general obligation bonds, which bear a lower interest rate.

"You're damned right it's a subterfuge," says one senator kindly disposed toward academia. "And if folks ever figure it out, we'll just think up another one."

EASY RIDERS
The Legislative Retirement Act

For years legislators begged Texas voters to give them a pay raise above the $400 a month provided in the State Constitution. For years the voters turned them down. If you were feeling guilty, don't. They got even. In fact, they may even be a little ahead, now that the public has finally relented and boosted their pay to $600 a month. You see, the Legislature has written itself one of the fattest, most comfortable, most outrageous retirement programs the mind of man has ever devised.

Most retirement plans are based upon a simple premise: you contribute a percentage of your salary now, you get back a percentage of your salary later, and the two should be roughly proportional. Not the Legislature's. Their benefits are tied to the liberal pensions of district judges, whose salary is $32,800 a year compared to legislators' $7200. That means that as judicial salaries go up (and with the Legislature setting them you can bet they will), so do legislative benefits. Even legislators who served before the act went into effect can qualify by taking a soft state job for a month or two, although they contributed nothing. If this sounds actuarially unsound, it is, but don't worry: the Legislature took care of everything. Their pension plan is part of the larger (and rock-solid) State Employees Retirement System. In addition to enduring the less than generous salaries set by the Legislature, the poor state employees must also subsidize the lawmakers' fat retirement program.

Legislators enjoy joking about their coup. Says one: "I hope to God A. M. Aikin [dean of the Senate with thirty years of service] runs again. If he ever quits, we'll have to pass a tax bill to pay for his retirement."

240 HOW SOME TEXAS BILLS BECOME LAW

THE GREAT TRAIN ROBBERY
The Franchise Tax Exemption

How would you like a nice tax loophole worth at least $4 million? Transportation companies—railroads, oil pipelines, truckers, and buses—have one, and you can bet they're not about to give it up.

Unlike most boondoggles, this one wasn't planned; it simply fell into their laps. Back in 1906 the Legislature was looking for a way to tax railroads, which were enormously profitable but had little property that stayed in a fixed location for taxing purposes. Eventually the Legislature hit on an elaborate levy called an intangibles tax, which amounts to a tax on the value of a business above and beyond its physical assets. (It is hard to define and even harder to administer.) A year later it passed a franchise tax on corporate capitalization, but since railroads were already tithing substantial sums, they (and later other transportation companies) were exempted from four-fifths of their franchise tax burden.

All this made good sense at the time, but in recent years the intangibles tax has brought in less and less revenue as the state tax rate, for unrelated reasons, dwindled. Meanwhile the franchise tax has evolved into one of the state's biggest money raisers. But the exemption for transportation companies remains on the books. This year, companies that pay the intangibles tax will contribute only $168,000 to the state treasury—a sum that barely covers that state's administrative costs—plus just under $1.2 million in franchise taxes. If their vestigial franchise tax exemption were revoked, they would pay $5.7 million in franchise taxes alone: railroad taxes would go up 111 per cent, motor carriers' 108 per cent, and oil pipelines' 71 per cent.

CROSSING THE BAR
The State Bar Act

Like all other states, Texas has an official agency that issues licenses to lawyers and on occasion takes them away. Unlike many states, though, Texas law provides for what is called an *integrated bar*: before a lawyer can practice in Texas, he must not only have a license but must also pay tribute to his professional trade organization. This is analogous to a city saying that before a licensed plumber can tap into its water mains, he must belong to a labor union. What's more, for lawyers, the public licensing agency and the union are one and the same: the State Bar of Texas.

What difference does this make to the general public? Just this: because it wears two hats, the bar can nimbly choose to wear whichever one suits it. It uses state employees on state time with state funds to further the private ends of the legal profession—which, though the bar would like for you to believe differently, are not necessarily synonymous with the best interests of the general public. The bar's legislative program is largely determined by a committee stocked with lobbyists for other interest groups—bankers, insurance companies, oil companies, and the like—who make certain that the bar never supports any proposal inimical to their clients' interests. The bar leadership is dominated by giant law firms who perform the same service for their corporate clients.

Either the bar should not be allowed to masquerade as a state agency, or it should be prohibited from lobbying before the Legislature. A state agency has no business doing anything other than issuing licenses and taking them away. If lawyers need a trade organization and a lobbyist, they can get them without the help of a state law. ★

A PENNY SAVED IS A PENNY EARNED

by Griffin Smith, jr.

Things you should know when they start ringing up the tax at the checkout counter.

Late one afternoon in early June, a chain-smoking, dark-haired man in his mid-forties idly watched an Austin convenience store cashier violate the law. Not until the man got home did he discover that the cashier had illegally charged him sales tax on his sack of groceries—on the milk, onions, and bread; on every single item, in fact, all of which happened to be exempt under the Texas sales tax law.

It was not the loss of the 25 cents that chagrined him; it was the firm suspicion that the store had a deliberate policy of tacking a phony "tax" onto every ticket, unless challenged by the customer. He suspected that, by his absentmindedness, he'd fallen victim to one of the countless petty sales tax rip-offs the State Comptroller has been trying to stamp out. He resolved to do something about it on his next visit. And that's bad news for the store. Because the customer's name was Bob Bullock, and he *is* the Comptroller.

The sales tax is Texas' most prolific source of government revenue; 38 per cent ($1.3 billion) of last year's state tax collections were derived from what the law books officially call the "Limited Sales, Excise, and Use Tax." The closest contender—oil and natural gas production taxes—brought in almost exactly half as much ($664 million), and the principal "business tax"—corporation franchise taxes—was far down the list with just $167 million.

If the adjective "limited" sounds like wishful thinking to describe a levy that seems to sprout like a weed at the foot of practically every sales receipt, keep in mind that the sales tax statute is an intricate tangle of exemptions. These are at best chaotic, often whimsical, at worst nonsensical—nothing so simple and clear-cut as the popular labels of "food" and "drugs" would make them appear. For the average Texan, the sales tax is the sole everyday rendezvous with the tax collector; and, because of its exemptions, it is also the tax you are most likely to overpay.

That danger has worsened lately—an unintended side effect of Comptroller Bullock's energetic campaign to crack down on retail stores that charge the tax to their customers and then fail to pass the money along to the state treasury. When the colorful Bullock—who has had several previous incarnations in Texas politics, including four years as a state legislator, five as a savvy, freewheeling lobbyist, one as an assistant attorney general in charge of antitrust, and three more as Governor Preston Smith's controversial secretary of state—arrived at the Comptroller's office in January 1975 he discovered that the collection procedures were dismayingly lackadaisical. Under departing Comptroller Robert Calvert, each bureaucratic section operated as an independent fiefdom, often issuing its own tax rulings without even consulting the department's legal division. Serious audits were a now-and-then/maybe affair; many retail establishments openly and with impunity refused to give the state the sales taxes their customers had already paid. Asked what his official priorities had been concerning the sales tax when he took office, Bullock explained: "Collect it. Just plain collect it." Thus began the hard-line policy against retail tax cheats—who, Bullock found, were disproportionately concentrated in certain types of highly competitive businesses like carpet stores, restaurants, appliance stores, tire companies, and lumber yards, though there was hardly any line of retail sales in which some merchant somewhere had not been tempted to convert his 5 per cent tax collections into 5 per cent extra "profit." Unscrupulous businesses skimmed off money belonging to the public, then put the illegal money to work against law-abiding competitors. "Give those people a five per cent advantage," says Bullock, "and they'll run their competition right out of business. A few dollars can make the difference in a tire sale or a TV sale."

Bullock's Raiders have already paid surprise visits to 285 delinquent businesses owing a total of $2.7 million in tax liabilities. Some have forked over their debt on the spot; others have been padlocked until their owners could produce the missing money. Bullock's sales tax division collected $993,000 in court judgments during the first sixteen months of his tenure—considerably more than Calvert had collected in his final eight *years*. His field auditors will, at their present brisk pace, bring in $33 million in otherwise uncollected sales taxes this year, compared to $9 million during the last full year under Calvert.

All of this has flustered retail businesses accustomed to the casual indifference of the Calvert era. For years they were willing to resolve ambiguous tax questions in a good customer's favor; even though stores are liable for tax on all taxable sales whether or not they collect it from purchasers, full-fledged audits were rare, so they got by comfortably. Now there is a discernible tendency to insist that customers pay

Photography by Michael Patrick

the "tax" whenever there is the slightest possibility it could be due. Result: Texas consumers are paying more and more "taxes" they don't owe. And the pennies add up. "If even one-half of one per cent of the sales tax revenue has been erroneously collected," says Garry Mauro, assistant comptroller for field operations, "that is still a hell of a lot of money"—more than $6.5 million last year.

Most of the confusion in sales tax collections results from the almost indecipherable glut of exceptions. Bullock has begun to eliminate some of the more spectacular absurdities that he inherited from Calvert. He has, for example, abolished the ruling under which tax was due on baling wire used to bale hay for one's own farm, but not due on baling wire used to bale hay for sale; he has discarded the ruling that made hand-held posthole diggers taxable and tractor-mounted posthole diggers untaxable. But others remain, either built into the statute by the Legislature or engrafted onto it by administrative fiat: the infamous Six Doughnut Rule, the Sliced Barbecue Test, the Complete Funeral Principle, and the Fudgsicle Savings Clause, to mention a few (see page 116).

The Comptroller has been called upon to decide such weighty questions as whether tax is due on candy sold at PTA carnivals (no), the electricity used in a doghouse at a mine (yes), tarragon herbs (yes if bought as a living plant; no if bought dried in a bottle), and worms (yes if bought as fish bait; no if bought by a farmer to improve his soil). He has ruled that sales tax is due on garage sales, that a Dairy Queen cone is taxable but a pint of Dairy Queen isn't, and that pet dogs are taxable but stock dogs are not. If, as has been reported, dog meat is considered a delicacy by the Vietnamese, he may soon be called upon to judge whether the purchase of a canine for, say, sweet-and-sour Doberman is a taxable transaction for our newest Texans. (Reluctant to prejudge his legal division, Bullock so far merely says he expects it would be regarded "like sweet-and-sour possum in East Texas.")

Both the sales tax rate and the number of exceptions have risen since the tax was first passed, over Governor Price Daniel's long and fierce resistance, in an embattled special legislative session in 1961. The rate, originally 2 per cent, rose to 3 in 1967, to 3¼ in 1969, and to 4 in 1971. In 1967 cities and towns were given the right to tack on an extra 1 per cent for local use, yielding the now-familiar 5 per cent tax in most urban areas of Texas. The tax itself, imposed on "the receipts from the sale at retail" of "tangible personal property" within Texas, was originally designed to exclude a host of items that the Legislature considered "essentials" rather than "luxuries," some of which were essential only to the special-interest groups that successfully persuaded the lawmakers to include them. Tax benefits went to such disparate groups as airlines, labor, and vending machine companies; the oil drillers got their gravy and as time passed, others added their own: in 1968, for example, racehorse breeders pushed through an amendment exempting their thoroughbreds from sales tax. By any reckoning, the most lavish tax breaks went to the farm and ranch lobby; unlike the city dweller, a farmer can, by tapping the right plug, run his home TV and air conditioners on tax-free electricity; feed the family dog tax-free pet food; put tax-free oil in his pickup; and enjoy myriad other privileges. Even the taxable bug spray which the city dweller uses on his home garden is not taxable for the farmer's crops. (The same is true of ladybugs and praying mantises, which the law considers "work animals" for the farmer.) Tax exemptions on farm machinery, in effect from the beginning, were broadened in 1968 to allow farmers and ranchers to include such machinery as road graders in the tax-free category—a major boon to large property holders in South and West Texas.

One of the biggest special-interest beneficiaries under the sales tax law is the retail merchant himself. Not only does he get to keep a collector's fee of 1 per cent of the total tax he owes (3 per cent if he prepays), but the law is designed to let him collect from customers considerably more money than he subsequently will be required to forward to the state treasury. He collects on each *individual* sale, but he pays only on the *aggregate* of all his taxable sales. Moreover, the "bracket" system which he can use to compute the tax on those individual sales is skewed to let him collect *more* than 5 per cent on many taxable items. The sales tax can be as high as *10* per cent—as anyone who buys a dime postcard or newspaper soon discovers.

It is possible to get a fairly accurate picture of the things a society values and does not value by perusing its tax structure. Texas' persistent reputation for anti-intellectualism is underscored by its decision, contrary to most states', to tax newspapers and magazines—though perhaps a magazine is not the place to point that out. (In England, even books are free of tax.)

The most important sales tax exemptions are the result of tenacious efforts by legislative liberals in the 1961 special sessions and in later years. The most well-intentioned exemption is "food for human consumption," which, however, does not include food "served, prepared, or sold ready for immediate consumption" by restaurants, drugstores, pushcart vendors, and similar businesses, nor does it include various kinds of food the Legislature disapproved of—candy, soft drinks, wine, and Popsicles, for example. By the time the Legislature finished granting special privileges allowing favored organizations like church groups and PTAs to sell even taxable items free of tax, the chaos caused by the food exemptions was extraordinary. "Texas has one of the most elaborate exemption structures in the U.S.," says Deputy Comptroller Buck Wood. "I grew up thinking the exemptions were a great idea, but now I'm not so sure. Everybody wants to look at the tax structure to accomplish some social purpose, but it doesn't do a good job of that. A lot of exemptions have just gotten out of hand. Food is the worst. Our number one audit problem is grocery stores that sell both exempt and nonexempt items."

Most states do tax food—but, as Wood points out, they generally cushion the impact of their food tax upon the poor by providing a corresponding rebate on personal income taxes—an alternative unavailable in Texas, which is one of only eight states without a personal income tax.

Because the grocery exemption is Texas' way of serving a widely recognized social purpose, it will likely be around for many years to come. Bullock, however, will ask the 1977 Legislature to consider reforming other exemptions, like the one which allows common carriers to purchase replacement parts tax free. He also would not be disappointed if the legislators repealed the sales tax on electricity, at least for residential users.

In the meantime, what should consumers do? There is, unfortunately, no ready summary of exemptions or your rights under the law. The sales tax is so complicated it can't be summarized: the statute and the official interpretive rulings form a sheaf of paper more than an inch high. Bullock has ordered the preparation of brochures that would explain in simple terms the exemptions applicable to various types of businesses, but according to Carlton Carl, director of tax information, "To try to be specific on everything would cause more confusion than we have now."

Instead of trying to devise a written explanation for every possibility, Bullock has installed a toll-free WATS line to answer individual taxpayers' questions, which goes into operation August 1. The number is 800-252-5555. "If you think you're being overcharged on something," says Carl, "tell the store to pick up the phone and ask us whether it's taxable or not."

If the whole thing seems like too much hassle, you may want to lie down and take an aspirin. OK. But it's taxable.

TEN SNEAKY SALES TAX RIP-OFFS

Back in 1961 when the Texas sales tax was new, consumers paid more attention to what was taxable and what wasn't than they do now. In fifteen years a whole generation has grown up thinking the words "plus tax" are part of the natural order of things. They are more inclined to pay up than to ask questions. The rest of us have been thoroughly confused—not only by the tangle of exemptions that were woven into the tax at the beginning, but also by the new items that come and go (mostly come) under its provisions. There is ample opportunity for overcharge, intentional or unintentional, in a wide array of commercial transactions. Some of the most bizarre are illustrated on these pages. With many nontaxable items—fertilizer, for example—your own knowledge is your only protection; many are the checkout clerks who have no idea what's taxable and what isn't, so speak up or pay what you don't owe. If you're uncertain, call the Comptroller's toll-free number or if you want to report a violation, contact the nearest local district office.

The Drinks-With-Dinner Trap

Even as the liquor-by-the-drink law brought the benefits of tequila sunrises to Texas' deprived millions, it created a tricky pitfall for the unwary diner. If the restaurant you're visiting has a mixed-drink permit, *all* its alcoholic beverages are exempt from the sales tax (they are taxed—at 10 per cent—under a different law, and that tax must be included in the menu price, not tacked onto the bill). Check to see if the sales tax you are asked to pay has been computed on the price of your dinner *and* drinks. If so, the management may be gambling that the customer is so used to seeing sales tax that he'll never notice. An extra 5 per cent on what may be $20 or $30 worth of cocktails and wine quickly adds up to a nifty profit margin for the management. At one top Dallas restaurant we sent back such a miscomputed bill; it was discreetly returned a few moments later with the tax computed correctly, but when we paid another visit six months later, the same game was still going on.

But keep in mind two *caveats*: (1) since 1975, if a restaurant adds a mandatory "service charge" to your bill, they can properly charge tax on that ("voluntary" tips are still exempt, of course), and (2) if the restaurant you visit does *not* have a mixed-beverage permit—say it just sells wine and beer—it falls under a different provision of the law and wine and beer *are* subject to sales tax.

Mail-order Swindles

Beware of mail-order forms from companies with out-of-state addresses. Nine times out of ten the companies are not registered to do business in Texas, which means that they are not authorized to collect Texas sales tax on the items they sell. Some, of course, don't even try to; but others have developed the "add applicable tax" ploy. Their order blanks have a line for you to fill in the price of the merchandise and then a line underneath marked "add applicable tax." The unwitting purchaser dutifully adds 4 or 5 per cent and mails away the money. The unregistered company simply pockets the "tax." They haven't broken any laws, because in truth there is no tax on sales of this type; you have just been suckered. But be careful: if the mailing address is in Texas, or if the company is registered to do business here, you *do* owe tax, and the company will let you know it in no uncertain words—the form will say clearly, "Texas residents add 5 per cent sales tax," or some other phrase to make it plain exactly what tax is being collected.

Another word to the wise: just because you don't owe Texas sales tax on mail-order merchandise from most out-of-state firms does not, alas, mean it's tax free. If the item would be taxable if sold in Texas, you are supposed to volunteer to pay the Comptroller a "use tax" in an amount equal to the sales tax. Few do; but on some big-ticket items, he will track you down. The taxman thinks of everything.

Fertilizer Flimflams

Fertilizer is exempt from sales tax in Texas, regardless of who the purchaser is or what he plans to use it for. But outside of farm and ranch stores in rural areas, this exemption is widely unknown and ignored. "Inadvertently paying tax on large exempt items like fertilizer is one of the most frequent mistakes a consumer makes," says Deputy Comptroller Buck Wood. The more urban the location, the more likely the error; recently we picked up a bag of fertilizer at our downtown Woolworth's, were charged tax, questioned it, and were told by the checkout girl, "Nobody ever told *me* it isn't taxable." True, nobody had; and since almost everything else Woolworth's sells is taxable, her assumption was a natural one. We decided to see how long it might take to get things straightened out; after talking with two supervisors, the manager, and waiting for him to telephone the comptroller, we got our tax-free fertilizer in about 25 minutes.

Tires and Fishing Gear

The federal excise tax is applied to a wide variety of items. In most cases—radios and batteries, for instance—the state sales tax is due on the entire purchase price, including the federal tax. Not so, however, with two privileged types of merchandise: tires and fishing equipment.

Tire dealers are fiercely competitive, and some of them are not above quoting you an attractive deal and then gigging you at the last minute with an inflated "sales tax." Study any tire bill closely: has the sales tax been figured on the price of the tires *after* deductions for any trade-in, and *before* the federal excise tax is added? If so, you're ok; if not, holler.

The same is true with fishing equipment, though in that case mistakes are more often the result of sales clerk ignorance than company trickery. We owe both these peculiar exemptions to the Legislature.

Convenience Store Chicanery

Convenience food stores sell so much that is taxable (anywhere from 30 to 70 per cent of their sales are beer), that they often charge tax on virtually anything you buy. Whether they do this because they don't stop to think or because they are confident *you* won't stop to think is a matter of some debate. Recently, at our neighborhood Seven-Eleven, a customer brought two 37 cent cans of tomato paste to the checkout counter. Nothing could have been more clearly "food." This exchange ensued:

Clerk: "That'll be seventy-four cents plus four cents tax, seventy-eight cents."

Customer: "But this is food, there's no tax on this."

Clerk: "Well, there *is* tax, but we won't worry about it, okay?"

Seven-Eleven is by no means the sole offender. At a local Utotem, the ice cream cabinets were brazenly festooned with large stickers reading, "Fudgsicles 17 cents plus tax" and "Ice Cream Sandwiches 20 cents plus tax"—despite the fact that both articles, being dairy products, have always been tax free when sold in grocery stores.

A familiar convenience store practice is to tax soft drinks in returnable bottles based on a lump sum that includes the deposit on the bottle. No way. Although soft drinks are taxable, bottle deposits are not. The gambit is not limited to convenience food stores—any time you go to your grocery without bottles, pick up a carton or two, and the clerk rings up a lump sum for the drinks and bottles together, you can be sure he has hit the "taxable" button for the whole amount. Bottle deposits should be added on at the bottom of your bill, after the tax has been computed, or else rung up as nontaxable "groceries."

Rural One-Percenters

City folks tend to forget that the Texas *state* sales tax is 4 per cent, not 5. The other penny goes to those municipalities which have elected to piggyback their own 1 per cent sales tax on top of the state's. Almost every city and town of any size has done so. But that extra penny stops at the city limits; stores in rural areas can charge no more than the basic 4 per cent.

Result: some rural businesses, especially those just outside the city limits, hit up unsuspecting city slickers for the extra 1 per cent and (unless the Comptroller catches them) pocket it. Few customers notice, because 5 per cent tax is so widely accepted.

"Rounding Off"

An increasingly common practice is to "round off" the sales tax to the nearest nickel. Somehow, it always seems to get rounded off up, not down.

Unlike most sales tax rip-offs, which are perpetrated either in ignorance or by sharpies who are obviously sharpies, this one is both deliberate and most likely to happen to you at a better-class establishment. If you question the extra three or four cents, the management will probably tell you, "Oh, we just don't like to fool with pennies here," implying by a suitably arched eyebrow that you must be some sort of Silas Marner for fooling with them yourself. For even noticing, in fact.

For better or worse, however, the U.S. government still mints pennies, and the Texas sales tax is still computed in them. Within 48 hours after Maryln Schwartz of the *Dallas Morning News* did a front-page exposé about "rounding off" in Dallas, Bullock issued a new regulation forbidding it and imposing civil penalties of up to $500 per day for violations. He also began audits of the offending businesses. But elsewhere, the practice still goes on.

Repair Contract Pitfalls

Repairs are one of the most complicated areas of the sales tax. Say you take your ragged old venetian blinds to be restrung. The repairman can either divide your bill into "materials" and "labor," or he can write your bill for one lump sum covering everything. If he does the former, he is entitled to charge you tax on the materials but not the labor; if he does the latter, the whole bill is free of sales tax. Obviously, then, it's to your advantage to get a lump-sum repair bill if you can—provided your repairman follows the rules and doesn't add sales tax onto *that*, as many unfortunately do.

Caveat: What makes the repair area so complicated is that some things which look like repairs aren't legally repairs. If you take an old upholstered chair and have it re-upholstered, that's a repair; but if you take a chair frame and have it upholstered for the first time, that's "processing" or "fabrication," for which a whole different set of rules applies. According to Tom Henderson, director of the sales tax division, "If the work substantially modifies the nature or purpose of the item, rather than simply restoring it to its original condition, then it's not a 'repair.'" Thus, if you bring a seamstress cloth to make drapes, her bill is fully taxable; if you ask her to mend the drapes you already have, she is performing a repair and a lump-sum bill from her should be tax free.

Mobile Home and Used Car Gimmicks

In sheer dollars lost, no sales tax rip-off can equal the game played by some unscrupulous used-car salesmen and mobile-home dealers. Neither automobiles nor mobile homes are subject to the sales tax. They are covered, instead, by the motor vehicle tax, an entirely separate levy which dates from 1941 and is payable not to the retailer but to the county tax collector directly. (You pay the 4 per cent motor vehicle tax at the time you register your car and pick up the tags.)

A fast-talking used car salesman can bamboozle unsuspecting purchasers out of a big chunk of money. "Some of these guys," says Buck Wood, "will tell you, 'Yessiree, this one's a beautiful baby, you bet, just nine hunnert dollars, that's all, just nine hunnert dollars plus tax,' and you'll listen to their pitch and wind up paying forty-five dollars you don't owe. Later, when you go to transfer your title, you'll find out you still owe the state the motor vehicle tax of four per cent. And when you go back to locate the guy who took your money, he's nowhere to be found."

The same sales swindle occasionally happens to unlucky mobile-home buyers, with even more disastrous results, since the phony "sales tax" on a $10,000 mobile home can be as much as $500. Because mobile homes are not issued tags except for highway use, moreover, the purchaser who buys one for a fixed residence may never learn that he has been had.

Use Tax Evaders

The tenth rip-off is one that hurts you primarily as a citizen, not as a consumer. It's the failure of many businesses (and individuals) to pay "use tax" on expensive items they purchase from out of state, thereby shortchanging the state treasury. Technically, of course, even the tiniest mail-order purchase may be subject to the use tax, but the cost of the paperwork required to process such a minuscule payment would exceed the revenue the state might get. Not so, however, with things like bank computers, printing presses, television towers, convenience store coolers, pleasure boats, and airplanes—all of which, the Comptroller has found, are being purchased out of state by Texans who bring them home and use them without paying tax. The revenue loss is substantial; an unpaid five per cent use tax on a $3 million printing press is an even $150,000. An $800,000 corporate jet involves $40,000.

Some businesses aren't even aware of the use tax. Others know perfectly well what they are doing. A common practice is to purchase, say, a Cessna out of state, fly it surreptitiously into Texas, and put it in a hangar. "How do we ever find it?" says Bullock. "We can go out and check the registration numbers with the FAA, but that's a tedious process." Nor are private individuals above cutting tax corners at the expense of their fellow citizens. "People in Galveston or Beaumont buy pleasure boats tax-exempt in Louisiana, bring them back, and don't pay the use tax," says Bullock. "We have a hell of a time finding them. But what they're doing is unfair to the Texas merchant; that Louisiana salesman has a $5000 advantage on a $100,000 boat. He can make you a pretty good deal on that boat."

Bullock has instructed his auditors to keep a sharp eye out for possible use tax violations. In so doing, he hopes to put a noticeable dent in the present multimillion-dollar losses for unreported and unpaid use taxes.

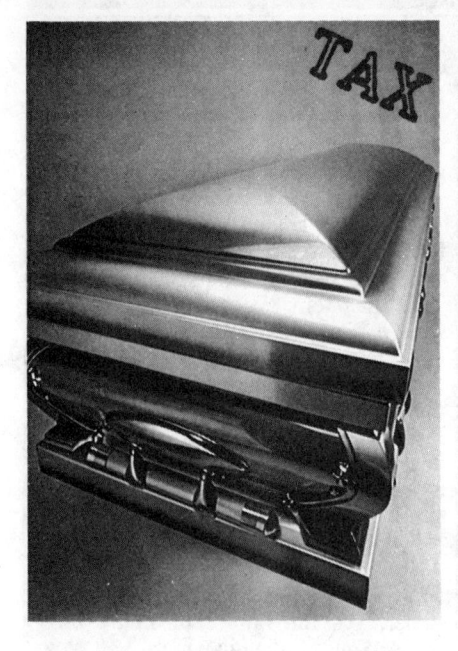

SIX REASONS
WHY YOU'LL NEVER UNDERSTAND
THE SALES TAX

1 **The Complete Funeral Principle.** So you want to buy a *casket*—never mind why. If that's all you buy from your friendly mortician, it's taxable. But if you go for the *complete funeral package*—flowers and choirs, say, plus his agreement to handle the funeral services, he can send you a lump-sum bill in which everything including the casket is tax free.

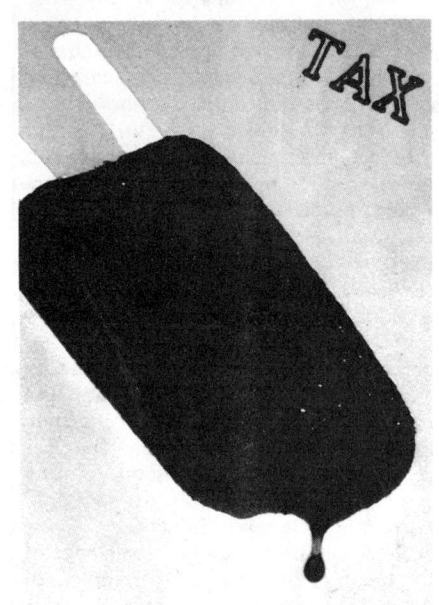

2 **The Fudgsicle Savings Clause.** Food sold in grocery stores is exempt from sales tax. But what is food? Dairy products are, says the statute. But not products made from "diluted juices sold in frozen form." Remember that when you buy a *Fudgsicle* (tax free) and hope the clerk forgets it when he sells you a *Popsicle* (taxable). Suppose, though, that you get a yen for that Fudgsicle at a movie, lunch counter, or street vendor's pushcart instead of at a grocery store; then what? Sorry, it's taxable. And you thought you had things all figured out.

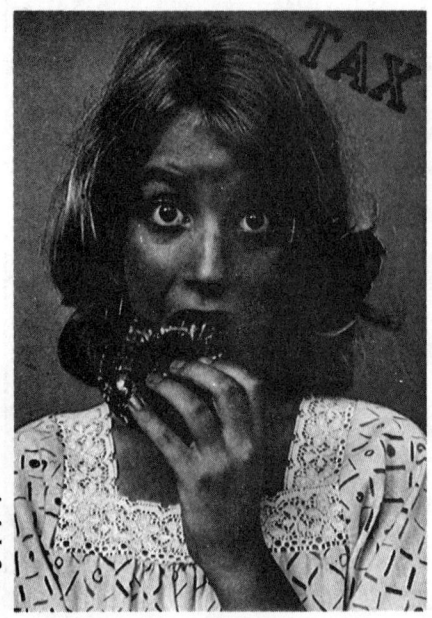

3 **The Six Doughnut Rule.** The distinction between plain old food and "food sold ready for immediate consumption" has created some of the zaniest quirks in Texas law. If you buy a doughnut at a bakery, it's considered tax-free food. But what if you buy it at Dunkin' Donuts "to go"? Says the Comptroller: *one to five doughnuts*, taxable; *six or more doughnuts*, no tax. The theory, which the author can attest is false, is that nobody can immediately consume six doughnuts. An even weirder corollary is the Sliced Barbecue Test: if you carry out some sliced barbecue, it's presumed to be for immediate consumption and is thus taxable. But if you carry out a big chunk, it's nontaxable, like a big smoked ham at the grocery store. What's a big chunk? If it's too big to get in your mouth sideways, it's tax free.

Photography by Michael Patrick

4 The Candy Criterion. Candy, says the Legislature, is bad stuff and ought to be taxed. Chocolate for cooking is good stuff, and shouldn't be. How do you tell the difference? Simple, rules the Comptroller: candy is "the product sold in a confectionary form." Fine. If you buy *chocolate bits* (nontaxable) instead of *Hershey kisses* (taxable), you'll save.

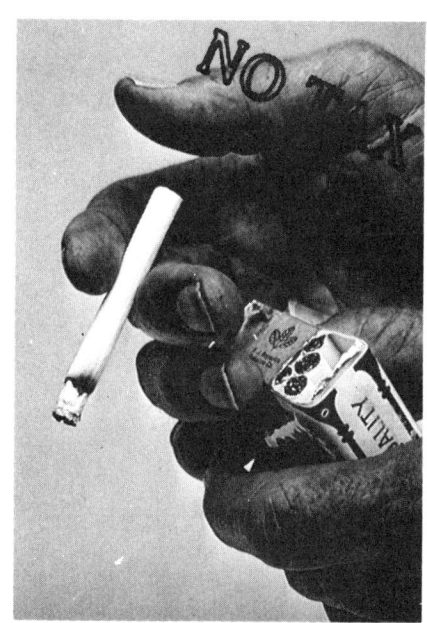

5 The Snuff Proviso. Specifically exempted from sales tax are all products taxed under the state's tobacco tax — which would, you might expect, include all things nicotinic. But you'd be wrong. The tobacco tax leaves out snuff, largely because former East Texas legislator (and later Land Commissioner) Jerry Sadler had a special personal fondness for dipping snuff. Result: if you *dip*, you pay sales tax; if you *smoke* or *chew*, you don't. (But before smokers rejoice, remember the tobacco tax is 18½ cents on a 50 cent pack of cigarettes, while the sales tax on 50 cents' worth of snuff is just 3 cents.)

6 The Alpo Anomaly. When the Legislature made groceries for human consumption nontaxable and pet food taxable, they thought they'd made themselves perfectly clear. But they also stuck in a tax exemption for "farm and ranch animals." As a consequence, the rancher's *stock dog* can dine tax free while a citified *pet dog* can't. But wait: it gets worse. What about poor folks who can't keep pace with inflation and have to eat cat food or Alpo now and then—appallingly enough it does happen. Do they owe tax? Says the Comptroller's legal division: in theory no (because it's food, of sorts, for human consumption) but in practice yes (because pet food isn't "ordinarily" eaten by humans). Small consolation for the humans who *do*. ★

HOW SOME TEXAS BILLS BECOME LAW 247

Texans and Energy

PART FIVE

The changes now taking place in Texas are fundamentally linked with oil and gas, for the discovery of those two energy sources sparked the growth of financial empires and industry in the state. Control and regulation of oil and gas reserves critically influence the power and wealth of the state's economic elite, as well as the jobs and economic well-being of its general citizenry. Thus regulation remains a central political issue in Texas. However, as the number of wildcatter strikes declines, reserves dwindle, and energy demands continue to expand, state government and industry must prepare to supplement oil and gas with other forms of energy. The historic concern with energy promises to remain a central issue in Texas politics for decades to come.

Conflict over Texas' energy resources and needs dominates both state and national politics. At the state level, lawmakers concern themselves with the policies most likely to secure reliable energy supplies for Texas. At the national level, Texas representatives attempt to weigh the needs and interests of Texans against those of other states and the nation at large. At the outset, it is often difficult to determine the real energy needs of any state and the trade-offs that are justified in fulfilling those needs at the expense of other states or interests.

The intensity of the energy conflict is linked to the perceived scarcity of energy supplies. A major influence on Texas politics is the activity of both private and public officials in discovering new energy resources and insuring the delivery of that energy. Along the way, businessmen attempt to corner markets for private gain, and politicians attempt to exploit energy reserves in order to guarantee energy independence and their own political careers. Fortunes are made and lost. Careers rise and fall. In the process, Texas and the entire nation search for the one energy source that will be inexhaustible, safe, inexpensive, and secure.

Texas has come a long way since the era of the cowboy. As the essays in Part V indicate, the state's future seems to be linked with the ability of government, business, and research technology to open new energy frontiers. Chapter Eleven examines the politics of energy battles within the state and national governments. Chapter Twelve focuses on business and energy. Chapter Thirteen takes a look at alternate energy sources that may eventually fashion a new environment for Texas—changing the political and social context of the state yet again.

Energy and Government

★

CHAPTER ELEVEN

Pipe Dream, Paul Burka (August 77)
So Close, So Far, Paul Burka (April 76)

PIPE DREAM
by Paul Burka

Is that what the coal slurry lobby sold the Legislature?

Back in 1891, ten years before Spindletop blew in, someone got the idea that coal could be pulverized, mixed with water, and transported through a pipeline. The idea was patented but no one would pay much attention to coal slurry pipelines for more than half a century; everyone was far too busy switching from coal to oil and gas.

The idea was resurrected in the 1970s when it became clear that everyone would eventually have to switch back. At least eight coal slurry pipelines have been proposed, but the only line in operation today runs from strip mines in the Arizona desert to a power plant in Southern California. Houston Natural Gas Corporation wants to build a second line stretching from Walsenburg, Colorado, to a site southeast of Houston near Angleton. Though not one inch of pipe has been laid, the Texas line has already crossed territory far more rugged than the builders of the Arizona line ever had to contend with: its course ran through the Texas Legislature and directly over the Texas Railroad Association, one of the oldest and most powerful lobbies in the state. To negotiate such terrain successfully was itself an engineering feat; the masterminds constituted one of the most powerful lobby coalitions ever seen in Texas politics. The session-long struggle between backers of the pipeline and the railroads was a classic of its type, matching two very different approaches to lobbying and at the same time offering a lesson in how a bill becomes law that can't be found in any textbook.

Why the railroads were so violently opposed to the pipeline can be summed up in just one word: money. Coal represents more than a fourth of all rail freight tonnage—and, except for the Arizona coal slurry line (owned, ironically, by a Southern Pacific subsidiary), railroads have a monopoly over coal transportation. The proposed pipeline, carrying fifteen million tons a year, could cost railroads at least $100 million annually—and that doesn't include the impact of competition on railroads' borrowing power. This was the real issue, though there was much debate over the need for a pipeline, which method would be cheaper for the consumer, and whether there was enough water in arid southeastern Colorado to keep the coal flowing. The economic stakes made it inevitable that the fight would be decided by political muscle.

The two sides could hardly have been less alike. The railroad lobby has been a potent force in Texas politics for more than a century; the coal slurry team was assembled specifically for this one battle. For all their influence in the Legislature, however, the railroads don't wield a big stick in the larger world of Texas politics. Their heyday is long behind them; in political clout they can't begin to measure up to Houston Natural Gas, the chief proponent of the pipeline. Unlike other special interest groups—doctors, lawyers, realtors—railroads are not known for lavish campaign contributions. The coal slurry team, on the other hand, had several top fund raisers.

The railroads have compensated for their lack of money by becoming the best organized lobby in Austin. They have seven full-time lobbyists, plus access to at least a dozen more who can come to town on a moment's notice. Their style is heavily personal: lots of contact with legislators, not necessarily about legislation, but rather just to build up friendships: lunch after the morning session, golf after committee meetings, drinks at night. They even have been known to take members' secretaries to lunch and bring them candy on Valentine's Day. When an issue comes up that isn't hot or philosophical—and most issues the railroads care about are neither—all that time invested pays off.

At the pinnacle of the railroad organization was Walter Caven, 56, a lanky, white-haired former legislator (1949-1951) who looks more like a retired admiral than the popular conception of a cigar-chomping lobbyist. Caven is universally regarded as one of the Big Three Austin lobbyists; the others are Bill Abington of the Mid-Continent Oil and Gas Association and Harry Whitworth of the Texas Chemical Council. Though Abington and Whitworth are able lobbyists, it is safe to say that anyone at the head of their organizations would rank atop the lobby hierarchy; Caven has gotten there on his own.

The coal slurry team was put together by former State Senator Searcy Bracewell, 59, a close associate of Houston Natural Gas (HNG) president Joe Foy and a bellwether in Houston conservative Democratic circles. Bracewell's participation brought in Dean Cobb, 41, the Austin-based lobbyist for Bracewell's law firm who had represented far-off Dumas in the House from 1969 through 1974. Houston's mammoth Vinson & Elkins law firm, which serves HNG as counsel, contributed Sandy Sanford, 36, one of the state's most respected independent lobbyists. Houston Natural Gas assigned Mark Gillaspie, 58, to unravel the mysteries of coal slurry technology for legislators. Construction unions and utility lobbyists provided additional support. But Bracewell still felt that something was missing. They had to combat the railroads' image as hail fel-

Illustrated by Michael Dean

lows well met: if the issue were viewed purely as a special interest fight, the pipeline bill was in trouble. Bracewell decided to add former presidential press secretary George Christian to wage a public relations campaign aimed at making coal slurry an energy/consumer issue.

Work began in earnest during June 1976 with a scouting trip to Arizona for a look at a slurry pipeline in operation. Christian was so impressed that he decided to bring members of the press for a later visit. Next the team set out to cement its political base—the Harris County delegation. (With the party primaries already over and few close races expected in the general election, the makeup of the 65th Legislature was pretty well set.) The reception was favorable: one firm No (someone from a railroad family), a few Maybes, and the others ranged from Probably to Where Do I Sign? And that was just the House; all six senators (of thirty-one) were solid. By the time the Legislature met in January, over half the membership had been contacted; the rest would be visited in the first month of the session.

Both sides regarded the outcome as a toss-up. The coal slurry team had money, clout, and a hot issue: energy. The railroads had experience, strong personal friendships, and the easier job: there are more ways to kill a bill than to pass one. "I'd rather have our job than theirs," Caven said.

The object of all this controversy was officially known as Senate Bill 185. It made for very dull reading. The bill itself had nothing to do with energy; it did one thing only—gave coal slurry pipeline companies the power to condemn private property. In Texas the pipeline would have to cross 28 railroad tracks, and one thing was certain: the railroads wouldn't grant the pipeline a right-of-way unless they were forced to.

In lobbying, as in football, each side has a game plan. For the coal slurry group, the plan of attack had three facets. Above all, speed was essential. The House inevitably bogs down in April over the appropriations bill and other time-consuming issues; the resulting logjam of bills has become an unhappy fact of life for lobbyists, more than a few of whom have watched the session run out with their projects not quite completed. The pipeline lobbyists knew that the earlier a bill gets out of committee, the better are its chances of beating the logjam. One way to guard against having the bill linger in committee is to let the chairman sponsor the bill—and so the coal slurry team entrusted their legislation to Max Sherman of the Senate Natural Resources Committee and Joe Hanna of the House Energy Committee.

The second vital aspect was Christian's department. He bombarded the press, city councils, and civic groups with material showing that Texas would need to import millions of tons of coal by 1985 (the exact amount was hotly disputed by railroads). Would the railroads maintain their monopoly, or would there be an alternate means of transportation? The beneficiaries of competition, the material stressed, would be Texas consumers. (One thing Christian did *not* stress was that Houston would be the only area served by the pipeline.) Everything was designed to give legislators a reason to tell Caven, "I'd like to help you, Walter, but we're in the middle of an *energy crisis.*" When he wasn't cranking out fact sheets and brochures or showing films, Christian was working on public officials; he was instrumental in getting the bill endorsed by the governor, lieutenant governor, attorney general, the Governor's Energy Advisory Council, the Railroad Commission, and assorted local groups.

Finally, the coal slurry team tried to focus the issue on the one thing the bill did: "Our job is to make legislators understand that the *only* relevant issue is whether it's in the public interest to give coal slurry pipelines the power of eminent domain," Sanford said. "All this talk about the cost and whether we can get the water is beside the point. If the pipeline isn't economically feasible, or we can't get the water, then we'll never be able to finance it."

Former *Texas Observer* editor Willie Morris once described the Texas Senate as resembling a mortuary parlor, which aptly fits its role in the legislative process. The reason the Senate has acquired its funereal reputation can be traced directly to Senate Rule No. 12, which requires a two-thirds vote before a bill can be considered out of the regular calendar order, and to Senate tradition, which holds that *all* bills are so considered. In effect, this combination allows one-third of the Senate— eleven of thirty-one—to block any bill from coming to the floor. Senators uniformly regard the rule with reverence, since it greatly enhances their individual power, while lobbyists either curse or embrace it, depending on whether they want to pass or kill a bill.

Because of the two-thirds rule, the Senate is often the first house to act on controversial legislation; House members would rather not go on record (making enemies on one side or the other) when a bill has no chance to pass the Senate. Speaker Bill Clayton let it be known early that coal slurry was one of those issues where he intended to shield his troops. So the first battleground would be the Senate—in particular, the Natural Resources Committee, where the bill was sent for a hearing. The bill had died there in 1975, because Houston Natural Gas lobbyists were much too involved in a utility regulation fight to worry about coal slurry. The only thing most senators knew about the issue then was that railroads looked upon coal slurry pipelines with an affection previously reserved for derailments and passenger trains.

Now Sherman was back for another run, but he had no illusions. "If you were betting on track records," he said a few days before the Senate hearing, "You'd have to go with the railroads." He wasn't at all comfortable about the sophisticated lobby effort behind the bill. To him it was just an energy issue; he had never been tagged as a lobby senator and didn't want to jeopardize his reputation. He seldom collaborated with the slurry team during the session.

The first prognosis of the committee vote was that it would be close. Each side's confidential count gave it a 5–4 edge with two undecideds; the contested senator was Ray Farabee of Wichita Falls, a thoughtful, almost professorial legislator with a reputation for approaching problems with an open mind. Farabee had opposed the pipeline in 1975, but unbeknownst to the railroads, he had been wooed and won by HNG's Mark Gillaspie. (A former Bill Hobby campaign manager, Farabee may also have been influenced by the lieutenant governor's strong support of the bill.) Of the two undecideds, it was futile to speculate what Bill Patman of Ganado was going to do: his is the most unpredictable vote in the Senate. Freshman Senator Carlos Truan of Corpus Christi was a different matter, however; both sides thought they had a good shot at his vote. ("I felt like the only girl at the party," Truan said later.) Caven was encouraged that Truan was locked in a bitter dispute with labor supporters of the pipeline over their hostile attitude toward illegal aliens. (He might have been less optimistic had he heard Truan refer to him as "Walter Craven.") Meanwhile, railroad workers were concentrating on Truan; even their wives were in Austin to warn that the bill would put their husbands out of work. But Truan had other things on his mind. His district was beset by energy problems; utility bills were soaring and industries were laying people off.

The night before the February 16 hearing, both sides were confident. One railroad lobbyist—not Caven—threw a $100 bill on a table at a local bar and offered to bet a coal slurry lobbyist that the bill would again die in committee (the challenge was rejected). Cobb went to bed at 1:30 a.m., then awoke at 3 and couldn't go back to sleep. He reviewed the alphabetical roster of the committee and realized that the roll call ended with Patman and Truan; his side would need one. He walked into the hearing telling himself he wouldn't be the least surprised if the vote was 6–5 either way.

The hearing itself was uneventful.

ENERGY AND GOVERNMENT 253

The previous day Caven had raised some eyebrows during the House hearing with an almost evangelical, arm-waving outburst, but he had known from the start that Hanna's committee would approve the bill. This was different, and Caven was all business. True to form, his presentation was extremely personal, punctuated by references to power plants and contract negotiations in individual senators' districts—especially Patman's and Truan's.

But it was futile. Halfway through the roll call the railroads lost the vote of Grant Jones of Abilene, one of their four stalwarts, and before the balloting reached Patman and Truan, the bill already had the six favorable votes it needed. Jones hadn't actually promised his vote to anyone, but even the coal slurry team had conceded his vote. His great uncle had come to this country with a load of dynamite to help build the Union Pacific; his father was a railway conductor who met Jones' mother on the Wichita Valley line. Jones was later to call the coal slurry bill "the toughest vote I've cast since I came to the Legislature"; in the end, he said he couldn't ignore something that possibly could help stabilize utility rates. Patman and Truan added their superfluous aye votes, and the bill was on its way to the floor.

Now the two-thirds rule came into play, but Jones' defection made it less of a factor. The coal slurry team's initial count of the Senate was 16 for, 7 against, 8 undecided—but since then Jones had switched and Patman and Truan had committed: 19–6–6, with two more needed. "We're a lot closer to our twenty-one than they are to their eleven," Sanford said after the hearing, and Caven knew it too. "My guess is that they'll get their twenty-one and pass it," he said. "But this thing isn't over yet."

One of the first things Caven did after the hearing was let Grant Jones know there were no hard feelings. Jones might still be some help on amendments, Caven hoped, and in any case, there were other battles to fight. His organization was locked in struggles over railway safety and wrongful-death laws; Jones could be counted upon in both. Perhaps lobbyists with narrow interests could afford the luxury of blood feuds with members of the Legislature, but not Caven: railroads were interested in everything from taxes to tort law. Their universal involvement was one source of their influence, but when things went sour, it was also a limiting factor: vengeance was out. No one issue was worth making a permanent enemy, not even this one.

The bill was out of committee now, but floor action was still a month away (Senate rules require a four-fifths majority for consideration of bills in the first 60 days of a session, and that was out of reach). The first day for floor action under the two-thirds rule would be March 14, and Sherman was determined to move immediately in order to beat the post-appropriations logjam.

The Senate debate turned out to be a formality. As expected, Sherman brought the bill up on the first day following the expiration of the four-fifths rule. The vote to consider it was 23–6: two to spare. With Caven and a large clump of railroaders watching stoically in the gallery, a series of amendments was beaten back effortlessly. Sherman was confident he had the votes and didn't waste time with lengthy rebuttals. Once he said simply, "I think this amendment is not designed to help this bill," and moved to table. The best the railroads could muster was twelve votes. Shortly after noon the Senate passed the bill on a voice vote. Now it was the House's turn.

Sandy Sanford walked up the east steps of the Capitol on the morning the House was scheduled to vote on Senate Bill 185, stopping to inspect the archway above the door carefully, as though he suspected a boxcar might topple on him if he proceeded through the doorway. He ran through the vote tally sheet in his mind one more time: with 76 votes needed, he counted 82 firm aye votes minimum, 96 probable, perhaps more. Still, he wasn't happy. He looked up at the archway again.

"The House is a funny place," he mused. "Some days, as they say, you can't even pass gas. It's very different from the Senate. In the Senate they just beat you straight; either you've got two-thirds or you don't. In the House you never know what they're doing to you; sometimes *they* don't even know."

If the Senate is where bills die, the House is where they are maimed. There is no two-thirds rule to require broad support before a bill can reach the floor; consequently, no bill is safe from attack and few escape it. Sanford was worried this morning, not about losing the bill, but about hostile amendments; a crippling phrase or two at this stage could still kill the bill. Now he was at the mercy of the mood of the House—something which can shift suddenly and violently, like tidal currents in an estuary. It was completely unpredictable: only a few days before, the House had inexplicably voted down a noncontroversial bill for no better reason than legislators had just finished the exhausting school finance bill and wanted to go home for the weekend.

To the uninitiated, watching the House at work would not be the best introduction to the democratic process. The decorum resembles a Moorish marketplace on a busy day. At any given moment half the members are likely to be out of their seats, buttonholing members about upcoming bills, currying favor with the Speaker or the press, plotting with lobbyists in the foyer, consulting with constituents in the gallery, or just meandering aimlessly through the aisles. In such a disorganized atmosphere, a legislator's only real guidepost to what's happening is to watch the personalities involved; he blocks out most of what goes on and focuses his attention on debate only when the known heavyweights—or members he personally listens to—get up to speak. There is a herd instinct in the House, and, like any herd, it can be stampeded. The best protection is to have one or more of the heavyweights firmly committed to your side. But not one of the handful of members whose presence at the microphone can overcome the din of confusion on the floor was a vocal backer of the pipeline. Most of them were from rural areas where railroads still have political clout, and many had been around long enough either to have personal ties to Caven or to want to avoid antagonizing him.

All the coal slurry team could do under the circumstances was instruct their votes to "follow the sponsor" and hope the coalition would hold firm. But Hanna, who had been invaluable in getting the bill through committee and onto the calendar, was now, if not a liability, certainly not an asset. He had neither fondness nor flair for debate; if brilliant oratory would be required to save the day, Sanford knew that they might as well start thinking about 1979.

It didn't take long for Sanford's fears to be confirmed. Early in the floor debate, Joe Hubenak of Rosenberg, who has his eye on the upcoming statewide race for agriculture commissioner, offered an amendment to prohibit pipeline companies from condemning agricultural land. Except for those 28 railroad tracks, there wasn't much else along the proposed 800-mile route of the pipeline, so obviously the amendment would have rendered the bill meaningless. But, as so often happens in the House, the amendment's author wasn't really concerned about the bill; he was trying to ingratiate himself with the farmers' lobby. It was purely a political gesture: no one expected the vote to be close. Hanna moved to table the amendment, and the familiar free verse announcing a vote was read over the microphone:

Mr. Hubenak sends up an amendment;
Mr. Hanna moves to table.
The vote is on
The motion to table.
Those in favor, vote aye.
Those opposed, vote nay.
This is a record vote.
The clerk will ring the bell.

On the electronic scoreboard in front of the House chamber, each representative's name is followed by three lights: green (for aye), red (for nay) and white (for present, not voting). The coal slurry forces in the gallery glanced at the board expecting to find it as green as the Capitol grounds outside, with close to 100 members voting to table the amendment, and got the shock of their lives. "My God," said Cobb. "*Look* at all that red."

"I still think it's a green board," someone said, and it was: 77–65 to table. An insignificant skirmish had taken on the look of a major battle. "It's going to be a long day," Sanford said.

The debate moved ahead, slowly. More amendments were proposed, mostly to give property owners every possible break in bargaining with the pipeline company. Some had been drafted by railroad lobbyists, who are old hands at eminent domain law, and distributed to friendly members. A few were tabled, but others were tacked on over Hanna's protests. Individually they were minor; together they had substantial nuisance value, adding to the time and expense of constructing the pipeline. And the big fights, the gutting amendments, were still to come. One of the House heavyweights observed drily, "If this thing keeps going the way it has been, that bill's going to have so much baggage the coal slurry boys are going to have to rent a train from Mr. Caven to haul it back to the Senate."

At 12:15 p.m. the House recessed for lunch. Cobb, Sanford, and two of their lieutenants hustled down from the gallery to huddle with Hanna and three floor leaders near the Speaker's podium. The railroads, not surprisingly, had proved a worthy adversary. Their strategy was a clever one: run with the minor amendments first, win a few, break the aura of invincibility the coal slurry team had enjoyed since the Senate committee vote. Many of the legislators committed to voting for the bill nevertheless didn't want to see Caven embarrassed: why not throw a vote his way on the little stuff? What harm could it do? It seemed to Sanford that all he'd heard from House members for the past week was, "Don't worry—I'm going to give a vote or two to Walter, but I'm for the bill." Well, that had gone on long enough.

Over a bowl of chili, Cobb talked about what had gone wrong with the count. "A lobbyist is a salesman," he said, "and like any salesman, his hardest problem is closing the deal. It's easy to explain a bill; what's hard is asking a legislator, 'Are you for me or against me?' You don't like to ask it, and a lot of them don't like to tell you, especially if they're against you. So they end up saying something like, 'I'll help you if I can,' and you hear what you want to hear, and the first thing you know, that guy is down as a favorable vote. In this business, you got to count conservative." He pulled out a blue pamphlet with each legislator's picture in it and pointed to a mug shot of a veteran legislator. "He's listed as a possible aye, but I *know* we never had him. I'm going by the feeling in my gut."

By the time the afternoon session began, both sides knew that the battle was up for grabs. The bill would pass, that was certain, but the killing amendments could go either way. After some heavy sparring over the water issue, won narrowly by pipeline adherents, the critical moment was at hand. It came in the form of an amendment by one of the House heavyweights, Bob Davis of Irving, and, as a good gutting amendment should, it sounded *so* reasonable. The problem, Davis explained, is that if the pipeline turns out to be hugely expensive —the trans-Alaska pipeline exceeded the original cost estimates by a factor of eight—consumers are stuck. Just as Lo-Vaca Gathering Company charges consumers for the cost of all that new gas it is forced to purchase, so will the pipeline company pass on cost overruns from pipeline construction. What if the railroads turn out to be right, and the cost of delivering coal by rail is less than the cost of delivering coal by pipeline? Should Houston Natural be allowed to gamble with the public's money? His proposed solution: set utility rates on the basis of whichever transportation cost is cheaper. "What's wrong with competition and why are the coal slurry people so afraid of it?" Davis rhetorically asked his colleagues, neatly standing on its head the pipeline lobbyists' argument that it is the *railroads* who fear competition.

The bill was really on the line now. If the amendment went on the bill, the pipeline company could never arrange financing for construction. This was the time when the slurry forces desperately needed a strong spokesman on the floor, but when Hanna took the microphone to fight the amendment, his monotonic rebuttal was greeted with shouts of "Can't hear you" from desks in the rear. He tried to point out that transportation tariffs don't always tell the whole story—railroads, for example, have recently forced coal customers to buy their own railway cars—but no one was listening. The House was out of control now. There was no need to wait for the computer to tabulate the vote on Hanna's motion to table the amendment; the board was unmistakably red.

When the 65–80 tally flashed on the scoreboard, cheering broke out on the floor. "No pass-through!" someone shouted. "Hurrah for the Lo-Vaca amendment!" Another member waved at Caven in the gallery and mulled over the irony of what was happening: "Ole Walter's been beat on all session in the Senate, and here he is in the House where he didn't think he had any friends and look what happens."

But while the railroad forces were celebrating, the coal slurry lobbyists were desperately trying to shore up their collapsing coalition. They abandoned the gallery and headed for the foyer outside the House chamber; they sent urgent messages inside (lobbyists are barred from the floor) asking their floor leaders and faltering supporters to come outside for conferences. One burly labor leader cornered Matt Garcia of San Antonio, a member with some influence in liberal circles, and told him that if he was going to help, now was the time. Meanwhile, other pipeline backers advanced to the microphone to rail against the amendment and stall for time. Finally, Garcia got up to speak, aiming his pitch squarely at liberals who had been lured into thinking that this was a "consumer" amendment. His argument was simple: if this amendment is adopted, there will be no pipeline and no competition—and what good does that do consumers? Then it was time for the vote on the amendment itself, and as both sides made their closing arguments, Caven was so keyed up that he couldn't stay seated. Once again the Speaker sounded the ritual chant, once again the lights flashed green and red, and . . . red again! The same House that had voted against tabling the amendment had voted against putting it on the bill. Twenty-one votes had switched; the tally was 59 aye and 86 nay: in the range of Sanford's early-morning estimate. At the back of the gallery, Caven took one last look at the board and left.

The debate would stretch out for several more hours, but for all practical purposes it was over. The turnaround had broken the railroads' momentum. On the next two amendments, pipeline supporters broke the 100–vote barrier, and a feeling of anticlimax seemed to permeate the atmosphere. The long lines of questioners at the back microphone had dissipated, and both the tone of debate and the level of activity on the floor was less feverish. A few members dozed at their desks.

Sanford later called Garcia's speech the turning point. "Most members know what they're supposed to do, but they don't always know when to do it," he said. "A lot of people had decided to give the railroads a few votes, and we needed someone to tell them when to stop. Garcia told them."

In the fading hours of the day one last amendment did get added to the bill, but it wasn't one the railroads had dreamed up; it required the pipeline company to pay attorneys' fees for landowners who went to court over the value of their condemned property. There are 56 lawyers in the House, and just enough (37) found the proposal irresistible regardless of their commitment to the bill. Loyalty stops at the pocketbook.

Finally there was nothing left to do but vote on the bill. Six hours after debate began the lights lit up and everyone started heading for the door—

ENERGY AND GOVERNMENT 255

but the tallying machine broke down and, to everyone's dismay, they had to do it over. As Cobb leaned over the gallery railing and issued a general invitation for libations that night at a local watering hole, the board flashed the final tally: 111–34.

There was still a little excitement left. Sherman could accept the amendment and send the bill to the governor, or refuse to concur and ask for a conference committee. That decision was neither his nor the lobbyists' but Houston Natural's, and the word came back: the lawyers' amendment had to go. It was an open invitation to tie up the pipeline in court. A decade ago Caven's close friendship with the Speaker might have earned him a pro-railroad conference committee, but times have changed since Sharpstown. Clayton doesn't try many power plays and this wasn't the spot for one. The conference committee quickly dropped the amendment—so quickly that one House heavyweight who favored it complained, somewhat inappropriately, that he'd been "railroaded."

The bill is law now, but that doesn't mean pipeline construction will begin any day. The obstacles ahead are still staggering: financing, of course, plus land acquisition, and then there's the water problem. Caven is convinced the pipeline will never be built, and even Sherman has his doubts.

Despite the uncertain future of the pipeline, it is easy to understand in retrospect why the bill passed. Christian's public relations campaign was successful; the railroads could never overcome the appearance that they were arguing only for their self-interest while the pipeline seemed to be a public interest project at a time when all Texas is worried about running out of energy. To that extent the bill's passage was a victory for the "new" style of lobbying over the "old," and a sign of the growing sophistication of Texas politics. And yet, one wonders whether it was that simple; whether, if the railroads will really be dealt another in a long series of financial blows, one pipeline will be worth it. Who knows? You can't worry about it; there are two thousand such decisions every session: you just punch red or green and go on to the next one. ★

SO CLOSE, SO FAR

by Paul Burka

A freshman congressman from New Braunfels almost convinced Congress to deregulate natural gas — but almost doesn't count.

Sam Rayburn couldn't do it, even though he was Speaker of the House for 17 years. Neither could Lyndon Johnson. Senators Russell Long and Bob Kerr, the two best friends the oil and gas industry ever had, failed too. And so, in the end, did Robert C. Krueger, although for a brief, tantalizing moment, victory was in his grasp.

For most of the Fifties and Sixties, Rayburn, Johnson, Long, and Kerr had tried to persuade Congress to deregulate the wellhead price of natural gas; and despite their accumulated years of experience and seniority, they had gotten absolutely nowhere. On a bitterly cold Washington morning this February, with the temperature languishing near fifteen degrees and an ill wind whipping off the Potomac, the latest leader of the deregulation forces brought his case before the House Democratic Caucus. Bob Krueger was as unlikely a successor to Rayburn and Johnson as could be imagined, except that he too is from Texas. Together Mister Sam and LBJ amassed almost three-quarters of a century in Washington; Krueger is a freshman congressman with no political background. Rayburn and Johnson were hardscrabble; Krueger is a rich man's son. They were not exactly intellectuals; he is a former Shakespeare professor with a doctorate from Oxford. They knew the petroleum business backwards and forwards; a year ago all Krueger knew was that the stuff came out of the ground. Politically Rayburn and Johnson were masters at the art of compromise, at going along to get along; Krueger is something of a purist.

Yet Krueger came agonizingly close to succeeding where his legendary predecessors had failed. Narrowly defeated in committee, he took advantage of an obscure procedural rule to get his deregulation proposal to the floor. After several hours of intense and acrimonious debate, he won the first test vote by a comfortable 48-vote margin, and for the next two days he kept on winning, until, stunningly, his support evaporated at the crucial moment. The battle had all the elements of a classic political drama: desperately close votes, intense lobbying campaigns, endless behind-the-scenes intrigue, last-minute revelations by the press, and a Young Turk challenging the system. It is the stuff of which movies are made and novels written, and for a few minutes on the last afternoon, as the scoreboard clock on the wall of the House chamber blinked its way from 15:00 down toward zero and the vote stood tied at 196-all, the tension in the huge room was almost insupportable.

The fight over deregulation dates back to the late spring of 1954. Less than a month after the Supreme Court had ruled that separate but equal is "inherently unequal," the Court handed down an opinion in *Phillips v. Wisconsin* that would also influence the course of American history. Unlike the school desegregation case, however, the *Phillips* decision hardly created a stir outside the petroleum industry. So the Federal Power Commission would regulate the wellhead price of natural gas; so what? Wasn't the country swimming in natural gas? Didn't wildcatters curse their luck when they found gas instead of oil? Some oilmen even thought so little of natural gas that they contemptuously burned it on the spot rather than accept the meager prices offered by the giant pipeline companies—in some cases, no more than a penny or two per thousand cubic feet.

The immediate effect of FPC regulation was to change the structure of the natural gas industry. The commission controlled only the price of gas produced and sold to interstate pipelines; gas destined for intrastate consumption was unregulated. This two-tiered market, as it is known, didn't really make much difference as long as natural gas remained plentiful. Gas sold for about the same price in both the interstate and intrastate markets. But in the late Sixties, the supply situation changed dramatically. Demand kept going up, but production leveled off, then started to decline. The intrastate price began to rise, but the FPC kept the lid on interstate prices to protect customers at the other end of the pipeline.

It is customary in the gas industry

Opponents in the battle over deregulation chose sides: captains Bob Krueger (left) and Charles Wilson v. Bob Eckhardt.

for producers to sign long-term contracts with pipeline companies, usually for twenty years at fixed prices. The escalating price of natural gas reflects not the cost of *all* gas, but the cost of newly discovered gas, much of which is recovered by increasingly costly methods. New intrastate gas that had been selling at the wellhead for 12 to 16 cents per thousand cubic feet in the late Sixties climbed rapidly over 20 cents, 50 cents, a dollar, and, unbelievably, over two dollars, while the FPC grudgingly raised the interstate price to 52 cents. It was small wonder that producers didn't even bother to explore for gas unless they had an outlet to an intrastate pipeline. Those who did drill refused to sell new gas finds to interstate suppliers and dealt instead with intrastate companies. The intrastate market today is therefore glutted with gas, while the interstate pipelines must survive on production from old fields which are slowly playing out.

No one likes the two-tier market. Northerners have low prices which won't mean a thing when there's no gas to buy. Texans generally (customers of Coastal State's Lo-Vaca Gathering Company being the notable exception) have all the gas they want but have to pay four times as much as anyone else to get it. Even the FPC, in an uncharacteristic move for a regulatory body, asked Congress to revoke the agency's jurisdiction over natural gas prices. The problem is that no one can agree on how to get rid of the current system. The industry, rallying behind the banner of free enterprise, argues for deregulation; they claim higher prices will give producers more incentive to drill and will mean more gas for everyone. But northern liberals, who proliferated in Congress after the Watergate-influenced elections of 1974, view the industry with attitudes ranging from suspicion to outright hostility. Some believe that producers are deliberately holding back gas and are falsifying reserves in an effort to scare Congress into eliminating price controls. Others argue just the opposite: our gas reserves are so depleted, they say, that increased production is impossible, regardless of price—so the only effect of raising the price will be to line the industry's pockets for no purpose. One thing is certain. Neither group of liberals is about to loosen price controls and transfer billions of dollars from consumers to gas producers. Instead, they want the FPC to regulate *intrastate* gas as well as interstate, so that all the gas that's currently going to Texans can be redistributed across the country.

That is the rather complex background of the fight over deregulation which took shape in the House Commerce Committee last fall and culminated on the floor during the first week of February. At first it appeared that deregulation had no chance. It is virtually impossible for a bill to survive a hostile committee, and Commerce was hostile from top to bottom. Chairman Harley Staggers of West Virginia and powerful subcommittee chairmen John Dingell of Michigan and John Moss of California were sworn enemies of the oil and gas industry. In the unlikely event they wavered, some of the more strident freshman liberals, men like Toby Moffett of Connecticut and Andy Maguire of New Jersey, were around to shore up their determination. So was Houston Congressman Bob Eckhardt, and that spelled very bad news for supporters of deregulation. Eckhardt's casual air and slightly disheveled appearance belie a brilliant legislative mind; he is one of the few liberals in the House who understands how the petroleum industry works. He fought the industry in the Texas Legislature for years, without success of course, and finally managed to escape to Congress in 1967. "I was so happy to get away from Austin," he recalls, "because I wouldn't have to fight the oil and gas lobby any more. And then I got to Washington, and you know what? I found they'd gotten here first."

Deregulation had its supporters, of course, but there was no one to carry the ball. Outnumbered 29 to 14, Republicans could do little more than wring their hands and cast their votes. On the Democratic side, northern anti-gas industry liberals had a heavy majority. Except for Eckhardt, Krueger was the only Democrat on the committee from a major producing state—and he was just a freshman. True, he had made something of a name for himself in an earlier battle over decontrolling oil prices, but there he had had Dingell's help in subcommittee. This time the leadership was firmly aligned against him. Still, it had to be Krueger; there was no one else.

A few months earlier no one would have been more surprised that he would be leading the fight for deregulation than Krueger himself. When he arrived in Washington to represent the vast 21st Congressional district—it extends from New Braunfels on the east to the Big Bend on the west, and north almost to Abilene, an area larger than Pennsylvania—Krueger had his eye on the Agriculture Committee. But another Texas freshman wanted that seat, former State Senator Jack Hightower of Vernon. Seniority, of course, was equal, but ties are broken alphabetically. So Krueger had to look elsewhere. He decided that energy might be interesting and opted for Commerce.

With the help of Bill White, a twenty-year-old Harvard undergraduate from San Antonio whom Krueger hired as a $400-a-month intern, the new congressman didn't remain a neophyte for long. Like most Texas congressmen, he learned the gospel as preached by the oil and gas companies—except that Krueger managed to make it palatable by interjecting a quote or two from Shakespeare along the way. The Bard of Stratford has many remarkable accomplishments far too numerous to recount here, but not the least of these was lulling northern liberals into thinking that Bob Krueger represented not just the 21st District of Texas, but reasonable men everywhere. For the first time since the Arab embargo, debate over energy policy took place in a relatively calm and rational atmosphere, thanks in no small part to the polished style of the former university professor. An Oxford man a tool of the oil companies? Impossible. (Well, not so impossible, it turned out later. But that's getting ahead of our story.)

By the time the Commerce Committee was ready to take up natural gas legislation, Krueger had already proved himself a force to be reckoned with. His proposal for decontrolling oil prices had lost by only one vote (22–21) in the full committee and had come within eleven votes of adoption on the floor. Staggers and Dingell weren't about to risk a repeat performance on natural gas, so they carefully prepared a narrow bill with only one purpose: to let interstate pipelines buy intrastate gas in emergencies for up to eighteen months. (Current law limits these "spot" purchases to 60 days.)

The Dingell bill was a clever maneuver. It gave congressmen an easy chance to look as though they were doing something to increase gas supplies, when in fact they were only paving the way for interstate pipelines to raid the intrastate market. It was, as one oil and gas lobbyist lamented, "exactly the kind of bill the House loves," a simplistic short-term approach to a complex long-range problem. The bill was so narrowly drawn, in fact, that Krueger couldn't even use it as a vehicle for his long-range deregulation amendment—which is exactly what Dingell intended. ("We crafted that bill to keep you out," one of Dingell's allies warned Krueger.) Sure enough, when Krueger offered his amendment in subcommittee, Dingell—who as author of the bill and chairman of the hearing was both player and referee—ruled it out of order and nongermane. Krueger tried again in the full committee, but Staggers merely reiterated Dingell's previous ruling. Finally Krueger resorted to a short-term deregulation amendment, more as a test of strength than as a viable proposal; surprisingly, it came close but lost on a tie vote. With no other obstacles in the way, the committee sent the original bill on its way to the floor. The entire episode was an object lesson in the power of the committee system, and Dingell made certain that Krueger got the point. "Even if you'd won on the deregulation amendment," the twenty-year veteran told the freshman, "we'd never have let the bill out of committee." Round One to Dingell.

The most surprising thing about Round Two is that it happened at all. When Krueger lost in the Commerce Committee, natural gas deregulation was written off as dead. But it turned out that the fight was just beginning.

Krueger's new lease on life began, of all places, in the House Rules Committee, a much vilified body better known for performing last rites than resuscitation. The committee acts as a giant funnel—or bottleneck—through which all legislation must pass before it gets to the floor. Theoretically Rules only determines the sequence and procedure for debate, but as more than one frustrated congressman has learned, the power to schedule carries with it the power not to schedule. For years Southern Democrats used Rules as a last line of defense to kill liberal bills that somehow managed to escape one of the substantive committees. Finally President Kennedy and Sam Rayburn broke the committee's near-absolute power in 1961 by persuading the House to go along with their plan to pack the membership. Nevertheless, southerners clung tenaciously to the chairmanship and the disappearing remnants of the committee's power for eleven years. Then Mississippian William Colmer retired and Indiana's Ray Madden, now 84 and the oldest member of Congress, took over.

Under Madden the committee's reputation has deteriorated to the point where it is now regarded mainly as the closest thing Washington can offer to the circus. His colleagues openly joke that the chairman is actively senile. When not humming idly during committee meetings, he departs from the business at hand to ramble at length on subjects like the Bank Panic of 1907. Not surprisingly, committee sessions often degenerate into shouting matches.

But John Dingell hasn't spent twenty years in Congress for nothing. He knew that Rules still holds the power of life and death over legislation, even if the committee hasn't tried to exercise it lately. He also knew that Speaker of the House Carl Albert has tremendous influence with the committee, and that Albert is from Oklahoma, which just happens to be a major gas producing state. In order to nail the coffin shut on deregulation, Dingell and Staggers tried to get their bill designated as "emergency" legislation—which would mean *no* amendments could be offered on the floor. It didn't work. Instead, Corpus Christi Congressman John Young proposed a rule declaring Krueger's long-term deregulation amendment germane, and Albert interceded on Krueger's behalf. On December 12, the Rules Committee voted 12–4 with Young, and Krueger was suddenly very much alive. True, the rule would still have to be voted upon by the entire House, but any chance was better than none at all.

Now the maneuvering began in earnest. That was the perfect situation for the very special talents of Congressman Charles Wilson of Lufkin, one of the most baffling figures in Texas politics. Wilson, who has not undeservedly acquired a reputation as a good time Charlie in both Austin and Washington, has been an enigma almost from the day he arrived in the Texas Legislature as a 25-year-old state representative in 1961. He was reputed to be a moderate liberal but somehow wound up sponsoring the state's first sales tax for conservative Governor Price Daniel. It passed, and Wilson has defied classification ever since. No one has ever accused him of being a great legislative technician—obstreperous State Senator Bill Moore once groused that Wilson had never read a bill in his life; for his part Wilson says only that he's read as many as Moore has—but as a strategist and as a pure political animal Wilson has few equals. He has Lyndon Johnson's uncanny knack of knowing exactly the right way to approach other politicians—an instinct which came in very handy when the House was trying to repeal the oil depletion allowance in 1974. When the depletion debate started, Congress was awash with hatred for the entire oil industry; Wilson waded in and managed to persuade his colleagues that independent producers should be treated differently than the multinational energy corporations known as the majors. Today this proposition ranks alongside mom and apple pie in the congressional pantheon of American institutions, and it was Charlie Wilson who put it there. What makes this accomplishment so startling is that Wilson became accepted as an expert on oil and gas matters without being on a committee that deals with them. In Congress, such things just don't happen.

Together Wilson and Krueger made a formidable team: while Krueger patiently explained the details of his amendment to his colleagues one by one, Wilson mapped out the strategy. Krueger had already decided that deregulation should be sold not simply as a solution to the energy crisis, but also as a benefit to consumers, an approach Wilson endorsed with enthusiasm. He put together a coalition of gas users, groups like the National Cotton Council, the American Paper Institute, the Society of the Plastics Industry, the Aluminum Association, and, irresistibly, the International Association of Ice Cream Manufacturers. They were joined by every agricultural lobby known to man: the International Apple Institute, the milk producers, the corn growers, the National Broiler Council, the corn refiners, the wheat growers, and on and on. Any industry that depended upon natural gas was brought in to hear Wilson's basic theme: ultimately the supply of gas is more important than the price, and only deregulation could bring about increased supplies by restoring the incentive to drill. It is better, Wilson argued, to go to a job at a factory paying $1.70 for gas than to be unemployed and paying 52 cents for gas at home.

Wilson's office on the fifth floor of the Longworth Building became a command center. Krueger, very much an intellectual purist, was convinced he could win on the merits alone, but Wilson knew better. Staff aide Candy Shy maintained a thick file of tally sheets, rating members from 1 (certain FOR) to 5 (certain AGAINST), then, as the vote on the rule neared, from 1 to 7. The first head count showed 137 firm votes for deregulation, with another 149 of the 435 congressmen listed as possible. Eventually even seven categories weren't enough; the final list, marked in ten different colors, looked like a road map, with lines and circles everywhere.

Wilson kept a tight rein on the lobbying effort and orchestrated it brilliantly. He made it clear to the big oil companies that their help wasn't wanted and concentrated instead on selling the idea that deregulation would benefit independents, who drill most of the new wells. (What Wilson didn't say was that although independents drill 80 per cent of all new wells, they find only 50 per cent of the new gas.) He rounded up independents not just from Texas, but from California, Colorado, even New York, and matched them with potential votes. Anyone who showed up wearing cowboy boots and diamond rings was politely sent off to talk strictly to Texas congressmen and otherwise kept out of sight. Meanwhile farmer groups worked Midwest and border-state delegations, and industrial users called labor-oriented congressmen like Fred Rooney of Pennsylvania to warn that if deregulation failed, plants like Bethlehem Steel would have to lay off workers because of natural gas shortages.

Slowly, gradually, the balance began to tip in favor of deregulation. By this time Dingell and Staggers wished they had never produced a bill at all. The projected shortages of the winter had failed to materialize and there was no need for an emergency bill. First they made an abortive attempt to kill their own bill; then Dingell and all the other Commerce subcommittee chairmen met with Krueger in the Speaker's office one week before the House would vote on the deregulation rule. All pleaded with Krueger to pull his amendment down out of respect for the committee system. "You're going to be around for a long time," they told the freshman. "You've got to learn to have respect for House traditions." But Krueger stood firm: hadn't Dingell already warned him that Staggers would never let a deregulation bill out of committee? "I'm just following your political advice," Krueger told Dingell.

The vote on the Krueger rule was scheduled for the afternoon of February 3, a Tuesday. That morning House Democrats caucused in the chamber. Krueger's strategy was evident from his opening statement: "I have a simple story of one who wants his case heard." He was determined not to argue the merits prematurely, but to stick to procedure, and above all, to show the proper deference toward the seniority system; Bob Krueger wasn't about to get labeled an uppity freshman. He stressed over and over how he was blocked from presenting his amendment in committee, but always softened his narrative with phrases like, "I understand the Chairman's prerogatives and I understand that he acted correctly." It was an intelligent, well-thought-out battle plan, for if Wilson's count was correct, Krueger's job was not to win votes but to avoid losing them.

Dingell counterattacked in a burst of outrage. He accused the Speaker and the Rules Committee of flouting the committee system and warned that the Krueger amendment had never undergone hearings or careful scrutiny. Staggers chimed in with a plea to "let it happen the orderly way." Krueger's side seemed to have the better of the argument, though, and most of the Democrats had tired of the debate and were chatting aimlessly when, at the very end, Eckhardt got up to speak against the rule.

"The trouble with this process," Eckhardt began in his soft drawl, "is that it's just like the Texas Legislature." The buzz of conversation stopped; comparisons with the Texas Legislature are not taken lightly. "There's virtually no committee action," he continued. "A bill springs full-blown from the lobby and makes it to the floor in the identical form. What's wrong with this is that it polarizes debate—you're either for the bill or against. There's no opportunity to compromise. Give us a chance to hammer out a solution between men of good faith. That's what the committee system is for." It was a compelling argument, but it fell on too many deaf ears. Dingell had erred badly by attacking the Speaker; he forced northern liberals (majority leader Tip O'Neill was one) who were against deregulation into voting for the rule to avoid embarrassing Carl Albert. Furthermore, Staggers was the wrong person to defend the integrity of the committee system; he is neither a powerful nor a popular chairman. When the vote on the rule was taken several hours later, it was surprisingly lopsided: 231 for, 183 against. Round Two to Krueger.

Facing a 48-vote deficit, opponents of deregulation could only play for time while friendly lobbyists mounted a counterattack. For the next three days Capitol Hill swarmed with representatives of consumer groups and the AFL-CIO, who were unmoved by Wilson's argument that less gas meant fewer jobs. Even actor Paul Newman showed up to announce his opposition to deregulation. (Unimpressed, Wilson noted that as a child he'd watched Gene Autry for 25 cents, but Butch Cassidy cost $3; maybe we ought to deregulate gas and regulate movie prices instead.)

Meanwhile, the Dingell forces adopted a three-pronged strategy in floor debate. The younger liberals protested that deregulation would cost consumers anywhere from $5 billion to $20 billion. "Regulation is the only thing which keeps this concentrated industry from dictating prices and decimating consumers," Andy Maguire warned. Richard Ottinger of New York called deregulation a "congressionally donated windfall." Their emotional arguments were balanced by the hard-nosed speeches of John Moss, who as chairman of Commerce's oversight subcommittee had discovered that some producers were holding back gas in hopes of profiting from deregulation.

Most of the burden of stopping Krueger, however, fell on Bob Eckhardt. For three days Eckhardt stood before the House, leading the direct assault on the bill, offering amendment after narrow amendment—all designed not to kill the bill, but to plant the suspicion that, in Dingell's words, "the Krueger amendment is an ambiguous piece of legislation with many internal defects." Most of Eckhardt's changes were minuscule—one merely changed the word "ceiling" to "ceilings"—but cumulatively they began to suggest that this proposal would benefit from a trip through the usual committee process. "I do think that if the Krueger bill should by some strange quirk of conscience on the part of the House become law, it should be written in a way that will work," the man who is reputed to be the best technical legislator in the entire Congress lectured his colleagues. By Wednesday afternoon, Eckhardt was clearly outmaneuvering his younger opponent. On one occasion Krueger was ready to accept a proposed Eckhardt amendment but wily Jake Pickle of Austin leaped up to continue the fight.

It was on Wednesday afternoon, too, that the fight turned deadly serious, with the mysterious appearance in the press gallery of an unsigned statement detailing Krueger's campaign contributions from the oil and gas industry. The next morning the *Washington Post* published a story headlined OIL INTERESTS AID KRUEGER'S DRIVE. The article pointed out that Krueger had run up a massive campaign debt by spending more money in his 1974 race than any other congressman; that he had to raise $200,000 in the last half of 1975 to balance the books by the December 31 deadline; and that he collected more than $50,000 from the petroleum industry. The paper was careful to point out that there was no evidence of any wrongdoing, but the story had made its point: Krueger's posture as a rational man, committed only to the more logical side, was irreparably damaged.

As Thursday morning turned into Thursday afternoon, the strategies of both sides remained unchanged. Opponents of deregulation continued their delaying tactics as labor lobbyists blanketed the Capitol. Krueger, still calm and deferential, continued to lace his arguments with factual evidence while Wilson ceaselessly navigated the floor, working to hold the coalition together. It was widely assumed by both sides that the outcome would be determined after the weekend, that no final vote would come until Monday. The House would debate an amendment by Neal Smith of Iowa for a few more hours but would recess for the weekend before taking a vote.

Everyone knew the Smith amendment would be the crucial test. It was really Dingell's proposal, but he had fallen into disfavor by attacking the Speaker during the caucus, so Smith—a moderate Democrat with no particular expertise in energy—was chosen as the front man. The amendment was a last-gasp attempt to stop Krueger by offering something to everyone: it deregulated independent producers, but put all majors, including those in the intrastate market, under regulation.

Suddenly, at 3:27 p.m., Dingell rose and called for an end to debate and an immediate vote on the Smith amendment. The move caught Krueger and Wilson by surprise. They didn't know—perhaps they should have guessed—that Dingell thought *he* now had the upper hand. They agreed to the motion, and immediately the bells announcing a record vote began to sound throughout the Capitol and the three House office buildings across Independence Avenue. Once more the concealed electronic scoreboard flashed into view above the gallery facing the House, and the twin clocks on the side walls began their countdown from 15:00. Members jockeyed for positions around the five doors to the chamber, ready to buttonhole any arriving member whose vote might be in doubt. Slowly the giant room filled with congressmen, and the running tally on the scoreboard began to mount. With four minutes to go barely half the members had voted, and Krueger led 116–112. As the clocks blinked into the final minute, Krueger led by eight votes, then seven, then five, then, at 0:00, none. It was a tie, 196–196. Theoretically Smith had lost—but this scoreboard was operated not by the National Football League or some other literal-minded organization, but by the House of Representatives. One or two congressmen wandered in late and voted after the deadline. Several announced their votes from the floor and were not recorded electronically. A growing clump—a hundred, a hundred and twenty—huddled around the Speaker's desk; what was going on? Finally the end of voting was announced—and the score stood at 204 for Smith, 202 against, 26 absent—most of them committed to Krueger. Liberal Democrats erupted into cheers, answered by victorious shouts from union and consumer lobbyists in the hallways outside the chamber. One vote, one person switching, was all Krueger had missed by. And one person did switch, Republican Millicent Fenwick of New Jersey . . . but she switched the wrong way, from nay to yea, making the official tally 205–201. Round Three to Dingell.

No one expects the Smith amendment to become law; it shows so little understanding of how the gas industry actually works that the Commerce Committee staff has called a leading oil and gas lobbyist for help in unsnarling its complications. Even if the bill somehow emerges from a conference committee (the Senate has already passed a deregulation bill) and goes to the White House, a presidential veto is certain. Krueger and Wilson hope that the Senate deregulation bill will be adopted by a conference committee, but that too is unlikely; Dingell will control the House conferees by at least a six to five margin. It looks as though deregulation is dead for the session, but then it looked that way once before.

Why did Krueger lose? One thing is certain: the bulk of the votes for the Smith amendment were against Krueger from the start. (Remember, Wilson's first head count showed 149 firmly opposed to deregulation.) These were congressmen who hated Big Oil, who refused to believe that gas couldn't be produced profitably at regulated prices, who would never consider total deregulation unless Congress first passed a windfall profits tax. They were congressmen who resented producing states like Texas that have been siphoning off industries and people and jobs from their section of the country, mainly thanks to cheap energy, and they didn't want to hear any Texas solutions to the energy crisis. Only six Democrats from states east of the Mississippi and north of the Mason-Dixon line voted with Krueger against Smith. (One of them was Charlie Wilson's target Fred Rooney.)

As for the others, many of them found the Smith amendment too attractive to resist. They didn't care about the mechanics—all they knew was that it let them vote for deregulation and against the majors, a combination too appealing to pass up.

These (plus a warm winter) were the substantive reasons for Krueger's defeat, but a far more interesting topic of discussion in Washington after the vote were the tactical issues: how crucial were the absent members, what difference did the *Washington Post* story make, and did Krueger blow it by getting outmaneuvered?

Most supporters of deregulation, including Krueger, blame the loss on absenteeism—specifically, on Republicans whom the White House had guaranteed would be on hand to vote. The charge is indisputable, but it raises an even more interesting question: how did Dingell know the absentees were gone when Krueger and Wilson didn't?

As for the *Post* story, it is hard to believe the article was not decisive; after all, if it affected just two congressmen, it made the difference. Even Krueger admits that the story changed one vote (probably liberal Republican Margaret Heckler of Massachusetts). One former administrative assistant to a northern liberal Democrat guesses that the story may have changed as many as eighteen votes—an estimate Krueger and other members of the Texas delegation scoff at. Even if it didn't decide the outcome, however, what the article did do was change the momentum of the debate; it put Krueger on the defensive. One oil and gas lobbyist says that Krueger agreed to Dingell's motion to vote on Thursday afternoon because he was worried about additional stories over the weekend.

In the end, his inexperience and naiveté cost him dearly: faced with the Dingell motion and feeling the pressure of the *Post* article, he lost his poise and made a bad decision. Talking to Krueger, one senses his frustration at having come so close, his bitterness at the *Post* article, his feeling of betrayal by the absentees and the advisors who told him to move ahead with the vote on Thursday. A friend described Krueger as "crushed" by his defeat and "really singed" by the *Post* story. The picture that emerges is not without irony: the Shakespearean scholar learning the lesson of Caesar's wife. ★

Slick Operators

CHAPTER TWELVE

Psst . . . Have I Got a Deal for You! Paul Burka (March 79)
Ten Giant Steps to Disaster, Paul Burka (August 79)
Ask Jett Rink, Paul Burka and Nicholas Lemann (August 79)
. . . The Mexican Gas Deal, John Bloom (November 79)

THE HIDDEN BYPASS PLOY

THE GREAT BROWNSVILLE TURNAROUND

THE MIRACULOUS DAISY CHAIN DODGE

THE FAMOUS FRAUDULENT STOCK GAMBIT

THE DASTARDLY DRY HOLE DUPERY

MEXICO

U.S.A.

Psst... Have I Got A Deal For You!

by Paul Burka

A swindler's guide to oil riches.

Hardly a month goes by that the Department of Energy doesn't haul some oil company into court for overcharging customers. Most recently DOE sued nine of the nation's oil giants for almost $1 billion in overcharges, and one DOE official has accused the industry of executing "the biggest conspiracy in U.S. history." Hah! These corporate types, trying to decipher subparagraph (iii) to exception (b) in order to come up with a loophole in the government's energy program are Boy Scouts compared to the promoters and hot oil runners and slant hole drillers who robbed customers and consumers of untold billions long before inflation, the Arab embargo, and arcane regulations made it easy for anyone to do it. Speaking of the Boy Scouts, things once got so rough in the oil patch that even they weren't on the level. But that's getting ahead of our story.

The oil business has always been fraught with peril for the unwary. The con man arrived here almost as soon as the wildcatter. Within a year after Spindletop blew in, five hundred Texas oil companies were doing business in Beaumont, few of them legitimate, many with alluring but deceptive names like the Rockefeller Oil Company. Their main business was selling stock, not producing oil. Four such enterprises, capitalized at $1 million each, shared as their sole asset one jointly held lease on a tiny 45-foot square of turf. Eight months after the discovery at Swindletop, as it came to be known, Texas oil companies were capitalized at $231 million, but actual investment in the oil fields totaled only $11 million. That's twenty dollars swindled for every dollar put to work, making today's oil scams look like penny-ante stuff.

Things are different now. Securities laws, energy regulations, and public sophistication have made life more difficult for those not content to play the oil game according to the rules. You will even find Pollyannas defending the industry with claims that it is no more laced with charlatans and mountebanks than any other business. Ridiculous! Will anything else enflame the passions in quite the same way after all the oil is gone? Will there be solar scams, geothermal scams, fusion scams? Somehow they just don't sound the same. No, there is something about the search for oil—its promise of immediate riches, its dark and misbegotten past, the fear that it will all be gone someday, the mysteries of the bowels of the earth—that inexorably attracts both the scoundrel and his victim. So those still itching to get rich in oil should reflect on these monuments to man's extralegal ingenuity—and consider whether they are more likely to be predators or prey.

The Dry Look

The problem: Anyone can make a fortune from a gusher. The drawback is that the current odds are five-to-one in favor of finding a dry hole. How do you get the odds on your side and turn a dry hole into a nifty profit?

The scam: The trick is known as *The Producers* scam, not because it involves the actual production of oil (which is the last thing the mastermind wants), but because a variation of the gimmick was the subject of a popular 1968 film by that name. In the movie Zero Mostel played an aging Broadway wheeler-dealer who sold more than 100 per cent of a terrible play, hoping it would fold so that he could pocket everything over the cost of the play. An oilman can do the same thing with a well.

The legitimate wildcatter frequently bankrolls a venture by selling investors, say, eighty 1 per cent shares at $2000 each. That provides enough working capital to cover drilling costs and still leaves him a 20 per cent interest in any oil that's found. If the hole comes up dry . . . well, the investors knew that oil is a risky business.

An oilman with larceny in his heart might do it a little differently: by selling, say, *two hundred* 1 per cent shares. As long as he drills a dry hole (and some of these wells have been drilled in some very unlikely places, just for insurance), no one is likely to ask any questions. In the movie, however, the terrible play turned out to be a smash hit, and in the oil patch an occasional oversubscribed wildcatter has been unlucky enough to strike oil.

One operator recently applied a new twist to *The Producers* scam. He located a likely formation along the Gulf Coast where one reservoir of oil lay under another, separated by a thin layer of rock. He proceeded to sell shares in two wells, one for the top reservoir, one for the bottom, and indeed he paid his happy investors their fair shares. There was just one catch: it is possible to produce at two depths from the same well, so he had to drill only one hole. The money he raised to cover drilling costs for the second "well" was pure profit.

Cross Over the Bridge

The problem: It hardly seems possible by today's standards, but back in the mid-fifties foreign oil was actually cheaper than U.S.-produced oil. This so alarmed major domestic producers like Exxon, whose rate of return had sagged 45 per cent in just three years, that they persuaded

Illustrated by Tom Ballenger

the federal government to put a quota on imports in 1959. But the regulations contained two minor exceptions: they did not apply to the insignificant amount of oil that passed over U.S. borders by truck and railroad car from Canada and Mexico, nor did they affect oil shipped in under bond for export. Could that tiny crack be widened into a major loophole?

The scam: Several East Coast industries had their eyes on some cheap oil produced by Pemex, the Mexican national oil company. But how could they get it? If the oil had to travel by rail, the transportation cost would be prohibitive. If it came by ship from Tampico, it would be subject to the quota. But suppose it came from Brownsville?

Pemex shipped the oil in Mexican tankers from Tampico to Brownsville, bonded for export to Mexico. The oil was transferred from ship to tank truck and driven across the Rio Grande. But no Mexican ever got his hands on it. The trucks simply made a U-turn within sight of the bridge and re-entered the United States with overland Mexican oil now exempt from the quota. The trucks headed right back to the port, unloaded their oil into an American tanker bound for the East Coast, then filled up again at the Mexican vessel to start the cycle over again. Eighty trucks a day kept up a continual parade back and forth across the river, bringing in 30,000 barrels a day of cheap Mexican oil for ten years. By the late sixties, traffic in downtown Brownsville was so snarled that one of the town's two bridges had to be completely rebuilt and expanded.

Keep On Truckin'

The problem: The best of all possible worlds is to have an oil well that also produces gas. If you operate in the Panhandle, though, you might run into trouble, because the practice in some fields has been to separate oil and gas leases and give them to different operators. You can still produce gas from an oil well, but when oil production falls below a certain level, the oil well becomes, according to law, a gas well. Must the oil operator then meekly abandon the site to the holder of the gas lease?

The scam: Oil production is usually gauged at the tank, not the wellhead, so all the operator has to do to maintain appearances is keep oil flowing out of his tank. Some operators bought crude and trucked it in during the dead of night to fill their tanks. That would keep the oil ratio up, and they'd recoup most of their costs by selling the purchased oil. Of course, the profits from the gas more than made up the difference.

Most of the Panhandle knew what was going on, but the Railroad Commission only stumbled upon the ploy by a fluke. A field investigator was invited to a party one night where a number of oilmen were present. Mistakenly assuming him to be in the business, one oilman was exchanging small talk with the investigator when the conversation turned to economic hardships. "If we don't get the Legislature to do something about losin' our oil wells to them gas folks," the oilman complained, "truckin' in all that oil is gonna break us yet."

Coming Out in the Wash

The problem: The world price of oil has more than quadrupled since the 1973 embargo, but the Arabs have made a larger bundle than American oilmen, thanks to rigid federal price controls. At the same time that we're paying OPEC nations $15 a barrel for imports, "old" oil (domestic oil discovered in 1972 or before) has a ceiling of around $6 a barrel; "new" oil (discovered after 1972) goes for around $13. To make matters worse, most American oil is old oil. Does an oilman unfortunate enough to have discovered oil before 1973 have to settle for peanuts while everyone else is getting fabulously rich?

The scam: Remember the slogan for the detergent that claimed to make old clothes look like new? The same can be done for oil—but you won't hear anyone bragging about it on television. Some oil laundries are little more than shell games: a broker buys old oil from a producer, shuffles the transaction on his books, and resells it to a refinery as new oil. Up to 300,000 barrels of old oil a day disappeared between the wellhead and the refinery in 1977. Most of it, DOE officials suspect, later emerged as new oil.

The more sophisticated oil laundries, however, resort to doubt rather than deceit. Say, for example, that Exxon drills a new well on the edge of a producing field. Is the oil old or new? The answer—and about $7 a barrel—depends on whether it comes from a different reservoir. Naturally Exxon is inclined to give itself the benefit of the doubt. If the company is lucky, government auditors will accept the decision, or better yet, overlook it. And if worse comes to worst and the case winds up in court, Exxon can take comfort in the fact that judges and juries have shown little inclination to penalize oil cheaters. The schemer behind the sixties' most notorious oil swindle, a $140 million Ponzi game, spent one night in jail and paid a $19,000 fine.

Working On a Chain Gang

The problem: Those federal regulations again. You're a producer with lots of oil, and there are people willing to pay a premium for it, but you can't charge a nickel more than the regulations allow. It doesn't seem fair that a broker can resell your oil above the government's ceiling price when you can't, but the regulations make allowances for him to take his cut. But that doesn't help you get more for your oil. Or does it?

The scam: This is just classic supply-and-demand economics. The seller has something the broker wants: oil. And the broker has something the seller wants: a way around the price ceiling. That the two should get together is inevitable.

Of course, some brokers perform legitimate services for their clients, matching buyers and sellers and reducing the likelihood of spot shortages. If the seller already has a customer, however, a broker can perform a service that is equally valuable, if not so legitimate: he can serve as a middleman solely to jack the price up, then split the bonus with the seller. The more links in the daisy chain, the higher the payoff.

And what about the buyer who's paying the higher price? Wouldn't he get suspicious? Well, in what DOE says is the archetypal daisy chain case, executives of Florida Power Corporation were charged with sharing in the scam by receiving finder's fees. As in finder's keepers.

Buried Treasure

The problem: In recent years the Railroad Commission has allowed Texas wells to operate at full capacity, but not too long ago production was strictly controlled. The monthly allowable output for most wells could be reached in just eight days; the rest of the month the well had to sit idle. That kept prices up, but it also offered a tantalizing inducement to keep the oil flowing. How could a cunning operator conceal his excess production from state investigators?

The scam: This one reads like a fourth-grade multiplication tables quiz: if one well can produce for eight days, how many wells do you need for a full month's output? Answer: four. So the operator would install three realistic-looking dummy wellheads, usually on nearby property where oil prospects weren't bright and leases were cheap. Now he had four wells, four storage tanks, and four allowables: 32 production days a month. Then he'd connect all of the tanks to a buried pipeline extending from his original well and let the oil flow.

The real problem lay not in concocting the scheme but in shielding the truth from Railroad Commission investigators, who knew all about this ploy. And the hardest part was concealing the telltale bypass valve that diverted oil from his original tank to the other three. Ingenuity was essential here: one operator with an office near the well secreted the valve in the neck of a toilet bowl.

Eventually investigators resorted to metal detectors to locate the buried pipelines. That helped put an end to the flow of hot oil, as production in excess of the allowable is known, but it didn't improve their chances of sending a cheating operator to jail. Whenever the state tried to prosecute, they would run into a canny East Texas lawyer named William Fletcher "Big Fish" Fischer. "Being equipped to run hot oil isn't the same as running hot oil," he'd instruct the jury. "Why, every man in this courtroom is equipped for rape, but nobody's prosecuting them for it."

There Was a Crooked Well

The problem: You have just bought an oil lease on the edge of a major field. You're close enough to see your neighbor's well pumping; you know there's oil all around you; but when you drill you find that there's none where it counts—under your lease. Has fate had the last word?

The scam: The slant hole is almost the perfect scam. It is easy to carry out (all you need is a whipstock, an ordinary piece of oil-field equipment designed for legitimate directional drilling) and virtually impossible to detect (above ground, a deviated well looks like any other). The only hard part is keeping it secret. The oil sands in East Texas lie between 3500 and 3700 feet underground; any well much deeper than that is cause for suspicion. Rumors about crooked holes circulated in East Texas for fourteen years before the lid came off, and no wonder: dozens of people had to be aware of a crooked hole, including the drilling contractor, the crew that pulled more than 5000 feet of pipe out of the hole, and the firm that measured the hole with sensitive instruments. And there were almost four hundred slant wells near the East Texas field. One suspect operation had been given to the Boy Scouts by a benefactor with a better nose for oil than public relations. "Oh, please," said a Railroad Commissioner when the scandal broke, "don't let the Boy Scouts' well turn out to be crooked." But it was.

Punishing slant hole operators proved even more difficult than catching them. Texaco sued a driller who'd stolen their oil, seeking $2 million. They collected $16,000. Altogether, slant hole thieves pilfered oil worth more than $1 billion, but not one spent even a day in prison. ★

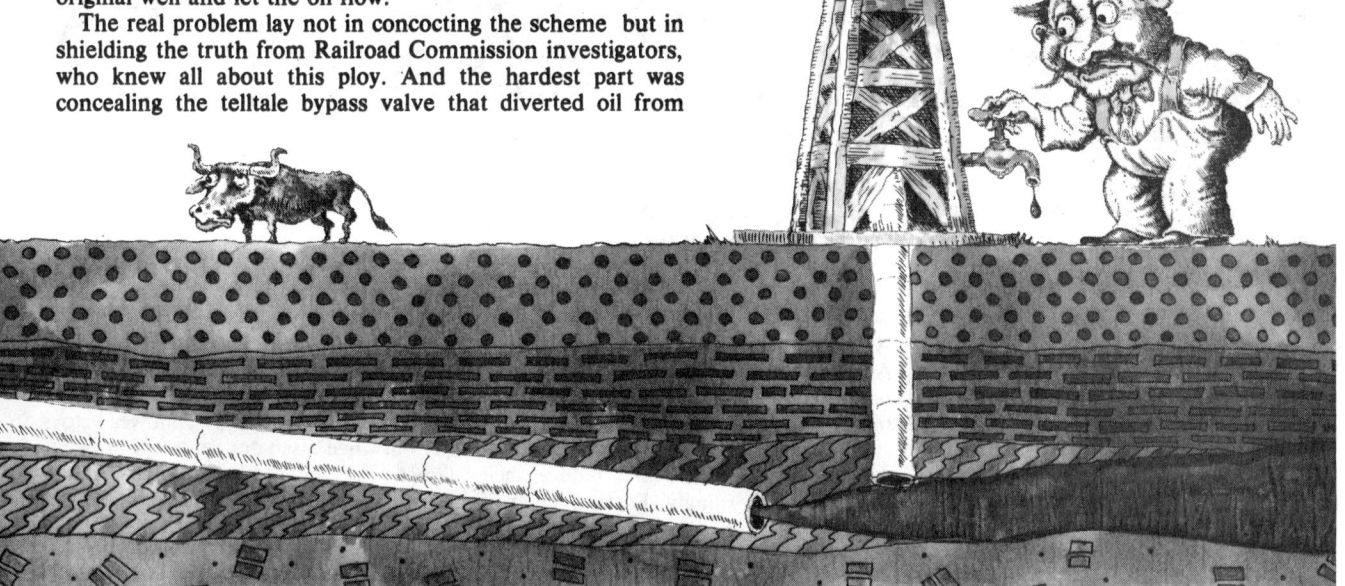

TEN GIANT STEPS TO DISASTER

by Paul Burka

Here's how we got in the fix we're in.

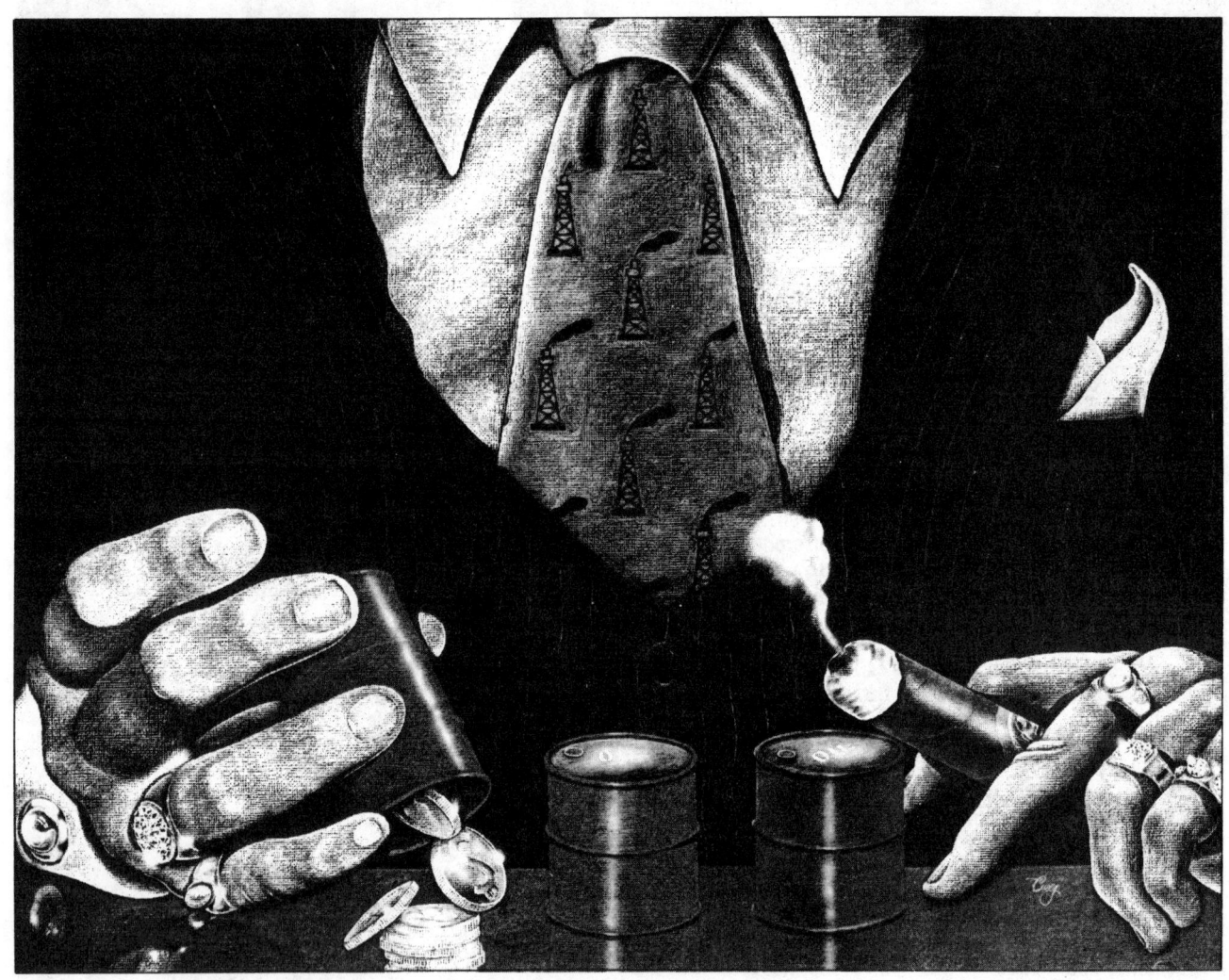

1848: THE TREATY OF GUADALUPE HIDALGO. After conquering Mexico, the U.S. decides to keep only what is now South Texas, California, and the American Southwest, and gives up the rest of Mexico—including what may turn out to be the world's largest oil field—without even demanding the mineral rights.

1938: MEXICO NATIONALIZES THE OIL INDUSTRY. Angered by oil company refusals to improve working conditions, Mexican President Lázaro Cárdenas nationalizes the oil industry. The companies respond by boycotting Mexican oil; the American ambassador predicts Mexicans "will drown in their own oil." Production that once supplied a fourth of the world's oil is lost, Mexico's economic development is stalled for decades, and the lingering bitterness affects U.S.-Mexico relations through the seventies.

1950: THE FOREIGN TAX CREDIT. The State Department, eager to funnel American dollars to anticommunist Arabs but fearful that foreign aid won't be approved by Congress, hits on a solution: let oil companies count their profit-sharing with foreign governments as foreign income taxes, and reduce their U.S. taxes accordingly. Foreign policy in the Middle East is thus effectively abdicated to the oil companies. For the next two decades, the fateful decisions that will determine the course of U.S. relations in the Middle East are made by the companies, not the State Department.

1956: EISENHOWER VETOES THE NATURAL GAS ACT. Congress tries to undo the Supreme Court's 1954 *Phillips* decision, which gave the Federal Power Commission the right to set the wellhead price of natural gas sold in the interstate market, but President Eisenhower vetoes the bill when a senator reports a bribe attempt. For the next twenty years Congress will fight over deregulation without passing a bill; meanwhile, the artificially low regulated price has the disastrous effect of encouraging profligate consumption while discouraging new exploration.

1958: THE OIL IMPORT QUOTA. Congress bows to pressure from smaller domestic producers and limits imports of cheap Middle East oil in order to keep domestic prices up. For the next thirteen years we use up our own oil when Middle Eastern oil is readily available at a much lower price; later, when domestic production starts to fall off, we have to increase imports—but the oil isn't cheap anymore.

1960: THE FORMATION OF OPEC. Faced with an oil glut, Exxon decides to cut what it will pay for Middle Eastern oil by ten cents a barrel. Offended at not being consulted as well as by the loss of hundreds of millions of dollars in revenue, five producing countries send representatives to a conference in Baghdad. Saudi Arabia, Kuwait, Iraq, Iran, and Venezuela agree to form the Organization of Petroleum Exporting Countries, a cartel aimed at upping the price of crude.

1969-1973: THE HUNTS CHALLENGE QADAFFI IN LIBYA. Dallas' Bunker Hunt, who has the largest oil concession in Libya, decides Libyan strongman Muamer Qadaffi's demands for a bigger share of the profits are excessive and his threats of nationalization a bluff. He finds out otherwise: Qadaffi nationalizes the Hunt concession, saying the U.S. needs "a good hard slap on its cool and insolent face." Qadaffi's success is a signal to other Arab nations that they can be as greedy as they want. The Libyans threaten to cut off all exports to the U.S. if American support of Israel continues; shortly thereafter OPEC meets to consider for the first time the use of oil as a political weapon.

1973-77: WASHINGTON PERPETUATES THE DREAM OF CHEAP ENERGY. The Nixon Administration's response to the Arab embargo is to keep domestic oil at an artificially low price, allowing demand for gasoline to keep rising and our oil reserves to keep falling. Relative to inflation, gasoline in 1977 is no more expensive than it was in the early sixties. Nevertheless Congress twice refuses to decontrol oil or deregulate natural gas. The controlled low price of energy defeats calls for sacrifice and conservation and makes the nation even more dependent on foreign oil.

1978: COLLAPSE OF THE MEXICAN GAS DEAL. The U.S. loses two billion cubic feet of natural gas a day—enough to meet this country's industrial gas needs for more than two months every year at current consumption rates—when energy czar James Schlesinger objects to the price agreed upon by U.S. companies and Pemex, the Mexican national oil company. Mexico abandons plans to complete a pipeline to the Rio Grande and decides to sell to countries that realize a guaranteed supply is more important than the lowest possible price.

1979: THE FALL OF THE SHAH. The Iranian revolution catches the U.S. by surprise. We can neither save the Shah (not worth the trouble) nor keep Iran's oil flowing (worth the trouble). At the very least, had the government or the oil companies caught on to the Shah's weakness, the companies could have stockpiled crude instead of letting their inventories dwindle, and we wouldn't have been worried about gas lines or talking about rationing until at least next summer. ★

Ask Jett Rink

by Paul Burka
and Nicholas Lemann

Straight answers from a straight shooter about your gasoline problems.

Dear Jett:

I live in Houston and I have to get up at six in the morning and wait in line for two hours to get a tank of gas. My brother-in-law in Beeville can get gas whenever he wants. Why's it been so hard to get gas in Dallas and Houston, and so easy everywhere else?

Frustrated, Houston

Dear Frustrated:

The problem is that every gas station in Texas has a monthly gasoline allocation set by the federal government that's based on 1977-78 figures, and Houston and Dallas have grown a lot more than Beeville in the last two years. You've got a lot more cars and a lot more service stations (the new ones get an allocation too) to divide up the same amount of gas. The more your city grows, the more you're going to get shorted.

Don't get the idea I'm blaming everything on the bureaucrats. The oil companies have been giving the stations even less than their allocations. Besides that, it's your own damn fault for living in a place that big. My daddy used to say he'd never seen a steer cut and run by himself—he's got to be with a lot of other steers before he'll panic. It's sort of like that with city folks. They get worried about shortages and they start hoarding and topping off their tanks and that only makes things worse.

Dear Jett:

Will there be gas lines this fall and winter?

Planning Ahead, Richardson

Dear Planning:

I'm just an old country boy, and all those smart folks in Washington are saying things are going to get better in the fall. Still and all, I wouldn't bet on it. The feds are pressuring the oil companies to refine more home heating oil and less gas so the Yankees can stay warm this winter, and if the President is serious about freezing imports, there's about as much chance of the gas supply increasing as there is of me going to a disco. Gas lines are going to get shorter, but a suburban sumbitch like yourself is still going to have to put more time and effort and money into filling your tank than you did last year.

Dear Jett:

How much is a gallon of gas going to cost in a year? Is the price now up to the station owners, the oil companies, or the government?

Penny Wise, San Angelo

Dear Penny:

There's no way a gallon of gas won't cost more than a dollar next year; the only question is how much more. Folks in the Department of Energy's Dallas office have been saying it'll be up to $1.50 by Christmas, but people in the business say it'll be less than that. Right now every service station's price is set by the government—the old boy who owns the station can charge whatever it takes to keep his profits at a constant level, but he can't raise his profits. If your neighborhood station charges more than most, it's because the owner operated below the government profit ceiling a couple of years ago and is making up the difference now.

As far as I'm concerned, all this regulation is the kind of thing that takes away a man's reason for getting out of bed in the morning. But in 1981, when decontrol takes full effect, the station owners will be able to charge what the market will bear—and that'll be a lot more than what they're charging now.

Dear Jett:

How's the oil and gas business? Do all the lines and shortages have any effect on a wildcatter like yourself? Are you going to find us some more oil so we'll be able to live normal lives again?

Curious, Waco

Dear Curious:

The oil business is just fine, thanks. What I'm selling, people want real bad, and that's always a good spot for a businessman to be in. The major companies' profits are up, and independents like me are happy about the government's letting us charge whatever we can get for any new oil we find. Drilling activity has been a little low lately, but Hughes Tool's count of running rigs jumped like a stuck pig in the last week of June. The way I figure it, everyone was waiting for price decontrol to start taking effect June 1, and now they're fixing to drill again. I'm going to make a little money, just like always, but I'm not going to find enough oil to make a difference to you—just enough to make a difference to me.

Dear Jett:

I own my Exxon station and it makes me sick to see cars pull up at the Seven-Eleven all day long when I only have enough gas to stay open two hours. Would I be better off without this allocation system?

Idle, Fort Worth

Dear Idle:

No, you wouldn't. The boys in Washington make sure Exxon sends you the same proportion of their gas they were sending you two years ago. If Exxon could do whatever it damn well pleased with its gas, in a crunch like we've got

Mr. Rink is a successful wildcatter. The movie Giant *portrayed his life.*

now it'd send its supply to the stations it owns and leave folks like you to buy on the spot market. If you could get any gas at all, you'd have to get it from weirdos and flakes in Rotterdam and places like that, and you'd have to pay—and charge—through the nose for it.

Dear Jett:

Is this situation going to change Texas in any major way over the next ten or twenty years?

Crystal Balling, Galveston

Dear Crystal:

You and I both got enough problems to where we should be worrying about next week, not ten years from now, but if you really want to hear the bad news, here it is: they just ain't making any more oil in Texas. Production of crude oil in Texas has been declining for the last seven years. Because the price has been going up, the oil business is healthy, but businesses that depend on oil consumption are going to be in big trouble. The folks in the tourist business are hurting already—Six Flags' business was off 15 per cent in June, and some resorts' as much as 40 per cent. Looking on down the long, dusty trail, I see less building and economic activity in the suburbs, more political pressure from the city folks for mass transit, and less moving around. 'Course, I'm never going to let any grass grow on my trail. But I'm special.

Dear Jett:

Is it true that this whole thing is an oil industry plot? That the big companies deliberately let their inventories get low so they could create shortages and raise the price? That refineries have been deliberately operating below capacity?

Suspicious, Marshall

Dear Suspicious:

I'm an old wildcatter, so I don't like anybody. I don't like the oil companies and I sure don't like the government. I go my own way in life mainly because everybody but me messes things up, and they messed this gas situation up, but it wasn't a plot. Yes, the oil companies misjudged this summer's oil demand and let their inventories of crude dwindle, but they'd have been able to cover their tracks if it hadn't been for Iran. Yes, everybody sort of lollygagged around in the early part of this year instead of drilling and refining at full steam, because they wanted to see what Congress would do about decontrol; but that's not a conspiracy, that's just sensible business. You would have done the same. ★

REPORTER
BY JOHN BLOOM

Letter from Washington
The real story behind the Mexican gas deal.

In the early morning hours of August 31, Bob Krueger was hunched into a phone booth in the teeming Mexico City airport, fighting against lackadaisical operators and bad connections and the prospect of missing his plane, which was scheduled to take off in fifteen minutes. He was trying, against all odds, to get through to Jimmy Carter, but he feared the worst. The last ten days of August had been the most dismal period yet for deteriorating relations with Mexico, and now it appeared that he wouldn't be able to head off the collapse of natural gas export talks and the imminent cancellation of President José López Portillo's visit to Washington.

But then Krueger got lucky. The distant voice of Carter advisor Stuart Eizenstat crackled onto the line, and Krueger breathlessly barked out his message. "Don't call off the visit yet," he pleaded. The Mexicans would sign a gas deal. He was sure they would. Eizenstat promised to reach Carter in Plains that day to relay his feelings. Krueger ran for his plane, and the formal invitation to López Portillo was cabled in time for his "Informe" (state of the union address) the following day.

Three weeks later the U.S. signed an agreement with Mexico to buy 300 million cubic feet of natural gas per day, beginning next year. The amount seemed minuscule—about one-half of one per cent of U.S. daily needs—and yet the symbolic value of the deal far outweighed all other considerations. Of late, the two countries' exchanges in all areas have resembled the backbiting and pouting of two prima donnas. But now they had struck a deal. It was universally praised in Washington and greeted with surprising tolerance by the fiercely nationalistic Mexico City press. The "Mexican albatross," as it was known in the State Department, had been removed. The agreement seemed to signify better times ahead for Carter and López Portillo—so much so that by the time the Mexican President arrived in Washington, the mercurial American press had all but lost interest. Enmity breeds more headlines than amity.

Yet the gas agreement was not all that it seemed, and the story of how it was concluded indicates that any future energy deals with Mexico will come slowly and dearly. That story begins in 1977 with the now legendary Schlesinger gas fiasco. The Mexicans had long been embarrassed about their practice of flaring off natural gas in the enormous Reforma oil fields of the south, so López Portillo spent his first year in office trying to sell that gas and improve the growing Mexican trade deficit at the same time. By the end of the year six U.S. companies, led by Houston-based Tenneco, had agreed to buy 2.2 billion cubic feet per day. Mexico spent $700 million building a pipeline from the southern fields to Monterrey—its final destination was to be Reynosa—but Energy Secretary Schlesinger told the Mexicans their price of $2.60 per thousand cubic feet (mcf) was too high and that their escalator clause—tying the price to home heating oil delivered at New York Harbor—was unacceptable. As it turned out, Schlesinger was right. If that deal had gone through, Mexican gas today would be the most expensive in the world at about $5 per mcf.

The Mexicans were furious, not so much because of Schlesinger's arguments, but because of his high-handed last-minute tactics. So, in a fit of pique, Mexico abruptly announced that the gas was no longer for sale. That's how matters stood for more than a year, until President Carter, visiting López Portillo last February, gingerly brought up the subject again. But López Portillo, still seething over the incident that had eroded part of his political support, was

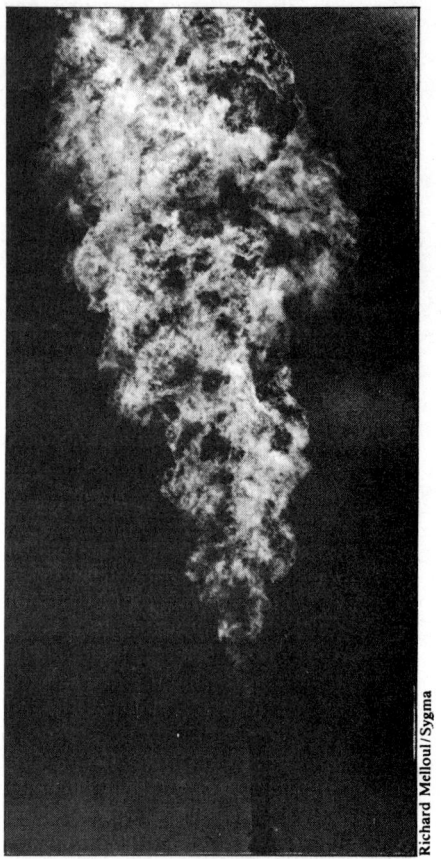

Our gas deal with Mexico should put a stop to flaring gas—and flaring tempers.

noncommittal. He agreed to talk about talking about it.

Julius Katz, an Assistant Secretary of State and a career diplomat, inherited the thankless task of trying to salvage something from the ruinous legacy of Schlesinger—and he was not optimistic. "Let's face it," he said, "we didn't have the strongest cards in the world. The Mexicans read our newspapers. And they knew how anxious we were to improve our energy position." Katz was selected to lead a team that also included representatives from the Department of Energy and the National Security Council, and in April the tug-of-war began at a meeting in Mexico City.

The Mexicans, it turned out, were

272 SLICK OPERATORS

prepared to meet but not prepared to talk. Juan Eibenschutz, an official in Mexico's Department of Patrimony (natural resources), was the titular delegation head, but he seemed to defer to officials from the Foreign Ministry whenever difficult issues were raised. The Mexicans would often sit silently for long, infuriating stretches—and only when pressed would they provide any information. At first, they didn't even know how much of a gas surplus Mexico had, but the figure of 800 million cubic feet per day was mentioned (about one-third the size of the 1977 deal). They also said they were willing to sell only "dry" gas (not associated with oil) from their northern fields—an odd position, since they were flaring 300 million cubic feet of "associated" gas per day in the south. And they were most insistent that the price, wherever it started, be linked to the rapidly escalating world price of number two fuel oil, the lightest and most expensive type. The meeting itself was confusing and unproductive. None of the Americans could tell exactly who was in charge. As the delegation returned to Washington, one of the negotiators turned to another. "We shouldn't assume," he said, "that their government knows any more about what it's doing than ours does."

By the time the Mexicans came to Washington for the third meeting in July, the U.S. had formulated a strategy: negotiate hard on every issue, but make major concessions on everything *except* the starting price and the escalator formula. A target was set: a maximum price of $3.40 tied to the cost of heavy number six fuel oil. But the U.S would start negotiating at rock bottom—$2.30, or less than the original 1977 contract. "When I heard we were actually going to offer $2.30," said one negotiator, "I almost had a heart attack. I expected the Mexicans to walk out altogether." But they didn't. They merely countered with their own price—an equally outrageous $5. No one took either figure seriously, and the Mexicans seemed indifferent to price negotiations. They were more interested in talking about the escalator formula and the contract terms—they wanted a six-year agreement, which the U.S. considered entirely too brief.

A wing and a prayer: Bob Krueger spent the dog days of summer bartering for Mexican gas.

The U.S. kept bringing the discussion back to pricing, but the Mexicans would listen indifferently even as the Americans continually raised the ante. Even when Katz offered $3.15, the Mexicans refused to make a serious counteroffer. "We just kept giving, giving, giving, giving," said one diplomat. "And they would just reel us in like a trout. I don't think they had authority to deal with us at all. It was a charade, and a little insulting."

That impression was reinforced when the Mexicans dropped several bombshells at a late-July meeting. First they said they had overestimated their surplus; only 300 million feet per day, instead of 800 million, would be available. Second, they were now offering only associated gas from the southern fields—not the more easily transported dry gas of the north. They were not prepared to compromise on the escalator formula. And finally, after casually mentioning a price in the $3.50 range, they returned the following day with a $4 demand. At least, said the diplomats, they were finally talking.

A dispirited U.S. team returned home to sort out the contradictions. The White House still badly wanted a deal, but most analysts in the State Department were convinced that Mexico would never settle. The American price, now raised to $3.30, was as high as they thought they could go without angering Canadian suppliers; Canada was selling gas to the U.S. for $2.80, but that was expected to rise to $3.30 by 1980. (Since the Mexican gas deal, the Canadians have raised their price to $3.45, effective in early November.) The Canadians, moreover, sell us ten times as much gas. "So every penny we gave the Mexicans," said a negotiator, "was going to cost us a dime in the long run."

The doldrums of late summer might have lasted for weeks had it not been for the personal intervention of López Portillo. In May the Mexican President had appointed a new foreign minister, Jorge Castañeda, and his first mandate was to expedite the gas deal. Castañeda called the State Department in Washington and asked to speak to Secretary of State Cyrus Vance. But Vance was out of the country, so the number two diplomat, Deputy Secretary Warren Christopher, fielded the call. The two career diplomats

Mexico's pipeline will bring the U.S. gas. Will it also bring a new era of amiability?

SLICK OPERATORS 273

established quick rapport, and after a brief discussion they both agreed to join the negotiators. Eibenschutz and the Department of Patrimony were removed from the Mexican team—a signal that López Portillo considered the talks more political than economic—and Bob Krueger, the new (and as yet unconfirmed) ambassador at large for Mexican affairs, was added to the American team. Meanwhile, the U.S. ambassador to Mexico, Patrick Lucey, managed to get an audience with López Portillo to discuss the gas deal, and early in August he sent an ecstatic cable back to Washington: López Portillo himself said the Mexicans would settle for a starting price of $3.40.

After four months of talks, this was the first sign of a breakthrough. The price was high, but only a dime more than the expected Canadian price—and the U.S. could probably live with it. The U.S. team, now led by Christopher, caught the earliest flight to Mexico and convened what they thought would be the final session. It was not to be. The Mexicans opened the talks by stating their price—$3.75—provoking howls of treachery from the Americans. (López Portillo now denies he ever offered $3.40.) The Mexicans finally did compromise on the escalator formula—agreeing to base it on crude oil prices—but little else was accomplished.

Oddly enough, it may have been the Mexican oil spill, which began washing up on Texas beaches about this time, that brought the talks back to life. On August 23, Krueger was told by the White House to hold a news conference on oil spill matters, mainly because the American press was clamoring for an explanation of the official U.S. position. Krueger held the conference and announced that the U.S. was asking Mexico to discuss damages. Mexico had received that request only the day before, so López Portillo was furious at Krueger for announcing it so soon. He was also peeved by Krueger's suggestion, in response to a question, that the López Portillo-Carter meeting might not be held.

After that incident, the negotiators met one more time in late August. But this visit was different. For one thing, the State Department was now convinced that López Portillo very much wanted a meeting with Carter. They were also convinced that the gas deal was perceived by the Mexicans as a prerequisite for that visit. (It was not.) And finally, one of the negotiators with ties to the U.S. gas industry brought some startling rumors. Gas wells in the deep Gulf waters offshore from Louisiana were due to begin production in January, with fixed contract prices of $3.79 (extremely deep offshore wells are exempt from normal regulations). The Mexicans didn't know about those contracts and presumably still don't. But once they found out they would want at least that much for their gas. Their price was looking better all the time.

On the plane going down to Mexico, one diplomat suggested what came to be called the Halfway/Walkaway Proposal. They would meet the Mexicans halfway between $3.75 and their own price of $3.40. If Mexico refused to accept $3.57, they would walk out. "I had noticed that this had always worked for me in the Mexican markets," the diplomat said, "and the talks had always had a sort of bazaar atmosphere anyway."

But Christopher wasn't so eager to try that tactic, so, as evidence of good faith, he opened the session at $3.50. Then the Mexicans offered their first and final concession: they would split the difference at $3.625. The State Department team was unanimous in its opinion: the price was still too high and it would infuriate the Canadians. The talks broke up again, and this time everyone assumed they were over for at least another month, and certainly until after the López Portillo visit—if there was a visit. Everyone, that is, except Lucey—he was convinced that the Mexicans were serious, and he also convinced Krueger they were.

On September 19, his birthday, Krueger walked into his State Department office, and one of his aides handed him a curious document—the daily horoscope from the *Washington Star*. "If September 19 is your birthday," it read, "you are in the midst of completing a major project or cycle. You can cash in on an idea or project germinated two years ago. You are on your way to recovery from trauma suffered last month." Krueger laughed, stuffed it into his pocket, and within hours boarded a military transport to Mexico City. Later that day he shared the horoscope with López Portillo, an astrology buff, and he too seemed to appreciate it.

The final gas agreement was signed the next day for the $3.625 price, with the stipulation that either side can cancel the deal with 180 days' notice. Krueger was happy. Carter was happy. López Portillo seemed happy. The State Department was exhausted and relieved. And nobody wanted to go through that again.

The next morning, Krueger made his phone call to Eizenstat from the Mexico City airport, and Lucey implored Vance to intervene personally with Carter. Their arguments were strong enough to result in a high-level meeting the following week, attended by Eizenstat, Energy Secretary Charles Duncan, Christopher, Katz, and Krueger. The decisions at that meeting hinged on a single question: could the expensive Louisiana offshore contracts be verified? They could be. ★

Jorge Castañeda's first task as Mexico's new foreign minister: cut a gas deal.

U.S. diplomat Warren Christopher: his job is to pull thorns from prickly issues.

Alternate Solutions

CHAPTER THIRTEEN

Behind the Lines, William Broyles Jr. (June 78)
Split With the Atom, John Bloom (June 78)
Solar on Ice, Robert Barnstone (October 77)

BEHIND THE LINES

Practical men, who believe themselves to be quite exempt from any intellectual influence, are usually the slaves of some defunct economist.

John Maynard Keynes

Keynes was a great economist who believed that ideas were powerful, and that none was more powerful than an idea whose time had passed. The energy program that Congress may yet approve in our lifetimes has its good points, but it is also a confused muddle of ideas whose times have passed. The program assumes that the interests of producers and consumers are fundamentally opposed, that coal and nuclear power can replace oil and gas, and that there is no more oil and gas, so a higher price won't increase their supply. All those assumptions are wrong.

The battle between producers and consumers is a phony issue. The dispute in Congress between so-called champions of producers and consumers of energy is like two ants fighting over a crumb of bread and ignoring the elephant's foot about to crush them both. Even taking an ambitious conservation effort into account, the national energy plan calls for massive increases in production by 1985: coal, up 84 per cent; nuclear power, quadrupled; oil and gas, new discoveries 60 per cent greater than recent rates. Simply to hold our import levels *constant* we will have to increase energy production in the next nine years more than in any other nine-year period in our history. The General Accounting Office, the Congressional Research Service, the Office of Technology Assessment, and the Congressional Budget Office all agree that given the provisions of the proposed energy plan we will in fact have to *double* our imports of foreign oil by 1985, when Arab oil production is expected to decline. "We've been telling everyone the result will be a global depression," said one economist, "but no one seems to listen." They don't listen because they are obsessed with energy producers "ripping off," in President Carter's words, the American people. But you don't sacrifice the fundamental need all Americans have for sufficient energy to discourage a few producers who might rip off consumers. An excess profits tax on energy revenues not plowed back into more production, combined with a fuel stamp program to help the poor meet rising energy costs, would be much more sensible than burning down the barn to kill a few rats.

Coal is the only immediate answer. No matter how quickly public happenings like Sun Day spur our technology to solve the hard problems of solar power and other energy alternatives, between now and 1985 only coal can close our energy gap, a fact that should hearten no one. Coal, our most abundant fossil fuel, cannot be produced without great danger to miners in deep mines or to the environment in strip mines; it cannot be transported without massive diversion of resources; and it cannot be burned without major health and environmental hazards. It is also beset by Stone Age operators and a belligerent work force, as the recent coal strike so abundantly proved. Until our technology allows us economically to convert coal into cleaner, transportable, efficient fuels like gas and gasoline (as the Germans did —at great cost—in World War II), coal will be at best an unpleasant necessity, its production constantly limited by its bulk and its manifest dangers to the environment.

Nuclear power is not the answer. On the other hand, the proposal that we quadruple our output of nuclear power by 1985 is not only wildly unrealistic, it is profoundly irresponsible. In the last 24 months, only one new nuclear plant was licensed and put into operation; thirteen were canceled; almost fifty were deferred, perhaps indefinitely. No matter how serious the energy crisis, this turn away from nuclear power could only be good news. After twenty years we have yet to come up with a way to dispose of the wastes from nuclear plants, wastes that remain dangerous to human life for 250,000 years. I doubt that any of the Texas cities now participating in nuclear power plants would continue if they were made responsible for disposing of the radioactive wastes. Today Texas is being considered as a dumping ground for hundreds of tons of such wastes. No new nuclear power plants should be built until we devise a satisfactory way to isolate and manage our current legacy of nuclear wastes.

We have plenty of energy resources. All energy experts agree that our oil and gas resources are plentiful; combined with coal and lignite, they provide enough fossil fuels to last a thousand years. The problem is not how much we have, but how long it takes to recover and how much it costs. In Texas, the easy oil and gas production discoveries were made before 1950. Since 1950 we have drilled two and a half times as many wells and found only a fourth as much oil. The oil and gas that we *must* produce between now and 1985, when alternative sources like coal gasification, methane, and solar can come into play, will come from deeper wells, from offshore, and from harder-to-find fields. So far the Carter Administration seems determined not to encourage the capital investment needed for this exploration. First the Administration dragged out the argument that a backlog in drilling rigs meant that higher prices wouldn't encourage production (although three hundred new drilling rigs were being produced every year); then they reprogrammed their computers (as the Governor's Energy Advisory Council discovered through the Freedom of Information Act) to distort the standard data that had originally shown more investment would be needed to find additional natural gas; then they fired the head of the respected U.S. Geological Survey, who was continuing to crank out reports showing that huge resources of gas and oil were still to be found. Since new fields take three to seven years to begin producing, this continued discouragement of new exploration could be disastrous.

The current energy "crisis" doesn't have to be a crisis. If we can rise above the petty politics of region versus region and producer versus consumer, then we can see the energy crisis for what it could be—a tremendous national opportunity, an economic frontier like the opening of the West and the building of the railroads. The $700 billion investment the University of Texas Council on Energy Resources calculates will be needed by 1985 to meet our goals of production, conservation, and environmental protection could soak up the persistent unemployment of the past five years, end regional stagnation, strengthen the dollar, and put our whole economy on a new and fundamentally sound footing. Outside of Washington, public officials are grasping the implications of this challenge. The Northeast governors, once implacable energy foes, are now pushing for the creation of the Energy Corporation of the Northeast, a public corporation funded to invest in energy projects. The Midwest governors are following suit. We need the same sort of leadership here, since it seems clear that Washington will not be providing it.

Texas is at the crossroads. For the immediate future our new energy base must be coal. Two years ago the Texas Railroad Commission ordered utilities and large industrial users to begin switching to coal. This switch has been accelerated by our high free market prices for natural gas, an incentive other states who get our gas at a cheaper, regulated price, unfortunately for the country, have not shared. This short-term regional inequity helped give Texas the jump on conversion to coal. The long-run contracts for the forty million tons of coal we will be importing by 1985 have been signed and the generating plants are coming on line. But already we are getting a taste of what it is like to be an energy importer. Montana has announced a 30 per cent severance tax on its coal, and the Burlington & Northern Railroad is on the verge of doubling its transportation rates to San Antonio. The combined result will cost Texas consumers hundreds of millions of dollars a year.

This imported coal must be a short-run solution, particularly if the national plan allows cities like Los Angeles to use the natural gas we save. If we think Houston has air pollution now, just wait until all its industries are burning coal instead of natural gas. All the specters of coal use, from acid rain to radioactive discharge to sludge disposal, will soon be our lot. Our only recourse is to push hard for new sources. This month a test well in Brazoria County is scheduled to begin drilling into the massive deposits of methane gas trapped in geopressured reservoirs like so many bubbles in champagne. Tests are underway to convert Texas' huge lignite fields into gas. If methane wells and lignite gasification become practical, then Texas will have a whole new base of clean and plentiful fossil fuel resources. We need to pursue solar alternatives as well, particularly the so-called "soft" approaches that provide home heating and cooling.

But Texas isn't alone at the crossroads. Energy is a fundamental world issue, and the world is looking to the United States for leadership. We still have a chance to set aside regional rivalries and political infighting so that we can face the challenges of conversion and production. We won't have that chance much longer. ★

William Broyles, Jr.

REPORTER
BY JOHN BLOOM

The Glen Rose power plant is due to open in 1981; Armadillo Coalition says no.

Politics
Split with the Atom

Jim Schermbeck had never heard of nuclear power until last summer. Home in Fort Worth after a year at Sherman's Austin College, he happened to watch a national newscast on the day 2000 chanting demonstrators staged a Gandhi-style sit-in at a nuclear reactor site in Seabrook, New Hampshire. "I couldn't understand why 2000 people would be willing to get arrested for some unheard-of issue like that." He didn't think much more about it until a few days later when a high school friend told him the "unheard-of issue" was thirty miles away—that giant Texas Utilities Company was building a nuclear plant near Glen Rose.

Today Schermbeck is thoroughly radicalized, the result of countless hours spent studying the history of the American nuclear power industry. As organizer and cofounder of the Armadillo Coalition of Texas (ACT)—with local organizations in Dallas, Fort Worth, Arlington, Austin, Houston, San Antonio, and Sherman—he intends to expose the Glen Rose plant as the first of several "utterly horrifying" environmental menaces in Texas. Like dozens of other ad hoc committees formed wherever reactors are proposed, ACT is prepared to picket, march, delay regulatory hearings, file lawsuits, and do whatever else is necessary to make nuclear power as unpopular and expensive as possible. Schermbeck has spent the better part of a year proselytizing on college campuses, but the real fight begins this summer.

The first symbolic ACT act will be the release of thousands of helium-filled balloons from the construction sites at Glen Rose. Each one will read, "If this balloon can reach you, so can radiation." That will be followed by statewide strategy sessions, teach-ins, civil disobedience seminars, leaflet brigades, and anything else Schermbeck can think of to stimulate grass-roots involvement. ACT, despite limited publicity, already numbers several hundred members statewide, a good many of them veterans of "old liberal causes." They publish a monthly newsletter from their Fort Worth offices, closely monitoring the oceans of government documents, environmental impact statements, and licensing regulations related to nuclear power in Texas.

When the federal government's national energy plan was drawn up a few years ago, it included 45 nuclear power plants in Texas—more than in any other state—but as reactors have proven increasingly costly, controversial, and inefficient that figure has been scaled down to seven—two at Glen Rose, two in Matagorda County (the South Texas Energy Project), two near the East Texas town of Jasper, and one at Wallis, about thirty miles west of Houston. The South Texas project has the earliest scheduled opening date (1980); the first Glen Rose reactor should begin operation a year later. ACT hopes to use Glen Rose and South Texas as springboards to head off the Wallis plant (hearings begin this summer) and the other two (scheduled for 1989 and 1991).

At issue are the familiar arguments of consumer activists who don't trust utility companies or the federal government to protect the public—namely, that no reliable safety system has ever been devised for a nuclear reactor, raising the prospect of massive radio-

Activist Schermbeck rebukes the nukes.

278 ALTERNATE SOLUTIONS

active leakage; that nuclear power is at least as expensive as coal-generated plants and almost as expensive as oil; that uranium supplies are limited; that alternative sources of energy are available; and that there is no safe way to store radioactive nuclear wastes.

That last issue may be the major source of concern for Texans, since the state has been selected as one of the prime storage sites in the nation. Palo Duro Basin in the Panhandle and the salt domes in East Texas are considered by the Department of Energy to be particularly excellent storage sites due to the high concentration of thick salt deposits below the earth's surface. Even if the waste were dumped in New Mexico, where a pilot project is already planned, Texans would have to worry about possible leakage into the underground water system for the next 250,000 years, which is how long it takes the waste material to lose its radioactivity.

The anti-nuclear protests, which have been slowly gaining strength for a year, spreading from New England to California, may turn out to be the most significant civil disobedience movement since the war rallies of the sixties. With President Carter firmly committed to nuclear power and Secretary of Energy James Schlesinger frankly opposed to the delaying tactics of consumer groups, the protesters must look for friends in state government and the Congress. They haven't found many. Schermbeck says it doesn't matter. "When we started this thing we thought, 'Well, there's no way in the world we're going to stop a nuclear plant. So we'll just try to educate the public to the danger.' But the way it's been growing—a combination of people getting involved in something for the first time and burnt-out liberals getting active again—we think it's just possible that we can do it after all."★

Citywise
by Robert Barnstone

SOLAR ON ICE

If you are looking to the sun for an immediate solution to all our energy woes, don't look now.

The Williamsons, a professional working couple in Austin, were determined to do something about the $200-per-month electric heating bills they received winter before last for their 2000-square-foot home. Progressive in outlook and concerned about energy resources, they decided to look into solar heating. But when they got an $8000 estimate for a solar system that would have saved them $300 to $350 per winter, their enthusiasm waned. "I was a natural candidate for solar," says Bill Williamson. "I'm the type of person who always wants to do the right thing. I drive small cars, eat fresh fruit, and stay away from white bread. But if I had spent $8000, the $300 I would have saved wouldn't even have paid the interest on the borrowed money." So they scrapped their plans for solar heating and instead bought four used gas space heaters for $80, which last winter saved them more on bills than the $8000 solar system would have.

The Williamsons aren't alone. Thousands of well-intentioned Texans are learning that solar heating and cooling equipment—and by this I mean the thermal systems now on the market—is costly and when installed too often fails to fulfill their expectations. Many other Texans are waiting either for the federal government to start handing out suitcases of money to give them the incentive to install solar systems, or for price reductions through mass production or technological breakthroughs.

Some of the well-to-do California chic are doing their bit for the energy crisis by installing solar-heated swimming pools, which is like trying to lose weight by drinking lots of diet Pepsi. "Converting to solar is a rich man's way of salving his conscience," says Bill Williamson. Others simply want to be the first on their block with a solar system.

A natural result of all this interest in solar is the growing number of people manufacturing or selling solar equipment. Texas has become a major manufacturing center, producing some of the best solar energy equipment in the nation, such as the Solarvac flat-plate collector (for low temperature uses like water heating) or the Northrup concentrating collector (for applications that require high heat, such as air conditioning). Texas also produces some of the worst, and the average consumer has almost no way of spotting the lemons.

Finding knowledgeable contractors to install and maintain the equipment is even harder. Two years ago the Austin telephone directory listed two contractors who installed solar equipment. The latest edition lists fifteen, and eight of those are already out of business. The 1975 Houston telephone directory listed three contractors, while the 1977 edition lists sixteen, six of which are now closed.

Some consumers have learned that, either because of ineffective equipment or faulty installation, the equipment doesn't meet their needs. A recent study conducted by a group of New England utilities found that the solar water heaters installed in 100 homes averaged a 17 per cent savings. "This was far below the fifty per cent savings that had been predicted," says John Stevens, a spokesman for a utility that participated in the study. "Solar energy is a victim of unreasonably high expectations."

George Smith, an Austin air-conditioning contractor, is a veteran in the solar energy industry, though he makes much more money lecturing on solar systems than installing them. "Malfunctions are mostly the results of honest mistakes rather than of con artists trying to make a quick buck," he says. "Recently another local solar equipment contractor had to replace a system he had installed because it wasn't even heating water to room temperature. He bought two of my collectors to replace the ones he had already installed but they didn't work either. I went out to inspect the job and saw the trouble before I even stepped out of the car. The pipes leading out of the collector weren't insulated. All the heat was being lost before it got into the house."

There is as much solar misinformation as illumination to be found in the press and in advertisements. Almost daily, newspapers carry a success story about some exotic application of solar energy. Very little real-world information can be obtained from what usually turn out to be demonstration projects. An article recently appeared in the *Fort Worth Star-Telegram* about a man who had installed a $30,000 solar air-conditioning system in his house (though he estimated that an "adequate" solar system could have been installed for about

Robert Barnstone is a financial analyst living in Austin, who has done feasibility studies on solar energy costs.

$17,000). A home builder's association official commenting on the installation gave the most optimistic forecast to date on solar energy, if he was quoted correctly. He said, "Costs of solar energy will be down by a hundred per cent within five years" (my math tells me solar systems will be free then) "and they may be down by another hundred per cent in another five years" (will they pay us to take the equipment?). Yet even allowing for the official's bad arithmetic, forecasting a 75 per cent reduction in cost within the next ten years is unrealistic. But there's more to this story.

An impressive full-page ad recently appeared in the *Wall Street Journal* with the banner: "Economical Solar Power for Air Conditioning Now!" The advertiser, a Texas producer of solar flat-plate collectors, claimed that a $16,850 solar absorption-type air conditioner could supply 72 per cent of the needs of the same area that could be cooled by a three-ton conventional air conditioner. Yet a knowledgeable contractor told me that it was very likely that the air conditioner would have to be powered by the supplementary gas burner, since flat-plate collectors are notoriously inefficient at collecting energy at the high temperatures necessary for cooling. Further, the ad claimed, "a computer analysis" showed that when amortized over twenty years, the cost of the solar unit would be as economical as the conventional electric unit. Checking their figures, however, I found that, even accepting their performance claim, the potential savings would amount to no more than $570 a year, while the interest charges alone on $16,850 exceeds $1500 per year—almost three times as much as the savings—not to mention depreciation costs. No explanation for the claim could be given by a company spokesman. When asked how many solar air-conditioning systems his firm had installed to date, he could recall only two: one was in its plant, the other in the home that was featured a few days earlier in the *Fort Worth Star-Telegram*. As it turned out, that home belonged to a distributor of its product—a fact the article neglected to mention.

Wise consumers will arm themselves with circumspection and knowledge before they jump in. The federal government has a solar information center (toll-free telephone 1-800-523-2929) that gives names of producers and installers of solar equipment, but it does not report on tests of equipment or comment on the reliability of the contractors who do the installations. Florida, which, with California, is one of the most advanced states in solar development, tests and certifies equipment (but not contractors) at the Florida Solar Energy Center. Until a national certification program is established, it is advisable not to buy equipment that the Florida center has not certified. They also sell the best layman's guide to solar energy, *A Floridian's Guide to Solar Energy* (available for $1.50 from Florida Solar Energy Center, 300 State Road 401, Cape Canaveral, Florida 32920). There are far too many books on solar energy to keep up with these days, and most are not relevant to Texas because they deal with areas of the country with greater space heating requirements. The advantage of the *Floridian's Guide* is that Texas is on the same latitude with Florida and has similar heating and cooling problems.

What, then, can the consumer realistically expect from solar energy? Not a great deal now, even if he buys cautiously, but considerably more in the future if some expected technological breakthroughs materialize.

On each day between March and October, 2100 BTUs of solar energy fall on each square foot of Texas soil; during the winter months this drops to 1800. Enough of the sun's energy falls on an average house to more than meet all its heating and cooling needs. Besides being virtually unlimited, solar power is nonpolluting. The trick, of course, is to harness this vast amount of clean energy. Excluding nuclear, all of our energy sources—fossil fuels and hydroelectric and wind power—are ultimately derived from solar energy. Solar equipment simply permits man to capture and store the energy delivered by the sun with no intermediate process—like cooking it up into oil for a few million years.

Energy, as you may remember from high school physics, is the ability to do work. The greater the heat-producing capability of a fuel, the more work it can do. Solar heat hits the earth's surface at a relatively low temperature, which is why it is best suited for low-temperature needs such as interior space heating and heating water for home use. Other applications, like air conditioning and producing steam for electric power, require higher heat and, therefore, a concentration of the sun's energy. The solar equipment presently available that can achieve this is very bulky and expensive.

A solar system has to do two things well. It must collect the energy (most good systems gather about 40 to 60 per cent of the sun's output) and it should be able to store the energy. Solar heat can be collected for only about six hours a day in Texas, and very little can be gathered when it's cloudy. Obviously, unless you restrict your uses of energy to sunlight hours, a storage capability is mandatory, and even the best storage set-ups on today's market cannot economically store heat over extended cloudy periods. Therefore, if you want your energy needs met at all times, you have to install as a back-up a conventional gas or electric system capable of carrying 100 per cent of the load.

In Texas, with present technology, the only truly practical application of solar energy is to heat water. To most consumers this seems unglamorous, yet heating water consumes 22 per cent of the total energy needs of an average Texas home. At today's prices solar water heating is cheaper than electric when you amortize the cost of solar equipment over twenty years. But natural gas prices would have to increase more than three times before solar would be cheaper than gas water heating.

Solar space heating is also at a disadvantage over natural gas heating in most of Texas because of the short winter season. Remember, you pay interest on the costs of the equipment all year, even when it's not in use. Your natural gas heating bill would have to increase more than four times before solar could be competitive. However, electric heat charges would have to increase only one and a half times to three times (if you have an electric heat pump) for solar to pay.

Unfortunately most Texans are concerned principally with cooling, and so far this is the least feasible application of solar energy. Electric rates would have to increase five to six times before solar air conditioning could be economical.

What about those who are waiting for federal tax credits before they consider solar equipment? If the tax credit is approved, its greatest impact will be in making solar water heating even more attractive than electric water heating (though it would still not be as economical as heating water with natural gas). Passive solar installations (see box page 156) are not eligible for the solar tax credit.

Finally, what are the prospects for cost reductions through mass production or technological breakthroughs? Dr. Jeff Moorehouse, professor of mechanical engineering at Texas A&M, who teaches a course in solar energy, says, "Since the raw materials of solar equipment account for about half of its cost, even as much as a fifty per cent reduction—highly unlikely—in labor charges through mass production, would reduce the total cost by only twenty-five per cent." As for advances in technology: today's equipment collects 40 to 60 per cent of the available energy; Moorehouse estimates that, even under theoretically perfect conditions, with the limitations of the materials now being used you could collect no more than 80 per cent. So a substantial reduction in flat-plate collector costs is improbable.

But Moorehouse believes that the most promising future use of solar energy is not in heat collection but in photovoltaics, which is the direct conversion of sunlight to electricity. Photovoltaics uses solid-state devices (solar cells) to convert solar energy to electricity. A photovoltaic cell is composed of crystals that change polarity when the sun strikes them, thereby giving off an electric charge. These are wildly expensive now—more than fifty times conventional electricity—but scientists working on photovoltaics expect to drop the cost substantially in the next few years, making this form of solar energy the best prospect for the cheap and endless energy that the sun tantalizes us with daily.

The solar energy industry has been launched, and many people are in a position to damn the dollars and install a solar system—we've all read about Robert Redford's house. It is obvious that what is motivating these people is less a need for cheap energy than a desire for an increasingly rare commodity these days—independence. And it's hard to put a dollar value on that.

ON THE OTHER HAND...

Active solar systems may have a way to go, but don't give up on the sun.

Passive solar design incorporates energy-conscious schemes into the structure itself without using pumps or fans or electricity. The most obvious device is a window on the south side of the house, shaded in summer and unshaded in winter. A more complicated passive system is the thermal chimney. In between these extremes, technological ingenuity is in full flower, with a host of magazines like *CoEvolution Quarterly* and *Mother Earth News* packed with passive solar tricks.

In new construction, passive devices can reduce substantially the need for mechanical heaters and coolers. Beginning with site location, the builder can choose to bury three sides of his house and the roof under a mound of earth. Because temperature changes of earth, unlike air, occur slowly and are never extreme, this admittedly radical step reduces the need for insulation.

The next consideration is orientation. Place the house facing south to catch the sun's heat in winter and the prevailing breezes in summer. To shade the south side in summer, use deciduous trees or a roof overhang that blocks the high summer sun but lets in the low winter rays. The north side of the house should present a solid front—few or no windows—and a sloping roof to channel the cold wind up and over the house.

Once solar heat is pouring through the windows into a well-insulated house in the winter, there has to be a way to store it for night use. This can be achieved by a massive concrete foundation slab or by tons of large stones, which will collect the heat all day and radiate it slowly at night. Another method is to store water under the floor, essentially to build on top of a pool. Mass is the secret. Thick adobe walls are a good traditional method.

In most of Texas, summer is a tougher problem than winter. The goal is to keep both temperature and humidity down. In dry areas of the state, ventilation is the key to keeping cool. One passive system for this climatic situation is the thermal chimney. Based on the principle that hot air rises, the thermal chimney in its many forms sucks air up and out of the house, eliminating the heat and creating a breeze without a motor, noise, or electricity. To control humidity, researchers are now trying various desiccants, or drying agents, in experimental construction.

In addition to these major architectural decisions, other simpler ones can help. By locating the kitchen on the north side of the house heat generated there in the summer will disperse on the cool side of the house, while in the winter the heat is needed on the cold north side. Passive rotating vents on the roof will pull hot air out of attics, and openings on both sides of a house (small intakes, large exhausts) will keep the breezes moving.

In the winter, fireplaces can be vented to draw the cool air they need from directly outside the house, instead of causing drafts around all the doors and windows. Greenhouses can be added to the south side of existing houses to provide warm, moist air in winter—although they must be profusely vented or they will provide the same thing in summer.

Radical climate differences across Texas require careful planning to solve the problems of the particular area.
David Crossley

TEN QUESTIONS TO ASK YOUR CONTRACTOR ABOUT SOLAR WATER HEATING

1. How many systems of the type you want has the contractor already installed? Check on his past work.
2. Has the equipment he sells been certified by an independent laboratory such as the Florida Solar Energy Center?
3. Does the system have storage capability? If not, find another contractor unless your needs occur strictly between 10 a.m. and 4 p.m. Hot-water storage should be at least twenty gallons per person.
4. If heat is collected by a liquid medium (as opposed to air), how are freeze-ups prevented in winter?
5. Since mineral build-up reduces efficiency, how does the system prevent such build-up in the collector pipes?
6. What are the maintenance requirements of the system? The industry is new, but good systems properly installed are currently averaging about two hours per year.
7. What size collector are you considering? No firm should sell less than 40 square feet of collector area to heat water.
8. Does the warranty cover performance as well as parts?
9. Does the proposal include reducing heat loss in the house? Solar equipment contractors should do everything to reduce the size and cost of solar equipment needed (a dollar spent on insulation is worth $10 in equipment in the average house). A substantial amount of energy can be saved simply by insulating hot-water pipes.
10. Have you kept track of your current energy costs so you know what kind of savings to expect? Be sure you understand the assumptions in computing the economic feasibility of a solar project. For any system more involved than water heating, consult an engineer. ★